THE NĀṬYA ŚĀSTRA

RAGA NRTYA SERIES No. 2

The Nāṭya Śāstra

of

BHARATAMUNI

Translated into English
By
A Board of Scholars

SRI SATGURU PUBLICATIONS
A Division of
INDIAN BOOKS CENTRE
DELHI-INDIA

Published by :
SRI SATGURU PUBLICATIONS
A Division of :
INDIAN BOOKS CENTRE
Indological and Oriental Publishers
40/5, Shakti Nagar,
Delhi-110007
(INDIA)

ISBN 81-7030-134-3
First Edition : Delhi, 1986
Second Revised Edition : 1989, 1993, 1996

Publishers are grateful to Sh. T.V. Parameshwar Iyer for his guidance in translation of this work.

Printed in India at :
D.K. Fine Art Press (P) Ltd., Delhi-110052

Contents

Introduction

The background—In 1789 William Jones brought out his translation of Śākuntala. This is a landmark in the Annals of Indological Research and the interest of Western scholars in Sanskrit works whether pure literature or technical works of the sort of the Nāṭyaśāstra. Scholars all over the world took great interest in the nature and origin of The Indian Theatre.

In the years 1826/27 H.H. Wilson published his select specimens of the Theatre of the Hindus in three volumes. He was afraid, he said that NŚ. of Bharata Muni had been lost. He said this because he could not find any Mss. of the work. Professor Hall the great Indologist edited Dhanañjaya's famous Dasarūpaka a splendid work on Dramaturgy. He published it in 1865. Till then he also could not find any Mss. of the famous NŚ. Later he was fortunate enough to come across a Mss, some chapters of which he published as a sort of supplement or Appendix to his Dasarupaka. As ill luck would have it even the best of the original Mss he had was full of lacunae. He had therefore to give up the idea of publishing a critical edition of the same. But the Scholars of oriental learning and literature were induced to search earnestly for other Mss material of NS throughout India. In 1874 the German Indologist Reymann wrote a lengthy paper on NŚ. He had elaborately shed light on its contents. This also acted as an inducement to many competent scholars in India and abroad. Various authors published separate chapters with translation in French, German etc. These several papers and pamphlets no doubt helped people to understand some aspects of Ancient Indian dramatic works. Ultimately it was the magnificent work on Indian Theatre by the celebrated author Sylvian Levi that shed considerable light on the exact nature of the ancient Hindu plays, especially the manner of their representation on the stage. **While expatiating on the various truths he discovered by** diligent research, he magnanimously acknowledged the different contributions of his predecessors. He had access to three different Mss more or less complete but major portion of the same had been corrupt and lacuna-ridden. . Hence he devoted more attention to the study of the literary form of the Hindu plays (Ch. 18 to 22) of NS which he discussed in greater details. Dhanañjaya, Viśvanātha and other earlier Indian writers had professed their indebtedness to Bharata and Levi's work contributed much to check the accuracy of the earlier Indian Authors' statements. It was Levi who focussed the attention of Indologists on the importance of NS.

In 1894 was published the Skt. text alone of NS. in the Kavyamala series as its 42nd title. This was edited by Pandits Sivadatta and Kasinath Pandurang Parab and in 1898 the French Indologist Grosset published his critical edition with Ch. 1 to 14. He consulted all the Mss. available till then. It is one of the best specimens of scholarship of the occidental Indologists. Later in 1926 the Chowkhamba edition and the Baroda edition were published. Thereafter many editions have come out with the local language translations and annotations. Unfortunately in almost all of these, printing mistakes editorial slips are too many. A comparatively error-free edition was published by the Kerala Sahitya Academy under the able editorship of Shri K.P. Narayana Pisharoti with the Malayalam translation written by himself. The text was in Mal. characters. Unfortunately this edition has become out of print. It behoves scholars in general to make use of the valuable data on the origin and nature of ancient Indian Drama found in NŚ and and subject them to the searching scrutiny they require.

Commentaries

The following are the best known commentators on NS viz ; Lollaṭa, Udbhaṭa, Śaṅkuka, and the most famous of the Abhinavaguptas. There is a mention of a Bhāṣya and a Vārtika, besides a Nāṭya Sūtra. This system of assigning Sūtras, Bhāṣyas and Vārtikas is common to all systems of Indian Philosophy. Hence the same has been introduced in the Nāṭyadarśana as well. Unfortunately our knowledge about these works except that of Abhinavagupta is very scanty.

(*a*) *Nanyadeva.* He is reputed to be the Bhāṣyakāra in this system. He has been quoted by Abhinavagupta and other early commentators.

(*b*) Bhaṭṭa Lollaṭa. It is conjectured that he lived in the 8th century. Abh. Gu. has quoted him often.

(*c*) *Sankuka.* This commentator has been quoted by Abh. Gu. many times. He has also been identified as the author of the poem Bhuvanabhyudays. He flourished in the period of the Kashmerian king Ajitapiḍa definitely known as reigning during 813/816 A.D.

(*d*) *Udbhaṭa.* Abhinava has referred to his opinions a few times. Possibly he is identical with the Alaṁkārika of the same name.

(*e*) *Bhaṭṭanāyaka.* He is the author of Hṛdayadarpaṇa a work on the Dhvani theory and can be placed between 9th and 10th centuries. Ab. Gu. makes respectful mention of this commentator.

(*f*) *Bhaṭṭāyantra.* Too has been mentioned by Abh. Gu. Nothing more is known about this author too.

(*g*) *Acārya Kirtidhara.* He probably flourished in the sixth century. He might have been a very early commentator. He is respectfully remembered by Abhinava.

(*h*) *Abhinavagupta.* He seems to be the same as the celebrated author of the learned treatises on Kashmirian Śaivism ; as well as the Locana commentary on Dhvanyaloka. His age is established as between 10th and 11th centuries. He is known as Nṛsimhagupta too. Despite some weak points such as faulty explanations here and there, this commentary has additional value inasmuch as there are profuse quotations from a vast number of dramatic and other works. Serious students of Indian poetics, aesthetics and dramaturgy are sure to be profited by the thorough perusal of this commentary. The author's background as a voluminous writer on abstruse philosophical topics has given to the work a peculiar charm in regard to the learned reader.

The Text of Nāṭya Śāstra

The work available now under the name of NŚ. of Bharata Muni contains about five thousand six hundred verses. There is a shorter version with a reduction of nearly two hundred verses. Both the recensions possess great antiquity ; which one is the earlier we cannot say for certain. The problem of the relationship between different recensions of all ancient works cannot be solved this way or that way in an off hand manner. The very fact that the longer recension has more verses need not make us think that there are interpolations. The changes may be intentional or unintentional ; scribes must have blundered by omitting verses here and there. Use of different metres etc. cannot be adduced as reasons for priority or posteriority.

Authorship. Bharata is reputed to be the author of this work. Originally the word Bharata was used in the sense of an actor in a drama. The treatise dealing with the activities of a Bharata, or intended as a guide to him came to be called Bharataśāstra. Later on the compound word began to signify the Śāstra propounded by Bharata. Bhavabhuti the dramatist is probably the first to mention Bharata Muni as the author and he calls him Tauryatrikasutrakāra.

The Contents. A mere perusal of the contents of the work will convince everyone as the variety of the topics discussed herein. The principal theme is the dramatic art which concerns the producers of the plays as well as those who compose them, the playwrights. There are certain plays which can be only read and appreciated; but our Bharata wants the plays to be a Dṛśya Kāvya that can be succesfully and profitably represented on the stage. This vital relationship between the literary and the technical aspects of a play has been analysed by him and justice has been done to both. The dramatic theory as well as practice has been elaborately dealt with. Hence manual gestures, facial expressions. Poetics, music with all ramifications whether vocal or instrumental, prosody, some points of grammar, costumes, ornaments, setting up of the scenes with proper background etc. etc. have been thoroughly dealt with.

The Style. In the main the style of the author is simple; but sometimes the technical details cannot be easily understood without a commentary or the exposition of an experienced sponsor of plays. In the main the work is in small Anuṣṭup Ślokas and those in Arya Metre. There are prose passages too. The author has treated the subject matter so very analytically as not to hesitate to repeat the things mentioned earlier in order to be more specific. A technical treatise aiming at meticulous completeness can avoid diffuseness only at the sacrifice of clarity. The traditional practitioners of dance, music, drama etc have preserved the rules sucessively handed down from teacher to the pupil and they are better commentators on the text rather than the scribes writing glosses. Defective Mss cannot smother their enthusiasm or success in the dramatic performance.

Cultural Projection. Besides the topics relevant for the dramatic art, many other things conducive to the understanding of the various landmarks in the cultural history of India are found included in NŚ.

(i) *Linguistic.* Prākṛta and allied native languages are thoroughly dealt with by means of examples. References have been made to the languages of ancient tribes such as Barbaras, Kiratas, Andhras, Draviḍas, Śabaras, Candalar etc.

(ii) *Literary.* Beautiful verses of very fine literary excellence have been given by way of examples, while dealing with Dhruva songs, metres etc. In many of these verses we find the innate charm divested of all the artifices and linguistic thickeries of the later classical age. Rasas, Bhāvas, Alaṁkāras etc. are potrayed well.

(iii) *Arts and Crafts.* Dance is inseparable from drama and our author has done full justice to it. The various Abhinayas mentioned herein have been portrayed by mural paintings, sculpture, architecture etc. in our temples. Various crafts are brought into play to create a suitable background in the stage in different scenes.

(iv) *Costumes and ornaments.* Ch. 23 NŚ gives detailed directions about the dressing material, modes of wearing the garments and jewellery, articles to be used by the different characters in a play in accordance with their social status, pro fession, the cult practised etc. Naturally this has great significance in the understanding of the social life in those distant times.

(v) *Mythological and legendary figures.* NŚ mentions mythological figures starting from the lowest stratum such as the Uragas, Patangas, Bhutas, Rākṣasa . Asuras etc. and ending with the gods and goddesses of the Hindu Pantheon Viz; th Daityas, Dānavas, Guhyakas, Kṣtadikpalakas, Gandharvas Apsarās, Aśvins, Manmatha, Rudra, Viśve Devas, Bṛhaspati Nārada, Tumburu, Ṛshis Mantradrastrs, Brahma, Vishnu Shiva, Lakṣhmi, Chandikā, Sarasvati etc. A significant omis sion is of Ganeśa and Avatārs of Viṣṇ

(vi) *Geographical details.* In the chapters 14, 18 and 2: there are references to cities and rural regions such as Aṅga Antagiri, Andhra, Āvarta, Kharta, Anarta, Uṣinara, Odra Kalinga, Kāśmira, Kosala, Tāmralipta, Tosala, Tripura Dakshinapatha, Dramida, Nepāla, Pulindabhumi, Paundra Pragjyotiṣa, Plavanga, Bahirgiri, Brahmottara, Magadha Madraka, Mahārāshtra, Mālavā, Mahendra, Mosala, Vaṅga Vatsa, Vartika, Vahlika, Videha, Surasena, Salaka etc rivers and mountains such as Sindhu, Gaṅgā, Carmanvati, Mahendra, Malaya, Sahya, Himālaya, Vindhya etc.

(vii) *Erotical, Psychological and economical sciences etc.* The necessity of learning the different sciences has been stressed in the NŚ. The qualities mentioned in regard to the Sabhāś-ātras (the members of the court hall) are exhaustive. Readiness to work always, alertness, absence of indolence, affectionate feelings, forbearance, modesty, impartiality, training in polity, good manners and customs etc. (Ch. 34) Knowledge of Psychology is essential for the successful portrayal of various emotions Rasas, Bhāvas etc. Enjoyment of the dramatic performance presupposes the peculiar reactions which the playwright's skill and the actors' adroitness can evoke in the spectators of diverse kinds of capacities and tastes Dogmatism and domineering attitude should be eschewed and the views of the common man should be taken into consideration.

Early writers on Indian Drama and Dance.

Pāṇini the celebrated grammarian of the sixth century B C. in his Aṣṭādhyāyi (IV/3/110-111) mentions the Naṭasūtras of Silalin and Kṛsaśva. It is a pity that we do not possess the Mss. of these Sūtras. They may be manuals for the actors (Naṭas) or perhaps sets of rules for dancers and pantomimists. It is possible that the ideas from the said Naṭasūtras had been incorporated in the present NS.

The sons of Bharata. In I/26 to 39 NS there is an enumeration of the hundred sons of Bharata. Some of these could in fact have been the authors of works on dramaturgy, histrionics, dance, music and other allied topical topical. The following viz: Kohala, Dattila, Salikarna, Badarāyaṇa, Nakhakuṭṭa, Asmakutta and a few others have been quoted by later writers as their predecessors in the field of **dramaturgy**, and histronics. Unluckily these references alone are our source of knowledge of **these writers.**

(a) *Kohala.* In 36/68 NS it is mentioned that Kohala would mention apparent omissions herein, in his Uttara Tantra (Later Compendium). In the commentary of Abhinavagupta and in the Bhāvaprakāśana of Sāradatanaya there are references to the effect that Kohala wrote on dance, dramaturgy, histrionics and music.

(b) Dattila (Dantila. Dhurtiia) is quoted by Abh. Gu. He was an author on histrionics and music.

(c) Śāṇḍilya and Vatsya (NS 36/75) are referred to herein as successors of Bharata for the propagation of the art of dramatic performance. If at all they had written any treatise it is lost to us.

(d) *Satakarni* (*Salikarna*) A reference to him is found in the Naṭakaratna-kośa of Sāgaranandin. Hence he might have been a writer on dramaturgy. It is possible that he is the king Satakarni mentioned in some inscriptions around the last years of B.C. and early period of A D. Kings and persons of royal descent were interested in fine arts, many had written works on dance and dramaturgy etc.

(e) *Asmakutta and Nakhakutta.* These two writers have been quoted by Sagaranandin and Viśvanātha the author of Sāhityadarpaṇa. Bahurupa a commentator on Daśarupaka mentions Nakhakuṭīa. They were probably writers on dramaturgy.

Badarāyaṇa. He is quoted by Sāgaranandin. Further, anothor mentioned by him as Badari may be the same. These two are reputed writers on Vedānta philosophy too.

(g) *Saṅgrahakāra.* In NŚ VI/10 a Nāṭyavedasaṅgraha is referred to, Abh. Gu mentions a Sangrahakāra. This treatise might have dealt with dramaturgy and histrionics.

Later Writers

There were many writers in the later period on dramaturgy histrionics etc. but prior to Abhinavagupta. They are Nandikeśvara, Tumburu, Visakhila, Carayana, Sadāśiva, Padmabhu (Brahma), Drauhini (perhaps Narada). Vyāsa, Anjaneya, Kātyāyaṇa (perhaps the grammarian), Rāhula, Garga, Sakaligarbha, Ghantaka, Matrugupta (perhaps a commentator on NS), Subandhu etc. Fuller details of these writers are not available,

Agni Purāṇa and Viṣṇudharmottara. These two works contain elaborate explanations of various topics connected with Nāṭya, Nṛtya, Rasa, Abhinaya etc. They are not early works as the name Purāṇa may lead us to suppose. Much of what is contained in NŚ are reproduced therein.

Later original writings on Drama. It will not be out of place here to mention briefly some writers who have acknowledged their indebtedness to Bharata but were not commentators. They are Dhanañjaya, Sāgaranandin, Ramachandra-Gunachandra, Ruyyaka, Sāradātanaya, Viśvanātha Kaviratna and Singhabhupāla.

Dhanañjaya. He is known to have flourished in the last years of 10th century A.D. during the reign of Vakpatiārjā of Mālavā. More than half of the chapter 20 of NS deals with the ten kinds of plays and the detailed explanation of things connected therewith. Dhanañjaya in his Daśarūpaka elaborates on this topic. Of course some other relevant connected topics too are dealt with. A noteworthy feature is his omission of histrionics and similar technical aspects of dramatic perfor-mence. He lays emphasis on the literary aspect of the drama. What we can conclude from this is that by his time the popularity of Sanskrit dramas had dwindled and only scholars took special interest therein, more as literary pieces than as Dṛṣyakāvyas. That Bharata wanted his treatise NS to be a guide to the playwrights and producers of plays was forgotten by Dhanañjaya though his veneration for Bharata is eulogistically acknowledged. As far as dramaturgy is concerned Daśarupa seems to have superseded even Nāṭya Śāstra later on. It supplanted all other works on dramaturgy in due course of time. Later writers like the author of Sāhityadarpaṇa, i.e. Viśvanātha Kavirāja benefited by the explanations in this work.

Sāgaranandin. He is the author of Nāṭakalakṣaṇaratnakośa, the Mss of which was first discovered in 1922 in Nepal by Sylvian Levi. Later in 1937, M. Dhillon edited it and published it from London. Besides dramaturgy, histrionics and allied topics are dealt with. In the course of his work he acknowledges his indebtedness to many of the earlier writers on the dramatic art, especially NŚ which he quotes verbatim or paraphrases.

Rāmachandra & Guṇachandra are collaborators of the work named Nāṭyadarpaṇa. Both of them were the disciples of the celebrated rhetorician Rāmachandra. They lived between 1100 and 1178. ND consists of four chapters in Anuṣṭup couplets. They themselves have written a Vṛtti (gloss) in prose elucidating difficult passages. Daśarupaka is subjected to severe criticism which is its unique value bordering on superiority over Daśarupaka.

Ruyyaka. He is otherwise known as Ruchaka. He was a Kāśhmirian Paṇḍit of the 12th cen. Various aspects of poetics have been elaborated by him in his works the chief of which is the commentary on the Vyaktiviveka of Mahimabhaṭṭa. In this latter work he mentions that he was the author of Nāṭakamimāṁsā, a work on dramaturgy which has so far not been discovered.

Sāradātanaya was a Dakṣinatya scholar who flourished in the 12th century. His Bhāvaprakāśana Illuminator of Bhāvas (mental emotions and fervour) is a more detailed work on dramaturgy than Daśarupaka and Nāṭyadarpaṇa. His preceptor Divākara is venerably mentioned as the Director of a theatre. Hence the practical aspects of dramatic performances as obtaining during his days have been expatiated in this work. Despite his indebtedness to the earlier writers his approach to the topics can be said to be very original in shedding light from fresher angles of vision. To be brief, it can be said that Sāradātanaya's treatment of the subject is more comprehensive than that of the Daśarupaka, Nāṭakalakṣana, and Nāṭyadarpaṇa. He mentions many of the earlier writers both as authorities for his views as well as the objects of his critical remarks.

Viśvanātha Kavirāja. He flourished in the 13th century. His Sāhityadarpaṇa deals with all branches of literature. The sixth chapter deals with drama. He has drawn materials from NS, Daśarupaka and its commentary Avaloka.

Singhabhupāla. His Nāṭakaparibhāṣa is known only by name. But Rasārnavasudhākara treats of drama in the closing section.

What is Nāṭya ?

A layman today understands by the word Bharatanāṭya only the Dance aspect with facial and manual gesticulations. We have separate words Nṛtta; Nṛtya, Abhinaya etc. to signify this restricted aspect, connot different shades in that meaning too. What Bharata had in view must have been a wider field including the theory and practice of the dramatic art. According to our Theorists, costumes, ornaments and general make-up of the actor or the actress are as important as the other items such as Vāchika, Aṅgika, Hastamudrā, Mukhavikāra etc. For an over all effect, the Nṛtta, Gita and Vādya are the *sine qua non.* NŚ. Ch I/117-121 gives full definition of Nāṭya as an all comprehensive term. Bharata wants his Nāṭya (we shall use the word Drama) to be a mirror of life, customs and manners of all sorts of people. He does not preclude the demons and gods from Nāṭya. NŚ. lays down very elaborate rules facilitating a drama to become a mimicry of the exploits of human, demoniac or divine beings. If the epic or the lyrics for that matter mirror life, wherein is the difference ? Bharata has an immediate answer. He states that Nāṭya is a Dṛśyakāvya (that which is seen and appreciated) Kālidāsa calls it Kantam Aratum Chakshusham (an attractive holy rite of visual depiction.)

How can Nāṭya be a mimicry (Anukaraṇa) ? The place of Realism in the representation of human activities is elaborated by what are called Lokadharmī and Nāṭyadharmī (Ch 14/62-76 and Ch 23/187-188). What follows the natural tendency and common behaviour, parlance etc. is Lokadharmī and deviation from it for some specific purpose is called Nāṭyadharmi where the dramatic conventions are to be scrupulously followed. Anukaraṇa does not mean a photographic representation of life. The tradition of the Hindu Theorists on dramaturgy the simple truth that unless a certain degree of artificiality is allowed or introduced no art can flourish in a deserving manner. Soliloquy, conversation of the type of of APAVARYA-Aside-are instances of these. A realist will laugh at the idea of one character being able to hear and the other being unable to hear what is openly uttered in the stage where all are simultameously present. To be brief, exacting demand for realism will cut at the very root of theatrical performances of aesthetic value.

Restrictions regarding time, place etc. In the Indian Dramas there is no undue restriction on the length of the period that extends between the events in the beginning and those in the end, except ofcourse the stipulation that longer periods should be indicated through the interludes such as Praveśaka, Viśkambha etc. There is no restriction as to the place where the events should take place.

Unity of Impression. This is an item about which the playwright must be very careful. It is for this purpose that the five Sandhis, Mukha, Pratimukha etc. are enjoined to be strictly observed so that the plot can have a uniform development in the various acts. Subsidiary events must be utilized to the minimum. They should not be allowed to affect the unity of impression adversely. They are to be indirectly hinted at or reported at or reported through the characters introduced in the introductory scenes of Praveśaka and Viśkambhaka. In addition to the maintenance of the unity of impression this device help in imparting to the plot the requisite rapidity of movement considered by the theorists on Dramaturgy to be very essential for every kind of dramatic representation and demonstration for the success therein,

DRAMATIC CRITICISM

The role of literary criticism is different from that of the dramatic criticism. A Nāṭaka is primarily a Dṛśyakāvya. As such the people who sit in the theatre to withess the performance is invariably referred to as Prekṣakas or Dṛṣhtaraḥ (Spectators) and not as Śrotarah (Rudience). The speech element of course is present there and it has to be listened to in order to do full justice to the visual aspect thereof. But the main part of the Drama is the spectacle (what should be visualised). This twin aspect makes it necessary to have a literary criticism besides the usual dramatic criticism. The words used, the ideas conveyed, the imagery etc brought in all these come under the literary criticism while importance of the representation the

Abhinaya of the Actor or actress comes under the dramatic criticism.

From the very early times we have been witnessing dramas produced in the stage but in the remote days, in the beginning stages actors and actresses were at liberty to use the dialogues of their own composition uttered by them almost *ex-tempore*. The folk plays in almost all the linguistic regions of India till very recent times there were such hotchpoch pieces. In the case of the works of the leading dramatists like Bhāsa Kālidāsa, Bhavabhuti etc the liberty referred to previously was curbed to a certain extent by the established conventions. Some of the vociferous actors and actresses should have made inroads there also in a desultory and deliberate manner. This accounts for the various readings in the passages preserved in Mss. Judgement of the worth of dramatic pieces should be the prerogatives of the laymen attending the presentation. This has been accepted even by the modern producers though the services of professional critics is being enlisted by them by way of propaganda and advertising devices. Unless the laymen are also impressed, the dramatic performance cannot be a box office success. In NŚ (Ch.27) the entire chapter is devoted to the success of dramatic representation and there is enough matter educating the Prekṣaka also in the manner and substance of the appreciation of the remarkable points on the part of the actors and the actresses. This chapter deals with the Ghaṭas (blemishes), Saṅgharṣa (Controversy), the method of rewarding the best performers and other topics too. It is the duty of the producers to cater to the varying tastes and inclinations of the medley persons, of ten of the incongruous variety. Nāṭyam Bhinnarucher Janasya Bahudhapyekem Samaradhanam says Kālidāsa. In NŚ (Ch. I/106-112) many points have been given importance such as imparting of duty to those who are duty-conscious, love to those who seek fulfilment, meting out punishment to the unruly, illbred riffraffs and similar things. Amusement and entertainment is supposed to be the ultimate objective.

It is a universally accepted insipid and platitudinous truism that no one can please all the people of diverse characteristics and varying tastes. A man seeking to please all, pleases none. But this need not make a playwright pessimistic about success.

Ch 27/59-62 recognizes this aspect and suggests ways and means to cater to the tastes of different persons successfully. Persons of great culture and eduation are of the superior order and they are responsible for the proper reaction to success or otherwise* in regard to the deeper aspects of the Nāṭaka presented. Ordinary persons are more concerned with the superficial aspects. Taking all these things into consideration we can assert that social amusement is the *sin qua non* of a drama and therefore the average spectator strikes the keynote of that success, The ultimate court of appeal concerning the dramatic practice, as well as the administrative set up in a democracy is the layman.

The role of Vṛttis in the dramatic performance

Vṛttis or Styles are four in number. They are (a) Bhāratī where importance is given to the diction, the choice of words in the Pāṭhya portion or the dialogue. (b) the Sattavati, the style where there is exuberance of joy, display of strength, rise of the spirits etc. predominantly. (c) In the Arabhaṭi or the energetic style there is the presentation of bold persons indulging in bragging, deception and falsehood and (d) thc Kaiśiki is the graceful and charming presentation through women characters in colourful costumes indulging in dances and music. The themes are based on the practices of love and enjoyment thereof.

The Ten Types of Rūpakas

Discussion on the Vṛttis naturally takes us to the different types of dramatic representations such as Nāṭaka, Prakaraṇa etc. They are ten in number. The Uparūpakas are excluded. Chapter 20 explains the ten types of plays and later on the chapter discusses the different aspects of Lāsya or graceful dance.

1. *The Nāṭaka.* The play with a wellknown story for its theme and a Prakhyāta (renowned) person as the hero is called Nāṭaka. His exploits are superhuman. The number of Acts (Aṅkas) is between five and ten. The Act in the Indian Drama has no clearly defined and divided scenes. Certain Do's and don'ts are included in the presentation of a Nāṭaka explanatory devices are to be utilized to depict less important details as well as prohibited representation.

The Development of the Plot. The Kathāvastu (subject natter) of a Nāṭaka may be either Adhikārika (Principal) or Prasāṅgika (casual chance occurrence). The Adhikārika theme is consciously developed by the dramatist himself while in the Prasāṅgika the characters further the main purpose of the Nāyaka even while they go on acting in their own interest, of course in the casual way. (NS 21/2-5)

There are five stages in the progress of the main Kathāvastu where the Nāyaka exerts himself in his endeavour to attain the result. They are Ārambha (beginning) Prayatna, (endeavour), Prāptisambhāvanā (possibility of attainment), Niyatapti (certainty of the achievement) and Phalaprāpti (Actual realization of the purpose). These five stages have five corresponding Arthaprakṛtis (elements of the plot). They are (a) Bīja (seed) (b) Bindu (prominent point) (c) Ptaka (the episode) (d) Prakarī (episodial incident) and the Karya (denouement).

In addition to these two sets of five things with respect to the action and the central theme of the Nāṭaka its furtherance depends upon five more called the Pañcasandhis (five junctions). They are Mukha (opening), thh Pratimukha (counter opening) i e. further progression ; the womb, the development), the Vimarsha or Avamarsha (ponderance, reflection, pause) and the Nirvāhana (Accomplishment, conclusion). The writers on dramaturgy, after careful analysis of all existing important dramas of master playwrights who had established themselves in the field formulated these and additional rules to be followed by the later aspirants for the fame of good playwrights. They had anticipated all sorts of difficulties they may have to face and had provided detailed hints for the purpose of the management of the events of the play irrespective of the fact that they occur at shorter or longer intervals. Kālidāsa's Śākuntala is the best specimen.

Other types of Plays are Prakaraṇa, Samavakara, Ihamṛga, Dima, Vyayoga, Utsrishtikāṅka, Prahasana, Bhana and the Vithi. We are not examining these in detail here. Reference may be made to Sāhityadarpaṇa etc. the authorities on these matters. A short notice with the salient features is given below :

Prakaraṇa. Main differences in Prakaraṇa from Nāṭaka are (a) less elexated range (b) Kathāvastu is original, drawn from real life (c) a brahmin or a merchant should be the hero (d) female character, a courtezan or a woman of depraved nature. Some call this a bourgeoise comedy. Mricchakatika, Mālatimādhava etc, are good examples.

Samavakara. The Kathāvastu is mythological. consists of three Acts. The subject matter should depict deception, excitement or love. No wellknown specimen. The NŚ mentions of a Samavakara written by Brahma, the theme being Amṛtamathana. The Samudramāthana of Vatsaraja belongs to the 12th century. This is perhaps a piece of fragment of a drama, a dramatic spectacle. The cause of the extinction of earlier Samavakaras, if at all there had been is the production of better literary dramas of Kālidāsa and others.

Ihamṛga. It is a play of four Acts with well ordered construction. The main theme, love, causes discord among females. It can be said to be a play of intrigue concerning only gods and goddesses. No old specimen is available.

Dima This is restricted to four Acts. Hāsya and Śṛngāra Rasas are eschewed. Bhukampa (earthquake), Ulkāpāta (fall of meteors), eclipses, deceit, jugglery etc are the events portrayed. The Sattvati and Arabhati Vṛttis abound. Different types of gods, nāgas, Rākṣasas, Yakṣas and Pisācas constitute the characters. (Ch. 20/87-89)

Vyayoga. This is a one-Act play with a wellknown hero. A small number of female characters. Battle, personal combat, challenge and angry conflict are depicted. (20/90-92) Bhāsa's Madhyama Vyayoga is the best specimen.

Utsrishtikānka. This is also a one-Act play. This is a predominantly pathetic piece with Karuṇā Rasa. The plot is wellknown including only human characters. This depicts despondent lamentations of the bereaved women after the cessation of hostilities. The downfall and discomfiture of one of the warring personalities should be clearly brought out. Urubhanga of Bhāsa seems to he the solitary specimen of this type of play. Tragic details in this play are well appreciated by Sahridayas.

Prahasana. This is a farce with predominant Hāsya. Usually it has only one Act. The impropriety of the vulgar characters such as rogues, courtezans, Vita etc. should be clearly depicted.

Bhagavadajukiya and Mattavilāsa are the old specımens of Prabasana type.

Bhāṇa. The entire piece is constituted by the soliloquy of one of the characters. He is supposed to repeat the answers of the invisible persons to whom he had been putting questions regarding the adventures of some hero or vulgar character by way of erotic escapades. The collection Caturbhāṇi gives four such old Bhaṇās.

Vithi. This may be a monologue or duologue. Uttama, Madhyama and Adhama characters can be introduced as the author desires. This is also a very short one-Act play. No specimen of this type of Rūpaka is available.

Language of the plays and allied matters. In all the Rūpakas both Sanskrit and Prakṛt are used. Refined and cultured male characters use Sanskrit. Ladies of even noble families use only Prakrit. Vulgar characters like Vita etc. use Prakṛt. Hence the linguistic conditions of the society when these dramas were written and staged is reflected.

Use of poetical pieces is allowed. There is restriction only on long compounds. obscure words etc. not intelligible to the laymen. Chapter 15 in NŚ deals with the different metres with specimens for the same.

Certain practical aspects regarding the staging of Dramas. Dramatic performances in India can trace their origin to religious rites and festivals. The early beginnings might have been dances and songs of eulogy by way of honouring Śiva and other deities. Śiva as the presiding Deity of dance is well known as Naṭarāja. His Tāṇḍava dance is described by many poets.

In course of time the range of subject matter might have been extended beyond the exploits of the deities concerned and the legends centring round those deities. Naturally the next step was the bold experiment with secular themes necessitating the loosening of the original affinities and dependence on the deities. Strong dosage of religious devotion and piety gave way to modes of moral edification and eagerness for aesthetic enjoyment. In those days the important plays never descenced to the level of means of vulgar amusement of everyday life. The occasion for the dramatic performance was usually some religious festival, the coronation of a king, celebration of his victory over ememies or some such important event in the life of the people. As in modern days there used to be competitions in the dramatic performances among rival dramatic troupes.

Diverse types of Playhouses. The various types of playhouse, their different parts and other details are mentioned in NS (Ch. 2) Whether the dramas were staged in the olden days in the specially constructed stages or in improvised ones with some semblance of a convenient place to demonstrate the histrionic skill of the actors and actresses is yet to be decided. Scholars differ from one another in this connection. Ordinary persons could not have afforded the expenses involved in constructing a playhouse answering to the specifications of NŚ. Only the kings and the rich gentry could own these playhouses. Of course Nāṭya Mandiras were in vogue. These were open halls in front of the temples or temporary structures with covering canopy and dramatic spectacles intended for the laymen were held in them.

In view of the fact that the audience in those days could not have been in such large numbers as now, NŚ envisages an ordinary playhouse that could have accommodated only about five hundred people. The smallness of the theatre may also be due to the special characteristics of the dramatic production technique. The utterances and the delicate sounds made by the players could not be heard if the theatre were very large, Mikes and other modern appliances had never been known then or even thought of and it is in the audibility of these that the success of the production depended. The readers are referred to the Chapter 2 for **further** elucidation in this regard.

The Representation. The technique of representation can be best understood if we bear in mind that stark realism is avoided by the ancient dramatists. They gave imagination and fancy utmost scope. Total absence of painted scenery from the stage is significant; but positive efforts to depict Rasa through suggestive use of colour in the costume etc. makes up for that want. The fourfold representation such as Āṅgika, Vāchika, Āhaṛya and Sāttvika should be studied carefully. (Ch. 6 to 12)

Theory and Practice of Music. The fine art of Music had been cultivated in India from time immemorial and the perfection reached by the Indians in this art has always been the wonder and the envy of the entire world. Volumes and volumes have been written about it. Hence it will be enough if we simply say that the entire edifice of the glory of India in Music rests on the foundation laid down in NŚ. The Gandharva Upaveda belongs to the Sāma Veda. The Ch. 28 to 33 have been devoted to a detailed survey. No further analysis thereof is necessary in this Introduction as the text is adequately illuminative.

1

The Origin of Drama[1]

1 I bow to the grandfather of the world (Brahmā) and the great lord Śiva and proceed to propound the Nāṭya Śāstra (the science of gesticulation and dance originally imparted by Brahmā).

The plea of the Sages

2—5 Formerly Ātreya and other noblesouled sages with great control over their sense organs approached the righteous Bharata the master of the science of drama and dance at the time when they had a short respite from studies. The sage had just concluded his Japa (repetition of holy names and utterance of prayers) and his sons too were with him. They asked him with great respect—"How did Nāṭya Veda on a par with the Śrutis originate? O Brahman, verily you had propounded it. For whom is that Science intended? How many parts does it have? What is its magnitude and how are we to apply the same? Kindly bless us with the full details.

Bharata replies

6 On hearing the request of the sages Bharata began to explain the Nāṭya Veda thus.

7 "Let the origin of the Nāṭya Veda evolved by Brahmā be heard by you all after being pure and attentive ?"

8—11 O Brahmins, the Manvantara of Svāyambhuva passed by and (later on) the Kṛtayuga of Vaivasvata Manu too passed. (Thereafter) when the Tretāyuga arrived people became victims of lust and covetousness, and were engaged in Rustic rites and activities, overwhelmed by jealousy and deluded by wrath, experiencing happiness and misery. When the Jambūdvīpa was over run by the Devas, Dānavas, Gandharvas, Yakṣas, **Rākṣasas** and great serpents it became well established by the guardians of the worlds (i.e. Indra and others) when

Mahendra and other leading Devas submitted to Pitāmaha—"We wish to have a pastime than shall simultaneously be visual as well as auditory."

12 The Vedic discussion and practice cannot be proclaimed among those born of the Śūdra caste. Hence evolve another Veda common to all the Varṇas (castes).

13 After saying to them "Let it be so" he dismissed the king of the Devas. Conversant with all principles he made use of the yogic power and recollected the four vedas.

14—16 The divine being resolved thus—"I shall evolve this Veda entitled Nāṭya Veda along with its historical basis. It shall be conducive to righteousness, production of wealth and diffusion of fame; it will have succinct collection of didactic material; it will serve as a guide in all (human) activities of future generations as well; it will be richly endowed with the topics dealt with in all the scriptural texts and it will demonstrate all types of arts and crafts." Fully recalling to his mind all the Vedas after this resolution the holy lord created Nāṭya Veda born out of the four Vedas and their ancillaries.

17 He took the Pāṭhyam (recitals) from the Ṛgveda, Gītam (music) from the Sāmans; Abhinayas (histrionic and gestural representation) from the Yajurveda and the Rasas (sentiments) from the Atharvaveda.

18 In this manner the charmingly graceful Nāṭya Veda having its origin and connection with the Vedas and Upavedas was evolved by the noble souled holy being Brahmā.

19—20 After evolving the Nāṭya Veda, the Creator instructed Indra as follows—"Historical legend has been got ready by me. Put it to practical use among the Suras. May this Nāṭya Veda be passed on to those among them who are proficient, shrewd, mature and indefatigable."

21 On hearing what has been mentioned by Brahmā, lord Śakra joined his palms in reverence, bowed down to Brahmā and replied thus.

22 "O divine Sir, the Devas are unworthy of the theoretical art because they are incapable of receiving, retaining, comprehending and putting it into practice."

23 These are the sages conversant with the esoteric mystery

of the Vedas and perfect in the observance of holy vows. They alone are capable of receiving, retaining and putting it into practical use.

24 On hearing the words of Śakra the lotus born lord said to me—"O sinless one, accompanied by your hundred sons you shall be the one putting this art to practical purpose."

25 Thus commanded I studied Nāṭya Veda from Pitāmaha and taught it to my worthy sons along with its proper practical application.

Names of the Sons of Bharata

26—39 The sons are Śāṇḍilya, Vātsya, Kohala, Dattila, Jaṭila, Ambaṣṭaka, Taṇḍu, Agniśikha, Saindhava, Puloman, Śāḍvali, Vipula, Kapiñjali, Bādari, Yama, Dhūmrāyaṇa, Jambudhvaja, Kākajaṅgha, Svarṇaka, Tāpasa, Kedāra, Śālikarṇa, Dīrghagātra, Śālika, Kautsa, Tāṇḍāyani, Piṅgala, Citraka (or Chatraka), Bandhula, Bhallaka (Bhaktaka), Muṣṭika (Muṣṭīka or Musṭhika), Saindhavāyana, Taitila, Bhārgava, Śuci, Bahula, Abudha, Budhasena, Pāṇḍukarṇa, Kerala, (Sukerala), Ṛjuka, Maṇḍaka, Śambara, Vañjula, Māgadha, Sarala, Kartar,Ugra, Tuṣāda, (Tuṣāra), Pārṣada, Gautama, Bādarāyaṇa (Bādarāyaṇi), Viśāla, Śabala, Sunābha (Sunālī), Meṣa, Kāliya, Bhramara, Pīṭhamukha, Muni, Nakhakuṭṭa, Aśmakuṭṭa, Ṣaṭpada, Uttama, Pāduka, Upānat, Śruti (Śrutika), Cāṣasvara (Ṣaṭsvara). Agnikuṇḍa, Ājyakuṇḍa, Vitaṇḍya, Tāṇḍya, Kartarākṣa, Hiraṇyākṣa, Kuśala, Duḥsaha, Jāla (Lāja), Bhayānaka, Bībhatsa, Vicakṣaṇa, Puṇḍrākṣa, Puṇḍranāsa (Pūrṇanāsa), Asita, Sita, Vidyujjihva, Mahājihva, Śālaṅkāyana, Śyāmāyana, Māṭhara, Lohitāṅga, Saṁvartaka, Pañcaśikha, Triśikha, Śikha, Śaṅkhavarṇamukha, Ṣaṇḍa, Śaṅkukarṇa, Śakranemi, Gabhasti, Aṁśumāli, Śaṭha, Vidyut, Śātajaṅgha, Raudra and Vīra.

40 At the bidding of Brahmā the hundred sons were engaged by me in such of the roles as suited them. My idea was to see that the people are benefited by it.

Three Styles at the outset

41—42 Every one was engaged in that activity where he was found most suitable.

O Brahmins, theatrical performance based on the three Vṛttis (Dramatic style) viz. Bhāratī (verbal utterance), Sāttvatī

(Grand conception of the mind) and Ārabhaṭī (Vigorous physical activity). Approaching and bowing down to him I submitted to Brahmā about my activity.

43 Then the leader of the Sikas said to me—"Add Kaiśikī too (the charmingly graceful). O excellent brahmin, tell me the material befitting it."

44 I had been asked thus. The lord then was replied to by me—"O holy sir, may the material contributory to the performance of Kaiśiki be given to me.

45—46 I have witnessed the Kaiśikī style during the dance of the blue-throated lord. It consists of Mṛdu Aṅgahāras (gentle gesticulation and movements of the limbs). Rasa (sentiment) Bhāva (states) and Kriyā (activity) constitute its soul. The dress should be charmingly beautiful and the erotic sentiment is its basis. It cannot be adequately portrayed by men. Excepting women none can practise it properly.

47 Then the highly resplendent lord mentally created the celestial damsels who were extremely proficient in heightening the beauty and charm of the dramatic art and dance performance. He then gave them to me for the purpose of performance.

The names of the celestial damsels

48—50 Mañjukeśī, Sukeśī, Miśrakeśī, Sulocanā, Saudāminī, Devadattā, Devasenā. Manoramā, Sudatī, Sundarī, Vidagdhā, Vividhā, Budhā, Sumālā, Santati, Sunandā, Sumukhī, Māgadhī, Arjunī, Saralā, Keralā, Dhṛti, Nandā, Supuṣkalā, Supuṣpamālā and Kalabhā.

Svāti and Nārada to assist Bharata

51 Along with his disciples Svāti was engaged by the self-born lord on the musical instruments Nārada and other Gandharvas were engaged in the Nāṭya Yoga (activity of dance) and Gāna Yoga (in singing songs).

52—53 After being convinced that this Bhāva Nāṭya (dramatic art and gesticulation of emotions) had been perfected because it is based on the Vedas and Vedāṅgas I approached the lord of the worlds (Brahmā) accompanied by all my sons as well as Svāti and Nārada with joined palms for the purpose of demonstrating it. "The dramatic art has been acquired. Tell me what shall I do?"

54–55 On hearing these words, Pitāmaha said—"A grand occasion for the production of the play has arrived. Here the festival of the flag of Mahendra is going on. May this Nāṭya Veda be produced here now."

The first production of a dramatic performance

56–58 In that festival of flagstaff boosting the victory of Mahendra after the annihilation of Asuras and Dānavas, when the delighted Amaras (Devas) had assembled in large numbers the Nāndī (Benedictory utterances) consisting of words of blessings having the eight fold aspects was made by me. It got the approval of the Devas because of the novelty and variety of the details in the depiction of the Daityas, being defeated by the Suras in the fight wherein the mutual. Cutting and wounding (of the soldiers) the angry and tumultuous altercations and challenges are also portrayed.

59 Brahmā and other Devas were delighted with the performance.

The Delighted Devas after gifts

60—62 Delighted in their minds they gave us all sorts of requisite articles by way of gift. At the outset the delighted Śakra gave away his splendid banner. Brahmā gave the Kamaṇḍalu (water pot) and Varuṇa a gold pot. Sūrya gave the umbrella; Śiva fulfil of desires; the wind god a fan; Viṣṇu the royal throne and Kubera a crown.

63—65 Goddess Sarasvatī bestowed the quality of audibility to what is to be seen, the remaining ones viz. the Devas, the Gandharvas, the Yakṣas, Rākṣasas and serpents in the assembly gave the sensitive feelings (Bhāvas), sentiments (Rasa), good form and the activity of a powerful (hero), all these intended (to be portrayed) based on different classes and possessing different qualities. Thus the performance portraying the slaughter of the Dānavas and the Daityas began.

Virūpākṣa and the Vighnas working havoc

The Daityas who had gatecrashed into the place of performance became excited. In citing the Vighnas (malignants spirits) creating obstacles under the leadership of Virūpākṣa, they said—"Come away. We don't like this dramatic peformance in this manner."

66 The evil Vighnas accompanied by the Asuras adopted the fraudulent power of Māyā and rendered the power of motion, memory and speech of the dancing players.

67—68 On seeing this affliction of the actors Indra said "Whence is this obstacle in the performance?" and began reflecting on it. Thereupon he perceived that the Sūtradhāra (stage manager) had been surrounded by the Vighnas along with the others and struck senseless and motionless.

69—70 He rose up angrily weilding the banner staff that dazzled brilliantly with the jewels set in them. With this Jarjara (banner) in his hand Indra looked ahead rolling his eyes and smote the Asuras and the Vighnas hovering round the stage (evidently for creating trouble) and beat them to death.

71—73 The Devas were extremely delighted all the death of the Dānavas and the Vighnas. They said—"Luckily (O Bharata) you have a divine weapon with which these mischief mongers disturbing the performance have been made Jarjara (smashed to smithereens). Hence this will be known by the name Jarjara

74 The rest of the hostile gang too will merit the same if they are to come here with violent intention.

Thereupon Indra said joyously to the gods—"May it be so, this Jarjara shall be a guarding spell and charm to all the players."

75—76 (Later) the play was resumed as the festivities of Indra gathered momentum when the surviving Vighnas began to strike terror and even intended to murder me.

77—78 On seeing these frequent attempts of the Daityas insulting to me I approached Brahmā along with my sons. I said—"O holy Sir, lord of the Suras, the Vighnas are bent upon the destruction of the dramatic display. Hence be pleased to instruct me as to how to accord protection to this."

79 "O fair one of highly perfect intelligence" said Brahmā to Viśvakarman "erect a dramatic hall endowed with all good characteristics."

Viśvakarman builds the dramatic hall

80—81 After erecting the playhouse in accordance with the instruction of the lotus born lord, Viśvakarman went to the assembly of Brahmā with palms joined in reverence (and said)—"O lord, the dramatic chamber is ready. It behoves you to have a look thereat."

Afterwards Brahmā hastened to the dramatic chamber to view it in the company of Mahendra and a chosen few of the best among the Suras.

Arrangement for the protection of the playhouse

82—88 After inspecting the playhouse Brahmā said to all the Suras—"This pavilion of dance and dramatic performance should be protected by you all taking up the responsibility of the different parts severally. The moon god will protect the main building, the guardians of the worlds the different sides, the wind gods the four corners, Varuṇa the interior, Mitra the green room, the fire god shall protect the altar; the clouds will guard the musical instruments; the four Varṇas have been engaged in the protection of the pillars, the Rudras and the Ādityas shall stay in the interstices of the pillars; the rows of the seats should be guarded by the spirits and the apartments by the celestial damsels. The Yakṣiṇīs shall be present in the entire house; the great sea shall guard the ground surface; Yama is employed in the entrance door. The powerful serpent kings shall guard the Dvāra Pārśva (the sides of the entry way), the staff of Yama shall be in the threshold and the trident shall be placed at the top.

89—93 Niyati and Mṛtyu were assigned the post of door keepers. Indra himself occupied the stage-side; the Mattavāraṇī was in the protection of the Vidyut (lightning) efficient in the annihilation of the Daityas. The powerful Bhūtas, Yakṣas, Piśācas and the Guhyakas were assigned the responsibility of guarding the pillars of the Mattavāraṇī.

In the Jarjara (Flagstaff) Vajra (Thunderbolt) was posted because it could curb the Daityas. The powerful gods were posted at the sections. Brahmā occupied its top portion, Śiva the second, Viṣṇu the third, Kārtikeya the fourth and the Nāgas Śeṣa, Vāsuki and Takṣa the fifth portion.

…is manner the Devas were assigned different …e Jarjar for dispelling the Vighnas. Brahmā occupied …entre of the stage. Hence flowers are regularly scattered there (before the performance starts).

95 The responsibility for the protection of the bottom of the stage was assigned to the residents of the Pātāla such as the Guhyakas, Yakṣas and and the Pannagas (Serpents).

96 May the actor who adopts the role of the Nāyaka (hero) be under the protection of Indra. Goddess Sarasvatī shall protect the actress in the heroine's role; Lord Oṁkāra shall protect the Vidūṣaka the jester and Lord Śiva shall protect the other characters in the play.

97 Brahmā further said that these gods would be the respective guardian deities.

The Vighnas pacified

98—99 The gods approached Brahmā collectively and said—"Method of conciliation should be used to subdue the Vighnas. It has to be used at the outset, secondly, offering of gifts should be applied; (In case this method is not effective) creating dissension among the **antagonists.** Only thereafter shall one employ **meting** out punishment directly for subduing them."

100 On hearing these words of the Suras, Brahmā addressed the Vighnas thus—'Why are you inclined to spoil the dramatic display?"

101—103 On being asked by Brahmā thus Virūpākṣa, the Daityas and the Vighnas said consolingly—"The Nāṭya Veda, introduced by you all at the request of the Suras has become adverse to us. You have done so to favour the gods. You are the grandfather, the progenitor of the gods as well as the Daityas. Hence you should not have done so.

104—105 When Virūpākṣa protested thus Brahmā replied—"Do not be angry, O Daityas. Do not have any grief too. This Nāṭya Veda has been evolved to portray both the good and the bad things that befall all whether gods or Daityas.

Characteristic features of the dramatic art

106 Being the representation of the states of all the worlds it does not exclusively depict Daityas or the gods.

107 In it there is reference to Dharma (piety), Artha (wealth), peace, laughter, fighting and even slaughtering. Lovemaking too is depicted.

108—109 The drama teaches the path of Virtue to those who carry on their duty; the modes of love to those eager to get it fulfilled; it admonishes the uncivilized and the ill natured ones.; encourages self control of those who are amenable to discipline; makes the coward bold; the heroic ones are given more incentives, the men of poor intellect are enlightened and the wisdom of the learned is enhanced.

110 The play entertains kings and the affluent ones, those who are sorrowing can receive solace therefrom; those who want to acquire wealth can understand ways and means thereof; and men who become agitated can derive composure and comfort from it.

111—112 Imitation of the conduct of the people full of emotional fervour while depicting different situations is the main item in the type of drama evolved by me. All sorts of people whether good or bad have been represented in it, in order to accord encouragement, amusement and pleasure along with sound advice to everyone.

113 Thus the play becomes an agent for educating people through the Bhāvas and Kriyās found depicted therein, through the Rasas expressed and implied.

114—115 Persons of bad fortune can overcome their afflictions due to sorrow and surmount the fatigue of over work and strain. Thereby the art of drama is conducive to the observance of duty, acquisition of fame, long life, intellect, all round good and learning in every aspect.

116 No wise utterance, no means to achieve learning, no art or craft and no useful device is omitted or ignored in it.

117—118 All the branches of learning find a place in the drama devised by me; different arts and actions converge therein. Hence O Daityas; do not become offended with the Suras because imitation of everything taking place in the world of seven continents is an invariable feature of the Dramatic art.

119 Vedic anecdotes, stories from Itihāsas and other sources are so utilised as to give pleasure to those who witness. This is the beauty of drama.

120—121 A close imitation of the gods, daityas, kings, householders etc. and their day-to-day activities represented through gestures etc. is called drama.

Adoration and flaral offerings

122—123 Brahmā then said to the gods—In the playhouse you must have adoration with offerings, performance of Homas with Mantras and Japas and Naivedyas (food offerings) should consist of all types of foodstuffs hard and soft.

124 There shall be a happy adoration of the world. The dramatic performance shall not be held without the stage-adoration.

125 He who conducts the dramatic performance without floral offerings and adoration will find his knowledge ineffective. He is likely to be reborn as a lower animal.

126 Producers of plays of entertainment shall not conduct them without a previous offering of Pūjās to the presiding deities of the stage. This is on a par with the Vedic Yajña.

127 Whether it is the Nartaka (dancer) or the Arthapati (lord of wealth), if he does not perform the Pūjā himself or through others he is found to sustain loss as a result of the omission.

128 Those who offer the adoration in accordance with conventions shall definitely attain splendid wealth and heavenly pleasures later.

129 Then Brahmā and the gods said to me—"May everything be thus. Offer the Pūjā to the stage.

NOTES

1 Obeisance is usually made to Vighneśvara for the purpose of getting obstacles eradicated. The favourite deity of the authors concerned is also **invoked** In this work Pitāmaha (Brahmā) and Maheśvara are bowed to because these two deities are closely associated with the science of dance. Lord Śiva is the primordial Naṭarāja (king of dancers) and Brahmā is the author of Nāṭya Veda.

2—6 The sages Ātreya and others approach Bharata on an Anadhyāya day when there will be enough time for a detailed discussion.

7—12 Fourteen Manvantaras constitute one day of Brahmā. Svāyambhuva is the first Manvantara. The Manvantara current now is Vaivasvata the seventh. There are seventy one sets of four Yugas in a Manvantara. The Yugas are Kṛta (or Satya), Tretā, Dvāpara and Kali. There is no Nāṭya performance in the Kṛta Yoga for it is a period free from all miseries and worries. Tretā Yuga is a period when there is happiness and misery. The purpose of Nāṭya is to dispel worries and derive pleasure.

Nāṭya Veda as composed by Brahmā is reputed to have contained 36000 verses. An abridged first version composed by Ādibharata is of 12000 verses. These two works are not available now. The present available text of Nāṭya Śāstra contains more than five thousand verses and some prose passages.

26—39 Hundred and old sons of Bharata—Many of these names are identical with those of some later authors on dramaturgy and allied topics such as Dattila, Śāṇḍilya, Vātsya, Kohala, Śālikaraṇa (Śātakarṇa), Bādarāyaṇa, Nakhakuṭṭa, Aśmakuṭṭa. Another thing to be noted in this connection is the very names of some of them give a veiled indication of the fact that some of them might have been specialists in some of the branches of dramaturgy.

41—43 The Vṛttis four in number refer to various activities such as all verbal activities fall within the jurisdiction of Bhāratī, mental activities in that of Sāttavatī and physical activities in that of Ārabhaṭī. The next one Kaiśikī Vṛtti functions in the domain of beauty in as much as it increases the sweetness of the Nāṭya adding grace and charm as well.

46—50 The creation of the celestial damsels is probably because the maidens among the Munis are too chaste to stoop to such display of voluptuous physical charms.

58 - 61 We follow the reading Kamaṇḍalu instead of Kuṭilaka.

78—79 Viśvakarman is the architect of the gods is frequently referred to in almost all classic Sanskrit literature. The deity of that name found mentioned in the Vedas also is to be taken into consideration.

101—103 The name Virūpākṣa referring to a demon occurs in the Rāmāyaṇa of Vālmīki. As an appellation of Śiva it is very frequently used in Sanskrit.

The *gist of the topics dealt* with in the First chapter.

The poet composing the literary piece for depiction in dance or drama should have the qualities and abilities of Brahmā the creator of the universe; the sponsor of the dramatic performance as well as the stage manager should be a man of organizing ability like Indra; the dramatic preceptor should be as versatile as Bharata himself; the sons of Bharata viz. Śāṇḍilya and others should the ideal for the ordinary actors; the celestial damsels for the women participants; the expert in charge of the musical instruments should have the vast knowledge, experience and ability of Svāti, the officer in charge of the music section should be like Nārada, it is the duty of the organizers of dramatic performance to accord all safeguards and means of security so that the performance concludes without any disturbance, occasions of jubilation should be utilized for the performance of dramas and dance items; the people who visit the theatre should not have prejudices this way or that way; they must have the full aesthetic sense in order to rise above petty personal gains or losses. Finally Raṅga Pūjā is an essential item in a society that meticulously follows the noble ideals of the Vedic seers of Mantras and philosophers irrespective of the schools of Darśana they may be specially interested in.

2

Characteristics of the Playhouse

1—2 On hearing the words of sage Bharata, the other sages said—"Holy sir, we would like to hear about the ceremonial offerings at the stage. Men of the future should have an idea of the adoration and similar practices connected thereto which is possible only after an accurate description.

3 Hence be kind enough to describe the playhouse wherein the protection of the play is to take place.

Three types of playhouse

4 On hearing their words Bharata replied—"O holy ones, listen to the description of the playhouse and the details of the floral offerings in this context."

5—6 In regard to houses and gardens the creations of gods are mental but those of men should necessarily be guided by rules and injunctions of the Śāstras. Hence, listen to the mode of erecting playhouses and the details of Pūjās and flora offerings at the place of building.

7—8 As devised by the intelligent architect of the gods there are three types of playhouses viz. Vikṛṣṭa (Rectangular) Caturaśra (square) and Tryāśra (triangular).

Dimensions

9—11 The sizes of these playhouses are various—very large, medium ones or small ones. The lengths may be 108, 64 or thirty two Hastas (30 cms) or Daṇḍas (120 cms). The corresponding widths may be had suitably. The large variety of playhouses are intended for gods, the medium ones for royal personages and the small sized ones for the ordinary people.

Details of measurements

12—16 Listen now to the details of the measurements as

laid down by Viśvakarman. The different units are—Aṇu, Raja, Bāla, Likṣā, Yūkā, Yava, Aṅgula, Hasta and Daṇḍa.

Eight Aṇus make one Raja.
,, Rajas ,, ,, Bāla
,, Bālas ,, ,, Likṣā
,, Likṣās ,, ,, Yūkā
,, Yūkās ,, ,, Yava
,, Yavas ,, ,, Aṅgula

Twenty four Aṅgulas make one Hasta.
Four Hastas ,, ,, Daṇḍa.

Based on this table of measurements. I shall describe the different types of playhouses.

Mortal playhouses

17 The rectangular playhouses intended for human beings should be sixty four Hastas long and thirty two Hastas in width.

Disadvantage of bigger playhouses are—

18—19 A playhouse bigger than this size shall not be erected because the play staged therein cannot be adequately expressive. Passages recited in large playhouses will lose the euphony. Thereby they may be indistinct.

20 Besides this the facial expression of the actors loses its distinct visibility when the playhouse is too big. It is in the facial expression that the representation of Bhāvas and Rasas depends.

21 Hence we wish the playhouses to be of medium size to facilitate the easy audition of the recited passages and sung songs.

22—23 In regard to houses and gardens, the creations of gods are mental but those of men should be well thought of and implemented in accordance with the Śāstras. Hence men should not compete with the gods. Therefore I shall now describe the characteristics of a playhouse suited for human activity.

Suitable sites

24 The adept in the art of building proceeds to examine the plot of land at the outset and then to measure the site.

25 The soil should be plain, firm, hard and black or white for the purpose of erecting the playhouse.

26 The ground should be cleared neatly. Then it should be ploughed well. Bones, pegs, potsherds, shrubs etc. should be removed.

Measurement

27 After clearing the ground the builder measures the site.

28 On a day with the Puṣya star the builder spreads a piece of white string of cotton, wool, Muñjā grass or the bark of a tree.

The string should not snap

29—31 A string that will not easily snap should be used for this purpose. If the string breaks into two pieces in the middle the sponsor of the dramatic performance will meet with his death. If the string snaps at a third of its length some political upheaval is bound to occur in the land. If it snaps at a fourth of its length the Nāṭyācārya (the preceptor) will die. If the string slips down some kind of loss is indicated. Hence the string is handled with great care. There shall be scrupulousness in the activity of measurement.

32—33 The measurement should be done when the moment is auspicious in regard to Tithi (lunar day) and Karaṇa (lunar conjunction). The **Brahmins** should be propitiated and the Puṇyāha Mantra should be recited.

Site plan

34—35 The builder then measures a plot of land sixty four Hastas long. This shall be divided into two equal parts. He shall then divide portion behind him into two equal parts. The hinder most of these two is again divided into two. One of these two is the stage proper and the other is the green room (Nepathya).

Foundation stone laying

36—37 After the division and measurement of the plot in accodance with the requisite rules, the builder should lay the foundation stone of the dramatic house when different kinds of musical instruments should be played such as Mṛdaṇga, Paṇava, Dundubhi and Śaṅkha.

38 All undesirable persons such as heretics Śramaṇas, recluses in ochre coloured robes and men with physical handicaps should be sent away from the places where the ceremonies are conducted.

39 During the night, offerings are made to the gods guarding the quarters, consisting of sweet scents, flowers, fruits and foodstuffs of diverse kinds.

40—41 The offerings made in the east consist of white cooked rice; of blue colour in the case of south; yellow in regard to the west and red in the case of the north. While making the offerings the requisite Mantras are to be uttered in regard to the deity presiding over the different quarters.

42 Ghee and milk pudding should be given to scholarly Brahmins at the time of the foundation laying ceremony; Madhuparka (honey etc. mixed together) to the royal personages and rice with treacle to the action participants.

43 The foundation stone should be lend during the auspicious lunar day with the constellation Mūla.

Erection of Pillars

44—45 The foundation stone having been duly laid the architect proceeds to build the walls and erection of pillars in an auspicious Tithi and excellent Karaṇa with an excellent asterism. Rohiṇi or Śravaṇa are the usual asterisms for this purpose.

46 The preceptor of dramatic art fasts for three days and nights with great faith and then erects the pillars at dawn when the auspicious moment arrives.

47—50 All the articles used in the ceremony regarding the Brahamin pillar are to be white in colour after purifying them with ghee and mustard seed. Brahmins should be offered milk pudding.

In regard to the Kṣatriya pillar the ceremony ought to be performed with red coloured cloth, garlands and unguents. Treacle-mixed cooked rice should be offered to the Brahmins. The erection of Vaiśya pillar is in the north-western quarter of the dramatic house with yellow articles. Brahmins are to be fed with rice mixed with ghee. The Śūdra pillar is erected in the north eastern quarter with offerings of blue articles. Kṛśara is offered to the Brahmins at that time.

51—53 At the outset white garlands and unguents and a piece of gold from an ear ornament are thrown at the foot of the Brahmin pillar. Copper, silver and iron are respectively to be thrown at the feet of the three other pillars. Gold piece also thrown at the feet of the other pillars.

54 Puṇyāha and Svasti Vācana ceremonies precede the placing of the pillars round which green leaves-garlands are tied.

55—57 Brahmins are propitiated with adequate gifts of jewels, cows and cloths. Thereafter the pillars are raised and fixed to prevent them from shaking, turning round or even moving slightly. If this is not so evil results follow. If a pillar after being fixed were to move the land will be afflicted by drought. If the pillar turns round fear of death befalls the person concerned. If it were to shake the land may be attacked by enemies. Hence pillar fixation should be performed with due care avoiding these.

58—60 As regards the sacred Brahmin Pillar a Dakṣiṇā (monetary gift) of a cow is given to the Brahmin and in the case of the other pillars the builders should be sumptuously fed. The Nāṭyācārya offers ghee purified with Mantra and he is also fed with Kṛsara and salt.

61—63 After scrupulously following these the participants in the ceremony sound the musical instruments the pillars are raised uttering the following Mantra—"Just as the Meru mountain cannot be shaken and the Himālaya remains firm so also thou shalt remain unmoveable ushering in the victory of the king."

Similarly the clever artisans shall erect pillars, doors, walls and the green room in accordance with the injunctions.

The Mattavārṇī

64—65 On either side of the stage a Mattavārṇī (side room) is built furnished with four pillars. It is as long as the stage and its plinth is one and a half Hastas high. The Raṅgamaṇḍala is of equal height with the two Mattavāraṇīs.

61—67 At the time of building these Bhūtas are to be offered garlands, incense, sweet scent, cloths of diverse colours etc. agreeable to them.

In order to ensure the steadiness of the pillars a piece of iron is placed below them. Brahmins are fed with Kṛsara and other items. These rules are to be scrupulously followed in building Mattavāraṇīs.

The Stage

68 Raṅgapīṭha (stage) should be constructed following the rules. There are six pieces of wood in the Raṅgaśīrṣa (stage head).

69—71 The green room is furnished with two doors. The ground marked for the stage is to be filled with black earth assiduously. No stone chip, gravel or grass should be mixed therein. Ploughing the place with a ploughshare yoked with two white draught cattle ensures this. Earth is to be carried in new baskets. All the workers engaged in these activities should be free from defects in their limbs.

72—74 The entire stage head is to be very carefully constructed. It should not resemble the convex backs of the fish or a tortoise. The ground shall be as flat and level as the surface of a mirror. Expert builders take care to lay underneath the stage head jewels and precious stones viz. diamond in the east, lapis lazuli in the south, crystals in the vest and Coral in the north. The central part is laid with gold.

Ornamental work over the stage

75—80 After the construction of the plinth of the stage, carefully throughout and planned wood work decoration should be arranged for consisting of ornamental designs, carved figures of animals such as elephants, tigers etc., and wooden statues. Niryūhas (a type of ornamental figurine) rows of good seats, latticed windows, numerous dovecots etc. should be fixed in the different parts of the floor. After the wood work is over the builders give a furnishing touch to the walls. It should be remembered that the pillars, brackets, windows, corners or doorways should be such as do not face the doors.

81—82 The playhouse should resemble a mountain-cave and consist of two floors of different levels with small windows. Too much of wind should not blow in it. It must enhance the acoustic quality so that the sound of the musical instruments and the utterances of the actors are perfectly audible.

83–85 After finishing the construction of the walls the plaster work and white washing must be undertaken. The plaster and lime should be smeared carefully. Thereafter painting work must be undertaken. Men, women, creepers, love play of folks etc. should be painted. In this manner the play house of the rectangular type is constructed (Vikṛṣṭa).

The Square house

86–92 Now the characteristics of the Caturaśra type of playhouse shall be described. A plot of land thirty two Hastas square is measured out on an auspicious moment. The playhouse is then constructed there by experts in the art of drama. Rules, definitions and ceremonies by way of propitiating deities etc. mentioned before hold good in the case of the square type too. It should be an exact square divided into the requisite parts by means of the measuring string. Strong bricks are to be used for the construction of the outer walls. They are to be set together very thickly. Inside the stage ten pillars are to be raised in the relevant directions. They should be capable of supporting the roof. Externally to the pillars seats are constructed in the form of galleries with brick and wood in order to accommodate the audience comfortably. Successive rows of seats are each one Hasta higher than the one before. The lowest row is one Hasta higher than the ground. These seats shall overlook the stage.

92–95 Inside the playhouse six more pillars strong enough to support the roof are ceremoniously raised. Eight more pillars are raised by their side. The plinth of the Raṅgapītha shall be eight Hastas square. More pillars are then raised in order to support the roof of the playhouse. Proper fastners are to be used to fix the pillars to the roof. They are then decorated with figurines (Śālabhañjikās).

96—100 Then the green room is to be constructed scrupulously. One door leads to the stage. The actors enter the stage through this door with their faces towards the audience. There must be another door facing the auditorium. The stage is eight Hastas square. Elevated plinth with plain surface is furnished. The Mattavaraṇī should be made in accordance with the injunctions laid down before on either side of the Raṅgapītha.

The stage can be equal to the plinth in height or somewhat elevated. In the case of the rectangular playhouse the plinth shall be higher than the stage. In the case of the square type the heights of both are equal to each other. These are the rules governing the square type of playhouse.

Triangular playhouse

101—104 Now the details of the characteristics of a Tryaśra type of playhouse are mentioned. The playhouse is built with three corners. The stage therein is also triangular. One of the doors is in a corner of the playhouse and the other should be at the back of the stage. Rules regarding the pillars and walls are the same in the case of triangular playhouses and square playhouses. These are the rules regarding the construction of playhouses. I shall now describe the propitiatory rites.

NOTES

The main topics dealt with in the II Chapter are as follows— Description of the playhouse in every detail beginning with the selection of the site and ending with the picturesque embelishments of the walls, ceilings etc. has been masterfully dealt with in this chapter. We find the description of three main types of Nāṭyagṛha viz. Vikṛṣṭa (rectangular), the Caturaśra (square in shape) and Tryaśra (triangular in shape). Each of these can be further divided into three in as much as it is large, medium or small. A large one has 108 Hastas for its length. A medium one sixty four Hastas and a small one thirty two Hastas. Instead of Hastas if the measurements is taken in as many Daṇḍas then we have eighteen different types of playhouses. Of course the large ones have been prohibited for performances intended for human beings. The selection of the site is very important. The soil shall be plain, firm and hard. The colour may be black or white laying of the foundation is very important. The pillars of the playhouse should be erected after due religious rites. Pillars representative of the different Varṇas and their different colours— Mattavāraṇī or side rooms. Their size and the adoration thereof. Then the construction of the Raṅgapīṭha (actual stage), Nepathya (green room) and the embelishments to be effected in the stage etc.

8-11 Meant for gods, kings and the rest of the people—Two interpretations are possible. Either the characters of the play are meant by the author or the spectators. The former seems to be more suitable. In Ḍima and other types of dramas where the Devas and demons are the characters ample space is essential for the purpose of their fighting, running about etc. to be represented suitably. Hence the large play-house of 108 Hastas or Daṇḍas.

20 Āsya Gato Rāgo Bhāva Sṛṣṭirasāśrayaḥ another reading is Nānā Dṛṣṭirasāśrayaḥ. The Bhāvas are mentioned in the VII chapter. The different Dṛṣṭis in the VIII chapter.

37—38 All types of undesirable persons to be excluded from the ceremony. The heretics, because they will object to the worship part of it. The ochre-robed ones are too devout to indulge in dramatic performances. Hence they have no place in the festivities. The Buddhist monks, are celibate people. Hence they are symbols of inability to produce or flourish.

43—45 Sukaraṇena. The Karaṇas are parts of the lunar day numbering eleven. The details can be found in the II chapter of the Sūryasiddhānta.

46--50 Brāhmaṇa Stambha—Sarvaśuklaḥ Vidhiḥ i.e. white mustard, white cloth and white garland because a true brahmin symbolizes purity of conduct, sound learning and wisdom Kṣatriya Stambha—Sarvam Raktam Pradātavyam. Because a true Kṣatriya symbolizes physical strength, valorous exploits etc. all the articles to be used in this pillar should be red in colour.

In Vaiśya Stambha everything is yellow in colour, yellow being the colour of gold and Vaiśyas being tradesmen this colour is justified.

3

Adoration of the Gods of the Stage

Consecration

1—8 Cows are to be kept in the splendid dramatic house duly constructed while Brahmins continue chanting the requisite Mantras. Nāṭyācārya has to consecrate the play house. He has to be initiated for the purpose. He will be wearing new clothes. Previously he should have observed fast for three days and have kept his senses under full control. He should have desisted from lying in comfortable bedsteads during those days of fast. Afterwards he shall be sprinkle his limbs with Mantra inspired water. He then makes obeisance to the great Lord Śiva the lord of all the worlds, the lotus-born lord, the preceptor of the Suras, Viṣṇu, Indra, Guha, Sarasvatī, Lakṣmī, Siddhi, Medhā, Smṛti, Mati, the moon god, the sun god, the winds, the guardians of the regions, Aśvins, Mitra, the fire god, the Svaras (vowels or notes of music), Rudras, Kāla, Kali, Yama, Niyati, the staff of Yama, the missiles of Viṣṇu, the serpent lord, Garuḍa, the thunderbolt, lightning, seas, the Gandharvas, the celestial damsels, the sages, Nāṭyakumārīs, Mahāgrāmaṇī (the great leader of the Groups), the Yakṣas, the Guhyakas and the groups of the Bhūtas.

9—10 After offering obeisance to all these as well as to royal sages he with palms joined in reverence shall invoke the gods seated in their respective positions saying—"O divine ones, it behoves you to take us all under your benign protection during the night. Accompanied by your followers extend to us all help in the dramatic performance."

Jarjara worship

11—13 Having worshipped the gods and sounded the

musical instruments the Nāṭyācārya adores the Jarjara (flag-staff of Indra) for the acquisition of grand success for the performance—"Thou art Mahendra's missile able to kill all the demons; thou best been created by all the Suras; thou court avert all hindrances; be glad enough to bring victory to the king and vanquishment for all his foes; welfare unto cows and Brahmins and steady progress to the art of drama."

14—15 After doing everything in accordance with the injunctions and spending the entire night in the premises of the playhouse the Ācārya begins the Pūjā early in the morning. The favourable constellation thereof is Ārdrā, Maghā, Bharaṇī, Pūrvaphalgunī, Pūrvāṣāḍha, Pūrvabhādrapada, Āśleṣa or Mūla.

16 The stage is lit brightly and the Ācārya with bodily purity and mental concentration performs the Pūjās after due initiation.

Installation of the deities

17 During the close of the day, when the Bhūtas are very powerful and preside over the period, it is likely that evils may befall (to avert them), the Ācārya installs the deities after the ceremonial rinsing of the mouth with water.

18—19 In this context the red auspicious threads, red unguents, red flowers and red fruits are to be honoured (by acceptance).

Barley, white mustard, raw rice grains, Nāgapuṣpa powder and **husked** Priyaṅgu should be used to make (the idols of) the deities.

The Maṇḍala of mystic diagram

20—22 In connection with this ceremony a mystic diagram is to be drawn in accordance with the injunctions at the due places. The overall dimension of the mystic diagram is sixteen Hastas square [Here Hasta = half of a cubit = 22.5 cm]. It has doors on all four sides. In the middle horizontal and vertical lines are drawn || to the sides. In the squares made by them different deities are installed for the purpose of adoration.

23—30 In the middle, Brahmā is to be installed seated in a lotus.

Then, at the outset, Lord Śiva is to be installed in the east.

The following deities too are installed there. Śiva with his hosts of Bhūtas lord Nārāyaṇa, Mahendra, Skanda. Sun god, the Aśvins, the moon god, Sarasvatī, Lakṣmī, Śraddhā and Medhā. In the south-east are to be installed the five god with his consort Svāhā, the Viśvedevas, the Gandharvas, Rudras and the sages. In the south are to be installed Yama, Mitra in the company of his followers, the Pitṛs (Manes) Piśācas, the serpents and the Guhyakas.

In the south-west are to be installed all the Nairṛtas and all Bhūtas (living beings spirits).

In the west the Ācārya should instal the oceans and Varuṇa.

In the north-west he shall instal the seven winds and Garuḍa along with the birds.

In the north Kubera is to be installed along with all attendants. So also the mothers of Nāṭya (Nāṭyasya Mātṛḥ) the Yakṣas and the Guhyakas.

In the north-east Nandin, the Gaṇeśvaras, and the groups of Brahmarṣis and Bhūtas in their allotted portions.

31 Sanatkumāra is to be installed in the eastern pillar, Dakṣa in the southern one, Grāmaṇī (leader of the groups) in the northern pillar and Skanda in the western pillar.

32 In accordance with these rules of procedure all the deities are to be installed in their conventional form and colour in their respective positions.

Pūjā to the deities

33 After installing the deities in their regular positions in the prescribed manner the Ācārya should perform their adoration in the manner suited to them.

34 With regards to the deities generally white garlands and unguents are in vogue but in the case of the Gandharvas, Agni and Sun god they should be offered red unguents and garlands.

35 After offering garlands, unguents and incense duly and in the prescribed order the Ācārya shall be offered oblations and adorations in accordance with the injunctions.

36—39 The devotee shall propitiate the different deities with the food offerings as follows:—

Druhiṇa shall be offered Madhuparka; Sarasvatī with milk pudding; Śiva, Viṣṇu, Mahendra and others should be honoured with sweet meats; the fire god with rice cooked in ghee, the moon god and sun god with cooked rice and treacle, the Viśvedevas, sages and the Gandharvas should be propitiated with honey and milk pudding, Yama and Mitra should be adored with sweet meats mixed with lentils, the devotee shall propitiate the Manes, the Piśācas and the serpents with ghee and milk. The groups of goblins are to be propitiated with raw or cooked meat, liquor, rum and fruit extracts and bengal grams soaked in milk.

Consecration of Mattavāraṇī

40—44 In the Mattavāraṇī or the side room too the procedure is the same in regard to the adoration of the deities. The groups of Rākṣasas are to be propitiated with raw or cooked meat. He shall propitiate the Dānavas by offering them liquor and meat. The remaining deities are to be propitiated with sweet pies, milk treacle and ghee preparations, and boiled rice. The oceans and rivers are adored with fishes and cakes. After due adoration Varuṇa should be given ghee and milk pudding. He should propitiate the sages with different kinds of roots and fruits, the winds and the birds are honoured with different kinds of edible foodstuffs. With sweet pies and lopikās (cakes) he should propitiate the Nāṭyamātṛs, Kubera and their followers.

45 Thus the above mentioned foodstuffs should be offered to the deities and the Mantras prescribed for utterance at that time are as followers.

46 O lord of the Devas, O highly fortunate one, O lotus born lord, O grandfather accept this oblation of ours sanctified by the Mantra [This is for Brahmā].

47 (Śiva) O great lord of the Devas, lord of the goblins, slayer of Tripuras, O great Yogin, accepting our oblation save us from the obstacles arising always, Accept this etc. etc.

48 (Viṣṇu) O Nārāyaṇa, the lotus-navelled lord, the most excellent one among the gods, O lord of unrestricted movement accept etc. etc.

49 (Indra) O Purandara who had performed a hundred sacrifices, O lord of the immortals holding the thunderbolt in the hand accept etc. etc.

50 (Skanda) O blessed lord Skanda, O six-faced favourite son of Śiva, O leader of the army of the gods accept this etc. etc.

51 (Sarasvatī) O goddess of excessive blessedness, O beloved of Hari accept this etc. etc.

52 (For various goddesses) O goddess Lakṣmī, O Siddhi Mati, Medhā, all of you are propitiated by all the worlds, accept this etc. etc.

53 (For Māruta) O Māruta O enliverer of the entire world, conversant with the might of all the living beings accept this etc. etc.

54 (Rākṣasas) O noble souled sons of Pulastya, born due to various causes accept this etc. etc.

55 (Agni) O Facial aperture of the gods, O best one of the gods, O smoke-bannered one, O Hutāśana (one who eats what is offered in the fire) accept this oblation offered unto you with great devotion.

56 (The Moon god) O lord of all the planets, O king of the twiceborn, O favourite of the world accept this etc. etc.

57 (The Sun god) O lord of the day time, O most-excellent one among all the planets, O mass of refulgence accept this etc. etc.

58 (Chiefs of the great Gaṇas) O great lords of the chiefs of Great Gaṇas with Nandīśvara as the leader accept this etc. etc.

59 (Pitṛs) Obeisance to all the Pitṛs. May they accept this oblation. I always bow to all the Bhūtas. This oblation appeals to them.

60—61 O Kāmapāla, I constantly bow to you and this offering is unto you.

O Gandharvas, with Nārada, Tumburu and Viśvavasu as the leaders, accept this excellent oblation.

62 O Yama and Mitra you two are the most adorned ones of all the worlds accept this etc. etc.

63 Obeisance, obeisance to all the serpents of the nether worlds. You whose diet consists of the wind, grant me success in the production of this play after duly being worshipped by me.

64 May Lord Varuṇa the lord of all waters, having the swan for vehicle, be pleased on being worshipped along with the seas and diverse kinds of rivers.

65 O lord of all birds, born of Vinatā, O highly powerful one let this oblation consecrated by Mantras and offered by me be accepted.

66 May the presiding deity of material wealth, the lord of the Yakṣas, the guardian of the quarters, the lord of riches accept my oblation along with Guhyakas and Yakṣas.

67 Obeisance be to the mothers of Nāṭya beginning with Brāhmī, obeisance. May the oblation be accepted by these good-countenanced delighted ones.

68 May the weapon of Rudra accept my oblation. Let the weapon of Viṣṇu too accept my oblations offered with devotion to Viṣṇu.

69 May Kṛtānta, the god of death, and Kāla, the twin lords under whose control are all the living beings. May Mṛtyu and Niyati accept my oblation.

70 May all those Vāstu deities (the deities presiding over houses and house sites) occupying the Mattavāraṇī (side room) accept this oblation of music duly sanctified by the Mantras.

71 This Bali is offered unto all other gods and the Gandharvas occupying the heavenly terrestrial or middle regions and all the ten quarters.

72 The Ācārya then shall place a water-filled jar embellished with garlands of leaves in the middle of the Raṅga (stage) and put a piece of gold therein.

73 He shall then cover all the musical instruments with cloths and worship them with sweet scents garlands, incense and different kinds of foodstuffs.

74 After worshipping all the deities in the order prescribed the Ācārya shall adore the Jarjara and thereby become free from obstacles and the state of being helpless.

75—76 The cloth at the top shall be white; blue at the joint pertaining to Rudra; it shall be yellow at the joint of

Viṣṇu; red at the Skanda joint and of variegated colour at the joint at the base. Garlands, incense and unguents shall also be given in the same suitable manner.

77—78 After performing all the rites through the incense garlands and unguents the Ācārya shall inspire the Jarjara with the Mantra for the purpose of starring off the obstacles :—

"It is for the purpose of subduing the obstacles that you have been created by the Devas with Brahmā as the leader. You have great potentiality. You are essentially adamantine. Your body (frame) is huge.

79 Let Brahmā protect your head along with all the groups of the Devas; Hara the second joint, Janārdana the third one, Kumāra the fourth one and the best of the Pannagas (serpents) the fifth (joint).

80—81 May all the gods protect you always become blessed yourself. You are the slayer of enemies. You are born under the star Abhijit (vega). Accord victory and prosperity to our king.

Procedure of Havana

82 After the performance of the adoration of the Jarjara in this manner and having offered all the oblations he shall perform Homa in the fire with ghee duly uttering the requisite Mantras.

83 After performing the Homa he shall perform the rite of Parimārjana (ritualistic cleaning) through the lighted torches which will bring about an increase in the splendour of the king as well as the dancing girls.

84 After brightening the dancing girls and the king along with the musical instruments he shall sprinkle them with water inspired with Mantras and speak thus to them.

85 You are born in a noble family and are embellished with many good qualities. Let that which you have been endowed with since birth be yours for ever.

86 After uttering these words for the prosperity of the king the sensible Ācārya shall pronounce these words of benediction for the purpose of making the dramatic performance a success.

87 "May all these Mothers viz. Sarasvatī, Dhṛti, Medhā, Hrī, Śrī, Lakṣmī and Smṛti protect you all. Let them be bestowers of fulfilment unto you all".

The rite of Kumbhabhedana

88 After the due performance of the Homa through Mantra inspired Havis (i.e. clarified butter) the Nāṭyāçārya shall scrupulously perform the rite of Kumbhabhedana (breaking the pot).

89 The lord may have to face danger from the foes should the pot be unbroken; if it gets broken, it should be known that the lord's enemies will become reduced.

The rite of Raṅgapradīpana

90 When the pot is broken the Ācārya can be without fear; he shall take up the lighted lamp and illuminate the entire dramatic hall.

91 In the middle of the hall he shall take the lighted lamp around making noise such as oral roar, snopping of the fingers, jumping up and running about.

92 With the production of sounds from Śaṅkhas and Dundubhis as well as Mṛdaṅgas and Paṇava drums and blowing all the other musical instruments he shall cause some fights in the stage.

93 (Let there be) bruises, cuts and lacerations spilling blood. A bright wound inflicted is an omen for the success in the play.

The benefits of the adoration and evils otherwise

94 Well consecrated hall and stage shall bring about splendid results to the lord, to the region and to the city including the old and the young.

95 Ill consecrated hall and stage will not be properly presided over by the deities and it shall ruin the dance programme and bring about calamity to the king.

96 He who sets at nought the rules of procedure and conducts the performance as he pleases will incure decline

soon. He will be reborn among the lower order of brutes.

97 This adoration of the deities of the stage is on a par with a Yajña (holy sacrifice). No one shall produce a play without the worship of the stage.

98 These deities worship others when they themselves are worshipped: when they are honoured they bestow honour to others. Hence one shall assiduously perform the rite of the adoration of the (deities of the) stage.

99 Five hundred by violent gusts of wind does not burn so quickly as the misdirected performance that burns instantly.

100—102 The worship of the stage should be performed by the Nāṭyācārya who is humble, pure and conversant with the theoretical texts, who is well trained and initiated into the art and who is always cool and calm. If he becomes dejected in mind and offers the oblations wrongly he shall perform expiatory rites like a Hotṛ (performer of sacrifice) bereft of Mantras. These are the procedures laid down in regard to the worship of the deities of the stage. It should of necessity be carried out by the producers (of plays) in regard to the performance in a newly built dramatic hall.

NOTES

In the third chapter the main topic is the detailed worship of the deities of the stage. These deities include the Rākṣasas, Dānavas, Piśācas, Bhūtas etc. In fact a detailed propitiation of all the beings of the Earth and heaven as well as the nether worlds is intended. A veritable Yajña is to be performed with Maṇḍalas (mystic diagrams) wherein the different deities are to be installed. Brahmā seated on the lotus is installed in the middle. Then Śiva with the attendant goblins, Nārāyana, Mahendra, Skanda, Arka (sun), Aśvins (physicians of the Devas) the moon, Sarasvatī (goddess of speech) Lakṣmī (goddess of fortune), Śraddhā (faith) and Medhā (Intellect). All these in the east, in the south-east the fire god with Svāhā, the Viśvedevas, the Gandharvas, Rudras and the sages. In the other directions the others in due order are to be installed and worshipped. The Mantras to accompany these consecratory rites are also given. There is a warning that if the requisite rites are not performed evils are sure to befall both the actors and the community too. Illumination of the auditorium is also a necessary feature. All these have been clearly described in the III chapter.

6 Svarān Varṇān. The Svaras may be the seven notes in the gamut of Indian music or the vowels. Varṇas may be letters or the different castes. The idea of worshipping them indicates that people of all castes should cooperate in making the performance a success.

9 Nāṭyakumārīśca. Another reading is Nāṭyasya Mātṛāśca (the mothers presiding over the dramatic art). In verse 5 Medhā (intellect), Mati (mind) and smṛti (memory) are conceived of as deities. Any devotional rite is bound to increase spiritual power if there is adequate faith.

36—39 The items to be offered as Naivedya to the different deities are worthy of note.

Madhuparka (mixture of honey, curd, ghee, water and sugar) to Brahmā; Pāyasa (milk pudding) to Sarasvatī.

42 Sāpūpotkarikodanaiḥ—Apūpa is fried sweet pie. Utkarikā is a mixture of milk treacle and ghee.

4

Characteristics of the Tāndava dance

1 After performing the rite of adoration thus Brahmā was addressed by me— "Command me quickly, O lord. What shall be the play to be produced?

Brahmā's Samavakāra play named Amṛtamanthana

2 Then I was told by the lord—"Perform the play on the churning of the ocean for the sake of the nectar. It is highly pleasing to the Suras and causes enthusiasm among them.

3 O learned one, let the play composed by me, a Samavakāra conducive to the achievement of piety, love and wealth be staged.

4 When the Samavakāra was staged, the Devas and the Dānavas became delighted by witnessing the actions and the emotions depicted.

5 After the lapse of some time the lotus born lord said to me— "We shall display our dramatic performance today to the three-eyed noble soul (Śiva)".

6 Then the grandfather went to the residence of the bull emblemed lord along with the Suras. After adoring Śiva he said.

7 "O the most excellent one among the Suras, it behoves you to grant me the favour of seeing and hearing the play Samavakāra composed by me."

8 " We shall witness it" said the lord of the Devas to Druhiṇa (Brahmā). Thereupon the lord said to me— "O highly intelligent one be prepared".

9—10 Thereupon on the summit of the Himālaya surrounded by many hills with beautiful caves and rivulets and filled with many groups of the goblins (attendants of Śiva), O excellent brahmins, this (Samavakāra of Brahmā) as well as a Ḍima named Tripuradāha was played after the prologue and the preliminary rites had been duly performed.

11 Then the groups of the spirits became delighted as the actions and emotions had been portrayed. Mahādeva too was extremely pleased and he spoke to Brahmā then.

12 "O highly intelligent one, this dance drama composed by you is very good. It is conducive to merit and reputation as the topics are splendid (theme is splendid) and the play makes the intellect keen.

13 This dance item is remembered by me as I performed the dance during the times of dusk. It is well embelished by the Aṅgahāras supplemented by various Karaṇas.

14—16 Let this be employed by you in the preliminary rites of the prologue properly with the application of Vardhamānaka in regard to the Gītas, Āsāritas and Mahāgītas. You will portray properly the themes (through gestures etc.).

The prologue that has just been performed by you is Śuddha (pure) but on being combined with these they will become Citra by name.

On hearing the words of Maheśvara, the following words were uttered by the self-born lord (Brahmā).

The Aṅgahāras

17—18 "O the most excellent one among the Gods advise us about the employment of the Aṅgahāras". Then the lord of the universe summoned Taṇḍu and commanded—"Instruct Bharata as to the proper employment of the Aṅgahāras."

I shall now expatiate upon those Aṅgahāras enumerated by the noble souled Taṇḍu along with the different Karaṇas as well as Recakas.

The names of the Aṅgahāras

19—27 The following thirty two are the names of the Aṅgahāras: — Sthirahasta, Paryastaka, Sūcīviddha, Sūpaviddha [Apaviddha], Ākṣiptaka, Udghaṭita [Udghaṭṭita], Viṣkambha, Aparājita, Viṣkambhāpasmṛta [Viṣkambhāpasṛta], Mattākrīḍa, Svastikarecita, Pārśvasvastika, Vṛścika, Bhramara, Mattaskhalitaka, Madavilasita, Gati-Maṇḍala, Paricchinna, Parivṛttarecita, Vaiśākharecita, Parāvṛtta, Alātkka Pārśvaccheda, Vidyudbhrānta, Uddhṛtaka, Ālīḍha, Recita, Ācchurita, Ākṣiptarecita, Saṁbhrānta, Upasarpita [Asarpita], and Arddhanikuṭṭaka.

Utilisation of the Aṅgahāras

28—29 I shall mention how they are to be utilized based on the Karaṇas. Moreover, O most excellent one among the Brahmins, I shall instruct you regarding the movements of the hands and feet as relevant to the Aṅgahāras.

Varaṇas

30 All the Aṅgahāras are evolved through Karaṇas and the names of these together with their actions shall be explained.

31—34 The simultaneous movements of hands and feet while dancing can be called Karaṇa. Two Karaṇas constitute one Mātṛkā; two, three or four Mātṛkās making up one Aṅgahāra. A Kalāpaka is evolved out of three Karaṇas, a Maṇḍaka [Ṣaṇḍaka] out of four and a Saṁghātaka out of five. There are well known Aṅgahāras consisting of six, seven, eight or nine Karaṇas.

I shall now expatiate the movements of the hands and feet for the evolution of the Karaṇas.

35—55 The Karaṇas one hundred and eight in number are as follows :—

Talapuṣpapuṭa, Vartita, Valitoru, Apaviddha, Samanakha, Līna, Svastikarecita Maṇḍalasvastika, Nikuṭṭaka, Ardhanikuṭṭaka, Kaṭicchinna, Ardharecita, Vakṣassvastika, Unmatta, Svastika, Pṛṣṭhasvastika, Diksvastika, Alāta, Kaṭisama, Ākṣiptarecita, Vikṣiptākṣipta, Ardhasvastika, Añcita, Bhujaṅga Trāsita, Urdhvajānu, Nikuñcita, Matalli, Ardhamatalli, Recakanikuṭṭita, Padāpaviddhaka, Valita, Ghūrṇita, Lalita, Daṇḍa Pakṣa, Bhujaṅga Trastarecita, Nūpura, Vaiśākharecita, Bhramaraka, Catura, Bhujaṅgañcitaka, Daṇḍakarecita, Vṛścikakuṭṭita, Kaṭibhrānta, Latāvṛścika, Chinna, Vṛścikarecita, Vṛścika, Vyaṁsita, Pārśvanikuṭṭana, Lalāṭatilaka, Krāntaka, Kuñcita, Cakramaṇḍala, Uromaṇḍala, Ākṣipta, Talavilāsita, Argala, Vikṣipta, Āvṛtta, Dolapāda, Vivṛtta, Vinivṛtta, Pārśvakrāntā,

Niśumbhita, Vidyudbhrānta, Atikrānta, Vivartitaka, Gajakrīḍita, Talasaṁsphoṭita, Garuḍaplutaka, Gaṇḍasūci, Parivṛtta, Pārśvajānu, Gṛdhrāvalīnaka, Sannata, Sūci, Ardhasūcī, Sūcīviddha, Apakrānta, Mayūralalita, Sarpita, Daṇḍapāda, Hariṇapluta, Preṅkholita, Nitamba, Skhalita, Karihasta, Prasarpita, Siṁhākrīḍita, Siṁhākarṣita, Udvṛtta, Upasṛta, Talasaṁghaṭṭita, Janita, Avahitthaka, Niveśa, Elakākrīḍita Urūdvṛtta, Madaskhalita, Viṣṇukrānta, Saṁbhrānta, Viṣkambha, **Udghaṭṭita** Vṛṣabhakrīḍita, Lolitaka, Nāgāpasarpita, Śakaṭāsya, and Gaṅgāvataraṇa. These Karaṇas are expected to be employed in the course of dance, fighting, indulging in personal combats, strolling and in all general movements.

56—58 Those movements of the feet allotted to the exercise of Sthānas and Cārīs must be considered so to the Karaṇas too. So also in the case of Nṛttakastas. These Sthānas, Cārīs and the Nṛttahastas are called Mātṛkās the variations thereof are known as Karaṇas.

59—61 I shall explain Cārīs pertaining to fight when discussing the details of Gati (movements). The dramatic preceptor shall make use of them in a manner befitting his histrionic skill. In the Karaṇa holding of the left hand on the breast is recommended. The right hand is to follow the right foot. Now pay attention to the movements of hands and feet while dancing in their connection with the movements of hip, sides and thigh and also their relation to the breast, back and belly.

The Karaṇas defined

62 Talapuṣpapuṭa—Hand is held on the left side the foot is in the position Agratalasañcara and the side is Sannata (bent).

63 Vartita—Hands bent at the wrist and place these hands on the thighs.

64 Valitoru—Hands in Vyāvartita and Sarivartita form and thighs in Valita (moving and turning).

65 Apaviddha—The right hand in Śukatuṇḍa gesture falls on the thigh, the left hand kept to the breast.

66 Samanakha—The two feet touch each other with the nails symmetrical, two hands hang down, the body in natural position.

67 Līna—The two Patākā hands are held together in the Añjalī position on the breast, the neck is held high and the shoulder is bent.

68 Svastikarecita—Two hands with Recita and Āviddha gesture held together in Svastika form then separated and held on the hips.

69 Maṇḍalasvastika—Two hands kept in Svastika gesture—palms turned upwards the body in the Maṇḍala Posture.

70 Nikuṭṭaka—The hands moved up and down in turns between the head and another arm—legs moved similarly.

71 Ardhanikuṭṭaka—Hands with Alapallava gesture bent towards shoulders—legs moved up and down.

72 Kaṭicchinna—The hip serially in the Chinna position—two Pallava hands held alternately and repeatedly on the head.

73 Ardharecita—Hand with Sūcīmukha gesture moves freely, feet move up and down in turns—side in Sannata posture.

74 Vakṣassvastika—Two legs on each other in Svastika form—two Recita hands joined together similarly on the breast kept bent

75 Unmatta—Feet to be Añcita and hands—Recita.

76 Svastika—Hands and feet respectively held together in the Svastika form.

77 Pṛṣṭhavastika—Two arms after being thrown up and down coming together as a Svastika with Apakrānta and Ardhasūcī Cārīs.

78 Diksvastika—Turning sideways and towards the front in course of a connected movement thereby forming Svastika with hands and feet.

79 Alāta—After making Alāta Cārī the hand is taken down from the level of the shoulder making Urdhvajānu Cārī.

80 Kaṭisama—Feet kept separated after Svastika Karaṇa, one hand placed at the navel and the other at the hip-sides in the Udvāhita pose.

81 Ākṣiptarecita—Left Hand on the heart right hand Recita—thrown up and sideways—then both the hands Recita with Apaviddha gesture.

82 Vikṣiptākṣiptaka—Hands and feet thrown up then down.

83 Ardhasvastika—The two feet make Svastika, right hand Karihasta gesture left one lying on the chest.

84 Añcita—In the Ardhasvastika the Karihasta alternately in Vyāvartita and Parivartita movement, then bent upon the tip of the nose.

85 Bhujaṅga Trāsita—The Kuñcita feet thrown up—thighs have an oblique Nivartana movement—the same movement in the hip and the thigh.

86 Urdhvajānu—A Kuñcita foot is thrown up—knee stretched on a level with the breast—hands in harmony with the dance.

87 Nikuñcita—Feet to be moved as in the Vṛścika Karaṇa—Both hands bent at the sides, right hand held at the tip of the nose.

88 Matalli—Make a whirling movement while throwing the two feet back—move hands on the Udveṣṭita and Apaviddha movements.

89 Ardhamatalli—Feet drawn away from the position in the Skhalita, left hand Recita and later part on the hip.

90 Recitanikuṭṭita—Right hand Recita, left foot Udghaṭṭita, left hand Dolā gesture.

91 Pādāpaviddhaka—The kaṭakāmukha hands with backs against the navel and feet to be in Sūcī and then Apakrānta Cārī.

92 Valita—Hands to be Apaviddha, beet to be in Sūcī Cārī —Trika turned round (lower part of the spine).

93 Ghūrṇita—left hand in Valita and moved round—right hand with Dolā gesture and the two feet to be drawn away from each other from the Svastika position.

94 Lalita—Left hand in Karihasta gesture—right turned aside (Apavartita) two feet moved up and down.

95 Daṇḍapakṣa—Observe Urdhvajānu Cārī, Latā hands to be placed on the knee.

96 Bhujaṅga Trastarecita—Feet in B.T. Cārī hands Recita to be moved to the left.

97 Nūpura—The lower spine gracefully turned round Bhramarī Cārī, hands showing Latā and Recita gestures and the feet the Nūpura Pāda Cārī.

98 Vaiśākharecita—Hands and feet to be Recita, the hip and the neck also and the whole body in Vaiśākha Sthāna.

99 Bhramaraka—Svastika feet in Ākṣipta Cārī, hands in Udveṣṭita. The sacrum turned round.

100 Catura—The left hand with Añcita gesture, right hand Catura gesture, right feet in Kuṭṭita pose.

101 Bhujaṅgāñcita—The feet in Bhujaṅgatrasita Cārī, right hand Recita, left hand Latā gesture.

102 Daṇḍakarecita—Hands and feet freely thrown about all sides like a staff and then Recita.

103 Vṛścikakuṭṭita—Assume the Vṛścika Karaṇa and make the Nikuṭṭita movement of the hands.

104 Kaṭibhrānti—The Sūcī Cārī, Apaviddha gesture with the right hand, hip to be moved round.

105 Latāvṛścika—A foot to be Añcita and turned backwards, Latā gesture with the left hand—palm and fingers bent and turned upwards.

106 Chinna—The Alapadma hand to be held on the hip in Chinna pose, Body in the Vaiśākha Sthāna.

107 Vṛścikarecita—Assume Vṛścika Karaṇa—the two hands in Svastika form gradually becoming Recita to show Viprakīrṇa gesture.

108 Vṛścika—The two hands bent and held over the shoulders and a leg bent and turned towards the back.

109 Vyaṁsita—Take up Ālīḍha Sthāna two hands to be Recita and held on the breast and afterwards moved up and down with Viprakīrṇa gesture.

110 Pārśvanikuṭṭaka—Svastika hands to be held on one side the feet Nikuṭṭita.

111 Lalāṭatilaka—Assume the Vṛścika Karaṇa or mark i to be made on the forehead with the great toe.

112 Krāntaka—Bending a Kuñcita leg behind the bac and the Atikrāntā Cārī—both the hands thrown down.

113 Kuñcita—Leg in Añcita and left hand held on the left side with palm upwards.

114 Cakramaṇḍala—The inner Apaviddha (Aḍḍitā Cārī) with the body bent and held down between the two arms hanging straight.

115 Uromaṇḍala—Two feet drawn away from Svastika position and then hands on the chest. Feet in Apaviddha Cārī.

116 Ākṣipta—Hands and feet thrown about swiftly.

117 Talavilāsita—Foot with toe and sole turned upwards, held high on the side, palm of hands bent.

118 Argala—Feet stretched backwards and kept two Tālas and a half apart. Hands moved in conformity.

119 Vikṣipta—Hands and feet thrown backwards or sideways in the same way.

120 Āvarta—The Kuñcita feet put forward—two hands moved swiftly to befit the dancing movement.

121 Dolapāda—Kuñcita foot thrown up two hands swinging from side to side in a manner befitting the dance.

122 Nivṛtta—Hands and feet thrown out—Trika to be turned round—hands to be Recita.

123 Pārśvakrānta—Observe the Cārī of the name, throw out hands forward, then move them in a manner befitting the dance.

124 Vinivṛtta—Observe the Sūcī Cārī sacrum to be turned round, hands to be Recita.

125 Niśumbhita—A foot bent towards the back, breast is raised high, hand held at the middle of the forehead.

126 Vidyudbhrānta—Foot turned backwards and the hands in Maṇḍalāviddha gesture stretched very close to the head.

127 Atikrānta—Observe Atikrāntā Cārī, stretch both the hands forward in a manner befitting the dance.

128 Vivartitaka—hands and feet thrown out Trika turned round, hands to be Recita.

129 Gajakrīḍita—Left hand bent and brought near the left ear, right hand in Latā gesture—feet Dolapāda Cārī.

130 Tala Saṁsphoṭita—Foot swiftly lifted up and placed forward—hands show Talasaṁsphoṭita gesture.

131 Garuḍaplutaka—Feet stretched backwards hands with Latā and Recita gestures breast raised.

132 Gaṇḍasūcī—Feet in Sūcī pose, side to be Unnata, one hand bent on the chest, other bent touching the cheek.

133 Parivṛtta—Hands raised in Āpaveṣṭita gesture, feet in Sūcī position, Sacrum turned round in the Bhramarī Cārī.

134 Pārśvajānu—One foot in Sama position and the opposite thigh is lifted up, one Muṣṭi (fist) hand on the chest.

135 Gṛdhrāvalīnaka—One foot stretched backwards and one knee slightly bent—both the arms outstreched.

136 Sannata—Leap forward, then place the feet forward in Svastika form, showing Sannata gesture with both the hands.

137 Sūcī—A Kuñcita foot raised and placed ahead on the ground, two hands in harmony with the performance.

138 Ardhasūcī—The Alapadma hand is held on the head, right foot in Sūcī Karaṇa

139 Sūcī Viddha—One foot of the Sūcī Karaṇa being put on the heel of the other, hands placed on the waist and chest respectively.

140 Apakrānta—Make the Valita thigh and perform Apakrānta Cārī, both the hands to be moved in harmony.

141 Mayūralalita—Assume the Vṛścika Karaṇa, keep hands in Recita, turn the Trika (Sacrum).

142 Sarpita—both the feet to be moved from Añcita position, head is in Parivāhita gesture, hands in Recita.

143 Daṇḍa Pāda—After the Nupura Cārī observe Daṇḍa Pāda Cārī and Āviddha hand is shown quickly.

144 Hariṇapluta—Observe Atikrānta Cārī the dancer should jump and stop. He then bends the shanks and throws them up.

145 Preṅkholitaka—After observing the Dolā Pāda Cārī, jump and let the Trika turn round and settle down.

146 Nitamba—Arms at the outset are thrown up with fingers pointing upwards. Baddhā Cārī is to be observed.

147 Skhalita—Observe Dolāpādacārī and then turn round the hands with Recita gesture in harmony therewith.

148 Karihasta—Left hand is placed on the chest, the other hand is Prodveṣṭitatala. The feet in Añcita.

149 Prasarpitaka—One hand in Recita and the other with Latā gesture; the feet in Saṁsarpitatala.

150 Siṁhavikrīḍita—After observing the Alāta Cāri, move swiftly making the hands to follow the feet.

151 Siṁhākarṣ'ta—One foot stretched backwards, hands to be bent and turned round in the front and again bent.

152 Udvṛtta—Hands, feet, whole body raised up—Udvṛtta Cārī to be observed.

153 Upasṛtaka—Employ Ākṣhipta Cārī and harmonize the hands therewith.

154 Talasaṁchaṭṭita—Employ Dolāpādacārī, clashing the palms together, left hand in Recita.

155 Janita—Keep one hand loose holding the other to the chest—employ Talāgrasaṁsthita Cārī.

156 Avahitthaka—After employing Janita Karaṇa raise the hands spreading out the fingers—Let them fall slowly.

157 Niveśa—Both the hands kept on the chest that is in Nirbhugna state—The dances then assumes Maṇḍala Sthāna.

158 Elakākrīḍita—Jump with Talasañcara feet and come to the ground with the body bent and turned.

159 Urūdvṛtta—A hand in Āvṛtta or Vyavartita state, keep it bent and place it on the thigh—shanks in Añcita and then Udvṛtta.

160 Madaskhalitaka—Two hands kept hanging down, head in the parivāhita gesture, feet turned round in Āviddha Cārī.

161 Viṣṇukrānta—One of the feet stretched forward and bent as though one is about to walk hands in Recita.

162 Saṁbhrānta—One hand in the Vyavartita movement is kept on the thigh in Āviddha.

163 Viṣkambha—One of the hands to be Apaviddha Sūcī Cārī, foot in Nikuṭṭita state—Left hand on the chest.

164 Udghaṭṭa—Feet in the Udghaṭṭita movement—hands in Talasaṁghaṭṭita and then placed on both sides.

165 Vṛṣabhakrīḍita—Employ Alātacārī both hands in Recita gradually taken to Kuñcita and Añcita.

166 Lolita—Hands in Recita on both sides then in Añcita—head lolita and Vartita.

167 Nāgāpasarpita—Draw back feet from Svastika position—Head in Parivāhita and the hands in Recita.

168 Śakaṭāsya—At the outset the body is in rest. Then advance with a Talasañcara foot—keep the chest Udvāhita.

169 Gaṅgāvataraṇa—Foot with the toes and the sole turned upwards—hands show the Tripatāka—fingers point downwards—Head in Sannata state.

Aṅgahāras

170 One hundred and eight Karaṇas having been explained, the different Aṅgahāras are being spoken of—

171—173 Sthirahasta—Stretch and throw up both the arms –Take up Samapāda Sthāna, then stretch the left hand upwards from the level of the shoulder. Pratyālīḍha Sthāna is then taken up. Then the following Karaṇas are respectively taken up one after the other—Nikuṭṭita, Urūdvṛtta, Ākṣipta, Svastika, Nitambha, Karihasta and Kaṭicchinna

174—176 Paryastaka—Employ the Karaṇas Talapuṣpapuṭa, Apaviddha and Vartita. Then take up Pratyālīḍha Sthāna. Thereafter the following Karaṇas to be employed—Nikuṭṭaka, Urūdvṛtta, Ākṣipta, Uromaṇḍala, Nitamba, Karihasta and Kaṭicchinna.

177—178 Sūcividdha—Show Alapallava and Sūcīmukha gestures employing these Karaṇas successively—Vikṣipta, Āvartita, Nikuṭṭaka, Urūdvṛtta, Ākṣipta, Uromaṇḍala, Karihasta and Kaṭicchinna.

179—180 Apaviddha—Appaviddha and Sūcīviddha Karaṇas are employed and then Udveṣṭita. Turn the Trika and the gesture Uromāṇḍalaka is shown while employing Kaṭicchinna Karaṇa.

181—182 Ākṣiptaka—Employ the following Karaṇas, successively viz.—Nūpura, Vikṣipta, Alātaka, Ākṣipta, Uromaṇḍala, Nitamba, Karihasta and Kaṭicchinna.

183—184 Udghaṭṭita—Hands is Udveṣṭita and Apaviddha and both the feet to be moved to Nikuṭṭita and then change to Uromaṇḍala gesture. Assume successively the Karaṇas Nitamba, Karihasta and Kaṭicchinna.

185—187 Viṣkambha—Hands to be made Udveṣṭita and one after the other feet successively to Nikuṭṭita and bent and then employ Urūdvṛttakaraṇa—Hands in Caturaśra and feet Nikuṭṭita employ Bhujaṅga Trāsita Karaṇa. Then hands in Udveṣṭita Employing Chinna and Bhramaraka Karaṇas even as the Sacrum is to be turned. Employ the Karaṇas, Karihasta and Kaṭicchinna Karaṇas.

188—190 Aparājita—Employ Daṇḍapāda Karaṇa hands in Vikṣipta and Ākṣipta; then employ the Vyaṁsita Karaṇa; the left hand moves along with the left foot hands remaining in Caturaśra and feet in the Nikuṭṭaka movement. Empoly Bhujaṅga Trāsita Karaṇa. Hands in the Udveṣṭita movement. Employ successively the two Nikuṭṭakas, Ākṣipta, Uromaṇḍala, Karihasta and Kaṭicchinna Karaṇas.

191—192 Viṣkaṁbhāpasṛta—Employ Karaṇas Kuṭṭita and Bhujaṅga Trāsita Karaṇas; Recita hand shows Patāka gesture—Employ the Karaṇas Ākṣiptaka, Uromaṇḍala, Latā and Kaṭiccheda successively.

193—195 Mattākrīḍa—Turn the Sacrum and employ Nūpura Karaṇa. Then successively Bhujaṅga Trāsita, Recita (right foot), Ākṣiptaka, Chinna, Bāhyabhramaraka, Uromaṇḍala, Nitamba, Karihasta and Kaṭicchinna Karaṇas.

196—197 Svastikarecita—Hands and feet in Recita. Employ Vṛścika Karaṇa and repeat this movement of both, then Nikuṭṭa Karaṇa and Latā gesture alternately with the right and the left hands. Finally Kaṭicchinna Karaṇa.

198—200 Pārśvasvastika—Employ Diksvastika from a side. Then Ardhanikuṭṭaka; then repeat all these on the other side. Āvṛtta hand is placed on the thigh. Employ the following Karaṇas successively Urūdvṛtta, Ākṣipta, Nitamba, Kārihasta and Kaṭicchinna.

201—202 Vṛścikāpasṛta—Employ Vṛścika Karaṇa holding Latā hand, held on the nose. Move the same hand in Udveṣṭita. Employ successively Nitamba, Karihasta and Kaṭicchinna.

203—204 Bhramara—The following Karaṇas are employed successively Nūpurapāda, Ākṣipta Kaṭicchinna, Sūcividdha, Nitamba, Karihasta, Uromaṇḍala and Kaṭicchinna.

205—206 Mattāskhalitaka—Employ Matalli Karaṇa. Move the right hand, bend and place it near the right cheek. The following Karaṇas in succession—Apaviddha, Talasaṁsphoṭita Karihasta and Kaṭichinna.

207—208 Madavilasita—Moving with Dolā hands Svastikā Pasṛta feet. Make Añcita and Valita in the hands. The following Karaṇas in succession. Talasaṁghaṭṭita, Nikuṭṭaka, Ūrūdvṛtta, Karihasta and Kaṭicchinna.

209—210 Gatimaṇḍala—Maṇḍala Sthānaka is assumed—Hands Recita—Feet Udghaṭṭita. The following Successively Matalli, Ākṣipta, Uromaṇḍala and Kaṭiccheda.

211-212 Paricchinna—Samapāda Sthāna with Paricchinna Karaṇa. Āviddha foot assumes Bāhya Bhramaraka—Sūcī Karaṇa in the left foot. The following Karaṇas successively—Atikrānta, Bhujaṅga Trāsita, Kaṭihasta and Katicchinna.

213—216 Parivṛttaka Recita—Hands in loose Svastika held on the head. Bend the body—left hand Recita. Raise the body. Again Recita in the same hands. Hands show Latā gesture. The following Karaṇas—Vṛścika, Recita, Karihasta, Bhujaṅga Trāsita and Ākṣiptaka. Svastika foot—Turn back completely and repect all. Then Karihasta.

217—219 Vaiśākharecita—Both the hands made Recita along with the body, Repeat this with bent body. Nūpura Cārī, Bhujaṅgatrāsita, Recita, Maṇḍalasvastika—to be employed. Shoulder is beck then Urūdvṛtta, Ākṣipta, Uromaṇḍala, Karihasta and Kaṭicchinna Karaṇas.

220—221 Parāvṛtta—Employ Janita Karaṇa—put forward a foot. Employ Alātaka Karaṇa. Turn the Sacrum afterwards. The bent left hand made Nikuṭṭita on the cheek. Employ Kaṭicchinna Karaṇa.

222—223 Alātaka—Employ the following Karaṇas in succession—Svastika, Vyaṁsita, Alātaka, Urdhvajānus Nikuñcita, Ardhasūcī, Vikṣipta, Udvṛtta, Ākṣipta, Karihasta and Kaṭicchinna.

224—225 Pārśvaccheda—Hands in Nikuṭṭita movement placed on the chest. Employ Ūrdhvajānu, Ākṣipta, and Svastika Karaṇas and turn the Trika (Sacrum). Then employ the Karaṇas Uromaṇḍala, Nitamba, Karihasta and Kaṭicchinna.

226—227 Vidyudbhrānta—Sūcikaraṇa with left foot—Vidyudbhrānta Karaṇa with right foot—Then change the order and Karaṇa. Chinna Karaṇa then. Turn the Trika. Latā and Kaṭicchinna Karaṇas.

228—229 Udvṛttaka—Employ Nūpurapāda Cārī hanging the hands by the side. Employ Vikṣipta Karaṇa. Assume Sūcikaraṇa and then turn the Trika in Bhramarīcārī. Latā and Kaṭicchinna Karaṇas thereafter.

230—231 Ālīḍha—Employ Vyaṁsita Karaṇa and strike the shoulder with the hands Nūpura Karaṇa with the left foot. Then Alāta and Ākṣipta Karaṇas with the right foot. Make Uromaṇḍala gestures with hands. Employ Karihasta and Kaṭicchinna Karaṇas.

232—233 Recita—showing Recita hand bending it on one side and making the same movement—Then repeating this movement after bending the entire body—Employ the following Karaṇa, successively—Nūpurapāda, Bhujaṅga Trāsita, Recita, Uromaṇḍala and Kaṭicchinna.

234—235 Ācchurita—Employ Nūpura Karaṇa turn the Trika round—employ Vyaṁsita karaṇa again turn the Trika. Then employ from the left side Alātaka, Sūci, Karihasta and Kaṭicchinna Karaṇas.

236—238 Ākṣipta Recita—Svastika feet in Recita, so too the Svastika hands. Then with the same movement they are separated. They are then thrown up. The following Karaṇas are employed successively—Udvṛtta, Ākṣipta, Uromaṇḍala, Nitamba, Karihasta and Kaṭicchinna.

239—241 Saṁbhrānta—Employ Vikṣipta Karaṇa—throw out the left hand with Sūcī gesture. The right hand is placed on

the chest—Turn the Trika. The following Karaṇas in succession —Nūpura, Ākṣipta, Ardhasvastika, Nitamba, Karihasta, Uromaṇḍala and Kaṭicchinna.

242—243 Apasarpita—Observe Apakrāntācārī and employ Vyamsita Karaṇa with the hands in Udveṣṭita movement. Then the following Karaṇas are employed successively—Ardhasūcī, Vikṣipta, Kaṭicchinna, Udvṛtta, Ākṣiptaka, Karihasta and Kaṭicchinna.

244—245 Ardhanikuṭṭaka—Observe swiftly Nūpurapādikā Cārī. Hands move in harmony with the feet. Trika is turned round. Hands and feet make Nikuṭṭita movement. The following Karaṇas—Uromaṇḍala, Karihasta, Kaṭicchinna and Ardhanikuṭṭaka Karaṇas.

The Recakas

246 The thirty two Aṅgahāras have been spoken of ; the four Recakas may kindly be attended to.

247 Of them the first is the Pāda Recaka (of the foot) ; then Kaṭirecaka (waist) the third Hasta Recaka (hand) and the last one Kaṇṭha Recaka (neck).

248 By Recita is meant moving the limb round separately or its drawing up separately.

249 Pāda Recaka—Movement from side to side with the feet wavering or having different movements.

250 Kaṭi Recaka—Raising up the Sacrum and turning the waist or drawing it back.

251 Hasta Recaka—Raising up, throwing out placing forward, turning round and drawing the back to the hand.

252 Kaṇṭha Recaka—Raising up lowering and bending the neck sideways and similar other movements.

253—254 On seeing Lord Śiva dance with Recakas, and Aṅgahāras the daughter of the mountain too danced with delicate features. This dance was followed by the playing of the instruments like. Mṛdaṅga, Bherī, Paṭaha, Jhañjhā, Ḍiṇḍima, Gomukha, Paṇava and Dardura.

255 After the annihilation of the sacrifice of Dakṣa Maheśvara performed the dance at the dusk employing Aṅgaharās in

conformity with proper beating of the time and the concordance of sounds.

256 On seeing the Piṇḍībandhas, Nandin Bhadramukha and other Gaṇas (attendants) gave the names and definitions of that Piṇḍībandhas.

257—263	Īśvara's	Vṛṣapiṇḍī
	of Nandin	Paṭṭiśī, (Pādasī)
	,, Caṇḍikā	Siṁhavāhinī
	,, Viṣṇu	Tārkṣya (Garuḍa)
	,, Svayambhū	Padma (lotus)
	,, Śakra	Airāvatī
	,, Manmatha	Jhaṣa (fish)
	,, Kumāra	Śikhi (Peacock)
	,, Śrī (Lakṣmī)	Rūpa (beauty)
	,, Jāhnavī	Dhārā (current)
	,, Yama	Pāśa (noose)
	,, Varuṇa	Nadī (River)
	,, Dhanada	Yakṣa
	,, Bala	Hala (Plough)
	,, Bhogins (serpents)	Sarpa (serpents)
	,, Gaṇeśvara	Dakṣayajñavimardinī
	,, the enemy of Antaka	Raudrī (in the form of the trident)

The Piṇḍīs of the other gods and goddesses shall be indicated through their emblems.

264 After evolving these Recakas, Aṅgahāras and Piṇḍīs lord Maheśvara imparted them to sage Taṇḍu who perfected the art of dance with vocal as well as instrumental music. This art of dance is known as Tāṇḍava.

The doubt of the sages

265 The art of Abhinaya (Indication through gestures) has been evolved by those conversant with the same to make the people understand the meaning (of the play). Why then was dance created ? On what feature does it depend ?

266 There is no apparent correlation with the music and the theme ; nor does it expand and reveal the literal meaning. Why is dance made an item in Gitas and Āsāritas.

267 Bharata said—This is to be mentioned here. Dance does not depend on any specific theme. It imparts beauty and splendour.

268 People spontaneously love dance. Further it is praised for its being auspicious.

269 Moreover it adds to the amusement and pleasure at the times of weddings, births of children, greeting a bridegroom, movements of joy and prosperity and general fetivity.

270 For the same reason the groups of the Bhūtas too have praised the Pratikṣepas (laudatory songs) used in songs regulating the developments of the dances.

271 The lord had said to Taṇḍu—Let this dance be performed in conjunction with the singing of songs.

272 Mostly the performance of Tāṇḍava is dependent on the eulogy of the deities but its more delicate production refers to the sentiment of love.

273 The rules and restrictions in regard to the performance of Tāṇḍava as laid down by Taṇḍu will be explained by me when we come up to Vardhamānaka.

274 It is called Vardhamānaka in as much as the increment of the Akṣaras causes the heightening of the Kalās and Laya.

The Procedure of Tāṇḍava

275 After duly arranging the musical instruments the rite of Āsārita (showering of flowers on the stage) should be performed by the sponsors of the play.

276 After performing the Upohana (humming or producing low sound as preliminary to a regular song) with the regular beating and playing of the dreams and stringed instruments the actress should be made to enter the stage to the accompaniment of beating the drums alone.

277 The playing of the instruments should be in the Jāti of Viśuddhakaraṇa. Then the Cārī is to be performed with the steps in tune with the song and the music of the instruments.

278 The female dancer shall enter the stage with a cluster of flowers in her hand. She shall be in the Vaiśākha Sthānaka and perform the four Recakas.

279 She shall then go round the stage scattering the flowers. After bowing to the deities she shall perform the Abhinaya (Gesticulation).

280 The players shall avoid instrumental music when the song is expatiated by means of gestures. Of course when the Aṅgahāras are performed the drums shall be played.

281 The playing of the instruments at the time of Tāṇḍava should be Sama (of proper level) Rakta (endearing), Vibhakta (of proper proportion) and Sphuṭa (distinct) with clear strokes. They shall be in consonance with the diverse aspects of the dance.

282 After singing the song the dancer makes her exit and other women enter the stage similarly.

283 The other women will form the Piṇḍīs duly and during that process perform the Paryastaka (Aṅgahāra).

284 These women shall depart after the formation of the Piṇḍīs. At that time the instrumental music with various Oghas and Karaṇas should be played similar to that at the time of Paryastaka.

285—287 Upohana and Āsārita are again performed as before. There shall be a song too and a female dancer enters as mentioned before. She should expatiate the song depicting the Vastu (theme) through the dance item.

288 The Āsārita having been concluded thus this dancer too departs and another Naṭī enters the stage for a similar performance.

289 Thus at every step the Āsārita rite is performed by the song stresses as well as the instrumentalists following the rules.

290 The first foot of the song is sung once, the second twice, the third thrice and the fourth four times.

291 The Piṇḍīs are of four sorts viz. Piṇḍī, Śṛṅkhalikā, Latābandha and Bhedyaka.

292 It is called Piṇḍībandha because it resembles a lump; Śṛṅkhalikā for it is held together in a cluster; Latābandha because the holding together resembles the cluster of creepers; Bhedyaka is the separate dance in a single person.

293 The application of Piṇḍībandha is in the shortest of the Āsāritas. Śṛṅkhalā at the transition of Laya, the Latābandha in the course of the middle one and the Bhedyaka during the Āsārita of longest duration.

294 The origin of the Piṇḍīs is of two types—(a) Yantra and (b) Bhadrāsana. They should be learned duly and relevantly employed by the producers.

The Procedures of Gītīs and Chandakas

295 Thus the producers of plays shall make use of dances in Vardhamānaka.

I shall later describe the rules pertaining to songs and Chandakas.

296—297 I shall explain the dance and the instrumental music that should accompany songs consisting of Vastus and Aṅgas. The female dancer enters the stage at the time of the performance of this item of song and music. All the drums should be sounded and the stringed musical instruments should be played with Kṣepa and Pratikṣepa.

298 Gestures should depict the Vastu (theme) of the song at the outset and this should be followed by the representation of the same by means of a dance item.

299 The subject matter of the songs in the Āsārita rite is to be governed by the same injunctions as the above in regard to the dance, gestures and the musical instruments.

300 This is remembered as the procedure with regard to the songs on the basis of Vastu. May the characteristic features of the songs on the basis of Aṅgas be listened to.

301 The Chandakas that are composed to their Aṅgas are governed by the same rules and procedures that apply to the dance, uses of gestures and the playing of instruments based on the words of the songs.

302 In the course of the Mukha and Upohana items the

players should be particular in employing heavy and light Akṣaras on the instruments by keeping the Varṇas aloof.

303 When it becomes necessary to repeat some of the parts as influenced by the course of the song the first ones are to be delineated by gestures and the remaining ones through dance.

304—305 The repetition of the parts in accordance with the course of the song is followed by the instrumental music observing the rules of three Pāṇis (such as Sama, Upari and Avara) and three Layas (Vilambita etc). This is the occasion where it is essential that the instrumental music should follow the proper Laya.

306—308 The Tattva, Anugata and Ogha refer to the Karaṇa. Of these the application of Tattva is in slow tempo (Laya) and of Ogha in quick. This is the procedure in regard to the instrumental music. Repetition of the different parts of the song in connection with Chandaka is in variably followed in joining dance, gestures and the song. There is Graha (commencement) at the end when songs are in simple stanzas but the Graha should take place from the beginning in the case of the large songs.

309—310 The foregoing is based on the eulogy of deities. Now understand the Sukumāra dance with the erotic sentiment based on a dialogue between a man and a woman in love.

Occasions befitting the dance item

311 Now listen Brahmins, to the occasions proper for the introduction of dance in the course of the songs.

312 The producer conversant with the procedure introduces dance at the close of the principal words and that of the Varṇa (Sthāyi, Ārohī, Avarohi, Sañcāri) or when the hero meets with success.

313 Dance item is also introduced on that occasion when something pertaining to the love of the married pair takes place because the dance will heighten the joy.

314 Also in that scene where the husband is near and the season is suitable with other things agreeable dance item can be introduced.

Prohibition of dance item

315 In the case of the heroine who is Khaṇḍitā (enraged), Vipralabhā (deceived) or Kalahāntaritā (keeping aloof due to quarrel) dance item is not introduced.

316 If a dialogue is going on, or if the lover is abroad or could not be near at hand the dance item is not to be introduced.

317 Further, if the heroine is conscious of the season or the like through the words of the female messenger and consequently overpowered by emotions of anxiety or wishful-longing no dance should be introduced.

318 But if the heroine gets pacified and restful gradually dance item is introduced with remaining Aṅgas (parts).

319 If the context pertains to the worship of any deity, a dance item with energetic Aṅgahāras as correlated to Śiva's dance should be introduced.

320 Where the song has the erotic sentiment as the basis covering a man and a woman in dance with gentle delicate. Aṅgahāras should be introduced as evolved by the goddess (Pārvatī).

Playing of the drums

321 I shall now explain the procedure regarding the beating of the drums following the four footed Narkuṭaka, Khañjaka and Parigītaka.

322 At the outset Sannipāta Graha inaugurates the playing of the drum when a foot of the Dhruva of the Khañja or Narkuṭa class has been already sung.

323 In the course of a Dhruva with even number of feet and having the syllables of equal number the drum can be beaten with the Graha by the forefinger after the first foot has already been sung.

324 Thereafter this should be repeated with proper gestures. At the close of the singing of the last foot drums are played again.

Prohibition of drums

325 When the song or its Varṇas have been concluded or about to begin a fresh drums should (not) be played.

326 When the Tantrīs or Karaṇas initiate the Antara Mārgas, the Tāṇḍava is accompanied by playing of the drums and the Sūcī Cārī.

327 One who performs this dance item as laid down by Maheśvara and practised by him shall be rid of all sins. He goes to the world of Śiva.

328 This is the procedure laid down as regards the performance of Tāṇḍava. O Brahmins, what more need be explained in connection with Nāṭya procedurē, may be kindly mentioned.

NOTES

The main topic discussed in the fourth chapter is the description of different kinds of dances and poses. It is revealed in this chapter that the first performance in the playhouse specially constructor by the divine architect was the composition of Brahmā himself—the story of the churning of the milk ocean. Later on at the instance of Brahmā, Bharata and his sons and disciples go to the Himālayan regions abounding in beautiful caves and waterfalls. Here they perform the Samavakāra on the churning of the milk ocean and a Ḍima named Tripura Dāha which pleased Śiva and his Bhūtas. The delighted Śiva informs them that he has himself evolved a dance item specially intended for his dance at the dusk. He has included 108 Karaṇas and 32 Aṅgahāras therein with this information the lord suggests that in the Pūrva Raṅga this special dance item should be included. What was Śuddha would then become Citra (Variegated). At the request of Brahmā for further edification and clarification of the dance item—Śiva calls Taṇḍu (probably Nandikeśvara) and asks him to explain Tāṇḍava dance to Bharata and others. Many letters joined together make words and many words joined together make sentences. Similarly the Karaṇas numbering 108 beginning with Talapuṣpapuṭa and ending with Gaṅgā Vataraṇa constitute Aṅgahāras by four or five joining together to make one

Aṅgahāra. These Aṅgahāras are 32 in number beginning with Sthirahasta. After the description of the Karaṇas the author mentions about four Recakas (or particular movements as distinct from the Karaṇas referred to above). The four Recakas are those of Pāda (foot), Kaṭī (hip), Hasta (hand) and Grīvā (neck). Then the Piṇḍībandhas are mentioned. They are seventeen in all pertaining to the different deities as follows :—

Lord Śiva (Aiśvarī or Vṛṣapiṇḍī), Nandin (Paṭṭasī, Pādasī or Paṭṭiśī), Caṇḍikā (Siṁhavāhinī), Viṣṇu (Tārasya Piṇḍī), Svayambhū (i.e. Brahmā) (Padma Piṇḍī) etc. etc. Then various rites are mentioned such as Āsārita, Upohana; when the female dance comes to the stage and scatter flowers making use of different gestures.

Then a group of female dancers enters the stage and form different Piṇḍīs such as Śṛṅkhalitā, Latābandha etc.

Then the author deals with those occasions when dances are prohibited and drums are not played.

4 Samavakāra—one of the ten dramatic types. The dominant sentiment is the heroic. There are twelve heroes, both Devas and Asuras.

10 Ḍima—is a drama with Raudra as the prominent sentiment. There are 16 Uddhata (haughty) heroes such as Yakṣas, Rākṣasas, Gandharvas etc.

59 Nṛttahastas are mentioned in detail in the ninth chapter about sixty seven in number of single hand gestures (24), combined hand gestures (13) and dance hands (30).

5

Procedure for the Preliminary Items

The sages' request

1—4 After listening to Bharata's explanation of the topic of Nāṭya, the sages were mentally delighted. They said—"The origin of drama and the Jarjara has been heard by us. We have understood the way of stopping obstacles and the adoration of the deities and have grasped the meaning. We would like to have the exhaustive details, O highly splendid one, of the Pūrvaraṅga (the preparatory rites). Kindly explain in a manner that we can understand everything.

Bharata's reply

5—6 On hearing the words of the sages, Bharata began to recount the procedure of the Pūrvaraṅga. He said—"O highly fortunate ones, even as I speak listen to the Pūrvaraṅga, the Kalās, Pādabhāgā, and Parivartanas (walking round).

Pūrvaraṅga

7 O excellent Brahmins, since at the outset (Pūrvam) this is performed on the stage (Raṅga) it is called Pūrvaraṅga (Preliminary item).

The parts of the Pūrvaraṅga

8—11 The following are the different items constituting the Pūrvaraṅga. They have to be performed along with Pāṭhya recitation of passages) playing of drums and other stringed instruments.

They are Pratyāhāra, Avataraṇa, Ārambha, Āśrāvaṇa, Vaktrapāṇi, Parighaṭṭana, Saṁghoṭana, Mārgāsārita, and Āsārita. The last one is of three types long, medium and short. These external songs are sung by the songsters sitting behind the curtain while drums and stringed instruments are played.

12—15 After raising the front curtain, dances and recitations are conducted while all the instruments are played. One song of Madraka class is sung. Vardhamānaka too may be used where Tāṇḍava shall be relevant. Thereafter the following items of Pūrvaraṅga shall take place viz.—Utthāpana, walking round, Benediction, Śuṣkāvakṛṣṭā, Raṅgadvāra, Cārī, Mahācārī, Trika (Joint talk of a set of three persons) and Prarocanā (incentive through laudation).

16 The characteristics of all these items in Pūrvaraṅga are being now explained by me.

17 Pratyāhāra—This is the neat arrangement of all the instruments of music.

Avataraṇa—This is the formal seating of the musicians and the instrumentalists.

18 Ārambha—The formal commencement of the singing.

Āśrāvaṇā—Adjustment of the instruments before actual playing.

19 Vakrapāṇi is the dividing and setting apart the various Vṛttis (styles) of instrumental music.

Parighaṭṭanā—Due adjustments to the strings of lute etc.

20 Saṁghotana—Practice of the different hand-poses for the purpose of indicating the time beat Mārgāsārita. The harmonious playing of drums and other instruments together.

21 Āsārita—The regular practising of the beat of the time fractions. The Gītavidhi (application of the songs) is intended for the glorification of the deities.

Utthāpana

22—23 Now the rite of Utthāpana is explained by me. The persons who are to recite Nāndī verses raise or inaugurate the performance of the play. Hence this rite is termed Utthāpana.

Parivartana

24 The director of the play begins to eulogise the guardian deities of the different regions by walking (Parivartana) all over the stage. Hence this item is called Parivartana Nāndī (Benediction).

25 This is invoking the blessings of the deities, the learned and the heads of government (kings etc.).

Śuṣkāpakṛṣṭa Dhruvā

26 Verses intended for the Jarjara composed of low worthless sounds and syllables are called Śuṣkāpakṛṣṭā.

Raṅgadvāra

27 Where from the performance of the play consisting of words and gestures actually commences in the Raṅgadvāra.

Cārī—Mahācarī

28 Cārī consists of movements depicting gentle and erotic sentiments and Mahācārī of those movements indicating the Furious Sentiment (Raudra).

Trigata (Set of three)

29 The conversation of the three persons viz. the Buffoon, the stage-manager and his assistant is called Trigata or Trika.

Prarocanā (Incentive laudation)

30 This is the laudatory talk of the stage manager suggesting the main theme and action of the play proposed to be staged by means of reasoning and arguments.

Bahirgīta—Its origin

31—36 The rite of Āśrāvaṇā included in the Bahirgīta shall now be described in detail. How it originated and how it is to be performed shall also be explained.

Nārada and other experts among the Gandharvas started the seven varieties of songs pertaining to Citra and Dakṣiṇa schools of music, together with Upohana and Nirgīta. These praised the gods and the Dānavas were compelled to hear the Nirgīta performed with proper Laya and Tāla. When they heard the happy songs in praise of the gods the Daityas and Rākṣasas became excited with jealousy and rivalry.

Consulting are another they said—"We are glad to hear this Nirgīta in accompaniment of the music of the instruments but not the songs in seven forms because they expatiate the exploits of the gods through they are delighted to hear it. We shall always hear the Nirgīta alone". Thereafter the Daityas pleased with the Nirgīta pressed the songsters for its repeated production.

Nārada requested to intercede

37—38 The furious gods said to Nārada—"These Dānavas and Rākṣasas appear to be delighted with Nirgīta alone. Hence we want this performance to come to an end. What do you think in this regard?"

Nārada consoles the gods

39—41 On hearing the enraged utterance of the gods Nārada said—"Let the Nirgīta based on the music of the stringed instruments be not discontinued but that combined with Upohana shall retain its seven forms in accompaniment to the musical instruments. Enshared by the other Nirgīta the Daityas and others will cease to be provoked. They will not then create obstacles."

42 Due to the rivalry of the Daityas this Nirgīta took its origin and to honour the Devas this is remembered as Bahirgīta.

43—44 Experts ought to play this in the Citravīṇā with metallic strings, making use of heavy and light syllables with due employment of Varṇas and Alaṁkāras , is Nirgīta since it is sung without words but only mere letters. It is termed Bahirgīta to smell the jealousy of the Devas.

45 I shall now explain the reason whereby Nirgīta has seven forms and the Utthāpana and the like.

46—54 The Pratyāhāra delights the Yātudhānas and the serpents while the Avataraṇa keeps the celestial damsels delighted. At the performance of the Ārambha the Gandharvas become pleased. The performance of Āśrāvaṇā increase the pleasure of the Daityas. Dānavas take delight in the Vaktrapāṇi. The hordes of Rākṣasas get pleasure in the performance of Parighattanā. The performance of Saṁghotanā satisfied the Guhyakas while the Yakṣas take delight in the Mārgāsārita gītas duly sung make the gods joyous. Rudra in the company of his Gaṇas is delighted at the performance of the Vardhamāna.

The rite of Parivartana delights the Lokapālas and Candra is pleased with the Nāndīnāgas are humoured by the singing of the Avakṛṣṭā Dhruvā while the Śuṣkāpakṛṣṭā thrills the groups of Pitṛs. Viṣṇu take delights in the Raṅgadvāra while the Vighnavināyakas take delight in the Jarjara ceremony.

If the Cārī rites are perfectly performed Umā becomes pleased while the Bhūtas become delighted in the excellent rite of Mahācārī.

55 Thus the propitiation of the different deities through the Pūrvaraṅga beginning with Pratyāhāra and ending with Mahācārī has been explained.

56 O excellent Brahmins I have made it clear which god is propitiated by which part of the Pūrvaraṅga.

57—58 The performance of the Pūrvaraṅga deserves the honour of all the deities, in fact it consists of the adoration of all deities, it is conducive to piety, renown and longevity. It delights the Daityas and the Dānavas as well as the heaven dwellers.

59 While explaining the Dhruvās I shall let you know the characteristics and the special function of the Vardhamāna and also of the performances with and without songs.

60—63 After the performance of the Gītaka and Vardhamāna the player shall sing the Utthāpanī Dhruvā It has eleven syllables in a foot with the first, second, fourth, eighth and the eleventh as long. It is sung in Caturaśra Tāla. It has four Sannipātas and all the three Layas. It has three Yatis (Caesurae) four Parivartanas and three Pāṇīs. The metre used shall be Viśloka and in the same kind of Tāla.

64 The Tāla mentioned here should have eight Kalās in the following manner: Śamyā of the two Kalās, Tāla of two Kalās, Śamyā of one Kalā and Sannipāta of three Kalās.

Parivartana I

65 Those conversant with it thus make use of eight Kalās. A walking round (Parivartana) is made of four such Sannipātas.

66 The first Parivartana in the Pūrvaraṅga should be performed in Sthitalaya. When the third Sannipāta is concluded drums should be played.

Parivartana II

67 At the conclusion of the first Parivartana when the second has started in Madhyalaya, the Sūtradhāra and the other two enter the stage.

68—69 With handfuls of flowers all the three of them should enter simultaneously. They shall be pure in complexion, excellent in mind and devoting mystery by means of eyes. Charms and auspicious spells should consecrate them. They should be in Vaiṣṇava Sthāna with perfection in physique.

70 The two assistants should carry a golden pot and the banner Jarjara. With them at his side the stage-manager takes five steps ahead.

71 It is for the specific purpose of adoring the lotus-born deity of Brahmā that the five steps are taken. I shall mention the taking of the steps in due detail.

72 The feet are to be placed three Tālas apart. They are to raise the feet one by one on each side and gradually set them down.

73 After going five steps the Sūcī Cārī should be performed by the three moving, the left foot at the outset and the right foot thereafter.

74 Then the stage manager should offer flowers in the Brahmamaṇḍala. Brahmā is well established in the centre of the Raṅgamaṇḍapa.

75—77 Afterwards he makes a respectful low bow to the grandfather of the world with Lalita gesture. During the process of salutation he should touch the ground thrice to measure the length of time. His steps shall therefore be suitably divided. The second Parivartana which has commenced with the entry of the stage manager and thus concludes with the salutation to the lotus-born lord accompanied by the necessary gestures should be performed in Madhyalaya.

Parivartana III

78 Thereafter the third Parivartana is undertaken by the stage manager who goes, round the Brahmamaṇḍala (i.e. the centre of the stage). He shall ritualistically drunk water thrice from his palm (i.e. Ācamana) and lift the Jarjara.

79—80 He should rise quickly from the Brahmamaṇḍala and perform the Vedhacārī (i.e. Sūcī Cārī) with his right foot placed forward first and the left foot thereafter. He then should raise the right foot and perform Cārī the order being the left foot first and the right foot thereafter.

81—83 Going around the stage-manager should summon the assistant with the Bhṛṅgāra in his hand and perform Śauca. He then performs the Ācamana rite and sprinkles himself with water. After duly performing the rite of ablution the stage manager assiduously takes up the Jarjara the remover of hindrances along with the beginning of the last Sannipāta.

84 The third Parivartana that had commenced with the circumambulation of the centre of the stage and just concluded with the taking up of the Jarjara should be performed in Drutalaya.

Parivartana IV

85—87 In order to ward off evils after taking up the Jarjara the stage manager should mutter some spells in eight Kalās. He should perform the Vedha Cārī by placing the left foot forward at the outset and the right foot thereafter. He shall then move five steps towards the Vādyas. Again he should perform the Vedha Cārī by placing the left foot at the outset and the right foot thereafter. Thus the Fourth Parivartana which had commenced with the taking up of the Jarjara and just concluded with an approach towards the Kutapas (musical instruments should be performed in Drutalaya).

88 In this rite sixteen Kalās are taken up by the movements of hand and feet. In case it is of the Tryasra type only twelve Kalās will be taken up by those movements.

89 Three salutations should be made by touching the ground. Sprinkling with water also should be undertaken. It is not undertaken in the Tryasra type.

Parivartanī Dhruvā

90 In this manner the rite of Utthāpana is to be performed. Thereafter the Parivartanī Dhruvā in Caturaśra Tāla, Madhyalaya and eight Sannipātas.

91 The Dhruvā that is in Atijagatī metre (thirteen syllables) with all the syllables except the last one, short is called Parivartanī Dhruvā. The last syllable is long.

92 Adopting the Vārtika Mārga the movement is directed leftwards with graceful steps in tune with the Vādya (instrumental music) and the deities are to be saluted in their respective quarters.

93 In the course of the movements every step consists of two Kalās and in every direction there should be two Sannipātas.

94 Then Vedha Cārī is observed with the left foot placed forward first and then the right foot placed at a distance of two Tālas.

95 Five steps are taken in Atikrānta Cārī. Thereafter the different deities are bowed to in their respective quarters.

96—97 He shall offer salutation to the eastern quarter at the outset wherein the deity is Śakra (Indra); the second quarter he should salute is that with Yama as its deity; then he should bow down to the Western direction that has Varuṇa as its deity. Fourthly he should make obeisance to the northern quarter supported by Dhanadā (Kubera).

98 After making obeisance to the quarters he should perform Vāmavedha (i.e. Sūcī Cārī with the left foot) and then the right foot is placed forward to perform the rite of Parivartana.

99 Turning his face towards the east the stage manager should make obeisance to Rudra, Upendra (Viṣṇu) and Brahmā taking three steps the "masculine", the "feminine" and the "Neuter."

100 The right one is the foot of men, the left that of the women and the right one not much lifted up is that of the enuch.

101 The stage manager should make obeisance to Śiva using the masculine foot (in placing forward at the outset) to Janārdana with the feminine foot and the lotus born lord with the neuter foot.

A fourth man enters the stage

102 Thus the Parivartana rite is concluded then enters the fourthman with flowers in his hand.

103 It is his duty to adore the Jarjara, the groups of muscial instru ments and the stage manager.

104 In the course of the adoration the foot movements of the stage manager should be in tune with the playing of the drums. Songs need not be sung then. There shall be Stobhakriyās (meaningless words should be uttered).

Avakṛṣṭā Dhruvā

105 The Caturthakāra (fourth man) makes his exit after the Pūjā has been duly performed. It is now that Avakṛṣṭā Dhruvā is to be sung in Caturaśra Tāla and Vilambitalaya.

106 Heavy syllables (Gurus) predominate in this Dhruvā consisting of eight Kalās (Mātrās). Avarapāṇi (Avapāṇikā). Sthāyi-Varṇa should be used (and not Ārohi, Avarohi or Sañcāri).

107 This Avakṛṣṭā Dhruvā consists of four Pādas each Pāda having ten syllables. Of these the fourth, fifth, seventh and the eighth are Laghu (and the other Guru).

The Nāndī

108 The stage manager reads out the Nāndī which may have eight or twelve Pādas. His tone shall be of the medium pitch.

109–112 The following is an example of a Nāndī of twelve Pādas (i.e. sentences)— "(1) Obeisance to all the gods (2) Welfare unto the twice-born ones (3) May the king Soma be victorious (4) Let there be auspiciousness unto the cows and Brahmins (5) Let there be progress of the Vedic study (6) May the enemies of Vedas perish (7) Let the great king rule over the ocean gridled earth (8) May the nation prosper (9) Let the stage flourish (10) May there be great piety to the sponsor of the play (11) Let the composer of the poem become renowned and righteous (12) May the deities be pleased with this Ijyā (sacrifice).

113 In the middle of these sentences of the Nāndī the two assistants should utter. "Be it so for ever" in land and distinct world

114 Thus the Nāndī recitation rite is to be performed duly.

Śuṣkāvakṛṣṭā Dhruvā

Verses in praise of Jarjara should be sung by means of Śūṣkāvakṛṣṭā.

115 There are nine Gurus at the outset; then six short syllables and three long syllables in the end and eight Mātrās in all.

116 As for example :—

Digle Digle Jhaṇḍe Jhaṇḍe Jambuka Valitaka Tete Jā

117—118 After the due performance of the Śuṣkāvakṛṣṭā Dhruvā, O excellent Brahmins he shall in a majestic voice utter a verse in praise of the diety currently being worshipped. It may be in the way of assenting loyalty to the king or praising the Brahmins.

Raṅga Dvāra

119 After the recitation of Jarjara śloka which is remembered in Raṅgadvāra rite he shall repeat another verse to glorify the Jarjara.

120 After duly honouring the Jarjara the stage manager should perform a Cārī when the two Assistants retrace their steps (the Sūtradhāra alone performs Cārī and Mahācārīs).

121 Madhyalaya is resorted to in performing the Aḍḍitā Dhruvā thereafter with Caturaśra Tāla and four Sannipātas.

Definition of Aḍḍitā

122 There are four feet of twelve syllables each. In all of them the first, fifth and the last syllables as well as the fourth are Aḍḍitā. The remaining ones are short. Such a Dhruvā song is long.

123 Formerly this was performed by Maheśvara along with Umā when he displayed different Bhāvas and Viceṣṭitas (movements). Following that same procedure I shall relate its application.

124—125 The Sutradhāra then assumes the Avahittha posture (Sthāna) [see 164-165 ch. 13]. He should keep the left hand on the navel with the palm pointing downwards. He should hold the Jarjara with the other hand and proceed five steps moving his limbs gracefully. The Pallava gesture should be shown by the left hand. He should proceed slowly so that he covers only a distance of one Tāla at every step.

126—127 Placing his left foot forward at the outset and the right foot thereafter the efficient Sūtradhāra should perform the Śuci Cārī. Then he recites a verse with love for its theme. After reciting the Cārī verse and performing the Parivartana rite he shall go back with the same steps as before but face the front.

Mahācārī

128 He should then handover the excellent Jarjara to the Pāripārśvikas (Assistants) and perform Mahācārī in accordance with the injunctions as follows.

Caturasrā Dhruvā

129—130 The Dhruvā song to be sung at the time of this Cārī is called Caturaśrā. It is in Druta (Quick) Laya with four Sannipātas and eight Kalās. Each of the four feet contains eleven syllables. The first, fourth, seventh, tenth and the last syllables are long ones. The remaining ones are short. Example of Caturaśrā Dhruvā-Pāda Talāhata Pātita Śailam etc. (meaning) —May this Tāṇḍava Nṛtya at the time of the annihilation of all living beings, of Hara protect you all. The kick from his sole has smashed the mountains and agitated the ocean with all the creatures therein. It is ever pleasing.

131—132 He should then advance towards the Bhāṇḍa (musical instrument) performing Śuci Cāri with an alteration in Vikṣepa. He shall then gracefully move his feet in Druta Laya keeping them three Tālas apart. Five steps are made by him performing the Sūcī Cārī in the order left first and the right thereafter.

133—135 He should then move backwards but with his face turned in front in the manner mentioned before. Thereafter he should proceed forward three steps in the same manner performing Śuci Cārī in the same fashion.

136—137 A verse with Raudra (Furious) sentiment should be recited by him bringing both the feet together. He should then proceed three steps and address his assistants making them sing a Narkuṭa Dhruvā, while this is being sung he should perform Śucī Cārī by putting forward the left foot at the outset and the right thereafter.

Trigata

138 The Trigata (conversation of the trio) should take place if the play follows the Bhārati Vṛtti (or the verbal style). The Buffoon should utter the Kathanikā (a discourse) consisting of split (non compound) words of irrelevant nature causing the Sūtra Dhāra to smile.

139 In this discourse a controversial topic may be introduced with an abrupt enigmatical remark but no false statement. Questions leading to a plot of the play (in the form of a poem) may be asked such as who stands? Who won? etc.

140—141 The prettle of the Pāripārśvika must be refuted by the Buffoon but approved of by the Sūtra Dhāra. It is thus that Trigata is conducted.

Prarocanā (Laudatory remark)

The Sūtradhāra who is highly efficient extends the formal invitation to the audience with laudatory remarks about the play in order to create enthusiasm in them.

142 After strictly adhering to the rules the trio should perform Sūcī Carī and make a simultaneous exit without undue shaking of the feet.

143 It is thus, O excellent Brahmins that the Caturaśra type of Pūrvaraṇga is conducted. Now the tryaśra type is described know it.

Tryaśra Pūrvaraṅga

144 The procedure is the same. The ancillaries are the same; the only difference in Tryaśra is the limited measurement of Tāla.

145—146 Two Kalās constitute the Śamyā and one Kalā the Tāla. Thereafter the Śamyā should be made of one Kalā and the Sannipāta of two Kalās. The Tryaśra Pūrvaraṅga is performed thus with Kalā, Tāla and Laya duly included. Of course Utthāpana and other items should be taken up.

Utthāpanī Dhruvā of the Tryaśra type

147 The song consists of four feet of twelve syllables each, the fourth, the eighth, the tenth and the last being long. This is called Utthāpannī Dhruvā of the Tryaśra variety.

148 The instrumental music, the walking about the Dhruvā songs and the Tāla need be made very short and simple by those of who know the art of dance.

149 The Aṅga Viceṣṭitas (movements of the limbs) should be in accordance with the nature of the instrumental music, elaborate or limited as the case may be.

150—151 The movement of hands and feet should take two Kalās for its duration and in the walking about (Parāvarta) in the Caturaśra Pūrvaraṅga the hands and feet move sixteen times whereas in the Tryaśra type they move twelve times. This is the measurement of both in the Pūrvaraṅgas.

152 In the walking round at the time of Parivartana, three steps are taken in the Tryaśra type and in the salutation to the quarters in Caturaśra, five steps are taken.

153 Tryaśra should be performed in accordance with the discretion of the Ācārya with due consideration for the Tāla Pramāṇa. Hence the detailed characteristics are not mentioned to avoid redundancy.

154 O excellent Brahmins the preliminary rites of Caturaśra and Tryaśra types relating to a play based on Bhāratī Vṛtti are performed in this manner.

155 Thus I have mentioned the Śuddha (pure) Pūrvaraṅga procedure. How Citratva (state of mixed or Variegated type) can be effected by the producers of the play I shall mention now.

Citra (Variegated) preliminaries

156—157 After the performance of the Utthāpana and the rite of Parivartana, the Caturthakāra (fourth man) embellishes with the flowers offered by him. The experts in music sing loudly and the Dundubhīs are played repeatedly.

158 The pure Devīs (dancers in the guise of goddesses) should scatter flower garlands all round. Then they should perform dance with all the Aṅgahāras duly adopted.

159—160 In the middle of the Nāndi Padas (the sentences in the benedictory verse) the various constituents of Tāṇḍava should be introduced by those who wish to turn the Śuddha Pūrvaraṅga into a Citra Pūrvaraṅga. They are to be fully accompanied by Piṇḍīs, Recakas Aṅgahāras, Nyāsas, Apanyāsas etc. etc.

161 After performing duly the Pūrvaraṇga rites whether Śuddha or Citra the actors should proceed ahead to the performance of the play. Thereafter the divine ladies shall vanish from the stage.

162 After the lady dancers have vanished the other items in the Pūrvaraṅga should be performed.

163 This is the procedure whereby the Śuddha becomes Citra.

One thing should be noted particularly whether the Śuddha or the Citra is adopted there should not be excess of dance or song.

164 If there is excess of dance and song there may be distress of the production-asistants and the audience as well.

165 The distressed ones can never have clarity of sentiments and Bhāvas. Thereby the remaining items in the programme cannot be conducive to pleasurable sensation.

166 Whether the Pūrvaraṅga is of the Caturaśra or Tryaśra type, whether it is of the Śuddha or Citra variety, after duly concluding their duties the Sūtradhāra and his followers should make their exit.

167 After the Pūrvaraṅga has been duly performed the Sthāpaka should enter the stage. He shall have the same features and characteristics as the Sūtradhāra.

Sthāpanā or introductory rite

168 The Sthāpaka adopts the Vaiṣṇava pose (Sthāna) with the requisite Sauṣṭhava (perfection) of the body. He shall then make use of the same types of foot movements as used by the Sūtradhāra.

169 After the entry of the Sthāpaka a Dhruvā relevant to the occasion should be performed by those who know these things. It may be Caturaśrā or Tryaśrā but the Madhya Laya should be invariably used.

170 Thereafter a Cārī in praise of gods and Brahmins is performed. Recitation of verses with sweet words and diverse

Tālas and Layas. They shall evoke the requisite sentiments and Bhāvas.

171 After propitiating the audience duly he shall announce the name of the poet who had written the play. Thereafter he proceeds with the Prastāvanā (Prologue) which refers to the theme of the work.

172—173 Then by mentioning a god in a divine play, a man in a human play and either a god or a man where gods and men assemble he shall announce in diverse ways the theme of the play by referring to its Mukhasandhi based on the Bīja (germ of the theme).

174 After introducing the play properly thus the Sthāpaka should make his exit. Thus the Pūrvaraṅga is to be performed duly.

175 If the sponsor of the play performs the Pūrvaraṅga in accordance with the injunctions nothing untoward shall happen to him and he will reach heaven.

176 If any one defies the rules and produces the play as he pleases he shall incur heavy loss and will be reborn as an animal of the low order.

177 If five these to be kindled by violent gusts of wind it cannot burn as quickly as the incorrect procedure in the performance of the play.

178 Thus people of Avantī, Pāñcāla, Southern regions and Odra deśa should perform the Pūrvaraṅga of the two types of extent (Tryaśra & Caturaśra).

179 O Brahmins, thus the procedure for Pūrvaraṅga has been recounted to you. Tell me what more shall I tell you about the rules and regulations in connection with Nāṭya Veda.

N.B. After this verse a few more verses are found in certain Mss. Many of those verses practically repetitions of some of the verses already included. The remaining do not seem to be genuine to many scholars. Hence we have not translated them here.

6

The Distinction betweer Sentiment and Emotional fervour

The query of the Sages

1—2 After listening to the explanation of the preliminary rites the venerable sages asked Bharata "We have five questions to be asked. It behoves you to clarify them." What have been recounted as Rasas in the dramatic art by those who are proficient in that art should be explained. How do these Rasas get their Rasatva ?

3 What have been mentioned as Bhāvas how do they make us feel the various emotions ? Kindly explain the terms Saṁgraha (Synoptic gist), Kārikā (Mnemonical Verse) and Nirukta (Etymological derivation).

Bharata begins to answer

4—5 On hearing the request of the sages Bharata resumed his explanation based on the distinction between Rasa and Bhāva "O saints, I shall expound in the due order the terms Saṁgraha, Kārikā and Nirukta."

6—7 It is impossible to reach the entire limit of the art of dance and drama. Why ? Since the lores are many and the arts and crafts are infinite. Even one branch of the Vast ocean of knowledge cannot be completed. Then where is the question of mastering the principles and meanings of all the Bhāvas ?

8 But I shall expatiate on the synoptic digest of Rasa, Bhāva etc. of the dramatic art embodying the main topics in a limited number of Sūtras (Aphorisms) but leaving ample scope for inference (for full comprehension).

Saṁgraha (Synoptic digest)

9 Learned men understand by the word Saṁgraha the

condensed summary of all the topics explained in detail into Sūtras and their Bhāṣyas (glosses).

10 [Another meaning of the word Saṁgraha is collection] That Saṁgraha in regard to the Nāṭyaveda comprises of the Rasas, Bhāvas, Abhinaya (Gesticulatory representation) Dharmi (Rehearsed practice), Vṛtti (Style), **Pravṛtti, (Action),** Siddhi (Achievement), Svaras (notes), Ātodya (instrumental music), Gāna (song) and Raṅga (the stage).

Mnemonical Verse (Kārikā)

11 The Kārikā reveals the meaning in full by means of limited utterance. Scholars explain the topics succinctly (in the form of verses) threading them together.

12—13 Nirukta (Text on etymological derivation of words). Learned men understand by the word Nirukta the body of glossary compiled on the basis of many substantives and strictly adhering to the scriptural (and other) texts. It contains adequate arguments for the specified meanings of the roots and they are justified by the different principles (in the Sāstras). The meaning shall be emphatically established by expressing the meanings of the roots.

14 O excellent Brahmins, what has been succinctly recounted by me a Saṁgraha shall be mentioned elaborately along with Nirukta and Kārikā.

15 *Rasas eight in number.*—Sentiments remembered in the dramatic art are eight viz. Śṛṅgāra (the erotic), Hāsya (Humorous), Karuṇa (Pathos), Raudra (Impetuous anger), Vīra (Heroic), Bhayānaka (Terrific), Bībhātsa (the odious) and Adbhuta (the mysterious).

16 These eight Rasas have been recounted by the noble-souled Brahmā. Now I shall enumerate Bhāvas (Emotional fervour and State) viz Sthāyi (Permanently dominant), Sañcāri (moving or transitory) and Sattvaja (originating from the mind, temperamental).

17 Sthāyi Bhāvas (Permanently dominant) are Rati (Love), Hāsa (merriment), Śoka (sorrow), Krodha (Fury), Utsāha (enthusiasm), Bhaya (terror), Jugupsā (disgust) and Vismaya (Astonishment).

18—21 *Vyabhicāri* [*Sañcāri*] *Bhāvas*.—They are thirty three in number viz. Nirveda (Despondency), Glāni (Weakness), Śaṅkā (Śuspicious), Asūyā (envy), Mada (Inebriation), Śrama (exhaustion), Ālasya (lethargy), Dainya (Depression), Cintā (anxiety), Moha (delusion), Smṛti (recollection), Dhṛti (fortitude), Vrīḍā (Bashfulness), Capalatā (in constancy), Harṣa (joy), Āvega (excitement), Jaḍatā (Stupefaction), Garva (Arrogance), Viṣāda (Despair), Autsukya (impatient curiosity), Nidrā (sleep), Apasmāra (Loss of memory), Svapna (Dreaming), Prabodha (Wakening), Amarṣa (indignation), Avahittha (Dissimulation), Ugratā (Cruelty), Mati (self assurance), Vyādhi (Sickness), Unmāda (madness), Maraṇa (death), Trāsa (fright) and Vitarka (deliberation).

Sāttvika Bhāvas (*Temperamental States of emotional fervour*)

22 The Sāttvika Bhāvas are eight in number. They originate from the physical form. They are Stambha (Paralysis), Sveda (Sweat), Romāñca (horripilation), Svarasāda (feebleness in the voice), Vepathu (Trembling), Vaivarṇya (change of colour), Aśru (Shedding tears), Pralaya (Loss of Sense).

Abhinaya (*Histrionic representation*)

23 The Abhinayas are four in number: (1) Āṅgika (Gestures from the limbs), (2) Vācika (Verbal utterance), (3) Āhārya (Embelishment through dress and ornaments etc.) and (4) Sāttvika (Temperamental).

Dharmis (*Rehearsed Practice*)

24 Dharmis are of two sorts in the dramatic portrayal (1) Loka Dharmi (Popularly realistic representation), (2) Nāṭya-dharmi (Theatrically conventional).

Vṛttis—The Vṛttis (Styles) are of four kinds (1) Bhārati [Pertaining to the goddess of speech (Verbal)], (2) Sāttvatī (The Grand one), (3) Kaiśikī (the graceful one) and (4) the Ārabhaṭī (the energetic or impetuous one).

25—26 *Pravṛtti* (Usage in local vogue)—They are four in vogue in the dramatic performances viz. (1) Āvantī, (2) Dākṣi-ṇātyā, (3) O Dramagadhi and(4) Pāñcālamadhyamā.

Siddhi (*Achievement*)

This is of various sorts but of two distinct kinds (1) Daivikī (divine) and (2) Mānuṣī (human).

Svaras (*Musical notes*)

27—31 The Svaras beginning with Ṣaḍja may be either Śārīra (Corporeal) or Vaiṇava (originating from Vīṇā or lute). The Ātodya (musical instrument) should be known as having four types, with special Characteristics for each viz. *Tata*, *Avanaddha*, *Ghana* and *Suṣira*. (1) *Tata* is the stringed instrument (with wire) (2) *Avanaddha* is drumlike instrument of percussion (3) *Ghana* is to be known as the instrument for beating time and (4) Suṣira (having holes) is the flute.

Gāna (Song) with the combination of Dhruvās is of five kinds (1) Praveśa (Entry) (2) Ākṣepa (Casual) (3) Niṣkrāma (Exit) (4) Prāsādika (pleasing) and (5) Āntara (Internal). *Raṅga* (Stage) is of three types (1) Caturaśra (Square) (2) Vikṛṣṭa (Rectangular) and (3) Tryaśra (triangular). This has already been explained.

Thus the Nāṭya Saṁgraha (the collection of component items in a dramatic performance) has been pointed out by means of Sūtra like brief words. Hereafter I shall expatiate on the details of the succinct statements.

Detailed explanation of Rasas

Prose Passage

In this connection we shall explain Rasas at the outset. No meaning has any function without any relish thereof. The combination of Vibhāvas (Determinants) and Anubhāvas (consequents) together with Vyabhicāri Bhāvas (Transitory states) produce Rasa. If you ask "Where is a specific instance thereof?" We shall say this—Just as there is the production of good taste through the juice produced when different spices, herbs and other articles are pressed together so also Rasa (Sentiment) is produced when various Bhāvas get together. Just as through molasses and other articles, spices and herbs six kinds of tastes are produced so also the Sthāyī Bhāvas in combination with different Bhāvas attain the state of Rasa.

The sages then asked—"What is that entity called Rasa ?"

Here it is explained (by us)—"It is Rasa because it is worthy of being tested (relished)." How is Rasa worthy of being relished ? If is explained thus—Just as noble minded persons consuming cooked food seasoned with various kinds of spices relish the tastes thereof and become excessively delighted so also sophisticated onlookers (theatre goers) relish the Sthāyī Bhāvas indicated through the gesticulation of the Bhāvas through Verbal, physical and temperamental activities and become delighted. Hence the Nāṭya Rasas are hereby explained this.

In this regard there are two traditionally handed over verses.

32—33 Just as the people conversant with foodstuffs and consuming articles of food consisting of various things and many spices enjoy their taste, so also the learned men enjoy the Sthāyī Bhāvas in combination with gesticulations of Bhāvas, mentally. Hence they are remembered as Nāṭya Rasas.

Here some one says—"Is the production and relish thereof of the Bhāvas from the Rasas or that of the Rasas from the Bhāvas ?" In this regard the opinion of some people is that the outcome and relish is due to the mutual contact. That is not the fact. Why ? It is experienced (perceived) that the relish of the Rasas is from the Bhāvas and not of the Bhāvas from the Rasas.

In this regard there are these verses :—

34—38 Dramatic experts call emotional fervour as Bhāvas because they bring about the outcome of Rasas by means of the impact of different Abhinayas. Just as the side dish is prepared by means of different articles of devise characteristics so the Bhāvas produce Rasas incombination with Abhinayas. There is no Rasa devoid of Bhāva nor Bhāva devoid of Rasa. Their effectiveness is mutual in regard to Abhinaya.

The combination of spices and herbs gives rise to taste and in the same manner. Bhāvas and Rasas contribute to the mutual development.

Just as the tree takes its origin from the seed and the flower and the fruit from the tree. So also the Rasas are the root and all the Bhāvas are stabilised therein.

Prose passage.—Therefore we shall explain in full the origin, specific colours, deities and specimens of these Rasas. Four Rasas are the main causes in the group of Rasas viz. Śṛṅgāra, Raudra, Vīra and Bībhatsa.

Rasa the cause and Rasa the effect

39—41 Hāsya (Humorous) Rasa originates from Śṛṅgāra

Karuṇa (Pathetic) from Raudra (Furious), Adbhuta (Marvellous) from Vīra (Heroic) and Bhayānaka (Terrible) from Bībhatsa (Odious). The imitation of Śṛṅgāra is termed Hāsya. The result of the activity of Raudra should be known as Karuṇa Rasa, the result of the activity of Vīra is glorified as Adbhuta; The sight of the odious (Bībhatsa) transforms into Bhayānaka (terrible).

The Varṇas (Colours)

42—43

Rasa	Colour
Śṛṅgāra	Śyāma (Green)
Hāsya	Sita (White)
Karuṇa	Kapota (Dove Coloured)
Raudra	Rakta (Red)
Vīra	Gaura (Wheatish Brown)
Bhayānaka	Kṛṣna (Black)
Bībhatsa	Nīla (Blue)
Adbhuta	Pīta (Yellow)

Deities

44—45

Śṛṅgāra	Viṣṇu	Hāsya	Pramatha
Raudra	Rudra	Karuṇa	Yama
Bībhatsa	Mahākāla	Bhayānaka	Kāla
Vīra	Mahendra	Adbhuta	Brahmā

Prose Passage. Thus the origin, colour and deity have been explained in detail. Now we shall explain their characteristics and specimens in conjunction with Vibhāva (Determinants), Anubhāva (Consequents) and Vyabhicārins (Transitory State). We shall point out how the Sthāyi Bhāva (Dominant State) transforms into Rasa.

Śṛṅgāra—The Rasa named Śṛṅgāra originates from the Sthāyi Bhāva of Rati (love) a bright dress is its soul. Whatever is clean, pure and worth looking at is connected with the Sentiment Śṛṅgāra. One who is brightly attired is termed Śṛṅgāravān (Don Juan). Just as the names of persons are assigned in accordance with the traditional customs and practice in the family so also the nomenclature of the Rasas and Bhāvas and other things in as much as they are concerned with the dramatic performance, proceeds along the tradition in vogue and the advice of persons in authority. In the case of the Śṛṅgāra Rasa too, it is so named because it goes along with an elegant bright dress and make up pleasant to all. It is enjoined by preceptors. Both male and female characters are behind its outcome. An excellent young woman is its Prakṛti (Source of origin).

It has two Adhiṣṭhānas (Bases) (*a*) Sambhoga (Love in Union) (*b*) Vipralambha (Love in Separation).

(*a*) *Sambhoga*—This love in union gets itself manifested through the Vibhāvas (Determinants) viz. the pleasant season, garlands, unguents, ornaments, people dear and near, sensual objects, excellent mansions, objects of pleasure, going to the garden, experiencing pleasures, listening (to sweet voices), seeing (beautiful things), play and sports etc.

Its production in the drama is by means of gestures through the Anubhāvas (consequents) viz. clever and significant glances of the eyes, movements of the eyebrows ogling looks, movements of limbs, sweet Aṅgahāras (major dance figures).

The Vyabhicāri Bhāvas in Śṛṅgāra are all those mentioned before excluding Trāsa (fright), Ālasya (lethargy), Augrya (ferocity) and Jugupsā (disgust).

(*b*) *Vipralambha* (*Love in Seperation*)—This should be displayed during the dramatic performance through the following Anubhāvas (consequents) viz. Nirveda (dejectedness and indifference to worldly joys), Glāni (languor), Śaṅkā (apprehension), Asūyā (jealousy), Śrama (weariness), Cintā (anxiety and worry), Autsukya (yearning), Nidrā (drowsiness), Supta (Sleep), Svapna (dream), Bibboka (feigned anger), Vyādhi (illness), Unmāda (insanity), Apasmāra (forgetfulness), Jāḍya (Sluggishness), Maraṇa (death) and other conditions.

One may say here thus—"You say that Śṛṅgāra originates from Rati (love); how do you account for its manifestation through the Bhāvas (emotional states and fervour) based on pathos?" It is mentioned in reply thus—we have already explained that Śṛṅgāra is of two types viz. (*a*) that induced by love in union and (*b*) love in separation. Ten States of Kāma (love) have been indicated in the authoritative texts on Vaiśika Tantra (Science of Amorous activities). We shall examine those states later in Sāmānya Abhinaya section (common histrionic presentation).

Karuṇa is distinct from Vipralambha. The former involves a desperate condition as a result of curse affliction, downfall, separation from the near and dear, loss of wealth, imprisonment, slaughter etc. The Vipralambha (love in separation) involves the condition of sticking to hopeful expectation (of reunion) out of yearning and anxiety. Thus Śṛṅgāra includes all the Bhāvas (of even other sentiments).

Further—(verses summarising the above discussion)

46 The term Śṛṅgāra refers to a man who is richly endowed with all desirable things and much interested in pleasure, who makes full use of the seasons gerlands etc. (for enhancing his pleasure) and who is accompanied by a youthful maiden. Two verses in Āryā Metre further clarify what is put in Sūtra form here.

47—48 Śṛṅgāra Rasa is the outcome of the following things and activities:—the favourable season, garlands, ornaments sweet music, poetry, persons dear and near, frequenting parks and gardens sporting activities.

Its presentation in the dramatic performance is through graceful movements of the limbs accompanied by sweet smiles, pleasing words, fortitude, delighted expressions, serene eyes, beaming face etc.

Hāsya Rasa (*Humour*)

Laughter is the Sthāyī Bhāva (dominant emotion) in the Hāsya Rasa. Its outcome is through the following Vibhāvas (Determinants) viz. Vikṛtaveṣa (Unseemly dress), Vikṛtālaṅkāra (misplaced ornaments), Dhārṣṭya (Impudance), Laulya (covetousness), Kalaha (quarrel), Asatpracāpa (near-obscene utterance), Vyaṅga Darśana (displaying deformed limbs), Doṣodā Haraṇa (Pointing out the faults of others) and other similar things. Its display in the dramatic performance is through the following Anubhāvas (consequents) like Oṣṭhadaṁśana (biting the lips), Nāsākapolaspandana (throbbing of the nose and the cheek), Dṛṣṭivyākośa (Opening the eyes wide), Dṛṣṭyākuñcana (contracting the eyes), Sveda (perspiration), Āsyarāga (colour of the face) Pārsvagrahaṇa (holding the sides) and others. The Vyabhicāri Bhāvas (Transitory

States) of this Rasa are Ālasya (Lethargy), Avahittha (dissimulation), Tandrā (drowsiness), Anidrā (Sleeplessness), Svapna (dreaming), Prabodha (waking up), Asūyā (envy) and other things.

Hāsya is of two kinds—Ātmastha (self-based), Parastha (Based in others). When the actor laughs to himself it is called Ātmastha when he makes another laugh it is called Parastha.

In this regard there are two Āryā verses traditionally handed down:—

49 The display of oddly placed ornaments, unseemly behaviour, unrelevant words, faulty dress, strange movements of the limbs etc. make people laugh to themselves. So this Rasa is called Hāsya.

50 The actor makes other people laugh through distortions of facial features, statements uttered irrelevantly, strange movements of the limbs, and odd dress. Hence the Rasa should be known as Hāsya.

51 This Rasa is most common to women characters and persons of the mean order. It has six distinct varieties which I shall explain presently.

52 They are (1) Smita (gentle smile), (2) Hasita (slight laughter), (3) Vihasita (open laughter), (4) Upahasita (Laughter of ridicule), (5) Apahasita (obscene laughter) and (6) Atihasita (Boisterous laughter). The superior types of persons, the middling ones and the base ones have respectively two of these.

53 Smita and Hasita belong to the people of high rank; Vihasita and Upahasita to the ordinary people; Apahasita and Atihasita to the mean people.

In this regard these are the following verses :—

People of high Rank

54—55 The cheeks are slightly blown, the glances are elegant, the teeth can not be seen—such is the Smita. The mouth and the eyes are blooming, the cheeks are blown and the teeth are slightly seen. Such is the Hasita.

The Middling ones

56—57 Vihasita should be befitting the occasion. It is a laughter when slight sound is produced sweetly. The actor contracts the eyes and the cheeks. There is cheerful lustre in the face. In the course of the Upahasita the nostrils become expanded. The eyes become strabismic and cross eyed. The shoulder and the head become bent a little.

Mean People

58—59 The Apahasita is usually unsuitable to the context. Tears trickle from the eyes. The actor violently shakes the shoulders and the head. The Atihasita is excessively boisterous. The eyes are expanded. Tears drop from them. Hands cover the sides.

60—61 When humorous interludes arise in the course of a dramatic performance the author shall so depict the smile or laughter as the case may be that the superior, middling and the mean do so befittingly. Thus the Hāsya Rasa is of two varieties either selfbased or based in others. It has three types of persons as the source. Hence on the whole the Rasa has of six kinds.

Karuṇa Rasa (Pathos)

Śoka (sorrow) is the Sthāyi Bhāva in the outcome of the Karuṇa Rasa. The Vibhāvas (determinants) are curse, distress, down fall, calamity, separation from the near and dear, loss of wealth, murder, imprisonment, flight, dangerous accidents and misfortunes. Its presentation in the stage is through the following Anubhāvas, viz. discharge of tears, lamentation, parched throat and mouth, pallor of the face, drooping of the limbs, gasping for breath, loss of memory and other similar things The Vyabhicāri Bhāvas are dejectedness, in difference, languor, anxiety, yearning excited state, illusion, loss of sense, sadness, ailments, lethargy, sluggishness, epileptic loss of memory, fear, death, paralysis, tremour, pallor in the face, shadding of tears, loss of speech and the kindred feelings.

In this regard there are two verses in the Āryā metre.

62—63 The Karuṇa Rasa takes its origin through different

Bhāvas either at the sight of the death (or murder) of the dear one or when unpleasant words have an adverse impact.

It is to be presented in the stage through sighs, lamentations, loss of sense, weeping bitterly and other guestures.

Raudra Rasa (Impetuous anger of wrath)

Prose Passage

The Sthāyi Bhāva of the Raudra Rasa is Krodha (Anger). It takes its origin in the Rākṣasas, Dānavas and very haughty human beings with a regular battle as its immediate cause. Its outcome is though the Vibhāvas much as Krodha (anger) Dharṣaṇa (violation of modesty), Adhikṣepa (abuse), Apamāna (insult), Anṛtavacana (uttering falsehoods), Vākpāruṣya (Harsh words), Droha (animosity), Mātsarya (jealousy) and kindred ones. The activities connected with this Rasa are beating, tearing, harassing, chopping off, breaking, piercing, striking hurling missiles, shedding blood, seizing of weapons and such like. Its presentation in the dramatic performance is through the Anubhāvas, making the eyes red, perspiring profusely, knitting of the eyebrows, clapping the hands, guashing of the teeth, biting of the lips, throbbing of the cheeks, hitting the palm with the fist etc. The Vyabhicāri Bhāvas of this Rasa are tumultuous battle, energetic enthusiasm, impetuosity, wrath, restlessness, ferocity, profuse perspiration, trembling, rising of the hairs etc.

Here some one may ask—"You said that Raudra Rasa takes its origin in the Rākṣasas etc. Does it not occur in the case of others? The reply is "Yes, there is Raudra in the case of others too. But here the special prerogative is to be taken into consideration. By nature the Rākṣasas are very furious. They are endowed with many hands and mouths. They have tawny dishavelled hairs standing up in an ugly manner. Their eyes are red and fearfully round. Their bodies are darkskinned and very huge. Whatever they undertake is naturally very furious, even their ordinary movements, utterance of words etc. are excessively fierce. Even those persons who imitate them are to be credited with the Raudra Rasa through the activities of fighting etc.

In this regard there are two Āryā verses—

64—65 Raudra Rasa is produced through these activities viz the excitement due to battles, hitting and striking, cutting and tearing, maining and mutilating. Its presentation in the the dramatic performance is by means of these special feats such as discharging different kinds of missiles, chopping off of the headless trunks, arms, heads etc

66 Thus the Raudra Rasa is seen as a fierce activity where there is much of the wielding of weapons and the movements and utterance of words etc are very terrible and frightening.

Vīra. Rasa (Heroic Sentiment)

Prose Passage. It is the exhibition of energy and enthusiasm with persons of high rank as the basis. The Vibhāvas (determinants) are Asammoha (Composure and absence of infatuation), Adhyavasāya (perseverance), Naya (good tactics) Vinaya (humility), Parākrama (Valour), Śakti (Power), Pratāpa (Aggressiveness), Prabhāva (mighty influence) and other similar one. Its presentation to the stage is through the Anubhāvas (Consequents) such as Sthairya (firmness), Śaurya (heroism), Dhairya (bravery), Tyāga (readiness to sacrifice), Vaiśāradya (Proficiency) and the like. The Sañcāri Bhāvas (Transitory States) are Dhṛti (fortitude), Mati (intellect), Garva (Pride), Vega (impetuosity), Augrya (ferocity), Amarṣa (indignation) Smṛti (Recollection), Romāñca (horripilation) and other features.

In this connection there are two verses in the Āryā metre traditionally handed down:

67-68 What is called Vīra Rasa is produced through enthusiasm, perseverance, absence of grief, absence of surprise and freedom from delusion. The Vīra Rasa should be depicted perfectly on the stage through statements scolding and censuring (the wrong doers), display of bravery, vigour, heroism, enthusiasms, aggressiveness and explorts.

Bhayānaka Rasa (The Terrible Sentiment)

Prose passage. In this Rasa the Sthāyibhāva is Bhaya (fright). Its outcome is through the Vibhāvas (determinents) such as Vikṛta Rava (terrific noise), Sattva Darśana (Sight of apparitions) Śivolūka Trāsodvega (pamic and worried state on hearing the cries of jackals and owls), Śūnyāgāra (Empty house), Araṇya Praveśa (entering a forest Maraṇa (deaths), Svajanavadha (murder of kingsmen), Bandhana (Imprisonment), seeing or hearing about or discussing any of these things and the like. Its presentation in the stage is through the Anubhāvas such as Pravepitakaracaraṅa (trembling of the hands and feet), Nayanacalana (movements of the eyes), Pulaka (hairs standing on ends), Mukha Vaivarṇya (Pallor in the face), Svarabheda (change of voice and tone) and the like. The Vyabhicārī bhāvas are Stambha (Paralysis), Sveda (Perspiration), Gadgada (Choked Voice). Romāñca (horripilation), Vepathu (trembling), Svarabheda (change of voice or tone), Vaivarṇya (lack of lustre), Śaṅkā (suspicion), Moha (fainting), Dainya (dejection) Āvega (Agitation), Cāpala (restlessness), Trāsa (fright) Apasmāra (epilepsy or loss of memory), Maraṇa (death) etc.

In this connection there are these verses in Āryā metre traditionally handed down :

69—72 Bhayānaka Rasa should be understood as produced through same offensive behaviour towards elders or Kings or by any of the following—hideous noise, sight of appartions, seeing a battle, entering the forest or an empty house. Fear is naturally produced and displayed by the various movements of the limbs, face and eyes, stunned sensation in the thighs, looking nervously and uneasily around, dejected feelings, tired face, dryness of the mouth, throbbing of the heart, and horripilation. The feigned fright is also to be displayed by these Bhāvas but the movements of the limbs are gentler. The Bhayānaka Rasa to be presented on the stage in variably through the trembling of the hands and feet, paralysis, palpitation, agitation in the limbs, parched lips. plate and throat.

Bibhatsa Rasa. (The Odious Sentiment)

Prose Passage. What is called Bībhatsa Rasa has Juguptsā (disgust) for its Sthāyibhāva. Its outcome is from the Vibhāvas such as Ahṛdya-apriya-avekṣā (seeing what is unwholesome or displeasing), Aniṣṭa-Śravaṇa-Darśana-Parikīrtana (hearing, seeing and discussing what is Undesuable) and similar things. Its representation on the stage is through the anubhāvas such as Sarvāṅgahāra (Squeezing up all the limbs), Mukhanetraghūrṇana (moving the face to and fro, rolling the eyes), Hṛllekha (heartache, grief anxiety), Niṣṭhīvana (spitting) Udvejana (expressing disgust) and the like. The Vyabhicāri Bhāvas are Apasmāra (loss of memory) Vega, (Agitation) Moha (delusion or loss of sense), Vyādhi (illness), Maraṇa (death) etc.

In this connection there are two verses in the metre Āryā traditionally handed down :

73—74. The Bībhatsa Rasa arises through many things causing disgust such as seeing what is not desirable, defects and abnormality in tcsts, smells touch and sound. Its presentation on the stage should be perfectly earned out by means of shaking the head, solling the eyes, closing the eyes, covering the nose, lending down the head and walking imperceptibly.

Adbhuta Rasa (The sentiment of wonderment Surprise).

The Adbhuta Rasa has as its Sthāyi Bhāva, Vismaya (Astonishment). Its outcome is through the Vibhāvas such as Divyadarśana (seeing a heavenly being), Īpsitamanorathāvāpti (Attainment of the cherished desire), Uttamavanadevakulābhigamana (proceeding towards excellent park, temple etc), seeing magical tricks and creations of things that can never be imagined about etc. Its presentation on the stage through the Anubhāvas such as Nayanavistāra (gaping of the eyes), Animeṣaprekṣaṇa (staring with winkless eyes), Romāñca (horripilation), Aśru (tears), Sveda (Perspiration),Harṣa (delight), Sādhuvāda (uttering words of Congratulation, Pradāna (making gifts), Bandhahāhākāra (senes of shouts of hā, hā), karacaraṇaṅgulibhramaṇa (movements of hands, feet) and the like. Its Vyabhicāri bhāvas are shedding tears, paralysis, perspiration choking of the voice, horripilation, excitement, flwury, sluggishness, sinking down etc.

In this connection there are two verses in the Āryā metre traditionally handed down :

75—76. The Rasa called Adbhuta should be known through these special features such as marvellous statement, conduct, acturty, form etc. Its presentation on the stage is through the perception of touch, earnest display of laughter, shouting of hā hā, Congratulatory remarks, tremour, choking words, perspiration etc.

77—83, *Adbhuta of two types and the other Rasas of three types.*

Sentiment—Varieties

Śṛṅgāra—based on (1) words (2) Dress (3) Acturities.

Hāsya, Raudra—based on (1) limbs (2) Dress (3) Statements.

Karuṇa (1) Dharmopaghātaja (2) Apacayodbhava (3) Śukakṛta.

(1) Arising from flouting prity (2) loss of wealth (3) caused by grief.

Vīrarasa—(1) Dānavīra (2) Dharmavīra (3) Yuddhavīra

(1) here the munificent (2) the pious one (3) the fighting one

Bhayānaka—(1) feigned (2) Arising from wrong ac (3) Apprehension of danger.

(1) Vyāja (2) Aparādha (3) Vitrāsitaka.

Bībhatsa—(1) Śuddha (the uneffected) (2) Udvegī (disgusting) through excrete, worms etc. (3) Kṣobhaja (Agitated) through blood etc.

Adbhuta—(1) Divya (divine) by seeing a divine being or celestial event (2) Ānandaja (born of delight) extremely delighted.

These are the eight Rasas explained with their characteristic in detail.

Now I shall explain the Bhāvas (emotions and traits) with their characteristics.

NOTES

Verse 6 The word jñāna is usually translated by using the word knowledge. Here it is used in the sense of "lores". Agnipurāṇa explains it by saying that all the Śāstras beginning with Vyākaraṇa are to be understood by the word Jñana.

Verse 11 Though the word Kārikā means mnemonic verse the metre used commonly is either Ārya or the Anuṣṭup

18. Vyabhicāri bhāva is also known as Sañcari bhāva

23 Āṅgika—Pertaining to the limbs Vācika (pertaining to the words). Chapters 8 to 12 explain these things in detail. Āhārya and sāttvika are explained in Chapters 23 and 24.

24 The two types, of Dharmis are explained in Chapter 14 verses 69 et sq. The various Vṛttis are explained in Chapter 22.

26 Nāṭyapravṛttis (Usage in local vogue) are explained in Chapter 14. The various geographical regions of India where different styles were popular accords interesting reading.

Siddhi (Achievement) is explained in Ch. 27.

27 Svaras the notes in the Indian gamut are explained in Ch. 28. The different kinds of musical instruments are also dealt with there.

29 The five kinds of Gānas explained in Ch. 32.

45 At the end of the prose passage Sāmānya Abhinaya section Chapter 24 verses 160—180 mentions the ten Avasthās (States) in detail.

7

Exposition on Bhāvas (Emotional tracts and states)

Now we shall explain the Bhāvas. One may ask in this context—"Why are these called Bhāvas? Is the derivation like this? Bhāvayanti (Fully compelend and pervade). It Bhāvāḥ? It is said in reply—"Those which "Bhāvayanti (Instil meaning) of the theme of the literary composition into the audience by means of Vācika, Āṅgika and Sāttvika means of presentation. The word Bhāva connotes the instrumental cause. The words Bhāvita, Vāsita and Kṛta convey the same sense. In common parlance we hear thus—Everything has been Bhāvita (pervaded assimilated) by the smell or juice of each other. So we can take Bhāvayanti to mean "pervade".

In this connection there are the following verse (Ślokas) — (1—3) when the theme conveyed by the Vibhāva is brought into realization through Anubhāva by means of the gestures whether Vācika, Āṅgika or Sāttvika, it is termed Bhāva. That which makes the idea of the poet revealed through words, gesticulations, colours of the face and temperamental represent-tion is called Bhāva. Since they make these Rasas related to different gestures pervade (the comprehension of the audience) they should be known by the sponsors of the dramatic performance as Bhāvas.

Vibhāvas

Prose passage. Why is this called Vibhāva? (It is said in reply)–The sense conveyed by the word. Vibhāva is special knowledge. It is synonymous with Kāraṇam, Nimittam and Hetu (cause). The Vācika, Āṅgika and Sāttvika gestures are known through this. Hence it is Vibhāva. Vibhāvita and Vijñāta (fully comprehended) are synonymous

In this connection there is a verse:—

4 Many things dependant upon the verbal and the physical gesticulations are determined by this. Hence it is called a Vibhāva (Determinant).

Anubhāva (Consequant)

Why is this called Anubhāva ? (Reply)—Since the dramatic presentations by means of words, gestures and the temperament are made to be felt by this it is called Anubhāva (consequent).

In this connection there is a verse :—

5 Since the meaning is brought to be felt by the spectators by means of words gestures and dramatic presentation it is called Anubhāva and it is remembered as relating to words, gesture, and ancillary Aṅgas.

Prose Passage

We shall explain the characteristics and examples of these Bhāvas accompanied by Vibhāva and Anubhāva. There the Vibhāvas and Anubhāvas are well known in the world. Their characteristic features are not being mentioned because they are closely connected with human nature. Further, Atiprasaṅga (prolixity) is to be avoided.

In this connection there is a verse.

6 Anubhāvas and Vibhāvas are to be known by learned men by means of Abhinaya. They are evolved by human nature and they follow the ways of the world.

Prose Passage.. There are eight Sthāyi Bhāvas, thirty three Vyabhicāri Bhāvas and eight Sāttvikas. Thus fortynine Bhāvas are to be known as the cause of the manifestation of the Rasa in the poem [or Play]. The Rasas arise from these when the Sāmānyaguṇas (common qualities) combine with them.

In this connection there is a verse :—

7 Just as the dry wood is pervaded by fire so also the physical body is pervaded by Rasa which is congenial to the heart and Bhāvas thus gives rise to the sentiment.

Prose passage. Here some one may put in a question—when the position is, this that all the fortynine Bhāvas come into mutual contact on being manifested by Vibhāvas and Anubhāvas and they become Rasas how do you say that the eight Sthāyi Bhāvas become Rasas. The reply is—It is so. How ? There are many men having hands, feet, bellis etc and having similar conceptions, notions etc, yet only a very few of noble birth, dignity, habits, learning and cleverness in arts and state crafts attain the royal states and others of meagre intellect become their servants. So also, the Vibhāvas, Anubhāvas and Vyabhicāri Bhāva, depend on Sthāyi Bhāvas and in view of that Sthāyi Bhāva become the lords. Similarly other Bhāvas are subordinates to the Sthāyi Bhāvas. Vyabhicāri Bhāvas have become attendents and depend on them. What is the example ? There is a leading man with many attendents but only he gets the name (king) and no one also albeit he may be very great. When many go along some one somewhere many ask "Who is this ?" He replies "Of course the king" So also Sthāyibhāva surrounded by Vibhāva, Anubhāva, and Vyabhicārin, gets the appellation Rasa like the appellation "King".

In this connection there is a verse:—

8 Just as the king is considered the greatest among men and the preception among the disciples so also the Sthāyī Bhāva is the greatest among all the Bhāvas.

Prose Passage

The definition of what are called Rasa has already been mentioned. Now we shall explain the characteristics of all Bhāvas. There at the outset we shall explain the Sthāyi-Bhāvas.

Rati (love)

What is called Rati is of the nature of Pleasure [Āmoda is its soul]. The Vibhāvas generating it are —— (favourable) seasons, garlands, unguents, ornaments, persons near and dear, lofty abodes, absence of antagonism (from others) etc. The actor shall represent it (on the stage) through the Anubhāvas like face beaming with, smiles, words of exquisite sweetness, knitting of the eyebrows, glances etc. In this context there is a Śloka.

9 Rati takes its origin through the requisition of the desired objects and sensations becouse of its being very delicate and gentle. It has to be represented on the stage through sweetness of words and suitable movements of the limbs.

Hāsa (laughter)

Prose Passage

What is called Hāsa is produced by the Anubhāvas such as closely imitating others' activities, inconsistent utterances, constiousness, foolish activities etc. The actor shall represent it on the stage by means of Hasita etc. explained before.

In this context there is a verse:—

10 Hāsa takes its origin from closely imitating others' activities. It has to be represented on the stage by learned men through gentle smile, broad laughter and boisterous out bursts.

Śoka (grief)

Prose Passage

What is called Śoka is produced by the Vibhāvas such as Separation from beloved ones, destruction of assets, murder, imprisonment, experience of private.

It has to be presented on the stage through the Anubhāvas such as shedding tears, lamentation, bewailing, pallor in the face, change of voice, sensation of looseness of limbs, falling on the ground, weeping loudly, writhing and squirming, deep sighs, sluggishness, madness, loss of sense, death etc. Rudita (crying) is of three types (a) born of joy (b) born of distress and (c) born of jealously.

Āryā verses in this connection.

11 That cry becomes one born of joy when cheeks bloom with delight, there is recollection through words without conceeling tears and the cheeks are marked with Romāñca (horripilation).

12 That cry becomes one arising from distress when there is much shedding of tears along with loud sound, the movement

of the limbs and the activities indicate uneasiness, there is falling on the ground, rolling and lamenting.

13 That cry of women becomes one arising from jealously when the lips and the cheeks throb violently, accompanied by deep sighs and shaking of the head. The glances and the eyebrows are curved and crooked.

14 Artificial sorrow is to be made to move with in the heroic sentiment. It expects adequate reasoning and generally it is accompanied by exertion as the main cause.

There is a verse too

15 This grief born of disaster has women and the base people for its Prakṛti (basis). In the case of the high ones and middling ones it is accompanied by courage. In the case of the base ones it is accompanied by shedding of tears.

Krodha (Anger)

Prose Passage

Krodha originates from the Vibhāvas such as insulting affront, abusive words, quarrel, dispute, adverse remarks, alter cations, etc. It shall be represented on the stage by means of the Anubhāvas such as swelling of the nostrils, haughtly elevated eyes, biting of the lips, throbbing of the cheeks etc.

In this context there are these verses in Āryā metre :—

16 One shall display anger on the stage in the following manner when there *is open resistance by the enemies* :— The eyebrows are knitted; there is ferocity in the face, the lips are bitten, the hand is touched with another hand; one touches the chest, head and the arms.

17 *Anger against venerable persons.* When there is restraint by venerable persons the actor indicates anger as follows :— he starts with slightly bowed head and down cast eyes ; he slightly wipes off the drops of Sweet ; violent activity is not remarkably displayed.

18 The actor exhibits *his anger towards his beloved* approaching him with love with very slight advance movement, shedding tears, frequently looking sideways and making the lips throb along with knitted eyebrows.

Anger against attendant

19 The gesticulatory presentation of the anger towards attendants is by means of threats, rebukes, opening the eyes widely and looking contemporaneously in diverse ways

Pretendent anger

20 The pretended anger should be exhibited on the stage as moving between two Rasas. It has its own motive to be realised and for that purpose effort is expressly made.

Utsāha (Energetic Enthusiasm)

Prose Passage

What is called Utsāha has persons of lofty nature as its basis. It is produced by Vibhāvas such as power, courage, heroism, readiness to sacrifice and absence of distress etc. Its Abhinaya on the stage is through the Anubhāvas such as fortitude, astuteness readiness to undertake much etc.

In this connection there is a verse:—

21 Manifesting from mental composure etc. Utsāha which has energic enterprise as its soul should be displayed on the stage by such activities as are devoid of bhinders etc.

Bhaya (Fear)

Prose Passage

What is called Bhaya has the mean type of persons for its basis. It is produced by such Vibhāvas as crimes committed against preceptors and kings, wandering through forests and vacant houses, seeing mountains, being rebuked, cloudy days, nocturual darkness, movements of owls., hearing the shouts of Rākṣaśas etc.

Its representation on the stage shall be through the Anubhāvas such as trembling of the hands and feet, palpitation of the heart, stupefaction, perched mouth licking with the tongue, perspiration, tremour of the heart, searching for a vantage point, flight, loud lamentation etc.

In this respect these are the verses: –

22 Fear takes its origin along with loss of sense due to an offence against elders and the king by seeing awful persons and things and by hearing terrible (shouts) etc.

23 Its presentation on the stage is by means of frights, tremblings of the limbs, agitation, dryness of the mouth, opening the eyes widely and similar actions and qualities.

24 Fear in men is produced by excessive bright. Dancers should represent it on the stage by means of loosened limbs and twinkling of the eyes.

A verse in Āryā metre on this point:—

25 Its gesticulatory presentation is by means of the trembling of the hands, feet and heart; paralysis of the limbs, licking with the tongue and dryness of the mouth, and slackened movements of the benumbed limbs.

Jugupsā (Disgust)

Prose Passage

What is called Jugupsā has women and persons mean of birth for its basis. It originates from the Vibhāvas such as hearing and listening to unpleasant things and other things. Its Abhinaya on the stage should be performed through the Anubhāvas such as contracting all the limb, spitting out, twisting of the mouth heartache etc.

Here too there is a Śloka (in support):—

26 The actor should exhibit Jugupsā (on the stage) by covering the nostrils, by shrinking the limbs, by manifestations of disgusts and heartaches.

Vismaya (Wonderment)

Prose Passage

What is called Vismaya is produced by Vibhāvas such as jugglery, magical illusion, superhuman activity of an extra-ordinary man, a wonderful and mysterious body, artistic and craft excellance and the like. Its production on the stage is by means of Anubhāvas such as dilating of the eyes, staring with winklers eyes, distortions of the eyebrows, horripilation, perspiration, expressions of "Bravo Bravo" etc.

In this regard there is a verse:—

27 Vismaya is produced by joy arising from an excellent and extraordinary work. This should be achieved in the place

of achievement (i.e. stage) by means of tears of joy, sinking down fainting etc.

Prose Passage

Thus these Sthāyi **Bhāvas** should be understood well. Now we shall explain Vyabhicārins. Here some one says—— "Why are ᵗhey called Vyabhicārins ?" (Reply). Vi and Abhi are prepositions. The root car is in the sense of "movement". Hence the word Vyabhicārinah means those that take the movement of different objects towards Rasas. That as they take the things that are connected with words, gesture, and the temperament towards Rasa. Caranti thus means carry. How do they carry? Just as the sun carries this star to this day. It is not carried by means of shoulders or arms. But it is the popular parlance. These Vyabhicārins are to be known as leading just like the sun leading. In the synoptic digest thirty three Vyabhicārins have been mentioned. We shall explain them in detail.

Nirveda (Despondency)

What is called Nirveda is produced through Vibhāvas such as advent of impoverised state, being insulted, abused by means of foul language, angry thrashing, separation from beloved persons and the acquisition of ultimate knowledge (of Brahman) and others similar. As far as this is concerned with women and with persons of mean nature it should be portrayed on the stage by means Anubhāvas such as crying, sighs, deep breaths, fraudulence etc.

In this regard there is the following verse :—

28 What is called Nirveda originates from poverty and separation from beloved ones. Its Abhinaya shall be through Sampradhāraṇa (elaborate thinking) deep sighing etc.

In this regard there are two verses in the Āryā metre traditionally handed over.

29 What is called Nirveda takes its origin due to the separation from the beloved ones, due to wretchedness and poverty, or due to sickness or excessive misery or on seeing another person's prosperity.

30 A person in the state of Nirveda is engrossed in meditation like a Yogin. His eyes are flooded with tears. His face droops down and his eyes are miserable. His sighs are deep and frequent.

Glāni (feebleness)

Prose Passage

What is called Glāni results from the Vibhāvas vomiting, dysentery, ailments, penances and observances, fasting, mental anguish, excessive drinking, over exercise, too much of travel, hunger, thirst, loss of sleep etc. Its Abhinaya is to be performed through the Anubhāvas such as feeble utterance, eyes without lustre, pale cheek,slow walk, absence of enthusiasm, thinness of the physical form, change of colour etc.

In this context there are two verses in Āryā metre :—

31 Glāni occurs when there is sickness, vomiting and purgation, while penance is performed and due to old age. It is depicted on the stage by the thinness of the body accompanied by slow steps and shivering sensation.

32 The actor shall portray Glāni through very very feeble utterances, distortions in the eyes, pitable movements, frequent slackness of the limbs etc.

Śaṅkā (Fearful Suspicion)

Prose Passage

What is called Śaṅkā has reference to women and persons of low status. Daubt is its basic feature. It is produced by Vibhāvas such as thieving, robbing, seizing, giving offence to the king, committing sinful deeds and the like. It is being depicted on the stage by means of constant (apprehansive) looks on all sides keeping the face veiled, dryness of the mouth, licking with the tongue, pallor of the face, tremors. parched lips, loss of voice etc.

There is a verse in the present context :—

33 Śaṅkā is usually pursued in the Bhayānaka Rasa if it arises from theft etc. and it is considered in the Śṛṅgāra Rasa if it arises from the transgencon on the part of the beloved.

Prose Passage

Some wish to include concealment of appearance. That should be propped up by means of clever adjuncts and hints.

In this regard there are two verses in Āryā metre.

34 Two types of Śaṅkā are pursued one arising from oneself and the other from others. What is called arising from oneself should be known through the movements of the eyes.

35 A person in the state of Śaṅkā experiences the trembling of the body. He glances either side very frequently. His tongue remains thick and stuck up. His face appears gloomy.

Asūyā (jealousy)

Prose Passage

What is called Asūyā is produced by Vibhāvas such as different kinds of offences, hatred, other people's wealth, blessedness, sportive display, learning and other assets and the like. Its presentation on the stage is by means of open proclamation of faults in the assembly, decrying good qualities, staring meaningfully, keeping face bowing down, distortions of the eyebrows, dirparagement, ridiculing and other Anubhāvas.

Here these are two verses in the Āryā metre :—

36. Asūyā arises on seeing other people's good luck, power and wealth, excessive intelligence and exuberance of sportive nature. The man will commit some offence too.

37 Its representation on the stage should be through crooked eyebrows, arrogant face, twining away the face with anger and envy and other activities. Indulgence in decrying good qualities (of others) and hated also to be displayed.

Mada (Inebriety)

Prose Passage

What is called Mada originates from the use of intoxicating drinks. It is of three types and has five Bhāvas attending upon.

In this regard these verses in Āryā are (to be considered)

38 Mada is considered to be of three kinds—Taruṇa (matine, excessive), Madhya (medium) and Avakṛṣṭa (low). Its cause is of five types. It shall be represent on the stage.

39 *The five functions of the inebrieted.* A certain intoxicated fellow sings, another cries, a third laughs the fourth ulters harsh words and one, the fifth, simply sleeps.

40 The man of excellent nature laughs and sings. The man of mean base nature utters harsh words and cries.

41 The man of mature inebriation is of the excellent nature. speaks smilingly, exhibits sweet passion, bold in physical appearance, slightly faltering in his words. His gait is unsteady but displays delicate charm.

42 The men of medium nature is a men of medium inbriety. His eyes roll unsteadily. His arms either droop down listlessly by or are thrown up in agitation. His gait is crooked and unsteady.

43 The man of mean nature utterly loses memory. His movement steads retarded. He is very disgusting due to biccups and coughs with vomiting to foot. His tongue is thick and stuck up and he spits frequently.

44 A character imbibing liquor on the stage must display increasing inebriety by adopting theatrical devices. If the character has entered the stage after imbibing liquor the decrease in his intoxication should be displayed.

45 His losts of intoxication should be shown by persons who know it well. Though adequate reasons it becomes reduced viz. through fright, grief. excessive fear etc. With effort too it can be reduced.

46 Through these special Bhāvas, Mada perishes quickly. So also grief becomes reduced through words indicating prosperity and happiness.

Prose Passage

Śrama (Exhaustion, fatigue)

What is called Śrama is produced through the journey along the road, indulging in physical exercises etc. as Vibhāvas. Its representation on the stage is through the Anubhāvas such as massaging of the body, hearing sights, twisting of the mouth, whinkling of the face, yawning, pressing of the limbs, placing steps slowly, rolling of the eyes, producing Sītkāra (hissing sound when one shivers etc.) and other.

In this connection there is a verse in Āryā :—

47 Fatigue occurs in men by means of travel physical exercise etc. Its Abhinaya is through deep breaths and tired mode of walking etc.

Ālasya (Utter lethargy)

What is called Ālasya is produced through the Vibhāvas natural inclination, sorrow, walking, satiety, pregnancy etc in the case of women as well as persons of mean nature. It is to be represented on the stage through the Anubhāvas such as distaste towards all types of activities, lying down, sitting quiet, drowsiness, going to sleep and the like.

In this regard there is a verse in Āryā:

48 Ālasya whether it arises from strain of sickness or occuring naturally should be represented on the stage by not resuming any activity except that of taking food.

Prose Passage

Dainya (Wretchedness)

What is called Dainya is produced by Vibhāvas such as pennilessness, mental distress etc. Its representation on the stage is by means of absence of fortitude, headache, paralysis of the body, mentally stunned state, avoiding cleansing of the body etc.

In this regard there is a verse in Āryā metre.

49 Men do experience wretchedness due to misery or excessive anxiety or too much of eagerness. There are various ways of representing it on the stage by avoiding all types of cleaning the body (and similar things)

Prose Passage Cintā (Anxiety)

What is called Cintā is produced through Vibhāvas such as loss of wealth, theft of a dear object, poverty etc. It should be presented on the stage by means of Anubhāvas such as deep breath, sighs, distress, contempletion, down cast face, pondering, enuciation of the body and the like.

In this regard there are two verses in the Āryā metre :—

50 Cintā is of various types. It is produced in men as a result of the theft of wealth or a favourite article or due to expectant eager heart.

It is to be represented on the stage by deep breaths, hearing of sighs, voidness of the heart, distressed states, absence of fortitude and avoidance of all sorts of cleansing activities.

Prose Passage

Moha (Delusion)

What is called Moha is produced by the Vibhāvas such a accidental mishap, adversity, sickness, fear, agitation, recollection of previous enmity etc. Its presentation on the stage is by means of the Anubhāvas such as absence of movements, whirling of the limbs, falling down, faltering etc.

In this connection there is a verse:—

52. On seeing thieves in a wrong place or when different kinds of frightening things occur, of a man does not find any means of remedy, Moha takes place there from.

In this regard there is an Āryā Verse:—

53. Moha is produced from adversity, accidents, fear and recollection of previous enmity. Its presentation on the stage is by means of loss of all senses.

Prose Passage Smṛtī (Recollection)

What is called Smṛti is produced by means of Vibhāvas such as health in utmost wretched state, disturbance to the sleep at night, frequent practice of thinking things of similar appearance and same examples etc. It is of the nature of remembering things producing happiness or misery. The actor represent it on the stage by means of the Anubhāvas such as noddings of the head, looking down, raising of the eyebrows, excessive delight etc.

In this regard there is a verse in the Āryā metre :—

54 He is called a man recollecting if he remembers everything that had happened in the past whether it is happiness or misery or what is imagined and forgotten as though that has really happened.

55 That Smṛti arising from what is heard and what is seen or what is within oneself and imagined by sheer practice should be represented on the stage by lifting up and nodding the head or by means of the movements of the eyebrows

Prose Passage Dhṛti (Fortitude)

What is called Dhṛti is produced by the Vibhāvas such as heroism, perfect knowledge, acquisition of Vedic knowledge, affluence, cleanliness, good habits, devotion to the preceptors getting surplus of funds, different kinds of sports etc. The player shall represent it on the stage by enjoying whatever is acquired and not regetting what is not yet acquired, or lost or has been destroyed. There are the Anubhāvas through which he shall exhibits.

In this regard there are two Āryā verses.

56 Dhṛti that arises from (the Vibhāvas) such as spiritual knowledge, cleanliness, good habits, power of Śruti should always be produced (in the drama) by good people omitting Bhaya (fear), Śoka (grief), Viṣāda (agony) etc.

57 That is Dhṛti which occurs to one when one enjoys what is acquired such as sound, touch, taste, beauty of form and fragrance and does not become sad when that is not acquired.

Prose Passage Vrīḍā (Bashfulness, Shame)

Doing what should not have been done is the basis of what is called Vrīḍā. It originates from such Vibhāvas as disobedience to the elders, insult to them, not keeping words of promise, denying what is done, regret over what is committed and other similar things. It should be represented on the stage by the Anubhāvas such as hiding the face, bending the head down, thinking and pondering drawning lines on the ground, touching the ring, clothes etc, biting or paring the nails etc.

In this regard there are two verses with Āryā metre.

58. A men who is observed by other pure men, in the act of committing an improper action and therefore regrets it should be known as one who is Vrīḍita (Ashamed).

59 The Vrīḍita conceals his face through shame, scretches the ground, bites the nails, tears something with the nails, and touches.

Prose passage

Capalatā (Inconstancy)

What is called Capalatā is produced by such Vibhāvas as passion, hatred, rivalary excessive anger, jealousy, absence of restraint etc. Its representation on the stage is to be had through the Anubhāvas such as harshness of words, rebuke, thrashing, killing, imprisoning, beating, reminding etc

A verse in Āryā metre in this connection :—

60 If one is in the habit of doing anything without proper

decision and so carries out such activities as imprisoning, killing etc. without pondering properly he is to be considered Capala (Inconstant) by learned men.

Prose passage

Harṣa (delight)

What is called Harṣa is caused by the Vibhāvas such as getting the denied things, union with the beloved, desired and trusted, mental satisfaction, divine favour, royal appreciation, preceptor's affection, obtaining good food, raiments and wealth as well as ability to benefit by them. That should be presented on the stage by the Anubhāvas such as facial brightness brilliance in the eyes, sweet speeches, embracing, horripilation, tears of joys, sweet, gentle stroke etc.

In this regard there are two verses in the Āryā metre.

61 Men become delighted when they realise their aims, obtain anything usually very difficult to get or meet their beloved one, or get cherished desires fulfilled.

62. The representation of delight on the stage is by means of brightness in the eyes and face loving speech, embrace, delicate movement of the limbs horripilation, perspiration etc.

Prose passage Āvega (Excitement)

What is called Āvega is caused by the Vibhāvas such as evil portents, gusts of winds, rains, arson, mad running of herds of elephants, hearing excessively good or bad[1] news adversity, etc. The words evil portents include full of lightning, meteors, comets, stars solar or lunar eclipses, appearance of Ketus etc. Āvega should be represented on the stage by the looseness of all limbs, sorrow, mental distraction, pallor in the face, surprise etc. The agitation due to gusts of wind shall be represented on the stage by covering the face with a veil, rubbing the eyes, folding of the clothes, hurried departure and other Anubhāvas. Agitation brought about by rains should be represented by the Anubhāvas such as dumping together all the parts of the body, running, holding umbrellas and the like. Agitation due to fire and arson cases by means of the Anubhāvas such as eyes afflicted by smoke are partially closed, limbs are squeezed together and shaken, running with wise steps etc etc. The agitation due to the running of wild elephants to be represented by the Anubhāvas of hertening the departune, unsteady walk, fear, paralysis, tremour, frequent look towards the rear, surprise etc. The agitation arising from hearing favourable news is represented by standing up by way of welcome, embracing, presenting garments and ornements, welling up of tears of joy, rising of the hairs with the body and the like. The agitation due to Apriyaśravaṇa is represents heering unpleasants thingsby means of falling down on the ground, lamentation, curious and distorted movements and sollings, running away, loud cry, Aparudita (erying out of tune) and the like. The agitation due to Vyasanābhighāta (adversity or sudden attack of people) shall be represented by hurried departure, seizing weapons and missiles, shields etc, wearing of coat of mail, mounting elephants, horses, chariots etc. striking and other Anubhāvas.

63 Thus Āvega the basis of which is agitation should be known as constituting eight types. In the case of the superior and the medium type, of persons it is controlled by Sthairya (steadfastness) and in the case of the mean type of persons by fleeing.

In this connection there are two verses in Āryā metre.

64 What is called Āvega results from hearing an intimation of what is unpleasant, to the person who understands the purport of those words because he becomes afraid of an attack with weapons.

65 If the Āvega is the result of hearing unpleasant news its Anubhāva shall be the resumption of a sad attitude. If there is the appearance of the enemy all of a sudden there should clash of weapons.

Prose passage

Jaḍatā (Stupor, sluggishness)

What is called Jaḍatā (sluggishness) is cessation or reluctance to resume all types of activities. It results from such Vibhāvas as—hearing or seeing what is desirable as well as undesirable, sickness etc. It has to be represented on the stage by praltting or not at all speaking, or speaking indistinctly, staring stead fortly or utter helplessness etc. etc.

In this regard there is an Āryā verse:—

66 A man is termed sluggish (Jaḍa) if he out of delusion does not become aware of what is undesirable, or conducive to happiness, or misery and remains silient and helpless.

Prose passage

Garva (Arrogance)

What is called Garva results from the Vibhāvas such as excessive affluence, nobility of birth, handsomeness and beauty of form, youth, academic distinction, influence and the like. Its representation on the stage by means of the Anubhāvas such as contempt for others, teasing and causing vexation to everyone, avoiding replying to others, or conversing with others, glancing at the shoulders, roaming about, derisive laughter harsh words, disobedience to elders, slighting them etc. In this regard there is a verse in Āryā metre.

67 The arrogance of the man follows due to academic achievements, youth, beauty, affluence, sudden augment of wealth etc. should be represented on the stage by means of the movements of the eyes and limbs.

Prose passage Viṣāda (Dejection)

What is called Viṣāda is produced by such Vibhāvas as fortune to complete the task on hand, accidents Calamities and adverse fate etc. With regard to the persons of superior and middling types of persons the representation of Viṣāda is by means of Anubhāvas such as searching for allies and collaborations, consideration of means of remedy, hindrance to enthusiasm, absent mindedness, deep sighs etc. etc. with regard to the persons of the mean order it is to be represented by flight, down cast look, dryness of the mouth, licking the sides of the mouth, drowsiness, sighs, contempletion etc. etc.

In this connection there is a verse in Āryā metre :

68 There shall be Viṣāda due to inbility to complete a task, being taken as prisoner by a person of superior valour, offence to the kings, inability to get what is desired because the fate is against, etc.

69 With regard to persons of the superior and medium types of persons, Viṣāda is to be represented by the consideration of diverse means of of remedy. In the case of the persons cf the mean type it shall be represented through drowsiness, deep sighs and contemplation.

Prose Passage

Autsukya

What is called Autsukya is produced through the Vibhāvas such as recollection of the separation from beloved persons, seeing parks ete. etc. Representation of this Autsukya is by means of the Anubhāvas such as deep sighs, drooping of the face, deep reflection, sleep, lethargy, desire to be down etc. etc. In this regard there is a verse in Āryā metre:—

70 What is called Autsukya is produced due to the reflection after separations from beloved persons. Its Abhinaya is by means of anxiety, sleep, lethargy and heaviness of limbs.

Prose Passage Nidrā (leep)

What is called Nidrā is produced by such Vibhāvas as delility, exhaution, inebriety, lethargy, anxiety, excessive intake of food, natural soporific tendency and the like. The players shall represent it by means of the Anubhāvas such as gravity of the face, rolling of the physical frame, movements of the eyes, yawning, massaging the body, deep sighs, noisy respirations relexed body, closing of the eyes, fainting etc. etc.

In this regard there are two verses in the Āryā metre.

71 Sleep overcomes a man through delility, indolence, exhaustion, wearness, overwork, too much of thinking, natural inclination, keeping awake at night etc.

72 Its representation is to be made by means of Anubhāvas such as gravity (or hearness) of face, closing the eyes, rolling the eyes, sluggishness, tendency to yawn massaging the body etc.

Prose Passage Apasmāra (Epilepsy, Loss of memory)

What is called Apasmāra is produced by means of the Vibhāvas such as malignant possession of an evil dirty, serpent, Yakṣa, Rākṣasa, Piśāca and others, recollection of such beings, partaking of the leavings of the foods of others, frequenting empty chambers, unclear forests etc. being crossed, derangement of the bodily harmons, etc. etc. Its Abhinaya is to be performed by means of the Anubhāvas such as difficulty, that bring, trembling, sighing, running, falling perspiration, boaming in the mouth, his cup, licking with the tongue, etc. etc.

In this regard there are two verses in the Āryā metre ;—

73 Apasmāra occurs to a person malignantly possessed by Bhūtas (evil spirits), Piśācas (Vampires) when he remembers them, partaking of Ucchiṣṭas (bearings of food), going to vacant houses, non-observance of proper timings and uncleanliness.

74 The following are the silent features of state of Apasmāra viz. falling down suddenly, shivering, forming in the mouth, getting up even in the state of loss of sense etc.

Prose passage Supta

(Dreaming-sleeping)

What is Supta,arises during sleep. The actor shall represent it by means of the Anubhāvas such as deep breathing, dullness of the body, closing the eyes stupor of all the senses, loss of senses, loss of sense and waking up after dreams etc. etc.

In this connection there is a verse in Āryā metre :—

75 The player shall represent Supta remaining motionless. The Anubhāvas such as deep sighs, long breath, partial closing of the eyes and senselessness in regard to all the sense organs occur. It is supplemented by deams too.

Prose passage Vibodha (Waking up)

What is called Vibodha is produced by such Vibhāvas as break of sleep, digestion of food, evil dreams, loud sounds etc. The player shall represent it through the Anubhāvas such as yawning, the eyes, learning the bed, seeing the limbs and face, throwing down the hands, snapping of the fingers etc. etc.

In this connection there is a verse in Āryā metre :—

76 Pratibodha (i.e. Vibodha) produced by the digestion of food, sound, touches etc. should be represented by means of yawning, writting of the body and rubbing of the eyes.

Prose passage Amarṣa (Anger, indignation)

What is called Amarṣa occurs to a person rebuked or insulted by other persons superior to him/her in learning, affluence, prosperity and strength. Its Abhinaya is to be performed by means of Anubhāvas such as shaking the head, perspiration, down cast face, reflecting, mental apprehension, meditation, looking for means of remedies etc. etc.

Two verses in this regard :—

77 What is called Amarṣa occurs to men along with

enthusiasm if they are rebuked and dishonoured in the open assembly by persons superior in learning, affluence and physical strength.

78 One conversant with the technique of Nāṭya shall represent it on the stage by means of enthusiasm mental apprehension, reflecting with downcast face, shaking of the head, perspiration etc. etc.

Prose Passage Avahittha (Dissimulation)

What is called Avahittha is in the nature of concealment of appearance. It is produced by means of the Vibhāvas such as shame, fear, defeat, deceit etc. It shall be represented on the stage by means of the Anubhāvas such as explaining away, looking elsewhere, pretending as though it has not been seen, breaking of talk etc.

A verse in this regard :—

79 Avahittha is produced by undue aggressiveness, deceit etc. It is terrible. It should be represented by indifference and also by speaking later.

Prose passage

Ugratā (Ferosity, cruelty)

What is called Ugratā is produced by means of the Vibhāvas such as incarceration of the thieves offence to the kings, speaking offencive words etc. It shall be represented on the stage by means of Anubhāvas such as slaying, arresting, lying up, bitting, threatening, rebuking, etc. etc.

A verse in Āryā metre in this regard :—

80 Ugratā occurs when thieves are caught and bound, arrested and kings are offended. Its Abhinaya is through the Anubhāvas of slaying, binding, bitting etc. etc.

Prose passage Mati (Self-assurence, intellect)

What is called Mati is produced by the Vibhāvas such as thinking about the purport of the scriptural texts, considerations and conjecting and inferences etc. It shall be performed on the stage by means of Anubhāva, such as imparting instruction to the pupils, ascertaining of the sense, clarification of doubts etc.

A verse in this respect.

81 Mati occurs to men when they are equipped with the master y of many scriptural texts. Its Abhinaya shall be by means of instructing disciples.

Prose Passage

Vyādhi (Ailment)

What is called Vyādhi originates from Vāta (wind) Pitta (bile), Kapha (phlegm) the three humours and their cumulative effect. Fever etc. are the special types of ailments. Javara (fever) is of two types Saśīta (with Cold) and Sadāha (with burning sensation). The Abhinaya of Saśīta is by means of the Anubhāvas such as shivering, shaking of all the limbs, squeezing and shrinking of the limbs, shaking of the jaws, distortion of the nostrils, dryness of the mouth, horripilation, tears, growning with pain, and the like. The represetation of the Sadāha fever is by means of the Anubhāvas such as throwing out the garments hands and feet, desire to roll on the ground eagerness for unguents and cool things, lamentation groaning etc. etc. The representation of the other types of sicknesses and ailments is by means of the Anubhāvas such as distortion of the face, paralysis of the body, deep breaths, shrill cries, tremour etc. etc.

A verse in this regard :—

82 The Abhinaya of ailments in general is to be performed by sensible persons by means of the looseness of the limbs, throwing out the limbs, distortion of the face and mouth etc.

Prose Passage

Unmāda (Insanity)

What is called Unmāda is produced by Vibhāvas such as death of a beloved, loss of wealth, accidental injury, upsetting of the bodily humour etc. etc. It shall be represented by Anubhāvas such as laughing, crying, lamenting, growning etc. without justification, irrelevant talk, misplaced lying lying down, sitting, standing up, running, dancing, singings, smeering the body with ashes and dust, wearing grass, Nirmālya etc., soiled cloth, rags polsterd, earthen tray as embellishments, senseless acts by way of imitating others etc. etc.

In this regard there are two verses in the Āryā metre :—

83 What is called Unmāda occurs due to the derangement of the humour Pitta in diverse ways. It results from the death or separation of beloved ones and the loss of wealth. It may result when struck suddenly and also due to the cumulative effect of the derangement of all the humours.

84 The portrayal of Unmāda is by means of laughter, cry,

sitting, running or crying without any relevance, and other equally senseless behaviour.

Prose Passage

Maraṇa (death)

What is called Maraṇa may be the result of ailment or violent attack. What is called Vyādhiprabhāvam (resulting from ailments) is caused by the Vibhāvas such as disturbance in the intestines, the liver, etc , colic pain, derangement of the humours, tumours, boils, fever, cholera etc. etc. What is called Abhighātasam (accidental of violent attack) is caused by weapons, serpent bite, drinking poison, beasts of pray, vehicles drawn by elephants, horses, chariots, and falls from these. I shall now describe the special mode of Abhinaya of these two. The death resulting from sickness is to be represented by means of Anubhāvas such as looseness of the body, immobility of the limbs, closing of the eyes Hiccup, deep breath, jumping up, not earing for or seeking help from attendants, speaking with indistinct voice etc.

A verse in this regard :—

85 The Abhinaya of Maraṇa is remembered as are Bhāva of a number of ailments. One point is that the body is kept loose and the sense organs in active

Prose Passage

In the case of death due to Abhighāta (attack) there are various kinds of Abhinayas e g. if the death is due to the injury from a weapon the representation is by means of Anubhāvas such as falling suddenly on the ground etc. But in the case of snake bite or drinking poison there is gradual development of the symptoms by stages such as Kārśya (thinness), Vepathu (tremour), Dāha (burning sensation), Hikkā (hiccup), Phena (froth from mouth), Skandhabhaṅga (acute pain in the shoulders as though they break as under), Jaḍatā (sluggishness) and Maraṇa (death).

In this context there are two verses traditionally handed down :—

86—87 The effect of person should represent as follows.

1st effect	(Symptom)	Kārśya (thiness)
2nd ,,	,,	Vepathu (Tremour)
3rd ,,	,,	Dāha (Burning sense)

4th	,,	,,	Hikkā (hiccup)
5th	,,	,,	Phena (froth)
6th	,,	,,	Skandha Bhañjana (Breaking of the shoulders)
7th	,,	,,	Jaḍata (Sluggishness)
8th	,,	,,	Maraṇa (death)

Two verses one in Āryā metre and one in Śloka form :—

88 In case of death due to beasts of pray or falling from the vehicles of chariot or other vehicles drawn by elephants horses etc. (or accident due to these) the Abhinaya is as in the case of wounds from weapons. There is no further movement of the body.

89 Thus Maraṇa is to be known as having various conditions. It should be properly represented by sensible persons by means of good words and appropriate activities of the bodies.

Prose Passage

Trāsa (fright)

What is called Trāsa is produced by the Vibhāvas such as lightning, comet fall, striking by thunder bolt, earth quake, clouds gathering together ominouly, seeking an unnatural being, cry of some wild animal etc. etc. It shall be represented on the stage through Anubhāvas such as contracting of the limbs, shaking of the limbs, shivering, paralysis, horripilation, choking words, prattling etc. etc.

There is a verse on this point :—

90 Trāsa is produced by loud sound etc. Its representation on the stage is through looseness of the limbs and half closed eyes etc.

Prose Passage

Vitarka (Deliberation)

What is called Vitarka is caused by Vibhāvas such as doubt, cogitation, belief etc. It shall be represented on the stage through the Anubhāvas as diverse discussions, deciding hints, hiding the manner of counsel aking etc. etc.

In this regard there is a verse :—

91 Vitarka originates from discussions. Its basis is the raising of doubts. Its Abhinaya is by means of the movements of head, eyebrows and eyelashes.

Prose Passage

There are the thirty three **Vyabhicarin Bhāvas** to be produced in plays by persons whether women or men of the superior medium or mean types with proper conformity to place, time and situation.

92 These thirty three Bhāvas are to be known as Vyabhicārins. I shall now explain in detail the Sāttvika Bhāvas (Temperemental feelings) in the proper order.

SĀTTVIKA BHĀVA

Prose Passage

Here some one may ask—"It is so that the other Bhāvas are mentioned bereft of Sattva ? Why do you call only these the Sāttvika Bhāvas ?" Here it is replied thus— In this context Sattva means originating in mind. It is caused by the mind when there is concentration. Through the mental concentration the Sattva is evolved. Its nature includes Stambha (Paralysis), Sveda (Perspiration), Romāñca (horripillation), Aśra (tears), Vaivarṇya (loss of colour). and other things. They cannot be properly portrayed by one with absent-mindeness. Hence Sāttvikas are desired in a play so that human nature can be properly imitated and not for any other purpose. Here the objecting one questions—"Is there any example for the same ?" In this connection we reply— Here it is the Nāṭya Dharma (theatrical activity) that is to be taken up. i.e. situations calling for happiness of misery. They should be portrayed in such a manner as to accord with the temperement behind them in order to become realistic. What is called Duhkha (misery) has crying for its basis. Sukham (happiness) has delight as its basis. How can sorrow be represented by one who is not sorry ? How can happiness be presented by one who is not happy ? Hence the explanation is that tears and horripilation should be displayed by a person mentally sorry or happy.

93 The eight Sāttvika Bhāvas are the following Stambha (Paralysis), Sveda (Perspiration), Romāñca (Horripilation),

Svarasāda (Afflication in the Voice), Vepathu (Tremour), Vaivarṇyam (Change of colour), Aśru (shedding tears) and Pralaya (sinking, fainting), Among them——

94 *Sveda* results from Anger, fright, delight, bashfulness, sadness, fatigue, sickness, heat, hitting, exercise, weariness, summer heat, and afflication (or harassment).

95 *Stambha* Results from joy, fear, ailment, wonderment, sadness, inebriety and anger *Kamia* (or Vepathu) results from chillness, fear, delight, touch and senility.

96 Aśrau results from joy, indignation, smoke, collyrium, yawning, fear, sadness, winklessness, stare, cold and sickness.

97 Vaivarṇya results from chillness, anger, fear, fatigue, sickness, toil and distress.

Romāñca results from touch, fear, chillness, delight, anger and ailments.

98 *Svarasāda* is produced by fear, delight, anger, fever, ailments, and inebriation.

Pralya is produced by toil, fainting, intoxication, sleep, injurious attack delusion etc.

99 Thus these eight Bhāvas are to be known as Sāttvika Bhāvas by learned men. I shall now mention the activity of these Bhāvas whereby they complete the experience.

100 The Abhinaya of Sveda should be performed by taking up fan, wiping off the sweat and exhibiting a desire for fresh wind.

101 The sensible man portrays Stambha by remaining in active, motionless, sluggish in appearance without a trace of smile, senseless and inert in body.

102 He shall portray *Vepathu* by means of trembling throbling, and shaking.

He shall portray *Svarabheda* by means of broken and choked voice.

103 *Romāñca* should be represented on the stage by repeated excitement, hairs rising from the body, and touching the body.

104/105 The sensible man portrays Aśru by means of rubbing the eyes and shedding tears.

Vaivarṇya that is situated on the body should be assiduously portrayed by changing the colour of the face and putting pressure on the blood vessels.

Pralaya The Abhinaya of Pralaya is by falling on the ground.

106 The forty nine Bhāvas have been explained by me to you duly. O leading Brahmins, it behaves you to listen to the explanation as to which of these Bhāvas are to be employed in which of the Rasas.

107 All these Bhāvas except Ālasya (lethargy), Augrya (ferocity), Jugupsā (disgust) further the development of *Śṛṅgāra* by their assignment.

108 These are glorified as the Bhāvas to be employed in Hāsya viz. Glāni (weakness), *Śaṅkā* (Suspicion), Asūyā (jealouy), Śrama (weariness), Capalatā (fickle mindedness), Supta (dreaming), Nidrā (Slumber) and Avahittha (dissimulation).

109 In the Karuṇa Rasa these are applicable viz Nirveda (despair, discouragement), Cintā (anxiety), Dainya (depression), Glāni (weakness), Aśra (tear), Jaḍata (sluggishness), Maraṇa (death) and Vyādhi (sickness).

110/111 These Bhāvas occur in the Vīra Rasa viz presence of mind, enthusiasm, agitation, delight, self assurance, ferocity, insanity, horripilation, awakening, anger, jealousy, fortitude, arrogance and deliberation.

112 In the Raudra Rasa these Bhāvas are to be employed viz——. Arrogance, jelaousy, enthusiasm, agitation, intoxication, anger, fickleminded inconstancy, delight and ferocity.

113 In the Bhayānaka Rasa the following Bhāvas are to be employed Viz—— Perspiration, tremor, horripilation, choking of the voice, fright, death, and change of colour (or pallor with face).

114 The following Bhāvas are applicable to the Bībhatsa Rasa Viz. Loss of memory (epilepsy), insanity, despair, inebriation, death, sickness and fear.

115 The following Bhāvas are applicable to the Adbhuta Rasa Viz.—— Paralysis, perspiration, loss of sense, horripilation, wonderment, excitement, sluggishness, delight and fainting.

116 These are then the Sāttvika Bhāvas included in the different kinds of Abhinayas with reference to the different Rasas by the persons who work in the Nāṭya performance.

117/118 No work can be presented on the stage with only one Rasa. If in the assemblage of many Bhāvas Rasas, Vṛttis and local usages any one item has multiple representation it should be considered the Sthāyi Rasa and the others are Sañcārins.

119 That which is based on the main theme of work on hand and is combined with Vibhāvas, Anubhāvas and Sañcārins is the Sthāyi Rasa.

120 This Sthāyi Rasa should be employed with an excessive quantity of the Sāttvika but the Sañcārin by mere gestures and postures for they are intended to support the Sthāyi Rasa.

121 Citras (on Variety of Sentiments) do not appeal and these are rarely to be seen in the world. Vimarda (a combination) does please if assiduously portrayed.

122 In the production of a performance the Sthāyi Sāttvika and the Vyabhicārins are to be assigned to male actors because they are accomplished through many objects.

123 Thus the Rasas and Bhāvas have been perfectly fitted in the Nāṭaka. He who knows this in this manner will attain the best success.

NOTES

Verses/-3 – The conception of Vibhāvas, Anubhāvas, Vyabhicāri Bhāvas and the Sthāyi Bhāvas is extremely unique in Indian Aesthetic, such deep study involves a lot of psychological experiments and analysis. The readers are requested to follow the explanations carefully. After explaining each of these by giving the corresponding English word once we have revertes to the Sanskrit terms to preserve this unique feature.

Unfortunately the text we have followed contains many printing mistakes and serious editorial blunders wherever it is possible we have corrected the text and translated. They are too numerous to enable us to cite all of them or even the most serious among them.

Prose Passage after 72

The conception of the three humrous in the body is found in ancient Greece also in an altered form. The humours are Vāta, Pitta and Kapha and the pathology of diseases found in ancient Āyurvedic works has stood the tests of time.

73 Ucchiṣṭa. This means not only leavings of the food. It has a wider connotation. If a man does not wash his mouth and gargle duly after his partaking of food he is still called Ucchiṣṭa and this considered a great lapse.

85 Grthodorp rhetoricians and whiters on the technique of dramaturgy were deed against portraying certain things on the stage death being one of them. But Bharata was in favour of it provided the procedure is followed duly. Some well known writers in India too have freely portrayed death on the stage,

83 *Nirmāla*. The flower offerings to the deity in Hindu temples are removed in the morning before the adoration begins. Orthodox devotees visit temples very early in order to see the deity in the previous day's florel offerings before they are removed. These flowers etc. are called Nirmālya These are usually allowed to get dried up in a special secluded spot in certain temples. Wearing these by devotees is some times prohibited. But an insane man does not come under its jurisdiction.

8

Procedure of the Ancillary Limbs

Request of the Sages

1—3 Thanks to your favour, O holy sir, every thing in regard to the out come of the Bhāvas and Rasas has been heard duly by us. We wish to understand further. How many types of Abhinaya Krama (seri:s of histrionic representation) are to be shown in Nāṭya by those who know them ? How is Abhinaya proceeded with ? How many varieties there of have been glorified ? It behaves your holiness to mention all this accurately. Which type of Abhinaya is to be apnlied where by one who wishes to be ‘uccessful ?

4 On hearing their words sage Bharata made this utterance in regard to the four types of Abhinaya.

Bharata begins the Explanation

5 O ascetics, I shall explain in its entirely the detailed procedure of Abhinya duly cited with examples.

Prose Passage

We shall explain what has already been mentioned as four types of Abhinaya Here some one says—— Where for is it Abhinaya ? Ic is **explained** here. Abhi is the preposition. Ṇīñ is the root in the sense of making some thing obtained. By juxta-position it becomes Abhinī. The suffix "Ac" is added there to and the form Abhinaya is the result. This has to be understood by considering the Dhātu carefully.

A verse in connection :—

6 The root Ṇīñ with Abhi prefixed is in the sense of "arriving at" or "taking on" face to face. Since this takes Padārthas (objects) [Another reading Prayogān (performances)] face to face it is remembered as Abhinya.

Explanation of abhinaya

7 Since it makes many kinds of objects clearly understood through performance along with Śākhā (branch—gesture), Aṅga (limb) and Upāṅga (Ancillary limb) it is remembered as Abhinaya.

Four types of Abhinaya

8 Abhinaya of Nāṭya can be of four types, O Brahmins Nāṭya, which is prolific in its ramifications, is well-established in this (Abhinaya).

9 The Abhinaya should be known, O learned ones, as Classified into four Viz Āṅgika (gestures of limbs), Vācika, (verbal display), Āhārya (representation through make up) and Sāttvika (Temperemental, conceptual).

10 Sāttvika has been explained by me before along with Bhāvas. Hence, even as I explain orally try to understand Aṅgābhinaya.

Āṅgika—three Varieties

11 Āṅgika is seen consisting of three types—(a) Śārīra (bodily) (b) Mukhaja (facial) (c) Ceṣṭākṛta (brought about by the movements). This is in combination with Śākhās, Aṅgas and Upāṅgas.

The Six Aṅgas

12 Nāṭya Saṅgraha has six Aṅgas in combination with the Aṅgas and Pratyaṅgas taking into consideration the head, the hand, hips, chest, sides and feet.

13 The Aṅgas are restricted to head, hand, chest, sides, hips and feet. The Upāṅgas, are the eyes, eyebrows, nose, lips, cheeks and the chin.

14 Themes (Vastus) of the Abhinaya are to be perfectly understood by the producers of dramatic and dance programmes viz. Śākhā, Nṛttam and Aṅkura (shoot).

15 What is mentioned before as Āṅgika is the Śākhā Aṅkura is the Sūcanā (Indication) or Dumb show Nṛtta (dance) is evolved out of Aṅga Hāras and it has Karaṇas for its basis.

16 Even as I explain the preliminary activity of the

Śiras (head), O learned ones, understand that it is included in the Mukhaja Abhinaya (Facial gestures) supporting many Rasas and Bhāvas.

Thirteen types of Śiras (and their uses)

17—18 Śiras (Movement of the head as Abhinaya) is of thirteen types viz.—Ākampita, Kampita, Dhūta, Vidhuta, Parivāhita, Udvāhitaka, Avadhūta, Añcita, Nihañcita, Parāvṛtta, Utkṣipta, Adhogata, and Lolita.

Ākampita

19 A slow movement of the head up and down is Ākampita. Quicker and too many movements of the head constitute Kampita.

Uses of Ākampita and Kampita

20—21 The Ākampita Śiras is employed in giving hints, instructing, asking, natural conversation, giving direction and bearing. The Kampita Śiras is accepted in displaying anger, argument, comprehension, averring, threatening, sickness and inability to brook.

22 Dhuta and Vidhuta. Slow bending and contracting of Śiras is called Dhuta. Should this movement be quicker it is called Vidhuta.

Uses of Dhuta and Vidhuta

23—24 The Dhuta Śiras is to be employed in expressing unwillingness, sorrow, wonderment, Self assured state, side glances, Voidness and prohibition.

The Vidhuta Śiras is applicable in cases of being affected by chillness, excessive fright, terrified situation, fever and preliminary stage of inebriation.

Parivāhita and Udvāhita

25 The head turned sideways successively is called Parivāhita. Once turned upwards is remembered as Udvāhita.

Uses of Parivāhita and Udvāhita

26—27 The Parivāhita is used in accomplishing, wonder

ing, enjoying, in getting angry, recollecting, reflecting deeply, in concealing and in dellience.

Udvāhita is to be adopted in showing pride, revealing desire, looking up and self confidence.

Avadhūta and its application

28 Avadhūta is that movement of the head when it is suddenly depressed down once (Use). It is to be applied in times of sending a massage, invocation of the deities, talking and beckoning people to oneself.

Añcita

29 That Śiras where the neck is bent towards one side slightly should be known as Añcita (use). It is employed in the course of ailments, loss of sense, inebriety, anxious vexation etc.

Nihañcita

30—31 Nihañcita should be known as the activity of one who lifts up the arms (shoulders) and the head when the neck is bent to a side. Its use is in regard to the women characters exhibiting pride, coquetry, light heartedness, feigned anger in love, hysterical laughter, silient expressions of affections; affected in difference, arrogance and jealous anger etc.

Parāvṛtta

32 When the actor imitates the turning of the face it is remembered as Parāvṛtta Śiras. That shall be employed in turining away the face looking behind etc.

Utkṣipta

33 If the head remains with the face looking up it should be known as Utkṣipta. While performing, Utkṣipta is to be employed when contacts with tall persons and divine weapons are to be depicted.

Adhogata

34 The head that remains with face turned down is called Adhogata. It is used in depicting bashfulness, veneration and sadness.

Parilolita

35 The head that rolls all round shall be Parilolita. It is remembered on occesions of fainting ailments, advanced state of inebriety, affiiction due to maligment planets. drowsiness etc.

36 Apart from these there are other varieties of movements of the head based on what we see in the world and witness being acted. They too can be employed by the sponsors of the programme of dances in accordance with the nature of the world.

37 Thus the activity of the head, of thirteen different types; has been recounted by me. Hence forth I shall explain the characteristics of the Dṛṣṭis (glances).

Rasadṛṣṭis (Glances expressing Sentiments)

38 These should be known as Rasadṛṣṭis viz. Kāntā, Bhayānakā, Hāsyā, Karuṇā, Adbhutā, Raudrī, Vīnā and Bībhatsā.

39 *Sthāyi Bhāvadṛṣṭis* (Glances in the dominant emotional fervours) They are Snigdhā, Hṛṣṭā, Dīnā, Kruddhā, Dṛptā, Bhayānvitā, Jugupsitā and Vismitā.

40—42 *Sañcāri Bhāva Dṛṣṭis* (Glances regarding Transitory States). They are Śūnyā, Malinā, Śrāntā, Lajjānvitā, Glānā, Śaṅkitā, Viṣaṇṇā, Mukulā, Kuñcitā, Abhitaptā, Jihmā, Lalitā, Vitarkitā, Ardhamukulā, Vibhrantā, Viplutā, Ākekarā, Vikośtā, Trastāis,Madirā, All the above together make up thirty six as I have enumerated.

43 I shall now mention in detail the salient features of the performance of these glances based on the different Bhāvas and Rasas befitting the actions during the performance.

44 *Kāntā.* This is the Drsti employed in Śṛṅgāra sentiment. This originates from excessive joy and delight when the person is extremely in love. The look involves contraction of the eyebrows and side long glances.

45 *Bhayānaka.* This is the Dṛṣṭi employed in Bhayānaka (Terrible) sentiment. It involves excessive fright. During this glance the eyelids are fixed and drawn up with the eyeballs turning up and gleaming.

46 *Hāsyā.* This is the glance with smiles. The eyelids are contracted one after the other. When the eyeballs move in agitation they too move. This is adopted when deception is to be portrayed.

47 *Karuṇā.* In this glance the upper eyelid becomes descended. Due to mental anguish the eyeball comes to rest. The gaze is fixed at the tip of the nose tearfully. It is adopted in Karuṇa (Pathos) sentiment.

48 *Adbhutā.* This is the Dṛṣṭi adopted in depicting Adbhuta (wonderment) sentiment. The tips of the eyelashes are a bit curved. Due to wonderment the eyeballs are slightly raised. The two extremities are gently distended.

49 *Raudrī.* This is the glance adopted in expressing the sentiment of fully. The Dṛṣṭi evinces pitilessness. The eyeballs are lifted up, rough and reddish in line. The eyelids are still and the eyebrows are kept crooked.

50 *Vīrā.* This is the heroic glance when the centre of the eye becomes blooming brightly. The eyeballs are kept in level. Agitated gravity is depicted by keeping the glance fully open. It is used in portraying the Vīrarasa.

51 *Bībhatsā.* This is the glance of disgust when the eyelids almost cover the corners, feelings of disgust make the eyeballs disturbed and due to arrogance the eyelashes are kept close together.

52 These Dṛṣṭis are to be known as Rasajās originating from Rasa (Sentiment). They have been explained along with their salient features. Hereafter I shall explain the glances based on the Sthāyibhāvas (Dominant emotional favour)

Sthāyi Bhāva Dṛṣṭis

53 *Snigdhā* (Loving glance) The centre is expanded and sweetness and loving nature is displayed. The eyeballs appear to be smiling. There are tears of joy. It originates from Ratibhāva (emotional fervour of love).

54. Hṛṣṭā (joyous). This glance is proclaimed to be used in the context of laughter and humour. There is a slight bend in the eye that rolls without disclosing the pupils. There is winking too.

55. *Dīnā* (Piteous) The lower eyelid is slightly fallen and the eyeballs are somewhat swollen. It moves slowly and it is a glance during the portrayal of sorrow.

56 Kruddhā (Angry) It is a rough glance with no motion in the eyelids that are kept drawn up the immobile eyeballs are turned up with knitted eyebrows. It is to be adopted in the depiction of anger.

57 Dṛptā (Haughty, arrogant). It originates from energetic enthusiasm. The glance is steedy and widely opened without moving the eyeballs. Prowess must appear to be coming out of it. It is Dṛptādṛṣṭi.

58 *Bhayānvita* (Endowed with terrified awe). In this glance the eyes are opened fully. The eyeballs move in fright from the central point. It is adopted in the Sthāyibhāva of terror.

59 *Jugupsitā* (Disgustful). The eyelids get contracted without coming together. The eyeballs are covered and turn away from the object kept in view. It is adopted when the theme is disgust.

60. Vismitā. (Astonished). It is a level glance fully blown up. Eyeballs get turned up; without any movement in the eyelids. It is used in portraying wonderment.

61 These Dṛṣṭis based on Sthāyibhāvas have been explained with their salient features. I shall now examine the characteristic features of the Dṛṣṭis based on Sañcārī Bhāvas.

Sañcāriṇī Dṛṣṭis (Glances Covering the transitory States)

62 Śūnyā (Vacant) The Śūnya glance is feeble and devoid of motion. It is turned towards the space without perceiving the objects clearly. The pupils and the lids are kept in level.

63 The Malinā (faded) glance keeps the eyelids half closed and the pupils appear to be in dismay. The eyelashes shake slightly and the eyes appear feeble and faded.

Śrānta

64. That glance is called Śrāntā (Tired) where the lids have become drooping down due to weariness; the corners are narrowed down and the pupils slip down.

65. Lajjānvitā (Bashful) This is called so because due to bashfulness the upper eyelid sinks down the eyeballs are lowered facing down and the ends of the lashes are slightly curved.

66 Glānā (Languid). That glance in which the brows and the lashes move very slowly and due to tired state the eyeballs are covered under the lids.

67 Śaṇkitā (fearfully uneasy). The glance kept hidden with movements and rests of intervals, sometimes lifted up and obliquely open with timid pupils is called Śaṅkitā Dṛṣṭi (fearfully uneasy glance)

68 Viṣādinī (Sorrowfully dejected). The glance appears to be bewildered. The lids are distended due to sadness and dejection. It is winkless and the pupils are motionless.

69 Mukulā (Budlike). Trembling eyelashes. The upper eyelids are bud shaped. Pupils wide open in happiness.

70 Kuñcitā (contracted). The ends of the eyelashes are bent after contracting the eyelids. There is contraction in the pupils too. This is called kuñcita glance.

71 Abhitaptā (Distressed) The movement of the eyelids make the eyeballs too move gently. Much distress and anguish, is indicated. This is the Abhitapta glance.

72. Jihma (Squinted). The crooked glance wherein eyelids bang down with the contraction not apparent. The concealed eyeballs during this glance give the glance the nature of a sky obligue look.

73 Lalitā (Lustfully charming). This glances is very sweet with contraction at the extremities. Smile is visible. There is the movement of eyebrows. All manifest significant lustful yearing.

74. Vitarkitā (Signifying conjectural guess). The eyelids are turned up for the purpose of guessing something. The full blown eyeballs move downwards. This is the Vitarkitā glance.

75 Ardhamukulā (Half bud). Thanks to the excessive joy the eyelids are shaped like half of a bud. The pupils too are half blown with slight movements. This glance is Ardhamukulā

76 Vibhrāntā (confused and excited). The middle of the eyelids make constant movements in agitation. This is the Vibhrāntā glance.

77 Viplutā (Distressingly disturbed). This glance there is the tremor of the eyelids suddenly followed by stunned immobile steadiness. The pupils are disturbed profusely. This is the Viplutā glance.

78 Ākekarā (Half-closed). In this glance the corner of the eyes together with the eyelids become contracted. They are joined together as it were in the nature of a half wink. There is repeated turning up in the pupils.

79 Vikośa (full floom). This is the joyous glance where the eyelids are wide open without the slightest winking. The pupils are not steady.

80 Trastā (frightened). The eyelids are down up due to fright. The pupils tremble. Panic makes the middle of the eye full blown. This glance is called Trastā.

81 The madirā (Inebriated) glance makes the eyeroll. with slight bent. The corners are fully widened. This is to be used when there is a slight intoxication.

82 In the medium inebriation the glance includes the contraction of the eyelids with a gentle movement in the eye-lashes and eyeballs.

83 In the excessive intoxicated state there is too much of winking with the eyeballs only slightly visible. There is a down-ward look when the winking may be absent.

84 Thus thirty six types of glances based on Rasa and Bhāva have been described by me. Now try to understand their application.

Application of the glances

85 The glances based on Rasas are to be applied when those Rasas are to be portrayed and the glances based on Sthāyi Bhāva should be used in representing them. Now listen to the mode of application of Vyabhicāri glances in the case of Sañcāribhāvas.

86–93

Glance—	Vyabhicāribhāvas
Śūnyā (Vacant)	Anxiety, Stunned State
Malinā (Pallid)	frustration, change of colour

Śrāntā (exhausted)	Weariness, perspiration
Lajjānvitā (Bashful)	Shame
Glānā (fatigued)	Loss of memory, sickness
Śaṅkitā (Apprehensive)	Weakness, Excessive suspicions
Viṣādinī (Dejected)	Desperate State
Mukulā (Bud shaped)	Sleep, dream, happiness.
Kuñcitā (Contracted)	Jealousy, undescrible object, minute objects difficult to be seen, pain in the eyes.
Abhitaptā (Distressed)	Distress, accidental hurt, great discouragement
Jihmā (Obliquely Squinted)	Jealousy, stupor, indolence
Lalitā (Lustful)	Contended love, joy
Vitarkitā (Guessing)	Recollection, delibeation
Ardhamukulā (Half bud)	Joy in experience, smell or touch
Vibhrāntā (Confused)	Excitements, burry, confusion
Viplutā (Distubed)	Inconstancy, insanity, affliction of misery, deaths
Ākekarā (Half closed)	In seeing an object difficult to be seen, things split between
Vikośitā (full blown)	Waking up, pride, indignation ruthlessness, complacency
Trastā (frightened)	great fear
Madira (Inebriated)	Intoxication

94—94 Thus the proper **description of the thirty** six glances basсd on Rasas and Bhāvas has been duly completed by me. Now listen even as I explain the activities of the pupils, eyelids and eyebrows.

The Pupils and their movements

95—98 The movement of the pupils is of nine types viz. (1) Bhramaṇa (circular movement) (2) Valana (Turning) (3) Pātaḥ (Letting it down relaxation) (4) Calanam (Trembling movement) (5) Saṁpravesanam (withdrawal, drawing within), (6) Nivartanam (Turning sideways) (7) Samudvṛttah (raising up) (8) Niṣkramaḥ (Going out, projecting forword) (9) Prākṛtam (Natural or usual position)

(1) Bhramaṇam is the random turning of the eyeballs

(2) Valanam is the triangular movement

(3) Pātanam is keeping them relaxed

(4) Calanam is trembling should be known as Calanam

(5) Saṁpraveśanam is the drawning of the eyeballs within

(6) Nivaratanam / Vivaratanam } It is the Kaṭākṣa when the eyeballs are turned sideways

(7) Samudvṛtta is the raising up of the pupils

(8) Niṣkrāma The coming out of the pupils i.e. the projecting forward is called so.

(9) Prākṛtam This is the natural position of the pupils

Application of these movements

99—101 Now listen and understand the mode of application of these movements of the eyeballs.

(a) In the presentation of Vīra and Raudra Rasas Bhramaṇam, Calanam, Samudvṛtta and Niṣktāma are to used. (b) Niṣkrāma and Valana are to be employed in the Bhayānaka Rasa. (c) In Hāsya and Bībhatsa Rasas Praveśana is to be used. (d) Pātana is to be employed in the Karuṇa Rasa (e) Niṣkrāmaṇa is to be employed in the Adbhuta Rasa (f) Vivartita is employed in the Śṛṅgārarasa (g) Prākṛta is employed in respect to the other Bhāvas.

102 These activities are natural to the eyeballs as found in the world. These movements of the pupils are to be properly applied in respect to all the Bhāvas.

Darśana types (Use of the pupils in diverse forms of looking)

103—107 I shall expatiate upon the vanrities of these special ways of looking there itself. They are classified into these lands viz. Samam (Level), Sāci (Askance), Anuvṛtta (following up), Ālokita (seeing over), Vilokita (looking round) Pralokita (careful observance), Ullokita (looking up) Avalokita (looking down).

Sama —This is the gentle look keeping the pupils in a level positions

Sāci —This is the look askance when the pupils are triangular, coming well within the eyelashes

Anuvṛtta —This is the scrutinising look following the form observed

Ālokita —Sudden looking over is considered as such

Vilokita —Looking round with the pupils turned back
Pralokita —This is the careful observance with the pupils turning from side to side.
Ullokita —This is the upward look
Avalokita —This is the downward look

This is the mode of looking based on all the Bhāvas

108—111 Understand the activity of the eyelids in their relationship with the pupils. They are (1) Unmeṣa (2) Nimeṣa (3) Prasṛta (4) Kuñcita (5) Sama (6) Vivartita (7) Sphurita (8) Pihita and (9) Vitālita.

(1) Unmeṣa (opening) Separating the eyelids is called Unmeṣa.

(2) Nimeṣa (closing) When the eyelids are brought together.

(3) Prasṛta (spreading) preading and separating widely

(4) Kuñcita (Contraction) The eyelids are contracted.

(5) Sama (Level) Keeping the eyelids in their natural position.

(6) Vivartita (Turned up). The eyelids are raised up.

(7) Sphurita (Throbbing) The eyelids continue to throb.

(8) Pihita (Concealed) The eyelids are closed as though resting.

(9) Vitālita (flapped) The eyelids get flapped.

112—115 Understand now the application of these in the different Rasas and Bhāvas.

Anger is depicted with the looks of Vivartita, Unmeṣa & Nimeṣa. In wonderment, delight and heroism—Prasṛta. In smelling, testing, touching and seeing undesirable objects Kuñcita is applied. In Śṛṅgāra Rasa the Sama mode of looking is employed. In cases of envy (jealousy etc.) Sphurita is applicable in depicting sleeping, dreaming, swooning, trouble due to blowing wind, hot air, smoke columns, rain etc., eyesore and seeking food (?). Vitālita (flapping) in depicting accidental hunts etc. Thus is the application of the pupils and eyelids in regard to Rasas and Bhāvas.

116—120 *Eyebrows.* Now understand the activity of the eyebrows befitting that of the eyelids and pupils. It is of seven types (1) Utkṣepa (2) Pātana (3) Bhrukvṭi (4) Caṭura (5) Kuñcita (6) Recita and (7) Sahaja.

(1) Utkṣepa (Lifting up) If the eyebrows are raised one by one or both together it is Utkṣepa (2) Pātana (Letting down). When the eyebrows are lowered one after the other or both together (3) Bhrukuṭī (knitting) The eyebrows are raised up from their roots (4) Caṭura (Ingeniously edroit) The eyebrows are pleasingly extended in a gentle slow movement (5) Kuñcita (contracted)—gentle bending of one of the eyebrows or both together is called Kuñcita (6) Recita (Loosening) when only one of the eyebrows is raised in a lovingly graceful manner it is called Recita of the eyebrows (7) Sahaja (Natural) this is the natural position of the eyebrows.

Application of eyebrow movements

121—125 Hereafter I shall mention their utility in regard to Rasas and Bhāvas.

In the act of Utkṣepa raise only one of the eyebrows in depicting anger, conjecture, sportiveness, natural playfulness, hearing and looking at. In wonderment, delight and anger raise both the eyebrows. Pātana is applicable in envious disgust, humour and smelling. The sensible man applies Bhrukuṭi towards the objects of anger and in illuminated articles. Caṭura movement occurs in Śṛṅgāra, graceful sport and gentle touch Kuñcita is applicable in displaying affection, pretension of anger, hilarious sportive behaviour etc. Recita movement of the eyebrows is applied during dances. In non complicated occasions and Bhāvas the sensible man employs the Sahaja position of the eyebrows.

126—128 The activity of the eyebrows has been explained. Now listen and understand the graceful movements of the nostrils.

The Nose and its activities

The nasal gestures are of six types viz. Natā, Mandā, Vikṛṣṭā, Socchvāsā, Vighūrṇitā and Svābhāvika.

Natā—(depressed). In this gesture the lobes cling together frequently. Mandā (Mild) The gesture is of the nature of resting lobes. Vikṛṣṭā (Expanded). The lobes are fully blown Socchvāsā (Having the respiration). The air is inhaled and drawn in Vighūrṇitā (rolling). There is manifest contraction of the nostrils. Svābhāvika (Natural). The nostrils are in level position.

Application of the nasal gestures

129—132 The nasal gestures have been described. Understand their application Natā is remembered in regard to mild cry accompanied by sighs broken now and then. While depicting Śoka (Sorrow) and despair, eagerness and anxiety Mandā form of nasal gesture is applicable. Vikṛṣṭā gesture is applicable in regard to strong smell, hearing sighs, anger fear and distress. Socchvāsā is applicable when the smell is mild and sweet as well as when the actor indulges deep breaths. Vighūrṇitā (Rolling) is applicable in humour, disgust and envious response Svābhāvikā gesture is applicable in regard to other types of Bhāvas.

Cheeks and their gestures

132—134 Gaṇḍa or the cheek is of six types viz. (1) Kṣāma (2) Phulla (3) Purṇa (4) Kampita (5) Kuñcita and (6) Sama (1) Kṣāma (Lean, enaciated) If the cheek is a bit depressed it is called Kṣāma (2) Phulla (blown up). If it is expanded and blown up it is called Phulla, (3) Pūrṇa (Full) If the cheek is raised up it is called Pūrṇa. (4) Kampita (Tremulous) When there is throbbing it is known as Kampita (5) Kuñcita (contracted). If the cheek is narrowed down it is called Kuñcita. (6) Sama (Level) This is the natural position of the cheek.

135—137 The characteristic features of the two cheeks have been explained Now understand their application Kṣāma is to be employed in miserable circumstances. Phulla is recommended when there is excessive joy. Pūrṇa is applicable when there is energetic enthusiasm and arrogant attitude. Kampita is useful when portraying Anger enthusiatic joy. Kuñcita is of utility depicting cold touch, fear, fever etc. and is to be accompanied by horripilation, Prākṛta or Sama is to be applied in regard to the remaining Bhāvas. Thus the gestures of the cheeks are to be used.

Lips and their gestures

137—139 The activities of the lips are of six types viz. (1) Vivartana (2) Kampana (3) Visarga (4) Vinigūhana

(5) Sandaṣṭaka and (6) Samudgaka. (1) Vivartana (Rolling, narrowing) The lips are narrowed down in this gesture (2) Kampana (Tremour) There is throbbing of the lips (3) Visarga (Spreading out) The lips appear to be spreading out (4) Vinigūhana (concealing). The lips appear to be drawing (5) Sandaṣṭaka (Biting) Teeth appear to bite the lips (6) Samudgaka (Closed up like a chest). The contraction of the lips makes them at rest.

140—142 Thus the characteristic features of the lips have been mentioned. Understand their application (1) Vivartana is to be employed in portraying envious jealousy, physical pain, contemptions disgust, laughter etc. (2) Kampana is to be employed when there is trembling, cold, fever, anger, victory etc. (3) Visarga is to be employed in women's graceful coquetry, pretended anger against lover, and painting of the lips (4) Vinigūhana is to be applied where there is exertion (5) Sandaṣṭaka in all the activities about anger etc. (6) Samudgaka is to be applied in the case of compassionate sympathy, kiss and congratulating

143—146 Thus the activities of the lips have been enumerated. Understand those of the chin.

The Chin and the gestures thereof. They are of seven kinds based on the activities of teeth viz. (1) Kuṭṭana (2) Khaṇḍana (3) Chinna (4) Cukṣita (5) Lehana (6) Sama and (7) Daṣṭa (1) Kuṭṭana. When there is clash of the upper row of teeth with the lower one (2)Khaṇḍana and Frequent throbbing of the lips (3) Chinna Close contact of the lips (4) Cukṣita When the lips are separated widely (5) Lehana this is the licking of the lips by means of the tongue. (6) Sama when the movement of the lips is very slight (7) Daṣṭa when the lower lip is bitten by the teeth.

Application of the gestures of the Chin

146—149 (1) Kuṭṭana is the activity of those afflicted by fright, chillness, old age, fever and chronic ailments. (2) Khaṇḍana is the activity during muttreing of the prayers, Vedic study and recitation, Conversation and taking food (3) Chinna is the activity of the Chin during sickness, fear, chillness, taking physical exercise and looking angrily.

(4) Cukṣita is to be applicable when one yawns (5) Lehana is applicable when the activity of licking is to be shown (6) Sama is applicable when natural state is to be portrayed and (7) Daṣṭa in connection with furious and angry activities. Thus the activity of the chin in association with lips, tongue and teeth.

149—156 *Oral gestures are of six types.* (1) Vidhuta (2) Vinivṛtta (3) Nirbhughna (4) Bhughana-Vyābhughna (5) Vivṛta and (6) Udvāhī.

(1) Vidhuta is spreading of the mouth obliqualy.
(2) Vinivṛtta—Turning and spreading backwards.
(3) Nirbhughna—The mouth is lowered down.
(4) Vyābhughna-Bhughna—Slightly spread out mouth.
(5) Vivṛta—When the lips are kept apart
(6) Udvāhi—mouth turned upwards.

Application of oral gestures

Sponsors of dramatic performance shall apply the Vinivṛtta gesture in feminine envious jealousy, anger motivated by rivalry, contemptuous and playful behaviour etc. Vidhuta is employed in preventing some activity or saying that something "is not so" and similar instances. Nirbhughna is to be employed in majestic and serious survey etc. Bhughna is to be employed in one feeing ashamed discouragement, impatience, anxiety, yearning contempletion etc. So also in taking counsel together. This is something natural in the case of ascetics Vivṛta is to be applicable in humour, grief, fear etc. Udvāhi is to be employed in playful behaviour of women, in their proud behaviour as though in saying "Go away" in their disrespect while saying "In this the way ?" and in angry words as well.

156—157 The varieties of glances mentioned before like Sama, Sācikṛta etc. are also to be employed by persons conversant with them along with the oral gestures.

Mukhrāga (Colour of the face)

157—158 This has been classified into four types (1) Svābhāvika (Natural) (2) Prasnna (Pleased) (3) Rakta (Reddish) and Śyāma (dark and moody) as based on the theme.

Application of the facial colour change

159—160 Svābhāvika based on the natural acting should

be applied in the case of Madhyastha (Neutral) Bhāva etc. Prasanna is to be employed in the Adbhuta Rasa as well as Hāsya and Śṛṅgāra Rakta is to be employed in Vīra and Raudra and also when there is intoxication etc. and Karuṇa Rasa. In Bībhatsa and Bhayānaka Rasas, the face becomes darkened.

161—162 The facial colour change should be thus applied in regard to themes, Rasa and Bhāvas. The gestures of the limbs in all their aspects may make an Abhinaya good but without the proper Mukha Rāga (Facial colouring) it will not be splended.

163—164 Even the slightest Abhinaya of the body and the limbs in collaboration with Mukharāga attains double splendour like the moon at night.

163—165 Glances mentioned before with due Mukha Rāga shall portray differents Bhāvas and Rasas because dramatic performance is based on this.

When the glances proceed along with the gestures of the mouth, eyebrows and Dṛṣṭi (peculiar look) the sponsor of the performance shall employ this Mukharāga too with due consi- deration for Bhāva and Rasa. Mukha Rāga has thus been explained duly.

Neck

166—167 O **Brahmins**, hereafter I shall explain Grīvā Karmans (activities of the neck)

167—171 *Gestures of the neck*. They are of nine kinds (1) Samā (2) Natā (3) Unnatā (4) Tryśrā (5) Recitā (6) Kuñcita (7) Añcitā (8) Velitā and (9) Nivṛttā (1) Samā is the natural posture of the neck. It is applicable in meditation, muttering of prayers and natural posture of the neck (2) Natā where the face is bent down. It is used to depict wearing of ornaments, placing hands round the neck etc. (3) Unnatā The face is turned up. It is used in reaching a high place (4) Tryaśrā (Triangular) face is turned sideways. Applicable in weight lifting by means of neck and depicting sorrow (5) Recitā (The neck is shaken and moved sideways). It is used in graceful charms and coquetry. Also in portraying churning and while dancing. (6) Kuñcitā (The neck with the head *kept* bent) In portraying the pressure of weight and protection of the neck. (7) Añcitā (The head is turned back). It is employed in portraying suicide by hanging, dragging of the hairs and looking higher up. (8) Velitā (Vāhitā) (The neck with the face turned **sideway** It is to be used in turning the face and looking behind (9) Nivṛtta (Face turned towards the front). Indicates proceeding towards one's own abode.

171—173 These are the diverse Varieties of the gestures of the neck based on their indicating customary practice of people. The gestures of the neck duly follow those of the head. The activity of the neck functions thanks to the activity of the head.

Thus the characteristics of the limbs, the Upāṅgas of the head, have been explained. Even as I explain listen to and understand the gestures of the remaining Aṅga.

NOTES

The translation is self explanatory. Hence no further notes.

9

Hastabhinaya (Gestures of the Hands)

Bharata resumes narration

1—3 The Upāṅga Abhinaya (Gestures of the minor limbs) as regards head, eyes, nose, eyebrows, lips and the cheeks has been explained to you by me along with the characteristics thereof. I shall now expatiate upon the activity of the hands in as much as they further the performance of a play. I shall clarify how and by whom they are to be shown, Even as I define listen to it. I am explaining the characteristics of the gestures of the hands, chest, 'sides, belly, waist, thighs, calves and feet and their application too as is commonly used.

4—10 *Asaṁyuta (non combined) and Śaṁyuta (combined)* Gestures of the Asaṁyuta hands are twenty four in number and those of Saṁyuta hands are thirteen.

Asaṁyuta (1) Patāka (2) Tripatāka (3) Kartarīmukha (4) Ardhacandra (5) Arāla (6) Śukatuṇḍay (7) Uṣṭi (8) Śikhara (9) Kapittha (10) Kaṭakāmukha (Khaṭakāmukha) (11) Sūcyāsya (Sūcīmukha) (12) Padmakośa (13) Sarpaśīrṣa (14) Mṛgaśīrṣa (15) Kāṅgula (Lāṅgula) (16) Alapadma (Alapadya, Alapallava) (17) Catura (18) Bhramara (19) Haṁsāsya (20) Haṁsāpakṣa (21) Sandaṁśa (22) Mukula (23) Urṇanābha and (24) Tāmracūḍa.

Saṁyuta (1) Añdali (2) Kapota (3) Karkaṭa (4) Svastika (5) Kaṭakāvardhamānaka (Khaṭakā) (6) Utsaṅga (7) Niṣadha (8) Dola (9) Puṣpapuṭa (10) Makara (11) Gajadanta (12) Avahittha and (13) Vardhamāna.

Nṛttahastas (Dance hand gestures)

11—16 The Nṛttahastas are thirty in number viz. (1) Caturasra (2) Udvṛtta (3) Talamukha (4) Svastika (5) Viprakīrṇa (6) Arālakhaṭakāmukha (Kaṭa) (7) Āviddhavaktra (8)

Sūcyāsya (9) Recita (10) Ardharecita (11) Uttānavañcita (12) Pallava (13) Nitamba (14) Keśabandha (15) Latā (16) Karihasta (17) Pakṣavañcitaka) (18) Pakṣapradyotaka (19) Garuḍapakṣaka (20) Daṇḍapakṣa (21) Ūrdhvamaṇḍalī (22) Pārsvamaṇḍalī (23) Uromaṇḍalī (24) Urahparśvār-Dhamaṇḍalī (25) Muṣṭikasvastika (26) Nalinī-Padmakośaka (27) Alapallava (28) Ulbaṇa (29) Lalita and (30) Valita.

17 There are thus sixty four [sixty seven] gestures of hands named by me. Now understand their detailed characteristics and applications.

18 Where all the fingers are extended keeping them close to one another with the thumb bent, the gesture is called *Patāka*.

19 This gesture is applied when it is required to represent continous shower of blows, warming near the fire, nudging others, excessive delight and proud indication of oneself. Those conversant with the [use of this gesture should place the hand with the gesture on a level with the forehead.

20 When it is required to represent flames of fire, shower of flowers, heavy downpour etc. both the hands with Patāka Mudrā are joined together and then the fingers are separeted and kept moving.

21 Presentation of flowers and sprouts, flourishing growth of grass and things arranged on the ground are represented by two Patāka hands separated from Svastika position.

22 If the hands with Patāka gesture are separated from Svastika position with the fingers pointing downwards the following can be represented viz. an object is opened, something is protected, another thing is covered and made dense and something indicated as a secret.

23 This same with the fingers pointing downwards but kept moving up and down is to be applied when the gust of wind, waves of water, agitation of the seashore and flood are to be indicated.

24 The gesture of Patāka hand with the combination of Recaka should be employed to represent incitement of people, a crowd of many participants, loftiness, beating of musical in-

strument of percussion, and upward flight of birds.

25 Two Patāka hands with the palms shriking against each other can represent the act of washing, breeding, pressing, cleansing, uprooting and lifting up of a mountain.

26 The manner of applying the gesture is the same whether a man or a woman stages it.

Here after I shall explain the characteristics of *Tripatāka*.

27 In the Patāka hand the ring finger is kept bent. This should be known as Tripatāka understand its application (function).

28—29 Invocation, stepping down, dismissal, obstruction, gaining access, lifting up, bowing down, observing similarity, putting out alternatives and suggestions, touching holy and auspicious objects or placing them on the head, wearing the turban or any head gear or putting on the crown, covering the nostril, mouth or ear etc are represented by this gesture.

30 The same Tripatāka had when the fingers are kept pointing downwards and moving up and down represents the flight of small birds, tortuous flow of a streem, wriggling movement of as make and fluttering of bees etc.

31 Wiping off of the tears, applying the Tilaka on the forehead, smearing of Rocanā and touching of the forelocks hairs should be represented by Tripatāka and the ring finger.

32 The Svastika formation of two Tripatāka hands is to be applied when the salutation to an elderly person is to be shown. For the representation of a marriage caremony the same with tips touching one another is to be employed.

33 When the hands are separated and moved from this position they indicate a royal personage. The Svastika formation carried out obliquely indicates the seeing of a planet.

34 To represent the appearance of an ascetic the hands are to be raised with the palms averted from each other. When the palms are kept facing each other it represents a doorway.

35 Two Tripatāka hands first kept supine near the face and the second face downwards represent the submarine fire or battle or the appearance of sharks.

36 Capering gambol of monkeys, surging of the waves, the wafting wind and the moving men are to be represented in a dance with this gesture by those who are adepts in gesture.

37 The hand should be kept with the thumb strectched forward when crescent moon is to be shown. The hand turned towards the back indicates the march of men (against enemies).

38 Kartarīmukha. In the Tripatāka hand if the index finger faces the back of the middle finger it is *Kartarīmukha*

39 This hand with face downwards indicates walking along the road; decorating the feet colouring them or dancing. With the finger pointing upwards the hand represents biting, blowing of horn or painting of a picture.

40 When the fingers in the hand are turned towards different directions (or different modes of folding) it represents falling down, dying, transgressing, reverting, cogitating and depositing of some (valuable) thing.

41 This hand is employed by persons conversant with it either as Saṁyutakaraṇa (with both the hands joined) or as Asaṁyuta (disjointed) in regard to black antelope, Camara deer, buffalo, divine elephant, bullock, ornamental gateway and peaks of mountains.

Ardhacandra

42 The hand wherein the fingers along with the thumb are kept bent depicting a bow is well known as Ardhacandra. Its application (function) is being mentioned.

43 Small plants the diget of the moon, the conch, the pot, bracelet, forcible forward thrust, excessive exertion, slenderness of the waist the girth etc. should be represented by means of this hand.

44 With this Ardhacandra alone should be represented the girdle, hips, waist, the face, the Talapatra (leaflike ornament for ears) and the Kuṇḍala (the ear ornment that hangs down suspended) of women.

Arāla

45 The index finger is bent like a bow; the thumb is kept urved and the remaining ones separate and turned upwards.

In the Arāla hand this is the position of fingers.

46 With this gesture inherent strength, pride, exploit, beauty, surage, divine objects, majesty, blessings and similar pleasing Bhāvas are to be represented.

47 Collecting together or scattering and separating the hairs and glancing all over the body as is done by women are also represented through this.

48—49 The initial rites connected with marriage ceremony, the circumambulation of the fire by the couple, etc should be represented by two Arāla hands waved round each other with finger tip, touching so as to form a Svastika. People moving round and round, the general assemblage of people in a circle, the object buried under the ground—all these should be represented by the similar hands.

50 Beckoning to others, preventing some one from coming in, creating something, uttering too many words, wiping off perspiration, smelling sweet scents etc. and all auspicious matter (too are to be represented like this),

51 The activities mentioned before as ones to be presented by means of Arāla hands by women equally well *Śukatuṇḍa*. (beak of a parrot).

52 When ring finger in the Arāla hand becomes bent it is called Śukatuṇḍa. Understand its function.

53 "Neither I nor you" "This should not be done" these ideas are to be represented with this gesture. So also invocation, dismissal, words in contempt such as "Fil upon you" etc. are represented by means of this land.

54 Muṣṭi (fist like). If the ends of the fingers are kept close to the palm and the thumb is placed above them it is termed Muṣṭi.

55 This hand is applicable in regard to the representation of striking, exercising (fighting), setting out, pressing (milk from the udders of cow etc), massaging, grasping of swords, lances and clubs etc.

Śikhara (Summit)

56 If the thumb of the Muṣṭi gesture lifted up it should

be known as Śikhara hand by those who employ the gesture.

57 This gesture is applicable in the representations of Raśmi (Reins rays), Kuśa grass, burling of Tomara, and javelin, wielding of goad and bow, the painting of lips feet etc. and stroking the forelocks of hairs.

Kapittha (Wood apple)

58 If in the gesture named Śikhara the forefinger is kept curved and pressed down by (? two) thumbs, it is then remembered as Kapitta.

59 Truthful and beneficient acts are to be represented by this Kapittha gesture. The weapons such as sword, bow, discuss, tomara, lance, club, Śakti, thunderbolt, arrows etc are also indicated by the gesture.

Kaṭakāmukha (Khaṭakāmukha)

60 When the ring finger along with the little finger of this Kapittha gesture is raised and bent it is ka (kha) Ṭakāmukha.

61—63 This gesture is applicable when the following are to be represented viz.—Hotra (Sacrifice), Havya (offerings into the fire), umbrella, pulling the rains, fanning, holding a mirror, cutting, powdering, holding a long baton, arranging the pendulous pearl-necklaces, long wreaths, flower garlands, tucking up the loose ends of robes, churning, drawing of arrows, gathering of flowers, poking with the goad, drawing up the goad, pulling a rope and seeing a woman.

Sūcīmukha

64 When the index finger in the Hasta named Kaṭaka is stretched that Hasta should be known as one named Sūcīmukha by those who employ (gestures).

65 I shall briefly mention the various applications of this when the forefinger is raised, bent, kept shaking, oscillating, expanded, lifted up and tremulous.

66—67 The following are to be represented by this gesture with the index finger kept moving after being raised—discus, lightning, flags and festoons, bunches of flowers, Karṇacūlikās (ear ornaments) and all types of crooked movements. So also should the expressions of approval, small serpent, tender sprout, incense, lights, Vallīs (creepers bearing bulky fruits like gourds, pumpkins etc), Latās (those having small fruits like grapes), Śikhaṇḍa (tufts of hair), falling down, obliqueness and globular things be represented.

68 In representing snouts, number one, clubs sticks etc. this hand should be employed with the forefinger raised further. It should be bent and made to come into contact with the mouth to represent beings with curved fangs.

69 By a circular movement of this band, the forfeit are of all the possessions can be represented. An alternate raising and lowering of the forefinger is this hand represents long study and long day.

70 In order to indicate the realization of the meanings of utterences, the forefinger is curved and moved up and down near the face.

71 The artiste stretches the forefinger, shakes it and moves it up in order to indicate "Do not" or "Do speak".

72—75 Anger is represented, perspiration is indicated if the forefinger is merely shaken. In the Abhinaya based on tresses of hair, earring, armlet and decoration of the cheeks, in representing egotism, or "I am" or pointing out on enemy the same gestures are followed. When asking "who is this ?" or while scratching, the hand is held very near the forehead.

Two Sūcīmukha hands are collectively made use of to indicate gathering together of the men and their separation is indicated when they are separated. The artiste crosses the two hands to represent a quarrel. When the hands press each other bondage is represented. To indicate the close of the day make the two sūcīmukha hands face each other and hold them separately on the left side.

76 When moved in the front this hand represents any form, stone whirlpool, some mechanical contrivance or a hill. Serving of food is represented when the same movement is made with the hand pointing downwards.

77. While representing Śiva this hand as, pointed downwards and closely held to the forehead; while indicating Indra the bend is to be raised into the forehead and held across.

78 Two such hands can represent the olb of the full moon

ana rising of the banner of Indra is indicated when they are held close to the forehead.

79 Moved around this same hand (single) represents the lunar area and Śiva's third eye is represented when held on the forehead. The artiste raises it obliquely to represent Indra's eyes.

Padma Kośa

80 All the fingers including the thumb are kept separately and the ends bent. They do not meet one another.

81 Breasts of women and the fruits of similar appearance viz. Bilva, Kapittha etc. are represented through this hand. Acceptance of these fruits, flesh etc. is indicated by slightly bending it at its end.

82 The same Padmakośa hand represents offering of Pūjā to a deity carrying tribute casket, offering of the Agrapiṇḍa (the chief of balls of rice as oblation), and a number of flowers gathered together.

83 The lotus in full boom and the lily can be represented with two such hands with the fingers kept **moving**. The hands meet at the wrist and then turn backwards.

Sarpaśirṣa

84 All the fingers not excluding the thumb are kept close to one another and the palm of the hand is hollow. This is called Sarpaśīrṣa.

85 In order to represent water offerings (libations as well as sprinkling), movement of reptiles, challenging persons to combats and the stroking of the frontal globes the elephant etc. this hand is used.

86 *Mṛgaśīrṣa.* All the fingers are kept permiting downwards except the thumb and the little finger which are to be kept raised up. This is called Mṛgaśīrṣā.

87 This hand is moved in order to represent "here" "now" "It is present" "today" "it is possible" and similar senses. Splendour throwing of dice, removal of perspiration and the affected displeasure of women against lovers etc. are also represented by this hand.

88 *Kaṅgula.* The little finger is raised, the ring finger is kept bent and the three other fingers viz. the middle the forefinger and the thumb are kept separated, like the holy fires. This hand is called Kaṅgula.

89 Insignificant fruits of diverse kinds, angry retorts of women etc. are represented by this hand when the fingers are kept moved.

Alapadmaka

90 The fingers are separated from one another and are kept turned towards the palm in a circular way. This is called Alapadmaka or Alapallava.

91 It is employed by artistes to indicate prevention, a woman's boasting about herself and such senses as "who are you ?" "It is not", "Absurd" etc.

Catura

92 Three fingers are spread. The little finger is lifted up The thumb is kept within them. This hand is remembered as Catura.

93 It is used in indicating the senses of policy, discipline, penances, cleverness, a timid girl, a sick person, spirit, deceit etc and also apt words welfare, truth and tranquillity.

94 Openness, delibration, movement conjecture, shame etc. can be represented with one or two such Catura hands kept moving round.

95 Two Catura hands combined together are employed to indicate **comparision** between the eyes and petals of lotus and also the ears of deer.

96—98 Apart from these, it is the practice of the artistes to employ Catura hand in signifying various things such as sports dalliance splendour, memory, intellect judgement forgiveness, nutritions, consciousness, hope, affection reasoning, union, purity cleverness, favourableness, softness, happiness, character, question livelihood, property, wealth, defeat, amorous coition, merit and demerit, youth, home, wife and various colours.

99. The colours represented thus. The Catura hand is held

up to indicate white, if it is moved round yellow and red colours can be represented and when one Catura hand is pressed with another it indicates blue,

100 *Bhramara* The middle finger and the thumb cross each other, the index finger is bent and the other two fingers are separated and raised. This is in the Bhramara hand.

101 By means of this hand the artiste indicates the plucking of flowers with long stems viz lotus waterlily etc. and the adornment of the ear is also indicated.

102 The Bhramara hand is allowed to fall down with a thud to indicate scolding, arrogance, rapidity, beating the Tāla and instilling confidence and comfort in some one.

103 *Hamsāsya*. Keeping the forefinger middle finger and the thumb without any intervening space. The remainnig fingers are to be kept stretched. This is Hamsāsya.

104 With the end throbbing slightly this hand should be used to indicate exquisitely fine, small loose and light things. Exit and Softness too can be displayed.

Haṁsapakṣa

105 Three fingers are kept stretched resembling the wings of a swan ; the small finger is kept raised and the thumb is kept bent.

106—108 Offering libations of water is indicated here by keeping the hand near the cheek the artist represents acceptance of gifts, ceremonious rinsing of the mouth, the feeding of the Brahmins, close embrace, too much of stupour, horripilation, gentle touch, massaging with unquents etc. The amorous actions of ladies in regard to the space between the breasts shall also be indicated by means of this hand with relevance to the Rasa concerned. Touching of the Chin and the mood of sorrow too can be thus indicated.

Sandaṁśa

109 The thumb and the forefinger in the position of Arāla hand are kept crossed like pincers. The palms is slightly hollowed. This is Sandaṁśa hand.

110 In as much as the hand is held in front, near the

mouth or on one side this **Sandaṁśa** can be classified into three. The due Rasa and Bhāvas are kept in mind.

111—115 (a) *Sandamśa in front.* This represents plucking of flowers, wreathing of garlands, taking up blades of grass, leaves, hairs or thread, holding or pulling out an arrow or removing thorn.

(b) Sandaṁśa near the mouth. This represents taking off of a flower from the stem gently, the wick of a lemp, the stick of collyrium, filling up of vessels with something, saying "Fie upon you!" and wreath in diverse forms.

(c) Sandaṁśa on one side. The left hand is used by slightly turning the tip to represent softness, abuse and envy. The combination of two or more of these is used to represent Sacred thread, piercing holes in pearls etc. bow string, fineness, arrow, objects aimed at yogic practice, meditation and small quantity. The Sandaṁśa is used to indicate painting colouring the eyes, deliberation, drawing the Patra Lekhā and squeezing of the Lākṣārasa.

Mukula

116 The fingers, are bent and kept close to one another in the form of a bud as it were when their tips meet together in the Haṁsāsya hand. This is called Mukula.

117—118 Making of offerings in the adoration of a deity, lotus bud, that of a lily, long distant kiss that of a vulgar lecher, contempt, diverse object, taking food, counting of coins, ponting the lips, donating something, quickness etc. are represented by this hand.

119—120 In the Padmakośa hand fingers are further bent. This is called Urṇanābha because it resembles a spider.

121/122 Tne Urṇanābha hand is usually employed to represent the combing of the tresses, receiving stolen property, scratching the head, the fell,disease of leprosy, lions, tigers and holding a stone.

Tāmracūḍā The middle finger crosses with the thumb, the index finger is kept bent, the remaining two fingers resting on the palm. This is called Tāmracūḍa.

In order to indicate rebuke this hand is allowed to fall down with a thud. Beating time, instilling self confidence, rapidity and gesticulation too are indicated hereby.

123--125 Small fractions of time viz. Kalā, Kāṣṭhā, Kṣaṇa Nimeṣa are represented by this hand. It also represents talking to and inviting a young girl. Even of the fingers are kept close to one another and made bent with the thumb set on them the hand is termed Tāmaracūḍa. With [this hand, hundred, thousand gold coins are indicated. If the fingers are quickly made to move freely it represents sparks or drops.

126 O excellent Brahmins, these hands explained are single (non-combined). Hereafter listen to the combined hands.

Añjali

127 Two Patāka hands are put together. This is called *Añjali*. It is employed to great friends, receive venerable persons and making obeisance to deities.

128 In regard to the deites Añjali is held on the head; to venerable persons near one's face, and in greeting friends Añjali is placed on the breast. With regard to the others there is no specific stipulation.

Kapota

129 Two Añjali hands meeting resembling a dove. Listen to its employment.

130—131 A ferocious approach with inimical intention is indicated by the Kapota hand. So also bowing down and talking to a venerable man. Women artistes employ this hand on their breasts to represent cold and fear. The Kapota hands released after the meeting of fingers are used to represent the ideas. "This much can be done" "Nothing more is feasible" or words expressing anxiety.

Karkaṭa

132 Interlocked fingers resembling Karkaṭa (Cref) constitute this hand.

133 Bee's wax, massaging of the limbs, yawning soon after getting up from sleep, a huge body, supporting the chin

and holding a conch shall in order to blow on it—all these are indicated by this hand.

Svastika

134 Two Arāla hands are kept upturned and held together at the wrists. This constitutes Svastika hand. Usually women employ this hand.

135 If the hands are separated from the Svastika position it will represent directions clouds, the firmament, jungles, oceans, the different Ṛtus,the earth and other vast things as well.

136 *Kaṭakā Vardhamānaka.* This is the combination of two Kaṭakāmukha hands i.e. one is placed on another at the wrist. This is employed to represent movements concerning wooing a lady or in bowing down to a venerable person.

137 *Utsaṅga* In this hand the Arāla hands are placed in a contrary manner. Its main use is to represent the feeling of touch.

138 Further its employment is to represent anything to be done with excessive effort, acts of anger and indignation, women's envious acts and squeezing of something.

139—140 *Niṣadha* If the Mukula hand is enturned with Kapittha hand it is Niṣadha hand. or The left hand holds the other arm above the elbow and the right hand touched fist. This also makes a Niṣadha hand.

141 Patience, intoxication, arrogance, magnanimity, eagerness, valour, conceit, haughtiness, absence of motion, steadiness etc. are indicated by this hand.

142 *Dola.* Both the shoulders are at ease in a Karaṇa and two Patākā hands long down. This constitutes the Dola hand.

143 This hand represents haste, sadness, loss of sense, swooning, inebriated state, excitement illness and weapon-inflicted wounds,

Puṣpapuṭa

144 Two Sarpaśīrṣa hands with the fingers close to one another meet on one side intimately. This constitutes Puṣpapuṭa hand.

145 It is employed to indicate receiving, carrying etc. of

rice, fruits, flowers, different kinds of foodstuffs as well as water.

Makara

146 Two Patākā hands are turned down and placed on each other with the thumbs kept raised. This is Makara hand resembling shark.

147 Its employment is for the representation of lion, tiger, elephant, crocodile, shark, fish and flesh eating animals.

Gajadanta

148 The Gajadanta hand is the combination of two Sarpaśīrṣa hands mutually touching the opposite arms between the elbow and the shoulder.

149 The carrying of the bride and the groom, excessive weight, clasping a pillar and the extermination of a hill or a boulder are indicated by the Gaja Danta hand.

150 *Avahittha.* This is the combination of two Śukatuṇda hands meeting each other on the breast. They are bent and slowly lowered.

151 This hand is to be employed to represent weakness, sigh, revelation of one's own body, thinness there of and the yearning for a beloved.

Vardhamāna

152 This is the combination of the Mukula hand and Kapittha in close clasp,

153 If one hand is pressed with the other this hand indcates grasping, receiving, preserving, convenion, truthfulness and compression.

154 The combination of two Haṁsapakṣa hands turned down is also known as Vardhamāna. It is utilized in representing the opening of objects like latticed windows.

155 The two types of hands single or combined described succinctly by me may be used elsewhere too bearing in mind the injunctions laid down here.

General rules governing the use of hand gestures

156 The personal judgement of the actor is the main guiding factor in the selection of the hand gestures while acting, who shall bear in mind their form, movement significance and class.

157 There is no gesture that cannot be used in representing something or some idea. I have adequately described the usual application of these gestures in their association with different ideas.

158 Besides these there are many other commonly used hands (i.e. gestures) pregnent with implied meanings. They are to be employed as one pleases in depicting Rasas Bhāvas and allied activities.

159 Both men and women artistes shall employ these gestures with adequate consideration for the place, occasion and the performances intended to be stayed in the context of the suitability of their meanings.

Movements of the hand gestures

160 I shall now explain the various movements of these hand gestures in as much as the revelation of Rasas and Bhāvas are concerned.

161—163 The said movements are Utkarṣaṇa (drawing up words), Vikarṣaṇa (dragging), Vyākarṣaṇa (drawing out) Parigraha (acceptance), Nigraha (killing or curbing), Āhvāna (beckoning), Todana (inciting), Saṁślesa (joining together), Viyoga (separation), Rakṣaṇa (protecting), Mokṣaṇa (letting out), Vikṣepa (throwing up), Dhūnana (shaking), Visarga (giving away), Chedana (cutting), Bhedana (piercing) Sphoṭana (Bursting), Moṭana (Folding up) and Tāḍana (beating).

164 There are three types of general movements viz. upwards, sideways and downwards based on the principles of histrionic revelation.

165 Sensible persons shall embellish these hand movements while they are being employed by means of befitting expressions in the eyes, eyebrows and the face.

166 The hand gestures are to be employed by those conversant with them in accordance with the general practice

in the society with adequate consideration for the Karaṇas (explained in IV Chapter), Karmans, Patāka and other Sthānas sphere, quantity, appropriateness etc.

167 The hand gestures of the Superior persons have their range (sphere) near the forehead, those of the middling sort around the breast and those of the inferior sort in regions below thereof.

Pracāra (quantity) of the gestures

168 There is scanty movement of the hand gestures is the superior Abhinaya, medium sort of movement in the middling Abhinaya whereas there are profuse movements of these gestures in the ordinary Abhinaya.

169 The superior and the middling types of persons shall indicate different objects and ideas theory hand gestures strictly following the injunctions in the Śāstras whereas the inferior ones need only follow the popular practice as well as their natural inclinations.

170 But, in exceptional circumstances wise people are at liberty to employ the hand gestures contrarily or not use at all.

171—174 There are certain situations which cannot or should not be represented by means of hand gestures e.g. when one is sad, about to faint, terrified, disgusted, excessively sorrowful, weak, asleep, incapacitated or beurldetted, in active, drowsy, inert, sick, feverish, panic strucken assailed by chillness, inebrieted, mad, thoughtful; performing penances, imprisoned, swiftly running speaking in dream, excited or pairing something with the nails. On those occasions the Naṭa should resort to Bhāvābhinya and Kākuviśeṣa (Change in the Voice befitting the circumstances in conformity with different Rasas and Bhāvas.

175 When verbal enunciation is done by the actor the eyes and the glance are directed to points where the hand gestures are expected to move with suitable pauses clearly implying the meaning.

176—177 In dance and acting the activity of the limbs is threefold (1) Uttāna (palm kept up ward (2) Pārśvaga (palm kept obliquely), (3) Adhomukha (kept downwards). But the

Hastapracara is of five kinds (1) Uttāna, (2) Vartula (moving in a circular motion), (3) Tryśra (Triangular i.e. obliquely) (4) Sthita (steady), (5) Adhomukha.

These are the hand gestures in regard to histrionic representation. I shall hereafter explain the Nṛttahastas (Dancehands).

Nṛttahastas

178 (a) *Caturaśra.* Two Khaṭakā Mukha hands are to be held eight Aṅgulas away from the chest while the shoulders and elbows are on the same level. This is called Caturaśra.

179 (b) *Udvṛtta.* Two Haṁsapakṣa hands are waved like Tālavṛnta (palm leaf fan). This should be known as Udvṛtta or Tālavṛntaka.

180 (c) *Tālamukha.* Two hands from Caturaśra position are held obliquely facing each other. This is called Tālamukha.

181 (d) *Svastika.* The Tāla Mukha hands when placed crossed at the wrists in the shape of a Svastika are termed Svastika, when they are released they are called Viprakīrṇa.

182 *Arālakaṭakāmukha.* Two Alapallava hands palms up wards changed into Padmakośa hands are called Arālakaṭakā Mukha or Arālākhaṭaka.

183 *Āviddhavakraka* The two hands are to have Kuṭila (oblique) movement after touching the opposite shoulder elbow and hands. Then the palms are moved and turned towards the back. This is known as Āviddhavakraka.

184 *Sūcīmukha* When two Sarpaśīrṣa hands have their tips stretched obliquely with the thumbs touching middle fingers it is remembered as Sūcīmukha.

185 *Recita.* Two Haṁsapakṣa hands moving swiftly with the palms facing upward is called Recita. This is like the ordinary Recita of the hands.

186 *Ardharecita.* The left hand is as in the Caturaśra and the right hand as in the Recita. This should be known by those conversent with the principles of dance as Ardharecita.

187 *Uttānavancita.* Two Tripatāka hands are slightly

bent obliquely and the shoulders and the elbows are moved. This is remembered as *Uttānavañcita*.

188 *Pallava* Two Patāka hands joined at the wrist termed Pallava.

Nitamba. They taken out from the shoulder to the hip are termed Nitamba.

189 *Keśabandha*. Two hands are moved out from the Keśabandha (hair knot) and held on the sides are termed Keśabandha.

190 *Latā*. Two hands to be obliquely stretched sideways are termed Latā.

191 *Karihasta*. The Latā hand held up and swung from side to side and the other hand Tripatāka is held on the ear. This is glorified as Karihasta.

192 *Pakṣavañcitaka*. A Tripatāka hand is placed on the waist and the other on the head. The sponsors of dance programmes know this as Pakṣavañcitaka.

193 *Pakṣapradyotaka*. The hands in the Pakṣavañcitaka change places (waist and head). Then they are rembered as Pakṣapradyotaka.

Garuḍapakṣa The same with the palm placed downwards is called Garuḍapakṣa.

194 *Daṇḍapakṣa* Two Hamsa Pakṣa hands moved alternately and then held out like a staff are called Daṇḍapakṣa.

195 *Urdhvomaṇḍalī* If the hands have circling movement near the upper part of the body they are called Urdhvamaṇḍali.

The same with the movement made on one side is called Pārśvamaṇḍali.

196 *Uromoṇḍali* One hand is to be raised up after the circling movements and the other is to be kept hanging down. Some movements are to take place near the breast. This is called Uromaṇḍalī.

197 *Uraḥpārīvārdhamaṇḍala*. The Alapadmaka and Arāla hands are moved by turns above the breast and on the sides. This should be known as Urahpārśvārdhamaṇḍala.

198 *Muṣṭikasvastika*. When two Khaṭakāmukha hands

are bent at the wrists and moved round they shall be called Muṣṭikasvastika.

199 *Nalinī Padmakośa.* The hands are moved by turns with Vyāvartita and Parivartita Karaṇa, from Padmakośa form. They should be known as Nalinī Padmakośa.

200 *Alapallava.* The hands have Udveṣṭita Karaṇa in their movements in Alapallava hand.

When they are stretched up and waved they are called Ulbaṇa.

201 *Lalita.* Two Pallava hands are to be moved above the head. It is remembered as Lalita. *Valita* When two Latā hands are crossed at the elbows they are called Valita.

202 The Nṛtta Hastas are to be employed in the formation of Karaṇas and Patāka and other hands are to be employed in representing the meanings of words.

203 Of course, at times the uses of the hands may get interchanged but the name given are based on their predominant use in dramatic programme and dance item.

204 Nṛttahastas are reputed to be of two types, single and combined. I shall now explain the hands in their kinship with the Karaṇas.

The four Karaṇas

205—206 Four classes of hand gestures should be noted carefully by the instructors in Nāṭyahasta. They are (a) Āveṣṭita (b) Udveṣṭita (c) Vyāvartita and (d) Parivartita.

207 (a) *Āveṣṭita* The index finger and after fingers gradually point inwards while the hand goes on moving round. The Karaṇa thus employed is called Āveṣṭita.

208 (b) *Udveṣṭita* The index and other fingers gradually point outwards while the hand goes on moving round. The Karaṇa thus employed is called Udveṣṭita.

209 (c) *Vyāvartita.* The small finger and other fingers gradually point inwards while the hand goes on moving round. The Karaṇa thus employed is called Vyāvartita.

210 (d) *Parivartita.* The small finger and other fingers

gradually point outwards while the hand goes on moving round. O Brahmins, the Karaṇa thus employed is called Parivartita.

211 White applying the hand gestures in their various movements in dramatic performance and dance item they should be accompanied by Karaṇas having relevant expression of the face the eyebrows and the eyes.

The Arm-movements

212—213 Persons practising and trying to be perfect in dramatic performance and dance items have reminded us of ten Prakāras (modes) of moving the arms. They are (1) Tiryak (2) Ūrdhvasaṁstha (3) Adhomukha (4) Añcita (5) Apaviddha (6) Maṇḍalagati (7) Svastika (8) Pṛṣṭhānusāri (9) Udveṣṭita and (10) Prasārita.

214 Thus, O Brahmins, I have concluded a succinct explanation of rules regarding the Karaṇa, Henceforth I shall expatiate upon the movements of the chest, stomach and the sides.

NOTES

Verses 4—10 The usage of Asaṁyuta hands is in reference to the realistic (Lokadharmi) practice on the stage. Padmakośa and other hands represent external forms of objects. This comes under the Nāṭya Dharmi or conventional practice. The usage of single bands is more in vogue but the combined usage is also in vogue to be more effective on the audience.

11—16 Nṛtta Hastas are generally in use in dance items. In the dramatic performance they are used singly or in combination with other gestures to give an ornamental effect.

There are certain extraneous items such as the deity, colour and caste pertaining to the Mudrās (hand gestures) found in commentaries. We give them below :

Name of the Mudrā	*Deity*	*Caste*	*Colour*
1 Patâka	The Supreme Brahman	Brahmin	White
2 Tripatāka	Śiva	Kṣatriya	Red
3 Kartarīmukha	Viṣṇu wielding discuss	,,	Copper

4	Ardhacandra	Mahadeva	Vaiśya	Smoky
5	Arāla	Vāsudeva	Mixed	Red
6	Śukatuṇḍa	Marīci	Brahmin	Red
7	Muṣṭi	Moon	Śūdra	Blue
8	Śikhara	Kāmadeva	Gandharva	Dusty
9	Kapittha	Padma Garbha-Visṇu	Sage	White
10	Kaṭakāmukha	Raghurāma	Deva	Copper
11	Sūcīmukha	Viśvakarman	,,	White
12	Padmakośa	Bhārgava	Yakṣakinnara	White
13	Sarpa Śīrṣa	Śiva	Deva	Yellow
14	Mṛga Śīrṣa	Maheśvara Śiva	Ṛṣi	White
15	Kaṅgula	Padma	Siddha	Golden
16	Alapadma	Sun	Gandharva	Dusty
17	Catura	Sun	Mixed	,,
18	Bhramara	Garuḍa	,,	Cloudy black
19	Haṁsāsya	Brahmā	,,	White
20	Haṁsapakṣa	Kāmadeva	Apsaras	Blue
21	Sandaṁśa	Vālmiki	Vidyādhara	White
22	Mukula	Candra	Sankīrṇa	White
23	Urṇanābha	Indra	Deva	,,
24	Tāmra Cūḍa	Incarnation as Tortoise	Kṣatriya	Red

The stories connected with the origin of these Mudrās are given in brief :

1. Patāka—Brahmā made use of this Mudrā while making obeisance to Viṣṇu. Patāka has reference to flags and banners.
2. Tripatāka—While holding the thunderbolt Indra kept three fingers separate.
3. Kartarī Mukh—Śiva is the sponsor of this Mudrā before slaying Andhakāsura.

4. Ardha Candra—Śiva in the form of Naṭarāja embellished his matted hair with crescent moon.

5. Arāla—Sage Agastya made use of this Mudrā before drinking up the ocean.

6. Śukatuṇḍa—Gaurī was in the state of feigned anger with Śiva. She made use of this Mudrā.

7. Muṣṭi—Lord Viṣṇu made use of this Mudrā at the time of slaying Madhu.

8. Śikhara—At the time of the churning of the milk ocean the moon-crested lord wanted to uproot Sumeru mountain when he made use of this Mudrā.

9. Kapittha—At the time of the churning of the milk ocean Lord Viṣṇu pulled out the celestral tree Mandāra and made use of this Mudrā.

10. Kaṭakāmukh—While learning the science of archery from Lord Śiva, Kārtikeya made use of this Mudrā.

11. Sūcīmukha—Brahmā made use of this hand gesture in order to reveal the principle "Ekoham" (I am one)

12. Padmakośa—In order to receive the discuss Sudarśana from lord Śiva, lord Viṣṇu made use of this Mudrā instead of floral offering.

13. Sarpa Śirṣa—When the demon king Bali was found the divine incarnation Vāmana assuaged the grief of the Devas by using this hand gesture.

14. Mṛga Śīrṣa—Pārvatī performed penance to gain the hand of lord Śiva. She applied sandal paste over her forehead making use of this Mudrā.

15. Kaṅgula—Before swallowing the Kālakūṭa poison Lord Śiva made use of this Mudrā.

16. Alapallava—While stealing butter from the huts of the cowherdesses Lord Kṛṣṇa made use of this Mudrā.

17. Catura—When Garuḍa went in search of Amṛta, Sage Kaśyapa gave him guidance making use of this Mudrā.

18. Bhramara—Sage Kaśyapa made use of this Mudrā when he wanted to make the earings for Aditi.

19. Haṁsāsya—Lord Śiva in Dakṣiṇāmūrti form was instructing the sages in the principles of Absolute Philosophy beneath the Vaṭa tree. Then be made use of this Mudrā.

20. Haṁsapakṣa—Taṇḍu who expounded the dance form Tāṇḍava made use of this Mudrā.

21. Sandaṁśa—This is also known as Jñāna Mudrā. At the outset this was made use of by the goodness of speech and musicology goddess Sarasvatī.

22. Mukula—The monkey god Hanumān attempted to gulp the rising sun. He made use of this Mudrā.

23. Urṇanābha—The divine incarnation of man-lion made use of thus Mudrā before slaying Hiraṇyakaśyapa

24. Tāmra Cūḍa—The three Vedas after being spelt out by Brahmā made use of this Mudrā in making obeisance to him.

10

Śarirābhinaya (Gestures of the limbs)

"*Uras*" (*Chest gestures*)

1 The chest is remembered as consisting of five types viz. Ābhugna (bent slightly), Nirbhugna (not bent, raised up), Prakampita (quivering), Udvāhita (lifted up) and Sama (level, natural).

2 (a) *Ābhugna.* The chest is kept lowered the back is raised higher, the shoulders are slightly bent and left loose at times without being stiff. This chest should be known as Ābhugna. Understand its application.

3 Its application is in embarressment, despair, fainting, sorrow, fright, ailment, heartache, coldtouch, rain and bashfulness (suitably).

4 (b) *Nirbhugna.* The Chest is stiff, the back depressed, shoulders are not bent but kept raised. This chest is Nirbhugna. Understand its use.

5 It is applicable in paralysis, expressing resentment, surprised look averring the truth, haughty expression and excessive arrogance.

6 (c) *Prakampita* The chest is incessantly heaved up and down. This is known by the sponsors of dramatic gesture as Prakampita.

7 Its application is in laughter, weeping, exhaustion, terror, asthmatic fit, hiccough and misery in accordance with the situation obtaining.

8 (d) *Udvāhita.* If the chest is kept raised up it should be known as Udvāhita by the dramatists. Its application is in

deep breathing, looking at the objects placed high above and in yawning.

9 (e) *Sama.* All the limbs are in the Caturaśra (symmetrical) state and the chest has Sauṣṭhava (excellance). This is called Sama.

The Pārśva (sides)

10 Thus the Varieties of the chest gestures have been properly described by me. I shall now explain the characteristics of the two sides.

11 The characteristics of the sides are of five types viz. (a) Nata (bent) (b) Samunnata (lifted up) (c) Prasārita (extended) (d) Vivartita (turned round) and (e) Apasṛta (withdrawn slightly).

12—15 (a) *Nata.* The waist is slightly bent. So also one of the sides is also slightly bent and a shoulder is drawn away slightly.

(b) *Unnata* (lifted up). The other side (i.e. that which is not Nata) will be lifted up. Similarly the waist, the side, arm and the shoulder will be raised.

(c) *Prasārita.* The sides are stretched in their respective directions.

(d) *Vivartita* The sacrum is kept turned round.

(e) *Apasṛta.* The side is restored to its original position from the Vivartita position.

These are the characteristics of the various sides understand their application.

Application of the side

16—17 The Nata should be applied while approaching some one; Unnata in going away; Prasārita is applied in delight etc; Vivartita is applied in turning about and the Apasṛta in returning. These are the activities of application of the sides in accordance with the theme displayed. Now understand the characteristics etc. of the belly.

Jaṭhara

18 *Belly.* The belly is of three bends viz. (a) Kṣâma (b) Khalva and (c) Pūrṇa. The slender and thin one is Kṣāma.

the depressed one is Khalva and the blown up one is Pūrṇa.

Applications

19—20 The Kṣāma belly is utilised in depicting laughter, cry, whalation and yawning. The Khalva is to be applied in displaying sickness, penance, weariness and hunger.

The Pūrṇa belly is to be applied in gasping out, stoutness, disease, excessive eating and the like.

Thus the activities of the Jaṭhara have been explained. Now understand those of the Kaṭi (hip)

21—23 In dance and drama Kaṭi is of five types viz. Chinnā (turned aside), Nivṛttā (turned up), Recita (moved about), Kampitā (Shivering) and Udvāhita (lifted up).

If the middle of the waist is turned aside it is called Chinnā; if the same is turned to the front from a reverse position it is called Nivṛtta, if the hip moves about in all directions it is called Recitā; if the sides of the hip are raised slowly it is called Udvāhitā and if it moves up and down obliquely it is Kampitā

These characteristic activities of the hip have been explained by me. Now understand their application.

Application of the hip movements

25—26 The Chinnā is applied in depicting exercises, agitated confusion and looking back turning round and other themes; the Nivṛttā is applied when taking an "About turn"; the Recitā in wandering etc. of a general nature; the Kampitā is to be employed in depicting the movement of hunch backs, dwarfs and persons of the inferior type, Udvāhitā is to be applied in depicting the movements of stout and bulky persons as well as the amorous and seductive movements of women.

Urū (Thighs). The *Urūs* have five types of movements viz. Kampana (quivering), Valana (turning round), Stambhana (rigidity), Udvartana (springing up) and Vivartana (turning).

Application of the Urū moments and their characteristics

31—32 The characteristics of Kampana are raising and lowering of the heels repeatedly. In Valana the knees are drawn inwards. Suspension of all movements characterizes Stambhana; after the inward drawing the knees are moved in the case of Udvartana; if the heels are drawn inwards it is Vivartana

Kampana is applied in the case of the movements of the dramatics personal of the inferior type as well as in great fright. Valana is applicable in the case of the uninhibited movements of women; Stambhana is employed in perturbation and despondency; the sensible man employs Udvartana in the case of physical exercise and the Tāṇḍava dance; Vivartana should be employed in the case of movements due to agitation etc.

33 By careful observation the actor shall pick up other types of the movements of the thigh as they are found in popular practice. Thus the characteristics of the thigh movements have been explained. Now listen to those of the shanks.

Jaṅghā (Calf, Shank)

34-37 The characteristic activities of the Jaṅghā are of five types viz. Āvartita (turned), Nata (bent), Kṣipta (thrown out), Udvāhita (raised) and Parivṛtta (turned back).

In Āvartita the left foot turnes to the right and the right one to the left. The Nata is effected by bending the knee; when the shank is thrown out it is called Kṣipta and when it is raised up it is Udvāhita: when the shank is turned back it is Parivṛtta.

Application

38—40 The Āvartita should be emplyed in the sauntering stroll of the Vidūṣaka (buffoon); Nata is to be applied in assuming Sthāna (Standing posture) and Āsana (sitting posture) etc; Kṣpita is employed in depicting the performance of exercises and the Tāṇḍava dance; Udvāhita is to be utilized in depicting Āviddha (crooked) movements; Parivṛtta too is employed by the sponsors of the drama in dipicting Tāṇḍava etc.

These are the characteristics and activities of the Shank. Now listen to those of the feet.

The feet and their applications

41—50 The characteristics of the feet are of five types viz.

(a) Udghaṭṭita (b) Sama (c) Agratala Sañcara, Añcita and Kuñcita.

(a) *Udghaṭṭita.* The actor stands on the fore part of the feet and then lets the heels fall on the ground. Its application is for the purpose of imitation in the Udghaṭṭita Karaṇas and that too either once or repeatedly in the high or medium speed,

(b) *Sama.* The feet are kept placed naturally on an even ground. It is based on the presentation of a natural posture. Its application is in representing the natural position of the body in relation to the different Karaṇas but in the Recaka movement of the feet they should be moved.

(c) *Agratalasañcara.* The heels are thrown up. The big toe is projected forward and the other toes are kept bent. Its application is in inducing, breaking, remaining in standing posture, hitting with (something like a hammer), striking the ground, wandering, casting off something, diverse kinds of Recaka movements and walking on the forepart of the foot due to some wound on the heel.

(d) *Añcita.* If the heels rest on the ground; the forepart of the feet is raised and the toes are kept spread, that foot is termed Añcita. It is to be applied in the representation of a movement when there is a wound at the forepart of the foot turning round in everyway, foot-being struck by something and in the diverse Bhramarī movements.

(e) *Kuñcita.* The heels are thrown up toes are all bent-down and the middle of the feet too is bent.

51 Its application. It has to be employed in Udātta (grand and majestic) going, turning round to the right and vice versa and in the Atikrānt Cārī.

The Cārīs

52—54 Persons wishing to practise the Cārīs shall take up simultaneously the movements of the feet, the shanks and the thighs because therein are included all the movements of the shanks and the things. The thighs follows the way in which the feet are moved and the Cārī of the feet is constituted by these two limbs. These are the characteristics and applications of the limbs. I shall now explain the system of the different Cārīs.

Notes

In this chapter the gestures of the vorious limbs other than dealt with in Chapter X are explained in detail. Different Mss. give different reading. We have followed what appeared to be geniune and to the point without unnecessary and verbose repetitions.

Verse 5 Here there is a Prakṣipta verse explaining the application of Nirbhugna namely deep breath, yawning, snapping the joints, and the feigned anger of ladies.

Verse 7 Another reading adds a couple of themes more such as Sambrama (excitement), Vyādhi Pīḍita (are afflicted by ailments).

Verse 14 Vivartita in some Mss. is shown as Nivartita (turned back).

Verse 20 According to a Prakṣipta verse the belly is of four kinds, one Sama (natural, level) is added.

Verses 31--32 In some Mss. we have Nivartanam for Vivartanam.

Verse 50 Instead of Pārṣṇikṛtāgamanam Some Mss. read Pārṣṇikṣatāgra Gamanam. This has been followed in our translation.

11

Cārīvidhāna (Explanation of the Cārī movements)

Definition

1 Cārī is that activity wherein the movements of the hands, feet, calves, thighs and the hip are kept in mutual concordance.

The Cārī can be called a Vyāyāma (exercise) because all the Cārī movements are governed by rules and the movements of the different limbs are in concordant relationship with one another when they stretch out to one another.

2—3 The word Cārī strictly connotes the movement with a single foot, the concordant movement of two feet is called a Karaṇa the combination of three (or more) Karaṇas is termed a Khaṇḍa and three or four Khaṇḍas combining together constitute a Maṇḍala.

Utility of Cārī movements

4 A dance item is pervaded by Cārī movements, in fact all movements in general do proceed from Cārīs; discharge of missiles is attended with Cārī movements; Cārīs are reputed to be in use while fighting (in the stage).

5 Everything concerned and projected as Nāṭya is included in the Cārī movements; no part of Nāṭya can function without a Cārī.

6 Hence I shall explain the characteristics of the Cārī movements and mention which one is to be employed in dance items, which in the fighting (on the stage) and which one in ordinary movement.

Two types (a) Bhaumī Cārī (b) Ākāśi Kī Cārī

7—9 There are sixteen Bhaumī (Earthly) Cārīs and they

are (1) Samapādā (2) **Sthitavarta** (3) Śakaṭāsya (4) Adhyardhikā (5) Cāṣagati (6) Vicyavā (7) Eḍakākrīḍitā (8) Baddhā (9) Ūrūdvṛttā (10) Aḍḍitā (11) Utsyanditā (12) Janitā (13) Syanditā (14) Apaspandita (15) Samotsārita Mattallī and (16) Mattallī.

Verses 10—12 The Ākāśikī (aerial) Cārīs are also sixteen and they are (1) Atikrāntā (2) Apakrāntā (3) Pārśvakrāntā (4) Urdhvajānu (5) Sūcī (6) Nūpurapādikā (7) Dolapāda (8) Ākṣiptā (9) Āviddhā (10) Udvṛttā (11) Vidyudbhrāntā (12) Alāta (13) Bhujaṅga Trāsitā (14) Mṛgaplutā (15) Daṇḍā and (16) Bhramarī.

Now listen to the characteristics of these.

Bhaumī Cārīs

Verse 13 *Samapādā*. Both the feet are kept close together and the nails are symmetrical. The actor stands on the spot.

14 *Sthitāvartā* One foot is in Agratalasañcara state It is drawn up in order to cross the other foot. Thereafter this movement is repeated with the other foot after keeping the feet apart. This is called Sthitāvartā Cārī.

15 *Śakaṭāsyā*. The actor keeps his body erect. One foot in Agratalasañcara state is put forward and he keeps the chest in Udvāhitā state This Cārī is called Śakaṭāsyā.

16 *Adhyardhikā*. The left foot is kept at the back of the right one and then the right foot is removed in 1½ Tāla time. This should be known as Adhyardhikā by sensible persons.

17 *Cāṣagati*. In the Cārī called Cāṣagati the right foot is put forward and then drawn back. At the same time the left foot is drawn back and put forwards.

18 *Vicyavā*. The feet are separated from the Samapādā state and the ground is struck with the forepart of the foot as through beating time.

19 *Eḍakākrīḍitā*. With the Tālasañcara feet the actor jumps up and falls down alternatively. This Cārī is called Eḍakākrīḍitā.

20 *Baddhā*. The two shanks are crossed in the form of Svastika. Then the thighs are moved sideways. That is cited as Baddhā Cārī.

21 *Urūdvṛttā.* The heel of a Tālasañcara foot is to be placed facing outwards ; of the shanks one is to be slightly bent and the thigh is turned up. This is remembered as Urūdvṛttā.

22 *Aḍḍitā.* Where an Agratala Sañcara foot rubs against either the forepart or the back of another foot it is Aḍḍitā-Cārī.

23 *Utsyanditā* (or Utspanditā). If the feet move gradually in and out (i e. sideways) in the manner of Recaka, the Cārī is called Utsyanditā.

24 *Janitā.* A Muṣṭi hand is held on the chest and the other hand is moved round. The feet are to be kept in Tāla-sañcara manner. This Cārī is called Janitā.

25 *Syanditā.* One of the feet is put forward five Tālas away from the other. This Cārī is called Syanditā.

Apasyanditā. If the other foot is put forward five Tālas away from the previous one it is Apasyanditā.

26 *Samotsarita-Mattallī.* Both the Talasañcara feet have a circular movement while going back. This is Samotsarita-mattalli cited in Vyāyāma (exercise).

27 *Mattallī.* If there is a backward step with a circular movement and the hands are Udveṣṭita and then Apaviddha, it is called Mattallī.

28 These are remembered as Earthly Cārīs employed in Niyuddha (Wrestling) and Karaṇas. I shall now explain the Ākāśikī Cārīs and their characteristics.

Ākāśikī (Aerial) Cārī movements

29 *Atikrāntā.* A Kuñcita foot is raised and stretched forward. After lifting up it is allowed to fall back. This Cārī is remembered as Atikrāntā.

30 *Apakrāntā.* If Valana (twisting and turning) is performa-med by both the thighs and then a Kuñcita foot is raised and immediately set down sideways it is Apakrāntā Cārī.

31 *Pārśva Krāntā.* A foot is raised in the Kuñcita state and stretched beyond the knee, Another is thrown up and

brought near the side. It is thus that Pārśvakrāntā Cārī is made.

32 *Ūrdhvajānu.* A Kuñcita foot is lifted up and the knee thereof is brought up to the level of the Chest and the other knee is kept free from movement. The second foot is thrown up in the manner of the first while the first foot is kept motionless. This is said to be Ūrdhvajānu Cārī.

33 *Sūcī.* The Kuñcita foot is thrown up and stretched above the knee of the other foot. Then it is allowed to fall on its fore part. That Cārī is called Sūcī.

34 *Nūpurapādikā.* An Añcita foot is lifted up and taken behind another foot. Thereafter it is quickly caused to fall on the ground. That Cārī is Nūpurapādikā.

35 Dolapādā Left up the Kuñcita foot and rock it from side to side. Thereafter let it fall on the ground as an Añcita foot. This is mentioned to be Dol apādā (Ḍolāpādā) Cārī.

36 *Ākṣiptā.* A Kuñcita foot is thrown up and immediately it is placed on an Añcita foot while the shank of the remaining leg is crossed like Svastika. This Cārī is called Ākṣiptā.

37 *Āviddhā.* A Kuñcita foot in the Svastika state is stretched out and it is let fall on the ground quickly as an Añcita foot. It is remembered as an Āviddhā Cārī.

38 *Udvṛttā.* If in the Āviddhā Cārī the Kuñcita foot is taken round the thigh of the other leg, thrown up and then caused to fall on the ground it shall be called Udvṛttā Cārī.

39 *Vidyudbhrāntā.* One foot is circled backwards and stretched so as to touch its top; then the head is moved in a circle. It is remembered as Vidyudbhrāntā Cārī.

40 *Alātā.* One foot is stretched backwards and then thrust in after being twisted. Thereafter it is caused to fall on its heel. It is cited as Alātā Cārī.

41 *Bhujaṅgatrāsitā.* After throwing up a Kuñcita foot there shall be a three cornered twisting round of the thigh hip and the knee. This Cārī is called Bhujaṅgatrāsitā.

42 Hariṇa plutā (Mṛgaplutā). The foot in the Atikrāntā Cārī is made to fall on the ground after a leap up. Then the Shank of an Añcita foot is employed in the Kṣiptā posture

43 *Daṇḍapādā.* The foot in the Nūpura Pādika Cārī to be stretched and quickly to turn. This is called Nūpurapādikā Cārī.

44 *Bhramarī.* The foot in the Atikrāntā Cārī is to be thrown up and the Sacrum is to be turned round. Thereafter the second foot is to be moved on its sole.

45 These are remembered as Ākāśikī Cārīs mainly dependent upon graceful movements of the limbs. They are to be employed in the discharge of missiles such as thunderbolt, sword bow etc.

46 O Brahmins both the hands should be employed as circumstances warrant, in wielding all these missiles, in such a manner as to go ahead, synchronize with or follow the feet. The sponsors of the dramatic performance should attend to it.

47 The hands should follow the movement of the feet and the sacrum should keep up with the movement of the hands. At every step the minor limbs should be utilized (Upāṅgas).

48 After the demonstration of a Cārī even as the foot comes to a rest on the ground, the hand too after the concerned display should be moved round and brought to rest on the hip.

49 I have concluded the explaination of the Cārīs in the form of graceful movements of the limbs. I shall now explain the Sthānas (the posture of standing in readiness) at the time of the release of all the missiles.

STHĀNAS

50 In the case of men there are six Sthānas viz Vaiṣṇava, Samapāda, Vaiśākha, Maṇḍala, Ālīḍha and Pratyālīḍha.

51—52 *Vaiṣṇava.* The feet are kept two and a half Tālas apart; one of them shall be in the natural posture; the other is obliquely placed with toes turning towards the sides; the shank is in the Añcita state and all the limbs have Sauṣṭhava. This is called Vaiṣṇava sthāna. The presiding deity here of is Viṣṇu.

53—57 *Its Application.* Natural conversation should be carried on by means of this Sthāna by men of Superior and middling types having many activities and duties. This shall be employed while discharging the discus, holding the bow when in excessive anger and also during the bold and stately movements of the limbs. After reversing it, it shall be employed in prevented anger in love, in rebuking and in love, anguish, suspicion, jealoustly, fierceness, anxiety, intellectual activity recollection, in wretchedness, fickleness, arrogance, yearning and power when the sentiments of Śṛṇgāra, Aḍbhuta, Vīra and Bībhatsa are prominently introduced this Sthāna has to be resorted to.

58 *Samapāda.* If the feet are kept in their natural posture and one Tāla apart; the body is in its natural Sauṣṭhava, the Sthāna is called Samapāda. The presiding deity here of is Brahmā.

58—60 *Its application.* This Sthāna is to be resorted to while receiving blessings from **Brahmins** and in portraying birds. The bride groom wearing the auspicious thread, persons moving in the sky, persons in a chariot or aerial cars, Śaiva devotees and persons observing vows have to resort to this Sthāna.

61—62 *Vaiśākha.* The feet are kept three and a half Tālas apart, the thighs remain steady and reclined; the feet are placed obliquely pointing sideways. This is Vaiśākha Sthāna. Kārtikeya is the presiding deity of this Sthāna.

63—64 *Its application.* Sensible persons make use of this Sthāna to portray riding of horses, performance of exercises, coming out of any place, portraying (or observing) large birds drawing of a bow and in Recakas of the feet.

65 *Maṇḍala.* The presiding **deity** is Indra in the Maṇḍala Sthāna. The feet are kept four Tālas apart. They are to be placed obliquely with sideward turn. The waist and the knee are to remain in their natural position.

66 *Its application.* Missiles such as the thunderbold and bow should be handled while remaining in this Sthāna. So also while riding elephants or observing large birds this Sthāna should be assumed.

67 *Ālīḍha.* In the Maṇḍala Sthāna itself the right foot is removed five Tālas apart. That will make the Ālīḍha Sthāna the presiding deity whereof is Rudra.

68—69 *Its application.* Whatever act is related to Vīra and Raudra Rasas should be performed in this Sthana; arguments are following the other resulting from anger and wrath the challanging utterances (Sampheṭa) of wrestling champions, observations and survey of enemies, **attack** on them and discharge of arrows—all should be portrayed in this Sthāna.

69—70 *Pratyālīḍha.* If the right foot in the Ālīḍha Sthāna is kept bent and the left foot is put forword it is Pratyālīḍha Sthāna.

71 *Its application.* The missiles kept in readiness for discharging while in the Ālīḍha posture should be discharged after assuming the Pratyalīḍha Sthāna. The discharge of diverse kinds of missiles is performed by the actors from this Sthāna.

The four Nyāyas (justifiable means)in welding weapons

72 In regard to the mode of discharging missiles, four Nyāyas are to be taken note of, viz. Bhārata, Sāttvata, **Vārṣagaṇya** and Kaiśika.

73 In the Bhārata Nyāya the weapon (is supposed to) strike the waist, in the Sāttvata at the foot, in the **Vārṣagaṇya** at the chest and in the Kaiśika on the head.

74 While displaying the use of the weapons on the stage employing these Nyāyas arising out of the various Cārīs, Pravicāras (Sauntering about on the stage) should be performed by the actors concerned.

75 The fights on the stage are carried on with the Aṅgahāras governed by the Nyāyas and directly resulting from them. Hence these means are called Nyāyas.

76—76 *Bhārata Nyāya* The Actor performs Pravicāra keeping the shield in the left hand and the weapon in the right. He stretches the hands fully forward and then draws them back. Thereafter be shall **whirl** the shield from side to side. Śiraḥparigama (waving arround the head) also should be performed by the fighting actors. The weapon shall be whirled between the cheek and the shoulder. Once more, with the sword in his hand and the shield gracefully flourished Śiraḥparigama is performed by the sensible actor. It is thus that Pravicāra should be performed while discharging (wielding) the missile in accordance with Bhārata Nyāya.

80—81 *Sāttvata.* I shall duly explain the Pravicāra in accordance with Sāttvata Nyāya. The movement of the weapon and the shield is the same as it obtains in the Bhārata Nyāya; but the flourishing of the weapon should take place at the back of the actor.

82 *Vārṣagaṇya.* The Gati i.e. Pravicāra in accordance with Vārṣagaṇya Nyāya is similar to that in accordance with Sāttavata. The flourishing of the weapon and the shield as well as the Śiraḥparigama shell also be the same but the Udveṣṭana (whirling) of the weapon should be performed at the chest or at the shoulder.

83—84 *Kaiśika.* In Kaiśika too the Pravicāra is the same as in Bhārata. But the weapon is whirled round and allowed to fall only on the head.

85 It is in this same manner that weapons like the bow, the thunderbolt, sword etc. are to be flourished at the time when they are used the Pravicāras are to be performed with graceful movements of the limbs.

86—87 No limb should be pierced or cut nor blood should be spilt during the fight on the stage. Nor should the striking be actual The discharge of missiles by sensible persons should be only by means of hints, gestures and postures.

88 *Vyāyāma* should be performed with the due embellishments with Aṅgahāras endowed with Aṅga Sauṣṭhava (Excellence of the limbs) to the accompaniment of music with proper tempo and Tāla (beating of the time).

89 -91 Endeavour should be made by those conversant with Vyāyâma towards Sauṣṭhava. Neither in Drama nor in the dance programme do those with their limbs devoid of Sauṣṭhava shine. When the limbs are still unbent, at ease, neither too upright nor bent much, when the waist, ears, elbows, shoulders and the head are in their natural position and the chest is lifted up it shall constitute the Sauṣṭhava of the body.

91 (A) (Prakṣipta). In this, endeavour should always be made by persons of middling and superior types.

Caturaśra

92 The actor is in Vaiṣṇava Sthâna. The hands move

about at the waist and the navel together. The chest is raised. This cumulative display is called Caturaśra.

The four Karaṇas (acts) *relating to the bow*

93 Four acts relating to the bow should be performed viz Parimārjana, Ādāna, Sandhāna and Mokṣaṇa.

94 Parimārjana is the stroking of the bow (and bending), Ādāna is the act of taking it up; Sandhāna is the fixing of the arrow to the bow and Mokṣaṇa is the discharge of the arrow.

Performance of Vyāyāma

95 For the purpose of practising Aṅgahāras and Cārīs the actor shall perform exercise on the Bhitti (Wall, ? ground) or in Ākāśika (upper att c) and prior to that smear his body with Gingerlly oil or Yavāgū (qruel) for the proper massage.

96 An ideal wall is befitting. Hence he shall resort to a Bhitti. The actor spreads his limbs over the Bhitti and (the attendants) make him perform the Vyāyāma.

97—99 For the sake of vitality the actor undergoes the treatment of Nasya and Bastividhi (sternutatory and diulectic) mentioned in medical treatises. He shall take delicious and nutritious food, gravy, beverages etc. The vital breaths are dependent upon nutrition and ability is based on vitality. Hence for the sake of maintaining the ability one should be scrupulous about ones diet. The instructor shall not make the pupil perform the exercise if his body is defiled, if he is tired, if he is excessively hungry or thirsty, if he has drunk (Water, liquor etc.) too much or if he has eaten profusely. The sensible instructor shall train a pupil with graceful body and square well shaped chest and steady limbs.

100 These are the rules govering the Cārī movements in connection with the performance of exercises. I shall hereafter explain the different Maṇḍalas.

Notes

1 Cārī is the cumulative movement of all limbs in a graceful way. The word "Step" may connote its general sense.

In the Naṭya Śastra there are sixteen Bhaumī Cārīs and sixteen Ākāśikī (aerial) Cārīs. According to Saṅgīta Ratnākara there are thirty five Bhaumī and twentynine Ākāśikī Carīs. Kohala a later Ācārya has encouraged additions in the Cārīs for the purpose of the instructors in dance. Readers who wish to know more details are referred to Seventh Chapter of Saṅgīta Ratnākāra eighth section of Bharaṭārṇavā as well as Abhinaya Darpaṇa. This verse is not found in some Mss.

2 Karaṇa. This term Karaṇa has various connotations in different contexts.

7—9 Different Mss. give different names Utsyanditā—Utspanditā, Apasyanditā—Apaspanditā.

Khaṇḍa, Maṇḍala etc. have not been dealt with in later treatises, nor are they in vogue now.

53 A Tāla=12 Aṅgulas (i.e. 24 cms)

Hence 2½ Tālas=30 Aṅgulas (i e. 60 cms)

12

Maṇḍalavikalpanam (Diverse Maṇḍala movements)

1 These cārīs have been duly explained by me in regard to the discharge of missiles. Now understand the maṇḍalas arising out of a combination of the cārīs.

2—3 The Ākāśaga (aerial) Maṇḍalas are ten viz. (1) Atikrānta (2) Vicitra (3) Lalitasañcara (4) Sūcīviddha (5) Daṇḍapāda (6) Vihṛta (7) Alāta (8) Vāmaviddha (9) Lalita (10) Krānta.

4—5 The Bhūmiga (Earthly) Maṇḍalas too are mentioned as ten in number viz. (1) Bhramara (2) Āskandita (3) Āvarta (4) Samotsārita (5) Eḍakākriḍita (6) Aḍḍita (7) Śakaṭāsya (8) Adhyardhaka (9) Piṣṭakuṭṭa and (10) Cāṣagata. I shall mention their characteristics.

The Aerial Maṇḍalas

6—9 *Atikrānta.* The right foot is in the Janitācārī and then the chest is made Udvāhita by taking Śakaṭāṣyā cārī, then the left foot takes up Alātā cārī and the right foot the Pārśvākrāntā cārī, then the left foot is in the Sūcī cārī and the right foot in the Apākrāntā cārī; then successively the left foot in the Sūcī cārī as well as the Bhramarī cārī by turning the Sacrum, then the right foot is in the Udvṛtta cārī and the left foot in the Alāta cārī which should be altered to the Bhramarī-cārī, again the left foot is in the Alātā cārī and the right foot in the Daṇḍapādā cārī. This constitutes the Atikrānta Maṇḍala.

10—13 *Vicitra Maṇḍala.* The right foot is successively moved in the Janitā cārī and in the Nikuṭṭana (i.e. Talasañcara) manner and then the left foot in the Āspanditā cārī, the right foot in the Pārśvakrāntā cārī, then the left foot in the Śūcīpāda and the right foot in Apakrānta, then the left foot in the

Bhujaṅgatrāsitā cārī foot in the Atikrāntā and Udvṛttā cārīs, next the left in the Alātā cārī then the right foot in Pārśvakrāntā cārī; then the left foot in sūcīpāda; then the right foot in the Vikṣiptā cārī and the left foot in Apakrānta Prakṣipta there is Bhramara externally as well as Vikṣepa]. In the Vyāyāma this should be known as Vicitra Maṇḍala.

14—17 *Lalitasañcara*; the right foot with the knee raised moves in the Sūcī cārī next the left foot in the Apakrāntā cārī and the right one in the Pārśvā krāntā cārī; again the left foot in the sūcī and the Bhramarī cārīs (this latter by turning round the sacrum and the right foot in the Pārśvākrāntā cārī and the left foot in the Atikrāntā cārī which is to be changed into the Bhramarī cārī. (Here according to some Mss there is Pārśvakrāntā in the right foot and Atikrānta in the left then the right foot in Sūcī and the left in Apakrāntā. This is the cārī Prayoga in the Lalita Sañcara Maṇḍala *Sūcīviddha* Maṇḍala.

18—19 The left foot is to be moved in the Sūcī and the Bhramarī cārīs while turning the sacrum during the latter movement, the right foot in the Pārśvakrāntācārī the left foot in the Atikrāntācārī next the right foot in the Sūcī, the left foot in the Apākrāntā, cārī and the right foot again in the Pārśvakrāntā cārī. This is the combination in the Sūcīviddha Maṇḍala.

Daṇḍa Pādamaṇḍala

20—22 The right foot to be moved in the Janitā and the Daṇḍapādā cārīs; the left foot in the Sūcī and the Bhramarī cārīs, the sacrum being turned during the latter movements next the right foot in the Udvṛttā cārī and the left foot in the Alātā cārī, again the right foot in the Pārśvākrāntā cārī and the left foot successively in the Bhujaṅgatrāsitā and the Atikrāntā cārī to meet the right foot successively in the Sūcī and the Bhramarī cārīs the sacrum being turned during the latter movement. Thus the combination of cārīs in the Daṇḍapāda Maṇḍala.

23—26 *Vihṛta Maṇḍala.* The right foot to be moved in the Janitā cārī, then its Nikuṭṭana next the left foot in the Āspanditā cārī and the right foot in the Udvṛttā cārī; then the left foot in the Alātā cārī and the right foot in the Sūcī cārī, again the left foot in the Pārśvakrāntā cārī and the right foot in the Ākṣiptā and the Bhramarī Cārīs, the sacrum being turned during the latter movement, then the Daṇḍapāda Cārī, then the left in the

Sūcī and Bhramarīs Cārīs with the turning of the Sacrum during the latter movement; again the right foot in the Bhujaṅgatrāsitā Cārī and the left foot in the Atikrāntā Cārī.

27—29 *Alāta Maṇḍala.* The right foot to be moved in the Sūcī Cārī and the left foot in the Apākrāntā Cārī, then the right foot in the Pārśvakrāntā Cārī and the left in the Alātā Cārī; after moving by turns in these Cārīs six or seven times with graceful steps, again the right foot in the Apakrāntā Cārī and the left foot successively in the Atikrāntā and the Bhramarī Carīs.

Vāmabandha (*Vāmaviddha*) Maṇḍala

30—33 The right foot is to be moved in the Sūcī Cārī the left foot in the Apākrāntā Cārī then the right foot in the Daṇḍapādā Cārī and the left foot in the Sūcī Cārī and right foot in the Bhramarī Cārī while the Sacrum is being turned; and then in the Pārśvakrāntā Cārī next the left foot is in the Ākṣiptā Cārī and the right foot in the Daṇḍapādā and Urūdvṛttā Cārīs; then the left foot successively in the Sūcī the Bhramarī and the Alātā Cārīs. While it is in Bhramarī the Trika is to be turned next the right foot in the Pārśvakrāntā Cārī. Thus is the combination of Cārīs in the Vāmabandha Maṇḍala.

34—37 *Lalita Maṇḍala.* The right foot is to be moved in the Sūcī Cārī and the left foot in the Apakrāntā Cārī; then the right foot in the Pārśvakrāntā and the Bhujaṅga Trāsitā Cārīs; then the left foot in the Atikrāntā Cārī and the Urūdvṛttā Cārīs; then the left foot in the Alātā Cārī and the right foot in the Pārśvakrāntā Cārī next the left foot in the Atikrāntā Cārī with graceful steps. This combination is in the Lalita Maṇḍala.

38—40 *Krānta Maṇḍala.* The right foot is to be moved in the Sūcī Cārī and the left foot in the Apakrāntā Cārī, then the right foot in the Pārśvakrāntā Cārī and the left foot too in the same Cārī, moving round alternately in these Cārīs in all directions, again the left foot in the Sūcī Cārī and the right foot in the Apakrāntā Cārī. This Maṇḍala should be known as Krāṇta by name. This is enjoined to be employed in the course of the natural gaint.

41 These ten Maṇḍalas are to be known as aerial Maṇḍalas. I shall henceforth mention the characteristics of the Bhauma (earthly) Maṇḍalas.

The Earthly Maṇḍalas.

42—44 *The Bhramara Maṇḍalas* The right foot is to be moved in the Janitā Cārī and the left foot Āspanditā Cārī (Āskanditā) then the right foot in the Śakaṭāsyā Cārī and the left foot to be stretched next the right foot in the Bhramarī Cārī by turning the Sacrum, again the left foot in the Āskanditā Cārī and the right foot in the **Sakatasya** Cārī, then the left foot in the Pṛṣṭhā Pasarpī (i e. Apakrāntā) Cārī and the Bhramarī Cārī by turning about the back. This is Bhramara Maṇḍala.

45—47 *Āskandita Mandala* The right foot is to be moved in the Bhramara Cārī and the left foot in the Aḍḍitā and the Bhramarī Cārīs while turning the sacrum; then the right foot in the Urūdvṛttā Cārī and the left foot in the Apasarpit (Apakrāntā) and the Bhramarī (the Sacrum is turned then) the right foot in the Skanditā Cārī, the left foot in the Śakaṭāsyā and the same foot is to strike the ground violently. This is the Āskandita Maṇḍala employed in the practice of battle.

48—50 *Āvarta Maṇḍala.* The right foot is to be moved in the Janitā Cārī and the left foot in the Nikuṭṭakā Cārī (i.e. Tāla-Sañcara, then the right foot in the Śakaṭāsyā and the Urūdvṛttā Cārīs, next the right foot in the Apasarpī (Atikrāntā) Cārī turning backwards and the Cāṣagati Cārī, then the right foot in the Āskanditā Cārī and the left foot in the Śakaṭāsyā Cārī, again the right foot in the Bhramarī Cārī with the sacrum being turned round and the left foot in the Apasarpī (Apakrāntā) Cārī. This shall be the combination in Āvarta Maṇḍala.

51—53 *Samotsārita Maṇḍala.* At the outset the dancer assumes the Samapāda Sthāna and stretches both the hands with their palms turned upwards; then their incessant Āveṣṭana and Udveṣṭana movements; then the left hand is placed on the hip the right hand is moved in the Āvartita manner; next the right hand is placed on the hip and the left hand is moved in the Āvartita manner moving round alternately with this cāri. This is to be known as Samotsārita Maṇḍala.

54—55 *Eḍakakrīḍita Maṇḍala;* the two feet on the ground to be moved suceessively in the Sūcī and the Eḍakākrīḍitā Cārīs; then moving the Āviddha Cārīs. This culminates in the Khaṇḍa Maṇḍala called Eḍakākrīdita.

56—58 *Aḍḍita Maṇḍala.* The right foot is to be moved in the Udghaṭṭita manner and then simply moved round; next to be moved in the Syanditā Cārī and the left foot in the Śakaṭāsyā Cārī, next the right foot to be moved back-wards in the Apasarpī (Apakrāntā) and the Cāṣagati Cārīs, then the left foot in the Aḍḍittā Cārī and the right foot in the Apaṣarpitā (Apakrāntā) Cārī, next the left foot in the Bhramarī Cārī and the right foot in Āskanditā (Syanditā) Cārī and thereafter the ground is violently struck.

59—60 *Śakaṭāsya Maṇḍala.* The right foot is to be moved in Janitā Cārī and thereafter it is to be moved in the Nikuṭṭaka manner (Tāla Sañcara), the same foot in the Śakaṭāsyā Cārī and the left foot in the Āskanditā (Syanditā) Cārī; moving round in this manner **alternately** with the Śakaṭāsyā Cārī. This should be known as Śakaṭāsvā Cārī Maṇḍala and is to be employed in fighting.

61—62 *Adhyardha Maṇḍala* The right foot is to be moved successively in the Janitā and Āskanditā (Syanditā) Cārīs; then the left foot in the Apasarpitā (Apakrāntā) Cārī and the Śakaṭāsyā Cārī. Moving arround alternately in these Cārīs this shall be the Cārī Maṇḍala named Adhyardha employed in personal duel.

63—64 *Piṣṭakuṭṭa.* The right foot is to be moved in the Sūcī Cārī and the left foot is in the Apākrāntā, then the right foot in the Bhujangatrāsitā Cārī and the left foot too in the same Cārī. Thus going round in the Bhujaṅgatrāsitā Cārī is to be known as the Cārī Maṇḍala entitled Piṣṭakuṭta known to be used in personal combat.

65 *Cāṣagata Maṇḍala.* Going round and round with the feet in the Cāṣagata Cārī is called the Carīmaṇḍala named Cāṣagata. It is to be employed in personal combat.

66 Here I have described in brief the Maṇḍalas arising out of the various Cārīs. Now I shall explain the Sama Cārīs.

67—68 Sama Cārīs in use are known as Sama Maṇḍala. The dancer who employs them shall follow the instruction of the Ācārya and employ them. These Maṇḍalas are to be used in fight and personal combat. They are to be performed with sportiveness and graceful movements of the limbs to the accompaniment of suitable instruments of music.

Notes

Combination of the Cārīs entitled Maṇḍalas is entitled a Maṇḍala. These Maṇḍalas are divided into earthly ones as well as aerial ones each ten in number.

The nomenclature is based on the main Cārī in which the dancer sets his fees.

10 Nikuṭṭana. Agnipurāṇa interprets this word as Tala-sañcara.

47 Āsphoṭana Agnipurāṇa interprets this word as "striking the ground with the sole of the foot".

13

Gatipracāra (The different types of Gaits)

1 Thus in the combination of the systems of Cārīs the Maṇḍalas should be formed. Hereafter I shall describe the Gaits (Gatipracāra) pertaining to the different characters in the dramatic performance.

Entry into the sage of the Dramatics—Personal

2—3 After the Upavahana (Preliminary humming of the tune before singing) to the accompaniment of instrumental music, has been gone through with the due observance of Kalās befitting the Mārga, after the commencement of the Dhruva songs specially for the entrance of the Dramatics personal the curtain has to be drawn. Then the characters of the play should enter the stage in order to display the sentiments and the themes.

The posture of the superior and the middling characters

4—7 The posture to be assumed is Vaiṣṇava Sthāna if the characters are of Superior type or middling one. They keep their chest raised in the Sama and Caturaśra order. The shoulders should be at rest **without** raising them inordinately. The neck is gracefully displayed like that of a peacock; the shoulders shall be eight Aṅgulas from the ears; the chin is kept four Aṅgulas apart from the chest and both the hands are respectively kept at the navel and at the left waist.

The Tāla, Laya and Kalā of the feet

8—9 In the posture the actor should keep his feet apart leaving an interspace of two and a half Tālas and the steps he has to take shall be four, two or one Tāla according to his own measure.

10—11 The time taken for the steps shall be four or two Kalās or even one Kalā. Superior characters takes of four Kalās, the middling one two Kalās and the inferior characters and women only one Kalā.

12 Three kinds of Layas (tempo) shall be adopted by the expert in the theatrical art viz Sthira, Madhya and Druta (Slow, medium and rapid) befitting the Gait of the different characters.

13 The Gati or gait of the Superior characters shall be Sthira (slow), that of the middling ones Madhya (medium) and that of the inferior characters Druta (rapid). The three tempos should be in accordance with the spirit of the characters.

14 This is the injunction regarding the Tāla, Laya and Kalā in regard to the steps, O sinless sages. Now listen further to the application of Gatipracāra (taking steps) in regard to the different characters.

15 *Svabhāvika Gati* (Natural gait). A superior character raises his knee upto the hip in his natural gait. When the Yuddha Cārīs (Cārīs at the time of battle) are adopted the knee is raised up to the height of the chest.

16—19 The actor then proceeds to a corner of the stage with graceful steps of the Pārśvakrāntā Cārī while the musical instruments are duly played. He takes five steps at the outset. Then he adopts Sūcī Cārī and moves ahead placing left foot first and the right thereafter. Then he takes an abrupt turning and takes five similar steps towards the other corner of the stage. He then takes Sūcī Cāri for the next movement. Here also the left foot is placed first ahead and then the right foot. For the third time he turns round and takes five similar steps towards the musical instruments. Thereafter he moves in the Sūcī Cārī by placing the left foot forward at the outset and the right foot thereafter. Thus he takes in all twenty one steps in the Course of these movements.

20 If the stage (Nāṭyagṛha) is of Vikṛṣṭ type (oblong) there are eleborate foot movements of the actor. In a square stage the foot movements are of the Caturaśra type and in a triangular Nāṭyagṛha they are of the Tryaśra type.

21 When an actor walks in the company of his equals

and takes level steps the Laya of his gait will be in accordance with his own rank adopting four or two Kalās or even one Kalā.

22 When an actor walks in the company of persons of the medium or inferior types, the Laya of the set of people will be in terms of four of two Kalā as the case may be

23 The sensible directors make the actors take the steps four Tālas wide where the Devas, Dānavas, Pannagas (Serpents). Yakṣas, kings and demons are concerned.

24 The Gati of all the heaven-dwellers is preferably of Madhyamā type. Those who are excessively haughty among them shall have the Gati on a par with that of the Devas.

Gati befitting the Pātras

25—28 The sages asked :- The kings are only human beings. Why should then they have the Devagati ? The reply thereof is thus why should not the kings have Gatis suitable for gods ? The dramatics personal of a play are of three types (a) divine, (b) half divine half human and (c) human. Among these the nature of the Devas is of course divine; that of the kings is half divine and half human and people do know that the nature of the others is but human. In the Vedas and others scriptural texts kings are glorified as born of the parts of the different gods. That being so how can there be any fault if kings imitate the Devas ?

29 This is the rule laid down in the case of Svacchanda Gamana (ordinary walking). In the case of excitement, chaotic upheaval of nature and anger the rule thereof is not applicable.

The Gati of the characters in special cases

30 In those special circumstances the sponsors of the dramatic performance shall assign to the different characters i.e. Superior, medium and base or inferior, Gatis with suitable modifications based on their special condition.

31 When conditions other than normal ones prevail their Gatis should have the duration of two Kalās or one Kalā (Caturārdha=two). Tadārdha (i.e. half of that—one)

32 While a Superior Character is assigned a gait of four Kalās and an inferior character—one Kalā.

33 While a middling character has the Gati of one Kalā an inferior character has the Gati of half a Kalā. In this manner one should make suitable reduction of Kalās for special cases.

34 The Gati that pertains to superior persons is not to be applied to the Gati of the middling type and that of the middling characters is not to applied to that of the inferior type.

Laya under special conditions

35—37 In the case of one distressed with fever, one overwhelmed by hunger, one weary due to penance, one who is frightened, when there is dismay, dissimulation or uneasiness, when love in separation is described or displayed, during grief and in ordinary walk the Gati shall be very slow in Laya with duration of more than four Kalās. In the case of characters with predominance of anxiety it shall be of four Kalas in duration.

37—40 In the case of Aśvasthakāmita (one afflicted by uneasy and concealed love), panic, terror, agitation joy, action done **hastily** hearing of unpalatable news, insult, seeing a miracle, urgent task, distressed condition, searching for the enemy, pursuit of a guilty person, chasing a ferocious creature, steps of two Kalās duration should be recommended by sensible actors.

Śṛṅgāriṇīgati (Gait in the sentiment of love)

41—44 Gracefulness marks the Gait in ordinary expressions and activities of love. The Dūtī (the lady conveying the messages of lovers) shows the path to the lover as both of them enter the stage. He acts his part through Sūcā (i.e. Idea is conveyed first through Bhāva and Mudrā. Verbal representation follows it). Lovely clothes, sweet scents jewels and garlands of fragrant flowers should adorn him. He adopts the Atikrāntā Cāri for walking thus. Sauṣṭhava in the limbs accompanied by proper Tāla and Laya is an essential feature. The movement of the hands follow that of the feet. When the foot falls the **hand raised and** *vice versa*

45—48 Understand the Gati when there is Pracchannakāmita (Concealment of love). The lover is expected to walk during the night with the Dūtī as his guide. Before that he dismisses the attendents and puts out the lamp. He is scumpulously dressed in accordance with the time of the day but not so particular with the ornaments. One with concealed amorous activities should walk with slow and silent steps. He is cautiously wary of the sounds heard but not a whiteless in his ardour he should be circumspect enough to look around. In his suspicious his body trembles and he falters frequently.

Gati in Raudra sentiment

48—54 In describing Gati in Raudra Rasa. I shall confine myself, O Brahmins, to the Daityas, Nāgas and Pākṣasas. One Rasa is excessively predominat in their case. The Raudra is of that types in this regard (a) Nepathya Raudra (b) Aṅga Raudra and (c) Svabhāvaja. The example for Nepathys Raudra is the demon with blood dripping down from his body and clothes; his mouth is moistered with blood and he has pieces of meat held in his hands.

An example of Aṅga Raudra is a tall demon with huge physical frame, many heads, many hands and fully equipped with weapons of various kinds. An example of Svabhāvata Raudra is a red-eyed one black in complexion. He has tawny coloured hairs. His voice is gruff and harsh. He is tall and bulky. He is prone to scold others at the slightest provocation. His feet are kept for Tālas apart when he stands and his steps are four Tālas in width. Characters resembling them too have the same Gati.

Gati in the Bībhatsa sentiment

55—56 Where the ground is gruesome because of a recent terrible battle or because it happens to be a cremation ground the Gati to be adopted is one of Bībhatsa sentiment. The feet fall in quick succession with Eḍakākrīḍitā Cārī, falling one over the other some times close to each other and sometimes wide apart. The hands necessarily follow the moments of the feet. This is the Gati for the Bībhatsa sentiment.

Gati in the Vīra sentiment

57—58 The Gati in the Vīra Rasa is attended with swift foot steps adopting various Cārīs. If there is impetuousness the footsteps to be adopted are those with relevant Kaḷā and Tāla adopting Pārśva Krāntā, Drvtāviddha and Sūci Viddha.

59 These are mostly for the Superior characters who adopt these Gatis. I shall now describe the Gati of the middlings and the base ones once again.

60 *Adbhuta and Hāsyarcsa* When they are astonised or hilariously **joyous** they adopt Vikṣipta Padavikramas (Swift and short steps) in all directions. When the Hāsyarasa is fully adopted similar movements are equally employed.

Gati in the Karuṇa sentiment

61—63 The Gati in the Karuṇa Rasa is marked with Sthira (slow) Padas and the general features are the eyes wetting with tears, limbs drooping down, the arms thrown up and let down to fall and there is loud weaping. When the event is excessively unpleasant (such as death etc.) this Gati is adopted. The Cārī adopted is Adhyardhikā. In the Sthita Laya one and a half times more Kalās are employed and the foot movements are repeated. In the case of women and persons of low calibre also this Gati is adopted

63—66 In the Karuṇa Rasa the superior characters are to possess excessive fortitude, tearful gasping for breath and sighs of long drawn. They should be looking up frequently not losing patience. There is no regular measure therein and the Sauṣṭhava of the body is not insisted upon. When the death of beloved persons occurs the character s bend down with droaping chest. The enthusiasm should wave and the consciousness is defiled due to grief. The characters walk without raising the feet very high. When beaten excessively, the shoulder and the arms are drooped down with the unsteadines in the movement. The walking is with **Cūrṇapadas** (Measured steps, raising a little and planting on the feet).

67—69 When the persons of the inferior type and women are tormented by cold and running of the nose or attacked by a sudden downpour are to squeeze their limbs and draw them together; they tremble excessively; the hands are placed over the chest, the body is bent forward, the teeth chalter the lips throb and the chin quivers. If the attack of cold is to be represented the Gati is very slow.

Gati in Bhayānaka Rasa (Sentiment of the dreadful)

70—75 Clever Sponsors of the play should make the Gati

of women and characters of the base type lacking in spirited activity, one with suitability to their nature. The eyes are kept wide open and roving tremulously. The gesture of the head is Vidhuta. The look is awe-strucken with glances to sides alternately. The Kapota Mudrā of the hands is shown when they walk with quick steps. The body trembles with faltering steps. When a person is pursued by an enemy this movemnnt is resorted to. The same is applicable when anyone is threatened or frightened; when anything dreadful is seen or when any dreadful sound is heard. In the Bhayānaka Rasa in regard to women and cowards the Gati consists of the movement of feet in Eḍakārīḍita Cārī falling in quick succession one over the other sometimes very near and sometimes at a great distance. The hands shall of necessity follow the feet.

Gatis of different characters of the play merchants and ministers

76—78 (a) The Gati of Vaiśyas and Sacivas should be made natural Atikrāntā Cārī with steps two Tālas wide should be adopted when they walk. The upturned Kaṭakāmukha is shown by the left hand kept on the navel and the first hand (i.e. the right) shows the upturned Arāla on one side away from the left one. The limbs should not droop down. They are neither motionless nor excessively moving.

79—86 (b) *Ascetics, Buddhist mendicants etc.*

Yatis, Śramaṇas, persons who practise penance or observe the vow of celibacy must have a special Gati. The sensible actor playing their part should have steady eyes looking only upto Yuga i.e. a distance of four Hastas. He must have a ready memory, the entire body being steady, the mind is kept at rest; he scrupulously adopts the marks belonging to his sect, clad in modest clothes generally dyed in dark red; he stands with Sama Pāda assuming Sama Sthāna. He shall then make two Catura hands stretching one of them. With natural limbs he performs the Atikrāntā Cārī scurpulously assuming a serene appearance in conformity with the performance. The qualities are in regard to the best ascetice of great vow. Those with contrary qualities these alone with opposite characteristics are employed in their case. Other Gatis of the Vibhrāntā (confused), Udāttā (stately), Nibhṛtā (sober) or Vihṛtā (mild) types are enjoined in the case of other types of ascetics. The ascetics of the Pāśupata sect should walk in the Śakaṭāsyā and Atikrāntā Cārīs. Haughtiness is evident in their steps.

87 (c) *Persons in darkness or blind man*

The Gati of persons moving about in darkness or blind men should consist of the feet being drawn over the ground and the hands should be groping for the way.

88—90 (d) *Persons moving about in a Chariot*

Cūrṇapāda steps mark the Gati of persons riding a chariot. They gesticulate the fact that they are being carried in a chariot. From Sama Pāda Sthāna the actor playing the part of a chariot rider takes up the bow with one hand and the pole of the chariot with the other. The charioteer remains busy with the whip and the reins; and the draught animals should be properly represented differently according to the class of the vehicle. The actor enters the stage with quick and simple steps.

(e) *Gati of those who move about in aerial Chariot*

91—92 The Gati of one in aerial chariot should be similar to the one of those riding in ordinary chariots. One who is ascending holds his body up and one who makes a decent has the opposite movement.

Ākāśa Gati

93—95 Aerial Cārīs should be adopted for his Gati by an actor moving through the sky. From Sama Pāda he proceeds to head with Cūrṇapadas (Simple Steps). If one descends from the sky his Gati is also similar. It consists of straight and wide high and low, crooked and round and round. One falling from the sky has recourse to Apaviddha arms, the ends of the clothes being scattered about and the eyes fixed to the ground.

Ascending a lofty mansion or palace etc.

96—98 In the course of the dramatic performance there occurs the necessity of going up the stairs of a palace, climbing a tree or proceeding to the top of a hill and similar lofty places. Then there is the further necessity of descending there from. Sometimes the actor has to imitate the walkdown into the river or the climb on to some mounds etc. The climbing in the place should be performed through Atikrānta Pādas. After holding up the body the actor places the steps in the flight of strairs. When coming down from those places the actor keeps his body slightly bent. One of the feet is in the Atikrāntā Cārī and the other in the Añcita motion.

99—100 While climbing the hills too the same Gati as in the case of ascending the flights of stairs in the palace is to be employed but the limbs are to be lifted up. The hands extend support to be lifted up. The hands extend support to the legs. When climbing the trees the actor employs Atikrāntā, Sūcī, Apakrāntā and Pārśvakrāntā Cārīs.

Avataraṇa Gati (Steps while descending)

101—104 The same steps are employed in depicting the descent from the trees or going down into a river But in the case of crossing a river the Gati employed as mentioned by me in coming down the palace holds good. The Gati in the water is based on the quantity of water therein. When the quantity of water is less the actor exhibits tucking up of the clothes and when there is plenty of water the hands are thrown on the sides keeping the fore part of the body slightly bent. When the person is carried away by the current the actor stretches out his arms one by one to push the water forward repeatedly. In the course of these activities all his limbs are busily engaged and there is water-filled mouth.

Cruise in the boat

105 Quick steps mark the Gati of the person in a cruise in the the boat Following this rule the actor employs the various Gatis and movements.

106—107 These displays are but indicative through hints. If you ask "Why should it be so" the reply is as follows. When the dramatic persons are said to be dead it does not mean than the actor too dies. The elephant is represented by the bridle bit and the chariot is represented by the rain. In the same way other vehicles can be represented.

Gati in mounting the horse (Adhirohaṇa)

108 When the horse is used as the Vehicle the Gati Consists of Vaiśākha Sthāna and simple footstep of diverse kinds.

Sarpagati (Serpentine movements)

109 Svastika feet shall indicate the serpentive movements. The actor has recourse to Pārśvakrāntā Cārī along with the Recaka of the Svastika feet.

Viṭa Gati (Lecherous one)

110—111 The Gati of the lecherous Viṭa should necessarily be graceful. The actor represents that by putting forward the Ākuñcita feet within one Tāla and displaying Khāṭakā and Vardhamana hands endowed with Sauṣṭhava. The hands should follow the feet.

Kāñcukīya Gati (Chamber loin)

112—113 The movement of Chamber loin is in accordance with his age and other conditions. If he is not old his Gati shall be as follows :—

The feet are kept raised half a Tāla high. He then takes simple steps and walks making his limbs appear as though he is treading upon mind.

114 If he is an old man he walks with quivering body raising the feet slowly and breathing deeply at every step.

Kṛsa, Vyādhigrasta etc.

115—117 When a lean person walks he takes slow steps. A person suffering from fever or other ailments, a person tired due to penance or starvation walks with lean, depressed belly; feels difficulty in breathing; has feeble voice, depressed cheeks; eyes with no glow; the movement of the hands and feet is very slow; there is tremor in the limbs; they appear afflicted.

Pathika Gati (Wayfarer)

118 A Long distance hiker walks with slow steps limbs tend to narrow down and the knees rub against each other

Sthūla Gati (Stout person)

119—120 The stout person walks with feet raised very slowly. He appears to dragon his body with great effort. In case he takes hurried steps he will breathe profusely and sweat excessively due to fatigue. His steps should be simple.

Mattagati (Inebrieted one)

121—122 If the intoxication is slight or medium the

person reels while walking with the feet swerving now and then. If the person is heavily inebriated the feet are unsteady; the body rells and there are staggering steps.

Unmattagati (Toe mad man)

123—130 A lunatic walks with irregular steps; taking many Cārīs in imitation of diverse types of men. Hairs are rough and dishevelled, the body is covered with dust; he babbles incoherently; sometimes he talks too much in an unnatural manner; now he sings, now he laughs, he refuses to go along with the others; sometimes he dances joyously; he beats on the objects in front of him as though drumming; now he runs swiftly, now he stands still; sometime he squats down firmly and sometimes he lies down on the ground; rags of all types constitute his clothes and the open high way his temporary abode. These are the characteristics of a lunatic; his Gati shall be as follows. He takes Baddhā Cārī and crosses his feet. He then performs Bhramara Maṇḍala outwards after going in all directions in this Cārī. He then goes to a corner in the stage. He then turns the Sacrum holding "Latā" hand; he moves the feet irregularly.

Khañja, Paṅgu, Vāmana Gati (Lame, crippled and dwarfs)

138—136 Hāsya Rasa can be developed by the display of the lame and others. Their physical defects are of three kinds was much as the Gati is concerned. In the first Gati the feet remain stiff; in the second the feet are in Agratala Sañcara and the body is raised by the stiff foot. In the third the body moves on one foot and takes rest on the other. The Khañjas are to go in this manner. When there is Talaśalya Kṣata (when the sole is pricked and wounded with thorn or spikes etc.) the same Gati is adopted. The Paṅgus have the Gati consisting of Agratala Sañcara and Añcita feet the body is kept steady and the shanks are Nata (bent down). All the limbs are contracted when dwarf walk. They never move quickly. The steps are never wide.

Vidūṣaka Gati

137—149 The Vidūṣaka too has the same Gati with simple laughter-provoking steps. The kinds of laughter result from his Gati i.e. Aṅgaja (provoked by the limbs) Kāvyaja (provoked by words) and Nepathyaja (provoked by the costume). Of these the Aṅgaja laughter consists of defects in limbs. If the Vidūṣaka has ugly and protruding teeth; if he is bald, if he is hunch backed, if he is lame or if his face is distorted he will provoke laughter in this manner. Aṅga Hāsya can also be in the following instances viz. when he walks like a stork with Ullokita (looking up), Vilokita, (looking down) and also wide strides.

141 Irrelevant incoherent talk, meaningless utterances ann obscene words provoke Kāvyaja Hāsya (laughter due to words).

142 O Brahmins if the person is clad in tattered clothes, or skin or bark garments, clothes sullied with ink and lamp black, ashes or yellow ochre it provokes Nepathyaja Hāsya (laughter due to costume and make up). The actor playing the part of the Vidūṣaka shall consider the characters he has to contend with and carefully assume one or more of these states.

143—146 The Gati of the Vidūṣaka should vary according to his conditions. In his natural mode of walking he carries the Kuṭilaka (thick staff) in his left hand and shows the Catura gesture with the right hand. In addition to this, he lowers his head, one of the sides, hands and feet etc. by turns maintaining proper Laya and Tāla. The other Gati of his is abnormal resulting from aberrations. His Gati is Stabdhā (puffed up, stubborn) when he gets food or some rare object.

Dāsagati (Menials, Servants)

147—148 In the case of the mode of walking of servents of very low order or persons of the inferior type the following facts should be noted. When servants walk, the head, one of the sides, the hand or the foot is kept lowered and the eyes move from one object to another in a fickle manner.

Śakāra Gati (King's brother-in law)

148—149 The Śyāla (or the brother of the king's concubine) is a proud and ruthless character. His Gati consists of ordinary steps. In the course of his peregrinations he continues fondling his ornaments and touching the clothes proudly and looking at them admiringly. In view of the unnatural movement of his body his garlands and loose ends of his clothes move to and fro.

Nīcapātra Gati (Lowly persons)

150 Persons of inferior characteristics walk cautiously looking around saving their limbs from the contact of other people by shrinking and contracting their limbs.

Mleccha Gati (Barbarous tribes)

151 Pulindas, Śabaras etc. form the Mleccha tribes. Their Gatis and Viceṣṭitas (activities) should be in accordance with the land of their nativity.

Paśupakṣi Gati (Animals and birds)

152 O excellant Brahmins the Gati of the animals birds and beasts of prey shall be in accordance with the character natural to them.

Lion, bears, monkeys

153 The Gati of these animals is to be adapted to what was assumed by lord Viṣṇu in the course of his incarnation as Narahari etc.

154—155 The Ālīḍha Sthāna is assumed at the outset and the limbs conform to it. One hand is kept over the knee and the other on the chest. The actor then looks all round, put his chin on his shoulder and walks with feet placed five Tālas apart.

156 At the time of duels and while entering the stage the Gati is assumed to represent lions and other animals.

157 In regard to the other animals the Gati and the Sthāna at the time of entering the stage and carrying persons or things on the back should be suitable to the occasion.

158—159 Wise actors make use of these different Gatis mentioned by me. Those that have not been mentioned can be adopted from the usual practice of the people. Henceforth I shall describe the Gatis and Viceṣṭitas of women.

Sthiti of women

160 The posture of women in walking and speaking to others shall be Āyata, Avahittha or Aśvakrāntā.

Āyata

161 In this Āyata Sthāna the right foot is in the Sama (level) position and the left foot is Tryaśra (in oblique position). The left waist is kept raised.

162—164 This Sthāna is to be employed in Āvāhana (in vocation), Visarjana (dismissal), careful observation thoughtful procedure and dissimulation. Further it shall be applicable at the time of the first appearance on the stage when the actor (actress) scatters flowers on the stage; in anger due to jealous, love, twisting the index finger, prohibition, pride, profundity silence, fit of resentment and looking up towards the horizen — these are to be represented from this Sthāna.

Avahittha

165 The left foot is in the Sama posture and the right is obliquely placed. The left wais is raised up.

165—167 This Sthāna is remembered as natural for women during their dialoque with anyone, indetermination, satisfaction and conjecture. In representing anxiety, amoroursness, sportiveness, grace, Śṛṅgāra and other similar Rasas and while watching the husband coming or going.

168 *Aśvakrāntā Sthāna* One foot is kept raised and the other rests on its forpart. It is ready for Sūcī or Āviddha Cārī. This Sthāna is called Aśvakrāntā.

169 *Application of Aśvakrāntā.* This Sthāna is to be adopted to take hold of the branch of a tree, plucking a cluster of blossoms, or when goddesses or ordinary women begin to take rest.

170--171 A dancer maintains this Sthāna till the movement begins. That is because, during a dance the Sthāna is at an end when the Cārī has begun. This is the rule govering the Sthāna for women and also for men. I shall now narrate their Gati in relation to their nature.

Yuvatī Strīgati (of young women)

172—176 The following Sthānas and movements are successively adopted. The Avahittha Sthāna at the outset, the left hand points down wards, the right hand with the Kaṭakā Mukha gesture is placed on the navel, the right foot is raised up gracefully by one Tāla and thrown on the left one. Simultaneously the left hand with Latā Mudrā is placed on the navel. The right side is bent then. Then the righthand is placed on the hip, The Udveṣṭita movement of the left hand follows. The left foot is put forward. Then the right hand with Latā gesture is shown. They then walk five steps with the body slightly bent and the head is gracefully held in the Udvāhita posture.

177 The rules that nad been prescribed in the case of men in connection with the movements on the stage are equally applicable to the women too.

178—179 The duration of the steps of women shall not be made for six or eight Kalās because such a step irks them much. This shall be the Gati of young women. I shall now speak about the Gatis of elderly ladies.

180—181 *Prauḍhā Gati.* Avahittha Sthāna is assumed. The left hand is put on the waist. The right hand with the Arāla gesture is kept upturned and placed between the navel and the chest. The women then walk gradually keeping their body neither relaxed nor stiff. They are not moved about much.

Preṣyā Gati (Slave girl running errands)

182—183 The Gati of Slave girls should be of the perturbed type (Vibhrāntā). While walking the body is raised slightly; the arms are flourished. Then Avahittha Sthāna is adopted with the left hand pointing downwards and the right hand showing the Kaṭakamukhā hand held on the navel.

184 *Napuṁsaka Gati.* The Gati of the eunuchs has an admixture of that of men and of women. The movement of the limbs is stately but none the less graceful. The steps are playful.

185—186 The time required for the Gati in the case of superior persons will be halved in the case of women and further halved in the case of eunuchs. The Gati of the superior the middling and the inferior types will apply in the case of women of these three types. But, of course the footsteps will be graceful.

187 *Bāla Gati.* (Children) Tne Gati of children shall be completely in accordance with their will and fancy. No Sauṣṭhava and specified measurement of time is requiied.

188 *Strīpuruṣalakṣaṇadhāri Gati.* A third type of persons shall be the her maphrodities with the twin characteristics of women and men but the Gati assigned to them shall be completely that of women to the exclusion of the male character.

189 *Gati when Bhūmikā (assigned role) is changed.* When the actor/actress changes his/her role the Gati previously allotted should be changed into that befiting the present role.

190—191 *Persons in disguise* Under a pretext or for playful teasing or deliberate deception a woman may assume the role of a man or vice versa. In those cases the original woman in man's role shall play his role with liberal spirit and intelligence. Her acts, dress, words and movements shalls be befitting the new character.

192 A man playing the role of a woman in similar circumstances shall wear her clothes, speak like her and behave in every respect like her looking at particular things in the same way as she or abstaining from the same. He further adopts delicate and slow Gati.

193 *Gati of Pulindās etc.* Women of lower castes as well as the women of Pulinda or Śabara clan must have Gatis befitting their community.

194 *Tapasvinī Gatī* (Ascetic ladies). In regard to ladies observing vows, practising penances or having the sectarian characteristics religions cults or traversing the sky the samapādā Cārī should be used.

195 An expert in the art of dram a turgy shall desist from assigning Uddhata (energetic) Aṅgahāras Cārīs or Maṇḍalas to women.

Āsanavidhāna (Sitting Postures)

196 Sitting postures in the case of men and women shall assigned in conformity with the Bhāvas they are in, and the same holds good in the case of their occupation of beds too.

Svastha Daśā (Relaxed State)

197 While in relaxed state, sitting at ease both the feet are at rest—(Viṣkambhita) and kept doubled up (Añcita), The Sacrum is raised slightly and both the hands are put on the thighs on either side.

198 *Vicārāvasthā* (Reflective mood) When a person is in the state of deep ponderance he is to stretch one of his feet slightly and the other foot rests on the seat. The head is bent on one side.

199 *Śokāvasthā* (Sorrowful mood) When a person is in excess of sorrow he is to put up his hands for supporting the chin. His head is to rest on a shoulder. He appears like one whose mind and sense organs are entirely upset.

200 *Mūrcchā State* (State of Surooning) when person is about to faint or is inebriated, weakened or sad he stetches his arms loosely and sits depending on some support.

Lajjā—Roga—Nidrā (Shame—Sickness—Sleep).

201 When a person is ashamed, ill, asleep or in decp absorption of the mind he keeps his limbs lumped together between the legs and knees.

202 *Ritualistic occasions* While offering a libation of water to the Pitṛs, while chanting Mantras or uttering Sandhyā Prayers, or Ācamana (ceremonial rinsing of the mouth) the person concerned assumes a sitting posture with the hump lifted up; the hip and the heels come together.

Pacifying the enraged beloved.

203 In pacifying the anger of an estranged beloved or while pouring ghee into the sacred fire or doing similar things the person places one of his stratched knees on the ground.

204—206 *During adoration of a deity.* As before the down cast face and the position of kneeling down is to be assumed at the time of the adoration of a deity, appeasing the angry superiors loud, lamentation, looking at a corpse, when frightened by persons of evil intentions, begging of something by base born ones and servants and watching Homas and Yajñas. This injunction regarding sitting shall be observed by sages practising penance.

207 *Vibhinnapātra* (of diverse characters) Rules regarding

seats for men and women in the dramatic performance are two fold viz. Bāhya (external—public) and Ābhyantara (internal—or exclusive). Ābhyantara concerns the being and the Bāhya the lay public outside.

208—210 *Seats for male characters.* O Brahmins, lion seat (throne) is to be allotted to kings and gods Vetra Āsana (Cane seat) to the priests and the ministers, the Muṇda-seat (or topless) to the Crown price and commander of the army the wooden seat, for the ordinary Brahmins and the carpet seat to the princes. This rule regarding seats is to be observed in the royal court.

210—214 *Seats for female characters* (and audience) I shall now explain the arrangement of sects for women. The chief queen deserve, the throne, the female relatives and other wives of the king, the Muṇḍa seat, the wives of priests and ministers the cane-seat the mistresses of the king seats made of cloth, skin, or carpet; the wives of brahmins and female ascetics the wooden planks, the wives of Vaiśyas the the Masūraka (cushioned pillows) and the bare ground for other ladies. So much about the rule of sets in the inner apartments as well as in public places. As for the seats in ones own house one may take any seat of one's choice.

215 *The seats for sages etc.* The rules of the sect or cult they belong to decide the seats to be allotted to sages and other observing vows.

216 While performing Homas into the sacred fire or other duties attending upon it or while offering libations of water to the Pitṛs one is to sit on a Bṛsī (seat made of Kuśa grass), the Muṇḍa seat or the Vetra seat.

General rule regarding seats

217—220 Local people of high birth and adequate learning must be honoured by the king with the offer of suitable seats. The king shall offer seats equal to his own to the people of equal states. To the people of medium importance he offers seats of middling height. To the superior people he offers an exalted seat. The lowly persons are seated on the ground. Sensible persons shall sit only on the ground or on wooden seats in the presence of the preceptor, the king or spiritual guide. Sitting together with all these viz. the Guru, the Upādhyāya and the king in a boat chariot or on the back of an elephant can not be objected to.

Śayanāvasthā (Lying down posture)

221 There are six lyingdown postures viz. Ākuñcita, Sama, Prasārita, Vivartita, Udvāhita and Nata.

222 *Ākuñcita* The limbs are contracted and narrowed down. The two knees stick to the bed. This is called Ākuñcita posture. It has to be adopted in the case of those distressed with chillness.

Sama

223 Lying down with the face upturned and the hands free and turning downwards is called Sama posture. It is the posture in sound sleep

224 *Prasārita.* Lying down with an arm as the pillow and the knees stretched is called Prasārita posture. It is to be adopted to depict one enjoying a sleep of happiness.

225 *Vivarita* Lying down with the face downwards is called Vivartita posture. It is to be assumed in representing wound from weapons, death, intoxication, vomiting and lunacy.

226 *Udvāhita* Lying down with the head resting on the hand and making a movement of the knee is called the Udvāhita posture. It is to be used in sports and when the master enters.

227 *Nata* Lying down with shanks slightly stretched and both the hands resting loosely is called the Nata posture It is to be adopted in laziness, fatigue and distress.

228 This is rule regarding Gati and movements and I have mentioned it. Whatever remains not expressly stated should be achieved according to the matter on hand. Hereafter I shall mention about the division of the stage into different Kakṣyas (zones) in regard to the movement thereon.

Notes

Verse 2. Upavahana. This is a kind of Ālāpa or singing of the tunes to the accompaniment of instrumental music. Agni Purāṇa explains it thus—Upohyante Samāsavyāsataḥ

Padakalā tāla Sambhihitāḥ Svarā Yaśminnange Tat Tathoktam. See Ch. 31/13 below and also 5—59 Saṅgīta Ratnākara-Kallinatha's Comments.

70—75 Vidhuta is explained already in VIII—22
Eḍakākrīḍitakā Cārī in IX—19
Kapota hand is explained in IX—8-10

106—107 Kasmāt etc. This passage indicates that in ancient India the dramatists did not consider it absolutely essential that painted sccnery should be used for stage effects. Agnipurāṇa has this passage—Tena Citra Paṭādiviyogepi Rathagamanādya Bhinayanam Nāyuktam Saukaryāttu Tatkaraṇampi Yuktam.

112 Kañcukīya—the Chamber loin.

The famous definition is as follows :

Akāmā Brāhmāṇāścaiva Kañcukoṣṇīṣa Vetriṇa; Jñāna Vijñāna Sampannāḥ Kāñcukīyāḥ Smṛta Budhaiḥ.

14

Kaksya Paridhi & Lokadharmi Nirūpana (Review of Zonal division and realistic Practice)

1 Three Nāṭya Maṇḍapas have been mentioned by me formerly. Only after knowing that division can one fix the zones of the stage.

2 The drums anddrum mens are to be kept between the two doors of the tiring room already explained by me.

3 *Kakṣyā-Vibhāga* (Division of the zones). If one walks round the stage one can indicate the division of the zones. By walking out of one's zone one can show the change in the zone.

Usefulness of the Kakṣyā Vibhāga

4—6 From the convention of the zonel division one is able to know whether the place in which the scene has been laid is a residential place, a town, a park, a place of recreation, a river, a penance grove a jungle, the earth the ocean, any region of the three worlds, any of the seven Varṣas or nine Dvīpas, different mountains, Āloka and Loka (Special Mountains, of twilight), Rasātala (the nether world, the abodes of Daityas and serpents).

7 The Kakṣvāparidih should be fixed with referencc to places such as the town the jungle, the Dvīpa or mountain in which the event takes place.

Indicating of the location

8 The divisions of the Kakṣyā on the stage should relate to the inside, outside or middle of the location or to a place far or near.

9 It should be the convention as regards the zonel division that those actors who had entered the stage before are within and those who are to enter afterwards are to be treated as standing externally.

10 The actor on the point of entering the stage for the specific purpose of visiting those already within should report himself turning to the right (Southern side).

Eastern direction on the stage

11 The dramatic convention lays down that the direction faced by the musical instruments and the green room doors is the east.

Regulation for going out

12 If any actor has to go out after carrying his work he shall go out by the way through which he had entered.

13 If after exist anyone has cause to enter once again he shall make the next exist by the door through which the man who entered later had entered.

14—15 If it becomes necessary for him to go along with the latter or to re-enter the house with the latter or himself alone, the two shall have and the Kakṣyā Paridhi shall be allotted. This other Kakṣyā shall be indicated by the order in which they walk on the stage.

Rules governing the rank of the dramatic personal

16 An actor walks side by side with his equals and surrounded by the base ones. The handmaids should be directed to go ahead (of the king etc.) in the stage.

Indication of distances

17 A distant land is indicated by walking over the same place much with many circumambulations.

Open or disquised movement of Gods

18—20 Based on the necessity arising from the plot of the drama gods and semidivine beings can be represented moving to cities, forests, seas or mountains through the sky in Vimānas thanks to their divine power or other activities of diverse kinds.

When they are disguised as human beings they must be represented as moving on the ground to be viewed like man.

21—21*A* *Movements in Bhāratavarṣa.* The Gods and the semidivine beings can have unrestricted movement in Bhārata, Haima, Harivarṣa, Ilāvṛta, in the beautiful Kimpuruṣa, or in the northern Kurus. They have been proclaimed to have free access there. But human movement is displayed only in Bhārata.

22 *Journey to a distant place.* If a person has to go to a distant place on some purpose the Act is closed at the time of his departure and his journey is indicated in Praveśaka (Interlude—middle scene).

23 *Restriction of time.* The achievement of the object is represented after traversing for the duration of a day. When the purpose is not served the Act is closed.

24 Pursuing the Bīja (seed—main plot) of the play a moment, a Muhūrta, a Yāma and a day are to be represented in the course of a single act through the incidents thereof.

25 What has occurred in the course of a month or a year should be represented before the close of the Act. Events transpiring after the lapse of a year should not be put in a single Act.

26 The Kakṣyās should be thus represented in the Bhārata Varṣa based on human movement. Now understand the movement of the gods and the semidivine beings.

27—32 On the excellent mountain Kailāsa situated on the Himālayas live the following semidivine beings viz. the Yakṣas the Guhyakas, and other followers of Kubera, the Rākṣasas, the Bhūtas and the Piśācas. All these are remembered as Haimavatas (residents of the Himālayas). The Gandharvas along with the group of celestial damsels should be known as residing on the Hemakūṭe. All the Nāgas are in the Niṣadha. They are Śeṣa, Vāsuki and Takṣaka (and others). The thirty three groups of Devas should be known by scholars as the residents of Mahāmeru. The Siddhas as well as the Brahmarṣis are on the Nīla full of Vaiḍūrya (Lapis Lajuli). Śveta Parvata is mentioned as the abode of the Daityas and Dānavas. The

Pitṛs (Manes) should be known as the residents of the Śṛṅgavān. These excellent mountains are divine abodes. Their zonel division shall be in the Jambūdvīpa.

Movements of the Devas

33—35 Their activities are to represented in accordance with their duties and explorts. The varieties of their dress and make up should be like those of the human beings. All their Bhāvas are to be made as based on human ones. Their well known winklessness should not be displayed by the producers of the play. The Bhāvas and Rasas depend upon the Dṛṣṭi (vision) alone. The Bhāvas are first indicated by visions to be represented later by the Aṅgas (gestures of limbs etc.). O excellent Brahmins thus the Kakṣyā Vibhāga has been explained by me.

Four types of Pravṛttis (Local usages)

36 I shall now expatiate on Pravṛtti which has been classified into four by the producers of plays. They are (a) Āvanti (b) Dākṣiṇātyā (c) Pāñcālī and (d) Oḍhra Māgadhī.

Prose Passage. A question is raised here. Why is it termed Pravṛtti ? The answer is Pravṛtti is so called because it gives the detailed information regarding dress types, languages used, manners and customs followed and professions engaged in the different regions of the land. Pravṛtti is in the sense of Nivedana (making it known). Another doubt may arise. How can there be only four Pravṛttis when there are many countries in the world ? These Pravṛttis have certain common characteristics prominently. The reply to this objection is as follows :— It is admitted that their common characteristics are patent. But, since people hail from different countries, wear different kinds of dress, speak many languages and follow many customs I have projected the fourfold classification. As there are four different styles (Vṛttis) such as Bhārati, Sāttvatī, Kaiśikī and Ārabhaṭī concerned with different sets of people and countries the Practical usages (Pravṛttis) are also similarly dealt with.

Dākṣiṇātyā Pravṛtti. The Southern people have maay kinds of dance styles songs and musical instruments ; they employ the Kaiśikī Vṛtti mostly and cultivate efficient gestures. They are :

37 Countries in and around the mountains of Mahendra, Malaya, Sahya, Mekala and Kālapañjara are known as Dakṣiṇāpatha.

38—39 Still all the areas between the Southern Sea and the Vidaya mountain adopt the Dākṣiṇātyā Pravṛtti viz. Kosala, Tosala Kaliṅga, Yavana, Khasa, the Dramiḍa Āndhra, Mahārāṣtra, Veṇṇa and Vanavāsika.

Āvantī Pravṛtti

40—41 Avanti, Vidiśa, Saurāṣṭra, Mālava, Sindhu, Sauvīra, Ānarta, Arbudeyaka, Dasārṇa, Traipura and Mārtikāvata always adopt the Āvantī Pravṛtti.

42 The dramatic performance by these inhabitants mainly concerned with Sāttvati and Kaiśika styles and the producers should not fail to adopt them.

Oḍhri-Māgadhi Pravṛtti

43—45 The eastern areas comprising of Aṅga, Vaṅga, Kaliṅga, Vatsa, Oḍhra, Magadha, Puṇḍra, Nepāla, Antargira, Bahirgira, Plavaṅgama, Malada, Mallavartaka, Brahmottara, Bhārgava, Mārgava, Prāgjyotiṣa, Pulinda, Videha and Tāmralipta take to the local usage known as Oḍhra Māgadhī.

46 The same is the case with the other areas mentioned in the Purāṇas as falling within the area eastern tract and Oḍhri-Māgadhi Pravṛtti is to be employed in their productions too.

Pāñcāla Madhyamā Pravrtti

47—48 The region including Pāñcāla, Śūrasena, Kaśmīra, Hastināpura, Vālhīka, Śākala, Madra, and Uśīnara, contiguous either to the Himālayas or the northern banks of the Gaṅga—adopts the Pāñcāla-Madhyamā Pravṛtti.

49 The Pāñcāla Māgadhi Pravṛtti goes in with Sāttvati and Ārabhati Vṛttis mostly. The production of these indicates paucity of songs, excessive movements and Gaits and steps of the Āviddha type.

Two fold modes of entry

50 These Pravṛttis include two fold modes of entry viz. Pradakṣiṇa Praveśā and Apradakṣiṇa Praveśā (entering clock-wise or anticlockwise).

51 The Āvanti and Dākṣiṇātyā Pravṛttis are Dakṣiṇa Praveśā and the Pāñcālī and Oḍhra Māgadhi are Apradakṣiṇa Praveśa.

52 In the case of the Āvanti and Dākṣiṇātya Pravṛttis the entry door is the northern side door is while in the case of other two entry door is the southern side door.

53 But in exceptional cases of special assembly, place or occasion or while expressing certain special theme these rules may be combined and unified.

54 Pravṛttis as laid down before for different regions should be adopted by experts while sponsoring dramatic performances.

55 These shall be unified (simplified) when applied to to short plays etc. In view of the multiplicity of Vṛttis one should practise these acts reasonably.

56 *Two types of plays.* In conformity with the rules of dramatic practice the production of plays can be of two types the Sukumāra (delicate) and the Āviddha (aggressive).

The Aggressive type

57—58 The play that requires Āviddha movements and gestures (Aṅgahāra) to represent, hitting, wounding, challenging and piercing and the use of charms and yogic powers and also painting and plastering work to the course of the make up and has more of men characters than women and adopts mainly Sātvatti and Ārabhaṭī Vṛttis is called *Āviddha*.

59 Sponsors of dramatic performances should know that the following forms of Rūpavam mainly Ḍima, Samavakāra, Vyāyoga and Īhāmṛga come under the Āviddha type of plays.

60 Production of Āviddha plays should be through Devas, Dānavas and Rākṣasas (represented by) actors who are haughty and endowed with heroism, vitality and prowess.

Tho Sukumāra type

61 The Nāṭaka, Prakaraṇa, Bhāṇavīthi, and the Aṅka types of Rūpakas come under the Sukumāra class of plays depending on the impersonation of humen beings for their production.

Loka Dharmī and Nāṭya Dharmi

62. I shall now mention the characteristic features O excellent Brahmins of Laukikī and Nāṭya-Dharmi, the two practices mentioned by me before.

Lokadharmī (Realistic Practice)

63-64 If a play depends on natural behaviour in its characters; is simple excluding artificiality, has professions and activities of the people in its plot; has simple acting avoiding playful flowerish of limbs and depends on men and women of different types it is called Lokadharmī

The Nāṭya Dharmi

65—66 If Speeches & activities are too many; if the Sattva and Bhāva are of the extra ordinary kind, if the acting necessitates playful flourish of limbs (Aṅgahāra), if the play has the characteristic features of dance items Svara and Alaṁkāra are employed in well arranged fashion and emotionally carried characters predominate it should be known as Nāṭya Dharmī

67 If things used by the common people appear in a play as endowed with Corporeal form and speech it is Nāṭya Dharmi.

68 If the words uttered very close by are expected to be not heard by the other characters (Apavārya etc.) and words not spoken are also supposed to be heard, it is remembered as Nāṭya Dharmī.

69 If objects like mountains, vehicles, vimānas, shields, armours, śastras, flagstaff and banner are personified and made appear on the stage in human form it is an example of Nāṭya Dharmī.

70 If after appearing in one role, a character assumes a different role in the same play because he happens to be an therein or if no one else is available for that role it is an example of Nāṭya Dharmī

71 If an actor/actress is employed in the role of a woman unfit for sexual union and later on is employed in the role of a

woman fit for such union, it is an example of Nāṭya Dharmī. The case reversed too is also an example of Nāṭya Dharmī.

72 If instead of walking in the usual manner a character dances or proceeds ahead with graceful movements of the limbs and steps it is an example of Nāṭya Dharmī.

73 The common features of men such as happiness and sorrow are displayed with Aṅga Abhinaya. This is also known as Nāṭya Dharmi.

74*a* (Prakṣipta) Brahmā has produced a play with the Vedic and Itihāsaic themes for humouring the Devas and human beings. It is called Nāṭya Dharmī.

74 The Kakṣyā vibhāga depending on different sets of rules when produced on the stage is also an example of Nāṭya Dharmi.

75 A dramatic performance should invariably have Nāṭya Dharmi items for without the use of gestures etc. by the actors, *the spectators are not adequetly used.* I.

76 The Bhāvas are congenital to all. The Abhinaya is done on purposes. Thus, the decorative movements of limbs in producing play have been considered Nāṭya Dharmī.

77 In this manner Kakṣyāvibhāga, Dharmī and Pravṛtti should be known properly by those conversent with the principles of Dramatic performance and employed realistically.

78 I have finished explaining the histronic representation through the Śākhās and Aṅgahāras. Henceforth I shall describe Vākyābhinaya (Verbal representation) based upon Vowels and Consonents.

Notes

Verse 3

Kakṣyāvibhāga or zonal division becomes essential to indicate the locality in which the different characters meet together. In the modern theatre this is possible throughs change of scenes and other devices. They were absent in the early Hindu Theatre.

17 This practice of representing doing journey by means of many circumambulations has been employed by various dramatists. Uttara Rāma Carita of Bhavabhūti Act II has a fine example.

43–45 Names of various regions mentioned here closely bellow the descriptions in the Purāṇas. Many of these are not correctly identified.

15

Chandovidhana (Rules of Prosody)

Vāgabhinaya

1 O the best of Brahmins, I shall now mention in detail Vāgabhinaya (Verbal representation) mentioned before, and its characteristic features based on Vowels and Consonants.

Importance of speech

2 Great effort should be taken in regard to words since 'word' is remembered as the physical form of Nāṭya. The gestures, the make up and the dress as well as Sāttvika Abhinaya reveal the inherent meaning of words.

3 Here in the world, words constitute Śāstras and support them. Hence there is nothing greater than words. It is the word that is the basis of every this.

4 Verbal representation is concerned with the knowledge of Nāma (Substantives), Ākhyāta (Verbal forms), Nipāta (Particle), Upasarga (Prefixes Prepositions), Taddhita (nominal suffix), Samāsa (Compounds), Sandhi (Phonetic Change) and the Vibhakti (Case terminations).

Pāṭhyas of two kinds

5 Pāṭhya (what is recited) in a play is remembered as of two kinds—Sanskṛta and Prākṛta. I shall explain these two duly.

Aspects of the Pāṭhya

6—7 The Sanskṛta Pāṭhya is characterised by the following aspects—the Vowels, Consonants, the Sandhis, the Vibhaktis, the Nāmans, Ākhyātas, Upasargas, Nipātas, Tadditas, the Compounds and various verbal roots. Now listen to their application.

Varṇas

8 Fourteen Varṇas beginning with A and ending with AU are to be known as Vowels Svaras. Learned man know Vyañjanas (Consonants) as beginning with Ka and ending with Ha.

Prose Passage

Vowels are fourteen A, Ā, I, Ī, U, Ū, Ṛ, Ṝ, ḷ, ḹ, E, Ai, O and Au.

Vyañjanas are Ka, Kha, Ga, Gha Ṅa, Ca, Cha, Ja, Jha, Na, Ṭa, Ṭha, Ḍa, Ḍha, Ṇa, Ta, Tha, Da, Dha, Na, Pa, Pha, Bha, Ma, Ya, Ra, La, Va, Śa, Ṣa, Ṣa, and Ha.

The consonants and their articulation

9 The first two consonants in each group are known as Aghoṣa (Unvoiced) and the remaining ones are called Ghoṣa (Voiced).

10 These consonants are classified as Ghoṣas, Aghoṣas, Gutturals, labials, dentals, Jihvyas (cerebrals), nasals, sibilants, palatals and Visarjanīya.

11 Among these Ga, Gha, Ṅa, Ja, Jha, N̄a, Ḍa, Ḍha, Ṇa, Ḍa, Dha, Na, Ba, Bha, Ma, Ya, Ra, La and Va are considered Ghoṣas, Ka Kha, Ca, Cha, Ṭa Ṭha, Ta, Tha, Pa, Pha, Śa, Ṣa, Sa are unvoiced.

12—14 Ka, Kha, Ga, Gha and Ṅa are Kaṇṭhasthas (gutturals), Ca, Cha, Ja, Jha, Na, I, Ya and Śa are palatals (Tālavya), Ṭa, Ṭha, Ḍa, Ḍha, Ṇa, Ṛ, Ra and Ṣa are (Mūrdhanyas) cerebral, Ta, Tha, Da, Dha, Na, La and Sa are (Dantyas) Dentals, Pa, Pha, Ba, Bha and Ma are Oṣṭhya (lebrals) A and Ha are Kaṭhaschas, O and Au are Kaṇṭhoṣṭhya (throat-labral), E and Ai are Kaṇṭhatālavya (throat-paletel).

15 The Visarjanīya is from the throat, Ka, Kha are from the root of the tongue. The places of articulation for Pa and Pha are the lips and the same will be for the closed (Avivṛta) vowels U and Ū.

16 The consonants beginning with Ka and ending with Ma are called Sparśa. Ṣa, Sa and Ha are Vivṛtas (open) while

the Antasthas (semivowels) are Samvṛta; Ṅa, Na, Ṇa, Na and Ma are the Anunāsikyas (Nasal sounds).

17 Śa, Ṣa, Sa, Ha are Uṣmans (subilant and the (Aspirate Ha) ; Ya, Ra, La and Va are Antaḥsthas (Semivowels) Ka≍ is Jihvāmūlīya and Pa≍ is Upadhmānīya.

18 Ka, CA, Ṭa, Ta and Pa are Svaritas (simply uttered), Kha, Cha, Ṭha, Tha and Pha are markedly uttered Kaṇṭhyas; Ga, Gha, Ja, Jha, Ḍa, Ḍha and Ba, Bha are Kaṇṭhorasya (throat and chest).

19 The Visarjanīya should be known as a sound produced from the root of the tongue. Thus the consonants have been termed and briefly explained. I shall now discuss the vowels with reference to their use in words.

Vowels and their Parimāṇa (Extent)

20 Of the afore-mentioned vowels fourteen in number, the first ten are Samānas (of Similar features). The previous ones are Hrasvas and the latter ones are Dīrghas in every pair.

21 What is called Śabda (word) is constituted by these vowels, groups of consonants and accompanied by Taddhita, Sandhi and Vibhakti are classified with Nāma, Ākhyāta, Upasarga and Nipāta.

22 The characteristics of the Śabda have been mentioned in detail by the ancient Ācāryas. I shall discuss this further when an occasion may arise.

Namān (Substantives)

23 The case terminations determine the functions of the Substantive since they have special meanings attached to them. It is of five types and the meaning of each Prātipadika (Substantive) is separate. It has gender also.

24 They say that the Nāman has seven divisions and on notes six Kārakas (such as object etc.) with their special terms Nirdeśa (Suggestion) Sampradāna (handing over), Apādāna (separating off) etc. Some of them are Prathita (well established) and others are Sādhya (yet to be derived).

25 The Nāman is used alongwith Kriyās (verbs) etc. denoting the present and past time, they are Prathita and

Sādhya. They are divided according to number and person.

Verb

26 Five hundred roots classified into twenty-five groups should be known as verbs as belonging to the text recited and having the speciality of resorting to the meaning of the noun. (i.e. qualifying it)

Upasargas

27 Those that change the meaning of the roots with respect to their own special senses are therefore called Upasargas in the treatise of Saṁskāra (consecration of words i.e. Grammer)

Nipātas (Particles)

28 The Nipātas (Particles) are so called because they fall in together on the word strengthening its meaning in combination with the verbal roots, metres and etymology.

Pratyayas (Suffixes)

29 Since the suffixs clarify the ideas and develop the root meaning and intensify the same or combine with another revealing the essential quality they are called so.

Taddhita (Nominal affixes)

30 Since the nominal affix completes the meanings or develops them through dropping off, or separation of the base and the termination and hints at the inner thought or sense it is called Taddhita.

Vibhakti (Case endings)

31 As they give distinctive meaning to an inflected word or words in relation to their roots or gender it is called Vibhakti (case ending).

Sandhi (Phonetic change)

32 Separare vowels or consonants combining together through nearness in a word or words bring about the Sandhi or Phonetic change.

33 Due to the meeting of two letters or words their order results in a combination and it is called Sandhi (euphonic combination).

Samāsas (Compounds)

34 O Brahmins, the combination of nouns into one unit of a single meaning by dropping the case terminations has been described as Samāsa by those who know the details thereof; it is of six kinds beginning with Tatpuruṣa (the coordinating) compound.

Two types of words

35 Word-groups should be made in the forms of Nibaddha Bandhas (Verses) or Cūrṇas (Prose) through these words having the quality of indicating extensive meanings.

36 Pada which is the unit (of letters) ending with the case terminations should be known as Nibaddha and Cūrṇa. Of them, understand the characteristic features of the Cūrṇa Pada.

Cūrṇa Pada

37 That group of Padas which is not meterically arranged, where the syllables are not regulated and which contains as many syllables as are essential to convey the sense, should be known as Cūrṇa Pada (Prose) by sensible men.

Nibaddha Pada

38 Where the syllables are arranged metrically with cessations and caesura and where the numbers are stipulated, should be known as Nibaddha Pada (Verse).

Chandas (Metre)

39 Chandas otherwise called Vṛtta is constituted of four feet embellished with words having diverse meanings.

Varieties of Chandas

40—42 Varieties of Chandas are twenty six in number based on the number of letters in each foot. Chandas or Vṛtta can be of three types viz. Sama (even), Ardhasama (semi even) and Viṣama (Uneven). This is remembered as the body of words arising out of the diverse kinds of Vṛttas. There is no word devoid of Chandas and no Chandas without word. Thus the combination of both is remembered as the illuminator of the dramatic performance.

Twenty six types of Chandas

43—49 **The Chandas with number of syllables stipulated as under is called respectively :**

one	syllables	Ukta
two	syllables	**Atyukta**
three	„	**Madhya**
four	„	**Pratiṣṭhā**
five	„	**Supratiṣṭhā**
six	„	Gāyatrī
seven	„	**Uṣṇik**
eight	„	**Anuṣṭup**
nine	„	**Bṛhatī**
ten	„	**Paṅkti**
eleven	„	**Triṣṭup**
twelve	„	**Jagati**
thirteen	„	**Atijagati**
fourteen	„	Śakvarī
fifteen	„	**Atiśakvarī**
sixteen	„	**Aṣṭi**
seventeen	„	**Atyaṣṭi**
eighteen	„	**Dhṛti**
nineteen	„	**Atidhṛti**
twenty	„	**Kṛti**
twenty one	„	**Prakṛti**
twenty two	„	**Ākṛti**
twenty three	„	**Vikṛti**
twenty four	„	**Saṅkṛti**
twenty five	„	**Atikṛti**
twenty six	„	**Utkṛti**

49—51 A Chandas with more syllables per foot is remembered as Mālāvṛtta. When tabulated suitably there can be many Chandas and so learned men say that Vṛttas are innumerable. The possible number of Vṛttas from the Gāyatrī Chandas and thereafter will be mentioned. Not that all of them are in practical application.

51—76 Sixty four Vṛttas have been mentioned in the Gāyatrī Chandas; Uṣṇik is said to have hundred and twenty-eight Vṛttas; two hundred and fifty six Vṛttas in Anuṣṭup, five hundred and twelve in Bṛhatī. One thousand and twenty four in Paṅkti, two thousand and forty eight in Traiṣṭubha, four thousand and ninety six Samavarṇa Vṛttas in Jagati, eight thousand one hundred and ninety two in Atijagati, sixteen thousand three hundred and eighty four in Śakvarī, thirty two thousand seven hundred and sixty eight in Atiśakvari; sixty five thousand five hundred and thirty six in Aṣṭi; One hundred and thirty one thousand and seventy two in Atyaṣṭi, two hundred and forty four in Dhṛti; five hundred and twenty four thousand two hundred and eighty eight in Atidhrti; one million forty eight thousand five hundred seventy six in Kṛti; two million ninety seven thousand one hundred and fifty two in Prakṛti four million one hundred and ninety four thousand three hundred and four in Ākṛti; eight million three hundred and eighty eight thousand six hundred and eight in Vikṛti; sixteen million seven hundred and seventy seven thousand two hundred and sixteen in Saṁkṛti; thirty three million five hundred and fifty four thousand four hundred and thirty two in Atikṛti (Abhikṛti), and sixty seven million one hundred and eight thousand eight hundred and sixty four in Utkṛti.

77—79 If we add together the number of possible Vṛttas in each of the Chandas, that comes to one hundred and thirty four million two hundred and seventeen thousand and seven hundred and twenty six.

Another method of grouping letters

79—81 The twenty six types of Chandas have been explained briefly. All the possible Sama Vṛttas based on calculations have also been mentioned. In all the Chandas the Vṛttas are to be constituted by means of Trikas (units of three syllables) whether the possible Vṛttas be one, twenty, thousand or ten million.

82—84 These Trikas (trieds) should be known as totalling eight. They have their own special terms. The syllables short or long constitute the Trikas named Gaṇas. This is the case in all the Vṛttas. The Bha-Gaṇa has a long syllable as the first (and the other two short); the Ma-Gaṇa has all the three long;

the Ja-Gaṇa has the long syllable in the middle and the Sa Gaṇa a long syllable in the end; the Ra-Gaṇa has a short syllable in the middle the Ta-Gaṇa has its last syllable short; the Ya-Gaṇa has a short-syllable as the first and Na-Gaṇa has all the syllables short. These eight Gaṇas have their origin in Brahmā.

85—86 For the purpose of condensation or for defining the Vṛtta these are used in treatises on prosody.

87 They can be used with or without the Vowel part e.g. a Guru should be known as Ga or G and a Laghu as La or L.

88—89 The regular stop or cessation of a latter to separate words is called Yati (Caesure). A prosodially long vowel is either the long one, the prolated one, one with Anusvāra, Visarga or a conjunct consonant following in or sometimes, even a Laghu when it comes at the end of a Pāda Rules regarding the metre relate to a regular couplet (Sampat), Cessation (Virāma), Pāda (foot) Devata (deity), Sthāna (location), Akṣara (Syllable), Varṇa (Colour), Svara (Accent) and Vidhi and Vṛtta (hyper metric pattern).

Sampat (Regular Couplet)

90 If the number of syllables does does not exceed or fall short of what is stipulated it is called Sampat in this treatise on metres.

Virāma (Stop)

91—97 Where the meaning comes to an end, is mentioned as Virāma (Stop).

Pāda (foot)

This word is derived from the root Pad and it means a fourth of the verse.

Deities. Agni etc. are called the deities.

Location. Sthāna is of two types-one arising from the parts of the body and the other relating to a particular region.

Akṣara (Syllable) is of three kinds Hrasva, Dīrgha and Pluta.

Varṇa (colour) like white etc.

Svara (Pitch, accent). The Svaras are Tāra (high), Mandra (low) and Madhya (medium). I shall explain their characteristics when explaining Dhruvā (Chapter 32)

Vidhi (rules). This is in relation to Gaṇa as well as Artha (theme).

Vṛtta is of three kinds, Sama, Ardharsama and Viṣama.

Nivṛt etc. If a foot is short of a syllable or has one syllable in excess it is called Nivṛt or Bhuruk. If there is a excess of two syllables it is Svarāṭ and if there is deficiency of two syllables it is Virāṭ.

98—102 Three classes should further be known among all the Vṛttas viz. Divya, Divyetara snd Divya Mānuṣa. The first class of Divya consists of Gāyatrī Uṣṇik, Anuṣṭup, Bṛhatī, Triṣṭup and Jagati. Similarly Atijagati Śakvari, Atiśakvari, Aṣṭi, Atyaṣṭi Dhṛti and Atidhṛti belong to the Divetara class. Kṛti Prakṛti, Ākṛti, Vikṛti, Saṁkṛti, Abhikṛti and Utkṛti belong to the Divya Mānuṣa (Semi divine) class.

These are the Chandas which I have now fully dealt with. How these Vṛttas are to be employed in the dramatic performance, you do understand now.

Notes

1 The four types of Abhinaya including that of Vāgabhinaya has been introduced in Chapter Six (See 6—23).

2 Words should be carefully noted not only by the actors but also the playwright. Abhinava Gupta sayṣ—Vāci Yatnastu Kartavyaḥ—Kavinā Nirmāṇa Kāle, Naṭena Prayoga Kāle.

3 The Śāstras are Vāṅmayas; The Vāg is the cause of everything. This is the view of all important Vyākaraṇa experts such as Bhartṛhari and others. See Vākyapadīya—Brahma Kāṇḍa Chanddbhya Eva Prathamametajviśvam Vyavartata etc.

8 In the Prātiśākhyas and earlier Vyākaraṇa treatises the the nomenclature, total number and classification of the Vowels Consonants etc. follows different methods. Pāṇini has given them a standard form and it is followed by all later Grammarians.

10 The term Jihvya is not adopted by later writers who prefer the term Mūrdhanya. But the Taittirīya Prātiśākhya reconciles both. See—Jihvāgreṇa Prativeṣṭya Mūrdhani Ṭavarhasya (II—37)

23 Pañcavidha Nāma Pada—They are (1) Uṇādyanta, (2) Kṛdanta, (3) Taddhitānta, (4) Samāsaja and (5) Śabdānukaraṇa.

26 Pañcaśata Dhātu. According to later Grammarians the number is more—even going to 2000. The grouping of Dhātus into twentyfive is not well known.

The technical terms used by Bharata are different from those of later Vaiyakaraṇas.

16

Chandoviciti (An inquiry into the Varieties of metres

1 *Tanumadhyā.* In the Vṛtta named Tanumadhyā coming under the Gāyatri Chandas (of six syllables in every foot) the first two and the last two are long example.

2. Saṅtyakta Vibhūṣā Bhraṣṭāñjananetrā
Hastārpitagaṇḍā Kim Tvam Tanumadhyā

(meaning) O Slender-waisted one, why have you set aside the ornaments ? Why are your eyes devoid of collyrium ? Why have you kept your cheek resting on the palm ?

3 *Makaraka Sīrṣā.* In the Vṛtta named Makarakaśīrṣā there are four Laghu (Short) syllables at the outset and two Gurus (long) in the end

(Example) 4 Svayamu Payāntaṁ Bhajasi Nakāntam
Bhayakari Kimtvam Makarakaśīrṣā

O terrifying one, are you an alligator headed one ? You do not resort to your husband who has himself come unto you.

5 *Mālati.* The Vṛtta where the second and the fifth are short syllables and all the remaining ones are long, is called Mālatī.

6 Śobhate Baddhyā Ṣaṭpadāviddhayā
Mālatī Mālayā Māninī Līlayā

The woman with feigned anger looks graceful with the Mālatī garland she is wearing where the bees hover round.

7 *Mālanī.* In every foot the second syllble has only one Mātra (i.e. short). That Vṛtta is well known as Mālinī.

8 Snāna Gandha Sragbhirvastra Bhūṣāyogaiḥ
Vyakta Mevāsautvam Mālinī Prakhyātā

It is manifestly clear that you are the well known. Mālinī (female florist) through your garland of sweet scents after the bath, the clothes and jewels.

9 *Uddhatā* If in every foot of seven syllables the second, fourth and the fifth are always short the Vṛtta is called Udonatā.

10 Dantakunta Kṛtāṅkam Vyākulāla Śobham
Śaṃsatīva Tavāsyam Nirdayam Ratayuddham

It is as through your mouth itself indicates an unrelating tussle of love because it has the distinct marks of the spear teeth and has excessive splendour with the forelocks of hair dishevelled.

11 *Bhramara Mālā.* If in each of the feet of seven syllables the first two and the last two syllables be long and the remaining ones short the Vṛtta is called Bhramaramālikā.

12 O dear one, as the Surabhi Month (Caitra) has arrived with diverse kinds of flowers the intoxicated cluster of bees have begun to hover arround.

13 *Siṁhalekhā.* If in each of the feet the first, third, fifth seventh and the last syllable of eight syllables in all were to be long the Vṛtta is called Siṁhalekhā.

14 O lady of splendid limbs, your secret activities with many Bhāvas (Emotional states) have penetrated my mind; the Vṛtta here is Siṁhalekha [it is the behaviour of the writing (with the claws) of the lion].

15 *Mattaceṣṭita* If in the feet of eight syllables the second, the fourth, the sixth and the eighth were to be long the Vṛtta is called Mattaceṣṭita.

16 The beloved lady is behaving like an inebrieted person keeping her restless eyes rolling, the tresses of hairs hanging down dishevelled and the footsteps unsteady.

17 *Vidyullekhā.* If all the eight syllables in a foot were to be long the Vṛtta is called Vidyullekhā.

18 The sky is pervaded by dark clouds rumbling along with the weight of waters this streak of lightning that vies with the sun travels in all directions.

19 *Cittav:lāsita.* If in every foot of eight syllables the fifth, seventh and the last were to be long the Vṛtta is called Cittavilāsita.

20 O lady of fair body, your face over laps the full moon with the teeth appearing due to your smile :

Smitavaśa Viprakāśairdaśanapadairamībhiḥ

Varatanu Pūrṇacandram Tavamukhamāvṛṇoti

21 *Madhukarī.* If in every foot of nine syllables the last three are long the Vṛttə .is called Madhukarī.

22 Kusumitamabhipaśyantī Vividhataru Gaṇaiśchannam
Vanamatiśaya Gandhāḍhyam Bhramati Madhukarī-
Hṛṣṭā

The delighted female bee is hovering round the forest in full bloom seeing it enveloped by diverse clusters of trees and having excellent fragrance.

23 *Utpala Mālā* (Kuvalaya Mālā). If in every foot of ten syllables the three in the beginning and the three in the end are long, the Vṛtta in Paṅkti Chandas is called Utpalamālikā.

24 Asmiṁsteśirasi Tadākānte Vaiḍūryasphaṭika
—Suvarṇāḍhye
Śobhṅm Svām Navahati Tām Baddhā Suśliṣṭā
Kuvalaya Māleyam

O beloved one, this well wreathed garland of Kuvalaya flowers does not have its well known beauty which it had at that time when it was fastened to your head having lapislazuli, quartz and gold.

25 *Mayūrasāriṇī.* If in every foot of ten syllables the second, the fourth, the sixth and the eighth are short it is called Śikhi (Mayūra) Sāriṇī.

26 Naiva Testi Saṅga Momanuṣyirnāpi Kāmabhoga
—Cihnamanyat
Garbhiṇīva Dṛśyase Hyanārye Kim Mayūrasāriṇī
Īvamevam

O lady of no noble features, you have not copulated with men, you do not exhibit signs of sexual enjoyment. Yet you appear to be pregment. Have you adopted the mode of the prefowl ?

27 *Dodhaka.* If in a foot of eleven syllables of the Traiṣṭubha Chandas, the first, the fourth, the seventh, the tenth and the last are long the Vṛtta is called Dodhaka.

28 Praskhalitāgrapada Pravicāram
Mattavighūrṇita Gātra Vilāsaṃ
Paśya Vilāsini Kuñjaram Etam
Dodhaka Vṛttam Ayam Prakaroti ll

O charming lady, look at this elephant which exhibits the behaviour of a Dodhaka (Cub of an elephant ?). The steps of his anteriori legs falter. The body is gracefully shaking as though it is inebriated.

29 *Moṭaka.* If in every foot of eleven syllables the first, the second, the fifth, the eighth and the last are long the Vṛtta is called Moṭaka.

30 Eṣombuda Nisvana Tulya Ravaḥa
Kṣībaḥ Skhalamāna Vilamba Gat l
Śrutvā Ghana Garjitam Adri Taṭe
Vṛkṣān Prati Moṭayati Dviradaḥ ll

On hearing the rumbling sound of the clouds on the ridge of the mountain, this elephant produces a trumpeting sound rivalling with the sound of the clouds. It is excited and its goes ahead with slow faltering steps and then crushes the trees.

31—32 *Indra Vajrā.* You are one unworthy of being looked at. You cannot be pacified easily; you can be won over only with great difficulty; you are exclusively hard of fellings. You are unfit for all states mentioned in the treatises on erotics. Why eleborate ? You are the very thunder bolt of Indra.

Tvam Durnirīkṣyā Durati Prasādā
Dhuḥkhaika Sādhyā Kaṭhinaikabhāvā l
Sarvāsvavasthāsuca Kāmatantre
Yogyāsi Kiṁ Bahunendra Vajrā ll

If in every foot of eleven syllables the third, the sixth, the seventh and the ninth are short the Vṛtta is called Indravajrā.

33 *Upendravajrā* If in every foot of eleven syllables the first, the third, the sixth, the seventh and the ninth are short the Vṛtta is called Upendravajrā.

34 Priye Śriyā Varṇa Viśeṣaṇena
Smitena Kāntyā Sukumārabhāvāt l
Amīguṇā Rūpaguṇā Nurūpā
Bhavanti Te Kim Tvamupendra Vajrā ll

O beloved lady, you are my beloved because of your glory, excellent complexion, smile, splendour and the graceful emotions. These qualities of yours are befitting your beauty of form. Are you akin to Indra Vajra ?

35 *Svāgatā.* If in a foot of eleven syllables the first, the third, the seventh, the seventh and the last are long the Vṛtta is called Svāgatā.

36 Adya Me Saphalam Āyata Netre
Jīvitam Madana Saṁśraya Bhāvam l
Āgatāsi Bhavanam Mama Yasmāt
Svāgatam Tava Varoru Niṣīda ll

O beautiful lady of large eyes, today my life is fruitful with the emotional fervour supported by Madana because you have come to my abode. Welcome to you. Sit here.

37 *Rathoddhatā.* If in a foot of eleven syllables the first, the third, the seventh, the ninth and the last are long the Vṛtta is called Rathoddhatā.

31 Kiṁtvayā Subhaṭa Varjitātamanā
Nātmano Nasuhṛdām Priyam Kṛtam
Yat Palāyana Parāyaṇasya Te
Yāti Dhūli Radhunā Rathoddhatā.

Why O excellent Soldier has neither your own nor your friends good been carried out by you who have neglected your self ? As you are bent upon fleeing the dust rises now scattered by the chariot.

39 *Śālnī.* If in every foot of eleven syllables the sixth and the ninth are short, the Vṛtta is called Śālinī.

40 Āryam Śīlam Sādhvi He Te' Nuvṛttam
Mādhuryāḍhyā Sarvathā Śālinī Tvam
Duśśīlam Vā Nirguṇam Pāpakam Vā
Saumyā Loke Nāpriyam Tvam Bravīṣi

O chaste lady, the noble bahaviour has been followed by you. Endowed with sweetness you are a well behaved housewife. Always gentle you never speak a displeasing word to any one in the word whether he be an impolite fellow, or a sinner devoid of virtues.

41 *Toṭaka.* If in a foot of twelve syllables the third, the sixth, the ninth and the last are long the Vṛtta is called Toṭaka.

42 Kimidam Kapaṭāśraya Durviṣaham
Bahu Śāṭhyamatholbaṇarūkṣakatham
Svajanapriya Sajjana Bhedakaram
Nanutoṭaka Vṛttami Dam Kuru Se

Why is this crooked and unbearable villainous conduct? Why these stubborn and harsh words? Why do you follow the work of cut-throat that creates split between the dear kinsmen and other good people?

43 *Kumudanibhā* If in every foot of twelve syllables the first four ones, the eighth and the tenth are short the Vṛtta is called Kumudanibhā.

44 Kumudanibhā Tvam Kāma Bāṇa viddhā
Kimasi Nata Bhrūḥ Śītavātadagdhā
Mrdunalinīvāpāṇḍu Vaktra Śobhā
Kathmapi Jātā Hyagrataḥ Sakhīnām

O woman of curved eyebrows, tender like the waterlily, why have you become like the delicate lotus assailed by chillness and wind when hit by the arrows of cupid? In front of your friends you have somehow become pale in the colour of your face.

45 *Candralekhā.* If in every foot of twelve syllables, the seventh and the tenth are short and the Yati falls at the end of fifth syllable, the Vṛtta is called Candralekhā.

46 Vaktram Saumyam Te Padmapatrāyatākṣam
Kāmasyāvāsam Subhruvoścāvabhāsam
Kāmasyā Pīdam Kāmamādhartukāmam
Kāntyā Tvam Kānte Candral Ekheva Bhāsi

O beloved one, your gentle face with eyes as large as the petals of the lotus, is the abode of Kāma and brightly illuminatles the excellent brows. It is desirous of generating love even to Kāma. With your splendour you shine like the digit of the moon.

47 *Pramitākṣarā.* If in every foot of twelve syllables the fifth, the ninth and the last are long the Vṛtta is called Pramitākṣarā.

48 Smitabhāṣiṇī Hyacapalā Paruṣā
Nibhṛtā Pavāda Vimukhī Satatam
Yadi Kasyacid Yuvatirasti Sukhā
Pramitākṣarā Sahi Pumān Jayati

If any one has a wife in the prime of youth with the following qualities, indeed that man fares well. She must be smiling when talking; she should not be harsh or fickle; she should not scandalise any one even secretly. She must render him happiness and she must speak only a few measured words.

49 *Vaṁśasthā.* In every foot of twelve syllables in the Jagatī Chandas, the second, the fourth, the fifth, the eighth, the tenth and the last are long. The Vṛtta then is called Vaṁśasthā.

50 Namepriyā Yad Bahumānā Varjitā
Kṛtāpriyā Te Paruṣābhi Bhāṣaṇaiḥ
Tathā Ca Paśyāmyahamadya Vigraho
Dhruvam Hi Vaṁśa-sthagatimkariṣyati.

Since you desist from honouring me you are not any beloved; through your harsh words you have already displeased me. I see that this disfavour will certainly envelope the whole family.

51 *Hariṇa Plutā.* If in every foot of twelve syllables in the Jagatī Chandas the fourth, seventh, tenth and the last are long the Vṛtta is called Hariṇaplutā

52 Paruṣavṇkyavaśābhihatā Tvayā
Bhayavilokana Pārśva Nirīkṣaṇā
Varatanuḥ Pratata Plutasarpaṇair
Anukaroti Gatairhariṇplutam

She has been struk with the whip of your harsh words; in fear she looks over the sides. With her movement of quick steps the lady of excellent physical form thereby imitates the gallop of the deer.

53 *Kāmadattā.* If in every foot of twelve syllables the seventh, the ninth, the penultimate one and the last one are long the Vaṛtta is called Kāmadattā.

54 O fawn eyed one, you are indeed given over to Kāma; since you are adorned with the imprints of nails; O lady of excellent teeth your lips have been wounded by some one's teeth; your gait is faltering and slow.

55 *Aprameyā.* If in every foot of twelve syllables of the Jagatī Chandas, the first, the fourth, the seventh and the tenth are short the Vṛtta is called Aprameyā.

56 Nate Kācidanyā Samā Dṛśyate Strī
Nṛlok Viśiṣṭā Guṇairadvītīyaiḥ
Trilokyām Guṇāgryān Samāhṛtya Sarvān
Jagatyaprameyāsti Sṛṣṭā Vidhātrā

In the world of the mortals no other woman is seen on a par with you or superior to you by means of unparalleled good qualities. After gathering together all the excellent achievements in the three worlds you have been created by Brahmā as one who is incomprehensible in the world (Aprameyiā in Jagati Chandas).

57 *Padminī* If in every foot of twelve syllables the sccond, the fifth, the eighth and the eleventh are short the Vṛtta is called Padmini.

58 Deha Toyāśayā Vaktra Padmojvalā
Netra Bhṛṅgākulā Danta Haṁsaiḥsmitā
Keśa Patracchadā Cakravāka Stanī
Padminīva Priye Bhāsi Mesorvadā

O dear lady, you always seem to me like a lotus lake; your body is a pool of water, shining by your lotus like face; your eyes are the resltercss bees, you smile with swanlike teeth and your hairs are akin to the lotus leaves and the breasts are like the ruddy geese.

59 *Puṭavṛtta* If in every foot of twelve syllables of the Jagati Chandas, the initial six ones, and the the tenth one are short and the rest long the Vṛtta is called Puṭavṛtta.

60 The month of full blown flowers indicates the pairing activity of the loving damsels through the tender lotuses in the waters of the park; the chirping songs of the bees and the Cuckoos and the graceful movements of the loveable ladies.

61 *Prabhāvatī.* If in every foot of thirteen syllables in the Atijagati Chandas, the second, the fourth, the ninths, the

eleventh and the last are long the Vṛtta is called Prabhāvati. There is Yati at the end of four syllables.

62 Katham Navidam Kamalaviśālalocane
Gṛham Ghanaiḥ Pihitakare Niśākare
Acintayantyabhinava Varṣavidyutas—
Tvamāgatā Sutanu Yathā Prabhāvatī

How is it that, O lady of excellent physical form, you have, like a lustrous one, come to this house, when the moon has been enveloped by the clouds without minding in the least the fresh down-pour and streeks of lightning ?

63 *Praharṣiṇī* If in every foot of thirteen syllables in the Atijagati Chandas the first three ones, the eightth, the tenth and the last two ones are long and there is Yati at the end of three syllables (in the beginning) the Vṛtta is called Praharṣiṇī.

64 Bhāvasthairmadhhura Kathaiḥ Subhāṣitaistvam
Sāṭopakhali Tavilambitairrataiśca !
Śobhāḍhyairharasi Manāṁsi Kāmukānām
Suvyaktam Hyati Jagatī Praharṣiṇī Ca

O lady, it is very clear that you are extremely enrapturing far ahead of the entire world sincc through your loving and sweet words, wise utterances, majestically graceful and faltering slow steps you attract the minds of the lovers.

65 *Mattamayūra*. If in every foot of thirteen syllables the sixth, seventh, tenth and eleventh are short the Vṛtta should be known as Mattamayūraka.

66 Vidyunnaddhā Ssendradhanūrañjita Dehā
Vātoddhūtāḥ Śvetabalākakṛta Śobhāḥ
Ete Meghā Garjitanā Dojvalacinhāḥ
Prāvṛṭkālammattama Yūram Kathayanti

These clouds characterised by the reverberations of thunder and splendid signs consisting of lightning and rainbow are lashed about by the wind. Adorned with white cranes they proclaim the rainy season abounding in intoxicated peacocks.

Vasantatilakā. If in every foot of fourteen syllables in Śakvari Chandas, the initial two syllables the fourth, the eighth, the eleventh and the final two syllables are long, the Vṛtta is clalled Vasantatilaka.

68 Citrairvasantakusumaiḥ Kṛta Keśa Hastā
Sragdāma Mālya Racanā Suvibhū Ṣitāṅgī
Nānā Vataṁsaka Vibhūṣita Karṇapāśa
Sākṣād Vasantatilakeva Vibhāti Nārī

Indeed this woman appears like the Tilaka (mark of adornment on the forehead) of the goddess of the spring season for she has embellished her hoard of hairs with the spring blooms of different colours; the body with various kinds of wreaths and the ears with diverse kinds of jewels.

69 *Asaṁbādhā* If in every foot of fourteen syllable the first five and the last three are long and the Yati is at the end of the fifth syllable the Vṛtta is called Asaṁbādhā.

70 Mānī Lokajñaḥ Śrutabalakula Śīlāḍhyo
Yasmin Sammānamna Sadṛśam Anupaśyeddhi
Gaccet Tam Tyaktvā Drutagatiraparam Deśam
Kīrṇā Nānārthairavaniriyamasambādhā

A self-respecting person conversant with the affairs of the world who happens to possess learning, prowess, good behaviour and parentage shall leave off that land where he does not find a befitting honour and go to another land. Indeed this earth is scattered over with riches of diverse kinds and is devoid of congestion.

71 *Śarabhā* If in every foot of fourteen syllables in the Śakvarī Chandas the initial four ones the tenth, the eleventh and the last two ones are long the Vṛtta is called Śarabhā.

72 Eṣākāntā Vrajati Lalitam Vepamānā
Gulmacchannam Vanamurunagai Hsampraviddham
Hāhākaṣṭam Kimidamiti No Vedmi Mūḍho
Vyaktam Karodhāccharabhalalitamkartukāmā

This beloved one goes gracefully but shivering to the sybran region infested with shrubs and great trees. I am foolish not to know why ? It is indeed a pity. Apparently she is desirous of playing the funny frolics of the cub of an elephant.

73 *Nāndīmukhī.* If in every foot of fifteen syllables in the Atiśakvarī Chandas, the six initial ones, the tenth and the thirteenth are short the Vṛtta is called Nāndīuukhī.

74 Nakhalu Tavakdācit Krodhatāmrāyātākṣam
Bhrukuṭi Valita Bhaṅgam Dṛṣṭapūrvammayāsyam

Kimiha Bahubhiruktairyāmamasihāhṛdisthā
Tvamasi Madhura Vākyā Devi Nāndīmukhīva

Never before have I seen your face with eyes red in ire with knitted eyebrows in frowning. O noble lady, of what avail is uttering too much. Are you the selfsame sweet voiced one residing in my heart like Nāndīmukhī (auspicious faced).

75 *Gajavilasita.* If in every foot of sixteen syllables the first, the fourth, the sixth and the last are long the Vṛtta is called Gajavilasita.

76 Toyadharaiḥ Sudhīraghanapaṭupaṭaharavaiḥ
Sarja Kadamba Nīpakuṭaja Kusuma Surabhim
Kandala Sendragopakaracitamavanitalam
Vīkṣya Karotya Sau Vṛṣabhagaja Vilasitakam

On seeing the upper layer of the earth embellished with the Kandala and Indragopa flowers and rendered fragrant through the flowers of Sarja, Kadamba, Nīpa and Kuṭaja blooming thanks to the loud and drumlike peals of thunder this fellow mimics the playful movement of the bull elephant.

77 *Pravara Lalita.* If in every foot of sixteen syllables the five ones after the first, the twelfth, the thirteenth and the last two ones are long the Vṛtta is called Pravara Lalita

78 Nakhālīḍham Gātram Daśana Khacitam Coṣṭhagaṇḍam
Śiraḥ Puṣponmiśram Pravilulitakeśālakāntam
Gatiḥ Khinnā Ceyam Vadanamapi Sambhrāntanetram
Tvaho Ślaghyam Vṛttam Pravara Lalitam Kāmaceṣṭam

The body has been pierced with nails; the lips and the cheeks have been bitten by teeth; the head is covered with flowers; the tips of hairs and forelocks are dishevelled; her gaint is painfully longuid; the face is disturbed with rolling eyes. Ah, the love dalliance has taken place in an extremely graceful and praise worthy manner.

79 *Śikhariṇī* If in every foot of seventeen syllables, the five ones after the first, the twelfth, the thirteenth and the last are long the Vṛtta is called Śikhariṇī.

80 Mahānandyābhoge Pulinam Ivatebhāti Jaghanm
Tathāsyam Netrābhyām Bhramara Sahitam Paṅkaja-
miva
Tanusparśaścāyam Sutanusukumāro Na Paruṣaḥ
Stanābhyām Tuṅgābhyām Śikhariṇi Mamā Bhāsi,
Dayite

Your hip is on a par with the sand bank at the extensive edge of the river; the face with the eyes resembles the lotus with fees; the touch of your body is soft not rough; with your elevated breasts. O lady, you appear to me like the hall with peaks

81 *Vṛṣabha Ceṣṭita.* If in every foot of seventeen syllables, the five intial ones, the eleventh, the thirteenth the fourteenth and the sixteenth are long the Vṛtta is called Vṛṣabha Ceṣṭita.

82 Jaladaninadam Śrutvagarjan Madoccaya Darpitaḥ
Pralikhati Mahīm Śṛṅgakṣepair Vṛṣaḥpratinardyaca
Svayuvativṛtogoṣṭhād Goṣṭham Prayāti Ca Nirbhayo
Vṛṣabhalalitam Citramvṛttam Karoti Ca Śādvale

On hearing the rumbling round of the clouds, the bull haughty at the peak of its rut strikes the earth with its horns and bellows in return. Surrounded by his young females (Cows) it goes undaunted from one coupen to another. In the green pasture land it exhibits the wonderfully variegated exploits of a bull.

83—83A *Śrīdharā* If in every foot of seventeen syllables the four initial ones, the tenth, the eleventh, the thirteenth, the fourteenth and the last are long and the remaining ones short the Vṛtta should be known by the name Śridharā.

84 Snānaiścūrṇaiḥ Sukha Surabhibhir Gaṇḍalepaiśca
Daūpaiḥ
Pūṣpaiścānyaḥ Sirasi Racitairveastra Yogaiścataistaiḥ
Nānāratnaiḥkanaka Racitairaṅga Sambhogasamsthair
Vyaktam Kānte Kamalanilayā Śrīdharevāti Bhāsi

Oh my beloved one, you indeed shine like the goddess of beauty residing in the lotus, by means of your ablutions, the scented powders, the pleasantly sweet smilling paste applied to the cheeks, the incense vapours, the different jewels set in gold, the flowers and other things embellishing the head, the various garments all readily adjusted for enjoyment in the limbs.

85 *Vamśapatra Patita*. If in every foot of seventeen syllable the first, the fourth, the sixth, the tenth and the last are long the Vṛtta is called Vamśapatra Patita, the yati falls on the tenth and the seventh (thereafter).

O beautiful lady, this elephant surrounded by cubs is playing near the ridge of the mountain in the thick forest of trees and shrubs drooping down with the weight of blossoms. It is delighted to bear the rumbling of the clouds. Like the swift blast of wind it causes the fall of the bamboo leaves.

87—87A *Vilambitagati*. If in every foot of seventeen syllables the second, the sixth, the eighth, the twelfth, the fourteenth and the last are long and the remaining ones are short, the Vṛtta should be known Vilambitagati by name.

88 Vighūrṇita Vilocanā Pṛthuvikīrṇahārā Punaḥ
Praḷambaraśanā Calat Skhalita Pādamandakramā
Namepriyamidam Janasya Bahumānarāgeṇa Yan-
Madena Vivaśā Vilambitagatiḥ Kṛtātvam Priye

O beloved one you have your eyes rolling; the necklace has got diplaced; the girdle is slipping down; your slow steps falter. Is this not pleasing to me that you have been made helpless with slow gait by the intoxication due to the honour and love of the people.

89 *Citralekhā*. If in every foot of eighteen syllables, the five initial ones, the eleventh, the twelfth, the fourteenth, the fifteenth, the eleventeenth and the last are long the Vṛtta in the Dhṛti Chandas is called Citralekhā.

90 Nānāratnāḍhyair Bahubhiradhikam Bhuṣaṇairaṅga Saṁsthaiḥ
Nānāgandhāḍhyaırmadana Jananairaṅgaiśca Hṛdyaiḥ
Keśaiḥ Snānārdraiḥ Kusuma Bharitair Vastra Rāgaiśca-Taistaiḥ
Kānte Saṁkṣepāt Kimihababahunā Citra Lekheva Bhāsi

O beloved one, you are resplendent with the different ornaments worn on your body, various unguents rich in love provoking scents, hairs wet after bath and embellished with flowers and the clothes of different colour. Why need I say more ? Succinctly put,you appear like one painted in a picture.

91–92 *Śārdūlavikrīḍita.* If in every foot of nineteen syllables the initial three ones, the sixth, the eighth, the twelfth, the thirteenth, the fourteenth, the sixteenth, the seventeenth and the last are long the Vṛtta is called Śārdūlavikrīḍitan.

93 Nānāśastraśataghnitomarahatāḥ Prabhraṣṭasarvā-
yudhāḥ
Nirbhinnodarapāda Bāhuvadanā Nirbhartāssatravaḥ
Dhairyatsāha Parākrama Prabhṛtibhistaistairvi
Citrairguṇaiḥ
Vṛttamteripughāti Bhāti Samare Śārdūlavikrīḍitam

The enemies have been repulsed after many have been killed with weapons of diverse kinds such a Śataghnī and Tomara, with their stomachs, hands, feet and faces pierced and being deprived of all their weapons. Your exploits in the battle are akin to those of the tiger, destructive of the enemies and distinguished by those excellant virtues such as bravery, enthusiasm, valour etc.

94—95 *Suvadanā.* If in every foot of twenty syllables in the Kṛti Chandas the four initial ones, the sixth, the seventh, the fourteenth, the fifteenth, the sixteenth and the last are long Vṛtta is called Suvadanā.

96 Netre Līlālasānte Kamaladalanibhe Bhrūcāparucire
Gaṇḍoṣṭham Pīna Madhyam Samasahitaghanāḥ-
Snigdhāśca Daśanāḥ
Karṇavaṁsa Pralambau Cibukamapi Natam Ghoṇā
Surucirā
Vyaktam Tvam Martya Loke Varatanu Vihitāsyekā
Suvadanā

Your eyes resemble the petals of the lotus, the bowlike brows enhancing its beauty and the ends thereof being grace fully lazy, the cheeks and the lips are plump in their middle, the teeth are all equal in a line, thickly set and shining; the ears are suspended down as it were as far as the shoulders the chin is bent and the nose is beautiful. O fair lady you are certainly the only fair faced lady whose face has been skilfully fashioned.

97 *Sragdharā.* If in every foot of twenty one syllables, the four initial ones the sixth, the seventh the fourteenth, the fifteenth, the seventeenth, the eighteenth the last two ones are

long and the remaining ones short, the Vṛtta is called Sragdharā.

99 Cūtāśokāravindaiḥ Kuravakatilakaiḥ Karṇikāraiḥ Śirīṣaiḥ
Punnāgaiḥ Pārijātairvakula Kuvalayaiḥ Kiṁśukaiḥ Sātimuktaiḥ
Eiairnānā Prakāraiḥ Kusumasurabhibhir- Viprakīrṇaiśca Taistair
Vāsantaiḥ Puṣpavṛndairnaravara Vasudhā Sragdharevādya Bhāti

O the most excellent are among men, the earth now looks like a lady wearing garlands as the following sweet smelling flowers are scattered around viz. Cūta, Aśoka, Aravinda, Kuravaka, Tilaka, Karṇikāra, Śirīṣa, Punnāga, Pārijāta, Vakula, Kiṁśuka and Atimukta.

100—101 *Madraka.* If in every foot of twenty two syllables, the first, the fourth, the sixth, the tenth, the twelfth, the sixteenth, the eighteenth, and the last are long and the rest short the Vṛtta is called Madraka.

102 Udyatam Ekahasta Caraṇam Dvitīyakara Recitam Suvinatam
Vaṁśa Mṛdaṅga Vādya Madhuram Vicitrakaraṇān- vitam Bahu Vidham
Madrakam Etadadya Subhagair vidagdhagaticeṣṭitairi Sulalitair
Nṛtyasi vibhramākulapadam viviktara Sabhāvitam Śaśimukhi

O moon faced one, to the accompaniment of sweet sounds of flutes and drums you perform the Madraka dance, raising one of your hands and bending the other and keeping the feet resltess in clever movements of great grace; you are making happy clever and graceful movements following the many Karaṇas of diverse kinds. Thus this dance is imbibed with distinct Rasas.

103—104 *Aśvalalita.* If in every foot of twentythree syllables in the Vikṛti Chandas, the seventeenth, the nineteenth and the last are long and the remaining ones are short, the Vṛtta should be known by learned men as Aśvalalita in name.

105 Vividhaturaṅga Nāgaratha Yodhasaṅkulam Alam
Balaṁsamuditam
Śaraśata Śakti Kuntaparighāsiyaṣṭivitatam Bahupraha
Raṇam
Ripuśata Mukta Śastra Ravabhītaśaṅkita Bhaṭam
Bhayākulamidam
Kṛtamabhivīkṣya Samyugamukhe Samīpsita
Guṇam Tvayāśvalalitam

Even after observing this perfectly assembled army comprising many horses, elephants, chariots and soldiers the numerous attacks effected by hundreds of arrows, spears, javelins, maces and swords, the infantry terrified on account of the loud report of the discharged missiles, you have practised in the vanguard the equestrian sportful activities the qualities whereof are appreciated.

106—107 *Meghamālā* If in every foot of twenty four syllables the six initial ones, the eighth, the eleventh. the fourteenth, the seventeenth, the twentieth and twenty third are short and the remaining ones are long the vṛtta is called Meghamālā.

108 Pavana Javasamāhṛtā Tīvragambhīra Nādā
Balākāvalī Mekhalā
Kṣitadhara Sadṛśoccarūpā Mahānīladhū-
Māñjanābhāmbu Garbhodvahā
Surapati Dhanurujvalā Baddhakakṣyā
Taḍiddyotasannāhapaṭṭojvalā
Gagana Tala visārṇī Prāvṛṣeṇyā Dṛḍham Meghamala
Dhikamśobhate

The mass of clouds of the rainy season has been carried over by the force of the gust of wind; it has a deep and piercing sound; lt has a flight of cranes to make up its girdle; it is huge and massive like a mountain; it has the lustre of the extremely blue-coloured smoke and collyrium; it carries within it plenty of water, the rainbow acts as its dazzling girdle; it has its armour plates illuminated by the streak of lightning; it spreads all over the sky certainly it shines very much.

109—110 *Krauñca Pādī.* If in every foot of twenty five syllables, the first, the fourth, the sixth the ninth, the tenth and the last are long and the remaining ones are short that should be known by the name Krauñca Pādī by those conversant with Vṛttas.

111 May the lord who is the enemy of the group of Daityas and who destroyed the sacrifice of Dakṣa in the following manner burn the entire host of the enemies like that sacrifice : He caused the Soma juice to be spilled everywhere; the Camasa was taken away, the Kalaśa was removed; the Yūpa was made to fall down, the Caṣāla was disrupted the Cayana was disturbed; the five was extinguished; the sacrificial animals were driven away; the Caru was removed; with the arrow discharged from his bow he quickly drove away the groups of Devas and Pitṛs.

112—113 *Bhujaṅga Vijṛmbhita.* If in every foot of twenty six syllables, the eight initial ones, the nineteenth, the twenty first, the twenty fourth and the last are long and the remaining ones are short the Vṛtta is called Bhujaṅga Vijṛmbhita

114 Rūpopetām Devaiḥ Sṛṣṭām Samadagajavilasitagtim
Nirīkṣyatilottamām
Prādakṣiṇyāt Prāptām Draṣṭumbahuvadanam
Acalanayanam Śirahkṛtavān Haraḥ
Dīrgham Niśśvasyāntargūḍham Stanavadanajaghana
Rucirām Nirīkṣya Tathāpunaḥ
Pṛṣṭhe Nyastam Devendreṇa Pravaramaṇikanaka
Valayam Bhujaṅgavijṛmbhitam

On seeing Tilottamā the beautiful one created by the Devas, whose gait had the graceful movement of an elephant in rut and who had come near in the course of her cricumambulation, Śiva made his head motionless and kept the eyes in all the faces steady to look at her. Looking at her again at the beauty of her breasts, mouth and hips be began to heave a sigh silently. Thereafter a gold bangle set with excellent gems and displayed by the serpents was placed (on her) back by the lord of the Devas.

The Viṣama and the Ardha Sama metres

115 O excellant Branmins there are Samavṛttas which have been explained by me so far. I shall now explain the characteristic features of the Viṣama (Uneven) and the Ardhasama (Semi-even) metres.

116—118 If in a verse the different feet consist of different metres the Vṛtta thereof is called Viṣama. In Ardhaviṣama Vṛtta two feet are disimilar and two are dissimilar. If all the feet are dissimilar, the Vṛtta is called Viṣama (Uneven). The Semieven metre is to have its even and odd feet dissimlar and the first of such groups of feet may be shorter or longer than the rest or one of them may be longer and the other shorter than the rest.

119 If one foot is defined the Sama (even) metre can be known while all the feet should be defined to know the Viṣama fully. By the definition of the two (different) feet, the semi even (Ardhasama) metre can be understood. This is the division of the feet.

120 I have described the Sama Vṛttas in regard to their divisions of feet. Henceforth I shall describe the characteristics of Viṣama Vṛttas by means of Trikas (Units of three syllables)

121 *Pathya.* If in every foot of eight syllables the first one contains 2 "Sa" Gannas and 2 long syllables and the second foot a 'Sa' Gaṇa, a "Ra" Gaṇa and short and a long syllable it should be known as Pathyā. The third and the fourth feet will be also like the above.

122 Priyadaivatamitrāsi Priya Samsandhibāndhavā
Privadānaratā Pathyā Dayitetvam Priyāsime

Deities and friends you like, Kinsmen and those related to you by matrimonial alliance are loved by you. You are aggreeable and are also found of making gifts. Hence O beloved one you are dear to me.

123 *Sarvaviṣamapathyā.* (Uneven) The first foot contains "Ma" Gaṇa and "Ra" Gaṇa and two long syllables; the second foot Ya, Sa, short and long; the third foot Ra, Bha, short and long the fourth Ja, Sa, Short and long. This is all uneven Pathyā.

124 Naivā Cāro Natemitram Na Sambandhi Guṇākriyā
Sarvathā Sarvaviṣamā Pathyā Na Bhavasi Priye

You do not practise good conduct; you have no friend; Your action is not decent in regard to relatives. In every respect you are rude; O beloved one you are one agreeable to me.

125 *Viparīta Pathyā.* The characteristics of the Ayuj when made contrary becomes the characteristics of the Viparīta Pathya i.e. the second and the fourth being of this description.

126 Kṛtena Ramaṇasya Kim Sakhi Roṣeṇatepyartham
Viparītā Na Pathyāsi Tvam Jaḍekenmohitā

O friend, of what avail is the anger perpetrated against the lover ? O foolish one, by whom have you been deluded ? Being antagonistic you are not agreeable.

127 *Capalā.* If in the first and the third feet there are three short syllables after the fourth one that Vṛtta should be known as Anuṣṭup Capalā.

128 If seventh syllable is short in the Yuk (i.e. 2nd and 4th feet) it should be known as *Vipulā.* In the opinion of some the seventh in every foot is short.

129 *Example for Capalā*

Nakhalvasyāḥ Priyatamaḥ Śrotavyamvyāhṛtam (Sakhyā)
Nāradasya Pratikṛtiḥ Kathyate Capalā Hīyam

He is not this girl's dearest lover. What should have been heard has been uttered by the female companion. This fickle one is said to be an image of Nārada (a quarrel monger).

130 *Example of Vipulā*

Saṁkṣiptā Vajravan Madhye Hemakumbhanibhastanī l
Vipulāsi Priyeśroṇyām Pūrṇa Candranibhānane ll

In the waist you are slender like Vajra, O beloved one with breasts resembling gold pot. You are expansive in your hips O beloved one with the face resembling the full moon.

131 *Another example*

Gaṅgeva Meghopagame Hyāplāvitavasundharā l
Kūlavṛkṣānā Rujatī Sravantī Vipulācalāt ll

You are like Gaṅgā when the clouds begain to arrive. Indeed you flood the earth, destroy the trees on the banks and flow down from a big mountain.

132 The feet of Pathyā can thus be of various kinds; in the remaining varieties of Anṣṭup even the odd and even feet can be made up with other Gaṇas of units of three syllables.

133 In this metre a Gaṇa ending with a long syllable (i.e. Ma, Ra, Ya and Sa Gaṇas) or a Gaṇa solely consisting of short syllables (i.e. Na Gaṇa) is not recommended after the first syllable. A short syllable is prescribed after the fourth one.

134 If in the Pathyā Pāda there are three long syllables at the end it is called (Pathyā) Vaktra by learned men.

135 Dantaksatādharamsubhru Jāgaraglāna Netrāntam
Rati Sambhoga Khinnam Te Darśanīyataram Vaktram

O fair lady of excellent eyebrows, thy lips are bitten by the teeth; eyes are lanquid in the extremities due to keeping awake; though exhausted after love play your face has become more charming

136 These are Sarvviṣama metres of the Anuṣṭup class. There is disagreement among those coversant with them in respect to the arrangement of the Gaṇas and syllables.

137 *Vānavāsika*. The metre where every foot consists of sixteen Mātrās as parts of Gāthā to be divided into four sections is called Vānavāsikā.

138 Asaṁsthitapadā Suvihvalāṅgī
Madaskhalita Ceṣṭairmanojñā
Kvayāsyasi Varoru Suratakāle
Viṣamā Kim Vāna Vāsikā Tvam

Where do you proceed to at the time of sexual dalliance, fair lady with unsteady gaits, overagitated limbs and faltering movements due to ardent passion, though you are extremely charming ? Have you become a perverse woman residing in the forest (Vānavāsikā).

139 *Ketumatī* The first and the third feet consist of the Gaṇas Sa, Ja, Sa and a long syllable the second and fourth of the Gaṇas Bha, Ra, Na and a long syllable. This Vṛtta is called Ketumatī.

140 Sphuritā Dharam Cakitanetram
Raktakapola Mambujadalākṣam
Kimidamruṣāpahṛta Śobham
Ketumatī Samam Vada Mukhamte

Your lips quiver. The eyes resembling the petals of the lotus are stunned. The cheeks are red. Due to anger your face is bereft of its splendour. Tell me why your face appears like the flame of fire.

141 *Aparavaktra* If the first and third feet consist of two 'Na' Gaṇas, 'Ra' Gaṇa, a short and a long syllable and the second and the fourth feet consist of 'Na' Gaṇa, two 'Ja' Gaṇas and a 'Ra' Gaṇa the Vṛtta is called Aparavaktra.

142 Sutanu Jalaparīta Lobanam
Jalada Niruddham Ivendumaṇḍalam
Kimidan Apara Vaktram Evate
Śaśi Vadanèdya Mukham Parāṅmukham

O moon faced lady, why is your face reverted now ? It has eyes filled with tears as though the moon's disc is obscured by the clouds. Is your face another one ?

143 *Puṣpitāgrā*

In Puṣpitāgrā metre the first and the third feet consist of two 'Na' Gaṇas, a 'Ra' Gaṇa and a 'Ya' Gaṇa. The second and the fourth feet consist of a 'Na' Gaṇa, two 'Ja' Gaṇas, a 'R' Gaṇa and a long syllable.

144 Pavanaraya Vidhūta Cāruśākham
Pramudita Kokila Kaṇṭha Nādaramyam
Madhukara Parigīyamāna Sabdam
Varatanu Paśya Vanam Supuṣpitāgram

O fair lady look at the top of the forest in full bloom. The beautiful branches of the trees are shaken by the gust of wind. It is rendered charming by the full throated songs of the joyous cuckoos. The humming sound of the bees appear like songs being sung.

145 *Udgatā.* In the Udgatā metre the first foot consists of 'Sa' 'Ja' 'Sa' and short syllable; the second foot of 'Na', 'Sa', 'Ja' and a long syllable; the third of 'Bha', 'Na', 'Ja' and a short syllable and a long syllable and the fourth of 'Sa', 'Ja', 'Sa', Ja and a long syllable.

146 Tava Roma Rajirati Bhāti
Sutanu Madanasya Mañjarīm
Nābhikamala Vivarotpatitā
Bhramarāvalīva Kusumāt Samugatā

O lady of good physical form, the cluster of hairs coming out of the cavity of the lotus like navel is on a par withthe

Swarm of bees coming out of the flower. It exceeds in lustre the blossoms of Kāma Deva.

147 The first foot Consists of Sa, Ja, Sa and a short syllable; the second foot of Na, Sa, Ja and a long syllable; the third foot of two 'Na's and two "Sa"s and the fourth foot of Sa, Ja, Sa, Ja and a long syllable.

148 O lady, you are resplendenl though fatigued by the sexual dalliance; your face has the splendour of the blooming lotus. Hurriedly but gracefully you tuck up the excellent clothes and move your sprout like hands.

149 These are Vṛttas of both Sama and Viṣama types to be employed by poets in the Drama and other forms of poetical compositions.

150 Besides these there are many other Vṛttas which have been collectively grouped here. They are not to be employed because they are lacking in lustre.

151 Those Vṛttas left out here may be employed in songs. I shall describe their detailed classifications while treating the Dhruvās.

152 Thus the characteristic features of the Vṛttas have been succinctly explained by me. Henceforth I shall mention the characteristic features of the Āryās.

153 The Āryā metre has been grouped into five divisions (1) Pathyā (2) Vipulā (3) Capalā (4) Mukha Capalā and (5) Jaghana Capalā.

154 Now I shall speak about their Yati and division of Mātrās and their varieties as well as the difference due to Guru and Laghu.

155 Yatī is to be considered as the severance, the Gaṇas have four Mātrās. Of the feet the second and the fourth are Yuks (even ones) and the first and the third are Ayuks (odd ones).

156 In an Āryā metre the odd Gaṇas consisting of four Mātrās should have no "Ja" Gaṇa and the even Gaṇas may be of any type according to the wish of the poet.

157 The sixth Gaṇa may be of two alternative types and the last one has only one Mātrā. The sixth Gaṇa in the latter half will have only one Mātrā.

158 In one alternative the sixth Gaṇa will be 'Ja' Gaṇa and in the other it will consist of four short syllables and these are related to Yati.

159 The Yati many occur when the second short syllable after the fifth Gaṇa has been completed or it may occur from first syllable or after the fifth Gaṇa is completed.

160 *Pathyā Āryā & Vipulā Āryā.* The Āryā metre where Yati occurs after the three Gaṇas (i.e. at the end of a Pāḍa) is called Pathyā. The Vipulā is distinct from this only in this matter that there is no Yati in it any where

161 *Pathyā Āryā*

Raktamṛdupadamanetrāhyasita Ḍīṛghabahula-
Mṛdukeśī

Kasya Na Pṛthumṛdu Jaghanātanubāhvaṁsodarī
Pathyā

To whom is not agreeable a lady with beautiful soft eyes resembling lotus, long profusely growing black hairs, large and soft hips, slender arms shoulders and belly ?

162 *Vipulā Āryā*

Vipulajaghana Vadanastananayanais Tāmrādharoṣṭha-
Kara Caraṇaiḥ

Āyatanāsāgaṇḍairlalāṭakarṇaḥ Śubhākanyā l

A maiden is splendid when her hips, face, breasts and eyes are large, lips, palms and feet are red and nose, cheeks, forehead and ears are prominent.

163 *Capalā Āryā.* Where the second and the fourth Gaṇas are the ones with the long syllable in the middle in both the halves the Vṛtta should be known as Capalā.

164 Udbhartṛgāminī Paruṣabhāṣinī
Kāma Cinha Kṛta Veṣā
Jānīhi Māṁsasaktā
Surāpriyā Sarvataś Capalā

The woman who goes against the wishes of her husband, who speaks rudely and harshly, who dresses herself with prominent signs of lust & who is fond of meat and liquor is inconstant in every way.

165 Mukha Capalā—Jaghana Capalā

If the first half of the verse has all the characteristics of of Capalā it is called Mukha Capalā. If the same pertains to the second half alone it is called Jaghana Capalā.

166 Hāryā Mukhetu Capalā Tathāpi
Caryā Na, Me Yataḥ Sā Tu
Dakṣā Gṛhakṛtyeṣu Tathā
Duḥkhe Bhavati Duḥkhārtā

My wife is talkative but her general behaviour is not bad because she is clever at household duties and becomes unhappy if I am miserable.

167 Vara Mṛganayane Capalāsi
Varoru Śaśāṅka Darpana Nibhāsye
Kāmasya Sārabhū Tena
Pūrṇa Mada Cāru Jaghanena

O lady of excellant thighs, with the eyes of the most excellent deer; O lady of moon like face resembling the mirror with the hips that can be called the quant essence of love and that are beautiful with the utmost intoxication you are really in constant.

168 If these characteristics are seen in both the halves that Vṛtta is to be known by those conversant with prosody as Sarvataś Capalā.

169 The first and the third feet should have twelve Mātrās, the second Pāda has eighteen Mātrās and the fourth one fifteen Mātrās.

170 Poetical compositions should be produced thus with these Metres explained thus as arising from the diverse Chandas. These Kāvyas should have the thirty six characteristic features.

Notes

2 In Nāṭya Śāstra the explanatory verses themselves are the examples of the metres defined such is the case in Vṛtta-Ratnākara and other well known works on prosody. Separate examples are also given under each definition.

7 The Mālinīvṛtta is different from the metre of that name explained by Piṅgala and others. The fifteen syllabled Mālinī of the later authors is called by the name Nandimukhi in Nāṭya Śāstra. Verses 73—74.

The Guru Laghu analysis of the Vṛttas is not given by us separately as that can be understood from any elementary treatise on prosody. Difference in the nomenclature of the Vṛttas is also not pointed out here for the same reason.

26 It is well known that peacocks, crows etc. among birds, elephants, lions etc. among animals do not copulate in the open (like cocks, dogs etc.)

28 Dodhaka we have translated as cub of an elephant following certain authors. But it is doubtful. There is a Vedic root Duḍḍ to injure or tease. Can Dodhaka mean one who teases"?

59 Puṭavṛtta is often written as Paṭuvṛtta

68 Srak and Mālya are usually translated "Garland" but Sraks are really cheplets worn on the head and Mālyas wreaths round the neck.

164 Jānihi seems to be the correct form and not Jānāti.

17

Kāvyalakṣaṇa (Characteristics of a Poetical Work)

1—5 The thirty six characteristic features of Kāvyabandha (poetical composition—here dramatic composition) are as follows :—(1) Bhūṣaṇa (ornateness) (2) Akṣara Saṅghāta compact non-brevity) (3) Śobhā (Brilliance) (4) Udāharaṇa (Example—Parallelism) (5) Hetu (causation) (6) Saṁśaya (Hesitation-doubt) (7) Dṛṣṭānta (precedent) (8) Prāpti (discovery-attainment) (9) Abhiprāya (fancy) (10) Nidarśana (Unfavourable precedent) (11) Nirukta (convincing explanation) (12) Siddhi (Persuasion) (13) Viśèṣaṇa (Distinction) (14) Guṇātipāta (Accusation of virtue) (15) Atiśaya (Excellence) (16) Tulyatarka (Inference from similitude) (17) Padoccaya (Multiplex predication) (18) Diṣṭa (Description) (19) Upadiṣṭa (Pointed utterance) (20) Vicara (Deliberation) (21) Viparyaya (Inversion) (22) Bhraṁśa (Slip of the tongue) (23) Anunaya (Mediation) (24) Mālā (Series of offers) (25) Dākṣiṇya (Clever manner) (26) Garhaṇa (Censure) (27) Arthāpatti (Presumption) (28) Prasiddhi (Celebrity) (29) Pṛcchā (Interrogation), (30) Sārūpya (Identity) (31) Manoratha (Indirect Expression of mental desire (32) Leśa (Wit) (33) Saṁkṣepa (Concealment) (34) Guṇakīrtana (Enumeration of merits) (35) Jñeyā-Bhyanukta siddhi (Semi-uttered Expression) and (36) Priyam Vacanam (Compliment).

6 Bhūṣaṇa (ornateness) is that quality whereby the composition is rendered beautiful with many figures of speech and Guṇas like jewels etc. by projecting many meanings.

7 *Akṣarasaṅghāta.* (Compactness-Brevity) A wonderful sense is conveyed through a small number of syllables with double entendie. This is called compactness (Akṣarasaṅghata). The literal sense of the term is a group of syllables).

8 *Śobhā* (Brilliance) An object not commonly known is

dealt with after comparing it to a popularly known object and a fresh idea emerges appealing to the aesthetic sense of the reader or audience (in the theatre) on account of the use of the double entendie. This is called Śobhā.

9 *Udāharaṇa* (Parallelism). This occurs when words denoting similar circumstances enables the adept-playwright to bring in a suggestion of accomplishing another object.

10 *Hetu* (Causation). When succintly put pleasing words achieve the desired object by m eans of clever usage it is called Hetu.

11 *Saṁśaya* (Hesitation) Thanks to the multiplicity of ideas and considerations a sentence is brought to a close even before fully expressing the intended theme. This then becomes an instance of Saṁśaya (doubt-hesitation).

12 Dṛṣṭānta. Justifying the case in hand and pleasing all the people, if a set of words and phrases adduces examples and reason it is called Dṛṣṭānta (Precedent favourable to the speaker).

13 *Prāpti* (Discovery, attainment). Prāpti is a main characteristic feauture of Nāṭaka. In this, on seeing certain parts alone the Bhāva is inferred.

14 *Abhiprāya* (Fancy, opinion). An entirely new object or theme is conceived on the basis of resemblance but of course interesting to the people. It is called Abhiprāya.

15 *Nidarśana* (Unfavourable Precedent) When well known examples are quoted for the purpose of rejecting the contrary view point. This quality in a drama is called Nidarśana.

16 *Nirukta* (Convincing Explanation, etymology). Some faullters statements made before are once again justified by means of after words. This constitutes the quality of Nirukta.

17 *Siddhi* (Successful achievement—Persuasion) Names of well known important persons are mentioned for the purpose of accomplishing the object aimed at. This is an instance of Siddhi.

18 *Viśeṣaṇa* (Distinction). After mentioning many well known important objects something special is mentioned distingusihing. This forms an instance of Viśeṣaṇa.

19 *Guṇātipāta* (Opposition to virtūe. Accusation of virtues)

Virtūes are enumerated with sweet words, with their import rather harsh in order to convey contrary impression. This is an instance of Guṇātipāta.

20 *Atiśaya* (Guṇātiśaya—Excellence) After mentioning many qualities present in ordinary men, of some speciality is mentioned, it is an instance of Atiśaya.

21 *Tulya Tarka* (Difference from Similarity) When an object not directly perceived is inferred from metaphor or simile applied in another similar instance it is to be known as Tulya Tarka.

22 *Padoccaya* (Multiplex Predication) When a number of words are used along with a number of other words to form different groups for the same purpose it is an example of Padoccaya.

23 *Diṣṭa* (Description) When any object or incident directly seen or not is described in harmony with place, time or form related to it constitutes the quality called Diṣṭa.

24 *Upadiṣṭā* (Utterance-Pointed utterance) The statement made on the basis of what is expressed in the Śāstras in order to attract the minds of the learned is an instance of Upadiṣṭa.

25 *Vicāra* (Deliberation) The statement establishing something not directly perceived but in harmony with the meaning expressed earlier including elimination of errors is called Vicāra.

26 *Viparyaya* (Inversion) Due to doubt the deliberation is changed in respect to what is seen or imported. This is to be known as Viparyaya.

27 *Bhraṁśa* (lapse, Slip of the tongue) Manifold deviation from the intended words and falling into a completely different thing is respect to persons of proud nature is called Bhraṁśa.

28 *Anunaya* (Imploring Mediation) Statement that pleases two persons of mutually contradictory desires and intentions and accomplisties the object constitutes Anunaya.

29 *Mālā* (garland, series of offers) When many needs and purposes are glorified by the learned men for the purpose of fulfilling the desired object it is an instance of Mālā.

30 *Dākṣinya* (Clever manners, chivelry) When another man's inclination is acted upon with joyous and pleased face

sweet speech and desirable movements it is an example of Dākṣiṇya.

31 *Garhaṇa* (Censure) When faults are mentioned and represented as merits or merits are belittled and called faults it is an instance of Garhaṇa.

32 *Arthāpatti* (Presumption) When something is mentioned with empharison sweetness of speech and another thing as expected to be implied it is an instance of Arthāpatti.

33 *Prasiddhi* (Calebrity) That which is expressed with excellent words enumerating many well known exploits fully expressing the intended purport is an example of Prasiddhi.

34 *Pṛcchā* (Interrogation) When same one addresses himself or others questioning as it were, through words proceeding from conventional courtesy it is termed Pṛcchā.

35 *Sārūpya* (Identity). If the inspected identity arising from the utterance of what is seen, heard or otherwise experienced causes some excitement it is termed Sārūpya.

36 *Manoratha* (Indirect Expreession of desire, Mental wish) If one pretends to refer to some one else's condition but actually gives expression to the secret desire in his heart of hearts it is called Manoratha.

37 *Leśa* (Wit) Words addressed in clever manner by expert disputants, relating to the accomplisment of similar objects give rise to Leśa.

38 *Saṁkṣepa* (Concealment, taking away) When being faultless, one declares to be taking oneself various faults of another it is an instance of Saṁkṣepa.

39 *Guṇakīrtana* (Enumerations of good qualities) When a single person is credited with the possession of all (and even more) the merits of human beings in the world it is an instance of Guṇakīrtana.

40 *Anukta Siddhi* (Unattared achievement—Semi uttered Expression). Though only commencement of a topic is made yet the rest of the topic is comprehended without actual expression in so many words it is an instance of Aunkta Siddhi.

41 *Priyokti* (Pleasing utterance—Compliment) When one

is in jovial mood and utters words in veneration of a venerable person giving expression to his joy as well it is an instance of Priyokti.

42 These are the thirty six characteristic features of the Kāvya meant of achieve the object in view. They add beauty to the composition. They should be employed by persons conversant with theme with due attention to the Rasas introduced.

43 *Four Alaṁkāras* Upamā (simile), Rūpaka (Metaphor), Dīpaka (Illumination through condensed Expression) and Yamaka (Alliteration).

44 *Upamā.* If in a poetical composition something is compared to another in view of some re-semblance in regard to quality or form it should be known as Upamā.

45—49 This comparison may be (1) of one with another one (2) of one with many (3) of many with one and (4) of many with many. Your face is like the moon. This is the comparison of one with another one. The lummaries shine like the moon—This is the comparision of many with one. He has an eye like that of a vulture, peacock and hawk. This is the comparison of one with many. The elephants are like the clouds. This is the comparison of many with many.

Five kinds of Upamā.

50 Upamā is further to be known as of five kinds—(a) Praśaṁsā (praise) (b) Nindā (censure) (c) Kalpitā (conceit), (d) Sadṛśī (similarity-uniqueness) and (e) Kiṇcitsadṛśī (partial likeness).

51 *Praśaṁsā* On seeing that large eyed maiden the king became satisfied as though she was the personification of the spiritual achievement of the sages after a great-deal of austerities.

52 *Nindā* The woman embraced that man devoid of every good quality and having rough features like a creeper in the forest turning round the thorny tree in the forest burnt down by the forest fire.

53 *Kalpitā* Elephants proceeding ahead slowely and gracefully and profusely exuding the ichor shine like moving mountains.

54 *Sadṛśi.* What has been done by you today with due deferance to another man's mental inclinations is comparable any to your superhuman activities.

55 *Kiñcitsadṛśī.* Here is my lady companion with the full-moon counterance, blue lotus-like eyes and intoxicated elephants' gait.

56 These are the varieties of Upamā to be known succintly by the learned ones. Those remaining ones not mentioned here with their characteristic features are to be understood from the common people as well as poetical compositions.

57 *Dīpaka.* When words having different meanings as the bases are combined into one sentence that illuminates all it is an instance of Dīpaka.

58 (Example) In that region the following are caused not to be devoid of these viz. the lakes are not devoid of swans, the trees are not devoid of flowers, the lotuses not devoid of inebriated bees, the gardens and parks not devoid of friendly groups of people.

59 *Rūpaka.* An usage of slight resemblance gives rise to a conception in the poet based on the objects having similar characteristic features. The product thereof is an instance of Rūpaka.

60 They have lotuses as for their faces, lilies for smiles; the full blown blue lotuses for the beautiful eyes ; when flocks of swans begin to chirp, the pools resembling women appear to shine talking to one another.

61 *Yamaka.* Repetition of sounds and syllables at the beginning etc. of the feet and at other places constitute Yamaka. Listen to their special features even as explain.

Ten Types of Yamaka.

62—64 Yamakas are of ten types (a) Pādānta (b) Kāñcī (c) Samudga (d) Vikrānta (e) Cakravāla (f) Sandaṣta (g) Pādādi (h) Āmraḍita (i) Caturvyavasita (j) Mālā.

65 *Pādānta Yamaka.* When the syllables are the same at the ends of all the four feet, that should be known by the name Pādānta Yamaka.

66 Dinakṣayāt Saṁhṛta Rasmi Maṇḍalam
Divīva Lagnam Tapanīyamaṇḍalam
Vibhāti Tāmram Divi Sūrya Maṇḍalam
Yathā Taruṇyāḥ Stanabhāra Maṇḍalam.

At the close of the day the copper hued orb of the sun with the cluster of rays drawn in shines like a golden disc in the heavens and looks like the heavy bosom of a young maiden.

67 *Kāñcī Yamaka.* Both at the beginning and at the end of every foot there shall be two similar words known as Kāñcī Yamaka.

68 Maya. Maya Candravatīnām Dravatīnām
Vyaktāvyaktā Sārajanīnāmrajanīnām
Phullephulle Sabhramare Vā'Bhramarevā
Rāmā Rāmā Vismayateca Smayateca

The watches of the nights full of moonlight pass swiftly in the company of young women. They are sometimes noticed and sometimes not, Flowers have bloomed. Whether they have been or not the fair lady looks at them admiringly and the park smiles with their beauty.

69 *Samudga Yamaka.* If half of the verse is repeated (with difference in meaning) it is an instance of Samudga Yamaka.

70 Ketakī Kusuma Pāṇḍura Dantaḥ
Śobhate Pravarakānana Hastī
Ketakīkusuma Pāṇḍuradantaḥ
Śobhate Pravara Kānana Hastī

The lofty forest elephant with its tusks grey and pale like Ketakī flowers appears splendid. The elephant like large forest appears splendid with Ketakī flowers constituting its pale white tusks.

71 *Vikrānta Yamaka.* If two feet are similar leaving a feet in the middle it should be known as Vikrānta Yamaka.

72 Sa Pūrvamvāraṇo Bhūtvā Dviśṛnga Iva Parvataḥ
Abhavad Dantavaikalyād Viśṛnga Iva Parvataḥ.

Having been like a mountain with two peaks formerly that elephant has become like a mountain with no peak since the tusks were impaired.

73 *Cakravāla Yamaka.* If the word or syllable at the end of a foot is repeated at the beginning of the next foot it is an example of the Cakravāla Yamaka.

74 Śaraistathā Śatrubhirāhatā Hatā
Hatāśca Bhūyastvanupuṅkhagaiḥ
Khagaiśca Sarvair Yudhi Śañcitāścitāś
Citādhirūdhā Nihatās Talaistalaiḥ

They were killed by the enemies with their arrows and they were struck again by the birds closely following the tail end of the missiles; the battle field was overspread with such birds by which dead bodies placed on the funeral pyre were pounced upon with their sharp latous.

75 *Sandaṣṭa Yamaka.* When two words at the beginning of every foot are similar it is an example of Sandaṣṭa Yamaka.

76 Paśya Paśya Ramaṇasya Meguṇān
Yena Yena Vaśagām Karoti Mām
Yena Yena Hi Mamaiti Darśanam
Tena Tena Vaśagām Karoti Mam

See, see the good qualities of my lover by which he puts me under his control and he entices me with those qualities with which becomes within my vision.

77 *Pādādi Yamaka.* When the same word occurs at the beginning of all the feet it is an example of Pādādi Yamaka.

78 Viṣṇuḥ Sṛjati Bhūtāni Viṣṇuḥ Saṁharate Prajāḥ
Viṣṇuḥ Prasūte Trailokyam Viṣṇurlokādhidaivtam

Viṣṇu creates all living beings. Viṣṇu destroys all the subjects; Viṣṇu gives birth to all the three worlds and Viṣṇu is the presiding deity of all the worlds.

79 *Āmreḍita Yamaka.* If at the end of every foot a word is repeated twice it should be known as Āmreḍita Yamaka by learned men.

80 Vijṛṁbhitam Niḥśvsitam Muhurmuhuḥ
Kathābhidhānam Smaraṇampadepade
Yathā Ca Te Dhyānamidam Punaḥ Punaḥ
Dhruvam Gatā Te Rajanī Vinā Vinā

You are repeatedly yawning and sighing. You indulge in

mentioning her story and remembering her at every step. As you meditate on her again and again it is certain that your night had passed without her.

81 *Catu Vyavasita Yamaka*

All the feet of the verse consist of the same words and syllables. That should be known as Caturvya Vasitayamaka

82 (Sa) Varaṇānāmaya Meva Kālaḥ in all the four feet. This is the time of the Vāraṇa flower. This is the season when elephants are free from illiness. This is the time for resistances and warding off the enemies; This is the time for compaign of war.

83 *Mālā Yamaka*

Where the same consonant recurs with different vowels many times it is an example of Mālā Yamāka.

84 Halī Balī Halimālī Śūlī Khelī Lalī Jalī
Balo Baloccalolākṣo Musalī Tvābhirakṣatu

May the powerful Balarāma, who is sportive and faltering in his gait, who has his eyes rolling and who wields a club, protect you.

85 Asau Hirāmā Rati vigraha Priyā
Rahaḥ Pragalbhā Ramaṇam Rahogatam
Ratena Rātrau Ramayet Pareṇa vā
Naceaudeṣyatyaruṇaḥ Puro Ripuḥ

This lovely maiden is fond of indulging in loving quarrels. She is unbashful in secret tryst. She will please her lover at night with the most excellent sexual alliance. If not, the sun will rise up in the east as her enemy.

86 Sa Puṣkarākṣaḥ Kṣatajokṣitākṣaḥ
Kṣaratkṣatebhyaḥ Kṣatajam Durīkṣam
Kṣatair Gavākṣairivasamvṛtāṅgaḥ
Sākṣāt Sahasrākṣa Ivāvabhāti

That lotus-eyed hero had his eyes bathed in blood. Blood no one would like to look at oozed out of his wounds. His body is covered as it were with window like wounds. So he appears like the thousand-eyed Indra vissible in person.

87 One shall produce poetical compositions with these Alaṁkāras having these characteristics with their objects and functions in view. I shall now speak about the Doṣas (defects) succinctly.

Ten defects

88 The ten defects in the poetical compositions are (a) Gūḍhārtha (Circulocution-didden meaning) (b) Arthāntaram (Conveying another sense-superfluous Expression) (c) Arthahīnam (Meaningless want of significance) (d) Bhinnārtham (conveying different meaning, Defective significance) (e) Ekārtham (Tantology) (f) Abhiplutārtham (Want of Synthesis) (g) Nyāya Dapetam (logical defect) (h) Viṣama (Uneveness—Metrical defect) (i) Visandhi (hiatus) (j) and Śābdhacyuta (lapse in a word—Slang).

89 Gūḍhārtha (circumlocution). If the object of description is indicated by a farfetched synonym the defect is called Gūḍhārtha.

When something other than the object of description is indicated it is called Arthāntara (Superfluous expression).

90 *Arthahīna* (Want of Significance). If the indicated theme is irreleventor if the expression is incomplete the defect is Arthahīna.

Bhinnārtha (Defective Significance). If the expression wants in refinement or if it is rustic in its setting the defect is Bhinnârtha.

91 If an idea different from what is intended is understood, that is also mentioned as Bhinnārtha by those who are experts in poetical works.

92 *Ekārtha* (Tantology is indiscriminate use of many words for a single idea.

Abhiplutārtha (Want of Synthesis). When the idea is complete in every foot and there is no correlation with the idea expressed in the adjacent foot,the defect is Abhiplutārtha.

93 *Nyāyādapeta* (Logical defect). What is devoid of reasoning, what is not supported by relevant authority or what is mentioned thoroughly contrary to sciences, arts, Śāstras etc. is called Nyāyādapeta.

Where there is lapse in the metrical structure the defect is *Viṣama.*

94 *Visandhi* (Hiatus). Where words liable to euphonic change are kept separate the defect is Visandhi.

Where the syllable or Savara (accent) is dropped the defect is Śabdacyuta (Slang).

95— Thus these defects in the poetical compositions have been described in detail by me. The Guṇas (merits) are contrary to these. They are significantly sweet and pregnant with meaning.

96 *Ten Guṇas.* The ten Guṇas in the poetical works are—(a) Śleṣa (union, combination, Synthesis) (b) Prasāda (Perspicuity) (c) Samatā (Smoothness) (d) Samādhi (Concentration) (e) Mādhurya (Sweetnesss) (f) Ojas (grandeur) (g) Padasaukumārya (delicacy of words, Agreeableness) (h) Arthavyakti (Clarity of meaning, Directness of Expression) (i) Udāratā (depth, nobility, Exaltedness) and (j) Kānti (Splendour Loveliness).

97 . *Śleṣa.* The combination of words related to one another by the desired meanings is called Śleṣa (Synthesis).

98 Prasāda (Perspicuity). Through the employment of easily comprehensible words and ideas, if even unexpressed word and idea are clearly brought home to the reader or member of the audience the Guṇa in the poetical (dramatic) composition is Prasāda.

99 *Samatā* (Smoothness). If the composition does not contain too many compounded words, words incapable of expressings ideas clearly or words of incomprehensible nature it is an example of Samatā because there is evenness.

100 *Samādhi* (Concentration). If the poetical composition expresses some special sense which the connoisseur and the critic can easily spot out the merit therein is called Samādhi.

101 *Mādhurya* (Sweetness). If the passage does not tire the reader or disgust him even when read or heard over and over again the quality there in is called Mādhurya.

102 *Ojas* (Grandeur). If a composition contains passages

consisting of many and varied compound words exalted in sense and agreeable in sound the Guṇa therein is Ojas.

103 *Saukumārya* (Agreeableness). When a poetical work has many passages where the words can be easily pronounced and are knit together compactly by means of phonetic changes and when the work leaves an agreeable impression (in the minds of readers etc.) it is an example of Saukumāya.

104 *Artha Vyakti* (Directness of Expression). If well known predicates give expression to common events, ordinary subjects, actions etc. in a poetical piece it is an example of Arthavyakti,

105 *Udāratā* (Exaltedness). When in a poetical piece superhuman characters are brought in with regard to Śṛṅgāra and Adbhuta Rasas and contains diverse Bhāvas it is an example of Udāratā (Udāttatā).

106 *Kānti* (Loveliness). Sportive movements etc. are being described by a passage and in doing so the composition delights the ear and the mind like the moon. The Guṇa therein is called Kānti.

Use of Alaṁkāras and Guṇas based on Rasa

107 Thus the Alaṁkāras, Doṣas ad Guṇas have been described. Now I shall mention the employment of these with reference to the Rasas.

108 A poetical composition expatiating on the Vīra, Raudra and the Adbhuta Rasas should contain short vowels and make use of Upamā and Rūpaka Alaṁkāras.

109—110 In the Bībhatsa and Karuṇa Rasas too the poetical should be so but long vowels are to be profusely and mainly employed. Sometimes when Vīra and Raudra are employed the same shall be the rule. Then the composition shall be in the Āryā metre and the Alaṁkāras used shall be Dīpaka and Rūpaka.

In the Śṛṅgāra Rasa the gentle metres shall be employed.

111—112 In the Vīra Rasa there shall be the graded employment of conjunct consonants. The Chandas employed shall be Jagati, Atijagati or Saṅkṛti.

While describing skirmishes and tumults the Utkṛti Chandas has been recommended by those who are conversant with them.

In the Karuṇa Rasa these shall be Śakvarī and Atidhṛti Chandas.

113 The Chandas recommended in the case of the Vīra Rasa can be employed in the Raudra Rasa too with regard to the other Rasas and contexts the use of the Chandas by the Sponsors of the composition shall be suitable to the meaning intended.

114 *Vowels and the Rasas*. Three types of vowels the short, the long and the prolated are to be employed by poets in the drama representing the different Rasas and Bhāvas.

115 While reciting the short vowel has only one Mātrā, the long vowel has two Mātrās and the Pluta (Prolated Vowel) three Mātrās.

116 *Use of Pluta*. In the case of recollecting something, in expressing indignation, in lamenting and in the Vedapāṭha of the Brahmins the Pluta vowel is recommended.

117 The long Ā in the case of recollecting, the long U in the case of indignation, Hā for lamentation and Om for the Vedapāṭha.

118 In all the poetical compositions the other vowels too are to be employed in short, long or prolated form in accordance with the Rasa and Bhāva.

119 Viṣama, Ardhasama and Sama Vṛttas mentioned before should also be used in these compositions with agreeable and soft sounds with due attention to the Rasas employed.

120 The poet should endeavour to use in his works based on dramas and dance performances sweet, exalted and agreeable words so that they can be easily pronounced even by women. Poetical works when embellished with them appear beautiful like the lotus pound in full bloom when adorned with swans.

121 With harsh words like Cekrīḍita etc. the gracefully delicate projects of Bharata do not apear beautiful in the same way as whores do not appear well in the company of Brahmins clad in deer skin and anointed with ghee, carrying water pots

and staff while Yajñakriyā (Sacrificial rite) shines with them no doubt.

122 A play consisting of pleasing sounds and agreeable senses becomes suitable for being presented to the spectators. No obscure and difficult words should be used. It shall be intelligible to even laymen. The structure should be proper. The paths of many Rasas should be properly done. There shall be dances befittingly used.

Notes

The *Lakṣaṇas* of *Kāvya*. The commentators do not agree with one another in the interpretation of the original texts of Bharata. There are many recensions. These characteristic marks are definitely different from Alaṁkāras (figures of speech) and Guṇas (excellance, merits). Many writers have dealt with these aspects in well known works and journals of oriental research and indological topics. There are two distinct versions of these Lakṣaṇas. We have given here that followed by Viśvanātha and Śingabhūpāla. Kīrtidhara, Abhinava Gupta and later writers adopt a different version. In the latter one only seventeen terms are the same as given here. In regard to the definition only eight are similar in both. We are not elaborating the latter version because the definitions therein have only an academic value.

The distinct terms used by the later writers are Abhimāna, Protsāhanā, Hetu, Mithyā, Dhyavasāya, Ākranda, Ākhyāna, Yācñā, Pratiṣedha, Nirbhāsana, Āśīḥ, Kapaṭa, Kṣamā, Paścāttāpa, Anuvṛtti, Upapatti, Yukti, Kārya & Paridevana.

As for examples of the well known characteristics we shall give some hints here because an elaborate treatment will make the book voluminous.

(1) *Bhūṣaṇa*—Ratnāvalī I—8.
(2) *Akṣara Saṅghāta*—Sākuntala VII—Saundalāvaṇṇa.
(3) *Śobhā*—Ratnāvalī I—7.
(4) *Udāharaṇā*—Prāveśikī Dhruvā in Devīcandragupta.
(5) *Hetu*—SixthAṅka in Tapasavatsarāja
(6) *Saṁśaya*—Sixth Act in Kundamālā

(7) *Dṛṣṭānta*—"Dhūrtaviṭa".
(8) *Prāpti*—Third Act Kundamālā.
(9) *Abhiprāya*—Tāpasavatsarāja—IV Act.
(10) *Nidarśana*—"Ubhayābhisārikā"
(11) *Nirukta*—Uatsarājacaritra I Act
(the words of Bharatarohaka to the king)
(12) *Siddhi*—Kaumudī Mahotsava IV Act.
(13) *Viśeṣaṇa*—Tāpasavatsarāja III Act.
(14) *Guṇātipāta* Dhūrtaviṭa—Jātyandhām etc.
(15) *Atiśaya*—Bhīṣma's words Etattehṛdayam etc. to Dhṛta-Rāṣṭra.
(16) *Tulyatarka*—VIII Act Vatsarāja Carita Navārkabhā-pallavita etc.—Kings words.
(17) *Padoccaya*—VI Act Vatsarājacarita. The kings words i.e. the minister's excellance.
(18) *Diṣta*—King's words Vāmam Sandhistimita Valayam Nyasya Hastam Nitambe" etc. in Mālavikāgnimitra.
(19) *Upadiṣṭa*—Avimāraka I Act. The king's words Dharmaḥ Prāgeva Cintyah" etc.
(20) *Vicāra*—Rākṣasa's words in Act V, Mudrārākṣasa "Sādhye Niścitamanvayena" etc.
(21) *Viparyaya*—Rāvaṇa is addressed by the minister
Udarkasiddhimicchadbhiḥ Sadbhir Nakhalu Dṛśyate
Caturthī Candra Lekheva Parastrī Phālapaṭṭikā
Rāvaṇa replies :
Parastrī Kucakumbheṣu Kumbheṣu Varadantinām
Nipatanti Na Bhīrūṇām Dṛṣṭayaḥ Śaravṛṣṭayaḥ
(22) *Bhraṁśa*—II Act Veṇīsamhāra.
(23) *Anunaya*—II Act Rāmābhyudaya Rāvaṇa's angry words to Mārīca.
(24) *Mālā*—Tāpasavatsarāja. The King's words "Dṛṣṭā Yūyam Nirjiva Vidviṣantah" etc.
(25) *Dākṣiṇya*—Ratnāvalī II Act. Vidūṣaka's action.
(26) *Garhaṇa*—Dhūrtaviṭa. The words Praṇaṣṭā Navyakti-rbhavati Vacasā Saiva Mṛdutā etc.
(27) *Arthāpatti*—Dhūrtaviṭa. "Ādaṣṭasphuritādhare Bhavati Yo" etc.
(28) *Prasiddhi*—Duryodhana's Words. "Yenendrasya Ca Pārijātakatarurmānena Tulyam Hṛto" etc.
(29) *Pṛcchā*—Hanumān's words looking at Sītā Sthāne Vasīdasi Raghūdvaha Kim Vidhātah etc.

(30) *Sārūpya*—"Chalitarāma" Lava's words.
(31) *Manoratha*—Vikaṭanitambā Prahasana. The words Anyāsu Tāvadupamarda Sahāsu etc.
(32) *Leśa*—Avimārak Act II.
(33) *Saṁkṣepa* (Saṁkṣobha)—Ratnāvalī Act III
(34) *Guṇakīrtana*—Vatsarājacarita Act IV Tenayroktam Dhairyagāmbhīrya Śaurya Prajñātejo Nīti Dākṣīṇya Garbham etc.
(35) *Anukta Śiddhi*—Yaugan Dharāyaṇa's words to Vāsavadattā in Tāpasavatsarāja.
(36) *Priyokti*—VII Act Tāpasavatsarāja Bharata Rohaka's words to Vatsarāja :— "Yāśetekaustubhasya Dyutikisalayite Śāradavyomanīle" etc.

Verse. 61–62 Bhāmaha the celebrated rhetorician defines Yamaka in II—9. According to him Yamaka is fivefold. In his opinion Bharata's ten Yamakas can merge into his five. Daṇḍin (III—51/52) also defines and gives examples.

89 Fōr circumlocution ancient rhetoricians stock example is Ekādhikanavavimāna for Daśaratha.

18

Bhasavidhana (Rules regarding the Use of Languages)

Prākṛta-Pāṭhya-Lakṣaṇa (Characteristics of Prakritaric recitation)

1 Thus the Samskrta mode of recitation has been explained succinctly by me. I shall now mention the characteristic features of Prākṛtic recitation.

2 This mode of Sanskṛt recitation if changed and deprived of its quality of refinement can be called Prākṛtic recitation and changes due to different conditions constitute its chief features.

Three types of Prākṛtapāṭhya

3 As far as the dramatic representation is concerned the Prākṛta Pāṭhya is of three types viz.—(1) the same set of words (Śamāna Śabda) (2) the corrupted ones (Vibhraṣṭa) and (3) those of native origin (Deśīgata).

4 Some Prākṛta compositions the words Kamala, Amala, Reṇu, Taraṅga, Lola Salila and others are used in the same way as in Saṁskṛta works.

5 Generally in the middle of a word etc. some sounds change their combined forms or vowels. Some of them sustain loss or deficiency. Such changed words are called Vibhraṣṭa (Corrupt).

6 *Vowels and Simple Consonants* : In Prākrta we do not have "ai" and "au" and that after the Anusvāra (i.e. Ḥ). The letters Śa and Ṣa and the nasals Na, Na and Na also do not occur.

7 Letters Ka, Ga, Ta, Da, Ya and Va are dropped and

their meanings are retained by the vowels left behind. The letters Kha, Tha, Dha and Bha change into Ha and the meaning is not given up.

8 In Prākṛta the letter Ra above or below other letters (i.e. preceding or following other letters) is not in vogue except in the case of the words Bhadra, Vodraha, Hrada, Candra etc.

9 Kha, Gha, Tha, Dha and Bha change into Ha in such words as Mukha, Megha, Hathā, Vadhū, & Prabhūta. The vowels following the dropped Ka, Ga, Ta, Da, Ya and Va represent them.

10 Ṣaṭpada etc. change their Ṣa into Cha [i.e. Chatpada]. The final La of Kila should be Ra and the word Khalu becomes Khu.

11 In words like Bhaṭa, Kuṭī, Kaṭaka, Taṭa etc. Ṭa becomes Ḍa. Śa and Ṣa are changed into Sa as in the case of Saṅkā (Saṅkā), Visa (Visa).

12 If it is not at the beginning of a word Ta changes into an indistinct "Da". The Ḍa in the words Baḍavā, Tadāga etc. becomes "La".

13 In words such as Śaṭha, Pīṭhi, Pāṭha etc. the letter Ṭha becomes Ḍha always and Na becomes Ṇa while pronouncing.

14—15 Āvāna becomes Āvāṇa with its Pa changed into Va. Excepting in the case of Yathā and Tathā Tha becomes Dha, Mṛga becomes Mao and also Mṛta becomes Mao.

Paruṣa should be known as Pharusa since Pakāra too becomes Pha.

16 Au used in words like Auṣadha etc. turns into O and 'Ca' in words Pracaya, Acira, Acala etc. will become Ya.

17 When they are not in conjunct use what changes the Prākṛta varṇas take have been explained thus. Now I shall describe them when they are in conjunct use.

18 Śca, Psa, Tsa, Thya > Cha
Bhya, Hya, Dhya > Jha
Ṣṭa > Ṭṭha, Ṣma > Mha, Ṣṇa > Ṇha.
Kṣṇa > Ṇha Kṣa > Kha.

19 Hence Āścarya > Acchariya; Niścaya > Nicchaya
Utsāha > Ucchāha; Pathya > Paccha, Vatsa > vaccha,
Apsarasa > Accharaam.

20 Tubhyam > Tujjham Mahyam > Majjham
Vindhya > Viṁjha Daṣṭa > Daṭṭha;
Hasta > Hattha.

21 Grīṣm > Gimha Ślakṣṇa > Sahṇa Uṣṇa > Uṇha
Yakṣa > Jakkha Paryaṅka > Pallaṁku

22 In the combination of Ha and Ma in Brahmā etc. there shall be metathesis (i.e. Ha+Ma=Ma+Ha). In the word Bṛhaspati the group Spa becomes Pha; Yajña > Jaṇṇa and Bhīṣma > Bhimha,

23 Ka and other letters in combination with other letters before or after are disjointed in their pronunciation Śakra > Sakka, Arka > Akka etc.

24 The pronunciation of Prākṛta and Saṁskṛta is to be known in this manner. Henceforth I shall explain the diverse classification of the local language (Deśabhāṣā).

25 The languages of four types are to be used in the ten kinds of play where the Pāṭhya is either Prākṛta or Saṁskṛta.

Four distinct linguistic units

26 The languages glorified in the dramatic performance are (a) Atibhāṣā (b) Āryabhāṣā (c) Jātibhāṣā and (d) Yonyantarī Bhāṣā.

27 Atibhāṣā (Superhuman language) is of the Devas and Āryabhāṣā (Language of the Nobility) is that of the kings. In these languages there is refinement and they are in vogue in all the seven continents.

28 Jātibhāṣā (Language of the laity) is of two kinds as used by the people. One is the language where Mleccha words (words of foreign origin) are profusely used and the other is confined to Bhāratavarṣa.

29 *Yonyantarī Bhāṣā* is the langnage of the animals whether domestic or wild and also of the various kinds of birds. This has to be used in the dramatic performances in the manner of Nāṭya Dharmi (Conventional Practice).

30 The Pāṭhya (Recitation) based on Jātibhāṣā and widely pervading over the four castes, is of two types the Prākṛta (the rustic and unrefined) and Saṁskṛta (the urban, the polished & civilized).

31 Saṁskṛta Pāṭhya is to be employed in the cases of the four types of heroes viz. Dhīrodātta (hero of the exalted type), Dhīroddhata (hero of the vehement haughty type), Dhīralalita (hero of the light-hearted easy-going type) and Dhīrapraśānta (hero of the serene cool type).

32 In the case of all these heroes too Prākṛta can be employed when circumstances warrant it.

33 Even in the case of the superior persons, no Saṁskṛta should be employed if they are maddened with prosperity or deprived of it through poverty, want of study or through sheer chance. So also when a mad man is represented as reading or reciting no Saṁskṛta is utilized.

34 Prākṛta Pāṭhya should be allotted to persons in concealment of identity, Śramaṇas, ascetics, mendicants, jugglers and spies.

35 In the same way, children, persons in the grip of evil spirits, persons of low character, inebriated ones, persons of low character, inebriated ones, phallus worshippers, women and men in the characters of women—Prākṛta should be employed.

36 In the case of itinerant ascetics, saints, Buddhists, pure Śrotriyas, and the remaining ones, well trained and wearing the prescribed dress and having other paraphernalia Saṁskṛta should be employed.

37 Saṁskṛta Pāṭhya should be allotted to queens, courtesans, female artistes etc. as befitting the occasion and the situations.

38—39 Matters pertaining to peaceful alliance or martial preparation, the movements of planets and star whether auspicious or inauspicious, the foreboding chirps of the birds—if the queen were to be informed of these Saṁskṛita should be employed in their cases.

40 To accord joy to all kinds of people and if the practice of fine arts demands it the courtezous should be allotted Saṁskṛta Pāṭhya that can be easily managed by them.

41 For being conversant with the practical application of fine arts and in order to entertain the king the female artisans and craft women have been allotted Saṁskṛta Pāṭhya in the dramatic performance.

42 Purity in speech of all the celestial damsels is sanctioned by tradition in view of their association with the Devas. The same is followed in the world as well.

43 To the Apsaras on the earth the Prākṛta Pāṭhya depends upon the will (of the playwright). If they act the role of any mortal woman the allotment should depend on adequate reasons and necessity of the occasion.

44 In the course of a dramatic performance the Barbaras, Kirātas, Āndhras, Dravidas and other communities should not be assigned their respective nature tongues.

45 O excellant Brahmins in regard to all these pure groups and societies the language employed in the poetical compositions should be based on the Śaurasenī Bhāṣā.

46 However, it is left to the option of the sponsors of the dramatic performance to make use of the regional language for the poetry part in the drama takes its origin in the different regions (for local production).

47 *Seven principal dialects*

The seven principal dialects in vogue here are (a) Māgadhī, (b) Āvantī, (c) Prācyā, (d) Śaurasenī, (e) Ardhamāgadhī, (f) Vahlīkā & (g) Dākṣiṇātyā.

48 Besides these there are many Vibhāṣās remembered in dramatic performances originating from the speeches of Śabaras, Ābhīras, Cāṇḍālas, Sacaras, Dravidas and Āndhras along with the lowly speeches of the foresters.

49 Of these, the guards and the inmates of the royal harem should speak Māgadhī; the menials, sons of the king, leader of merchants guilds should speak Ardhamāgadhī.

50 Prācyā should be allotted to Vidūṣaka and others; Āvantī for the Dhūrtas (rogue gamesters). To the heroines and the female companions, Śaurasenī if there is no impediment,

51 To the Soldiers, Nāgarakas (Citizens, police constables) the language allotted shall be the Dākṣiṇātyā. So also to the gamesters, Vāhlīka dialect is to be assigned to northerners. To the Khasas the language of their own region is to be assigned.

52 *Minor dialects.* Śākārī should be assigned to the

Śakāra and Śakas and other groups of the same nature. Cāṇḍālī is to be assigned to the Pulkasas and the like.

53 To charcoal makers, hunters and those who earn their livelihood by collecting wood and leaves the Śābarī tongue and a little of the speech of the forest dwellers can be assigned.

54 For those who live in places where elephants, horses, goats, sheep, camels or cows are kept in large numbers the Āmbhīrī or Śābarī can be allotted and the Drāviḍī tongue is to be allotted to the forest dwellers.

55 Oḍrī is to be assigned to diggers of sub terranean passages, prison warders, horsemen. Heroes and others like them while in difficulty are also to use Māgadhi as a means to protect themselves.

Distinguishing features of the local dialects

56 In regard to the regions well known between Gaṅgā and the ocean the sponsor of the dramatic performance shall employ a language abounding in the letter "E".

56 In regard to the regions renowned between Vindhya and the ocean the language allotted by those who are conversant with the same shall be abounding in "Na".

58—61 To the Regions like Surāṣṭra and Avantī lying to the north of Vetravati the language allotted shall be abounding in CA. To the people who live in the Himālayas, Sindhu and Sauvīra a language abounding in "U" should be assigned. To those who live on the banks of the Carmaṇvati river and around the Arbuda mountain a language abounding in "O" should be assigned There are the rules governing the allotment of dialects in plays what has not been mentioned here should be learned from popular usage by the sensible persons.

Notes

3 In later Grammatic works Samānaśabda is known as Tatsama, Vibhraṣṭa as Tadbhava and Deśī is retained.

12 This type of smoothening of hard sounds is a regular feature in the Dravidian languages where the hard sounds in the middle of a word are invarably Mṛdu or soft. Mutal meaning Principal is invarialy pronounced as though Mudal; So also

Aviṭe (there) is aviḍe; Itu (This) Idu; Kuṭai (Umbrella) Kuḍai.

There are hundreds of such words.

27 According to Bhoja, Atibhāṣā is Vedic language, Āryabhāṣā is Paurāṇic language and Jātibhāṣā the popular Laukika language.

29 Yonyantarī Bhāṣā. This has not been practically exemplified in any of the extant plays or works on dramaturgy.

31 Chepter 36 of Nāṭya Śāstra explains the different types of heroes.

19

Vākyavidhāna and Kākusvara Vyañjana

Modes of address, intonation etc.

1—3 Different modes of address :—

The foregoing, O best of Brahmins, constitutes the rules on the use of languages in a drama. Now listen to Vākyavidhāna (popular modes of address) and the manner in which men of exalted, similar and lower status should be addressed by the others in a Nāṭaka.

The noble-souled saints are the Devas (venerable ones) or even the Devas, they are to be addressed as Bhagavān (Holy highness) and their womenfolk too are to be suitably addressed (Bhagavatī).

4 *Gods, Teachers etc.* The Gods, leaders of the cults and persons of diverse types of learning are to be addressed as "Bhagavān" by men and women.

5 The Brahmin is to be addressed "Ārya" the king is to be addressed "Mahārāja" the preceptor is to be addressed "Upādhyāya" and an elderly person "Tāta".

6 The kings can be addressed by their names or by the term "Rāja" by the Brahmins. This has to be tolerated by the rulers of the Earth because Brahmins are remembered as those worthy of adoration.

7 The minister is to be addressed by the Brahmins as Amātya or Saciva. He is to be addressed always as "Ārya" by all the other people and even the base ones.

8 Equals are addressed by the names with which they are styled. A superior person may be addressed by name even by inferior persons as though of the same family.

9 All employees whether men or women, servants, artisans and craftsmen also can be addressed so.

10 A venerable person is to be addressed as "Bhāva" (honoured sir) and some one slightly less so can be addressed "Mārṣaka" (worthy one). A person of same or similar status should be addressed "Vayasya" (comrade) and a lowly one "Ham Ho" (Hey ho).

11 The person taken in the chariot should always be addressed by the charioteer as "Āyuṣmān" (Long lived) one. An ascetic of tranquillity is to be addressed "Tapasvī" or "Sādhu" (Blessed one).

12. The heir-apparent is to be addressed "Svāmī" and the other princes Bhartṛdāraka (Son of our lord). Inferior persons are to be addressed as a "Saumya" (gentle one) or Bhadramukha (Auspicious Counternanced) with He (Oh) prefixed to it.

13 In a dramatic performance a person can be addressed by a term appropriate to his brith or the profession, art or craft practised by him.

14 A disciple or a son shall be addressed by the precepto or father as "Vatsa" (dear one), Putraka (son), Tāta (father) or by his name or after his Gotra.

15 Buddhist and Jain (Nigrantha) monks should be addressed as Bhaḍanta. Persons of other sects are to be addressed by terms as laid down in their canons.

16 The king is to be addressed by his servants as well as subjects "Deva" (Lord) but when he is an Emperor he is to be addressed by his servants "Bhaṭṭa".

17—18 When addressed by saints, asceties etc. the being is addressed "Rājan" or by his patronymic name (such as Paurava, Bhārata Rāghava etc. The Vidūṣaka is to address him Vayasya or Rājan. The Queen and her maid servants are to be addressed by him Bhavatī (your ladyship). The Vidūṣaka is to be addressed Vayasya by the king or by his name.

19 In their youth the husband should be addressed by all women "Āryaputra" (noble one's son). On other occasions the husband is simply addressed Ārya. If he were to be a king Mahārāja is the term to be used.

20 The elder brother is to be addressed Ārya and the younger brother like the son. It is in this manner that male characters are to be addressed in the drama by the actors.

21 I shall now speak of the manner of address of female characters in a play. Female saints and goddesses are to be addressed as "Bhagavati".

The wife of the preceptor and any other lady of the same Status should be addressed "Bhavati"—A rustic woman should be addressed "Bhadrā" (good lady) and if she is elderly "Ambā" (mother).

23 All the moves of the king should be addressed by the attendants "Bhaṭṭinī", "Svāminī" or "Devī" as the drama as laid down by learned people.

24 The crowned queen should be addressed by the king and by the attendants "Devī", the remaining ones to be addressed "Bhaṭṭinī" or "Svāminī"

25 Young princesses should be addressed by the maid-servants as "Bhartṛdārikā (daughter of the lord), the sister is to be addressed "Svasṛ" and the younger ones "Vatsā"

26 A Brahmin lady, a woman in a monastery or observing vows (Liṅgasthā) (wratasthā) should be addressed "Āryā : One's own wife can too is to be addressed "Āryā" or by the name of her father (i e. daughter of so and so) or son (mother of so and so).

27 Equals shall address one another as "Halā". A superior lady shall address her servant maid as "Hañjā".

28 A courtezan shall be addressed by the attending servants by the word Ajjukā and the mother of the courtezans by the wotd Attā.

29 In the scene of love, the wife is addressed by the king or anyone else by the word "Priyā". The wives of priests and leaders of caravan shall always be addressed with the word "Āryā".

30 If the characters are minor ones, not well known the poets shall assign them names signifying their traits of character or alluding to their origin.

31 The Brahmins and the Kṣtriyas should be given names pertaining to their clan or special assignments the names ending with Śarman and Varman respectively.

32 Names of Vaiśyas should end in Datta and heroic characters should be given names signifying vigour and exaltedness.

33 The names of the king's wives shall always be indicative of victory. The names of the courtezans shall be so assigned as to conclude with Datta, Mitrā or Senā.

34. The errand-girls should be given names associated with flowers. Ceṭas (menials and personal attendants) should have names auspicious in character.

35 The exalted persons should be assigned such names, as are of deep significance and these names should be in harmony with their activities and vice verse.

36 Remaining persons should be given such names as are befitting their naturity and activities. Thus the names to be allotted to men and women have been explained factually.

37—38 Names in a dramatic work should always be of this nature. After knowing all the details concerning the rules regarding languages one can proceed to employ Pāṭhya equipped with the six Alaṁkāras.

Prose Passage

Qualities of the Pāṭhya. We shall explain now the qualities of the Pāṭhya. They are the seven Svaras (notes), the three Sthānas (locations) the four Varṇas (manner of utterance), two ways of intonation (kāku); six Alaṁkāras (embellishments) and the six Aṅgas (limbs). Now we shall expatiate up on the characteristics of these.

The seven Svaras are—Ṣaḍja, Ṛṣabha, Gāndhāra, Madhyama, Pañcama, Dhaivata, and Niṣāda. They are to be employed relevantly in the Rasas e.g.

38—40 The Svaras Madhyama and Pañcama should be used in the Hāsya (Comic) and Śṛṅgāra (Erotic) Rasas. Ṣaḍja and Ṛṣabha are the notes to be employed in the case of the Rasas Vīra (heroic), Raudra (terrible) and Adbhuta (wonderment); the Svaras Gāndhāra and Niṣāda are the notes to be employed in the Karuṇa rasa (Pathos) and the note Dhaivata isto be employed in the Bībhatsa and Bhayanaka Rasas (Contemptible, and the frightening).

The three Sthānas (Locations) There are three locations) (1) the chest (Uras), (2) throat (kaṇṭha) and (3) the head (Śiras).

41—43 Whether it be the note or pitch from the body (Vocal) or in Vīṇā the Sthāna for the same shall be the chest, throat or the head. The beckoning and the address of one far off shall be made ·through the notes from the head (Śiras Sthāna); the same in regard to one not very far off, shall be through the notes from the throat whereas notes from the chest will suit the beckoning of a person at one's side. In regard to the Pāṭhya the following injunctions shall hold good always. The sensible one shall illuminate by the head Sthāna the statement uttered through the chest Sthāna and finally brought to a calm down through the throat.

O Ascetics, there shall be four types of Varṇas (accents) namely Udātta (Acute), Anudātta (grave), Svarita (circumflex) and Kampita (Quivering).

Prose Passage. In Hāsya and Śṛṅgāra Rasas the accents Svarita and Udātta are to be employed in the recitation. In Vīra, Raudra and Adbhuta Rasas the accents suitable are the Udātta and Kampita. In the Rasas Karuṇa, Bībhatsa and Bhayānaka the accents are Anudātta, Svarita and Kampita.

Two types of Intonation. The Kāku (Intonation) is of two types viz. Sākāṁkṣā (full of expectation) and Nirākāṅkṣā (devoid of expectation) since a statement can be related to expectation or not.

44 A sentence wherein the intended idea is not fully expressed is termed Sākāṅkṣa and a sentence that has fully expressed the idea is one entailing no expectation (Nirākāṅkṣa).

Prose Passage. A Sākāṅksa sentence therefore comes to thus—It starts with a high pitch (Tāra) and comes to an end with a low pitch (Mandra); the meaning or idea is not expressed fully; Varṇas and Alaṁkāras have not been fully employed; it has notes from the throat and the chest. The Nirākāṅkṣa is one that starts with a low pitch and comes to an end with a high pitch; the varnas and Alaṁkāras have been fully employed; the notes are from the head the idea has been fully expressed (kāku is of two types because in as much as it is based on these two types of sentences).

45 The six Alaṁkāras (embellishments) may are (1) Ucca (of the high pitch) (2) Dīpta (excited, illuminated) (3) Mandrá (of the grave accent) (4) Nīca (low pitch) (5) Druta (fast) and (6) Vilambi(a (slow).

Prose Passage. The Ucca note proceeds from the Śiras Sthāna (head location). It is of the high pitch. It is to be employed while speaking to some one far off, when there is wonder or dismay; when there is spirited assertions and counter replies; when some one is frightened and when there is affliction.

The *Dīpta* note originates from the location of head; the the pitch is more than in the case before (Tāra-Tara); it is employed in reproach, quarrel, dispute annoyance, seize, anger, exhibition of arrogance due to heroism, defiance, sharp and harsh words, repulsion, lamentation etc.

The *Mandra* notes originate from the location of the head. They are to be emp loyed in utter desperate state, gloominess, weakness, anxiety, impatience, eagerness, wretchedness, sickness, playfull spirit, deep wound due to weapons, fainting, inebriety, whispering secret words etc.

The Nīca note proceeds from the chest with a lower pitch than in the case before. It is to be employed in the natural regular conversation, ailments, weariness, tranquility, exhaustion due to austerities, panicky state, falling down, frightened posture etc.

The Druta note proceeds from the throat and proceeds swiftly. It is to be employed in the pacification of children by women, inability to accept a lovers overtimes and advances, fear, cold, fever panic, secret emergent activity, pain etc.

The Vilambita note arises from the throat It is of slightly low pitch (Tanu Mandra). It is to be used in Śṛṅgāra and Karuṇa Rasas, in deliberation, discrimination, jealous anger, envy, inadequately expressed speech, bashfulness, anxiety, threatening, surprise, censure, chronic illness, squeezing etc.

In this context there are the following Verses traditionally handed down.

46—48 To fit in with different Rasas the Kāku should always be made Ucca, Dīpta and Druta in the contexts of repartee, confusion, harsh rebuke, representation of sharpness and roughness, agitation weeping, calling or challanging absent persons out of view threatening some one etc.

49—50 Kāku should be made Mandra and Nīca in ailments, fever, grief, hunger, thirst, distress due to chillness, observation of simpler vows, deliberation, deep wound from a weapon, whispering secret words, anxiety and state of penance.

51 The Kāku is rendered Mandra and Druta by the sponsors of the dramatic performance while representing soothing of children by women, slighting of overtures of lovers, panic and distress due to chillness.

52—55 The Kāku should be made Dīpta and Vilambita as well as Mandra in the case of the pursuit of an object lost from view after being seen momentarily, hearing unpleasant things about the dear and near, announcing what is desired, ponderance and meditation, lunatic state, envy censure, saying something regarding inadequately expressed or expressible, narration of aneedotes, continuous speech by way of argument and counter argument, something extraordinary that has happened, wounded and deformed, anger, misery, dismay, indiguation, excess of joy and lamentation.

56 Kāku of Mandra and Vilambita types are recommended in cases pertaining to pleasant situation and sense associated with pleasant and happy emotions.

57 Kākus of Dīptā and Uccā types have been recommended in the case of words that express sharpness and roughness. In this manner the Pāṭhya based on different intonations should be employed by the sponsors.

Kākus and the Rasas

58—59 In Hāsya, Śṛṅgāra and Karuṇa Rasas the Vilambitā (Slow) intonation is desired. In the Virā, Raudra and Adbhuta Rasas the Uccā and the Dīptā intonations are recommended. In the Bhayānaka and the Bībhatsa Rasas the Drutā (quick) and the Nīcā (low) Kāku is glorified. In this manner the Kāku should be employed by the sponsors with the relevant Bhāvas and Rasas.

Prose Passage

The *Six Aṅgas* (limbs). There are six Aṅgas (limbs, ancillary adjuncts) viz. (1) Viccheda (separation) (2) Arpaṇa (Presentation) (3) Visarga (Closure) (4) Anubandha (Continuity) (5) Dīpana (Brightening, brilliance) and (6) Praśamana (Calming, Subduing).

Viccheda is due to Virāma (Pause).

Arpaṇa. If any Pāṭhya is recited in a note that appears to be gracefully playing and sweetly modulated to be filling as it were the entire auditorium.

Visarga means the Completion of a sentence.

Anubandha means want of separation between words or refraining from inhaling while uttering them.

Dīpana means gradual augmentation of notes proceeding beautifully from the three locations.

Praśamana means the lowering of the notes of Tāra (higher pitch) without making them discordant. Their use in the different Rasas—In the Hāsya and Śṛṅgāra Raṣas the Pāṭhya should be made equipped with the Aṅgas— Arpaṇa, Viccheda, Dīpana and Praśamana. In the Karuṇa Rasa it shall be equipped with Dīpana and Praśamana. In Vīra, Raudra and Adbhuta Rasas the Pāṭhya shall abound in Viccheda, Praśamana, Dīpana and Anubandha. In the Bībhatsa and Bhayānaka it shall be equipped with Visarga and Viccheda.

All these are to be used in dramatic performance from the three locations. In addressing one far off the Tāra notes should be used proceeding from the head; if the person adressed be not very far off the Madhya notes should be used proceeding from the throat; if the person addressed is near at hand the Mandra notes should be used proceeding from the chest. One shall never proceed from the Mandra to Tāra or from Tāra to Mandra.

The three Layas (tempo) these notes viz. the Druta (quick) Madhya (medium) and Vilambita (slow) should be employed in regard to different Rasas. The Madhya Laya is employed in Hāsya and Śṛṅgāra Rasas; the Vilambita in the Karuṇa Rasa and the Druta in the Rasas Vīra, Raudra, Adbhuta, Bībhatsa and Bhayānaka.

Virāma—Characteristics

60 Virāma (Pause) in statements is at the conclusion of the idea. It depends on the function and not on the metrical exigencies. Why? It is the personal experience of all of us that there is pause-even after one, two, three or four syllables, as kim? Gaccha, Māviśa Durjana Vārito'si Kāryam Tvayā Na Mama Sarvajanopabhukta. What? Go away. Come not within, O wicked one. You are banned from entering. I have nothing to do with you O Wretched one enjoyed by all and Sundry. In a poetical composition the Padas contain only a few syllables in regard to Sūcā and Aṅkura Abhinaya.

Prose Thus one should be assiduous in regard to Virāma. Why? Application of Virāma clarifies the sense. A verse in this context.

61 In the Vācika Abhinaya (Verbal representation) care should be taken by the producers in the matter of Virāma for on it depends the idea indicated.

62 In the course of the dance the eyes should be directed towards the spot where the hands are busily engaged in showing the Gestures and the Vācika Abhinaya is to be proceeded with by observing the relevant Virāmas that indicate the idea intended to be conveyed.

63—64 Mostly in the Vīra and Raudra Rasas the hands are employed in handling the weapons; in the Bībhatsa Rasa they are kept bent due to contemptuous attitude; in Hāsya Rasa they simply point out something; in Karuṇa they are kept dangling and in the Adbhuta Rasa they remain motionless due to wonder and dismay.

65 On similar occasions too when there is the movement of the hands the idea is clarified by means of Alaṁkāras and Virāma.

66—67 In Vṛttas Virāmas (Caesura etc.) are prescribed. Alaṁkāras should be used there; when the idea is concluded there should be Virāma in a word. If breath calls for it, there should be Virāma. When words and syllables are combined into a big compound, when the utterance is rapid, when there is the predicament due to multiplicity of meanings, pause should necessarily be made. Virāma is essential at the end of a foot or if breath calls for it. In other cases the Virāma depends on the idea conveyed.

Prose. In this context the Kṛṣya (likely to be drawn) out syllables should be understood with respect to the Bhāvas and Rasas.

68—69 The consonants ending with long vowels such as ā, e, ai or au are termed Kṛṣyākṣaras. In sadness, disputes, queries & indignation they are to be employed taking one Kalā time.

70 In regard to the remaining syllables they are to be uttered with Virāma called for by the idea conveyed. Such a Virāma shall be of one, two, three, four, five or six Kalās' duration.

71 In the case of delayed pause, the syllable uttered shall be long, but in no instance should the duration be more than six Kalās.

72 Or, the pause should be observed in a manner befitting the Rasas after taking into account the practice as required by any cause or action.

73 Well may there be Virāmas in Pāṭhya arising from the injunctions regarding the Vṛttas or the position of the metrical foot. But that order can be slighted (by stage managers) conversant with them to suit the meaning of the passage cocerned.

74 One conversant with the requistite practice shall not read, mispronouncing the words or against the meterical mode; there shall not be pauses where there is to be none; in expressing wretchedness the Kāku shall not be Dīpta (excited).

75 One shall recite the Pāṭhya possessing all the characteristics, equipped with Guṇas (qualities) and Svara and Alaṁkāras and also devoid of defects—one shall recite it in accordance with the injunctions thereof.

76 Alaṁkāras and Virāmas that have been prescribed in

the case of Saṁskrita shall also be observed in non- Saṁskrta (i.e. Prākṛta) pāṭhyas of the women.

77 Thus in the representation of the ten types of dramatic works, Pāṭhyas should be used by the sponsors subject to the observance of proper notes, Kalā, time and tempo.

78 The Kākuvidhāna has been explained by me duly and in the proper sequence. I shall now explain the classification of the ten Rūpakas.

Notes

2 The rules regarding the mode of address to venerable persons, equals, inferiors etc. are not comprehensive. We find numerous and diverse kinds of cases in the Saṁskrta Dramatic literature not covered by Nāṭya Śāstra.

9 Abhinava Gupta explains Kārukas as architects erecting sacrificial posts, columns etc. Śilpins are craftsmen, painters and the like.

30 Significant names—Śākuntala I. Anasūyā and Priyaṁvadā (the female companions of Śakuntalā have very significant names.

37—38 Some playwrights have over looked the injunctions regarding the names and addresses. But probably changes in the society over the centuries are responsible for these alterations.

Some of the prose pieces that follow may be the notes of stage managers or playwrights for general guidance. What Bharata has himself given in verse forms are therefore later introduced as traditionally handed over pieces.

20

Daśarūpavidhāna (Rules regarding the ten types of Dramas

1 **O Brahmins** I shall now describe the ten classes of plays in regard to their names, functions and the manner of their production on the stage.

2—5 As distinguished by their characteristics the dramas fall into ten classes viz. (1) Nāṭaka (2) Prakaraṇa (3) Aṅka (Utsṛṣṭikāṅka) (4) Vyāyoga (5) Bhāṇa (6) Samavakāra (7) Vīthī (8) Prahasana (9) Ḍima and (10) Īhāmṛga. I shall enumerate their characteristics duly.

Vṛttis (styles) are reputed to be the constituent factors of all dramatic works. If we take into account their production the ten types of dramas can be considered to have been evolved from these. The Svaras constitute the Grāmas (Scales) through Jātis and Śrutis. In the same manner the Kāvya Bandha (composition) is evolved through the different kinds of Vṛttis.

6—7 The Nāṭaka and the Prakaraṇa should be understood to have been evolved from all the vṛttis and these two make use of the different kinds of Bandhas (constructions). Just as the Ṣaḍja and Madhyama Grāmas are comprised of all the Svaras so also these two poetical works are evolved from all the Vṛttis (styles).

8—9 Plays of these names viz Vīthī, Samavakāra, Ihāmṛga, Utsṛṣṭikāṅka, Vyāyoga, Bhāṇa, Prahasana vṛtti (Graceful Style). Hence forth I shall mention the classification of Kāvyas (dramatic poems).

Nāṭaka explanation till verse 47

10—11 A play of the following type is styled Nāṭaka the theme is well known story. **The hero is a celebrated person** of exalted nature. The conduct of a saintly king is to be elaborated. He must have the support and succour from celestral beings. The exploits detailed should be many. There shall be prosperity, grace, elegance and other good points. Adequate number of Acts and introductory scenes (Praveśaka) must enrich it.

12 The conduct and activities of the kings, their movements representing the different Bhāvas and Rasas. and the effect of their personal joys and sorrows when represented in a play constitute a Nāṭaka.

13 *The Aṅka (Act).* The Act is to be constructed by elaborating the Bindu (turning Point, the nucleous) after first selecting the kārya (the main plot) befitting the stage. The persons well versed in the principles of dramatic productions should make each Act furnished with a group of characters.

14. The Aṅka makes the topics of the play grow (√Ruh- to Grow) through the Bhāvas and Rasas following certain rules and techniques. Then it has become a Rūḍhi word (Traditionally sense).

15 An Aṅka can be brought to a termination by a division of the play but the Bīja (seed) should not be got rid of. The Bindu originating from the poetical composition shall always be made to pervade the Vastu (the plot of the play).

16 That part of the play where the meaning is fully expressed but the Bīja is not got rid of is to be known as an Aṅka. It is here that Bindu clings to atleast to a certain extent always.

17 In an Aṅka the explorts of the persons pointed out before as the heroes, are to be displayed directly in the course of their various states but the Aṅka should not be made too long.

18 It should also be known that the Aṅka must contain the diverse Rasas from the speech and deeds of the queen, the hero, his elders, the priest, minister, the leader of the caravans etc.

. 18 (A) There shall be more than five and less than ten Aṅkas in a Nāṭaka and a Prakaraṇa. It the end of an Aṅka all the characters go out. This also should be noted.

19 Acts of wrath, favour, grief, pronouncing a curse, running away, marriage, the outcome of some miracle and its appearence—these should not be directly visible in an Aṅka.

20 A skirmish loss of kingdom, extinction of life, and the siege of a city are not to be presented directly visible. They should be indicated through the Praveśakas (Introductory scenes).

21 The bulling of the character introduced as the well known hero shall not be displayed either in the Aṅka itself or in the Praveśaka.

22 The flight, the treaty or capture should be presented through poetical pieces and the Praveśaka shall do that.

23 The Aṅka should be made to cover the incidents of only a single days based on the Arthabīja and proceeding without any obstacle to the essential incidents.

24 A sensible playwright shall not introduce far too many incidents in an Aṅka. The incidents introduced too shall avoid clash with the essential incidents.

25 People entering the stage in an Aṅka will go out after performing things connecting with the Bīja and the theme of the play with the Rasas befitting them.

26 Realizing the usual length of the day consisting of kṣaṇas (moments), yāmas (watches) and muhūrtas (24 mts) are should spread out the different incidents in a play to different Aṅkas.

27 *Praveśaka* If the incidents expected to be finished in the course of a single day cannot be fully dealt with in the Aṅka they should be presented through Praveśakas after terminating the Aṅka.

28 Events taking up a period of time extending to a month or more but any up to a year shall also be presented in the same manner after terminating the Aṅka, but those taking up more than a year, never.

29 If any man travels a long distance on an errand there also the Aṅka is to be terminated as before by those conversant with the same.

30 The Aṅka in Nāṭaka or Prakaraṇa shall be so made up as to be closely linked with the Nāyaka. The Praveśaka should be known as one associated with the attendants talking together.

31 In Prakaraṇa and Nāṭaka the Praveśaka should be made to closely follow the other Aṅkas based on the essentials of the Bindus.

32 The Praveśaka shall not contain the superior or middling characters nor should the speeches therein be of the exalted type. The language shall (mainly) be Prākṛta adopting the mode of speech of the laity.

33 The Praveśaka can have multiplicity of purposes. The advent or passage of time can be hinted at. Change of Rasas, the initial theme and the subject can be alluded to by mentioning the fact.

34 Events depending on many characters should be condensed by means of Praveśakas or in the Sandhis. A play consisting of many prose passages creates fatigue in the minds of the audience as well as the actors at the time of production.

35 Sometimes the items to be produced may be too many to be completed in one Aṅka. In that case the multiplicity of items should be produced through Praveśakas consisting of very few words.

The Viṣkambha (Explanatory Scene).

36 The Viṣkambha is to be produced through middling characters by persons aware of the procedure thereof. The language shall be **Saṁskṛta** It shall be brief and to the point like the Praveśaka.

37 The Viṣkambha of two kinds is to be produced. The Śuddha (Pure) one with middling **characters** and the Saṅkīrṇa (Mixed) one with both inferior and middling characters.

38 An Explanatory Scene (Viṣkambha) may be at the beginning of an Aṅka or between two Aṅkas in the drama called Nāṭaka or Prakaraṇa. It should invariably include the middling and the inferior characters.

39 Niether the Nāṭaka nor the Prakaraṇa should have too

many characters acting the role of the attendants or the commonalty. The number of workers should be limited to four or five

40 Poetical compositions such as Vyāyoga, Īhāmṛga, Samavakāra and Ḍima should contain ten or twelve characters.

41 There shall not be the direct introduction of the chariot, elephant, horse or aerialcart on the stage. The injunction is that they shall be presented through their imagss or costumes of the characters as well as their Gatis or Pravicāras (mode of walking or movements).

42 Model works of elephants, horses, aerial chariots. mountains, vehicles and weapons of dummy character can be made use of by those who known thc procedure.

Introduction of army

43 If for some reason it has become necessary to represent a royal camp or a division of the army the said marchpast can be represented by five or six man.

44 The introduction thereof shall be with very few persons, very few conveyances and very few accounterments all moving very slowly. Everything is to be made to show or hint in a veiled manner. The actors are not expected to behave like Kṣatriyas and rule over a kingdom.

45 In the composition of a poetical nature such as the drama the *denouement* shall be like the tip of a cow's tail. The exalted situations and Bhāvas should be at the end.

46—47 At the close of the play in the Nirvahaṇa Sandhi where different Rasas and Bhāvas manifest themselves, the Adbhuta Rasa must invariably be employed by the expert playwrights. In this manner I have succinctly but duly explained the characteristics of Nāṭaka. I shall hereafter explain the Prakaraṇa with all its characteristics.

48 *The Prakaraṇa.* By using his imaginative faculty the poet creates an original plot, the body of the work and its hero and makes the entire thing proceed ahead. This should be known by learned men to be a Prakaraṇa.

49 Sometimes a playwright writes a drama with purely invented Bīja (Seed) and (Vastu) these not at all connected with the epics of Saintly scholars (i.e. Vyāsa & Vālmīki) or the story may be taken from some other well known works (like Bṛhatkathā). He introduces marvellous qualities also therein We can call that too a Prakaraṇa.

50 The theme, body of the work, different Vṛttis etc which have been explained by me as adjuncts to a Nāṭaka can also be applied in the case of a Prakaraṇa too in all its Sandhis together with all the characteristic features.

51 That work also can be called a Prakaraṇa where in the different activities of **Brahmins** merchants, ministers, priests, counsellors and leaders of caravans are introduced.

52 It has no exalted personage as its hero. No divine conduct of life is dealt with therein. The king's pleasurable pastimes and enjoyments do not find a place there. It is solely produced by external ones (not connected with the palace) Persons conversant with that should make a note of this fact that it is the characteristic feature of a Prakaraṇa.

53 In a Prakaraṇa the theme of the poem shall move round servants, lechers, leading merchants, incidents connected with the activities of courtezans and very little of the conduct of the women of noble families.

54 In Prakaraṇa no courtezan is to be brought in and around the domestic domain of the ministers, leading merchants, **Brahmins** priests, counsellors and leaders of the caravans.

55 In a Prakaraṇa if the theme centres round the conduct of a youthful courtezan, no woman of a noble family should be brought into that scene. If, on the other hand it abounds in the activities of women of nobility no youthful courtezan treads her foot therein.

56 If, due to some exigency there happens a simultaneous appearance of the chaste women and the harlots in a scene, the Pāṭhya should contain the respective language and mannerism undisturbed and unchanged.

57 In the Nāṭaka as well as Prakaraṇa the playwright should compose not less than five and not more than ten

Aṅkas. They are fully embellished with different Rasas and Bhāvas.

58 The Praveśakas are to be composed between two Aṅkas with due consideration for the need and action of the plot. For the sake of brevity the events are to be compressed in the Sandhis.

59 *The Nāṭikā.* In a play of the Nāṭikā type the producers bring in a new type mingling these two (Nāṭaka and Prakarana) the hero (or theme, wellknown or otherwise.)

60 Since it is different from both Prakaraṇa and Nāṭaka the plot is something that has to be invented. The hero shall be a king and the Nāṭikā is to be based on the story of a girl in the harem well-versed in music.

61—62 Thd Nāṭikā should be known from the following features :—Female characters abound in the Nāṭikā consisting of four Aṅkas, graceful Abhinaya constitutes its soul; its constituents are excellently arranged it abounds, in dances, songs and passages of recitation and love in union forms its essence. The royal manners and customs are displayed in it; fits of anger, pacification thereof, acts of hypocrisy and deceit and the interrelation of the hero, the queen, the female messenger and the attendants find their fullest expression in the Nāṭikā.

63 The characteristic features of the Nāṭaka and Prakaraṇa also of the Nāṭikā have been mentioned. Hence forth I shall mention the characteristic features of Samavakāra.

64—65 *The Samavakāra.* The exploits of the Devas and the Asuras constitute its subject matter. A well known exalted personage is its hero. It has three Aṅkas depicting the three Kapaṭas (deception), three Vidravas (excitements) and the three Śṛṅgāras (lives). There shall be twelve (or there-about) characters. The duration of the play is eighteen Nāḍikās (18 × 24 mts). I shall now explain the rule regarding the number of Nāḍikās to be set apart for the different Aṅkas.

66 A Nāḍikā is half of a Mahūrta (48 mts). As a measure of time it is known to all. The Aṅkas in a Samavakāra should be of the duration of as many Nāḍikās are will be stipulated.

67 The first Aṅka of Samavakāra has a duration of twelve

Nāḍikās (4 hrs 48 mts). It contains humorous elements, running about here and there, deception and the elements of Vīthī (Vīthyaṅga thirteen in number. See 115 below).

68 The Second Aṅka has a duration of four Nāḍikās. The third Aṅka has two Nāḍikās within which the plot is brought to a successful end.

69 While engaged in the poetical Composition the playwright introduces different topics in the different Aṅkas. The topics in a Samavakāra are only loosely related to one another.

70 The *three Vidravas* (Excitements) are (a) due to war or flood of waters (b) due to stormy blasts of wind, raging fine and elephant run amuk and (c) due to the siege of a city.

71 The *three Kapaṭas* (deception) are (a) due to a devised plan (b) due to an accident and (c) due to the stratagem of an enemy.

72 The three Śṛṅgāras (Love) to be presented are (a) that which is based on Dharma (piety) (b) that which is motivated by profit of wealth (Artha) and (c) that actuated by passionate attachment (Kāma).

73 *Dharma Śṛṅgāra* (Love based on piety) while discharging his duty if one attains desired welfare and one adopts means like observing of vows, austerities and penance this is to be known as love based on piety (Dharma Śṛṅgāra).

74 *Artha Śṛṅgāra* (Love actuated by profit motive). If through wealth anything desired is obtained by diverse means or if women's love and enjoyment of pleasure with them is for some material gain it is an instance of Artha Śṛṅgāra (Love activated by profit motive).

75 *Kāma Śṛṅgāra*. Where there is seduction of a Virgin or the mutually consented intercourse between a man and a woman giving them excitement and pleasure, it is called Love due to passion.

76 Metres of complex construction should be used by the playwright in the Samavakāra. They should not be of Uṣṇika and Gāyatrī and other smallar Chandas.

77 Thus Samavakāra equipped with different kinds of

Rasas should be composed by those who are aware of their procedure. Hence forth I shall explain the characteristic features of Īhāmṛga.

78 *The Īhāmṛga*. Male ones of divine origin are the characters in an Īhāmṛga. There is fight over a celestial woman. It should be convincingly constructed with a well arranged plot.

79 The heroes are of the Uddhata (haughty and vehement) type. The basis for the composed poetical piece is the anger of women. There are incidents causing Saṁkṣobha (commotion), Vidrava (running about excitedly) and Saṁpheṭa (mutual conflict).

80 The Īhāmṛga has a well ordered structure in which the plot of love causes dissension among ladies and their abduction and also suppression of enemies.

81 Whatever has been prescribed in the case of vyāyoga shall be followed in Īhāmṛga too such as the male characters, the Vṛttis and the Rasas. The only difference is the association with the celestial woman (as heroine etc.).

82 In the Īhāmṛga when the killing of those desired to be killed becomes intense and unbearable the fight should be subdued under some pretext.

83 O Brahmins the characteristic features of the Īhāmṛga have been mentioned by me succinctly. Now I shall mention the characteristic features of Ḍima.

84 Ḍima is a play in four Aṅkas *displaying six Rasas*. The theme is well known and the hero is a renowned personality of exalted nature.

85–86 Excluding the Hāsya and Śṛṅgāra the other Rasas are represented. The theme has the different Rasas and Bhāvas brightly displayed. Incidents like Nirghata (thunder storm, earthquake), fall of meteors, eclipses of the moon, fights, wrestling, challenging and mutual conflict should be included.

87—88 Acts of deceit, jugglery ete. are brought in profusely, there are the energetic activities of many characters with dissension among themselves,. Devas, serpent lords, Rākṣasas, Yaksas and Piśācas predominate; as many as sixteen heroes should be introduced; Sātvati (Grand) Vṛtti are richly used, different Bhāvas, are to be resorted to supplement these.

89 Thus succinctly the characteristic features of the Ḍima have been described by me I shall now explain the essential features of the Vyāyoga.

90—93 *The Vyāyoga* is a short play with incidents of a single day. One well known personality is its hero. There are only very few female characters. In this was should it be composed by experts. As in the Samavakāra many male characters do take part in it but not so extensively because it has only one Aṅka. No divine personage acts as the hero here. A saintly king is the hero. It presents fights, duals, challenges and angry mutual conflicts. Such a Vyāyoga with its poetical theme resplendent with Rasas should be composed with all the characteristics. I shall now explain the characteristic features of the Utsṛṣṭikāṅka.

94 The plot in Utsṛṣṭikāṅka is a well known one. Sometimes it can be otherwise. The male characters are other than than the divine ones.

95—96 The Karuṇa Rasa predominninates in it. The incidents are after the cessation of hostilities and violent fightings on the part of the soldiers. Lamentations of women and utterances of utter despair and loss of hope abound in it. Different agitated activities and the termination of prosperity and glory are presented. The Utsrstikāṅka should be composed thus.

97 The scene is to be laid in Bhāratavarṣa if the poetical composition has celestial personages for heroes and scenes of fights, imprisoning and killing for its theme.

98 What is the reason for selecting Bhāratavarṣa of all the Varṣas allotted to the Devas ? That is because the land is wholly charming fragrant and golden coloured.

99—100 The scenes of their frequenting the parks enjoying sports and pastimes and sexual dalliance are to be laid in those Varṣas since there is neither sorrow nor misery there. Their residences mentioned in the accounts of the Purāṇas the mountains etc. should be set apart for must be held here (Bhārata Varṣa).

101 The characteristic features of Utsṛṣṭikāṅka have thus been explained by me in full. Henceforth I shall explain Prahasana with all the characteristic features.

101 *The Prahasana* too should be known to be of two kinds the Śuddha (Pure) and Saṅkīrṇa (mixed). I shall mention the essential features of either separately.

103—104 *The Śuddha Prahasana* contains comic disputations by saints of Śaiva cult and other Brahmins; cowardly and ignominions persons indulge in jocular remarks giving undistorted language of the laity full expression; the conduct of all the characters is described in passages with picturesque expressions of all their special Bhāvas.

105 *The Saṅkīrṇa Prahasana* is that wherein the characters are harlots, eunuchs, lechers (touts), rogues and women slaves indecent in appearance and dress and movements, uncouth in their activities.

106—107 Popular topics, slanderous rumours, incidents of hypocracy etc. should be introduced in the mixed Prahasana through arguments and disputes of rogues and pretenders. This Prahasana should contain the Vīthyaṅgas as well in accordance with suitability.

I shall hence forth describe the characteristics of Bhāṇa.

108 *The Bhāṇa* has only a single character. It is of two Kinds in as much as (a) one recounts ones own experience or (b) describes another person's activities.

109 The Bhāṇa of the latter variety including the words of another addressed to the speaker should be presented by means of replies in course of the conversations with imagined persons through Ākāśa Bhāṣita (Unembodied aerial speech) along with relevant movements of the limbs and gestures.

110 A Dhūrta (cheat, rogue) or a Viṭa (lecher) should present the play with many movements. The play consists of only one Aṅka. The different conditions of rogues and lechers should be alluded to.

111 All the essential features of Bhāṇa have been described by me as traditionally handed down I shall now describe the charaterstics of Vīthī O Brahmins

112—113 The Vīthī is a one-Act play where there may be one or two characters. It may have superior middling or the inferior character. Any Rasa can be displayed. Any of the thirteen Aṅgas can be included. I shall now mention the essential features of these Aṅgas as laid down (by tradition).

The Thirteen Aṅgas (*Ancilliaries*) of Vīthī

114—115 They are (1) Udghātyaka (2) Avalagita (3) Avaspandita (4) Asatpalāpa (5) Prapañca (6) Nālikā (7) Vākkeḷī (8) Adhibal (9) Chala (10) Vyāhāra (11) Mṛdava (12) Trigata and (13) Gaṇḍa.

116 In Vīthi these thirteen Aṅgas should alway be used (suitably). I shall mention the characteristics of these in the due order.

117 *Udghātyaka* (Accidental Interpretation). If men connect words very difficult to interpret with words not necessarily intended by the speaker for the purpose of explaining them it is an example of Udghātyaka.

118 *Avalagita* (Transference). When any thing occurring in relation to something is made to accomplish something else it becomes Avalagata.

119 *Avaspandita* (Ominons Significance). If any one utters something without thinking indicating auspicious or inauspicious sense and if it is explained away in another sense due to cleverness it shall be an example of Avaspandita.

120 *Asatpralāpa* (Incoherent chatter). When an irrelevant question is followed by an equally irrelevant answer it is an example of Asatpralāpa.

121 When a learned man speaks the rightwords but the foolish one does not pay heed to them it is also an example of Asatpralāpa.

122 *Prapañca* (Compliment). When comic and untrue words purporting to be mutual praise of two persons are uttered in the interest of one of them it is example of Prapañca.

124 Nālikā (Enigma) and Vākkelī (Repartee). An enigmatic remark followed by laughter is Nālikā. That which has a single or two fold reply is a Vākkelī.

124 *Adhibala* (Out vying). When somebody else's words and those of one's own in the course of a dialogue lead to their mutual modification it is example of Adhibala.

125 Chala (Deception). When after alluring one by replies, something opposite is done through those very replies being considered meaningless it is an example of Chala.

126 Vyāhāra (Declaration). If any thing likely to occur is described vividly as though seen actually in the presence of the hero and it does happen undoubtedly, it is an example of Vyāhāra.

127 *Mṛdava* (Crushing contrasting). That due to an altercation one represents another's merits as demerits by showing cause for the same or vice versa is called *Mṛdava.*

128 *Trigata* (Three men's talk). When exalted words with Hāsya Rasa are shared by three characters it should be known as Trigata.

129 *Gaṇda* (Undue combination of words). Due to excitement, confusion) quarrel, reviting and many people's abusive words an undue combination of words occurs. Those who know it call the same Gaṇḍa.

130—131 If in a play any of these thirteen Aṅgas occurs with clear meanings and these Aṅgas possess all the characters Rasas and Bhāvas enjoined by the treatise, it is called Vithī. It is presented by a single actor or two actors.

132 *Lāsyāṅga.* There are other ancillaries to attached to Nāṭaka in connection with the performance of Lāsyāṅga (a type of play) and they over their origin to this (i.e. Nāṭaka). They are to be acted like the Bhāṇa by a single person.

133 The Lāsya has a form similar to that of the Bhāṇa and it is to be acted by one person. Its theme is to be inferred like that of the Prakaraṇa and should relate to loving intimacy with anyone.

Twelve types of the Lāsya (Lāsyāṅgas)

134—135 The Lāsyāṅgas are (1) Geyapada (2) Sthitapāṭhya (3) Āsīna (4) Puṣpagaṇḍikā (5) Pracchedaka (6) Trimūḍha (7) Saindhava (8) Dvimūdhaka (9) Uttamotiamaka (10) Viçitrapada (11) Uktapratyukta and (12) Bhāvita.

136 *Geyapada.* The heroine is seated in the midst of her musical instruments but the singers go on singing the Geyapada (Sample Song) without playing on the instruments. This is called Geyapaḍa.

137 If a woman sings a song in praise of her beloved, in the posture of sitting, but with the gestures of the various limbs it is also called Geyapada.

138 *Sthitapāṭhya.* Burning with the fire of love if a woman in separation from her lover recites a composition in Prākṛta while seated on her seat it is an example of Sthitapāṭhya.

139 *Āsīnā.* The lover or the beloved sits overcome with anxiety and sorrow without caring for any make up or embelishment of the body looking askance. This is an example of Āsīna.

140 *Puṣpagaṇḍikā* If a women dressed like a man recites a simple poem in **Saṁskṛta** for amusing her female companious it is an example of Puṣpagaṇḍikā.

141 *Pracchedaka.* Where the moon struck women prepare to hasten to the side of their lovers even if they had committed infidelity and done them wrong the Lāsyāṅga should be known Pracchedaka.

142 *Trimūḍhaka.* A play composed of wods neither harsh nor large in number is called Trimūḍhaka if it is embelished with even metres and abounds in manly Bhāvas.

143 *Saindhavaka.* When a lover is represented as are who has not kept his tryst and one who uses Prākṛta to express his chief through well performed Karaṇas it is an example of Saindhavaka.

144 *Svimūḍhaka.* Delineating a song of the Caturaśra type with auspicous meaning, clear Bhāvas and Rasas is called Dvimūḍhaka if activities are pursued under pretants.

145 *Vicitrapada.* If any women burning with the fire of love consoles herself by looking at the portrait of her lover it is called Vicitrapada.

146 *Uttamottamaka.* The Uttamottamaka is composed of

diverse kinds of Ślokas including many Rasas and adorned with the Bhāva of Helā (Sportive passion).

147 *Uktapratyukta.* This is set to music with diverse kinds of ideas implied. It is a combination of speeches and curt replies arising from either Anger or eageroness to pacify It contains words of censure and rebuke.

148 *Bhāvita.* If a woman in separation, scorched with the fire of love sees her lover in the dream and expresses her feelings and emotional fervourit is an example of Bhāvita.

149 These are the characteristic features of the Lāsyāṅgas explained in detail by me. If anything is excluded here it is because of the fear of exceeding the limits of the context.

150 The rules regarding the ten kinds of dramatic compositions with their essential features in detail cannot be adequetely dealt with completely. Only a succinct accounts given here.

150a Everything connected with the ten Rūpakas has been explained by me along with their definitions etc. I shall now seak about their physical forms and their Sandhis (Junctures) with their characteristics.

Notes

1 Ancient writers onthe subject of drama and allied ones mention more types of plays such as Saṭṭaka, Toṭaka etc. They have differences of opinions too.

2 The word Nāṭaka sometimes is used in a general way indicating all types of plays.

3 The play Aṅka is distinct from the division of the play, Aṅka (Act). Hence the nomenclature of Utsṛṣṭikāṅka.

18 Sārthavāha is interpreted as Senāpati by Abhinavagupta. This has no Kośa sanction.

24 Routine duties—taking food, offering prayers etc.

45 Gopuccha perhaps means the necklace with many strings and a pendant. Hence the prominence given to the tips.

114—127 Examples for these thirteen Vīthyaṅgas are many in extant dramas such a Ratnāvalī, Veṇisaṁhāra etc.

134—148 The twelve Lāsyāṅgas. These also can be clearly understood through the examples in extant dramas. Sāhityadarpaṇa, Bhāvaprakāśa and other works give ample quotations.

21

Sandhyanga Vikalpa
Classification of the Constituents of Sandhis (Junctures)

1 The Itivṛtta (story, plot) is glorified as the physical form of the dramatic composition. It is classified into five Sandhis (junctures, joints).

2 The story or the plot is of two kinds; one is Ādhikārika (the main one, the principal theme) and the other one is Prāsaṅgika (subsidiary).

3 That aspect of the story where the activities are evolved and elaborated with a view to the achievement of some particular result is to be known as Ādhikārika and the other one they say is the Prāsaṅgika.

4—5 Based on the attainment of the result the plot and the event becomes Ādhikārika. The Ānuṣaṅgika (i.e. Prāsaṅgika) is that incident mentioned for the purpose of helping another main incident in it. Through the effort of the poet as well as the adherence to the rules by the heroes the attainment of the result and its exaltation becomes possible.

6 *Five stages of Action.* The activity of the Sādhaka (the striving hero) in respect to the attainment of the result should be understood by the producers to have five stages in due order.

7 [The verse is Prakṣipta]. Those stages are considered to be arising in the Nāṭaka and Prakaraṇa. The Phalayoga (Attainment of the fruit) is in relation to Dharma (piety), Kāma (love) and Artha (wealth).

8 The five stages are (1) Prārambha (2) Prayatna (3) Prāptisambhava (4) Niyatā Phalaprāpti and (5) Phalayoga

9 Prārambha (Beginning) is that part of the composition where the eagerness (of the hero) for the attainment of the great fruit with reference to the Bīja (seed) is merely recorded.

10 *Prayatna* (Effort) Although unable to see the attainment of the fruit the hero is eager for the same and strives towards it. This is called Prayatna.

11 *Prāptisambhava* (Possiblity of attainment). If the attainment of the desired fruit is slightly suggested it is to be known as the Prāptisambhava.

12 *Niyatā Phalaprāpti*. (Certainty of attainment). If the hero (or others) mentally visualises that the attainment of the fruit is assured it is called *Niyatā Phalaprāpti*.

13 *Phalayoga*. (Ultimate attainment). At the end of the story or plot, of the fruit desired fruit appears in full and that too befittingly it is called Phalayoga.

14 These are the five successive stages of every effort on the part of the persons seeking the desired benefits and friut.

15 These different stages are intrinsically different from one another. Yet the playwright shall set-them together with a single minded attention for the purpose of producing the fruit. That is glorified as the cause of the attainment of fruit.

16 Ādhikārika plot has already been explained. The composition should be with that at the beginning so that it shall end also with it.

17 The composition shall have the full complement of all the Sandhis or be deficient in one or two. It is the general rule that all should be employed but if reasons warrant if, some of them may be dropped.

18 *Guidance for omitting* Sandhis. The guidance for omitting Sandhi is as follows If one of them is to be dropped then it shall be the fourth; if two Sandhis are to be dropped the third and the fourth are excluded; if three Sandhis are to be dropped then the second, third and the fourth are to be dropped..

19 This guideline is not applicable in the case of the Prāsaṅgika plot for it is to serve another plot, Without coming into clash with any rule and event can be introduced therein.

20 *Artha-Prakṛti.* (Elements of the plot). Just as five stages in the plot have been enumereted there are also five Artha-Prakṛtis (essential elements bringing about the results) beginning with Bīja (Seed).

21 *Bīja* (*Seed*). Bindu (Prominent point) Patākā (Episode), Prakarı (Episodical incident) and the Kārya (denouement) are the five Arthaprakṛtis. They must be properly understood and employed suitably.

22 *Bīja.* Scattered at the outset in a very small measure it expands and spreads in many ways and ultimately comes to fruition. That is called Bīja.

23 *Bindu.* Even the aimed objectives tend to break up there is something that supports the continuity till the end of the composition. It is called the Bindu.

24 *Patākā.* The incident introduced as subsidiary to the main plot but actually treated like the main plot is called Patākā.

25 *Prakarī.* When the result of subsidiary event is merely presented for the purpose of another (i.e. main story) because its itself has no continuity it is called Prakarī.

26 *Kārya.* The endeavour put in earnestly by the characters for the purpose of the main plot introduced by the sensible play wrights is called the Kārya.

27 Of these five Arthaprakṛtis that which has others to supplement it and to which others are mere subsidiaries should be treated as the chief one and-the others merely as adjuncts.

28 *Anubandha* (*Patāka*). When the Sandhi applied to Patāka is one or more but if it serves the purpose of the main plot it is called Anubandha-Patākā.

29 *Its limit,* The Patākā ceases to exist either at the Garbha Sandhi or at the Vimarśa Sandhi why ? Because its inclusion is for the sake of something else (i.e. main plot).

30 Patākāsthāna (Episode Indication). When some matter has already been thought of, if another matter having similar characteristics is suggested through a casual idea it is called Patākāsthāna.

31 *Prathama Patākāsthāna* (There are four Patākā-Sthānas). Of them the first one is the sudden development of a novel idea (Arthasamāpatti) due to an indirect suggestion.

32 *Dvitīya Patākā Sthāna.* The second one is the assemblage of words fully consisting of *double entendre* expressed poetically.

33 *Tṛtīya Patākā Sthāna.* The third one is that which politely suggests the subject matter but in a veiled manner along with a continuous and connected dialogue.

34 *Caturtha Patākā Sthnāna.* The fourth one is the utterance of words with double meaning in a well structured poetical language referring to something else.

35 The poetical composition in the form of a Nāṭaka should have the Kārya extending over the four Patākā Sthānas. It shall contain five Sandhis. Henceforth I shall mention them.

36 The *five Sandhis* in the Nāṭaka are (1) Mukha (opening) (2) Pratimukha (Progression) (3) Garbha (Development) (4) Vimarśa (deliberation, Pause) and (5) Nirvahaṇa (conclusion).

37 The principal plot is reputed to have been endowed with five Sandhis. The remaining ones are Anusandhis supporting the principal Sandhis.

38 *Mukha Sandhi* (The Opening Juncture). That part of a play where the Arthaprakṛti called Bīja (Seed) takes its origin along with the manifestation of many features and Rasas and is closely connected with the body of the plot (especially at the Prārambha stage) is called Mukha Sandhi.

39 *Pratimukha Sandhi* (Progression). That part of the play where the Bīja that had been previously placed is uncovered is called Pratimukha after being perceptible for a while and then getting lost as it were.

40 *Garbha Sandhi* (Development). The manifestation of the Bīja, its attainment and want of attainment and the search for it, is called Garbha Sandhi.

41 *Vimarśa Sandhi* (Pause and deliberation). The pause and reflection over the seed that has sprouted in the Garbha

Sandhi, due to some temptation, anger or vicious indulgence is called Vimarśa Sandhi.

42 *Nirvahaṇa Sandhi* (Conclusion) is that part of the play where the objects of Mukha and other Sandhis, along with the Bīja (seed) are brought together when they have attained fruition.

43 These Sandhis should be understood by those who produce Nāṭaka and Prakaraṇa. Understand the Sandhis of the remaining types of plays.

44 Ḍima and Samavakāra shall have only four Sandhis. Vimarśa Sandhi should never be included in them by the poets.

45 Vyāyoga and Īhāmṛga have been proclaimed as having only three Sandhis. There shall be no Garbha or Avamarśa Sandhi. Kaiśikī style too has no place in them.

46 The Prahasana, Vīthī, Utsṛṣṭikāṅka and the Bhāṇa have only two Sandhis viz the Mukha and the Nirvahaṇa and their style shall be Bhāratī.

47 Sandhis should be included in this manner in the ten Rūpakas by the producers. Now understand the adoption of the Aṅgas in these.

48—50 There are twenty one special Sandhyantaras of the Sandhis. They are (1) Sāma (Conciliation, pacification) (2) Bheda (Dissension) (3) Pradāna (Making gifts) (4) Daṇḍa (Chastisement) (5) Vadha (killing) (6) Pratyutpannamatitva (Presence of mind) (7) Gotraskhalita (Blunder in addressing (8) Sāhasa (Rashness) (9) Bhaya (fear) (10) Dhī (Intelligence) (11) Māyā (deceit) (12) Krodha (Anger) (13) Ojas (Strength) (14) Samvaraṇa (Concealment) (15) Bhrānti (Error) (16) Hetvavadhāraṇa (Ascertainment of the cause) (17) Dūta (Messenger) (18) Lekha (letter) (19) Svapna (Dream) (20) Citra (Portrait) and (21) Mada (Inebriety).

51. The events of the Sandhis in their respective parts will in due order support those limbs of the junctures by means of their own qualities.

52—53. *Six uses of Sandhyāṅgas* have been mentioned in the Śāstra viz. (1) Iṣṭasya Arthasya Vacanam (Expressing the desired object) (2) Vṛttāntasya Anupakṣaya (non-omission of essential features in the plot) (3) Rāgaprāptiḥ Prayogasyam (accession to feeling in production) (4) Guhyānām Gūhanam (Concealment of the objects to be concealed (5) Āścaryavadabhi khyānam (telling tales of surprise) and (6) Prakāśyānām Prakāśanam (disclosing things to be disclosed).

54 Just as a men devoid of his limbs is unable to take up any work so also a play without the limbs (Sandhyaṅga) will be unfit for successful production.

55. A poetical composition may be poor as regards its theme; but when furnished with the Aṅgas perfectly it will attain beauty because of the splendour of the production.

56. A poetical composition may be exalted in its theme. But when benefit of the Aṅgas it will never captivate the mind of the good critics because of the deficiency in production.

57. Hence in employing the Sandhis the poet should provide them with their relevant limbs. Now listen to and understand them.

The Sixty four Sandhyaṅgas

58—59 The Aṅgas of the Mukhasandhi are (1) Upakṣepa (2) Parikara (3) Parinyāsa (4) Vilobhanam (5) Yukti (6) Prāpti (7) Samādhāna (8) Vidhāna (9) Paribhāvanā (10) Udbheda (11) Karaṇa and (12) Bheda. Hence fourth listen to the Aṅgas in Pratimukha.

60—61 The following are the Aṅgas in the Pratimukha. Sandhi : (1) Vilāsa (2) Parisarpa (3) Vidhūta (4) Tāpana (Tāpana)(5) Narma (6) Narmadyuti (7) Pragamana (8) Nirodha (9) Paryupāsana (10) Puṣpa (11) Vajra (12) Upanyāsa and (13) Varṇa Saṁhāra.

62—64 The following are the Aṅgas of the Garbhasandhi :— (1) Abhūtāharaṇa (2) Mārga (3) Rūpa (4) Udāharaṇa (5) Krama (6) Saṁgraha (7) Anumāna (8) Prārthanā (9) Ākṣipta (10) Toṭaha (11) Adhibala (12) Udvega and (13) Vidrava.

65—66 The following are the Aṅgas in the Vimarśa Sandhi :— (1) Apavāda (2) Sampheṭa (3) Vidrava (4) Śakti (5) Vyavasāya (6) Prasaṅga (7) Dyuti (8) Kheda (9) Niṣedhana (10) Virodhana (11) Ādāna (12) Chādana and (13) Prarocana.

66—69 Listen to the Aṅgas of the Nirvahaṇaya Sandhi:—(1) Sandhi (2) Vibodha (3) Grathana (4) Nirṇaya (5) Paribhāṣaṇa (6) Dhṛti (7) Prasāda (8) Ānanda (9) Samaya (10) Apagūhana (11) Bhāṣaṇa (12) Pūrvavākya (13) Kāvyasaṁhāra and (14) Praśasti. These are the sixty four Aṅgas of the Sandhis to be known by learned men. These are to be employed by poets in the Nāṭaka after dividing the meanings. They are conducing to the attainment of the Bīja. I shall menti on their characteristics in due order.

69—75 *Mukhasandhi* (1) Upakṣepa (Suggestion—origin of the object originated (2) Parikara (Enlargement) Amplification of the object originated (3) Parikara (Establishment) Descr.bing the object thoroughly (4) Vilobhana (Allurement) Mentioning of good qualities. (5) Yukti (Decision) Settling the issues. (6) Prāpti (Accession) Summing up the purpose of the Mukhasandhi (7) Samādhāna (Settling) Summing the purpose of the Bīja (8) Vidhāna (Conflict of feelings) Joys and Sorrows occur in a Situation (9) Paribhāvanā (Surprise) Excitement gives rise to curiosity (10) Udbheda (Disclosure) Sprouting of the purpose of Bīja (Seed) (11) Karaṇa (Activity) Taking up the matter in question (12) Bheda (Incitement) That meant for disrupting a Union.

These are the Aṅgas of the Mukha Sandhi.

76—82 *Pratimukha Sandhi.* (1) Vilāsa (Amorousness). Eagerness for the pleasure of love play. (2) Pariśarpa (Pursuit) following the object lost after being seen (3) Vidhūta (Refusal) Not complying at the outset with a request made (4) Tāpan (Pessimism) Visualising danger and brooding over it. (5) Narma (Joke) Playful laughter. (6) Narmadyuti (Flash of joke) Laughter trying to hide faults. (7) Pragamana (Moving forward) Speaking words followed by words (8) Nirodha (Hindrance) Advent of some calamity (9) Paryupāsana (Pacification) Conciliating an angry person (10) Puṣpa (Sweet Words) Mentioning favourable peculiarity (11) Vajra (Thunderbolt) Harsh words uttered directly (12) Upanyāsa (Reference) a remark that is justified (13) Varṇasamhāra (Meeting of castes) Four castes coming together.

These are the Sandhyaṅgas of Pratimukha.

83—89 *Garbhasandhi* (1) Abhūtāharaṇa (Mis-statement)

Relying on decent (2) [Mārga (Indication). Speaking out the fact and real intention (3) Rūpa (Supposition) Hypothesis combined with novel meanings (4) Udāharaūa (Exaggeration). Over statement (5) Krama (Progress) Foreseeing what is about to follow (6) Saṁgraha (Propitiation) Use of pacifying words and gifts (7) Anumāna (Deduction) Perceiving something by the name of a thing similar to it in form (8) Prārthanā (Supplication) Request for sexual delliance delight, festivity etc (9) Ākṣipta (Revelation) The unfolding of the Garbha (10) Toṭaka (Quarrel) Speech with great anger (11) Adhibala (Out witting) Outwitting a deceitful person (12) Udvega (Dīsmay) Fear from the king enemy or robber (13) Vidrava (Panicky commotion) Flurry caused by fear of the king or conflagration.

These are the Aṅgas of the Garbhasandhi.

90—96 *Avamarśa Sandhi* (1) Apavāda (Censure) Proclaiming some are; fault (2) Saṁpheṭa (Angry words) Words spoken in anger (3) *Abhidrava* (Insolense) Transgression of the elders (4) Śakti (Placation) Allaying of disagreement with others (5) Vyavasāya (Assertion) Activity based on some reason or an account of a promise (6) Prasaṅga (Reverence) Eulogising the elders (7) Dyuti (Rebuke) Rebuking words spoken in contempt (8) Kheda (Lassitude) Weariness resulting from mental effort (9) Niṣedha (opposition) obstruction to one's desired object (10) Virodhana (Altercation) Arguments and counter orguments due to excitement (11) Ādāna (summing up) The act of bringing together all aspects of the Bīja (12) Chādana (concealment) Enduring insulting words for some purpose is called Chādana (13) *Prarocanā* (Foresight That which represents the conclusion in advance.

These are the Aṅgas of Vimarśa Sandhi. Now listen to the Aṅgas of the Nirvahaṇa.

97—103 *Nirvahaṇa Sandhi* (1) Sandhi (Junction). The coming up of the Bīja of the Mukha Sandhi (2) Vibodha (Awakening) Looking duly for the Kārya (3) Grathana Assembling) Intimation of the Various aspects of the Kāryas. (4) Nirṇaya (Ascertainment) Declaration of facts personally experienced (5) Paribhāṣaṇa (Accusation) That which is said in order to blame some one (6) Dhṛti (Confirmation) Turning to use the object gained (7) Prasāda treating one with waiting upon etc. and the pleasure desired therefrom. (8) Ānanda (Joy)

Attaining the objectives (9) Samaya (Deliverance) Passing off of all misery (10) Upagūhana (Surprise) Appearance of the mysterious (11) Bhāṣaṇa (Clever speech) Words expressing conciliation, gift and the like (12) Pūrvavākya (Retrospect) Reference to something spoken (13) Kāvyasaṁhāra (Termination) Receiving a boon (14) Praśasti (Benediction) Eulogy and blessing of the king and seeking welfare of the country.

104 Keeping in view the Rasas and the Bhāvas these Saṅdhyaṅgas must be introduced in theNāṭaka befitting the respective Sandhi by the poets clever in the poetical compositions.

105 Considering the extent of the Action or the stages a mixture of all or two or three of these Aṅgas should be introduced into the Sandhis at times.

106 *Arthopakṣepas five in number* Explanatory devices The āre (1) Viṣkambhaka (Supporting scene (2) Cūlika (Informatory speech) (3) Praveśaka (Introductory scene) (4) Aṅkāvatara (Transitional Scene).

107 The Viṣkambhaka shall consist of only the middling characters and that too Males it shall be introduced only in the Mukhasandhi of a Nāṭaka. The characters are preferably priest, the minister or the chamberlain.

108 *Viṣkambhaka* should be understood to be of two types the Śuddha (Pure) and the Saṅkīrṇa (mixed). Of these the Śuddha consists only middling characters while the Saṅkīrṇa of the middling as well as inferior characters.

109 *Cūlikā* Some secret points or events are explained from behind the curtain by the charioteer or others. It is called cūlikā (Informatory Speech).

110 *Praveśaka* (Introductory Scene) Based on the summary of the Prominent points the Praveśaka is to be introduced in between two Aṅkas in a Nāṭaka or Prakaraṇa.

111 *The Praveśaka* should be understood to have the following features. Neither the superior nor the middling male characters take part in it. No exalted speech finds place there. The language shall be Prākṛta.

112 *Aṅkāvatāra* This occurs in the course of the dramatic performance either between two Acts or at the end of an Act.

It adduces argument for the main purpose of the Bīja (Transitional scene).

113 *Aṅkamukha* (Anticipatory Scene) At the beginning of an Act if a male or a female character summerizes the events about to take place it is called Aṅka Mukha.

114–117 *An ideal Nāṭaka.* The poet must compose a Nāṭaka having different Vṛttis (Styles) minor limbs, Patākāsthānakas, Arthaprakṛtis (elements of the plot) arising from the five Avasthās, having the five Sandhis the twenty one Sandhyantaras, the sixty four Aṅgas, the thirty six Lakṣaṇas the Guṇas, the Alaṁkāras, many Rasas, topics of enjoyment of pleasures, exalted speeches, many excellent characters, description of good conduct, having popular appeal, well knit in junctures, easy for performance on the stage, composed of sweet words and competent to give aesthetic pleasure

118 All the stages and conditions of life existing in the world (i.e. society) as a result of happiness or misery and those related with different kinds of people find a place in the Nāṭaka.

119 There is nothing of wisdom, five arts, no lore, no art, no craft no device and no action that is not available in a Nāṭaka.

120 The very nature of the human beings in the form of different stages and states is represented through Aṅga Abhinayas (gestures of the limbs) etc. and it is called Nāṭya (dramatic performance).

121 An imitation of the previous activities of the Devas, sages and kings of excellent intellect shall become a Nāṭaka.

122 Since this is represented and interpreted by the characters who eschew their real nature but adopt different orders of movements of limbs it is remembered as Nāṭaka (from the √Naṭ to show gestures etc).

123 The Nāṭaka is made io include different stages, Rasas, predilections, activities and conditions of men and nature.

124 The different kinds of arts and crafts nay the manifold activities and enterprises of human beings should be applied wholly by those who produce.

125 After observing human nature completely after taking into consideration the strength and weakness of human beings as well as their ways of reasoning and enjoyment of pleasures one should attempt the composition of a Nāṭaka.

126 In the future eras men shall usually become senseless. Those who are yet to be born will be people of small learning and intellect.

127 Arts and Crafts, Śāstras, Strength and Cleverness—all these will become reduced. Then the world shall perish.

128 Hence the poet shall compose a Nāṭaka after carefully observing the strength and weakness of the people and their languages. It shall be full of soft words and pleasing topics.

129 If the poetical compositions abound in (harsh) words lakes Cekriḍita etc. they do not shine like harlots in the company of brahmins holding water pots.

130 O Brahmins I have explained the theme of the poetical composition along with its Sandhis and Aṅgas. Henceforth I shall explain the essential features of Vṛttis (styles).

Notes

The numerous technical terms in this chapter regarding the Sandhyaṅgas etc. have been later adopted by various rhetoricians with suitable alterations and additions too.

Some of the names are misspelt in different Mss. We have followed readings from all these and adopted whichever was found to be correct.

We do not give here cross references from Nyāyalakṣaṇa, Sāhityadarpaṇa, Daśarūpa and other standard works of which there are many excellent editions available edited by scholars of great erudiction.

22

Vrttivikalpa [Divisions of Vrttis (Styles)]

The origin of the Vṛttis

1 I shall now explain fully aud duly the outcome of Vṛttis. Incidentally I shall explain the origin formation and divisions of kāvyas (poetical and dramatic compositions).

2–3 When Lord Acyuta converted the entire universe into a vast expanse of water and compressed all the worlds through his Māyā (Super natural power of concealing and revealing differently) and lay thereafter on his serpent-conch two Asuras named Madhu and Kaiṭabha who became haughty due to their virility and prowess challenged the Lord vigorously with an ardour for fighting.

4–5 They made various gestures of challenge like rubbing both the hands together and pressing the arms. They fought the imperishable Bhūtabhāvana (the creator of all living being, Lord Viṣṇu) by hitting him with their fists and knees. Rushing at him by turns they indulged in harsh words and words of rebuke appeared to stir up the entire ocean.

6—7 *Bhāratī Vṛtti* (*Verbal style*) Hearing the words of rebuke of various kinds of those two, Druahiṇa (Brahmā) became distressed in mind and said—' Does this Bhārati Vṛtti (Verbal Style) starts with the words and increase step by step. Lead them to their death.

8—10 Hearing the words of the grandfather (Brahmā) Madhusūdana (i e. Viṣṇu) said—"It is with some special object that the Bhāratī Vṛtti has been evolved by me, O Brahmā. It will be the Bhāratī Vṛtti of those who speak. Words will prevail therein. I shall kill these two today." said Hari. With perfect gestures of the limbs and undistorted Aṅgahāras he fought assidiously with those two Daityas who were experts in the path of warfare.

11 At that time Hari's stepping with the Sthānakas on the ground caused a great burden (Bhāra) on the ground (Bhūmi). Therefore the Vṛtti named Bhārati was evolved. (Verbal Style).

12 *Satvatī Vṛtti*. At that very time the Valgitas (Vauntings) issuing from the Śārṅga bow of the lord became intensely brilliant, unagitated and full of Sattva (latent strength). Thus the Sāttvatī Vṛtti was evolved (Grand Style).

13 *Kaiśikīvṛtti*. The Deva moved Gracefully and sportingly with diverse Aṅgahāras and tied up his tuff (Śikhāpāśa or Keśapāśa). Thereupon the Kaiśikī Vṛtti was evolved (Graceful Style).

14 *Ārabhaṭī Vṛtti*. From the various personal combats (duals) full of energy and excitement and accompanied by different kinds of cārīs was evolved the Ārabhaṭī Vṛtti (Energetic Style).

15 Druhiṇa allotted ardently words befitting the meanings of the activitics (of Visnu) on seeing them arising out of the Vṛttis.

16 When the Asuras Madhu and Kaiṭabha were killed by Hari (i.e. Viṣṇu), the lotus born lord (i.e. Brahmā) said to Nārāyaṇa the suppressor of enemies.

17—18 The destruction of the Dānavas has been effected by you, O lord, through the various clearly expressive and graceful Aṅgahāras, hence this method of dual fighting shall be termed Nyāyainias much as they are related to the discharge of all sorts of missiles.

19 Since the fights are being pursued with the Aṅgahāras arising from Nyāya and based on it they are glorified as Nyāyas.

20 Thereafter this style (Vṛtti) was handed over to the Devas by the noble souled Druhiṇa for the purpose of using it in the production of dramatic and dance programmes because it was full of the various kinds of Bhāvas and Rasas.

21—22 These repositories of poetical compositions were named Vṛttis. The sages fashioned the Vṛttis along with the

Pāṭhyas out of the exploits of the lord Viṣṇu whatever they were in whatever manner they have been made. The words gestures had their origin in materials taken from the four Vedas (or Nāṭya Veda). The Vṛttis had the words and gestures as their essential characteristics.

23 These desirable and well-evolved Vṛttis full of various Cārīs were accepted and deposited by me (i.e. Bharata) at the bidding of Druhiṇa for the purpose of making poetical compositions (dramas).

24 The Bhāratī Vṛtti was from the Ṛgveda; the Sāttvatī from the Yajur Veda; the Kaiśiki from the Sāma Veda and the remaining one i e. the Ārabhaṭī from the Atharva Veda.

25 The Vṛtti that gives a preliment position to speeches with Saṁskṛta Pāṭhya is called Bhāratī Vṛtti. This is solely adopted by male characters excluding women. The Bharatas (actors) called it after their own name.

26 *Four varieties of Bhāratī style.* It has four varieties that had become its Aṅgas. Viz. (1) Prarocanā (Laudation) (2) Āmukha (Introduction) (3) Vīthī and (4) Prahasana.

27 Prarocanā is that introductory part where the name of the composition is announced and through adequate reasons and arguments the audience is invited to witness the same.

27a This laudation in the Pūrvaraṅga is for the purpose of attaining success, prosperity, good luck and victory and for the elimination of all sins.

28—29 *Āmukha* is that part of the play at the outset where the Naṭī, Vidūṣaka or Pāripārśvika (Assistant) is engaged in earnast conversation with the Sūtradhāra (Stage manager). The topic of conversation shall be relevant. The words used are of diverse kinds employing Vīthyaṅgas or other things. Sensible persons know it to be Āmukha or Prastāvanā.

30—31 Henceforth I shall explain the Āmukhāṅgas (Ancillaries of Āmukha) duly and in the proper order Udghātyaka, Kathodghāta, Prayogātiśaya, Pravṛttaka and Avalagita are the five Aṅgas of the Āmukha. The characteristics of the Udghātyaka and Avalagita have been already mentioned by me. I shall now speak in detail of the characteristics of the remaining ones.

32 *Kathodghāta* Taking up a remark of the stage manager or its meaning the character in the play enters. This is called Kathodghāta (opening of the story).

33 *Prayogātiśaya* When the stage manager imposes another production over the introduction and the character enters thereafter at is called Prayogātiśaya (Particular presentation).

34 *Pravṛttaka* The stage manager speaks of some matter taken up by him. The character in the play takes up the opportunity to enter on that very basis. This is called Pravṛttaka (Personal Business).

35 The playwright shall compose the Āmukha by employing one of the varieties mentioned above. He shall skilfully use Ślesa (double entendio) so that there is no hindrence to the entry of the characters nor is there any conflict with the authoritative texts.

36 The wise people are to know thus the different bases of Āmukha. The characteristics of the Vīthi and Prahasana have already been mentioned.

37 These are the eight different aspects of the Bhārati Vṛtti. I shall now explain the rules regarding Sāttvatī Vṛtti with all its essential features.

38 *Sāttvatī Vṛtti* This is endorved with the Sāttvata quality, the Nyāyas and metrical pattern. There is an exuberance of joy and the emotional fervour of sorrow is completely curbed. This is called Sāttvatī Vṛtti (Grand Style).

39 This Vṛtti is also to known to consist of representation of words and gestures and of power in the speeches and acts showing the rise of spirit.

40 This Vṛtti has the Vīra, Adbhuta and Raudra Rasas. It excludes Śṛṅgāra and Karuṇa Rasas. There is no place for despendency. The characters therein are mostly the majestic and the defiant ones.

41 *Four Varieties* of the Sāttvatī Vṛtti are (1) Utthāpava (2) Parivartaka (3) Sallāpaka and bv Saṁghāta.

42 *Utthāpaka* (Challenge) "I am getting up now for fighting. You may show your strength" Such a challenge arising from the spirit of rivalry is called Utthāpaka.

43 *Parivartaka* (Change of Action). If one sets apart the causes that made him rise and adopts other things out of necessity it is called Parivartaka.

44 *Sallāpaka* (Harsh discourse) Various kinds of words of abuse and insult caused by a challenge or otherwise are called Sallāpaka.

45 *Saṁghāta* (Breach of Alliance). If for the sake of a friend or some monetary gain or due to a chance occurrence or due to one's own fault an alliance is broken off it is called Saṁghāta.

46 These eight types of Sāttvatī Vṛtti have thus been explained by me. Henceforth I shall explain the characteristic features of the Kaiśikī Vṛtti.

47 *Kaiśikī Vṛtti* (Graceful Style) They call it Kaiśikī Vṛtti if it is extremely interesting thanks to the delicate costumes worn by the characters mostly women; and if it comprises of diverse types of dances and songs and the themes are the activities conducive to the enjoyment of love and sexual pleasures.

48 Four varieties of Kaiśikī Vṛtti have been mentioned namely (1) Narman (2) Narmasphūrja (3) Narmasphoṭa and (4) Narmagarbha.

49 *Narman* (Pleasantry) is the utterance that abounds in remarks made in jest. With regard to love in union it is of three kinds (1) Āsthāpita Śṛṅgāra (that by which love is stabilized) (2) Viśuddhakaraṇa (that with pure laughter) (3) Nivṛttavīrarasa (that which excludes Vīra Rasa).

50 **Savipralambha** Narman (Pleasantry in regard to love in separation) is also of three kinds (1) Īrṣyākopaprāyam (full of acts of jealousy and anger (2) Sopālambhakaraṇānuviddha (full of words of rebuke and taunt) and (3) Ātmopakṣepakṛtam (made through self reproach).

51 *Narmasphūrja* (Sudden burst of pleasantry). At the time of the first meeting of the lovers if at the outset words and dresses excite love but at the end causes fear. Then it is called Narmasphūrja.

52 *Narmasphoṭa* (Unfoldment of pleasantry) That which is embellished with fragments of various Bhāvas of diverse excellences should be known as Narma Sphoṭa. In it all the Rasas are not fully employed or revealed.

53 *Narmagarbha.* (Covert pleasantry). The hero endowed with the qualities of intelligence, beauty, affluence etc. behaves incognito for some ulterior purpose. Then it is called Narmagarbha.

54 These are the eight varieties of Kaiśikī Vṛtti and I have explained them. Hence forth I shall explain the Ārabhaṭī Vṛtti where haughticness dominates the Rasas.

55 *Ārabhaṭī Vṛtti* (Energetic Style) The style which includes mostly the qualities of a very courageous person is called Ārabhaṭī Vṛtti. There is much of deception and fraud. Hypocritic bragging and falsehood abounds in it.

56 They call that style Ārabhaṭī if there is representation of falling down, jumping, crossing over, deeds of magic and jugglery, and different kinds of fighting.

57 Four Varieties of Ārabhaṭī Vṛtti are (1) Saṁkṣiptaka (2) Avapāta (3) Vastūtthāpana and (4) Saṁpheṭa. I shall mention their essential features.

58 *Saṁkṣiptaka* (Compression) That which is called Saṁkṣiptaka is furnished with work manship in the literal sense of the term. Presentation of the model works, drawings and dresses is its main feature. The subject matter is also extremely condensed.

59 *Āvapata* (Commotion) is in those affairs causing fear and jubilation, panic, flurry, tumbling down and excited activities as well as quick entries and exists.

60 *Vastūtthāpana* (Raising the theme). Nāṭya where there is brief combination of all Rasas, with or without panicky running about is to be known as Vastūtthāpana.

61 *Sampheṭa* (Conflict) That which is actuated by excessive excitement and includes many fights, duals, deception, split, dissension and clash of weapons is called Sampheṭa.

62 Thus the Vṛttis should be known in their relationship with dramatic performances by the learned ones. Now listen to their application in regard to various Rasas as being narrated by me.

63 64 Kaiśikī Vṛtti is said to abound in Śṛṅgāra and Hāsya Rasas; Sāttvatī should be known in Vīra, Raudra and Adbhuta Rasas; Ārabhaṭī occurs in Bhayānaka, Bībhatsa and Raudra and Bhāratī should be understood as based on Karuṇa and Adbhuta Rasas.

65 I have duly explained the histronic representation based on words, bodily gestures and Sāttvika Bhāvas and ending with Vṛttis. Now I shall deal with continues and make up in the Āhārya Abhinaya as employed in the production of plays.

Notes

2. The Paurāṇic story of the final deluge and Nārāyaṇa's fight with the demons Madhu and Kaiṭabha finds mention in all early works of importance. But connecting it with the Vṛttis is an invention of Bharata.

11 Connecting Bharata with Bhāratī is an instance of synonymous pursuits very common all over the world.

211 Tracing important technicals terms to the Vedic source is as wide an occurrence as those of the lores too, Vedāṅgas etc. Āyurveda,Gāndharva Veda etc.

37 The eight aspects are Prarocana, Vīthī, Prahasana and the five varieties of Āmukha.

46 The eight meanings are Utthāpaka, Parivartaka, the two types of Sallāpaka and the four types of Saṁghāta.

49 If the definition of Narman is the following Parāpavādaiḥ Paruṣairaślīlaiścavivarjitamśuddhamantargatākūtamnarma syācchadmagarbhakam.

54 The eight aspects are the three kinds of Narman, three kinds of Narmagarbha, the Narma sphūrja and Narmasphoṭa.

23

Āhāryābhinaya
Costumes and Make up

1 I shall now explain in due order the Āhāryābhinaya (revelation through costumes and makeup) because production of play depends on this.

2 Extraneous representation should be known, O Brahmins as the rules regarding costumes and make up. Effort should be made in this regard by one who wishes splended success for the dramatic performance.

3 Characters in a play are of different types. If they are duly made ready with the requisite costumes etc. at the outset they shall accomplish the representation through gestures etc. without undue effort.

4 *Four kinds of Nepathya* are (1) Pusta (model work) (2) Alaṁkāra (Embellishment) (3) Angaracanā (painting the limbs of the body) and (4) Sañjīva (Living creatures).

5. *Three kinds of Pusta* (Model work) are (a) Sandhima (Joined objects) (b) Vyājima (Indicating objects and (c) Veṣṭima (wrapped objects).

6. The Pusta used in Nāṭakas make by sensible persons, out of mat, hide cloth etc. is called Sandhima.

7 Objects made through mechanical devices are known as Vyājimas. That which is produced by wrapping is called Veṣṭima.

8 Hills vehicles, aerial chariots, shields, armours flagstaffs, trees etc. constructed for the use in the production of a play are called Pustas.

9 *Alaṁkāra* (Embellishment) consists of floral wreaths, jewellery, garments etc. as well as the various unquents etc. applied over the limbs.

10 *Mālya* (Garland) This is of five types—(i) Veṣṭina [Veṣṭima] (Encircling) (2) Vitata (Spread up) (3) Saṅghātya (Grouped together) (4) Granthima (Tied up) and (5) Pralambita (Suspended down).

11 Ābharaṇa (jewellery) in the dramatic performance should be understood by sensible persons as consisting of four kinds – (i) Āvedhya (Limbs are pierced and worn) (2) Bandhanīya (that which is tied up) (3) Prakṣepya (Worn over) and (4) Āropya (Put around).

12—13 Āvedhya ornaments are ear rings etc. which embellish the ears; Bandhanīya ornaments are the girdles, arm bands etc; Prakṣepya ornaments are the anklets wearing apparel etc. Āropya ornaments are golden chains necklaces etc. of various kinds.

14 I shall now explain the different kinds of ornaments that men and women use in accordance with the conventions of their tribes and regions.

15 *Head ornaments.* Cūḍāmaṇi (crest jewel) and the crown (Mukuṭa) are remembered as head ornaments.

Ear ornaments. Kuṇḍala (Earning), Mocaka (earpendants) and Kila (eartops) are ear orgaments.

16 *Neck ornaments.* Muktāvali (Pearl necklace) Harṣaka (Serpent shaped ornament) and Sūtraka (gold thread) are the neck ornaments. Vetika (a bangle shaped ring) and Aṅgulī-Mudrā (ring) are the ornaments of the fingers.

17 Hastalī and Valaya (types of bangles) are the ornaments of the forearm. Rucika (bracelet) and Uccitika are ornaments *of the wrist.*

18 *Ornaments over the elbow are* Keyūra (armlet) and Aṅgada (Armband). Trisara (Three stringed necklace and the Hāra (chain) are the ornaments of the chest.

19. The hanging down pearl necklace and the flower garland are *ornaments for the whole body.* Tarala and Sūtraka are *waist-bands.*

20 These are the ornaments of the males kings and gods. I shall now explain the *ornaments* of the female characters.

21—22 The ornaments of the head are Śiknāpāśa·Śikhājāla, Piṇḍīpatra, Cūḍāmaṇi, Makarikā, Muktājāla (pearl-net), Gavākṣa, Śīrṣajāla (hair net) etc.

23 The Tilaka on the forehead applied with several artistic designs, the Guccha (bunch) above the eyebrows imitating flowers. These also are ornamental.

24—25 *Ear ornaments* are Kaṇḍaka, Kuṇḍala (ear-rings), Śikhipatra, Khaḍgapatra, Veṇīguccha (braid of hair) with the string attached thereto, Karṇavalaya, Patrakarṇikā, Karṇa-Mudrā, Karṇotkīlaka (ear tops), the different kinds of Danta-patras set with gems, ond Karṇapūra. The Tilaka and Patra-lekhā are ornaments of cheeks.

26—27 The pearl necklace, the Vyālapaṅkti (Snake group), the Mañjurī, Ratnamālikā (jewel string) the Ratnāvali and the Sūtraka are ornaments of the neck. The Dvisara (two stringed), Trisara (three-stringed) and Catussara (four stringed) necklaces and a gold chain too constitute the neck ornaments

28 *Breast* ornaments The necklaces made artistically fine are the ornaments of the breasts. The jewelled net is the ornament for the back as well as breasts.

29 *The ornaments* of the upper-arms are the Aṅgada and Valaya (bangles). , The ornaments of the forearm are the Varjura Kharjuraks and the Svecchitika Socchitika.

30 The Kaṭaka, the Kalasākhā, Hastapatra, Pūraka and the Mūdrā as well as Aṅgulīyaka are the binger ornaments.

31 The Kāñcī with a net of pearls, the kulaka (Talaka) Mekhalā, the Raśanā and the Kalāpa are the ornament of the hips.

32 The Kāñcī is a girdle with a single string, the Mekhalā is eight-stringed one and the Kalāpa has twenty five strings.

33 The necklaces of pearls for the goddesses and queens shall consist of thirty two, sixty four and one hundred and eight strings.

34 The ornaments over the ankles are the Nūpura, Kinkiṇī,

Rajnajāla (jewel net) and the Ghaṇṭikā as well as the Saghoṣa kaṭaka (sounding kaṭaka).

35 The Pādapatra is the jewel for the shanks, the toe-rings for the toes and the Tilaka for the big toes—These are the jewels for the feet.

36 There is an extra ornamental embellishment for the feet viz. Alaktaka-Rāga (the red-lace) which has to be applied in various designs to give them the natural colour of the flowers of the Aśoka tree.

37. These constitute the decorative oıuaments for the women characters from the tresses down to the nail, O excellent Brahmins these have to be employed to the different limbs in accordance with the Bhāvas, Rasas and the conditions,

38 These ornaments have to be worn in accordance with the injunctions in the Āgamas (traditional treatises). The measurements in accordance with the wearers but should bring forth the beauty amply. All in accordance with the views of Viśvakarman.

39 In a dramatic performance no one is empowered to embellish the limbs in accordance with his will by using gold, pearls and jewels.

40 Employed suitably to the different parts of the body these ornaments set with jewels will accord ample beauty to them.

41 In none of these items of dance and dramatic performances should the character be heavily burdened with jewels. They are sure to stiffen the movements and cause distress to them.

42 The weight of the ornaments prevents one from moving freely and pressing one down cause exhaustion and even fainting.

43 Hence in the dramatic performances ornaments made of pure gold should not be used. A thin layer of gold shall cover lad and other materials. This set with jewel cannot cause fatigue.

44 The rules regarding embellishment with jewels shall be optional in the case of the divine beings. The embellishment

of the human beings must be assiduous in accordance with the Bhāvas.

45 The celestial beings, especially the women characters are to be distinguished for their own roles by means of ornaments and costumes suited to the various states. With regard to human beings the arrangement for the jewellery shall be in accordance with the conventions of the regions concerned.

46 Costumes should be the distinguishing factor for the womenfolk of the Vidyādharas, Yakṣas, Nāgas, the celestial ladies and the daughters of the sages.

47 The women of the Siddhas, the Gandharvas, the Rākṣasas, the Asuras and the human beings also are subject to the same rule.

48 An entirely white dress and make-up should be assigned to the Vidyādharīs. Their hairs are tied in top knot decorated with the strings of many pearls.

49 The dress style of the Yakṣīs and the celestial ladies shall be similar. They should have jewels for ornaments. But the Yakṣa women must wear simple Śikhā (Tuft of hair).

50 The Nāga women have hoods mainly embellished with pearls and jewels. In other respects their ornaments should be made like those of the celestial ladies.

51 The young maidens of the sages have dress style befitting the sylvan atmosphere. They should not have much of ornamentation. Their hairs have a single Veṇī (braid of hair).

52 The embellishment of Siddha young women is mostly of pearls and emeralds. Their garments and attire should be of yellow colour.

53 The jewellery of Gandharvīs is of rubies mostly. They should be represented as holding Vīnās in their hands. Their clothes are of saffron colour.

54 The Rākṣasīs have ornaments mostly of sappliers. They have white curved teeth. They should be represented as clad in black clothes.

55 The celestial damsels should be represented as adorned with pearls and *lapis Lazuli* and clad in the attire resembling the feather of parrots.

56 The ornaments of the women of the celestial beings and the monkeys should be of topaz and jewels and in some places of *lapis lazula*. Their attire is of blue colour.

57 Thus, love-raising should be the costumes and the make up of the celestial damsels the occasion of Śṛṅgāra topics. On other occasions they should be made pure and white.

58 The dresses and the ornaments of human ladies should be in accordance with their respective native regions. Even as I enumerate them listen and understand.

59 The maidens of Avanti shall have wary hairs and also Śikhāpāśa and Veṇī.

60 The Ābhīra maidens shall have two-plaited tresses of hair with a ribbon going round the head. Their garments are mostly blue in colour.

61 The women of the North-East have rising Śikhaṇḍas and while dressing themselves they cover up to their hair.

62 The Southern women shall have Ullekhya (? tattoo marks) along with Kumbhīpadaka (a special tattoo mark) and Āvarta on the forehead (some kind of circular mark).

63 The embellishment and make up of the courtezans shall be in accordance with their idiosyncrasies. The dresses, ornaments, hair dressing etc. of the remaining characters shall be in accordance with their habitation naturty etc.

64 An ornament or make up out of place does not add to the splendour. The girdle worn over the chest-only provokes laughter.

65 The dress and make up of women in calamities or with husbands abroad shall be made untidy. The hair has single plaited Veṇī.

66 In love, inseparation the dress and make up of a woman shall be of white colour without much of jewellery. They shall not have the regular tidying up and cleansing.

67 Thus is the mode of make up and costume of the women in accordance with their native region as well as the conditions. Now I shall explain the make up and dress of the male characters.

68 In their case the painting of the limbs shall be carried out at the outset by the sponsors of the dramatic performance. Only thereafter should the make up in accordance with the native region be carried out.

69 The four natural colours are white blue, yellow and red. Aṅgavartana (painting of the limbs should be carried through these colours.

70 There are other colours produced by the mixture of these colours. There are also Upavarṇas (derivative secondary). I shall mention them and explain how they are to be carried out by the producers.

71 By mixing the white with the yellow colour the Pāṇḍu (yellowish white) colour is made. The white and the blue mixed together yields Kāraṇḍāva (species of duck) colour.

72 By mixing the white with the red the Padma (lotus) colour is produced and by mixing the yellow with the blue the Harita (green) colour is made.

73 The blue and the red mixed together yields the Kaṣāya (dark red) colour, The red and the yellow if mixed together Gaura (pale red) colour is produced.

74 These are the primary derivative colours. Besides there are many Upavarṇas (secondary colours) by mixing three or four primary colours.

75—76 Of these, if the colour is strong it forms only one part. If the colour is weak then two parts are taken but the blue colour has exceptions in being employed. The blue forms only one part and the other colours four parts. The blue is reputed to be the strongest of all colours.

77 After these principles underlying the mixing of colours have been understood the painting of the body of the character can be proceeded with.

78—80 The painted body together with the change of the costume should be considered the result of Nāṭyadharma (conventional practice) affecting the characters. A creature that enters and the body renounces its previous nature of the previous body and assumes another character. In the same way a person with different costume and colours adopts the behaviour of the person concerned.

81 In the Nāṭaka the Devas, the Dānavas, the Gandharvas, the Yakṣas, the Rākṣasas and the serpants are called Prāṇins because they breath.

82 Hills, Palaces, Yantras (machinery), shields, armours, bannerstaffs and the different kinds of weapons are to be known as Aprāṇins.

83 But, for adequate reasons, they may become embodied ones with befitting dress and speech according to Nāṭyadharma.

84 Only after understanding the rules for mixing the colours should one paint the limbs of the characters in accordance with their native region, community and the age.

85 The Devas should be known as Gauras (pale red). So also the Yakṣas and the celastial damsels. Rudra Arka (Sun), Druhiṇa and Skanda are remembered as having the golden lustre.

16 Soma (Moon), Bṛhaspati, Śukra, Varuṇa, the stars the oceans, the Himālayas and the Gaṅgā as well as Balarāma are white in complexion.

87 The Mars should be known as red. Budha and the fire are yellow. Nārāyaṇa, Nara, and the serpant Vāsuki should be dark in colour.

88 The Daityas, the Dānavas, the Rakṣasas the Guhyakas, the Piśacas, deities of mountains, water and the sky are dark blue in colour.

89 The Yakṣas, the Gandharvas, the Bhūtas, the Pannagas, the Vidyādharas the Manes and the monkeys are of various colours.

90 Human beings who dwell in the Sapta Dvīpas are to be painted in the colour of the molten gold.

91 In Jambūdvīpa there are man of diverse colours. But excluding the northern Kurus all of them should be represented as golden complexioned.

92 The men of Bhadrāśva should be represented white complexioned, those of Ketumāla blue in complexion; those in other Varṣas Gaura (Rose colour) complexioned.

93 The Bhūtas and the Vāmanas are remembered as having various colours. They have hideious faces like those boars, sheep, buffaloes and deer.

94—96 Listen to the different colours of the people of Bhārata Varṣa. Kings therein are of lotus complexion so also of dark and Gaura complexions. The ease loving happy men among them should be represented as Gaura complexioned by sensible persons. Men who are engaged in vile actions, those who are afflicted by malignant planets, sickly ones, those who are engaged in severe austerities without Yajñas and those of low naturity should be painted dark in colour, saints should be given the colour of Badara (plum) sages engaged in penance should always be represented as dark complexioned.

97—98 For adequate reasons, but not out of fanciful **whims** colours of persons may be varied according to the native region, birth and age. An expert in the dramatic performance should paint persons after understanding their place of action, time of action, birth and the region they live in.

99—100 Kirātas, Barbaras, Āndhras, **Draviḍas** Kāśis, Pulindas and the inhabitants of the south are mostly remembered as Asitas (brownish in colour) Śakas, Yavanas, Pahravas, and Vāhlīkas who dwell in the north should be made Gaura complexioned in general.

101 The Pāñcālas, Śūrasenas, Oḍhras, Māgadhas, Aṅgas, Vaṅgas and Kaliṅgas should always be represented dark blue complexioned.

102 The Brahmins and the Kṣatriyas should always be represented as Gaura complexioned. Vaiśyas and Sūdras are to be shown deep blue complexioned

103 After painting the face, the limbs etc the actor should be provided with moustache, beard etc. with due consideration for their native region, activity, time and age.

104 The beard and the moustache are of four kinds, according to the change of states Śuddha (pure, white) Śyāma (black) Vicitro (smarthy trimmed) and Romaśa (hairy, bushy).

105 The beards of religious medicants, ministers, priests and persons averse to sensual pleasures and those that have taken up initiation for rites should be **represented** clean shaven.

106–107. The beards of divine male beings like the Siddhas and the Vidyādharas, kings, princes, officers of the king and persons behaving like vain dandies, those who are proud of their youth—these should have smartly trimmed moustache provided by the producers.

108 Dark coloured moustache shall be provided for those who could not keep their promises, who are vexed on that account, those who have been afflicted by calamities.

109 Bushy Romaśa moustache and beard shall be assigned to sages, ascetics and persons observing long-standing vow with bark garments.

110 Thus the moustache and beard should be of diverse kinds as provided by the producers. I shall now explain the costumes suitable to different occasions.

111 The drapery siuted to different occasions can be of three kinds Śuddha (pure), Vicitra (Variegated) and Malina (Untidy).

112 Costumes are of three kinds too white red and variegated as used at the time of painting the limbs.

113—114 While visiting the temples of deities observing some auspicious rite, at the time of the conjunction of specified Tithi and star, at the time of the celebration of a marriage, at some consecratory rite, etc men and women shall have white costumes. The same is true in regard to a trader (Prāpaṇika).

115 Costumes of gods, the Dānavas, the Yakṣas the Gandharvas, the Nāgas, the Rākṣasas, kings and people of lascious temperament should have Vicitra Veṣa.

116-117 Costumes of the following persons shall be Śuddha elderly **Brahmins** Śreṣṭhis, ministers, priests merchants chamber loins, sages, men of an equal footing with **Brahmins** Kṣatriyas and Vaiśyas.

118 Costumes of lunatics, inebriated persons, travellers and persons in adversity should be of Malina type.

119 Costumes and embellishments of the sages, the Nirganthas, the Śākya monks, the Tridaṇḍins and Śrotriyas (those well versed in the Vedas) should be such as agree with the conventions in their societies.

120 Costumes of the Parivrājakas (way faring sages) great sages, and ordinary ascetics should be made according to necessity with Kaṣāya (dark red) cloth.

121—124 Parks of trees and hides of animals as well as tattered cloths should be allotted to the sages. So the Pāṣupatas variegated costumes are to be given persons of very noble family should be provided with the costumes befitting them. To the persons engaged in guarding the harem, armour and clothes of Kaṣaya (dark red) colour should be given. Costumes of the females in special positions should be the same costumes of the warriors should be befitting the battles they are engaged in. Brilliant weapons, armours, quivers and bows must form part of them.

125 Many coloured drapery should always be allotted to the kings except during the ominous appearance of the comets or meteors when it shall be Śuddha.

126 Thus does the dress and drapery confine to the native region, class of naturity and age of the men and women of the types of superior, middling and inferior.

127 These are the rules regarding costumes and drapery in a dramatic production in accordance with the different conditions and the practice of good or bad of the persons concerned.

128 Use of marks is also a necessary item in the dramatic production for gods and men in accordance with their native region, class of nativity and age.

129 Crowns of gods and kings are of three types a Pārśvagata (side head gear), Mastaki (forehead coronet) and Kirīṭi (Crowned).

130 For the gods in general, the Gandharvas, the Yakṣas the Pannagas and the Rākṣasas, the Pārṣvagata (head gear at the sides) has been prescribed.

131 The superior among the gods are to be given the Kirīṭi coronet, the middling among them are given Mastakī *type and the inferiour are assinged Pārśvagata types of headgea*

132—133 The head gear of the kings must be of the Mastaki type. The Vidyādharas, the Siddhas, and Cāraṇas are to have Granthimatkeśa-Mukuṭas (i.e. crowns made up of locks of hair).

134—139 The masks of ministers, Kaṇcukins, leaders of the merchants, guilds and priests should be furnished with turbans. The masks of the army—captains and the crowned prince must have an Ardhamukuṭa (half-coronat) fitted in. The remaining persons shall be assigned with such headgear as fit into them according to the exigencies by the producers as determined by the native region, class of nativity and age. The heads of boys shall be embellisted with Śikhaṇda (tuft of hair) and those of the sages should have crowns of matted hair (Jaṭā Mukuṭa). The masks of the Rākṣās, the Dānavas, and the Yakṣās should be provided with brown hairs and tawny beards. The masks of the Piśācas, lunatics, the Bhūtas (evil spirits), Spiritual aspirants ascetics and those who have not completely observed their vows must have long hairs.

139—141 The head in the masks of the Buddhist monks, Śrotriyas, Nirgranthas wandering sages and those who have been initiated for special sacred rites should be shaven clean. In regard to the remaining ascetics should be represented as having their heads shaven or with curly hairs or loosely hanging hairs in accordance with their practice in their respective cults.

142—144 Married women, those who are dependants of the king, men of foolish nature should have curly hairs on their heads. The menials are provided with three fold Śikhas on their head or their heads may remain clean shaven. The Vidūṣaka may be bald headed or there may be a Kākapada (incision in the skin) therein. In this manner the condition and nature of these persons should be represented through ornaments, costumes, inlands etc. after carefully distinguishing them in diverse ways. At the time of the production of the play the requisite Rasas should be displayed properly.

145 After man and woman have been treated like this their limbs should be painted to suit their different roles.

146 Sañjīvas (living objects) have been mentioned by me before. Of those I shall mention the characteristics now.

The introduction of living animals on to the stage is remembered as Sañjīva.

147—148 The animals are of three types viz Catuṣpada (four footed), Dvipada (two footed) and Apada (having no foot). Serpents should be known as Apadas; birds and human beings are Dvipadas. The domestic and the wild animals should be known as Catuṣpadas-

149—155 The characters in the play are to be provided with different weapons for use while representing fights angry conflicts or siege of a city in a drama.

Weapons should be made proportionate to the measurements of the characters. I shall now explain them along with the rules governing their measurements. The Bhiṇḍi (javelin) shall be twelve Tālas (i.e. 12×12=144 Aṅgulas) in length; the Kunta (spear) ten Tālas; the Śataghnī (hundred-kitler) Śūla (Trident), the Tomara and the Śakti shall measure eight Tālas. The bow measures eight Tālas in length and its width is two Hastas (i.e. 4 Tālas) Arrow, club and the thunderbolt should be four Tālas each. The sword is forty Aṅgulas long and the discus twelve Aṅgulas. The Prāsa (spike) shall measure half the last one. The Paṭṭisa shall be on a par with the Prāsa. The Daṇḍa (baton) shall measure twenty Aṅgulas and the Kaṇapa (Kampana) shall also measure twenty Aṅgulas. The Earma (shield) must be sixteen Aṅgulas in width and two Hastas in length. It shall have Vālyas (hairs) and bells fitted to it. The Kheṭaka (riders shield) shall be thirty Aṅgulas in width.

156—161 The Jarjara, Daṇḍakāṣṭha, masks, umbrella, chowries, banner staffs, waterpots and every other thing that people usually employ in their daily routine, can be employed in the productions of a play. The characteristics of these should be inferred as and when they come into use (by the actors). Now I shall explain the essential features of the Jarjara and the Daṇḍakāṣṭha. Trees planted under the constellation Puṣya on the sake of Indra's flagstaff as ordained by Viśvakarman. One of those trees should be turned into Jarjara by the work of a carpenter. The branch of any of those trees may be fashioned into the Jarjara. But the bamboo is the best one to be used. I shall mention its characteristics. Its length is one hundred and eight Aṅgulas.

162—167 It should have five knots and four joints. It shall be as tall as a palmyra. The joints shall not be very prominent; no branch should proceed therefrom. It should not be worm eaten also. The bamboo shall not have the joints worm eaten. It shail not be inferior to the other bamboos.

168—170 The Daṇḍakāṣṭha should always be made of the Bilva or the Kapittha tree or the bamboo. If should be curved and have three bends and should posses all the essential features. That whieh has very poor branches is called Daṇḍakāṣṭha. One who gets the Jarjara and Daṇḍakāṣṭha made devoid of of these salient features will certainly attain great loss.

171—175 *The Paṭī of the masks* should be prepared in their requisite measurements or (at **best**) thirty two Angulīs. The Paṭī should be prepared by using Bilva paste on cloth. Marks should be made with ashes or husks of paddy being mixed up with Bilva Paste or some watery form thereof after covering these with cloth smeared with thick Bilva paste The Paṭī made out of cloth smeared with Bilva paste should be neither too thick nor too thin; nor should it be too soft. After getting it dried up by fire or the sun one should pierce holes in it according to the rule by means of a sharp instrument and these holes should be made after dividing into two halves.

176—178 In the Paṭī so prepared, and opening six Aṅgulas long and one Aṅgula wide should be made in the form of the forehead and it should have two angular points at either end. Then a pair of openings two Aṅgulas wide should be made for the checks and after this has been done another opening three Aṅguias in length should be made for the ears. The opening for the ears being three Aṅgulas long the same should be the length for the opening of the month and the Avaṭu (symmetrical neck should be made twelve Aṅgulas long.

179 These are the rules regarding the cutting of openings in the Paṭī for the mask. Various forms of crowns set with diverse kinds of jewels are to be fixed to them.

Nāṭyopakaranas (Accessories to the dramatic production) are to be employed in regard to the persons taking the different roles. Whatever is created in this world of mobile and immobīle beings, excluding the fine specimens artistically produced çan be an Upakaraṇa (in dramatic production). *One should go to* persons whose special knowledge in respect to these Upakaraṇas is well known. There is no other means. A person professionally qualified to devise these things can decide its measurement large objects requiring much iron are not re-commended by us for the use on the stage; since those heavy things cause fatigue. Imitation of all the objects found in this world in different varieties is possible, those imitations are the accessories to be used in the dramatic performance. Palaces, houses, vehicles etc. are Upakaraṇas but they cannot be produced for the stage realistically.

Naṭya Dharmi and Loka Dharmi

188—192 Some Upakaraṇas are Lokadharmis (realistic) and others Nāṭyadharmi (conventional). If a thing follows its natural form it is called Lokadharmi and those deviating from the same are Nāṭyadharmi (conventional). Accessories for use on the stage should not be made with iron, stone ete. for they cause fatigue.

Light objects should be made with lac, wood, leather, cloths, leaves of trees bamboo sticks (splinters) etc. for use as Upakaraṇas in the Nāṭaka. Skeleton frames of armours, shields banner staffs, palaces, temples, elephant, aerial chariots and houses are made at the outset with bamboo splinters. Such frames are then covered with painted cloth to produce likeness of such objects.

193—196 If cloth is not readity available then palm products and mats are to be used instead simiiarly weapons are to be made with grass and bamboo splinters. Other objects should be represented with lac, and Bhāṇḍa (gourd etc. shaped like Vessels). Imitations of legs, heads, hands and skin should be made with grass, mat and Bhāṇda. Other objects too can be made by way of imitation using clay and bringing likeness.

197—198 Different kinds of hills, shields, armours, flag staffs etc. are to be made with Bhāṇda, cloth, bees, wax, lac and sheets of Abhraca (Mica) fruits and flowers growing in different regions and the various utensils should be made with lac.

199—200 *Ornaments* should be made with Bhāṇḍa, cloth, bees wax, their copper foils and mice sheets of blue or other suitable colours and their bases should be polished copper sheets.

201—208 The different kinds of crowns mentioned by me before should be made shining with splendour by using pieces of mica. In regard to these objects instructions in the Śāstras have not been quoted. The directions of the Ācārya concerned shall be the guiding factor. These are the rules after taking into consideration the mortels of the future, what of sufficient strength in whom is sure. Mortals of poor physical strength shall not extert themselves unduly. So it is not recommended that their crowns and ornaments shall be made with pure gold. In the course of battles, wrestings dance, glancing around etc. persons burdened with heavy weight are sure to be fatigued. They may even faint when the actor is over fatigued or about to swoon his performance on the stage is spoilt over acting may end in death. Hence ornaments are to be made with thin sheets of copper, coloured sheets of mica, Bhāṇḍa and bee's wax. Thus one shall produce theatrical Upakaraṇas properly, either by following the popular practice by using his discretion.

209—211. No missile is to be discharged on the stage and none should be strick or pierced. They shall just touch a spot and the weapons are to be used only as gestures. Or the producers can introduce real discharge of missiles etc. by means of Yogic power or Māyā on the stage.

Any relevant detail not mentioned by me should be gathered from the general public. Thus is the Āhārya Abhinaya that I have mentioned succinctly. I shall now explain the Sāmānya Abhinaya (Basic Represention).

Notes

Āhārya Abhinaya is very important because the other types of Abhinaya viz. Āngika, Vācika etc. depend upon this. The effect of costume make up etc. on the audience lasts even after he disappears from the stage.

15 Cūḍāmaṇi is to be worm on the top of the head Mukuṭa is to be worn above the forehead Kuṇḍala is worn in the lower lobe of the ear. Mocaka is to be worn in the hole in the middle of the ear.

16 Harṣaka is a snake shaped ornament.

17 Hastavī—This ornament is not mentioned in the well known plays or even Kāvyas.

18 Keyūra is worn above the elbow, Angada is worn above the Keyūra Trisara—three stringed necklace.

19 Tarala is worn below the navel. Sūtra to be worn below the Tarala.

22 Śikhāpāśa is the same as Cūḍāpāśa referred to in Megha-Sandeśa II-2.

Gavākṣa as a head ornament is rarely met with in the extent literature.

25 In some Mss. additional verses are to be found which can be translated thus—Triveṇi is an ornament worn over the breasts. Collyrium should be rendered sparkling. The four prominent teeth in both the rows may be rendered whiter or coloured with different paints to enhance their beauty. Teeth shining like pearls enhance the charm of the smile. Loveliness increased when painted with lotus-colour.

41 This suggestion or rather warning is of universal application.

119 Tridaṇḍins are Sannyāsins who carry three pieces of sticks tied together to imply that they have full control over the mind speech and body.

157 Jarjara, Daṇḍakāṣṭha, Bhṛngāra etc. are previously explained in I and III Chapters.

24

Samanyabhinaya (Basic Representation)

1 Sāmānya Abhinaya should be known as originating from words, gestures and Sattva (temperament). Out of these the actor should take specials care about Sattva because the dramatic production has this as its basis.

2 The Abhinaya in which there is exuberance of Sattva is superior, the one with level Sattva is middling and that with no Sattva is inferior.

3 Sattva is something not manifest but is the main basis for Bhāva and Rasa through Romāñca (horripilation), tears and other significant features displayed in proper places in harmony with the Rasas.

4—5 Alaṁkāras (graceful features) should be known by those conversant with Nāṭya as the features and changes in the faces and the limbs, all the more very prominent during the youth of ladies. They are the supporting factors of the Rasas. At the outset the change of the limbs (Aṅgajas) is of three kinds next, the Svābhāvikas (congenitel) are the natural changes of ten kinds and then Ayatnajas (effected easily, even involuntary) are of seven kinds.

6 *Physical graces of women.* Bhāva (feeling) arises from Sattva that partakes of the nature of the body while Hāva (Emotion) arises from Bhāva and Helā (Passion) from Hāva.

7 Thus feelings, emotions and passions this arise from one another since they are only different aspects of Sattva. They are the physical graces of women.

8 That which reveals the innermost idea of the poet through words, gesturess and facial expressions by the Sattva and Abhinaya is called Bhāva.

9 Temperament with excessive feeling manifests itself in relation to persons of the opposite **sex** And Hāva (Emotion) should be marked as relating to its various conditions.

10 In this regard, Hāva should be **understood** as coming forth from the mind manifesting itself in the Vikāṛas of eyes and eyebrows and the Recaka of the neck giving rise to the Śṛṅgāra Rasa.

11 Helā (Passion) comes forth from the Śṛṅgāra Rasa. It is the same as Hāva when expressing itself as graceful movements [Lalitābhinaya].

12—13 *Natural Graces* [Svabhāvaja Alaṁkāra] of women should be understood to be ten. They are Līlā (Sportive Mimicry), Vilāsa (Amorous gesture), Vicchitti (**Disability**) Vibhrama (confusion), Kilakiñcitam (Hysterical Mood), Moṭṭāyita (Manifestation of Affection), Kuṭṭamita (Pretended Anger), Bimboka (Affected coldness), Lalita (lolling), and Vihṛta (Want of Reponse)._ Now listen, O **Brahmins** to their characteristic features.

14 *Līā* is the playful imitation of the behaviour of a lover through relevant words, gestures and graceful movements, all delightful and induced by excessive love.

15 *Vilāsa* is the name given to those changes in the bodily movements in relation to standing sitting and mode of walking, and the activities of hands eyebrows and the eyes (while meeting with the lover or in his presence).

16 *Vicchitti* is the increase in the beauty resulting from even slightly careless wearing of garlands, clothes, or ornaments and applying unquents.

17 *Vibhrama* is that alteration of various items such as words, gestures, dresses, make up and Sattva as a result of inebriety. passion and excess of joy.

18 *Kilakiñcita* is the combination of isolated states of smiling, weeping, laughter, fear, sickness, fainting, sorrow and fatigue on account of excessive joy.

20 *Kuṭṭamita*, is the feigned anger arising on account of the hilarious mirth and perplexity on being touched in the hair, brests, lips and the like by the lover when the girl in question

pretends to be distressed when actually she was experiencing delight.

21 *Bimboka* is a sort of indifference and affected coldness that girls show to their lovers due to vanity and pride after the realization of the cherished desire of winning over the heart of the lover.

22 *Lalita* is the lolling reclining posture of women with graceful movements of hands, feet, brows, eyes lips etc.

23 *Vihṛta* is the want of response, willful or otherwise due to bashfulness or natural instinct displayed by a timid girl even after hearing the loving words of the lover.

24 *Ayatnaja Alaṁkāra* (Graces not forced). These graces, involuntary and effortlessly achieved by women are seven in number—Śobha, (beauty), Kānti, (charm) Dīpti, (radiance) Mādhurya, (delicacy, sweetness), Prāgalbhya (courage, Maturity) and Audārya (dignity, exalted State).

25 *Śobhā* is that beautiful embellishment of the limbs on account of seductive physical form, youth and loveliness being manifested and heightened through sexual enjoyment.

26 *Kānti* is the increased Śobhā as a result of the fulfilment of the desire for sexual pleasure Dīpti or radiance is a high degree of charm.

27 *Mādhurya* or delicacy is the moderation of the movements in all conditions especially iṇ Dīpti and Lalita.

28 *Dhairya* is the selfcontrol, a natural bent of the mind utterly devoid of rashness and bragging.

29 *Prāgalbhya* or maturity is the quality of courage resulting in avoidance of agitation in speaking or in practical demonstration.

Audārya or dignity is the courteous deportment in every situation.

30 These graces are tender in connexion with the performance of a delicate nature but in other cases they are brilliant excepting Vilāsa and Lalita.

Eight Aspects of Male temperament.

31 Śobhā (Brilliant character), Vilāsa (Graceful Bearing), Mādhurya (Self-Possession), Sthairya (Steadiness), Gāmbhīrya (Gravity), Lalita (Sportiveness), Audarya (Nobility) and Tejas (Spiritedness) are the different aspects of the Male temperament

32 *Śobhā* or Brilliant character comprises of skill in various things, heroism, energy, aversion to mean acts and competitive emulation of the best virtues.

33 *Vilāsa* is that graceful deportment where the eyes boldly move forward, the gait is graceful like that of a bull and talking is attended with smiles.

34 *Mādhurya* is that sweet self possession as a result of constant and habitual practice in retaining the firmness in the sense organs despite great Vikāras (upsetting tendencies).

35 *Sthairya* is the persevering tenacity of not giving up any task undertaken in regard to piety, wealth and enjoyment of pleasures whether the result be adverse or favourable.

36 *Gāmbhīrya* is that quality of gravity thanks to the influence of which no visible reaction takes place in spite of occurrence of anger, joy and fear.

37 *Lalita* (Sportiveness) is that tendency to be playful with erotic movements and changes of features resulting from a natural tenderness but not wantonly or deliberate.

38 *Audārya* is the quality of nobleheartedness wherein there is readiness to make gifts and acceptance thereof from others, speaking sweet words to one's own men and others" as well.

39 *Tejas* is that spirited feeling which makes the man intolerant of the words of reproach and insult uttered by some one with enmity even when the life may be at stake.

40 O excellent Brahmins, thus I have explained the Sāttvika Abhinaya. I shall now explain the Śārīra Abhinaya (histrionic representation through physical activities).

41 The Śārīra Abhinaya is of six types viz. Vākya (words), Sūcā. Aṅkura, Śākhā, Nāṭyāyita and Nivṛttyankura.

42 *Vākya* Abhinaya comprises of pieces of recitation in Saṁskṛta and Prākṛta, whether in prose or verse. They shall be meaningful and display various Rasas.

43 *Sūcā* is that type of Representation when the meaning of a sentence or the sentence itself is indicated at the outset by Sattva and Aṅga and thereafter the Vākya Abhinaya.

44 *Aṅkura* When the actor skilfully represents the inner feeling by gestures in the manner of Sūcā along with the words, it is called Aṅkura Abhinaya.

45 *Śākhā* The Abhinaya made in due order by the head, face, shanks, thighs, hands and feet in the manner of the Śākhā (i.e. Vartanā see ante 11-90).

46 *Nāṭyāyita* The intimation of histrionic representation made at the beginning of a drama through different practices for enlivening the time and which lasts till all the dramatis personce come together on the stage is called Nāṭyāyita.

47 The Abhinaya of the Dhruvās relating to Bhāvas and Rasas made by means of delineating joy, anger, grief and the like is also to be known as Nāṭyāyita.

48 *Nivṛttyaṅkura* When one represents words of another person by Sūcā as if announcing the event connected therewith it is called Nivṛttyaṅkura.

49—51 *Twelves forms of Vācika Abhinaya.* There shall be twelve ways of presenting the Vācika Abhinaya with proper Bhāvas and Rasas in connection with the subject matter of plays—(1) Ālāpa (Accosting, (2) Pralāpa (Prattling, (3) Vilāpa (Lamentation) (4) Anulāpa (Repeated utterance) (5) Saṁlāpa (Dialogue) (6) Apalāpa (Change of words) (7) Sandeśa (Massage) (8) Atideśa (Agreement) (9) Nirdeśa (Command direction) (10) Vyapadeśa (Pretext) (11) Upadeśa (Instruction, Advice) and (12) Apadeśa (Statement).

52 *Ālāpa* is the sentence used in addressing someone.

Pralāpa means the utterence of meaningless and irrelevant words.

53 *Vilāpa* consists of words issuing forth from a pathetic situation.

Anulāpa is the repetition of what is uttered over and over again.

54 *Sāṁlāpa* is made up of utterence and counter utterance.

Aplāpa is the alteration of words uttered before.

55 *Sandeśa* comprises of utterances like this—"Speak this to him".

Atideśa is that statement of agreement saying "You have said what was uttered by me".

56 *Nirdeśa* is a commanding assertion—"I alone am speaking.

Vyapadeśa is a pretext in speaking with the purpose of deception.

57 *Upadeśa* is instruction like "Do this" "Take this" etc.
Apadeśa is Anyārthakathana or mentioning an other meanning or speaking on behalf of others.

58 These are the forms of sentences for the purpose of all shorts Abhinayas through words. I shall speak of the characteristics of seven forms which too it may have.

59 Those seven are Pratyakṣa (Visible), Parokṣa (Invisible), present, past and future and Ātmostha (one's own) and Parastha (Another's).

60 "O this person is speaking. I am not speaking" is a statement which treats a visible act, affects another person (Parastha) and relates to the present.

61 "I am doing", "going" or "speaking" is the statement that affects oneself, relates to the present time and treats of a visible object or act.

62 "I shall do, go, or speak" is a statement which affects one's ownself, treats an invisible act and relates to future time.

63 "All my enemies have been killed by me" is a statement which affects one's ownself as well as others and relates to the past time.

64 "The enemies have been killed by thee" is a statement which treats an invisible act, affects others and relates to the past time.

65 "This person is speaking, doing or going" is a statement which affects another relates to the present time and treats a visible act.

66 "He is going or doing" is a statement which affects another, relates to the present time and treats a visible act".

67 "They will do, go or speak" is a statement which affects others, relates to the future time and treats an invisible act.

68 "That work is to be done today by me together with you" is a statement which affects one's ownself as well as another and relates to the present time.

69 Anything that is spoken on the stage in the drama under the cover of the hand, will affect one's ownself, relate to something at one's heart or will relate to an invisible (Parokṣa) act.

70 The seven forms of this Verbal Representation will have many more varieties when they are modified according to time and the persons affected.

71 These are the ways of the Histrionic Representation known to producers of a drama. Different kinds of representations are to be made through these.

72 *Sāmānya Abhinaya* is that which is made simultaneously by the head, the face, the feet, the thighs, the shanks, the belly and and the waist.

73 Abhinaya should be carried out by persons conversant with Nāṭya through graceful movements of hands and delicate efforts of limbs in general displaying the Bhāvas and the Rasas.

74—75 The Nāṭya which is performed through physical efforts that are not violent, hurried or complex, that rest on proper Laya, Tāla and the measurement of the Kalās and in which words are distinctly uttered with out harshness and hurry is called Ābhyantara (Regular, conforming to the rules).

76 When it is of the opposite kind and observes free movements and is not in harmony with songs and instrumental music accompanying it, is called Bāhya (Irregular, not conforming).

77 The Abhinaya is called Ābhyantara (Regular and conforming) when it is within the Lakṣaṇa or rule and Bāhya when it is beyond the ken of the Śāstra,

78 *The definition of Lakṣaṇa.* It is through this Lakṣaṇa that a dramatic performance is recognized (Lakṣyate). It is of much use in a drama.

79 Those who have not received regular instruction from any Ācārya or those who have no access to the treatises resort to the irregular ways which depend on the practices above.

80 A wise actor should represent the sense organs and their objects such as sound, touch, form, taste and smell through the concerned Bhāvas.

81 The sensible man represents Śabda (sound) by making a sidelong glance, bending the head side ways and placing the index finger near the ear.

82 The actor shall represent Sparśa (Touch) by slightly narrowing down the eyes, raising the eye brows in the like manner as well as by touching the shoulder and the cheek.

83 The sensible man represents Rūpa (Form) by holding on the head the Patāka hand with the fingers slightly moving and looking intently at something with the eyes.

84 He shall represent Rasa and Gandha (Taste and Odour) when favourable by slightly narrowing down the eyes and expanding the nostrils in the like manner and taking in a deep breath.

85 These are 'the gestures through which the activities of the five sense organs viz the ears, the skin, the eyes, the nose and the tongue are displayed.

86 When the object of a sense organ is contemplated in the mind it becomes represented outwardly. A person out of his mind cannot know the object of the senses perceptible through five sourees.

87 In regard to the Abhinaya, there are three attitudes towards the objects viz. Iṣṭa (favourable), Aniṣṭa (Unfavourable) and Madhyastha (non-committed).

88 One should represent the favourable through the joyous movement of the limbs, horripilation and the blooming of the face.

89 In regard to the favourable sound, touch, form shall or taste the actor shall display a happy face by taking the concerned senses up to the mind.

90 He shall display the unfavourable by the head turned back, eyes averted and eyes and nostrials distorted.

91 The actor displays the indifferent attitude by expressing neither excessive delight nor too much of abhorrence, by keeping himself in the middling state.

92 The representation of words like "It is done by him" "It is his", "He does so" in relation to invisible acts is an example of Madhyastha attitude.

93 *Ātmastha* (Personal) is that object which a person himself experiences. *Parastha* (Extraneous). Anything described by another is called Parastha.

94—95 Almost all the Bhāvas originate from Kāma (passionate attachment). In combination with particular desires it has many forms such a Dharma Kāma (desire for piety), Artha Kāma (monetary desire) and Mokṣa Kāma (desire for Salvation).

97 *Śṛṅgāra.* The union of man and woman causing a sexual intercourse and the pleasure thereof is known as Śṛṅgāra. It is auspicious if proper services are rendered mutually.

98 Most of the people in the world keenly desire hapiness always. Indeed the source of happiness is the woman. Women are of diverse natures.

99—100 Women are remembered as passing the nature of Devas, Asuras, Gandarvas, Rākṣasas, Nāgas, birds, Piśācas, Yakṣas, Vyālas, men, monkeys, elephants, deer, fish, camel, Makara (alligator), donkeys, horses, buffaloes, goats, dogs, cows etc.

101—102 *Devaśīlā* (of divine type). A women of divine type shall have the following characteristics :— She has steady and soft looks, delicate limbs, is free from sickness, has lustre, munificence, straight forwardness, produces very little perspiration, of middling sexual desire, takes less food, loves scent and is engaged in vocal and instrumental music.

103—104 *Asura sīlā.* A woman of demonaic nature has the following characteristics :— She transgresses laws of piety, practises trickery, is confirmed in anger, very crual, fond of wine and meat, always irritably hot tempered, very proud, fickle minded, very greedy, harsh, fond of quarrel jealous and in constant in affection.

105—106 *Gandharva Śīlā.* A woman is said to be possessing the nature of a Gandharva if she has the following characteristics :—She is fond of sports, she has beautiful eyes, good nails and teeth, she speaks steadily; is slim bodied, she has few children, fond of sexual dalliance, is always desirous of listening to songs and musical instruments, fond of dance; is careful about personal cleanliness, has soft skin, glossy hairs and lustrous eyes.

107—108 *Rākṣaśa Śīlā.* A woman is said to be possessing the nature of a Rākṣasa if she has large and broad limbs, red wide eyes, hard hairs; if she is fond of sleeping during the day time, she speaks loudly, fond of wounding others with nails and teeth, disposed to anger, jealousy and quarrel and likes to roam at night.

109—110 *Nāga Śīlā.* A woman is said to possess the nature of a Nāga (Serpent) if she has the following characteristics :—She has a pointed nose, sharp teeth, slender body, copper coloured eyes, blue lotus like complexion; she is fond of sleep, she is irritable, wobbling in walking, unsteady in efforts, takes fraquent breath, too proud, loves sweet scent, garlands and wine.

111—112 *Pakṣi Śīlā.* A woman of the nature of a bird has the following characteristic features :—She has a very large mouth, energetic character; she loves rivers, enjoys spirituous beverage and milk, has many offsprings, is fond of fruits, breathes too frequently, fond of gardens and forests, is very fickle and talkative.

113—114 *Piśācaśīlā.* The following are the characteristics of a woman of Piśāca nature :—fingers are less or more than the usual number; roams about in the gardens and parks at night; frightens children, is treacherous, speaks in double entendre, behaves atrociously during sexual dalliance, has hairy body and loud voice and is fond of liquor, meat and oblations.

115–116 *Yakṣa Śīlā.* A woman is said to possess the nature of a Yakṣa if the following characteristics are prominent. She perspires during sleep, loves quiet rest in bed or seat; is very intelligent, fearless and fond of wine, sweet smell and meat, takes delight on seeing persons after a long time, feels grateful to them and approaches them. She is not habituated to long sleep.

117 *Vyāla Śīlā.* A woman is said to have the nature of a Vyāla (Pythen, tiger) if she takes honour and insult in the same spirit, has a rough skin and harsh voice, is wily, speaks untruth and haughty words and has tawny eyes.

118–119 *Manuṣya Śīlā.* A woman is said to have the human nature when she possesses these predominant characteristics. She loves straight forwardness, is always clever and virtuous, has symmetrical limbs, is grateful (to those who help her) disposed to adore elders, gods and scholarly Brahmins prudent in regard to wealth, dutiful, loving, is free from pride, fond of friends, and possesses good character.

120–121 *Vānara Śīlā.* A woman is said to possess the nature of a monkey when she has the following characteristics: She has a compact small body, is impudent, has tawny hairs, is fond of fruits, talkative, fickle and energetic, loves to roam about among trees in the parks and forests esteems even the slightest generous act and is aggressive in sexual act.

122–123 *Hasti Śīlā.* A woman is said to possess the nature of an elephant if she has a large chin, and forehead, is flashy and plump, has tawny eyes hairy body, is fond of sweet scent, garlands and wine, has irritable temperament and steady energy, loves water gardens, forests, sweet things and sexual dalliance.

124–125 *Mṛga Śīlā.* A woman is said to have the nature of a deer if she has a small belly, flat nose, thin shanks, large red eyes; she is fickle; habituated to move quickly, frightened even during the day, fond of singing, musical instruments and sexu al dalliances, irrescible in temperament and unsteady in efforts.

126–128 *Matsya Śīlā.* A women is said to possess the nature of a fish if she has long, large and high breasts, is fickle and without any winking in her eyes, has many servants and offsprings and has liking for water.

Uṣṭrasattvā A woman of the Camel type has protruding lips, too much of perspiration, somewhat awkward mode of walking, slender belly, fondness for flowers, fruits, salt, sour and pungent tastes, waist and sides loosely bound, harshness and cruelty in speech, a high and rough neck and liking for forests.

129 *Makara Śīlā.* A woman endowed with all fishy characteristics with these in addition is said to possess the nature of an Alligator. She is cruel. She has a large head a steady neck, wide open mouth and very loud voice.

130—131 *Khara Śīlā.* A women with the following qualities is reputed to be of the nature of a donkey. She has a thick tongue and lips and large teeth; rough skin and very harsh words; she is violent during sexual intercourse, impudent, fond of nail scratches and bitings from the lover, jealous of the co-wives, clever,, fickle, slow in her gait, angry by nature and has many offsprings.

132—133 *Sūkara Śīlā.* A woman of the following characteristics is said to possess the nature of swine. She has a large back, belly and mouth, hairy and strong body a very narrow forehead; she is found of ordinary bullows roots; she has black teeth and ugly face large thigh and thick hairs, mean habits and many offsprings.

134—135 *Haya Sīlā.* A woman of the following qualities is remembered as possessing the nature of a horse she is faithful; she has symmetrical side, thighs hips and neck, straight and thick hairs; she is charming, munificent, lean, fickle minded, sharp tongued and quick in movement. She is prone to be angry and sexually passionate.

136—137 *Mahiṣa Śīlā* A women of the following characteristics is said to have the nature of a buffalo. She has broad back, bones, teeth sides, belly and rough hairs; she is faithless, turbulent and fond of sexual intercourse; she is hated by the common people. She has a slighly raised mouth, large forehead and excellent hips. She is fond of forests and sports in water.

138–139 *Ajā Śīlā.* A woman is remembered as possessing the nature of a goat if she has the following characteristics —She is lean. She has small arms and breasts, almost motionless red eyes, short hands and feet; she is covered with fine hairs; she is timid, foolish, mad, fond of forests, restless and of swift movements. She begets many offsprings.

140—141 *Śva Śīlā.* A woman with the following qualities is said to possess the nature of a dog. She is alert in eyes and limbs; is disposed to frequent yawning, talkactive and grateful; she has a small beaming face, short hands and feet, loud voice, viasable temper and low manners.

142—143 *Go Śīlā.* A woman with the following qualities is said to be of the nature of a cow. She has large plump and high hips, thin shanks, short hands and feet; she is kind and friendly to those who are near and dear, favourable to children, engaged in adoring gods and ancestors, always clean, respectful to superiors, faithful and patient at her sufferings.

144—145 Thus women should be known to possess different kinds of nature One should attend upon them after knowing their nature properly courteous attentions to them in accordance with their nature even if they were to be meagre, shall please them. A great deal of the same but provided otherwise will not at all satisfy them.

146—147 Intimate sexual love will arise in a woman if she gets whatever she desires. Certain Upacāras (ways of attention) have been prescribed for the purpose of generating amorous pleasure in man and woman. Austerities are practised for the sake of piety. Acquisition of piety is for the sake of happiness women constitute the source of happiness. Enjoyment of their company is desired by all.

148 *Kāmopacāra* (Loving attention) mentioned in the dramatic convention in relation to women and men is of two types the Bāhya (External) and the Ābhyantara (Intimate, internal).

149 Of these two the intimate attention is to be employed by kings in the Nāṭaka. The enternal one is to be observed by courtezans in the Prakarana.

150 In this connexion I shall describe in detail the loving attentions, on the part of Kings as laid down in the Kāma Tantra (treatises on love).

151 Women of various natures are of three types viz. Bāhyā (external. public), Ābhyantarā (Internal, domestic, homely) and Bāhyābhyantarā (mixed). A woman belonging to a very noble family is Ābhyantarā (internal) and a courtezen is Bāhyā (External).

152 A Kṛtaśaucā (a woman of inviolated chastity) if the is a maiden of very noble family is of the mixed type.

153 A maiden of very noble family has opportunity to receive the royal attention. A public woman is never desired by the king. Hence she too does not receive the royal service of love.

154 The Ābhyantarā shall be the object of royal attention and the Bāhyā that of the layman's attention. Union of a celestrial courtezan with the king is also possible.

155 The conduct approved of the case of married women of noble family holds good in the case of the virgins also. In the matter concerning love a courtezan too behaves like a lady of the noble family.

156 Whether in the case of men or women love is generated from various Bhāvas (emotional fervours) and it is three fold viz. superior, middling and inferior.

157 Love towards anyone is generated through hearing about the person, seeing the person, the beauty of the person, sportive movements there of and charming conversation therewith.

158 A person conversant with these affairs should observe the various indications of love in men and women desirous of one another.

159 A woman becomes overcome with love at the sight of a young man endowed with handsome features and good qualities, prime of youth and knowledge of various fine arts.

160 At this time the Dṛṣṭi shall be what is called Kāmyā (loving) when it is charming with tears, slightly drooping, with the eyelashes throbbing and the upper eyelid languid.

161 The glance in which the corner of the eyes moves and has sportful expressions is called Lalitā. It is to be employed in women's partial glances.

162 There is colour in the face with cheeks turned slightly red and made wonderful with a fear drops of sweet and hairs in the body stand on their end.

165—165 A courtezen can be understood as overcome with love when she expresses her passion with various loving movements of the limbs. She looks with sidelong glances, frequently touches the ornaments, scratches the ears, draws lines on the ground with the big toe, displays the breasts and the navel, rubs over the nails and engages herself in trying up the braid of hairs.

166—167 Similarly I shall mention the indications of love in a noble born lady. She looks continuously with blooming eyes, conceals her sweet and facial features smiles, and speaks with downcast face, replies with a smile, with the lips throbbing. She appears to tremble slightly.

168 The lady who has not yet received the experience of the consummation of loves pleasures reveals the love in its ten stages through the following signs.

169—171 *The ten stages of love.* Abhilāṣa (lcnging) in the first stage; Cintā (Anxiety) is the second stage; Anusmṛts (Recollection) in the third stage; Guṇakīrtana (glorification of the qualities of the lover) is the fourth stage; Udvega (Annoyance, distress) is the fifth stage; Vilāpa (Lamentation) is the sixth one Unmāda (Insanity) is the seventh stage; Vyādhi (sickness) is the eighth stage; Jaḍatā (Stupour) is the ninth stage and Maraṇa (death) is the tenth. This holds good in the cases of both men and women. Understand the characteristics of these.

172 Abhilāṣa arises from efforts induced by the wish and desire for the beloves and turns towards the means for the meeting.

173 The girl in the first stage of love goes out of the places where the lover is present and enters it frequently stays within his sight and shows signs of love,

174 *Cintā* (Anxiety) is to be displayed by speaking to the female messenger such words as—By what means and in what manner can there be the acquisition of the beloved ?"

175 In the second stage of love the actress should look with help closed eyes and touch or handle the bangles the girdle, the knot of the underwear and the navel.

176 *Anusmṛti* is characterised by frequent sighing, thinking deeply of the desired one and disliking other activities.

177 This third stage should be represented like this, that the loving one does not attain composure in sitting or lying in bed because of being engrossed in thinking about him. Hence she neglects her other duties.

178 *Guṇa kīrtana* is that stage where the loving one tries to express the idea that there is no one else on a par with him" through sportful movements of the limbs, smiles, words and glances.

179 The representation of the fourth stage is through horripilation, wiping the tears and sweets and talking in confidence to the female messenger for the relief from the pangs of separation.

180 *Udvega* is that stage where the loving one always eagerly expects the beloved one and is not pleased or satisfied with sitting or lying in bed.

181 This stage is displayed in drama by representing anxiety, sighs, lassitude and heart-burn in an exaggerated manner.

182 *Vīlapa* A woman in this stage is excessively anxious on account of eagerness and want of fortitude and laments excessively. She moves from place to place uneasily.

183 Lamentation is to be represented on the stage by speaking sorrowfully the words such as—"He stood here, he approached me here" etc.

184 *Unmāda* (Insanity) is that stage where the loving one is solely engaged in talking about her lover and hates all other men.

185 The Abhinaya of this stage of Unmāda is as follows : He (she) stands looking with a steadfast gaze, heaves a deep

sigh, becomes absorbed in himself (herself) and sometimes weeps while walking around (on the stage).

186. *Vyādhi* is the result when other means fails such as cajoling words, monetary and other gifts etc. and all the things. sent have been refused.

187 The eighth stage is to be represented thus. The person concerned swoons, or goes elsewhere; there is acute pain of the head; he (she) is unable to gain steadiness.

188 Jaḍatā is that stage where the person concerned does not reply when questioned does not see or hear anything. It is a pathetic situation when the victim loses memory and remains silent or simply repeats "Ha! Alas!"

189 While representing Jaḍatā (stupour) one is to utter "Hum" suddenly and is to have the limbs relaxed and sighs pass over the face.

190 *Maraṇa.* If even after trying all the methods possible the desired union does not take place the death befalls the lady consumed by the fire of love.

191 These are the stages to be portrayed in regard to love when there is no realization of what is desired. But the last stage should be avoided (should not be directly represented).

192 A man too, on being separated from his beloved, will make a manifestation of love in diverse ways through the different Bhāvas.

193 The sensible man shall carry out the Abhinaya through the common characteristics of men and women in love.

194—196 All the stages of love should be represented in different ways through anxiety, sighs, lassitude, wearness of the body, gestures of the heart-burn, gazing vacantly at the sky, following the beloved or looking up, touching or twisting various objects or ornaments worn or clinging to some support and similar conditions arising from want of contact with the beloved.

197 A person being consumed by the fire of love shall make use of these cooling objects such as garlands, jewels, scents and unguents, rooms and gardens.

198—199 Being overcome with the burning love and afflicted through the several stages of love one should willingly send a female messenger to speak of one's conditions. He shall send a love-message through her. She shall politely say "such is his condition" (to her).

200 After the substance of the message has been communicated one should think of the means of fulfilling love. This is the rule where love is secretly indulged.

201 I shall now explain the rules regarding the practice of kings in relation to Ābhyantara women as based on the science of love (Kāmatantra).

202 The people follow whatever the kings do in regard to the Bhāvas, causing, happiness or unhappiness as a result of various habits.

203 Means of pleasure can be commanded by kings. They are not inaccessible to them in virtue of their royal power but Kāma that issues forth and gets developed through chivdlrous qualities are conducive to better pleasure.

204 Thanks to the deference for the queens and out of fear for their favourite women secret love should be indulged in by a king in respect to the attendant girls.

205—206 Although the kings have many modes of enjoying love, it is the secret love that is the most pleasing of all. The fact that men are enamoured of women who oppose them initially, because they are forbidden from doing so and the fact that a woman is usually inaccessible is the perfect point in Rati (sexual love).

207 In the case of the women of the harem the kings, sexual intercourse with them is usually desired during the day time; but in dealing with external women the union at night is glorified.

208 The following six are the Vāsakas for a king [reasons for indulging in sexual intercouse]. Paripāṭī (specified days by turns), Phalārtha (for the sake of fruit i.e. progeny), Navatva (Newness of acquaintence), Prasava (because of the confinement of the queen), Duḥkha (sorrow) and Pramoda (Joy).

209. When the Vāsaka is relevant the kings shall freely approach attendant girls or beloved ones at the prescribed period after menstruation.

210—211 In this connection Nāyikās (heroines) are classified into eight types: Vāsakasajjikā (readily dressed up for Union), Virahotkaṇṭhitā (distressed due to separation) Svādhīnabhartṛkā (One having the husband under control), Kalahāntaritā (one estranged due to quarrel with the lover) Khaṇḍitā (one annoyed with her lover), Vipralabdhā (jilted by the lover).

Proṣita Bhartṛkā (one whose husband is in exite) and Abhisārikā (one who approaches the husband or lover herself).

212 *Vāsakasajjā* is that woman who embellishes herself in eager expectation of love when Vāsaka is relevant.

213 *Virahotkaṇṭhitā* is the woman whose lover does not turn up at the place of tryst on account of his preoccupation with many other engagements and she has become excessively sad.

214 *Svādhīna Bhartṛkā* as the woman whose husband stays by her for ever on being captivated by the way in which she has given him the plea, was of love and the pleasing qualities she possesses.

215 *Kalahāntaritā* is that woman who is separated from her lover due to a quarrel or jealousy and who is excessively angry and impatient.

216 *Khaṇḍitā* is that woman whose beloved one does not honour the Vāsaka on account of his attachment for another woman and who is distressed due to his non arrival.

217 Vipralabdha is that women, who is deceived by the lover not arriving at the place of tryst on account of some reasons despite the fact that a Dūtī had been sent by him.

218 *Proṣitabhartṛka* is that woman whose husband is in exiles or lives abroad on account of very responsible duties and who wears her hair hanging loose.

219 *Abhisārikā* is that woman who hastens to the plea of tryst due to love or inebriety for saking all manners and conventions of modesty.

220 Heroines of the Nāṭaka should be known in these Avasthās (stages). I shall mention their diversified activity of love.

221 The Khaṇḍitā, Vipralabdhā, Kalahāntaritā and the Proṣita Bhartṛkā heroines should be represented through anxiety, sighs, lassitude, heart-burn, conversation with the female companions, looking at one's own situation, weakness, depression tears, appearance of anger, giving up of ornaments and toilet, misery and lamentation.

224 A *Svādhīnabhartṛkā* should be represented with gaudy radiant dresses, face beaming with pleasure and having excess of physical charm.

225 The manner of the heroine's hastening to the place of tryst to meet the lover should be represented by means of the following special Bhāvas whether she be a courtezan, a lady of noble birth or a maid servant.

226 While hurrying to the place of tryst the courtezan is to have her body beautifully adorned with various ornaments and to walk slowly in the company of her attendants with a display of passion and joy.

227 In a similar situation the woman of a noble family is to cover her face with a veil and walk timidly with the limbs contracted, looking back very frequently.

228 The situation remaining so the hand maid will walk with uneven steps, the eyes beaming with amorous joy. Her talk shall be distorted and incoherent through intoxication.

229 After going there, if she were to find the lover sleeping she has to awaken him with the following mode of attention.

230 The noble lady shall awaken him through the jewels (making them tinkle), the courtezan through the sweet cool scents and the hand maid by fanning him with her clothes.

231 On this occasion the scolding words of the female companions shall be strong but sweet and conducive to consoling her.

232. This is the rule regarding love making and allied attentions with respect to the women of noble family and others, for the Nāṭaka is to respect all the Avasthās (stages, situations).

233 For a woman newly in love or for an enraged woman when she does not come of her our accord the Vāsaka services should be arranged through some feigned means or excuse.

234 The lover shall be joyously making use of the various ornaments, unguents and garlands worn and enjoyed by his beloved.

235 Unable to get a beloved lady a man does not become much infatuated with love as be becomes doubly delighted in close contact with his beloved.

236 At the time of conjugal intimacy there should be amorous feelings, gestures, words and sportful movements of the sweetest kind and especially looking at each other with love.

237 *Preparation for the Conjugal intimacy.* In the context of the visit of the lover (hero), a woman on her part should make some special preparation for the conjugal union to give rise to pleasure.

238 After wearing sweet garlands and clothes scented with powder, mirror should be sportfully held (and the face seen) again and again.

239 In the preparation for conjugal union one should not put on too many ornaments. The girdle and the anklet that produce a tinkling sound should be preferred.

240 *Acts forbidden on the stage.* In representing the various activities of women there should not be the wearing of clothes, nor bath nor use of unguents and collyrium, nor arrangement of the braid of hair.

241 Women of the superior and the middling type should not be ungainly draped or clad in a single cloth. They should not use any colour for their lips.

242 All these may be relevant in the case of the women of the inferior type, In regard to them too.what is obcene should not be presented by the producers.

243 In the drama (Nāṭaka) the men and women of the servant class should be shown wearing (simple) ornament or flowers.

244 If a woman with the embellishment of her body awaits the arrival of her beloved she should cleverly finish it so that nothing contrary to propriety finds expression.

245 After finishing the preparation for the conjugal intimacy the Nāyikā should sit down and wait for the arrival of the lover while listening to the sound of the striking of the Nāḍikās.

246 Afrer hearing the sound of the Nāḍikā the heroine who is overpowered by the joy of the assured arrival of the lover should run towards the gate with the body trembling.

247 Holding the doorframe with her left hand and a door blade with the right one she should look up with straight eyes for the arrival of the lover.

248 Over come with apprehenston she should show reasonable signs of fear when she is not able to see him. For a moment she remains sad.

249 After hearing a deep sigh she shall shad tears from her eyes. With a motionless heart she shall drop down her limbs on a seat.

250 Due to a delay of the beloved she shall ponder over his arrival with considerations of causes auspicious or otherwise.

251 She will think thus—Could my lover have been held up by oneroes duties, by the friends or by the ministers engaged in affairs of the state or could he have been detained by some favourite woman ?"

252 She should represent appearances connected with the various good or bad causes by means of personal omens like quivering or throbbing of a particular limb.

253 *Personal omens* indicating occurrence favourable to women will occur to their left side while omens in case of all undesirable happenings will take place on their right.

254 If there is (certain) union there shall be the throbbing of the left eye, eyebrows, forehead, lips, arm, breast or thigh.

255 If these throb otherwise, it will indicate something calamities. When such bad omens are perceived she should at once faint.

256 On the non-arrival of the Nāyaka, the hand should be made to rest on the cheek. She shall display disregard for ornaments and than weap.

257 If the omens were to be auspicious in regard to the arrival of the hero, the heroine should indicate that the hero is nearby, through the intake of the odour.

258 *Reception and honour to the hero.* On seeing him arrive she shall joyously get up and proceed to receive the lover and took at him with eyes beaming in delight.

259 *Reception of the guilty lover.* If the lover comes with the signs of meeting another woman and green wounds received from her, the heroine should point out the man after assuming the Āyata Sthāna, keeping her hand in the hand of her female companion.

260 On the lover being found guilty he should be censured duly by means of appropriate gestures and reproachful words as well as jealous anger (Māna), insult (Avamāna), fainting (Sammoha) and dissimulation (Avahittha).

261—264 Due to reasons like the application of dissimulation, the use of hidden words, or of laughter, curiosity, flurry calamity and acceding to a situation of fun and to his concealting any fault the heroine should speak to the lover even if his guilts require that he should not be spoken to. Where there is affection, there is fear also. Where there is jealousy here occurs love. The causes of jealousy are four viz Vaimanasya (Depression), Vyalīka (Mixed feeling), Vipriya (disgust) and Manyu (anger).

265 *Vaimanasya* arises from seeing the lover walking lazily due to sleepiness and lassitude and discovering signs of his union with another lady such as green wounds received from her.

266 This should be represented with an intensely jealous face, great trembling of limbs due to anger and utterance of words like "Excellent". "It is well-done" "It is splendid".

267 *Vyalīka* arises due to jealousy mixed in joy when the lover stays nearby even after being treated with insult.

268 In Vyalīka the Abhinaya is as follows :—She keeps her left hand on the breasts and gesticulates the right hand violenthy. She then stands planting the feet firmly.

269 *Vipriya* arises when the lover says—"I live while you are alive" "I am your slave" "You are my beloved" And behaves in a different manner thereafter.

270 Representation of Vipriya should be made by means of a cold treatment to the Dūtī disregard for the letters and indifference about replying to the questions (made by the lover or Dūti) and also by means of the shaking of the head.

271 *Manyu* arises in a woman when the lover comes to her after his union with a rival woman and boasts about his good luck in this matter and reveals the signs of such a union.

272 *Manyu* should be represented by giving up the bangles and throwing up the girdle in a loose manner and by timid and tearful eyes.

273 *Behaviour towards the guilty lover*. On seeing the lover standing ashamed and afraid due to the revelation of his guilt the Nāyikā should harass him with rebuke made up of words spoken in jealous indignation.

274 But cruel words should not be uttered and angry taunting words should be avoided. The Nāyikā should speak things referring to herself tearfully.

275—277 This attitude should be represented by the middle finger touching the edge of the lower lip and a hand placed on the breast and by looking with eyes up turned or by a Karaṇa in which a hand is placed on the hip and the fingers are separated or by moving the head and bending it to see the nails or by a look of dissimulation or by beautiful finger gestures indicating threat.

278—279 The actress then says "you are excellant," "You have been found out well" "Go away, why do you delay?" "Do not touch me" "Go to your beloved who is there" "Go to" After saying these she should turn back and make jokes with words and try to make him plead.

280 If she is taken forcibly by the dress, hand, or head the woman should be softened despite seeing the guilt.

281 When taken by her hand or dress or hair the act of releasing herself should be done by the woman very showly moving towards the lover.

282 When taken by her hair, hand or dress the women should experience (joyously) his touch in such a way that the lover does not perceive it.

283 The releasing of the hair should be done by the woman slowly by standing first on her toes with limbs bent and then taking to the Apakrāntā Cārī

284 When the had does not get release the woman should experience a little of perspiration and pretending to be languid due to the joy of touch shall say "Hum Hum leave it off had away".

285 Going at first on hearing the angry words "Go away" he should first go and then come back to start talking to her under some pretext.

286 Then the woman should make movements of her hand uttering "Hum Hum" and during these movements should speak to him with an imprecation.

287 If her cloths are taken away by the lover, the woman should either cover her eyes or look back covering her Nīvī (land of the clothes over the waist).

288 The lover should be harassed till he falls at the feet; but once he has fallen at her feet she should glance at the Dūtī (meaning fully).

289—291 The Nāyikā should embrace the lover. With loves enjoyment as the object she should joyously walk with him to the bed. All these should be represented only by means of songs, with a gentle dance. When there is Ākāśabhāṣita (addressing some one not present) in the Nāṭaka depending on other mans speech and related to love's pleasures and Śṛṅgāra Rasa than this same line of representation should be followed by the woman.

292 The same rule regarding the Abhinaya holde good in all those cases in a play having reference to the inner apartment (Zenana) and Śṛṅgāra Rasa.

293 *Prohibitions* Sleeping should not be openly depicted on the stage by one conversant with Nāṭya Dharma (dramatic convention and practice) but the Aṅka is brought to a close under some excuse.

294—295 If out of any necessity anyone sleeps alone or with some one else, no kissing or embracing or any other private action such as scratching with the nails, biting, loosening of the Nīvī, pressing of the breasts and lips should be presented on the stage.

296 Taking food, sporting in water and doing any obscene or inmodest act should not be presented on the stage.

297 Since a Nāṭaka is to be witnessed by the father and son, mother in law and daughter in law, all sitting together, these acts should be assiduously avoided.

298 Nāṭakas should be written with extremely pleasant sweet words, not at all harsh, by the poet conversant with them. These shall be advices on what is wholesome.

299 *Endearing terms of address.* Listen to and understand the words of women to be addressed to dear ones at the time of union.

300 These words are Priya (dear), Kānta (shining or loving one), Vinīta (cultured one), Nātha (lord), Svāmī (master), Jīvita (the very life), Nandana (joygiver).

301 *Angry term.* When angry the lady refers to the lover Duḥśīla (ill-natured), Durācāra (ill-doing, tyrant) Śaṭha (deceitful), Vāma (Antagonistic), Vikatthana (Boasting one), Nirlajja (Impendent) and Niṣṭhura (cruel).

302 *Priya* is one who is upright and straight forward in his behaviour, who does nothing undesirable who does not speak in proper words.

303 *Kānta.* That man is spoken of as Kānta in whose lips or other parts of the body there is no visible sign arising from another lady.

304 *Vinīta.* That lover is spoken of as Vinīta (desciplined, cultured) who, even when angry does not reply defiantly nor speaks harshly.

305 *Nātha* is one who is a well wisher, capable of according protection, neither concerted nor jealous and who has no delusion in regard to any activity.

306 *Svāmin.* That lover is spoken of as Svāmin who attends to his woman through Sāma (gentle and sweet words)

Dāna (gifts), Artha (monetary help) and Sambhoga (Sexual dalliance) as well as fondling and affording maintenance.

307 *Jīvita*. That lover is remembered as Jīvita who skilfully manages the arrangement for bed in accordance with the views and wishes of the woman at the time of love's enjoyment.

308 *Nandana*. That lover is called Nandana who is of noblefamily, courageous, efficient, chivalrous, eloquent in speech, praiseworthy in the midst of female companions.

309 These modes of address are to heighten the charm of love's enjoyment. I shall now explain the words of displeaure Hear them.

310 *Duḥśīla* is one who is ruthless, intolerant, arrogant, impudant, braggart and fickleminded.

311 *Durācāra* is one who is indiscreet; beats and binds his beloved and who uses harsh words.

312 *Śaṭha* is that man who speaks sweet words but does not demonstrate love in practice or does not give money to women.

313 *Vāma* is that hostile man who does everything he is forbidden to do and who acts contrary to the wish of the beloved.

314 *Vikatthana* (Virūpaka) is one who boasts about his good fortune when taunted as a result of revealing greenwounds received from another woman. He is stubborn and concerted also.

315 *Nirlajja* is that shameless lover who hovers round a woman despite being forbidden. He bears the marks of illegitimate love and guilt.

316 *Niṣṭhura* is that cruel one who aggressively tries to enjoy a woman despite being guilty towards her and never thinks of conciliating her.

317 These are the words indicating pleasure or otherwise or whether one is dear or not. In different circumstances the opposite words are to be used in *Ulluṇṭhana* (irony)

318 There should be the rules of address in songs with a gentle dance and also where anything is to be expressed in words for the Śṛṅgāra Rasa.

319 This is the way in which Abhinaya is carried out in regard to the incidents in the Antaḥpura. I shall now describe in detail the rules regarding celestial ladies.

320 The dress of the celestial damsels is always brilliant; their mind is perpetually delighted; their time passes happily in sports.

321 Celestial males have no jealeousy, anger or malice and so there is no necessity for them to propitiate their females in the activities of Śṛṅgāra.

322 When celestial women unite with human beings they have to be accorded all human Bhāvas.

323 Contact of the celestial ladies with human beings on a Śṛṅgāra basis is to be effected as a fall due to a curse or an urge to beget children.

324 The invisible celestial damsel shall tempt (the human lover) through flowers or the sounds of jewels. After revealing her self for a short while she should become invisible.

325 The Nāyaka is to be maddened by these attentions and services such as dresses, ornaments, garlands etc. and by sending epistles.

326 Love arising from being maddened is more conducive to love's pleasures. What arises naturally may not be so moving or emotional.

327 O Brahmins, after attaining human form celestial males should assume all the Bhāvas common to human beings, even their mode of walking and acting.

328 This should be the practice in connection royal etiquette (Rājopacāra) as related to Ābhyantara women. The Upacāra as related to Bāhyas will be treated in the rules regarding Vaiśika.

Notes

1 According to Bharata Sāmānya Abhinaya should be a combination of Āṅgika, Vācika and Sāttvika. As explained by

Abhinava Gupta it is the result of the combination of all Abhinayas in the same manner as scent results when various sweet-smelling substances are combined together in a certain proportion.

10 According to Nāṭyadarpaṇa the Bhāva relates to a slight manifestation of erotic feelings through words and gestures while Hāva relates to a very clear expression of one's emotion through various gestures. Hāva depends on the Bhāva depends on the Bhāva and Helā on the Bhāva.

25 It is the common experience that a young maiden's loveliness is augmented after her early experiences of sexual dalliance. This augmented loveliness is called Śobhā.

40 Fourfold division of Abhinaya is mentional in VI-23. (ante).

156 Three kinds of love have been defined by Śāradātanaya in his Bhāva Prakāśa 113-1 (10-14).

169 Two more stages viz. Icchā (Wish) and Utkaṇṭhā.. (Anxiety) are mentioned by others.

235—239 There are lacunae apparently in the Mss. at this place.

261—263 According to another Mss. Women's outbust of speech should be in Gāthā in the following cases such as affection. suspicious love, satisfaction, joy, courtesy, and infliction of abuse.

283 Apakrāntā Cāri is explained in XI—30 ante.

294—295 This dictum is characteristic of the Hindu mind that views everything from the Dharma angle.

300—301 Later rhetoricians had added more terms

25

Vaisikopacara (Services of the Gallant)

1 A Vaiśika (Gallant) is one who excels in all fine arts or one who is an adept in regard to the services of harlots.

2 One who is equipped with the knowledge of all arts, who is an expert in all crafts and who is conversant with the technique of captivating the hearts of women is called a Vaiśika.

3 Briefly put his qualities are thirty three that are be classified into three types (a) Corporeal (b) Extraneous and Corgenitel.

4--7 He is conversant with the Śāstras, richly endowed with craftsmanship, handsome of pleasing appearance, powerful, possessing fortitude, of desirable age, well dressed, of noble pedigree, Surabhi (bond of scents), Madhura (sweet in temperament), ready to forego personal things, able to endure, not prone to boast about himself, unsuspecting, speaking pleasing words, clever, bestower of auspiciousness, clean in habits, expert in amorous services, chivalrous, aware of the proper place, aware of the proper time, not indulging in piteons cringing words, smiling, eloquent, adept, Sweet tongued, not covetous, ready to share things with others, having faith, firm in resolve, distrusting even accessible women and self respecting.

8 His friend too has his qualities but especially these six viz he is devoted, clean in habits, self-possessed, chivalrous intelligent and capable of talking on various topics.

9—10 The following types of women can become the female messenger—one endowed with knowledge and good qualities, one who can narrate tales, a saintly woman, a woman whose means of sustenance is the stage or dyeing of clothes, an intelligent woman, a woman of the neighbourhood, a female companion, a maid servant, a virgin, a woman of crafts and fine arts, a foster mother or wet nurse, a heretical nun or a female fortune-teller.

11 The female messenger shall also be any woman with the following qualities : One who is an expert in convincing and encourag̀ng (the beloved or the lover) one who can narrate sweet stories, one who is courteous, one who is aware of the proper time, one who is charming in her behaviour and one who is capable of keeping secrets.

12 One shall never engage a man or a woman as messenger if he or she is foolish, extremely beautiful, wealthy or sickly.

13—18 *The functions of a messenger.* She should encourage the lovers with the adequate reasons pointed out and she must communicate the actual words used by the other one and also clarify the emotional fervour. Besides this the messenger should make exaggerated statements about his nobility of birth, affluence and ability to give amorous enjoyment. She must explain the various acts to be pursued to facilitate union. If the girl is a beginner in amorous activities or if she is in a huff or if she is excessively petulant it is the female messenger who has to bring about her union or re-union with the man through various means. The first meeting of men with women may be made on a festive occassion, during the night, in a garden, in the house of a friend, a foster mother or a female companion or in a dinner party, under the pretext of seeing a sick person or in an empty house. After bring about the union thus duly through various means (the messenger) should ascertain whether she is in love or averse through distinct signs.

19 *The Madanāturā* or woman overcome with love is that one who is naturally and emotionally smitten with love and does not conceal her amorous behaviour (on seeing the lover).

20—23 *Anuraktā* (Affectionate woman) is that woman with the following ways and behaviour she enumerates the good qualities of the lover in the midst of her female companions, she freely gives him (her) money, adores his friends, hates the enemies, solicits union (with him), becomes pleased when he is pleased, looks delighted after a talk about him, sleeps after he has gone to sleep, looks at him with affection, on being kissed, kisses in return, rises in the morning before he gets up, puts up with sufferings remains the same in happiness and misery, and never gets angry.

24—27 *The Viraktā* (hostiles) woman has the following distinguishing marks : on being kissed she wipes of the mouth, speaks unpleasant words, gets angry even after being addressed sweetly, hates his friends, resorts to his enemies, lies on the bed with averted face, goes to bed first, does not become satisfied despite a great deal of respect has been shown, never brooks the slightest pain, becomes offended even without any reason, does not even glance at him nor greets him. One should point out a woman with these characteristics as Viraktā.

28—29 The following measures may lead to the winning back of a woman's heart—constant effort in this respect, display of wealth, showing of good will, suggestion of offering money, giving up the inter-mediaries, and transferance of affection.

30—31 *Causes of hostility* in a man or a woman are the following—poverty, ailments, excessive misery, harshness, absence of education, exite, wounded pride, avariciousness, transgression of good conduct, arrival long after the due time, and resorting to undesirable activities.

32—35 *Bhāvagrahi* (Capable of regaining lost love) activities should be resorted to towards women in connection with love play so that the woman becomes pleased and is won over. A greedy lady should be won over by gifting money, an educated woman by means of the knowledge of arts, a clever woman through graceful sportive activities, a woman in a buff by acting up to her desire, a man-hating one by means of anecdotes humouring her and such activities desired, a girl in her teens by a present of toys, a terror-stricken girl by cheering her up, a haughty woman by servility and noble woman by displaying familiarity with fine arts.

36 By nature women can be classified into three types the Uttamā, Madhyamā and Nīcā. The nature of a harlot depends upon her intrinsic features.

37—39 Uttamā (superior) is that lady who exhibits the following characteristics—She does not speak displeasing words to her lover even when he does something to tease her, she has a short lived annoyance, she is skilled in fine arts, she is liked by men in view of her noble birth, affluence and ability to give sexual satisfaction etc; she is an adept in the love lore, courteaus, equipped with physical beauty, becomes angry only for adequate reasons, speaks without malicious rivalry, she is aware of the proper opportunity for everything and she is an all round beauty.

40—41 *That woman is remembered as Madhyamā* who displays the following characteristics :—She is liked by men and she desires the company of men, she is skilled in the amorous art, she is jealous of her rivals, she is overcome with jealousy, her anger is of short duration, she is proud but can be pacified quickly.

42 *The Adhamā* (inferior) woman is angry without proper reason. wicked by nature, fickleminded, harsh and her anger continues for a long time.

43 *Yauvanabheda* (Stages in the growth in adult-hood) of all these types of women are four is regarded to their behaviour after testing pleasures of love manifesty through dress, physical form, activity and inner qualities.

44 The first stage in the adulthood is the time when she is very enthusiastic about sexual activities the thighs, cheeks, lips, and breasts become plump and stout contributing to the pleasures of sexual dalliance.

45 The seeond stage affords the best pleasure of love. It is characterised by full and round limbs, plump breasts and slander waist.

46 The third stage is rich in various qualities, it excites sexual activities, it is full of the qualities of the amorous exercise; the beauty is enhanced by the enjoyment of love.

47—48 The fourth stage in adulthood can be termed (somewhat) inimical to love's enjoyment. It comes when the first second and third stages have passed duly. The physical charm is slightly reduced due to sunken cheeks, hips, lips and breasts. There is marked want of enthusiasm in sexual dalliance.

49 A woman in fresh youth can be recognized as one who cannot take much pains; she is neither displeased nor too

delighted with her female rivals. She attached to persons of mild qualities.

50 A woman in har second stage of adulthood takes offence very lightly; her anger and malice is not prolonged; she becomes silent when angry.

51 A woman in the third stage of adulthood is highty efficient in the art of sexual dalliance. She is excessively jealous of her rivals; she is not eager to hide her pride.

52 A woman in the fourth stage of adulthood is capable of attracting people; she does not feel envious of her rivals equally efficient in love's play; she craves for non-separation from her lover.

53—54 These are the four stages of the adult hood of the women characters in a drama. I shall now explain the different types of men in respect to their love life. In the matter of their dealings with women they are of five types—(a) Catura (Very clever, excellent), (b) Uttama (Superior) (c) Madhya (Middling) (d) Nīca (Inferior) and (e) Pravṛddhaka (too advanced in age).

55 That man should be known as *Catura* when he is sympathetic, sharing misery and pain; is skilled in pacifying anger feigned due to love, when he is efficient in amorous attendance and very chivalrous.

56—57 *The Uttama* man displays the following characteristics—he does not do anything displeasing to the woman, he is courageous and magnanimous, sweet tongued, and thoroughly conversant with the mysteries of human emotions, he is sweet in manners, liberal minded, experiences love but does not succumb to it, when jilted by a woman he too gets disgusted with he.

58 *The Madhyama* (Middling) man calmly accepts the different emotional states of the woman. He is disgusted with her on finding out faults.

59 He makes gifts at the proper time, even when insulted slightly he is not very angry but on finding out deceitful behaviour he gets disgusted with the woman thoroughly.

60—61 The Adhama (i.e. Nīca inferior) shamelessly approaches a woman with steady love even when insulted by her. When she indulges in deceit initially he loves her all the more. Though friends may dissuade him by saying that she has her affections elsewhere he retains his composure and perseveres in his advances.

62—63 *Saṃyravṛddhaka*. A men who does not care for fear or anger; is foolish, naturelly attracted to women, obdurate, shameless in sexual dalliance rough in love quarrels, he is a laughing stock and a toy in the hands of women. Such a man is to be known as Sampravṛddhaka (too advanced in age).

64 Women are of differant natures and their hearts are mystifying. Hence a sensible man tries to study her properly before approaching (then).

65 By means of different methods of approach a man should measure the feelings of a woman and deal with her in accordance with the treatises on love.

66 Thə methods of approach are Sāma (Conciliation), Pradāna (Gift), Bheda (Dissension) Dāṇḍa (Chastisement) and Upekṣā (Indifference).

67 *Sāma* Expressing attachment by saying "I am yours" "you are mine" "I am your servant" "you are my beloved" is called Sāma (conciliation).

68 *Pradāna* (gift) giving of money as occasions rise, in accordance with one's capacity and sending it under some pretext is called Pradāna.

69 *Bheda* (dissension) showing the faults of the dear one by means of some device is called Bheda. *Daṇḍa*-Imprisonment and actual beating is called Daṇḍa.

70 An indifferent woman is to be won over by conciliation, an avaricious woman is to be won over by monetary gifts; a woman attached to some other person can be won over by means of dissension.

71 If a woman begin to behave wickedly as a result of her being attracted by another person Daṇḍa should be employed

beginning with mild beating and restraint to physical movement.

72 A sencible man should be indifferent to a woman who does not come round even after all the four other means have been employed.

73 From the expression of a woman's face, from her eyes and from the movements of her limbs one can understand whether she hates a man, loves him or is indifferent to him.

74—76 Harlots are always available for money to a man whether he is dear to her or not. This is not applicable to those courtezans attached to temples and kings. They call a man worthy of being hated as "my dear" a man already dear to them as "dearer", a wicked man as "one well behaved" and a man devoid of good qualities at "one full of good qualities" On seeing these persons their eyeballs rolls in dancing fashion; they begin to smile and their faces put a pleasant colour by the simulation of proper feelings.

77 Hence, one should approach women with due regard to the tenets of the Kāmatantra (Science of Erotics) after understanding the emotional fervour or the absence thereof in them.

78 Passion arises in them after they have been treated properly or after they have been separated after the first union just as fire comes out of the firewood.

79 This is the traditional method of dealing with women as far as the Vaiśika is concerned. This shall be utilized in suitable manner in the Nāṭaka and Prakaraṇa.

80 This is the method of dealing with courtezans to be followed by those who are conversant with them O excellant Brahmins Now listen to my explanation of Citra-Abhinaya (Special Representation).

Notes

2 Fine Arts are sixty four in number as traditionally accepted. Many of them are of course utilitarian arts or actual crafts. The Jainas enumerate seventy two Arts.

9 Abhinava Gupta explains Raṅgopajivanā as a washer women who dyes clothes as well.

28—29 Vyavadhīnām may mean obstacles also but here it is intermediary i.e. the Messenger.

56—57 The word Dhīrodātta is used as the term for a special type of Hero in later works on dramaturgy.

66 The terms Sāma etc. are the terms for political expediencies as explained in Arthaśāstra and otherworks.

26

Citrābhinaya (Special Representation)

1 Citrābhinaya is the special representation which has not been mentioned before as related to Aṅga and other Abhinayas.

2--4 *Representation of day, night, season etc.* Two hands raised with Patāka and Svastika gestures; Udvāhita head looking upwards with glances of various kinds fitting each occasion constitute the Abhinaya of the following viz. morning, evening, night, the sky, the day, the seasons, the clouds, Vanāntas, (forest region), expansive water shads the directions, planats and stars and every thing in the heaven.

5 *Objects on the ground.* The same gestures of the hands and of the head but the eyes turned towards the ground are used to indicate objects resting on the ground.

6 *Moonlight etc.* In order to represent moonlight, happiness air, flavour and small one has to make use of gestures usually adopted for representing touch and horripilation.

7 *The sun, dust etc.* To indicate the sun, dust, smoke and fire one is to cover the face with clothes. Heat of the ground and also of other objects should be represented by showing the desire for a shady place.

8 *The mid day sun* is to be indicated by looking upwith half closed eyes and Sun rise and Sunset through the display of wonder etc.

9 *Pleasant objects.* In order to represent anything pleasant and happy the Abhinaya is touching the body with indications of the hairs risen.

10 *Sharp, hard objects*. In order to indicate things of sharp or hard features one is to use gestures for representing touch of one's limbs and uneasiness together with the narrowing down of the mouth.

11 *Deep and Exalted* feelings shall be represented with Sauṣṭhava of the limbs and a display of concert and pomposity.

12 Necklace flowers can be represented if one holds the two Arāla hands in the place where sacred thread is worn and then separates them from Svastika position.

13 To represent the idea of grasping the whole or omniscience one moves the index finger, looks round and presses the Alapallana hand.

14 In order to represent something audible or visible whether that is related to the speaker, the person spoken to or one spoken of, one shall point to the ears and eyes respectively.

15 *Lightning, meteor etc*. Lighting, meteors, comets thunder, sparks of fire and flame should be indicated by the producers through limbs and eyes of frightened features.

16 *Repugnent* (*Undesirable*) objects are to be represented by practising Udveṣṭita and Parāvṛtta Karaṇas of hands and bending the head looking obliquely to avoid contact.

17 *Hot wind heat etc*. from the sky, warding of the dust, rains, insects and bees are indicated by covering one's face.

18 *Lions etc*. such as bears, monkeys, tigers and other beasts of pray should be indicated by Svastika and Kaṭakāmukha hands (or Padmakoṣa turned up side down).

19 *Adoration of elders*. To indicate worshipping the feet of the elders are shaded display Tripatāka and Svastika hands. Taking up the goad or whip can be represented by Svastika and Khaṭaka hands.

20—22 Numerals from one to ten should be indicated by the fingers of equal number. Multiples of tens, hundreds, thousands etc. are to be indicated by the two Patāka hands. Any number above ten should be indicated indirectly alongwith the general meaning of the sentence thereof.

23 Umbrellas, banners, bannerstaffs and the different weapons should be indicated by representation of the holding of some staff.

24 Memory meditation etc. should be represented by indicating attention, downcast eyes, slightly bent head and the left hand with Sandaṁśa gesture.

25 In indicating offspring, the head is made Udvāhita and the hands Haṁsapakṣa and lifted up.

26 In order to indicate what is past, receding or lost and the words of a weary person, the Arāla left hand is carried up tothe place of the head.

27 The autumn is indicated by presenting a composure of all the sense organs, pleasant appearance of the quarters and the views of different flowers.

28 Hemanta (Early Winter) is to be indicated by the superior and the middling characters by means of narrowing down their limbs and resorting to sunlight, fire and warm clothing.

29 The inferior character shall represent the coolness through the trembling of the head and lips chattering, of the teeth, squeezing of the limbs and through groaning with the clicking of the tongue.

30 Coming to such a miserable plight due to ill fate the superior character also indicates the coolness in the same manner.

31 The sensible man shall indicate Śiśira (the late winter) by smelling the flowers, drinking wine and feeling the touch of the impleasant wind.

32 Vasanta (Spring) is to be indicated by the representation of acts of rejoicing enjoyments and festivities and a display of various flowers.

33 Grīṣma (Summer) is to be indicated through the representation of the heat of the Earth, fanning actions, wiping away the sweet and the feeling of the hot wind.

34 *Prāvṛṭ* (Rainy Season) is to be indicated through the presentation of the Kadamba, the Nimba, and the Kuṭaja

flowers, green grass Indragopa (glowworm) insects, clouds and the winds of pleasant touch.

35 The rainy nights should be indicated by the loud sound of the masses of clouds, falling torrents of rain as well as lightning and thunder.

36 Every season should be indicated by the sign, costume, activity of scenery which is proper to it or whatever is particularly desired or avoided in it.

37 According to the necessity of the theme these seasons should be indicated with proper Rasas as being full of happiness for those who are happy and full of distress for those afflicted.

38 He who is imbibed with a Bhāva whether pleasant or not looks under its influence everything as pervaded by it.

38A The Bhāvas should be indicated by the representation of the Vibhāvas. The accomplishment of the Bhāvas is through the representation of the Anubhāvas.

39 Acts connected with the Vibhāva should be represented by means of the Anubhāvas and the Bhāvas relate to the feeling of one's own self and the Vibhāvas relate to the display of another person.

40 A preception, a friend, an intimate associate, a relation of the mother's side or one of the fathers side who may enter and be announced is called a Vibhāva.

41 *Anubhāvas.* The honour shown to him by rising from the seat, by offering him Arghya, Pādya Āsana etc. and other means of devotional services is called Anubhaāva.

42 Similarly in other instances also one should find out the Vibhāva and the Anubhāva from an observation of different incidents in the play or from actions related to them.

43 Reply to a message given to the messenger should be known as Anubhāva as indicated as another man's (person's) message.

44 In these ways the Bhāvas, Vibhāvas and the Anubhāvas are to be represented by men as well as women.

45 In the representation of their own nature, men should assume the Vaiṣṇava posture (Sthāna) and the women the Āyata or the Avahittha postures in relation to appropriate actions.

46 But when special need arises, other postures too may be introduced for the representation of different Bhāvas in different ways.

47 Efforts of men should be characterised by cour:ge and steadiness as well as sportive limbs (Līlāṅgahāra) and those of women by delicate Aṅgahāras.

48 Women's movement of hands, feet and other limbs should be graceful while men's movements should be Dhīra (bold) and Uddhata (Vehemently energetic).

49 Representation of the meaning of words is to be made differently by men and women. I shall explain them in detail with reference to the Bhāvas and Anubhāvas.

50 A man should indicate his joy by embracing another's body, by smiling eyes and horripilation.

51 The Actress should indicate joy by sudden horripilation, tearfilled eyes, smiling words and loving attitude.

52 The man shall indicate anger by upturned red eyes, biting of the lips, trembling limbs and deep breaths.

53—54 *Jealous anger of woman.* The jealous anger of a woman should be indicated by tearful eyas, throbbing of the chin and the lips, shaking of the head, knitting of the eyebrows, keeping silent, twisting and curling the fingers, eschewing garlands and ornaments and assuming the Āyata posture.

55 *Men's sorrow* should be indicated by profuse breathing and sighing, thinking with downcast eyes or by looking up towards the sky.

56 Women's sorrow should be indicated by lamenting, sighing, the head, falling on the ground and hitting part of the body against the ground.

57 Crying, mentioned before as arising from tear of joy and from jealousy should be applied in the case of women as well as inferior male characters.

58 *Fear* of men should be indicated by acts of consternation and dismay fall of the weapons from the hands and loss of self control and similar features.

59–60 Women's fear should be indicated by eyes with moving eyeballs, throbbing and shaking limbs, glancing sideways with terrified heart, looking for someone to rescue them, weeping loudly and putting the hands round the lover by way of embrace.

61 *Women's* inebriated conditions mentioned before should be applied to men also of the inferior type. Adoption of gestures in such cases should be delicate and graceful.

62 Women's intoxication should be represented by rolling of the eyes, uttering of irrelevant words and shaking of the limbs.

63 These are the rules to be followed in a theatrical, production for representing men's and women's Bhāvas when occasions arise.

64 In a theatrical production the Bhāvas of the women are to be made graceful and those of men endowed with self control and equanimity.

65 *Parrots*, *Śārikās* and other small birds are to be indicated by two moving fingers to the Tripatāka hand.

66 Big birds like peacocks, cranes and swans are to be indicated by proper Recakas and Aṅgahāras.

67 Asses, camels, elephants, tigers, cows, buffaloes and the like should be indicated through their Gati Pracāras and limb gestures suited to them.

68 – 69 Bhūtas, Piśācas, Yakṣas, Dānavas and Rākṣasas when they are not visible should be indicated by the Aṅgahāras; but when they are visible they should be indicated by the representation of fear, dismay and atonishment.

70 The vissible Devas are to be indicated according to the necessity by making obeisence to them and by movements suitable to the Bhāvas.

71—75 Greeting an invisible man is to be indicated by touching the head with the Arāla hand raised from the left side. Greeting gods superiors and ladies, should be indicated by the

Kaṭakāvardhamāna or the Kapota hand touching the head similarly. Devas and venerable persons when they physically appear should be indicated by obeisance to them and by the deep influence they wild over others. A big crowd, friends, Viṭas and rogues are to be indicated by the Parimaṇḍala (Uro-maṇḍala) hand. Mountains together with their height and tall trees are to be indicated by lifting upwards the out stretched hands.

76—80 A vast expanse of water of the sea is to be indicated by two Patākā hands thrown side ways. The Arāla hand placed over the forehead is to be used for indicating heroism, courage, pride, haughtiness, magnanimity and loftiness. Two Mṛgaśīrṣa hands turned away from the breasts and held out quickly at a distance indicate anything made open. A house, darkness a hole or a cave is to be indicated by holding slightly the stretched hands which have their palms upturned and slightly tilted downwards. Sensible person should represent through suitable movements of their face and other limbs, persons who are lovesick or under a curse possessed of some evil spirit or enfeebled in mind by fever.

81—85 A swing should be indicated by the representation of its movement, agitation of the limbs and the holding of the strings. It is by acting like this that the moving swing will be perceptible to the audience and persons occupying their seats will be taken as moving in a swing I shall now explain the terms Ākāśa Bhāṣita (Speaking to the sky), Ātmagata (Speaking to oneself), Apavāritaka (Concealed Speaking) and Janāntika (Addressing particular person).

Ākāśa Bhāṣita Addressing someone staying at a distance or not appearing in person and words indirectly addressed to some one who is not near at hand is called Ākāśabhāṣita. This mode of speaking will present the substance of a dialogue by means of replies related to various imaginary questions arising out of the composition.

86 When overwhelmed with excessive joy, intoxication, madness, fit of passion, repugnance fear, astonishment, anger, and sorrow one speakes out words present in one's mind. This is called Ātmagata. Apavāritaka is that utterance which is related to secrecy. (Speaking Aside).

87—91 When, out of necessity, persons standing close by are supposed not to hears what is spoken to someone else this constitutes what is called Janāntika. What is related to something within the heart and is a matter of deliberation and feeling indeed Ātmagata. Words in a play which are connected with secrecy should be spoken into one's ears preceded by the words Evam (This). When one is to speak from necessity of something that has occurred earlier it also should be spoken into the ears least it should appear to be redundant.

92—94 Without making any confusion one should resort to Ākāśa Bhāṣita, Janāntika and Ātmagata whether it refers to a visible or invisible person or to one's own self or others Janāntika and Apavāritaka should be indicated by a Tripatāka hand covering the speaker. Words uttered due to fright, uttered due to fright, calamity, anger and intense sorrow are to be repeated. In those circumstances words such as Brūhi (Hell) Aho, (Ah), Sādhu (Welldone), Hā Hā (Alas), Gaccha (Go), Kim (what), Muñca (Leave off), Māvada (do not speak) should be repeated twice or thrice.

95—99 Distorted or incomplete words used in a play need not be represented by gestures for the sake of explanation. The Bhāva proper to a superior character should not be applied to a middling one. What is proper to a middling character should not be applied to an inferior one. A play will attain attractiveness only through the different Bhāvas and Rasas arising from the movements proper to the superior, middling and inferior characters. In the Svapnāyita condition (Somnolent) the Bhāvas are not to be represented by any movement of the hands. As in the representation of the Sattva this should be done through speech. Pāṭhya in the Svapnāyita condition should proceed with a slow voice; words therein are sometimes distinct and sometimes indistinct. The sense may be repeated twice but it should depend on the recollection of the past events.

100—103 Declamation of old people should be made with a faltering voice and dropping of syllables now and then. Declamation of children should be made with a lips leaving syllables incomplete. Declamation at the time of dying should be made indistinct with syllables produced by relaxed and heavy speech organs; it should be a faltering voice resembling the sound of small bells and it should be accompanied by hiccough, hard breathing and the after effects of phlegm. Occurrence of a swoon when accompanied by hiccough and hard breathing is considered similar to death. So indicate the same, the declamation should contain repetition. Representation of death which may arise from various causes shall be of different nature. Sometimes it is indicated by throwing out all the hands and feet and sometimes by a paralysis of the movement in all the limbs.

104—108 Death from drinking poison should be represented by throwing out the hands and feet and other limbs. The power of the poison may lead to the quivering action of the different parts of the body. Death from an attack of some illness should be represented by an occurrenee of hiccough, hard breathing and imperceptible movements of the relaxed limbs.

Eight stages of death due to person

The first stage in the series of actions of the person is the general weakness (Kārśya) of the body; the second ones is Vepathu (tremour) the third one is Dāha (burning sensation), the fourth is Hikkā (hiccough), the fifth Phena (foam froth), Grīvā Bhanga (Breaking of the neck) is the sixth stage and the seventh stage is Jaḍatā (Paralysis). The eighth stage is death itself (Maraṇa).

Kārśya The Abhinaya of the first stage of weakness should indicate eyes with sunken eyeballs, depressed cheeks, lips, belly and shoulder accompanied by feebleness of arms.

109—114 *Vepathu* should be represented by shaking simultaneously according to the situation the head, the hands and the feet or severably.

Dāha is to be represented by shaking the entire body violenthy, scratching the different limbs and throwing out the hands and other limbs.

Hikka should be represented by repeated blinking of the eyes, belching, vomiting, convulsion and uttering of indistinct sounds.

Phena in the mouth should be represented by shaking the head with different kinds of shaking of the head accompanied by belching and vomiting. There shall be licking of the extramities of the mouth, senselessness and winkless of the eyes.

Grīvābhaṅga should be represented by the shoulder touching the cheek and lowering the head.

Jaḍatā should be represented by the inaction of all the sense organs.

Maraṇa may be due to the acuteness of an ailment or to snake-bite. It should be represanted according to dramatic convention, by closing down the eyes.

115—120 These special modes of Abhinaya should be Combined with suitable Sāttvikas and Bhāvas.

The other ordinary activities of the laymen should be represented as they exist in the society. Just as the garland maker wreathes garlands with various kinds of flowers, the Nāṭya should be produced similarly by gestures of the different limbs in accordance with the Rasas and Bhāvas. Movements and Gatis that have been prescribed by the rules for a character who has entered the stage should be maintained by the actor without giving up the Sattva till he makes his final exit.

Now I have finished speaking about the representation to be made through words and gestures. Things omitted here by me should be gathered from the usage of the people.

The three Pramāṇas of the Naṭya. The people, the Vedas and the soul within are known as the three Pramāṇas (authorities). The drama is mostly based on objects related to the last two the Veda and the Adhyātma. The drama originating from the Vedas and the soul within and consisting of proper words and metre succeeds when it is approved of by the people. Hence the general public is considered as the ultimate authority on the drama.

121 An imitation of the exploits of Devas, sages, kings as well as householders in this world is called Nāṭya.

122 The activitiet of laymen with all the different conditions and situations are represented with suitable gestures. The same is called Nāṭya.

123 Thus the events relating to the people in all their different conditions and situations should be included and produced by those well versed in the canons of Nāṭya.

124 All the Śāstras, virtues, arts and activities connected with the human usage may be produced in the form of a drama.

125 It is not possible to arrive at a final decision regarding the internal feelings and emotions as well as the external activities of the world whether mobile or immoble solely through the Śāstra (Treatise).

126 The people have different dispositions and on their dispositions the drama rests. Hence playwrights and producers should take the people as their authority as regards the rules of the art.

127 Hence attention should be paid by the Prayoktṛs to the feelings, gestures and the Sattva representing the Bhāvas of the characters in the drama.

128 The man who knows these rules of Abhinaya perfectly and applies it on the stage receives in the world the highest honour for the practical application of the principles of drama.

129 These are to be known as the modes of representation dependent on words, costumes, makeup and gestures. An expert in dramatic production should adopt these for success in the dramatic production (Nāṭya Siddhi).

Notes

1 Citrābhinaya. This word has been defined and analysed by the commentators exhaustively. It is probably a limb at the "pictorial" effect of the direct or indirect use of gestures. See anta (24.1) Patāka, Svastika and Udvāhita have been explained in VIII-27 & IX chapters.

11 Sauṣṭhava is explained IX-88-91.

13 Alapallava IX-90.

16 Udveṣṭita & Parāvṛtta in IX-208/210.

18 Padmakośa IX-80.

19 Kaṭakāmukha IX-61-64.

Other technical terms may be seen in these two chapters.

54 Āyata Posture in XIII-157-170.

27

Nātya-Siddhi-Nirūpana (Review of fulfilment and success in dramatic production)

1 I shall now explain the characteristic features of success with reference to Nāṭaka since its production is aimed at achieving success in it.

2 Siddhi (Success) in the dramatic production is based on Rasas and Bhāvas and arises from words Sāttvika Abhinaya and gestures. It is of two kinds (a) divine and (b) human.

3 The human Siddhi has ten features and the divine two. It is based on various Sattvas and generate through words, costumes and physical action (expressed vocally and physically).

4 Smita (Slight-smile), Ardhahāsa (Smile), Atihāsa (Boisterous laughter), Sādhu (Well done), Aho (How wonderful), Kaṣṭam (How pathetic) and Pravṛddhanādā (Swelling uproar) are the signs of the success expressed vocally.

5 *Physically expressed.* Joy expressed in horripilation, the rising up from the seat and the giving away of clothes and of rings are signs of the success physically expressed.

6 When the actors display the Hāsya Rasa slightly dependent on words of *double entendre* the spectators should always accept it with a smile.

7 When they have a laughter not very clear or words which do not directly cause laughter the spectators are always expected to receive the same with an Ardha Hāsya.

8 Laughter created by the bragging of the Vidūṣaka or through some artifice (such as comic make up) should always be received by the spectators with a boisterous laughter (Ati Hāsya).

9—10 Representation of deeds which relate to the practice of virtue and is endowed with excellence should be greeted by the spectators with the word Sādhu (Well done). Similarly "Aho" (How wonderful) should be uttered by the spectators in regard to Vismaya and other Bhāvas and also in regard to themes of excessive delight.

11 But in the pathetic sentiment they should utter with tears—"Kaṣṭam" (How pathatic). In regard to themes exciting wonderment there should always be a tumultuous (Pravṛddha Nādā).

12 In cases of insulting words used in acting a play, they should be attentively received with horripilation by the spectators whose curiosity has been evoked.

13—14 If the play is a brilliant one with a plot containg cutting and piercing of limbs, fight, portentuous calamity, terrific happening or minor personal duals it should be received by the clever spectators with tears and rising up from the seat with shaking shoulders and head.

15 This is the manner in which the human success gets expressed. I shall now explain the divine success factually.

16 The success in a dramatic production which includes an excessive display of Sattva and clear expression of the Bhāvas is to be taken by the spectators as divine (Daivī).

17 The success is remembered as divine if there is no commotion, noise or unusual calamities phenomenon and it is a case of "House full" in the auditorium.

18—19 *Three kinds of Ghātas* (inauspicious features). These are the varieties of the successes to be known by the spectators as human and divine. I shall henceforth speak of the inauspicious features originating from divine and human beings. These inauspicious features are to be understood by sensible persons to be of three kinds originating from (1) gods (2) themselves and (3) enemies. Sometimes, a fourth one occurs originating from calamities phenomenon.

20 *Daiva Ghāta.* Inauspicious features with Devas as causes are violent gust of wind, fire, torrential rains, fear from an elephant or a serpent, falling of the pavilion, stroke of lightening, appearance of ants, insects and entry of ferocious animals.

27 *Śatru Ghāta. Onslaught by enemies.* Troubles and harassments created by an enemy are boisterous derisive laughter, crying, buzzing and booing, noisy clapping, throwing of cow-dung, hurling of abuses, clods of earth, grass and pebbles on to the stage.

22 Obstacles and troubles created by the enemies should be considered by the sensible due to jealousy, hostility, partiality (to the enemy) or receipt of bribe from the enemy.

23 Blesmishes and obstacle resulting from portents are those due to earthquake, storm, fall of meteors etc. *Ātma Samuttha Ghāta* self inflicted obstacles arising from the actors themselves shall be described by me.

24—25 Unnaturalness in the acting, wrong movement of the actors, unsuitability of a particular role to an actor, loss of memory of the actors, speaking of other words (outside the text), bewilderment (Vihastatva), falling off of the crown and other ornaments, defects in the playing of the drum (Puṣkara Doṣa), nervousness (Vāgbhīti) laughing too much, crying too much etc. contribute to the obstacles in success.

26 Attack of insects and ants completely spoils the success while the falling off the crown and other ornaments will spoil the tumultuous applause which the actor would have received from the spectators by way of appreciation.

27 Blemishes in the shape of an appearance of animals can be ignored. But shy speech and nervousness of the actors as well as the wrong playing of the drums will completely spoil the success.

28 Two kinds of blemishes cannot be remedied in the production of a composition. They are faults due to natural calamity and the running out of water from the Nāḍkā.

29—30 Easily noticeable blemishes in a play are redundancy, defective use of compound words, wrong use of case endings, want of proper euphonic combination, use of incoherent words, faulty use of the three genders, confusion in the direct and indirect implications of words, lapse in metre, mixing up of prosodially long and short vowels and non-observance of Yati (Caesura).

31 Absence of proper notes [Visvara], Want of sweetness in notes (Viyukta Rāga), ignorance of voice registers (Sthāna) tempo (Laya) and being deficient in the wealth of Varṇas and Svaras will disturb the musical rules in the production of a play.

32 Non observance of Sama, Mārga and Mārjanā giving discordant strokes, ignorance about Graha and Mokṣa will spoil the sweetness of drum music.

33–36 Omission due to loss of memory and defective enunciation in the declamation, wearing ornaments in the wrong place, balling off of the crown, not wearing the requisite ornament, perplexed state, ignorance about mounting or dismounting. chariots, elephants, horses, asses, camels, palanquins, aerial chariots and vehicles in general, wrongly holding and wielding weapons and armours, entering the stage without the crown, headgear or clothing or entering too late—the blemishes due to these lapses should be carefully observed by the clever experts but they may ignore the lapses regarding fixing of Yūpa, taking up the sacrificial tings, arrangement of fire, Kuśa grass, Sruc and other vessels pertaining to the sacrifice.

37 Blemishes should be recorded as Miśra (mixed Sarvagata (total) or Ekadeśaja (Partial) by experts in dramatic production but they should not record merely the success or the obstacle without detailed information thereof.

38 The total success or utter failure due to obstacles expresses itself in many ways. But the matter affecting only one aspect should not be reckoned as of poor quality.

39 After the putting down of the Jarjara in a dramatic production, the Prāśnikas (Assessors) should always achieve in due manner the Nāḍikā Siddhi (accuracy of the timing) and the Lekhya Siddhi (recording) of all good points and lapses.

40 When during a divine festival anyone foolishly recites a Benedictory Śloka in honour of the wrong god it is to be recorded as his lapse in the Pūrvaraṅga.

41 When anyone interpolates the composition of one playwright into that of another it is also to be recorded by the experts as his lapse.

42 When anyone wilfully interpolates in his play the name of another author then his lapse therein, being definite should be recorded in due order.

43 When anyone produces a play using costumes and languages in violation of the rules regarding the same laid down in the Śāstra then his lapse about the same should be recorded.

44—46 Who is competent enough to observe scrupulously the rules regarding the composition or the production on the stage of a play? Who can be sufficiently been or alert in mind to understand fully everything that has been mentioned duly. Hence one should include in plays words which have deep significances confirm to the Vedas and are approved of by the people and can be comprehended and appreciated by the layman. No play can be utterly devoid of any merit or totally free from faults. Hence faults and defects in a play should not be made much of.

47 But the Naṭa too should not there upon be indifferent o words, gestures and cstumes Sāttvika Abhinaya, Rasas, Bhāvas, songs, instrumental music and popular usages.

48 Thus the salient features of the Siddhis are to be understood by sensible persons. Henceforth I shall mention the characteristics of the Prāśnikas (arbitrators, Assessors) or Prekṣakāṇām (of the spectators).

49—52 Persons of the following characteristics should be made arbitrators, umpires, judge in the performance of drama. They must have good moral character and nobility of birth, of quiet behaviour ready to exert themselves, desirous of renown and piety, impartial, advanced in age, experts in the art of Nāṭya having six ancillaries, alert, of pure habits possessing equanimity, experts in the four types of musical instruments, conversant with different kinds of metres, costumes. Make up etc. sees of reality, well acquainted with different languages regions and modes, experts in different arts and crafts, and the four types of Abhinaya, having fine sense of the Rasas and Bhāvas, conversant with the rules regarding words and prosody and well versed in all the Śāstras.

53—57 One is remembered as the genuine spectator (Prekṣaka) if one has unruffled senses, is pure, clever in discussing and weighing pros and cons, devoid of faults and fond of merits. He who attains gladness on seeing another glad, sorrow on seeing another sorry and experiences wretchedness on seeing the wretchedness of another is considered fit to be a spectator in a drama. All these qualities are not expected to be present in a single individual. Objects of knowledge are numerous and the span of human life is brief. An assembly of persons in the auditorium consists of all types of people the superior, the middling and the inferior. *No Lay Man Can be* therefore expected to appreciate the performance of the superior. Hence that individual to whom a particular dress, profession, speech and act belong as his own should be considered fit to apprcciate only that upto that extant.

58. Different are the the dispositions of women and men young and old and possessing superior, middling and inferior talents. A drama rests on such dispositions.

59 Young people are pleased to see the representation of topics of love, the learned, a reference to some religions or philosophical doctrine, the seekers of wealth topics regarding aquisition thereof and persons devoid of passion the topics related to salvation.

60—61 Heroic persons are always pleased to witness the Bībhatsa and Raudra Rasas depicted and also personal combats and battles and the old people to witness Purāṇic legends and talas of virtue. The common women, children and unrefined men are always delighted with the Hāsya Rasa as well as brilliant colourful costumes and make-up.

62—68 Thus the man who is fit to assume a particular role by imitating the Bhāvas of the latter can be considered a Prekṣaka possessing these qualities. Prekṣakas are to be known thus in connection with a drama. Should there be any controversy about the performance of individual actors understand the following to be the Prāśnikas (judges) viz Yajñavit (an expert on Yajñas), Nartaka (a dancer), Chandovit (one conversant with prosody), Śabdavit (a grammarian), a Nṛpa (king), an Astravit (an expert in missiles), Citrakṛt (painter) Veśyâ (courtezan), Gāndharva (musician) and a Rājasevaka (king's officer).

An expert in Yajña will be a judge regarding matters concerning Yajña, Nartaka in dramatic representation; a Chandovit in complicated metres a, Śabdavit in a lengthy declamation; a Astravit in Sauṣṭhava; Citrakṛt in regard to the costumes and make up, a courtezan in regard to services and attentions during love scene, a Gāndarva in the application of notes; a Rājasevaka in regard to showing courtesies; a Nṛpa in connection with royal roles and in dealings with the harem. These are the ten judges (Praśnikas) of a dramatic performance.

69 When there is a controversy among the persons ignorant of the Nāṭya Śāstra the Prāsnikas are to pronounce justly the faults as well as the good points of the individual actors. Then only can they be the genuine Prāsnikas of whom I have mentioned.

70 When there occurs any learned controversy about the knowledge of the Śāstra the decision should be made on the testimony of the books.

71 Controversy arises when the Bharatas (actors) have the desire of mutual contest at the instance of their masters or for winning Patākā as rewards or even monetary prizes.

72 In the course of deciding a controversy one should observe the performance of the parties without any partiality. The decision about the award of the "Patākā" should be according to the stipulation made before the performance had started.

73 Blemishes affecting the success should be recorded with the help of reckoners (Gaṇakas) by the Prāśnikas who are comfortably seated, have clean intentions and single-minded attention.

74 The Prāśnikas (Preāṣakas) should neither be too near the stage nor too far from it. Their seats should be twelve Hastas (12×45 cms) away.

75 They are to observe the points of the success mentioned before, as well as the blemishes which may occur during the production of a drama.

76 Blemishes which are accidental, caused by the divine intercession, the portents or the enemies are not to be recorded

by the sensible judges. But the blemishes arising from the actors themselves or arising from their performance should be recorded.

77 After informing the king, the banner should be given to a person whose blemishes have been reckoned as the fewest in number but points of success are many.

78 If expert actors are found to be of equal merit in the production of a play the Patākā is to be awarded first to one whose success is greater or in case of equal success the award is to be made at the king's behest.

79 If the king adjudges both of them to be on a par, both should be awarded the banner with an eye on all these rules one should provide in the production of a play for the recitation, the distribution of roles and the Rasas.

80 Thus cultured persons who are well acquainted with the rules of theatrical production and capable of appreciating merits should out at ease with an unruffied mind and see to the proper judgement in regard to the award.

81 Then the Prāśnikas are to point out the measure of achievement as well as the slightest of faults which may relate to the theory of theatrical production.

82 Hence producers of plays should know properly about Samatva (co-ordination), Aṅgamādhuryam (charm of the limbs), Pāṭhya (passage for declamation), Prakṛti (role), Rasa (sentiment), Gāna (song), Vādya (Musical instrument) and Nepathya (costumes and make up).

83 Gestures which are simultaneously made in a play in harmony with the different aspects of the arts in course of the Dhruvā songs and of dances is called Samatva (co-ordination).

84 When in course of the performance of a play gestures of the different limbs major and minor are accompanied by songs with proper time (Tāla) and tempo (Laya) and by the playing of the drums it is called co-ordination.

85 *Aṅgamādhurya.* The position in which the chest is not bent, the two hands are Caturaśra and Āyata and the neck is Añcita gives rise to Aṅgamādhurya (charm of limbs).

86 In regard to the other subject (Pāṭhya, Nepathya and Rasa) which are to be mastered by the actors they have been discussed before. But they are to look after the instrumental music the roles and the songs.

87 The success arising from the gestures and the various Rasas should be expressed out of joy through all the signs of the same.

88 Producers of plays should know the time for a performance which depends on various considerations to be generally day and night. Listen now when a performance may take place during these two periods.

89 The performance in the evening, mid-night and the dawn belongs to the night.

90 The performance in the forenoon, midday and the after noon belongs to the day.

91 I shall now speak how these times are suited to different Rasas after mentioning the time to which a performance belongs.

92 The performance which is pleasant to the ears and is based on a tale of piety whether it is Śuddha (pure) or Vikṛta (mixed) should be held in the forenoon.

93 That which is rich in instrumental music includes the story of strength and energy carries the likelihood of abundant success should be performed in the afternoon.

94 That which relates to the Kaiśikī style, Śṛṅgāra Rasa and is full of dances, vocal and instrumental music should be performed in the evening.

95 The drama which relates to the magnanimity of the hero and contains mostly the Kruṇa Rasa should be performed in the morning and it will scare away sleep.

96 The drama should not be performed in the mid-night or midday or at the time of the Sandhyā proper or of taking meals.

97 Thus after looking into the time, place and the basic plot of a play one should bring about its production according to the Bhāvas and Rasas.

98 But when the master or patron the time and place are not to be taken into consideration and the performance is held without hesitation.

99 Coordinated production, brilliance of pageant and actors capable of good production are the three points of merits in a performance.

100—105 *Qualities of an actor.* The requisite qualities of an actor are intelligence, physical handsomeness, conversant with Tāla and Laya, appreciation of Rasas and Bhāvas, proper age, eagerness to act, acquisition of knowledge of arts, their retention, vocal music, dances, suppression of stage nervousness, and enthusiasm.

An ideal performance is that which includes good instrumental music, good songs, good declamations, as well as co ordination of all acts prescribed by the Śāstra.

Brilliance of pageant arises by the use of proper ornaments, good garlands, clothes, proper painting or make up. When all these factors combine together the performance should be considered by the producers as the ornament of all performances.

Thus I have spoken to you, O Excellant Brahmins, the characteristics of success. Now I shall explain the classification of Ātodya (Musical instruments).

Notes

The proof of the performance is in the appreciation of the audience and spectators. The assembly of the spectators in the auditorium includes persons of all sorts the good the bad and the middling not necessarity the in different. There must be something to humour these diversified sections. This chapter gives many useful tips to the producers in this line.

5 This is an agelong custom in India. Rich patrons when delighted with performances did not hesitate to reward the talented actors with whatever they had on their person when Kuśa and Lava delighted the audience consisting of sages with their sweet recitation the latter rewarded the youngsters with their water pots and Langotlc !!

15—17 The reaction to a splendid dramatic performance in persons with different culture background should necessarily be different.

21—23 Competition and rivalry when healthy brings about better productions but human nature being what it is, even in those hoary days as well as in the modern period there are unhealthy trends. There are persons who wish to get rid of what they cannot excel !

31 See chapter 28 for explanations of the musical terms.

46 Critics of arts and crafts must bear this in mind.

54 The Prekṣaka must have the Tanmayībhāva to appreciate the performance properly. He must identify himself with the character in the play as represented on the stage to appreciate the histrionic skill.

62—68 The elaborate arrangement with Prāśnikas is really landable.

28

Atodya Vikalpanam (Classification of Instrumental Music)

I shall now explain the general features of the instrumental music (Ātodya).

1 Common instruments of music can be classified into four kinds (1) Tata (or stringed) (2) Avannddha(Avanaddha) Instrument of percussion (3) Ghana (Solid) and (4) Suṣira (hollow).

2 The Tata instruments have strings, the Avanaddha means drums, the Ghana is cymbal etc. and the Suṣira consists of flutes.

3. As far as the dramatic performance is concerned these have three fold application (1) That in which Tata instruments are mainly used (2) that in which Avanaddha instruments are mainly used and (3) the general application during the dramatic performance (Nāṭyakṛta),

4—5 In the orchestra of the Kutapa (stringed instruments) the Gāyana (singer) and his wife, the players of Vipañcī, Vīṇā and flute appear.

Players of Mṛdaṅga, Paṇava and Dardara are collectively called Avanaddha Varga (orahestra of covered instruments)

6 The orchestra pretaining to actors and actresses of the Uttama, Adhama and Madhyama types occupies various places on the stage at the time of Nāṭya Prayoga.

7 *Embellishment of Nāṭya through different kinds of music.* In this manner Gāna, Vādya and Nāṭya. that depend on diverse things should be made by the sponsors of the play like the Alātacakra (fire brand) constituting a brilliant entity.

8 *Gāndharva* The playing on the stringed instruments accompanied by various other instruments should be known as Gāndharva. It includes Svara, Tāla and Pada (verbal theme).

9 It is very much liked by Devas and it pleases the Gandharvas. Hence its is called Gāndharva.

10 *Its Source* Its source is vocal music, the Vīṇa and the flute. I shall explain all the aspects depending on the notes.

11 *Three kinds.* Gāndharva is of three kinds; that of the Svara, that of the Tāla and that of the Pada. I shall describe the characteristics and the function of these three.

12 *Two bases of Svaras.* The Svaras have two bases (Adhiṣṭhānas), the human body and the Vīṇā. I shall speak about the formal aspects of the notes arising from the two.

13—14 *Formal Aspects of the Gīta of Vīṇā.* Svaras, Grāmas Mūrcchanās, Tānas, Sthānas (Voice Registers), Vṛttis Sādhāraṇa Svaras, Varṇas Alaṁkāras, Dhātus, Śrutis and Jātis—all constituted by the regular Svaras are available in the Dāravī Viṇa.

Those of Vocal Music. Svaras, Grāmas, Alamkāras, Varṇas, Sthānas, Jātis and overlapping notes are available in the Vīṇā of the human throat (vocal music).

16—17 *Verbal theme in Music* Vyañjanas, Svaras (vowels), Sandhis, Vibhaktis, Nāmans, Ākhyātas, Upasargas, Nipātas, Taddhitas as well as syllabic and moric metres always relate to the verbal themes of music (Pada) which are of two kinds Nibaddha and Anibaddha (See XV-9).

18—20 (*Tālas*) I shall now speak of the Tāla. There are twenty formal aspects of Tāla to be described later on. They are Āvāpa, Niṣkrama, Vikṣepa Praveśaka, Śamyā, Tāla, Sannipāta, Parivarta, Vastu, Mātrā, Vidārī Aṅga, Laya, Yati, Prakaraṇa, Gīti, Avayava Mārga, Pādabhāga and Pāṇi. Briefly these constitute Gāndharva (Music).

21 *Seven Svaras* The Seven Svaras are Ṣaḍja (sa), Ṛṣabha (Ri), Gāndhāra (Ga), Madhyama (Ma) Pañcama (Pa), Dhaivata (Dha) and Niṣāda (Ni).

22 In accordance with their relation to an interval of Śrutis they are of four kinds such as Vādī (Sonant), Samvādi (consonant), Anuvādi (Assonant) and Vivādī (Pisonant).

Prose Vadī and Samvadi That which is an Aṁśa (important part) anywhere, can in this connection be called Vādī. Those two Svaras which are at an interval of nine or thirteen Śrutis from each other are Samvādins such as Ṣadja and Madhyama, Ṣaḍja and Pañcama, Ṛṣabha and Dhaivata, Gāndhāra and Niṣāda in the Ṣaḍja Grāma. In the Madhyama Grāma Ṣadja and Pañcama are not Samvādīs but Pancamas and Ṛṣabha are so. In this connection there is a traditional verse.

23 Pañcama and Ṛṣabha are Samvādīs in the Madhyama Grāma while Pañcama Ṣaḍja are so in the Ṣaḍjagrāma alone.

Dissonant Notes

Prose. If the notes be at an interval of two Srutīs they are Vivādīs e.g. Ṛṣabha and Gāndhāra, Dhaivata and Niṣāda.

The Anuvādī notes. Now that Vādī, Samvādī and Vivādī notes have been determined, the remaining ones are to be designated Anuvādins e.g. Ri, Ga, Dha and Ni to Sa; Ma, Pa, Ni to Ri; Ma, Pa, and Dha to Ga Ḍha, Pa and Ni to Ma; Dha and Ni to Pa; Ri, Pa and Ma to Dha. All these foregoing ones are in the Ṣaḍja Grāma; In the Madhyama Grāma, Pa, Dha and Ni are Anuvādīs to Madhyama; Ri, Sa and Ga to Pa; Sa, Ri and Ga to Dha; the same to Ni. Since Svara sounds prominently it is called Vādī, as it sound in consonance with another it is Samvādī, as it sounds discordantly to another it is Vivādī and as it follows another Svara it is called Anuvādī. These notes becomes low or high according to the adustment of the strings and the diversity of the Dnda of the Vīṇā and of the sense organs. So much about the aspects of the four classes of Svaras.

The two Grāmas. There are two Grāmas viz. Ṣaḍja and Madhyama. Each of these two include twenty two Śrutis as follows.

24 Śrutis in the Ṣaḍja Grāma are shown in the following manner—three, two, four, four three, two and four [beginning with Ri and ending in Sa].

25—26 In the Ṣaḍja Grāma Ṣaḍja includes four Śrutis Ri—three; Ga—two; Ma—four; Pa—four; Dha—three and Ni—two.

Prose. In the Madhyama Grāma, Pañcama should be made deficient in one Śruti.

27—28 In the Madhyama Grâma, Ma consists of four Śrutis PA—three; Dha—four; Ni—two; Sa—four Ri—three and Gr—two. Thus the system of mutual intervals (Antara) has been explained.

Prose. The difference that occurs in Pa when it is raised or lowered by one Śruti and when the consequential Mārda (slackness) or tenseness of strings (Āyatatva) occurs will indicate a typical Sruti. We shall explain the system of these Śrutis. Two Vīṇās should be made ready with the Daṇḍas strings with similar measure and with similar adjustment of the latter in the Ṣaḍja Grāma. Then one of these should be tuned in the Madhyamagrāma by lowering Pa by one Śruti. The same Vīṇā by adding one to Pa will be tuned in the Ṣaḍja Grāma. This is the meaning of decreasing a Śruti. Again due to the decrease of one Śruti in another Vīṇā Ga and Ni will merge with Dha and Ri respectively when there is an interval of two Śrutis between them. Again due to the decrease of one Śruti in another Vīṇā Ri and Dha will merge with Sa and Pa respectively when there is an interval of three Śrutis. Similarly the same Śruti being again decreased, Pa, Ma and Sa will merge with Ma, Ga and and Ni respectively when there is an interval of four Śrutis between them. according to this system of Śrutis each of the two Grāmas should be taken as consisting of twenty two Śruti, now about the Mūrcchanās (Modes). They are of fourteen kinds in the two Grāmas.

Mūrcchanās in the Ṣaḍjagrāma

29—30 There are seven Mūrcchanās in the Ṣaḍjagrāma viz. Uttara Mandrā, Rajanī, Uttarāyatā, Śuddhaṣaḍja, Matṣarīkṛtā, Aśvakrāntā, and the seventh Abhirudgatā. The initial Svaras of these are respectively Sa, Ni, Dha, Pa, Ma, Ga and Ri.

Mūrcchanās in the Madhyama Grāma

31—32 In the Madhyama Grāma the following Mūrcchanās occur. There are seven Mūrcchanās viz. Sauvīrī, Hariṇāśvā, Kalopanatā, Śuddhamadhyā, Mārgī, Pauravī and Hṛṣyakā.

The initial notes of these are respectively Ma, Ga, Ri, Sa, Ni, Dha and Pa.

Initial Notes (further explained)

The initial notes in the Ṣaḍja Grāma are Sa in Uttara Mandrā, Ni in Rajanī, Dha in Uttarāyatā, Pa in Śuddhaṣaḍja, Ma in Matsarīkṛta, Ga in Aśvakrāntā and Ri in Abhirudgatā.

In the Madhyamagrāma—Ma in Sauvīrī, Ga in Hariṇāśvā, Ri in Kalopanatā, Sa in Śuddhamadhyama, Ni in Mārgī, Dha in Pauravī and Pa in Hṛṣyakā.

Four classes of Mūrcchanās. Combined thus in different orders the Svaras constitute four classes of these fourteen Mūrcchanās viz. Pūrṇā (full or Heptatonic), Ṣaḍavakṛta (Hexatonic), Audavitīkṛta (Pentatonic) and Svarasādhāraṇakṛtas (overlapping notes).

33—34 The seven Svaras combined in different orders are called Pūrṇā Mūrcchanās. Tānas consisting of six and five Svaras are respectively Ṣāḍava and Auḍavita. Besides these there is another kind of Mūrcchanā which includes the overlapping notes or is combined with the Kākalī notes or the intermediate notes (Antara Svaras) and this is the case in both the Grāmas.

Prose. The same Mūrcchanā is produced in two ways. In this connection, Gāndhāra being reduced to Dhaivata by an increase of two Śrutis in it, the two terms the Grāma and the Murchhana become differentiated in the Ṣaḍja Grāma and due to that, Madhyama and the notes following it become serially reduced to Niṣāda and the notes following it. In the Madhyama Grāma too. Dhaivata being softened (contailed in Śrutis) and Niṣāda being augmented the two terms are differentiated. In the case of this Grāma too there being an interval of the same number of Śrutis the difference of terms becomes justified. The interval between Pañcama and Dhaivata is of four Śrutis; Similarly due to an increase of Gāndhāra the interval will be of four Śrutis. The remaining Madhyama, Pañcama, Dhaivata, Nisāda, Ṛṣabha and Ṣadja become reduced serially to Madhyama and the notes following it. This is due to an interval of the same number of Śrutis. The system of intervals has been explained in connection with the system of Śrutis.

Eighty four Tānas Tānas depend upon the Mūrchanās and are eighty four in number; the Ṣāḍavas are forty nine and the Aupavitas thirty five.

The Ṣāḍavas consist of seven type e.g. four in Ṣaḍja Grāma excluding Ṣaḍja, Ṛṣabha, Niṣāda or Pañcama; three in the Madhyama Grāma excluding Ṣaḍja, Ṛṣabha or Gāndhāra. Worked properly in all the Mūrcchanās,these produce forty nine Tānas.

The Auḍavitas consist of five types e.g. three in Ṣaḍja Grāma excluding (a) Ṣaḍja Pañcama (b) Ṛṣabha and Pañcama or (c) Gāndhāra and Niṣāda; in the Madhyamagrāma there are two Tānas excluding (a) Ṛṣabha and Dhaivata or (b) Gāndhāra and Niṣāda. Worked properly in all the Mūrcchanās these produce thirty five Tānas.

Two Tānakriyās (Ways of Tānas) There are two types Kriyās through Praveśa (entrance) and Nigraha (Arrest). The Praveśa is made by sharpening (heightening) the preceding Svara and softening (lowering) the succeeding Svara. Nigraha means avoiding the middle note. The Mūrcchanā is indicated by the middle note of the Vīṇā because it does not perish. Thus Nigraha and Praveśa become possible. The variety of the Tānas and Mūrcchnnās thus gives entertainment to the producer. The purpose of Mūrcchanās and Tānas is the attainment of the Sthānas which are three [i.e. chest, throat and head XIX-37ff] as explained in the context of Kākuvidhi.

Sādhāraṇas (*Overlapping, Common to two*). We shall now explain the rules regarding Sādhāraṇas. Sādhāraṇa means Antarasvaratā (quality of a note rising between two consecutive ones). Why ? Sādhāraṇa is that which occurs between two seasons.

35 *Verse*. There is chillness in the shadow but perspiration comes when one is in the sun. Not that the spring has not arrived; nor has the winter season completely passed off. This is Kāla Sādhāraṇatā. There are two types of Sādhāraṇa (overlapping) (a) Svarasādhāraṇa and Jāti Sādhārāna (overlapping in notes and Jātis) Svara Sādhāraṇa comprises of Kākalī and Aatarasvara Niṣāda when augmented by two Śrutis is called Kākalī. Similarly Gāndhāra becomes an Antarasvara.

Why is Niṣāda called Kākalī ? Because it is an indistinct sound. Since it has very fineness (Saukṣmya) it has a second name Kaiśikā. This being Vikṛta it cannot be an Aṁśa Svara. As accepted by trustworthy Ācāryas it is not different from the seven Svaras just salt among the six types of taste is called by another name Kṣāra (corrosive) so also Niṣāda itself is called by the name Kākali and Gāndhāra is designated Anta. In this connection there are two Ślokas.

36—37 *Verse.* The Antara Svara (transitional note) should always go with the Ārohi (ascending) scale. It should also be made weak but it should never be in the Avaroha (Descending) scale. In case it is employed in the descending scale whether Alpa or Bahu the Antarasvara will spoil the Jāti Rāga and the Śruti.

Jāti Sādhāraṇa arises when notes belonging to the minor limbs of two or more Jātis of one Grāma are observed in another Grāma. They may have common Aṁśas too. The Svara Sādhāraṇa pertaining to the two Grāmas i.e. Ṣaḍja and Madhyama is of two kinds. In the Ṣaḍjagrāma it is the overlapping Ṣaḍja note and in the Madhyagrāma it it is the Madhyama note that overlaps. This Sādhāraṇa is a special nature of the note in either Grāma. The delicacy of its production (Prayoga Saukṣmya) gives the note the name Kaiśika (capillary) suitably. Thus is the Svarasādhāraṇa as produced in Jātis where Niṣāda and Gāndhāra are Alpa (weak, sparing).

38—39 The Jātis concerned with the Svarasādhāraṇa are three in number viz. Madhyamā Pañcamī and Ṣaḍjamadhyā Their Aṅgas (components) Ṣaḍja, Madhyama and Pañcama of which the Pañcamī will be manifest though weaker than the rest in its own note.

40—41 *Seven types of Jātis in the Saḍjagrāma* are (1) Ṣaḍjī (2) Ārṣabhī (3) Dhaivatī (4) Naiṣādī (5) Ṣaḍjodīcyavatī (6) Ṣaḍja Kaiśikī and (7) Ṣaḍja Madhyamā.

42—43 *Eleven types of Jātis in the Madhyamagrāma.* Henceforth I shall enumerate the Madhyamagrāma born Jātis. They are (1) Gāndhārī (2) Raktagāndhārī (3) Gāndhārodīcyavā (4) Madhyamodicyavā (5) Madhyamā (6) Pañcamī (7) Gāndhāra Pañcamī (8) Āndhrī (9) Nandayantī (10) Karmāravī and (11) Kaiśikī.

44 These are the eighteen Jātīs mentioned by me before. I shall explain them further along with Nyāsa and Apanyāsa (The terminal and semi terminal note).

Prose Passage. Of these eighteen seven derive their names from the seven Svaras. There Jātis can be otherwise group as Śuddha and Vikṛta (Pure and Modified). The Śuddhas in the Ṣaḍja Grama, Ārṣabhī, Dhaivatī and Niṣādavatī in the Madhyama Grāma they are Gāndhārī Madhyamā and Pañcamī. The name "Pure" in this regard connotes that it consists of all the notes without be deficient in anything and also has Aṁśa Graha Nyāsa when some of these Jātis are deficient in two or more characteristics excepting the Nyāsa they are termed Vikṛta. Thanks to this they are indeed pure or modified. In the observation of the Nyāsa in the case of pure ones the note shall be invariably Mandra. There is no such rule in the case of the Vikṛta Jātis. These are eleven in number growing from mutual conbinations. Verse in this connexion.

45 Jātis are Śuddhas as well as Vikṛtas. Vikṛtas are born due to the combination. Seven are Śuddhas and eleven are Vikṛtas.

46 *Vikṛta Jātis.* I shall now explain in the proper order and with adequate succinctness, the Jātis which grow out of Svaras and Aṁśas of the pure Jātis.

47 The Ṣaḍja Madhyamā Jāti is formed by the Ṣaḍja and Madhyama. The Ṣaḍja Kaiśikījāti is formed by the Ṣaḍja and Gāndhāra.

48 The Ṣaḍjodīchyavatī is formed either by the combination of Ṣaḍja, Gāndhāra and Dhaivata or mutually associated.

49—52 The Gāndharvodīcyavā is formed by Ṣaḍja, Gāndhāra Dhaivata and Madhyama. The Madhyamodīcyavā is formed by the Gāndhāra, Pañcamī Dhaivatī and Madhyamā. The Raktagāndhārī is formed by the following four viz the Gāndhārī the Pañcamī the Naiṣādī and the Madhyamā. The Āndhrī is formed by the Gāndhārī and the Ārṣabhī. The Nandayantī is formed by the Gāndhārī the Pañcamī and the Ārṣabhī.

53—55 The Gāndhāra Pañcamī, originates from the Gāndhāra and the Pañcamī. The Karmā Ravī is evolved out of the Naiṣādī, the Ārṣabhī and the Pañcamī. It is Pūrṇā (Hepta tonic). The Kaiśiki is formed by the Ṣāḍjī the Gāndhārī, the Madhyamā, the Pañcamī and the Naiṣādī after excluding Dhaivatī and the Ārṣabhi. These are the different Jatis evolved out of the mutual combination of the Svaras in the two Grāmas.

56 It should be known that four out of these are inivariably Saptasvarās (full); ten out of these are Pañcasvarās and the remaining four and Ṣatsvaras.

57 *Saḍja Grāma—Jāiis.* The Madhyamodīcyavā Ṣaḍja Kaiśikī the Karmā Ravī and the Gāndhāra Pañcamī are Pūrṇā Jātis.

58—60 The Gāndhārī, the Raktagāndhārī, the Madhyamā, the Pañcamī the Kaiśikī—all these belonging to Madhyama-Grāma and the five belonging to Ṣaḍjagrāma viz the Ārṣabhī, the Dhaivatī, the Naisādī, the Ṣaḍjamadhyamā and the Ṣaḍjodīcyavatī—this ten altogether are Pañcasvarās always.

61—62 *Madhyagrāma Jātis* The following three of the Madhya Grāma along with Ṣādjī of the Ṣaḍjagrāma are Ṣaṭsvarās viz Gāndhārodīcyavā, the Nanda Yantī and the Āndhrī. Those Jātis now described Pañcasvarās and Ṣaṭsvarās may on occasions be changed into Ṣaḍavas and Auḍavas.

63—64 The Karmā Ravi, the Madhyamodīcyavā and the Gāndhāra Pañcamī are Pūrṇās in the Madhyama Grāma and the Ṣaḍja Kaiśikī in the Ṣaḍjagrāma.

65—69 *Aṁśas in the Jātis.* This much about the Jātīs in the two Grāmas. I shall now explain their various Aṁśas. The Ṣaḍja Madhyamā should have not Ṣaṭsvara treatment including the seventh note viz. Niṣāda. There should not be Gāndhāra because the Samvādī note (Consonant) is eliminated. The Gāndhārī, the Rakta Gāndhārī and the Kaiśikī should have no Pañcama; the Ṣāḍjī should have no Gāndhāra and the Ṣaḍjodīcyavā should have no Gāndhāra—these in the case of their Ṣaṭsvara treatment. These seven notes are to be discarded in the Ṣaṭsvara treatment of the Jātis because of the elimination of Samvādī notes.

70—71 The following twelve notes should be discarded in the Pañcasvara treatment :—The Gāndhāri and the Rakta Gāndhārī Jātis should have no Ṣaḍja, Madhyama, Pañcama and Niṣāda. The Ṣāḍjī and the Madhyamā should not have Gāndhāra and Niṣāda. The Pañcamī should not have Ṛṣabha and the Kaiśikī has no Dhaivata.

72—73 Therefore these Jātīs should always be without Pañcasvara treatment. From the Jātis all the notes may be left out except Madhyama. Since the great sages who chanted the Sāmans have expressed, this in the Gāndharva Kalpa that Madhyama is the best of all notes and is Avināśī (imperishable).

74 *Ten characteristics of the Jātīs* They are Graha, Aṁśa, Tāra, Mandra, Nyāsa, Apanyāsa, Alpatva (deficiency), Bahutva (abundance) Ṣāḍavita and Auḍavita (Ṣaṣṭvara and Pañcasvara treatment).

75 *Graha* Grahas have been like the Aṁśa (part) of all the Jātis. That note with which the song begins is the Graha and it is an alternative term for Aṁśa.

76—78 *Aṁśa* (Key note) This has ten characteristics as follows, Amśa is that Svara on which the Rāga of the songs depends, it is from that the charm proceeds; it is the basis for the variation into Mandra (low) and Tāra (high) pitches depending on the initial five Svaras; in the combination of many notes it is perceived remarkably; it being strongs it has other Svaras related as Samvādī or Anuvādī. It is related to the Graha, Apanyāsa, Vinyāsa, Sannyāsa and Nyāsa notes. It lies scattered throughout the song.

79 *Aṁśas of the Jātis* The Jātis in the two Grāmas have always sixty three Aṁśasi as well as Grahas. We shall now discuss the rule regarding the Aṁśa and Graha as far as Jātis are concerned.

80 The Aṁśa and the Graha of the Madhyamodīcyavā, the Naivdayanti and the Gāndhārapañcamī is Pañcama.

81—82 The Aṁśa and Graha of the Dhaivatījāti are Dhaivata and Ṛṣabha; while those of Pañcamī Jāti are the Ṛṣabha and Pañcama.

82 Those of the Gāndhārodīcyavā are Ṣaḍja and Madhyama; while Ṛṣabha, Dhaivata and Nisāda are the Aṁśa and Graha of the Ārṣabhī.

83—84 Those of the Naiṣādī are Ṛṣabha, Gāndhāra and Niṣāda, Saḍja Gāndhāra and Pañcama are the Ạṁśa and Graha of the Ṣaḍjakaiśikī. Thus we have described the three Aṁśas and Grahas of the three Jātis.

84 Ṣaḍja, Madhyama, Dhaivata and Niṣāda are the four Aṁśas and the Grahas of the Ṣaḍjodīcyavati.

85 The Niṣāda, Dhaivata, Pañcama and Ṛṣabha are the four Aṁśas as well as Grahas of the karmāravī.

86 Those of the Āndhri Ṛṣabha, Gāndhāra Pañcama and Niṣāda.

87—91 The five Aṁśas and Grahas of the Madhyama are Madhyama, Ṣadja, Ṛṣabha, Pañcama and the Dhaiva. Those of the Ṣaḍjī are Ṣaḍja, Gāndhāra Madhyama, Pañcama and Dhaivata. The Aṁśas of the 'Gandhāri Rakta Gāndhārī are Gāndhāra, Ṛṣabha, Madhyama, Pañcama and Niṣāda.

All the Svara, except Ṛṣabha are the six Aṁśas and Grahas of the Kaiśiki.

All the Svaras are the seven Aṁśas and Grahas of the Ṣaḍjamadhyamā. Thus the sixty three Aṁśas and Grahas in the Jātis; Aṁśas themselves are the Grahas in all these Jātis.

The Tāra Gati (High Pitch movement). The High pitch movement depends on the five notes.

94 The rising movement of the ditch from any of the Aṁśa notes shall ordinarily be upto the fourth note there from or it may be even to the fifth note but never beyond it.

The low pitch movement (*Mandra*)

There are three kinds of the Mandra Gati, that pertaining to the Aṁśa or Nyāsa or on the Apanyāsa.

95 There is no pitch which becomes lower than that of the Aṁśa as pertaining to the Nyāsa such a pitch will be separated by two notes and when Gāndhāra is adopted as the Graha and the Nyāsa, Ṛṣabha and Dhaivata are seen having the low pitch.

Prose

Alpatva and Bahutva (Reduction & Amplification) Alpatva is of two kinds that due to Laṅghana (skipping over a note) and that due to Anabhyāsa (non-repetition) of the note. Of these the Alpatva by means of Laṅghana leads to Ṣāḍavīkarṅa and Auḍavīkaraṇa of the Aṁśas of songs when they come to Antaramārga; and that by means of Anabhyāṣa consists of enunciating them once according to the Jātis.

Bahutva. The Bahutva is the opposite of Alpatva The Sañcāra of the other notes which are string is of two kinds.

96 The Alpatva and Bahutva occur through early fixation in accordance with the convention in relation to particular notes of the Jātis. Alpatva therefore is of two kinds.

97 The movement of notes relates to the strong Aṁśa notes and the Alpatva to the weak notes. These are the two treatments of the Antara Mārgas which give character to the Jātis.

Ṣāḍavīkaraṇa. The Hexatonic treatment relates, to six Svaras in a Grāma. They are of fourteen kinds and have forty seven subdivisions. These have been described before in their Jātis and Aṁśas.

98 The Auḍavīkaraṇa (Pentatonic treatment) refers to five Svaras in one Grāma and should be understood to be of ten varieties. Its subdivisions, as already mentioned come to be thirty.

99 Groups of these five and six Svaras have their own respective application. In respect to Avakṛṣṭa Dhruvas groups of four Svaras are in use.

Nyāsa & Apanyāsa. Nyāsa akin to caḍence (of Western music) occurs at the conclusion of the song and consists of twenty one varieties. Thc Apanyāsa occurs at the conclusion of each of the divisions of the song and is of fifty six kinds.

101—102 *Jātis and their characteristics.* I shall now explain the characteristics of the Jātis together with their Nyāsa and Apanyāsa.

103—104 In the Ṣaḍjī Jāti the Aṁśa is of five notes after excluding Niṣāda Ṛṣabha. Gāndhāra and Pañcama constitute the Apanyāsa and Ṣaḍja its Nyāsa. Niṣāda the seventh note is

Lopya (worthy of omission). Ṣāḍava is without the seventh note. The Dhaivata and the seventh note are reduced. The Saḍja and Gāndhāra should move together while Gāndhāra is amplified.

105—107 *Ārṣabhī*. In this Jāti the Svaras Ṛṣabha, Dhaivata and Niṣāda constitute the Aṁśa. These are the Apanyāsa too. Ṛṣabha is the Nyāsa note. Ṣāḍava treatment is without Ṣaḍja and the Auḍavita treatment is without Ṣaḍja and Pañcama.

108—110 In the Dhaivatī Jāti the Nyāsa is Dhaivata; the Aṁśa is Ṛṣabha as Dhaivata; Ṛṣabha, Madhyama and Dhaivata constitute the Apanyāsa. The Pāñcasvarya is by excluding Ṣaḍja and Pañcama and Sāḍava treatment by eschewing Pañcama alone. Both these treatments should be in the Āroha (ascending scale). Ṛṣabha and Niṣāda are to be skipped and there is Bāhulya amplification of Gāndhāra.

111—112 *Naiṣādījāti*. Here Ṛṣabha, Gāndhāra, ano Niśāda constitute the Aṁśa, the Apanyāsa too being the same. There is Nyāsa in Niṣāḍa. The Ṣāḍavīkaraṇa and Auḍavitī Karaṇa are like those of the Dhaivati. The Alpatva and Bahutva (i.e. reduction and amplification of notes) are also similar.

113—114 *Ṣaḍjakaiśikī*. In this Ṣaḍja constitutes the Aṁśa. along with Gāndhāra and Pañcama; constitution of the Apanyāsa, is by Ṣaḍja, Pañcama and Niṣāda; Gāndhāra constitutes Nyāsa. There is no omission of any note because it is a complete Jāti. Reduction is Rṣabha and Dhaivata is inevitable.

115—117 *Ṣaḍjacīcyava*. In this Jāti three notes Sa, ma, Dha are the Amss; Ma is Nyāsa and Sa and Dha form Aparyāsa. The Amśa notes here are prescribed to come together with one another. It Auḍava treatment excludes RI and Pa and Ṣaḍava form excludes Ri. There is amplification in Ga.

118—120 *Ṣaḍjamadhyā*. All the notes constitute the Aṁśa. Auḍava, Ga and Ni are excluded. Ni is excluded in Ṣādava. Sañcāra of all the notes has be prescribed.

120—121 In the Ṣaḍja Grāma the above seven are the Jātis. I shall now mention the Jātis of Madhyama Grāma.

122—123 *Gāndhārī Jāti.* Five notes excluding Dh and Ri constitute the Aṁśa; Sa and Pa constitute Apanyāsa Gā constitutes Nyāsa. In the Ṣāḍava treatment Ri is excluded; Ri and Dha excluded in Auḍava treatment Ri and Dha should be skipped over. Ri always goes to Dha and there is amplification in Sa and Ma.

125—126 *Rakta Gāndhārījāti.* In respect to Nyāsa, omission of notes in Ṣāḍava and Auḍava and Amśa this is similar to Gāndhārī. There is amplification in Dha and Ni; Ga and Sa come together with the notes except Ri. Ma is its Apanyāsa.

127 *Gāndhārodīcyava.* In this Jāti Sa and Ma constitute the Amśa. There is no Auḍava treatment. Its Ṣāḍava on its Ri. Reduction, Amplification Nyāsa and Apanyāsa are like those of Ṣaḍjodīcyavā.

128—130 *Madhyamā.* The Aṁśa and Apanyāsa are constituted by Sa, Ri, Ma, Pa and Dha. Ma is Nyāsa. Ga and Ni are weakened. In Auḍava Ga and Ni are excluded. In Ṣāḍava Ga is omitted. Amplification of Ṣaḍja and Ma and reduction of Ga have been prescribed

131 *Madhyamodıcyavā.* Pa is Aṁśa. All the other features as in Gāndharodīcyavā.

132—134 *Pañcamī.* Ri and Pa form the Amśa; Ri, Pa and Ni form the Apanyāsa and Pa forms Nyāsa; Ri and Ma are dropped from it. The Ṣāḍava and Auḍava and Auḍava as in Madhyamā. There is reduction in Sa, Ga and Ma. Ma and Ri come together and go to Ga, Ni should be weakened.

135—136 *Gāndhārā Pañcamī.* In this Pa is Aṁśa. Ri and Pa form Apanyāsa and Ga forms Nyāsa. No Svara is wanting. Ga and Pa come together.

137—139 *Āndhrī.* Four Svaras namely Ri, Pa, Ga and Ni constitute Aṁśa and Apanyāsa. Ga is the Nyāsa Ṣaḍja is omitted in Ṣāḍava treatment. Ga and Sa come together in it. Amplification in the Āroha order of Dha and Ni. Reduction in Ṣaḍja. There is no Auḍava treatment.

140—143 *Nandayantī* Aṁśa is always Pa; the Apanyāsa—Ma and Pa. Ṣāḍava without Sa which is reduced. Notes coming together as in Āndhrī. There is reduction in Ri also. Mandra

Gati (Low pitch) in Ri and Tāra Gati in Sa. There is no Avaroha Krama. Its Graha is Ga; so also the Nyāsa.

144—145 *Karmāravī*. The Graha and Aṁśa constituted by Ri, Pa, Dha and Ni; so also the Apanyāsa. Pa is its Nyāsa. No note is left out. Notes other than those in Aṁśa are to be amplified. Ga comes together with all other notes.

146—149 *Kaiśikī*. Aṁśa consists of Svaras other than Ri. So also the Apanyāsa. Nyāsa is formed by Ga and Ni but when Dha and Ni are the Aṁśa, the Nyāsa shall be Pañcama. Ri is weak and should be skipped over. Sometimes Ri is its Apanyāsa. In Ṣāḍava Ri is omitted, and in Auḍava Ri and Dha, Sa and Pa being strong Svaras should be amplified. Ri is to be weakened and specially skipped over. The coming together of the Svaras as in the case of Ṣaḍja Madhyamā.

150—151 These are the Jātis with their ten characteristic features. These should be applied in the Pada with Karaṇas (dance movements) along with suitable gestures. I shall now speak of their distinction in respect to Rasas and Bhāvas Be pleased to listen

Notes

1 Nāṭya Śāstra considers only the well known musical instruments as auspicious.

4—5 The Kutapa is interpreted by some commentators as Kutam Śabdam Pāti.

Vipañcī originally was a Vīṇā with nine to twenty one strings.

Dardura is a large gong made of bell metal. Some take it to be a flute. In fact it must be considered as a kind of drum.

7 Nāṭya includes "dancing", not meraly "acting".

8 Gāndharva—a combination of vocal and instrumental music.

16—17 The various terms have been defined in Chapter Fifteen.

22 Vādi Svara is the melodic centre of the melody.

23 The word Grāma is usually translated as "Scale".

The Greak word Gamma in the musical sense is derived from the Sanskrit word.

24 Śruti means "interval". Viśvāvasu mentions that there are two Śrutis. Other authorities variously consider their number between three and sixty six and even infinite.

Of Kohala's verse

Dvāvimśatim Keciduda Haranti

Śrutīḥ Śruti Jñānavicāra Dakṣāḥ |

Ṣaṭṣaṣṭi Bhinnāḥ Khalu Keciāsām

Ānantyamanye/Pyupapādayanti ||

27—28 The Gāndhāra Grāma as expounded by Nārada had beome obsolete at the time of Nāṭya Śāstra.

29

On Stringed Instruments

1 *Application of Jātis to the Rasa.* The Ṣaḍjodīcyavatī and the Ṣaḍjamadhyā are applicable in the Śṛṅgāra and Hāsya Rasas respectively because Ma and Pa are amplified in them.

2 The Ṣāḍjī and the Ārṣabhī should be applied in the Vīra, Bhayānaka and the Adbhuta Rasas when Sa and Ri respectively make their, Grahasvara.

3 The Naiṣādi with Ni as its Aṁśa Svara and the Ṣaḍjakaiśiki with Gāndhāra as its Aṁśa Svara should be the Jāti sung by expert singers in the Karuṇa Rasa.

4 The Dhaivatī with Dha as its Aṁśa Svara is to applied in the Bībhatsa and Raudra Rasas. Further Dhaivati is applicable in the Karuṇa Rasa. Ṣaḍjamadhyā is to be applied in connection with lunacy.

5 The Jātis should be adopted in the application of Dhruvās by the sponsors with due consideration of the Rasas the action and the Bhāvas in the Drama.

6 The above are the Jātis of the Ṣaḍjagrāma as explained by the wise ones. I shall now explain those of the Madhyama Grāma.

7 The Gāndhārī and the Raktagāndhārī should be applied in the Karuṇa Rasa when they have Ga and Ni as their Aṁśa Svaras.

8—9 The Madhyamā, the Pañcamī, Nandayantī, Gāndhārī Madhyamodīcyavā Jātis should be applied in the Śṛṅgāra and the Hāsya Rasas when Ma and Pa are amplified.

9—10 In the Vīra, Raudra and Adbhutarasas the Karmā Ravi, Āndhrī and the Gāndhārodīcyavā should be applied with Sa and Ri as their Aṁśa Svaras. In the Bībhatsa and the

Raudra Rasas the Kaiśikī with Dha as the Aṁśa Svara should be applied.

11 The only Pāti that accommodates all the Rasas is the Ṣaḍja Madhyā. All the Svaras of the Grāma constitute its Aṁśa. This has already been explained.

12 When a particular Svara in connection with a particular Rasa is strong in a Jāti the Prayoktā should combine the song therewith according it due prominence.

13—14 A song the Śṛṅgāra or Hāsya Rasa should have many Ma's and Pa's in the Jāti concerned while songs with Vīra, Raudra and the Adbhuta Rasas should be made with many Sa's and Ri's. The song in Karuṇa Rasa should abound in Ga and Ni. A song in the Bībhatsa and Bhayānaka Rasas should have many Dha's.

15 In all the Aṁśas the application of these svaras in accordance with the rules with suitable Kākalī and Antara-Svara is recommended where they are made strong too.

16 The wise should understand these Jātis pertaining to the dramatic performance. Henceforth the Svaras presented in the musical instruments will be explained.

Prose Passage. Ma and Pa in Hāsya and Śṛṅgāra Rasas Sa and Ri in Vīra, Raudra and Adbhuta. Ga and Ni in the Karuṇa and Dha in Bībhatsa and Bhayānaka. I shall now speak of the Varṇas and the Alaṁkāras.

17—18 Varṇas on which Alaṁkāras depend are of four type, the Ārohin (ascending), Avarohin (descending) Sthāyin, (Persistant staying, and Sañcārin (moving together, mixed).

19 In Ārohin the Svaras go up; in Avarohin they go down in the scale, in the Sthāyin the Svaras are the same with the same pitch and in the Sañcārin the various of Svaras come together.

20 The Varṇas with clear cut features arise from physical voice with relation to the quality of the three Sthānas (voice registers).

21 The Varṇas give rise to the Rasas when atleast there are two Varṇas in a Pada (song) with a characteristic identity.

22 These four Varṇas are applicable to the songs. Now I shall describe the Alaṁkāras that depend on them.

23—28 *The Thirty three Alaṁkāras* are (1) Prasannādi (2) Prasadnānta (3) Prasannādyanta (4) Prasannamadhya (5) Sama (6) Bindu (7) Veṇu (8) Nivṛttapravṛtta (9) Kampita (10) Kuhara (11) Recita (12) Preṅkholitaka (13) Mandra Tāraprasanna (14) Tāramandraprasanna (15) Prasvara (16) Prasāda (17) Udvāhita (18) Avalokita (19) Krama (20) Niṣkūjita (21) Udgīta (22) Hrādamāna (23) Rañjita (24) Āvarta (25) Parivartaka (26) Udghaīṭṭita (27) Ākṣipta (28) Sampradāna (29) Humkāra (31) Sandhipracchādana (32) Vidhūna and (33) Gātravarṇa.

29—30 *The Sthāyi Alaṁkāras.* The Prasannādi, Prasannānta, Prasannādyanta, Prasannāmadhya, Sama Recita, Prasvāra, and Prasāda. Now about the Sañcārin (mixed) Alaṁkāras.

31—32 *The Sañcārin* Alaṁkāras are Mandra, Tāra, Prasanna, Bindu, Prenkholita, Nivṛtta, Recita, Kampita, Krama, Kuhara, Veṇu, Rañjita, Avalokita Āvartoka and Parivartaka.

33—34 The Ārohin Alaṁkāras are Niṣkūjita, Humkāra, Hasita, Bindu, Recita, Preṅkholita, Ākṣipta, Vidhūṇa,Udghaṭṭita, Hrādamāna, Sampradāna, Sandhipracchādana, Prasannādi and Prasannānta.

35 The Avarohin Alaṁkāras are Vidhūna, Gātravarṇa, Udvāhtta, Udgita and Venu.

36 Avarohin Alaṁkāras are attached to the songs of seven forms as known to the wise. It is not desirable to use them in the Dhruvās because they give importance to the Varṇas of Jātiṣ.

37 If at all Bindu and Veṇu are applied in the Dhruvas they are then not used in the Dhruvās they are then not used in their own Pramāṇas.

38—39 While the Dhruvā conforms to the meaning of the play and suggests the same, the Varṇalaṅkāras soften the Pada and therefore obscures it. The following are the Varṇas commonly used.

39—43 The following Alaṁkāras belong to all the Varnas viz. Prasannādi, Prasannānta, Prasannādyanta, Prasanna Madhya, Bindu, Kampita, Recita, Tāra, Tāramandra, Tāratara, Preṅkholita, Maṇdra, Mandratāra, Saṃa Nivṛttapravṛtta,

Prasāda, Apāṅga, Avaloka, and Veṇu, Excepting Sthāyin all the other Varṇas are utilized in song. Now I shall describe in full the *distinct features of these Alaṁkāras* as born of the Varṇas. The Alaṁkāra in which the Svara rises from the low pitch gradually and becomes brilliant.

44—47 The former one enunciated in the reverse order becomes Prasannānta. If the initial and the concluding Svaras are in low pitch and the middle one is in the high pitch it is Prasannādyanta. If the note in the middle is in the low pitch but those in the beginning and end are in the high pitch, it is Prasannamadhya. That in which a Svara is repeated in the same pitch and is equal in all the parts is called Sama If Svara of one Kalā of low pitch touches, the high pitch and comes back to the original pitch it is called Bindu. If a Svara of one Kalā of high pitch touches the low pitch and comes back to the original pitch it is called Vivṛtta Pravṛtta. If the Laya (Tempo) is play-like the Alaṁkāra is Veṇu. If the wind is in the medium pitch having stopped in the vocal passage and the notes are in a playlike tempo it is called Kuhara.

48—53 Svaras appearing to tremble in their vibration, with three Kalās in high pitch constitute Recita Alaṁkāra. Trembling notes of three Kalās in low pitch in the breast constitute Kampita, Preṅkholita is that Alaṁkāra in which Svaras occur in each Kalā in both the orders the Āroha and Avaroha. A note of medium pitch in the throat make Tāra. A Svara of low pitch in the breast makes Mandra. A Svara of very high pitch in the head makes Tāratara. If in a Kalā the fourth or fifth Svara gradually falls assuming a low gait from a high pitch it is Tāramandraprasanna. If in a Kalā four or five Svaras gradually rise to a high pitch from the low pitch and skip over other low Svaras it is Mandratāraprasanna. If in a Kalā the Svaras ascend note by note it is Prasvāra. If in a Kalā the Svaras descend gradually note by note it is Prasāda. If in a Kalā notes come together first in Āroha and then in Avaroha it is called Apāṅgika.

54—59 The consecutive, Svaras move Aroha in Kalā, Two such Kalās constitute one unit. This is called Udvāhita. In the previous one if the repeated Kalās are in Avaroha order it is Avalokita. When successive Kalās include one, two, three four, five, six or seven consecutive notes in the Āroha order it Krama. If Kalās have notes that proceed in the Āroha order omitting one Svara in the middle and come back to it is called Niṣkūjita Kalās in the Prasvāra, in the beginning and in the end ascend and descend alternatingly and constitute Udgīta Svaras as in the Udgīta constitute pairs of Kalās conisting of at least two or at most six Svaras with alternate Svaras coming together make Hrādamāna. After staying in two consecutive Svaras of two Kalās at proceeds in Āroha half a Kalā and then goes in Avaroha.

60—63 There are eight Kalās of four consecutive Svaras in the Āroha order. This is called Āvartaka. It may be formed with two alternative Svaras. Then four Kalās shall have Āroha and Avaroha Svaras. There are eight Kalās in which one Svara proceeds in Āroha Krama to the third one from it and then skips over the adjacent one in order to ascend in the following Svara. The Svara then proceeds in the Avaroha Krama in the same manner in the next Kalā. This is Parivartaka. There are eighteen Kalās which take Āroha Krama for two Svaras. Leaving out the next note it has an Āroha to the following Svara. This is Udghaṭṭita.

64—71 The Ākṣiptaka contains six Kalās of three Svaras. If it contains Kalās of four notes alternating with Kalās of three notes it is Sampradāna. Alternate notes are included in this. The Alaṁkāra, Hasita is constituted with double Kalās of two consecutive notes like laughter as in the Ākṣipta. As in the Hasita there are a minimum of two and a maximum of four Svaras in Āroha order in each Kalā. This is Huṁkāra. Alaṁkāra Sandhipracchādana has groups of four Kalās in the Āroha Krama from the original state to a high pitch and proceeding there from to the original one without any throwing up. The Pada containing two short Svaras is produced at first, then two consecutivee Svaras will proceed in the Āroha Krama in each Kalā. This is Vidhūna. In the Gātravarṇa Alaṁkāra as in Huṁkāra, Svaras proceed in the Āroha order in the alternate Kalās of four Svaras of which the first two appear to vibrate and tremble while the next two are of low pitch.

72—76 Long vowels like E-O etc. are to be added to the Svaras in the Alaṁkāras. This rule governs the Karaṇas of the Padas and Alaṁkāras. Songs are embellished with the Alaṁkāras that do not clash with the rule regarding the Varṇas. Alaṁkāras of the body are intended to be worn in the respective parts. The Kāñcī (gridle) is not to be fastened to the breast. Without Varṇa, one shall never make use of many Alaṁkāras so much for Alaṁkāras depending on Varṇas. Now I shall explain the Alaṁkāras depending on Chandas (Metre Rhythm and Akṣara (syllable of proper quality). A song devoid of Alaṁkāra resembles the night bereft of the Moon, river deprived of water creeper that has not blossomed, and a woman unadorned. The above are the thirty three Alaṁkāras. Now listen to the characteristics of the Gītis.

77—81 *Alaṁkāras based on the Gīti.* Gītis are of four kinds : Māgadhī, Ardhamāgadhī, Sambhāvitā and Pṛthulā. The Māgadhī is sung in different Gativṛttis. The Ardhamāgadhī revises its tempo (Gativṛtti) after half-time. The Sambāvita is known to be constituted with long syllables and the Pṛthulā with short syllables. There Gītis are not at all connected with the Dhruvās but have to be applied by the songsters in the Gāndharva only. I have explained Gītis adequately. Now listen to the expending of Dhātus as I speak about the playing of the Dhātus.

82—102 *Dhātus in the stringed instruments.* They are Visāra (Expansion), Karaṇa (Production), Āviddha (Breaking up) and Vyañjana (Indication). *Vistāra*-Consists of four kinds of strokes (a) Saṅghātaja (growing out of contrast), Samavāyaja (growing out of the combination), Vistāraja (growing out of amplitude) and Anubandhaja (growing out of mere succession). Its rules have been cited as follows—the Vistāraja is of one stroke; the Saṁghātaja and the Samavāyata consist of two and three strokes. The first is of four kinds and the second is of eight kinds. In accordance with the special ways of their production they have different rules. Svaras we know are of low and high pitch in as much as they come out of mild or strong strokes. Players of Vādita stringed instrument should know these rules. The Saṁghātaja strokes have the following varieties—two high, two low, low-high, and high-low. The Samavāyaja strokes have the following varieties—(a) three high (b) three low (c) two low and one high (d) two high and one low (e) one high two low (f) one low two high (g) one low, one high and one low (h) one high, one low and one high. The Anubandakṛta is irregular due to its formation by breaking up and combining of the groups of strokes explained before. Thus the fourteen kinds of the Vistāra Dhātus. *The Karaṇa Dhātus.* They are of five kinds as applicable to the play on the Vīṇh viz. Ribhitauccaya, Nīraṭita, Hrāda and Anubandha. The Karaṇa Dhātus will consist respectively of three, five, seven and nine light strokes and then, being combined all end in a heavy stroke. *The Ābiddha Dhātus* are of five kinds :—Kṣepa, Pluta, Atipāta, Atikīrṇa and Anubandha. They have respectively two, three, four and nine strokes made slowly and gradually and finally a combination of these. *Vyañjana Dhātus* are of ten kinds in respect to the playing on Vīṇā. They are Kala, Tala, Niṣkoṭita, Vnmṛṣṭa, Repha, Avamṛṣṭa, Puṣpa, Anusvanita, Bindu and Anubandha. (a) *Kala.* The string is touched with both the thumbs simultaneously (b) *Tala.* The string is pressed with the right thumb and struk with the left thumb (c) *Niṣkoṭita*—When the string is struck only with the left thumb (d) *Unmṛṣṭa*—when the string is struck with the left index finger (e) *Repha*—one single stroke with all the fingers of a hand (f) *Avamṛṣṭa*—three strokes low down in the string with the little finger and the thumb of the right hand (g) *Puṣpa*—one stroke with the little finger and the thumb (h) *Anusvanita*—the stroke is lower in the string than in the Tala ("b" above) (i) *Bindu*—one heavy stroke in a string, (j) *Anubandha*—one irregular combination after a break up of all these. It is in relation to all the Dhātus. Thus the ten Vyañjana Dhātus have been explained. These are therefore the four Dhātus with their characteristics features relating to the three Gativṛttis on which the playing of stringed instruments depends. *The three Vṛttis* (Prose Passage) styles of procedure to be mainly considered are three (a) Citra (Variegated), Vṛtti (Simple movement) and Dakṣiṇa (dexterous). For the determination of their characters we have instrumental music, timemeasure, Laya (Tempo), Gīti (rhythm), Yati (Pause) and Graha Mārga (Way of beginning). In the Citra the Māgadhī is the Gīti, the instrumental music becomes concise without being elaborate, the unit of Tāla is one Kalā, the Laya is quick (Druta) and Yati (Pause) is Samā. Anāgata Grahas are predominant. In the Vṛtti, the Sambhāvitā is the Gīti the instrument for music is Vīṇā the Laya is Madhya (medium) the Yati is Srotogatā (flowing like a current). The Sama Graha

Mārgas are prepoderant. In the Dakṣiṇa, the Gīti is Pṛthulā, the unit of time measure is four Kalās; the Laya is Vilambita (Slow), the Yati is Gopucchā (Cow's tail) and the Atīta Graha Mārgas are predominant.

103—104 The names of the three styles of procedure are Citra, Dakṣiṇa and Vṛtti. They accord good quality to the instrumental music and also to the vocal one. They have been defined in due order. The Jātis (such as Udātta, Lalita etc.) of all these styles of procedure when in combination with the Dhātus will become richer in quality.

105—107 *The Jātis.* Jātis issue from a mixture of the Dhātus. They are Udātta, Lalita, Ribhita and Ghana. The Udātta relates to the Vistāra Dhātus (many other things). The Lalita (graceful) relates to Vyañjana Dhātus. The Ribhita relates to the Ābiddea Dhātus and is characterised by a multitude of strokes. The Ghana relates to the Karaṇa Dhātus and depends on their aggregate of long and short Svaras.

108—110 *Three types of Vīṇā music.* Three distinct types of music can be produced by experts on the Vīṇā viz. Tattva, Anugata and Ogha. There is a combination of many Karaṇas. That types of music wherein the Laya, Tāla, Varṇa, Pada, Yati and Akṣara are expressed suitably is called Tattva. That type of instrumental music which closely follows the Pada (Song) is called Anugata. That type of music wherein Ābiddha Karaṇas prodominate is called Ogha. It has Uparipāṇi, Graha Mārga, Drutalaya (quick tempo) and is indifferent towards the meaning of the song.

111—113 According to rules Tattva is to be applied in Vilambita Laya (slow temps); the Anugata in Madhyalaya (medium) and the Ogha in Druta (quick) Laya. The expert in the instruments of music observes Laya and Tāla adequately and applies Tattva in the first song to be sung in the performance, the Anugata in the second and the Ogha in the third. These are the Dhātus in the music of the Vīṇā which all adepts should master. I shall now explain the Karaṇas in regard to the rules governing Vipañcī play.

114—117 *Karaṇas of Vipañcī.* Rūpa, Kṛtapratikṛta, Pryatibhedsa, Rūpaśeṣa, Ogha and Pratiśuṣka constitute the Karaṇas in regard to the rules governing Vipañcī play. It is

Rūpa when two heavy and two light syllables are placed on the Vīṇā. If this Rūpa is performed in the Pratibheda it is called Kṛtapratikṛta. What is called Pratibheda occurs when two different Karaṇas are played side by side on the Vīṇā showing heavy and light syllables. After the play in the principal Vīṇā has been stopped if the artiste continues the music in another Vīṇā it is called Rūpaśeṣa. The Ogha includes the Ābiddha Karaṇas performed in the Uparipāṇi Graha Mārga. If the Vipañcī is played, by means on only one string the Karaṇa then is Pratiśuṣka.

118—121 The adepts generally have to use plectrum [Koṇa] while playing on two Vipañcīs and there is the application of the Dhruvās when a song or others instruments are accompanied. The Artiste should equally reflect the place or character together with the song on the strings and in the Vipañcī it will be something like the Karaṇa named Ogha. The Vīṇā with seven strings is called Citra and one with nine strings Vipañcī. Citra is to be played only with fingers while Vipañci is to be played with plectrum. Thus the adept artiste should understand every thing about the Karaṇas of the Vipañcī. I shall now explain the Bahir-Gītas together with their fixed characteristics.

122—125 *The Bahir-Gītas.* These are included in the Preliminaries to the performance of the regular play. All these Pūrvaraṅga should be applied with or without Tālas and also in the styles of procedure called Citra and Vṛtti. They are Āśrāvaṇa, Ārambha, Vaktrapāṇi, Saṁghoṭana, Parighaṭṭana, Mārgāsārita, Līlākṛta and Āsārita. This last one is of three kinds, short, medium and long. These are to be applied first by the producers. The necessity for all these has already been mentioned in fifth chapter while describing the rules for Pūrvaraṅga. I shall now describe their characteristic features with examples. [Many passages are very corrupt. Hence we have not translated them.]

126—130 *The Aśrāvaṇa.* Karaṇas of the Vistāra Dhātu are repeated twice in successive Kalās and then they are increased gradually by two repeated Karaṇas. This is Āśrāvaṇa. It will include a pair of twenty four Varṇas (syllables) of which the first two, the eleventh, the fourteenth the fifteenth and the twenty fourth are heavy and a three fold fifteen syllables of which the first is light, the next seven (including the eighth) heavy, the next six again light and the last three syllables being heavy. The Tālas in the Āśrāvaṇa will be as follows :—three Śamyās and a Tāla in the Upari Pāṇi, two Śamyās and two Tālas and again a Śamyā and two Tālas in the Samapāṇi and suitable Uttara and Cañcatpuṭa Tālas of two Kalās.

131—136 *The Ārambha.* The first eight syllables are heavy the next twelve and the final one are light in the first section. In the second section the beginning four are heavy, next eight light, one heavy, four light and four heavy; in the third section the first eight and the final one are light and the others heavy This is Ārambha. It should be performed in three sections with the Karaṇas such as the Tāla the Ribhita and the Hrāda in which the Vistāra Dhātus prdominate; and ascent is followed by a descent. The Karaṇas will be in the Avaroha order twice or thrice. Thereafter it should be played in the reverse order. In the end all these are repeated. Its first Tāla is of three Kalās; there will be a Śamyā of one Kalā; a Tāla of two Kalās; then a Śamyā of two Kalās, a Tāla of two Kalās, and a Sannipāta of two Kalā and a Ṣaṭpitāputraka and a Cañcatpuṭa of two Kalās.

137—142 *The Vaktrapaṇi.* The music of the Vaktrapaṇi includes the Karaṇas of the Ābiddha Dhātu and it has two members, Ekaka or Vṛtta (Pravṛtta) and it is to have in its music half the member of the Vyañjana Dhātus. The syllabic scheme of the Vaktra Pāṇi is as follows :—five are heavy (Prosodially long), six are light (short), fourtimes heavy two heavy, one light, four light, three heavy, eight light and one heavy. The scheme of the Śamyā and the Tāla used in the Madraka song of two Kalās, will be used in the Vaktra Pāṇi; but at the Mukha (beginning) it will consist of eight Kalās. The Tāla in the Mukha and Pratimukha of the Vaktrapāṇi will be as follows :—a Śamyā, a Tāla, a Tāla, a Śamyā and a Tāla; a Śamyā, a Tāla and a Sannipāta and four Pañcapāṇis.

143—147 *The Saṁghaṭana.* The music of the Saṁghaṭana will be by means of three Karaṇas of the Vistāra Dhātu class and it will observe the Citra and the Vṛtta styles of procedure and three such Karaṇas will be repeated and will gradually rise. The sequence of prosodically long and short syllables of the theme of the Saṁghaṭana will be as follows :—2 long, 8 short,

2 long, 1 short, 1 long, 1 short, 4 short, 8 short and 1 long in the end. In the Saṁghoṭana the Vīṇā is taken with both the hands by its Daṇda (beam) and played with fingers of the right hand and both the thumbs. Saṁghaṭana is so called because of the playing together of the Samvādi and Viṣama Vādi notes together with the remaining Asamvādi ones. Its Tāla as in the Śīrṣaka will consist of the Pañcapāṇis.

148—151 *The Parighaṭṭanā.* The syllabic scheme of the Parighaṭṭanā is as follows :—8 long, 24 short, 1 long, 16 short and 2 long. Its music should consist of many Karaṇas of the Vyañjana Dhātu and should be performed with Upavahana (Upohana) by skilful hands. Its Tāla will be Sampakveṣṭāka as it will stand combined with the Karaṇa of the Dhātu (i.e. Vyāñjana) due to the syllabic scheme of the Parighaṭṭanā.

151—153 *The Mārgā Sārita.* The syllabic scheme of the Mārgā Sārita in its Vastu will be as follows : 4 long, 8 short, 8 long, 8 sort and the last one long. The instrumental music in the Mārgā Sārita will consist of Karaṇas of the Vistāra and Ābiddha Dhātus and it will observe all Tālas agreeing with its syllabic scheme.

154 It may also be 4 long, 8 short, 3 long, 3 short and 1 short in the end.

155 *The Līlākṛta.* The skilful producer shall perform the Līlākṛta as well as Abhisṛta and Parisṛta according to the rules of the Short Āsārita and it should observe Tālas sweet to hear. The Āsāritas may be Jyeṣṭha (long), Madhya (Middling) and Kaniṣṭha (Short). In relation to their Tālas and Pramāṇas they will be explained in the rules on Tālas (Chapter 31).

156 These should be learnt in regard to the notes arising from the body of the Viṇā. I shall now explain the features of the Suṣirātodya (Flute etc.).

Notes

1 Songs included in the performance of a Nāṭaka have the evocation of the Rasas as its principal purpose. Jātis can be applied for that purpose. The author discusses the process in this chapter. Formation of Rāgas in the later Indian music owes its origin to this. The melody types act on the hearers'

emotion in such a way as to make them experience in imagination the situations described in songs.

17 Varṇa means production of Svaras in a particular order, pitch or special grouping. Varṇa Paricaya is the technical term used when the student practises these.

23 Without Alaṁkāras a song does not distinguish itself from a mere chant. There is no unanimity among authorities regarding their number definition, features etc.

36 Seven types of songs are explained in Chapter 31 verses 220 ff.

92 Anubandha literally means "that which gets associated". Here we can take it to mean "Combination".

102 The word Laya signifies the speed at which a piece of music is performed. They are Druta, Vilambita and Madhya.

Yati usually means Caesura, pause etc. Here it may be taken to mean "Succession of different kinds of speed.

Mārga in the text should be taken here as Graha Mārga meaning the manner of following a song or a piece of music by an instrument of Tāla.

120 This Citrā Vīṇā probably developed later into Persian Sitār. The Guitar of Western origin has also seven strings intended for the seven notes of the gamut. The nine strings of the Vipañcī may have been intended for two Kākalī notes in addition to the usual seven.

30

On Susirātodya [Hollow Musical Instruments (Flute etc.)]

1 The Suṣira musical instrument is made of bamboo as all wise men already know. The rules regarding their Svaras and Grāma are the same as those of the Vīnā.

2 The Svaras of the Vaṁśa flute) have two three and four Śrutis. They are Kampita (shaken), Ardha-Mukta (half-liberated) and Vyakta Mukta (clearly liberated).

3 If it is increased (beyond that the Svara of the Vīṇā is changed into another. Similarly in the flute also it does so.

4 The number of Śrutis in notes produced in a flute will be two, three or four and by prolonging the blow the remaining notes may also be produced.

5 Notes have their features determined by the Śrutis numbering four three or two produced by the application of fingers while playing the flute. Listen to it attentively.

6—10 The note produced from a flute hole thoroughly free from a finger consists of four Śruti, and that from a hole on which a shaking finger is placed consists of three Śrutis and a note consisting of two Srutis is produced from a hole which is partly (Ardhamukta) free from a finger. All these are the notes in the Madhyama Grāma. Notes of the Ṣaḍjagrāma will be as follows. Sa, Ma and Pa will arise from a hole Vyaktamukta (fully open). Dha and Ri from a hole Kampita (covered by a quivering finger); Ga and Ni will arise from a hole Ardha-Mukta (partially liberated) Ni and Ga respectively coming in juxte position with Sa and Ma and modifying themselves in characteristic Śrutis will give rise to the Svara-Sādhāraṇa (overlapping note) and the Kākalī notes.

11—13 The notes of the flute should be perfected and accomplished with the help of the Vīṇā and of the human throat. The very notes the songster attains should be sung to the accompaniment of a flute. A unison of the human throat the Vīṇā and the flute is specially praised. The music of the flute, which is steady not very loud and furnished with the Varṇas and the Alaṁkāras and following the rules is sweet and soothing. These should be known regarding musical notes by persons playing flutes. I shall now speak of the Ghana class of musical instrument.

Notes

1 At the outset bamboo had been used in making the Indian flute even now bamboo is the most common material for flute. Hence the name Vaṁśa for flute also. Sāhityadarpaṇa mentions flutes made of horn, wood (Khadira and Candana), ivory and metals such as iron, brass, silver and gold. The Saṅgītaratnākara also mentions these things. The conch shell can be called a Suṣira, but its use for musical purpose is not known although for rituals and Pūjās it was and inevitable ancillary.

7—9 Abhinava Gupta mentions the mode of the production of the various notes in detail—

Left hand ring finger—Ṣaḍja

Left Middle ring finger—Ṛṣabha

No finger—fully open—Gāndhāra

Shaken finger —Madhyama

Right hand—ring finger—Pañcama

Right hand—Middle —Dhaivata

Right hand—Index finger—Niṣāda

Shaken finger—Madhyama

31

On Tālas [Time-measure and the Ghana instrument of Tāla]

1—3 The Tāla instrument belongs to the Ghaṇa (Solid) class and it relates to the division into Kalās and to the adaptation of the Laya. Those who apply Tālas in a musical demonstration must know Kalās as the measured time (Tāla). In popular parlance Kalā, Kāṣṭhā and Nimeṣa are used by scholars in a different sense. The word Kalā with reference to Tāla is utterly different. One Mātrā is made up of five Nimeṣas. Grouping of Mātrās gives rise to Kalaās. The interval between two Kalās at the time of singing is also made up of five Nimeṣas.

And from these again the Laya is made in accordance with the time of the Kalās in to which Mātrās have been divided.

4—6 The Laya is of three kinds Druta (Rapid), Madhya (Medium) and Vilambita (slow, delayed). It is the Madhya Laya which determines the Pramāṇa Kalā (normal Kalā). Kalā is to be understood to be of three varieties. The wise base thus difference on the three Mārgas (i.e. Pāṇis). In the Citra procedure there are two Mātrās, in the Vṛtti procedure there are four Mātrās and in Dakṣiṇa procedure there are eight Mātrās. These are the three types of Kalās. The Tāla is so termed because it measures time by a division of songs into Kalās.

7 Tāla is of two kinds viz. Caturaśra and Tryaśra. Both of them have the same source of origin.

8 Understand their two fold sources viz. Cañcatpuṭa and Cācapuṭa.

9—10 From each of these the Tāla proceeds whether it

has two Kalās or four Kalās. The Cañcatpuṭa is to be known as Caturaśra and Cāpapuṭa is Tryaśra. They have long or short syllables.

10—14 The Cañcatpuṭa has two long syllables followed by one short syllable and then the final Pluta syllable. The Cāpapuṭa which is Tryasra consists of one long syllable, followed by two short syllables and the last one is a long syllable. When these two are combined it is Miśra Tāla. The Miśra includes Ṣaṭpitāputrakaḥ and the Pañcapāṇi constituted according to long and short syllables occurring in their names. Thus the three kinds of Tālas are succinctly explained.

15—18 Their Pātakāla is as follows :—(1) Sannipātādi viz. Sannipāta, Śamyā, Tāla, Śamyā (2) Śamyādi viz Śamyā, Tāla, Śamyā Tāla and (3) Tālādi viz. Tāla, Śamyā, Tāla, Śamyā. The Cañcatpuṛa is of three kinds thus. The Sannipātādi will be Caturaśra in the Nāṭya and the Śamyādi is to be applied in the Āsāritas. Similarly the Tālādi is to be applied in Pāṇika etc. The three kinds of the Cañcatpuṭa viz. Sanhipātādi etc. are equally applicable in the case of Cāpapuṭa also.

19—22 The Sannipātādi and the other two as well are strong in this Cāpapuṭa. Tālas of six or eight Kalās proceed there from. Due to the Śamyā Tāla and Praveśa another Tryaśra is also produced. It is called Pañcapāṇi effected by Ṣaṭpitāputraka. Its Pātakāla is as follows :—The first syllable is Pluta, the second short and the third and fourth are long the fifth is short and the final one is Pluta. This is Ṣaṭpitāputraka with its long and short syllables. It is also called Pañcapāṇi and consists of six Pātas and six syllables.

23—25 Its six Pātas are these—Sannipāta, Tāla, Śamyā-Tāla, Śamyā and Tāla. There is another type of the Tālādi in Tryaśra. It is termed Sampakveṣṭāka It has five long syllables including the one at the beginning and the one in the end which is Pluta. The Pātas, thereof are as follows : Sannipāta, Śamyā-Tāla, Śamyā and Tāla. In case the Tryaśra consists of all three heavy (Prosodicallylong) syllables its Kalās shall be as follows : Niṣkrāma, Śamyā and Śamyā. It is termed Udghaṭṭaḥ.

26—29 So there shall be the pure Cañcatpuṭa etc. or one Kalā. The three varieties of the Tālas then are Yathākṣara

Dvikala and Catuṣkala the latter one being twice as long as the former. The Caturaśra Tāla is of three varieties with four, eight and sixteen Kalās. The Tryaśra Tāla has six special varieties with three, six, twelve, twenty four, forty eight and ninety six Kalās.

30—34 Thus Tryaśra Tālas are of nine types. Tāla in general can be of two kinds (1) Niśśabda (Silent) and Śabdavān (audible). Understand the two uses to which they can be put as described now. The Nisśabda Tāla has four varieties viz. Āvāpa Niṣkrāma, Vikṣepa and Praveśaka. The Śabdavān Tāla is also of four varieties viz Śamyā, Tāla, Dhruva and Sannipāta. The movement of hands and fingers in relation to them are now mentioned to due order with their characteristics and measure.

35—38 By Āvāpa, curving of fingers are spread out with the palm facing downwards, it is Niṣkrāma; if it is swiftly moved to the right side it is Vikṣepa; by Pravesh we mean the drawing away of the palm facing down wards. After the Āvāpa has been shown the dancer makes the Niṣkrāma and Vikṣepa and Pravesana in the end. If the combination of the Tālas consists of four Kalās this rule is followed. Niṣkrāma and the Praveśa are reputed as Dvikalās (having only two Kalās).

39—42 The alternate placing of these is known as Pāta. The Śamyā is of the right hand, the Tāla of the left hand and when the two hands come together it is Sannipāta. Dhruva is is the falling for a Mātrā and it makes for the way of the Rāgas and the Pāta of the three Kalās mentioned before is also called Dhruva. In the Yathākṣara Tāla the Dhruva is a long syllable. The Tāla with Yathākṣara Pātas is Yathāsthita (ordinary) type. With doubled long syllables it consists of two Kalās. The doubling of two Kalās will make it consist of four Kalās.

43—48 The description of the Pāta arising in the Yathākṣara Tāla is concluded. Similarly the Cañcatpuṭa, Cāpapuṭā and Pañcapāṇi have three varieties. There are five kinds of Tālas besides Tryaśra and Caturaśra types. They are termed Udghaṭṭaka etc. and are of the Miśra kind and they relate to different limbs of songs. The mixed Talās etc. may consist of five, seven, nine, ten or eleven Kalās. They are called Saṅkīrṇas.

They are not of any particular use in the seven kinds of songs and in the Dhruvas. The singers should use them in the Pravṛtta etc. I am speaking factually. The Dhruvas have the Catura-Śra and the Tryaśra Tālas consisting of eight and six Tālas respectively.

49—53 The Tāla of eight Kalās—the Niṣkrama through the litter finger, so also the Śamyā through the little finger and the ring finger, the Niṣkrama, the Tāla and the Śamyā through the middle finger, while the Niṣkrama and the Sannipāta through the forefinger. This is the method of showing Kalā and through fingers in the Caturaśra Tāla. The Tāla of the six Kalās will be like thus—through the little fingers the Niṣ-krama, the Śamyā, the Tāla, and the Śamyā, through the forefinger, the Śamyā and the Sannipāta are to be shown. This is the method of showing Kalās in a Tryaśra Tāla. The following is the rule regarding the Tāla of four Kalās in terms of Āvāpa and Vikṣepa shown through fingers as follows. Through the little finger the Niṣkrāma and the Praveśa; through the little and the ring fingers the Tāla and the Śamyā through the middle finger the Niṣkrāma and the Tāla through the little finger the Praveśa, through the forefinger the Niṣkrāma and the Sannipāta.

59—61 The Pādabhāgas consisting of two or four Kalās have been described. The four Pādabhāgas are called Mātrās. These are the different varieties of the Cañcatpuṭa, the Cāpapuṭa and the Pañcapāni Tālas. Thus I have described in brief the Tālas related to the Āsārita and the Vardhamāna and to the body of other songs.

62—66 *The Āsārita.* The characteristics of the Āsārita are being mentioned. The person who knows the technique of production first takes up the Cañcatpuṭa with its long, short and Pluta syllables another the twofold Pañcapāṇi. In the preceding Tāla he puts the syllables as indicated by the latter. Thus we get the same Pāta viz. Tāla, Śamyā, Tāla.

In the first syllable of Pañcapāṇi one should put in Sanni-pāta, then Tāla, Śamyā and Tāla. In the second syllable also this is the rule in the Pañcapāṇi. The Sannipāta is to occur in case of the final Pluta. This is the short Yathākṣara Āsārita. Understand the distribution of Pāta as described in the name of thc Tālas. Cañ indicates Śamyā, Cat the second indicates Tāla; the "Pu" indicates Śamyā and the Ṭa the Tāla. Thus one should know the Cañcatpuṭa and the Pañcapāṇi thereafter.

69—70 Ṣaṭ indicates Sannipāta, "Pi" the Tā' Śamyā Pu— the Tāla, the "Tra" the Śamyā and "Ka" the Tāla. The same will hold good in case of the second and then ones Sannipāta.

71—73 *Madhyama and Jyeṣṭha Āsārita.* On combining here the long syllables the short Āsārita will come Madhyama Āsārita. The Kalā that will follow the doubling of the combined long syllables should be applied in due order as before. The Madhyama Āsārita when doubled as called Jyeṣṭha Āsārita. Their Vastu is charactered by the Sannipāta and Nipāta.

74—75 *Layāntarita*. The characteristics of Layāntarita. It is that which has the shortest Tāla. The Kalā effected in another period of time becomes Kalāntara (different Kalā). The application of these Tālas gives special success and in the Layāntarita there occurs a difference there in words and the tempo (Laya).

76—82 *Vardhamāna*. A combination of the Āsāritas is called the Vardhamāna. After lulling the beautiful chance called the Tāṇḍava. The noble souled Bhūtas at that time created Vardhamāna embellished with the Piṇḍībandhas (group-dances?) On seeing this along with his wife, Siva was much pleased. Maheśvara and the goddess gave them the excellent boon. Those who perform the Vardhamāṇa dance as defined by him according to the traditional rules and order will attain the proximity of Śiva. This was witnessed by me for the sake of the Piṇḍībandhas. Listen, O Brahmins to the characteristics. If the Vardhamāna is performed in the three Mārgas viz Vṛtti, Dakṣiṇa and Citra it is to be constructed according to its own measure. Then it shall be of two kinds.

83—88 Its measure has two aspects with Tāla and without it. In all the Āsāritas there should be four Kaṇḍikās (Parts). The Kaṇḍikās are evolved by the gods through Dhruva composed of Kalās. The Mārgas are available in the Vardhamāna. The first group is made up of nine Kalās the second of eight

Kalās the third of sixteen Kalās and the fourth of thirty two Kalās. Thus in the Vardhamāna each part is made of fixed number of Kaḷās. It arises from proper Mārgas and is devoid of Laya and its minor or limbs. The Kaṇḍikās are made up of one, two, three and four Kaḷās and by them are made the proper Mārga and the limbs of the Tālas.

89–92 *Kaniṣṭha Āsārita*. The short Āsārita has the second half deficient in one Kalā. It is to be made up after finishing the first part combined with Bālatāla (short Tāla). If after completing the second part one adds to the first part in all its Kalās in the previous Tāla it becomes Layantarita in the Vardhamāna which should be performed any in the Citra-Mārga and not with the Vṛtti.

There is no Kaniṣṭha Āsārita in the Dakṣinṇa Mārga whether in the Vardhamāna or outside it. From the short Tāla (Bālatālə) the Layāntarita proceeds when it doubles the syllables and applies other Mārgas and regulates the time of dance.

93–98 *Madhyama-Āsārita & Jyeṣṭha Āsārita*. The Tāla I have prescribed in the case of Kaniṣṭha Āsārita is to be completaly observed in the first two parts. The third, second and first will have the Madhyama Āsārita. If the fourth part is made the first i.e. the parts are taken in an inverted order and all the four parts have an addition of four Kalās to them it is called the Jyeṣṭha Āsārita. When their application is taken in connection with the Piṇḍī Bandhas, then each of their limbs is to be made distinct. Mukha, Pratimukhadeha and Saṁharaṇa are the four Aṅgas (limbs) in all the Āsāritas. The Upohana is the Mukha; the Yugma is the Pratimukha, the Ojas in the Śarīra and the Saṁharaṇa. This the serial order of the Aṅgas and hence the Āsāritas consist of four limbs.

99—101 *Vardhamānaka*. A song composed of the four Āsāritas is called the Vardhamānaka. It is so called because of the gradual increase in it of the Varṇa (syllable), Tāla, Laya, instrumantal music and gestures which lead to the embellishment of the performance of the dancers. The body of the Vardhamāna and the Āsārita being mutually related as result and reason constitute each other. Just as the seed grows from the tree and the tree in its turn from the seed here too the same law of mutual causal connection is applicable.

102 *Layāntarita.* One Kalā being added to the Kaniṣṭha Āsārita it gives rise to Layāntarita and two Kalās being added it becomes the Madhyama Āsārita and four Kalās being added it becomes the Jyeṣṭha Āsārita.

103—109 The rule of the Pāta for the Kaniṣṭha Āsārita is as follows:—Śamyā, Tāla, Śamyā Tāla, Sannipāta, Tāla, Śamyā Talā (i.e. two Pañcapāṇis beginning with Śamyā). This is the scheme of Tāla in the Layāntarita and its characteristic growth has been mentioned before and these will be here a difference of words and Laya (tempo). This in the Pāta Vidhāna (scheme of falling) in Madhyama Āsārita, three Kalās at the beginning are to be acheived. In the Jyeṣṭha Āsārita these shall invariably be Mātrā of four Kalās. Those who have the Kaniṣṭha Āsārita consisting of nine Kalās are not approved of by the good authorities. The placing of the Sannipāta therein has been made according to the rule of the Kalā. For them the two Tālas at the Mukha of the Kaniṣṭha Āsārita are regulated by the Dhruva Pāta. I shall now explain the full Māna (measure) and the sequance of Guru and Laghu Varṇas. The Mukhas of the Jyeṣṭha Āsārita will respectively consist of eights, seven, six and five Kalās.

110—113 In the Upavahanas of the Āsārita of all kinds Āsāraṇas to be employed are of eight syllables, two long four short two long, [this is for the Kaniṣṭha]. Of twelve syllables—two long eight short two long [this is for the Layāntarita]. Of sixteen syllables two long, twelve short, two long [this is for the Madhyam Āsārita] and of twenty syllables, two long, sixteen short two long [this is for the Jyeṣtha Āsārita]. I shall now mention those syllables formerly sung by Brahmā. [The example thus cited is corrupt text in the Mss. & printed Books]. This rule of Upavahana has been prescribed in the case of the Mukhas of the Āsāritas in as much as they depend on the arrangement of syllables in Kalās and in the sequance of their being Guru or Laghu. Thus I have explained the extent and measurement of the Upavahana. In the Caturaśra there are four Gaṇas and in the Tryaśra there are six Gaṇas.

114—116 *Examples for Madhyama and Kaniṣṭha Āsāritas.* In the Pañcapāṇi and the Cāpapuṭa their number shall be six and a half. Translation of the example beginning with Devam Devaih etc. I have come to take refuge in Hara the terrible one, the benifactor of the three worlds who is worshipped as the lord God by the Devas and to whose feet the Daityas and Yakṣas low down. In the Cañcatpuṭa there shall be eight regular Gaṇas. In the Ṣaṭpitāputraka the Gaṇas should be twelve and in the third part of the Vastu there should be thirteen and half Gaṇas. This is the arrangement of syllables in the Madhyama Āsārita [Translation of the Example beginning with Bhūtādhipatim Bhaganetra Haranam, etc etc]. I have come to take refuge in Maheśvara the bestower of boons, the lord of the creatures, who removed the eyes of Bhaga, who is worthy of being adorned by the Deva, who destroys the sacrifice of the Suras, who is terrible and fearful, who is clad in the hide of an elaphant, who is the source of bliss, who is three-eyed, who wears matted hairs shining like fire who has serpants as his girdles, who is surrounded by the Devas, whose exploits are always recited by the Daityas, who is loved to by the lord of the immortal ones who bestows pleasures of our own choice, who is terrible and yellow, who dwells in the cremation ground and whose beautiful matted hairs are drenched by the waters of the Gaṅgā.

117—118 *Jyeṣṭha Āsārita.* At the outset there shall be the Cañcatpuṭa Tāla of sixteen Gaṇas, next the Cāpapuṭa Tāla of twentyfour Gaṇas and in the third there should be twenty four and half Gaṇas. This is the arrangement of syllables in the Jyeṣṭha Āsārita. [Translation of the example beginning with Amara Pravaram Madanāṅga Haram etc. etc.] I bow down to that lord the foremost among the immortal ones, the destroyer of the limbs of Madana, the sole lord of the Universe, the bestower of freedom from fear and the destroyer of the three Puras. I always make my obeisance to the lord whose feet are bowed down to by the Suras, Pitṛs, and the groups of Sages, whose creations have bean mentioned by the sages as eight in number named-Earth, Water. Fire, Air the other the master of Yajñas, the sun and the moon, who is the preceptor of the three worlds, who is beyond comprehension, who is unborn who is the abode of all lores, who is terrible in form, who holds

Khaṭvāṅga (skull topped club, the cause of sustenance, creation and annihilation, who is subtle-visioned, who is unthinkable, who holds half crescent, half Tilaka, half an eye, half the breasts, half the beloved and who is surrounded by various awful shaven headed ugly and strange Pramathas.

119—122 The three varieties of Āsārita have been described viz. Yathākṣara (literal), Dvisaṅkhyāta (doubled in number) and Trisaṁkhyāta (tripled in number). Gaṇas of equal Varṇas constitute the Yathākṣara Āsārita, doubled in the observance of the Tālas without the repetition of the syllables. This Yathākṣara Āsārita is called Dvisaṁkhyāta when it is repeated once and is called Trisaṁkhyāta when repeated twice. In the Tāla of the Āsārita songs one should make its Kalā of four etc. consist of Gaṇas made up of four Mātrās, their long and short syllables being as prescribed before.

123—128 Four Mātrās in Akṣaras amount to two Mātrās in Varṇas. The Kalās in the Vṛtti Mārga will be twice that in the Citra Mārga. Hence that Kalā which is of four Mātrās in the measure of Varṇa in the Vṛtti Mārga will be doubled in the Dakṣiṇa Mārga. In regard to the syllables indicated by the name of the Tālas no change of Mārga is available. It is only due to doubling the Mātrā that the variation of Varṇas has been described. This is mostly the rule relating to the Varṇa and the Tāla in Āsārita songs of the literal class [Yathākṣara]. In the Dvisaṁkhyāta Āsārita the repetition should be made by adding half a Gaṇa to the Yathāksara and in the Trisaṁkhyāta Āsārita the double one should be augmented by half a Gaṇa. The double Āsārita should not be performed in the Citra Mārga and the triple one in the Vārtika Mārga.

129—135 The Trisaṁkhyāta Āsārita should be in the Dakṣiṇa Mārga, the Dvisaṁkhāta in the Vārtika Mārga and the Yathākṣara in the Citra Mārga. This is the fixed rule relating to Mārgas. The rule of observing the Mārga in the Trisamkhyāta is, that it should begin in the Dakṣiṇa and in repetition the Vṛtti and the Citra are to be adopted serially. The double Āsārita is desired a according to this principle. Its performance may be in the Vṛtti or Dakṣiṇa Mārga. After considering the relative strength of the different limbs of a Vastu the expert musician should observe the repetition at its beginning, middle or conclusion. When there is a deficiency of a Kalā due to the composition of the Vastu, the singer should prolong the Varṇa till the Kalā is completed. The needs for repetition are as follows :—enrichment of the Varṇas and the Alaṁkāras rest for the producing organs and the application of the Tattva etc. Thus I have explained the mutual connection between the Varṇas, Tālas and Syllables in the course of performing the Āsārita and the Vardhamāna.

136—141 *Four Kaṇḍikās of the Vardhamāna.* There are four Kaṇḍikās or limbs in the Vardhamāna song namely Viśālā, Saṅgadā, Sunandā and Sumukhī. The first one consists of nine Kalās, the second of eight, the third of sixteen and the last of thirty two Kalās. The Upohana of the Viśālā consists of five Kalās that of Saṅgatā of six Kalās, that of Sunandā of seven Kalās; the Upohanā of the Sumukhī is always eight Kalās. I shall now speak of the sequence of their long and short syllables. In the Upohana of the Viśālā there should be two long syllables first, then fourteen short ones and finally a long syllable—Ex.—"Ṛm Dum Jagati Avalitaka Digini Kucakṛtatiti Cā". The sages have said that in order to make the Upohana of the Saṁgatā four more short syllables and three long ones should be added to the Upohona of the Viśālā *Example* "Jhaṇṭum Jagati Yavalitaka Digi Nigiti Tijhalatitivā".

142—145 The learned should note that in order to form the Upohana of the Sunandā four more short syllables and three long syllables should be added to that of Saṁgatā. Ex. Ṛm Dum Jagatiavalitaka Digiti Ṛla Kucala Titi Vā. In regard to the Upohana of the Sumukhi it should be known that it consists of twenty eight short and three long syllables Ex. Ṛm Dum Jagati Avalitaka Digi Vigititi Ṛla Ṛca Kulatiti Jagatiti Vā. *Definition of Upohana.* Since the notes in a song are carried forward from this (i.e. Upohana), since Songs proceed from this and since this consists of Śuṣkākṣaras (Meaningless letters) it is called Upohana. *Another definition.* Because a performance is carried forward by means of acts beginning with Sūcanā, this song that depends on musical instruments is called Upohana.

146—150 The Tāla of the Upohana in Viśāla is as follows Śamyā, Tāla, Śamyā, Tāla, Sannipāta. The Tāla in that of the Saṁgatā is the Cañcatpuṭa of two Kalās and this in its Tālādi variety proceded by the Tāla of three Kalās (Udghaṭṭa) will be the Tāla of the Upohana of the Sunandā. The Tāla of the Sumukhi will be the Cañcatpuṭa of two Kalās. Upohanas twice repeated in each case will make up the Kaṇḍikā. Thus I have explained the four Upohanas. Now understand the performance of the limbs (Kaṇḍikās) from the beginning. The Tāla of the Viśālā is as follows—Tāla, Śamyā, Tāla and Sannipāta of three Kalās.

151—156 The Tāla of the Saṁgatā is Cañcatpuṭa of two Kalās and that of the Sunandā is the same of the four Kalās. The Tāla of the Sumukhī should be the double Cañcatpuṭa of four Kalās together with two Sannipātas. I have thus spoken of the Tālas in the separate Kaṇḍikās of the Vardhamāna songs. Now understand their collective usage. First the Viśālā is produced with the shortest *Tāla*. The Tāla which has its end consisting of the three Kalās is the short Āsārita. When after making the Graha of the Saṁgatā, Viśālā is applied in all its Kalās and is coupled with the previous Tāla it is Layāntarita. Then one should perform the Sunandā and again the Saṁgatā and again Visālā and next the Sumukhī.

157—161 The Tāla that has been mentioned in the Kaniṣṭha Āsārita is wholly to be applied first at the beginning of the Kaṇḍika. Then after taking up the Graha of Sunandā one should perform Sunandā, Saṁgatā and Viśālā. The Tāla that has been prescribed by me in the case of the Madhyama Āsārita should be observed in the three Śamyās in case of the Sunandā and what follows Sumukhī, Sunandā and Saṁgatā should be performed and they should be performed and they should be applied beginning from the Sumukhī etc. Further, the conclusion and the repetitions of Viśālā should be known. The Tāla in the Jyeṣṭha Āsārita is either Niḥśabda or Śabdavān.

162—165 The same should be performed in till the Kaṇḍikās. Four Tālas are prescribed in the combination of these limbs wherefrom the Vardhamāna is made. The Pāla Āsārita consists of nine Kalās; the Layāntarita of seventeen Kalās, the Jyeṣṭha of sixty five Kalaās and the Madhyama of thirty three Kalās. This is the rule about the Tāla in all the Āsāritas. The Vardhamānakais so called because of a gradual increase of Kalās; thanks to gradual increase of syllables and because of an increase in the tempo in its successive phases. In all the Āsāritas and the Vardhamāna songs the law of the syllables relates to an application of double the usual Tāla.

166—170 When Sannipāta comes at the close without it being terminated the final Kalā should be of two Mātras. This is the characteristic feature of Vardhamāna as described by me. I shall now give a tabular statement of the characteristics of the Āsārita in brief. The wise prescribe the Dhruva Tāla in a Kalā which is not deficient. The remaining and final Tālas should be conforming to the syllables of the Tālas (names of the Tālas). There is no equality in Pluta (Sāmya) and the short syllable. This Samatva is prescribed through three Pātas. The Kaniṣṭha, Madhyama and Jyeṣṭha Āsāritas are to be made with Tālas viz. Sannipātas, Śamyās and Dhruvas.

171—176 By doubling afterwards the Kalās of this Kaniṣṭha Āsārita, the Madhyama Āsārita should be made as it consists of Śamyā in the intervals of Tālas. There should be Saṭpitāputraka Tāla leaving out three Kalās in the first Vastu of the Madhyama Āsārita. Further there shall be two complete repetitions. The Pāta of the Madhyama Āsārita is as follows :— Śamyā Tāla of two Kalās, Śamyā of two Kalās, Tāla of a Kalā, Sannipāta of three Kalās Tāla of three Kalās, Tāla of two Kalā, Sannipāta of three Kalās, again. In the third Vastu, Sannipāta of twelve Kalās at the end. The first part of the Madhyama Āsārita should consist of eight Kalās, the second part should consist of twelve Kalās and the third part should consist of twenty four Kalās ending in a Sannipāta.

177—180 The Praveśa, Vikṣepa and Niṣkrāma made with fingers already mentioned before should be observed by those conversant with it. In the Jyeṣṭha Āsārita the sensible artiste makes the body made up of Śamyā and Tāla with proper Laya and also of sixty five Kalās. Therein the Āvāpa, Niṣkrāma, Vikṣepa and Praveśaka of the fingers should consist of groups of four Kalās. The Jyeṣṭha Āsārita should have groups of four Kalās with its Āvāpa, and Vikṣepas and the Vastu in other places should consist of seventeen Kalās beginning with Śamyā.

181--188 The Pāta of this Āsārita may be as follows:— Śamyā and Tāla of four Kalās, Śamyā of four Kalās, Tāla of two Kalās, Sannipāta of six Kalās, Tāla of six Kalās, Śamyā of two Kalās, Tāla of two Kalās and Sannipāta of six Kalās. This is the rule on the whole in regard to the Tālas in the third Sannipāta but at the conclusion. I shall speak of the Aṅgulī Vikṣepa (throwing up gesture with the fingers) (a) With ring finger Āvāpa Śamyā, Niṣkrāma Vikṣepa, Tāla, Āvāpa and Niṣkrāma (b) with the middle finger—Vikṣepa, Śamyā, Āvāpa Tāla, Vikṣepa & Praveśa (c) with the index finger—Āvāpa and Niṣkrāma again Vikṣepa and Sannipāta. These constitute the seventeen Kalās in the first Sannipāta.

189—196 *In the Second Sannipāta*—(a) with the little finger—Āvāpa, and Niṣkrāma (b) with the ring and the little fingers—Vikṣepa, Praveśa, Āvāpa and Tāla (c) with the littlc and ring fingers—Tāla and Vikṣepa (d) with the fore finger—Śamya, Āvāpa and Niṣkrāma, Vikṣepa and Śamyā. These constitute fifteen Kalās (d) winh the forefinger Āvāpa, Tāla, Vikṣepa, Praveśa, Āvāpa Niṣkrāma and Niṣkrāma Vakṣepa, Sannipāta. These will make up twentyfour Kalās.

In the third Sannipāta. This is the rule in the third Sannipāta. Thisis the arrangement of fingers in showing the Tāla in the Jyeṣṭha Āsārita.. Sixteen Kalās in the first Sannipāta, twenty four in the second and one more (i.e. twentyfive) in the third Sannipāta. In each of these there would be ten or seven groups made of Śamyā Tāla and Sannipāta.

197—204 In the first Vastu of the Kaniṣṭha and Madhyama Āsāritas the other two should be applied as prescribed before. The three Vastus in them will consist of six Śamyās, eight Tālas and three Sannipātas. The Āsārita consists of seventeen Pātas (Kalās), Eight Tālas. six Śamyās and three Sannipātas are to be known as used in each of the Āsāritas. This is the description of the Āsāritas. I shall consider the application of the uses of the Vastus of songs. Thereafter I shall speak about the characteristics of songs. In the Vastus bodies of the songs there are limbs such as Vivadha, Ekaka and Vṛtta. In the Ekaka there is one Vidārī in the Vivadha there are two Vidārīs and in the Vṛtta not less than three and not more than six. Vidārī is that which consists of Padas or Varṇas, concluding there in Vastu is that which concludes in the Nyāsa, Apanyāsa and Amśa. Vidārī is so called because it splits the Padas and the Svaras in the middle. It imitates the long syllable.

205—209 The Vivadha and Ekaka are generally used in the Madraka songs, in each half Vastu of the Prakarī and in each quarter of the Rovindaka Bahirgītas and Lāsya it is the Vṛtta that is used. The Vṛtta is of two kinds viz Pravṛtta and Avagāḍha is in the ascending scale and the Pravṛtta in the descending scale. The Ārohaṇa (Ascending) as well as Avarohaṇa (descending) is of two kinds (1) that which is prescribed in connection with the Nyāsa and the Apanyāsa and (2) that which is made in the Antara Mārga. Vidārīs in a song are atleast three and at the most even usually. In rare cases the highest number may be twenty four.

210—214 In the case of the Ullopyaka and the Vaihāyasa, the number of Vidārīs will be half as much more in the third Sannipāta. They are to be performed there with the Vivadha or the two fold Vṛtta and the Aṅga will not come to a close in a half of the Sannipāta. The Vivadha said to have been of three kinds namely Sāmudga, Ardhasāmudga and Vivṛtta. The Vivadha is always found ending the Nyāsa note except in the case of the Geyaka, in the beginning of the Madraka the Sāmudga has been prescribed. The Geyaka in the Sāmudga should be in short syllables. It is called Geyaka because it is placed in the end of the third Vidārī.

215—219 While in application if one half of a Vidārī is similar to one half of another Vidārī, the other half is dissimilar to the remaining half of it it is called Ardhasāmudga. The Vidārī is uneven is the Nyāsa and the Apanyāsa and its copious use is called the Vivṛtta. The Vivadha, Ekaka and Vṛtta are respectively to end in the Nyāsa the Apanyāsa and the Aṁśa notes. The Sanyāsa and the Vinyāsa notes occur in the middle of the Aṅga and the Vinyāsa is known to occur in the middle of the Vidārī. The Vinyāsa may rarely be at the end of a word in a Vidārī but too much of it has not been prescribed by the experts.

220 *Seven types of Gīta.* They are Madraka, Ullopyaka, Aparāntaka, Prakarī, Oveṇaka, Rovindaka and Uttara.

221 *Madraka.* Madraka is of two kinds, one with four Vastus and the other with three Vastus. One with three Vastus includes a Śirṣaka.

222 *Aparāntaka.* There should be five, six or seven

Śīrṣakas in the Aparāntaka. *Prakarī* they should be four and three and a half (seven and a half in all).

223 *Rovindaka*. This consists of seven limbs in the minimum and sixteen limbs in the maximum. Ekkakas in them should consist of two consecutive Pādas consisting of equal Varṇas.

224 One is to apply in the beginning the Pravṛtta and Vivadha and then the body and the limbs are to be placed in their proper position.

225 The syllable (a) Ākāra should occur in its middle and in the end too the same. A clear Śīrṣaka should come in its end.

226—230 *Oveṇaka*. The Oveṇaka is known to be consisting of seven or twelve limbs. The seven limbed one may also be called Dvyaṅga and the twelve-limbed one Tryaṅga. The twelve lambs (Aṅgas) of the Oveṇaka are Pāda, Sandhi, Māsaghāta, Vajra, Sampiṣṭaka, Śīrṣaka, Caturaśra, Upavartana, Upapāta two Praveṇīs, and Saṁharaṇa. When Sampiṣṭaka, Upapāta, two Praveṇīs and Upavartana are left out from among the twelve limbs the Ovenaka is called a seven-limbed one [Saptāṅga]. The seven limbs common to the both Oveṇakas having similar Varṇas and Padas are called Vivartana. In the twelve limbed Oveṇaka Padas in other limbs are to be different.

231—234 *Ullopyaka*. The rule about the limbs of the Ullopyaka is this. Its three limbs are Avagāḍha, Pravṛtta and Mahājanika. It becomes Dvyaṅga when Mahājanika is left out. When Sthita is combined with Pravṛtta the Ullopyaka is called one-limbed and the Mahājanika also may constitute the one-limbed Ullopyaka. The Sthita and Pravṛttaka may constitute a two limbed Ullopyaka or a one limbed one separately. In the two limbed Ullopyaka the rule of the Dhruvās and the Dhātus.

235—240 The Two limbed Ullopyaka will exclude the Mahājanika and it alone will constitute the single-limbed Ullopyaka. These are separately and in combination. This is the rule regarding the Aṅgas. There shall be three types viz. Caturaśra, Tryaśra and Miśra. The Saṁhāra of the Oveṇaka is made up of two limbs or one. This should not be used at the beginning or in the middle. The Ekaka or the Vivadha should always be used in the end and the Ullopyaka should not have less than six and more than twenty limbs. Of these limbs the Saṁharaṇa will have the Mukha and the Pratimukha (as its two parts and it may be with the Vaihāyasaka or without it. It will not have less than three and more than twelve limbs, Vaihāyasaka will consist even of one limb and not more than six limbs.

241—244 The sponsors should proceed with the performance after the three Aṅgas (limbs) are over. The limbs Mukha and Pratimukha have been prescribed for the Ullopyaka and the Uttara. Then the other limbs may be compressed or extended. The Mukha and the Pratimukha are to be known as the Vivadha. The Vṛtta occurs in the Pratimukha and may shortly be in other limbs as well and the Sākhā in the Ullopyaka, the Uttara and the Aparāntaka as well as the Pratiśakha will have kinds of Varṇas and Padas as the Mukha and the Pratimukha have.

245—246 *The Uttara.* The Uttara will not have less than six and more then twelve limbs. Its Sīrṣaka should specially be placed at the end along with Rovindaka without "Ā" (Ākāra). This is the rule of limbs to be observed in the case of the songs of the seven forms. Henceforth I shall speak of the measurement of Vastus in the songs.

247—250 *Madraka.* In all the Vastus, the Kalās should consist of sixteen Mātrās. Each quarter of it is a Pādabhāga. In the beginning there should be eight long syllables. Then the next eight should be short. Upavahana is made in the two long Mātrās in the beginning. The third is long to facilitate Pratyupohana. In the fourth and the fifth long syllables there should be two Śāmyās. The sixth and the seventh will be Tāla and then the eighth will be Śamyā. All these are in the long syllables. Then a Pāda of eight Kalās is to be made with short syllables.

251—256 In the Tālas of long syllables Pādas will consists of one entire Kalā. The Patakalā will be as follows:—Śamyā Tāla, Tāla, Śamyā, Tāla and Sannipāta. Thus the Śīrṣaka is to be constructed with the Cañcatpuṭa and this will be the system of Tālas of are Lalā in the Madraka song. When Guru syllables are separated in a Pāda they will be considered as consisting of two Kalās. After separating them the Kalās are to be arranged as previously. In the Madraka of two Kalās, the Upohana will consist of three Kalās and the Pratyupohana of one or two Kalās. Four Kalās make one Mātrā and the Vastu will consist of three Mātrās. Each of these three Vastus will consist of two Kalā. This is the rule of Pāda in the Pāta.

257—259 The Pātas such as Śamyā Tāla etc. which have been prescribed in the case of Guru syllables should be used in the Pādabhāga of two Kalās. The eighth, the tenth and the sixteenth will have Śamyā and in the twelfth and fourteenth there shall be Tāla. The rule of Pāta in the case of eight Laghu syllables has been mentioned before. In three Vastus of two Kalās too, these Pātas should be applied. The Śīrṣaka of six Kalās should be made with Pañcapāṇi.

Translation of Example : I seek shelter in Thee, the peaceful lord Śiva whose matted hairs have been tied up with the king of serpents, who is bowed to by the Munis who is constantly engaged meditation, and is full of wisdom; who has destroyed the body of Madana; who is supreme and all powerful, who is adorned by the Daityas and serpents; who is the creator and Lord of the world and is bowed to by all the people. To thee who is praised by the Ṛg and Yajur Veda, who carries Gaṅgā (on the head), the spike in his hand, the lord of Serpents, I bow my head to Thee who art bliss and art clad in the skin of the lord of beasts, whose gait is prodigious and is comparable to that of a bull. Whose tawny matted hairs are like the burning fire. (This portion marks the end of Madraka).

I bend *my head* to Śiva the pure god who removes the afflication of persons bowing to him, who is the container of Māyā and is himself the Māyā in form and who wears matted hairs. (This marks the end of the Madraka of two Kalās).

260—264 I shall now speak properly of the Catuṣkala Madraka which will be characterised in terms of Pādabhāgan of four Kalās. Four Kalās will make one Mātrā and three Mātrās will make one Vastu. In giving the Pādabhāgas I shall speak of the Pāta in due order. In the first Vastu there will be

Śamyā at the end of the fourth, fifth, eighth, tenth and the eleventh Kalās and in the beginning of the ninth Kalā. At the end of the sixth, seventh and ninth and in the beginning of the tenth and seventh there will be Tālas. At the end of the twelfth, first of all there will be Sannipāta. Thus there will be the rule Pāta and thus one should apply all the Vastus.

265—270 In the first Vaṣtu, the eight Kalās in the beginning will constitute the Upohana; and the Pratyupohana in the second Vastu will be of two Kalās. In the third Vastu there will be three Kalās and in the fourth, four Kalās; the Śīrṣaka at its end will be made up of Ṣaṭpitāputraka. In the Vastu of two Kalās there should apply a time-measure consisting of four Yathākṣara Pañcapāṇi and in the third and the fourth Vastu there should be Dvigeyaka in due order. In the fourth Vastu the Parivarta should come to an end. In the first and the second Vastus there shall be Upohana and parts of the Madraka. They will include three Vastus of three different lengths arising out of the Tryaśra Tāla. The double of a Vastu of two Kalās will make up a Vastu of four Kalās. In it the seventh and final syllables will be Laghu and the doubling has been prescribed here. So the four Kalās are regular here and the Upohana will then consist of eight Kalās and the Praiyupohana will consist of one, two or four Kalās.

271—273 Śīrṣaka of the ordinary Madraka should be in Yathākṣara Pañcapāṇi. This Pañcapāṇi will consist of four Kalās in the Madraka of four Kalās and of two Kalās in the Dvikala Madraka. It will consist of three Vastus of different measures and these measures will arise from the Tryaśra Tāla. Thus the Madraka will have thirteen Pātas.

274—280 *The Aparāntaka.* It will have four Guru Syllables. In the second syllable which is Guru there will be Śamyā and in the third it will be Tāla. In the third and the fourth there will be Śamyā and Tāla for the Laghu syllables and Tāla, Śamyā two Tālas and Sannipāta are to be applied to these and in the Laghu syllables there will be Pātas consisting of eight Kalās. The Aparāntaka is to be known as originating in the Tryaśra Talā represented by Tāla, Śamyā, Tāla and Sannipāta. After separating the Guru (long) syllables one should apply the Tālas of two Kalās. These Tālas of two Kalās and of four

Kalās are to be represented by six Pādabhāgas as follows:—Śamyā, Tāla, two Tālas, Śamyā and Tāla. Arrangement of the Pāta will be as before. in the case of the fifth and the sixth Kalā. The Tāla of four Kalās includes Āvāpa and Vikṣepa. It is furnished with the Pādabhāgas of four or six Kalās. Vastus five six or seven in number should be applied here. In the end of the second and fifth Kalās there should be two Śamyās.

281—285 In the end of the third, the second and the fifth and at the beginning of the sixth there should be Tāla and then the Sannipāta should be at the end. There are Pātas relating to the previous Vastus in case of the Aparāntaka of four Kalās. This is the application of Tālas in the Aparāntaka of four Kalās. This is to be known as the Aparāntaka in the Pātas of Yathākṣara Tālas. In the beginning, the Upavahanas of the Kalā will be doubled due to Viśleṣa. In the Aparāntaka of two Kalās the Upahana consists of one or two Kalās and similarly in the Aparāntaka of one Kalā the Upohana will be of one Kalā. The being doubled is to be known as the Aparāntaka of four Kalās. In this third Aparāntaka of Laghu syllables the last Kalā will be doubled.

286—288 This is the Aparāntaka in which the Vastu arising from the Tryaśra Tāla represented with six Kalās is called Śākhā. Its Pratiśākhā is similar to its Śākhā. It is like its latter half and consists of different words. Its Śīrṣaka is to be made with the Pañcapāṇi of one Kalā.

289—292 In the course of the performance of four Vastus it should apply the Nivṛtta in the Vṛttimārga. The following is the special rule. Then there will be two Tālikās of six Kalāpātas. By means of the Yathākṣara Pañcapāṇi one Kalā, there will be an Upavartana of these two. The Upohana of the Aparāntaka of four Kalās will consist of half the number of Kalās in the Vastu and its Pratyupohana will be of two Kalās. The Aparāntaka of two Kalās is to be performed in the Dakṣiṇa Mārga and that of four Kalās in the Vṛtti Mārga. And in the case of the remaining ones there shall be no Upohaṇa here. This is the time measure prescribed by me for the Aparāntaka.

Ullopyaka. The Vastu of the Ullopyaka will consist of two Guru syllable two short syllables and a long syllable.

293—297 Its Kalās will be as follows :—Samyā, Tāla, Śamyā, Tāla and Sannipāta. These represent the five Pātas indicated by the syllables of the Yathākṣara Caturasra Tāla. According to the rules mentioned before the Ullopyaka shall be of two and of four Kalās. After its three limbs have been sung the Vaihā Yasika is desired. It shall not be less than one Aṅga nor more than twelve Aṅgas. There shall be twelve Kalās or seven Pātas—Śamyā of two Kalās, Tāla of two Kalās, the Śamyā, Tāla and Sannipāta, each of one Kalā one after another. This is the Śākhā the Pratiśakhā will consist of different words.

298—301 When this is nearby the Antā Haraṇa takes place. The Saṁhārya is regularly to be made of the Yathākṣara Pañcapāṇi. The Saṁhāra of that which does not come to a close is to be carried on in its own Tāla. The Nivṛtta of two kinds consists of three Aṁśas and are again of three kinds. The three kinds of Nivṛtta are Tryaśra, Caturaśra and mixed. The three Aṅgas there of are Sthita, Pravṛtta and Mahājanika. There shall be Antāharaṇa with the Pañcapāṇi Tāla and similarly Sthita with the Yugma Tāla. Its rule of Pāta shall be as follows :—

302—306 Śamyā of two Kalās, Tāla of two Kalās, Sannipāta of four Kalās. Then comes Pravṛtta. It has Śamyās of two Kalās, Tāla of one Kalā, Cañcatpuṭa of Talādi class and Sannipāta. Mahājanika should be performed with the Sthita, Tāla and the Nivṛtta should truely be in the Vivṛtta Tāla. Of Sthita and Mahājanika these should be mostly Upavartana and before it Udghaṭṭaka and Parivartaka should be performed. Yugma is a mixed Tāla. Hence it should be applied in the Anta Tāla Vivadha with Ekaka is the entire rule in Anta Tāla.

307—310 In this way I have duly described the Anta Tāla which is Yugma as well as mixed. Now for the Tryaśra Tāla which is Śamyā of two Kalās, Tāla, Sannipāta of three Kalās. Then comes Pravṛtta. Here Pravṛtta should be made into Parivartana with Yathākṣara Pañcapāṇi. Its Mahājanika should be in the Sthita Tāla and Nivṛtta Tāla should be observed in its Anta Nivartana.

311—314 Mixed Tāla is a combination of Yugma and Ojaḥ Tālas. So it should be the Antaḥ Pravartana. Vivadha with Ekaka is the entire rule of Anta Tāla. Sthita should briefly be made up of two limbs or one. That with Yugma Tāla should be of two limbs or one. That with Yugma Tāla should be of two limbs and that with Trysaśra of one limb Pravṛtta also will be of one limb with Saṁharaṇa of two limbs. In the Ullopya this is the Anta beginning from Sthita and ending with Pravṛtta.

315--322 *The Prakarī.* The Vastu of the Prakarī consists of six Mātrās and nineteen Pātas and it should be of four Kalās in length. There is no Yathākṣara Tāla or Tāla of two Kalās. After the initial three Mātrās there shall be Śamyā and Tāla. Then the Vastu should be serially made of Pātas consisting of six Mātrās. The Upohana will be in the first half of the Vastu. Its second Mātrā will be Śamyā with Tāla and Śamyā again will be at the end of the three Mātrās. In the fourth Mātrā there should be Twelve Tālas and in the fifth eight Tālas. In the sixth there should be Śamyā of two Kalās and Śamyā, Tāla, Tāla, Śamyā and Tāla, Śamyā, Tāla and Sannipātta. When four and a half Vastu's constitute the Prakarī it will be the latter half of the Pada and its half should be placed before. Its Saṁharaṇa should be made with Kaniṣtha Āsārita.

323—328 *The Ovenaka.* The first Pāda of the Oveṇaka is to be made equal to that of the Śākhā of the Aparāntaka and its second Pāda is to be made equal to that of its Pratiśākhā. The same will be its Pāta Kalā and Māṣaghāta afterwards. The rule of its Pāta will be six Pātas of twelve Kalās viz.—Śamyā of two Kalās, Tāla of two Kalās, Tāla of two Kalās Śamyā of two Kalās, Tāla of one Kalā, Sannipāta of three Kalās and its Māṣa Ghāta generally will be a limb of Vivadha. At its end should be Sandhi and sometimes Upavartana and its Ogha will be made up of Pañcapāṇi of one Kalā and the Sandhi should be made of Yathākṣara Pañcapāṇi and Ekaka Vivadha are its limbs.

329—333 As in the case of Upavartana its rule is different. The rule which is applicable at the beginning of the final Caturaśra is to be wished as the Caturaśraka according to the same limb of Vivadha. The Saṁpiṣṭaka will be of two kinds—

Sandhivat and Vajratāla. They will consist respectively of seven limbs of twelve Kalās and of twelve limbs of ten Kalās. One should use here Niṣkrāma, three Śamyās, three Tālas and a Śamyā and a Tāla, a Śamyā and Tāla, then a Sannipāta. This is the Sampiṣṭaka in the Oveṇaka of seven limbs.

334—338 After adding two Śamyās and a Tāla to it thus should be made into Saṁpiṣṭaka of twelve limbs. Nine or eleven Pātas are called Saṁpiṣṭaka and the Upavartana is to be applied like Vajra. Combined with Vivadha and Vṛtta the Praveṇī is of two kinds. The application of the Praveṇī should be made the Yathākṣara Pañcapāṇi and it should consist of two Kalās or mixed Kalās according to the limbs and some times Upavartana should be made at its end and the same should be according to the prescribed use of the Pañcapāṇi. The second Tāla falling from it is called Apapāta. Its Antāharaṇa should be made in the Vajratāla,

339—343 *The Rovindaka.* In the Rovindaka, there should be six Mātrās with the Pāoabhā Ga of four Kalās. Here the Pāta is desired after the half of the five Matrās viz Tāla Śamyā, Tāla, Śamyā, Tāla, Śamyā. This is the rule of five Mātrā's in due order. Fourteen are the Tālas desired in the Mātrās of the fifth similarly the sixth will have four Kalās as in the Madraka. In the begining there should be Upohana consisting of eight Kalās. Then there should be the Pratyupo Hana of two Kalās. The Pātas should end in a Sannipāta and include Vivadha and Ekaka. In the end its collection of Varṇas will consist of eight Kalās. This is the Tabular view of the first Pāda of the Rovindaka.

344—349 The second Pāda will also have similar Varṇas in its Upohana. Its tabular view should give the Tālas in its body. This should be represented by Pañcapāṇi of two Kalās and its total length shall be twelve Kalās one. In the body of the Rovindaka there should be the Upohana of six Kalās and in its beginning these should be Vivadha and Pravṛtta. It should begin with Āvāpa (? Ākāra ?) and is to consist of four or of three Kalās, according to one's option and joining of limbs is to come afterwards. Its Śīrṣaka should not be of any special kind and it should be made up of Yathākṣara Pañcapāṇi. In its beginning there should be Ekaka and at the end

Pravṛtta. This is the Rovindaka. The Uttara comes thereafter.

350—356 (*The Uttara*) I shall explain Uttara with all its characteristics duly. It should have Mukha and Pratimukha As in the Ullopyaka it should have in the beginning a Mātrā made up of four Kalās and as in the Rovindaka it should use at the beginning a group with Āvāpa (? Ākāra). Its Śākhā shall have not less than six limbs and not more than twelve limbs. The Śākhā has six Pātas consisting of twelve Kalās viz. Tāla of two Kalās, Śamyā of one Kalā, Tāla of two Kalās, Tāla of one Kalā, Sannipāta of three Kalās. The Pratiśākhā will be just like the Śākhā and only it will have a different Pada though it is performed without any speciality it should have some rule at the end. At its end the Śīrṣaka should be observed with the Yathākṣara Pañcapāṇi. The Pratiśākhā should also be performed with the Pañcapāṇi of two Kalās having Pātas mentioned before.

357—360 This is the Tāla of the Dakṣiṇa Mārga in the seven types of songs. The time which is suitable in the Dakṣiṇa Mārga will be used also in the Vārtika Mārga. The same is the case in the Citra Mārga when there is nothing special. This is the rule of time in dance due to Ardhayoga at that time will consist of two Kalās. Similarly in the case of the Rovindaka and of the Ullopyaka as well as of the Madraka. Of the Uttara the second syllable will consist of two Kalās or of four Kalās.

361—364 This is the rule in the bodies of songs and in the remaining case there should be Prakṛti and in the Prakṛti too four Kalās should be used alongwith two Kalās. In the case of the Vārtika Mārga the Ardhayoga in time will consist of groups of four Kalās. The Yoga (combination) of four Kalās available in the Vṛtti Mārga will also occur sometimes in the Dakṣiṇa Mārga. The rule of Tāla in the Dakṣiṇa Mārga mentioned in case of the Mukha and the Upavahana of the Madraka and the Ullopyaka will also be available in the Vṛtti Mārga. In the Citra Mārga whether it is used by itself or alongwith another, both these rules of Kalā have been prescribed. In the Citra the rule about the Śākhās may end in any of the three Mārgas.

365—370 These are the songs of the seven types sung in three Mārgas and they are of two kinds:— Kulaka and Chedyaka. A song of one sentence is Kulaka and that of different sentances is Chedyaka. The songs of seven types are again of three kinds—Niryukta, Padaniryukta and Aniryukta. The Niryukta is that which has Śākhā from outside the body of the song. The Padaniryukta is that which is partially free from such elements, outside the song and the Aniryukta is quite free from such elements. These are the two classes of the songs of seven types. These seven types of songs uttered by Brahmā have come out of the Sāma Veda. Songs and instrumental music performed in the worship of deities bring limitless merit and at the conclusion of all such songs Chedyaka has been prescribed.

371—374 This is the rule of the Ṛk Gāthā and Pāṇikā having forms consisting of two, four, three or nine Caturaśra Tālas. According to this rule ons should prescube Caturaśra and Tryaśra Tālas, The group mentioned before should have one Kalā at its beginning. This Kalā should consist of four Mātrās. The Madraka, the Pāṇikā and the Catuṣpadā songs connected with the praise of a deity should be made up of eight or of six limbs in Tālas of Caturaśra or Tryaśra forms. Such songs with one, two or three limbs are to be made up of four Pādas.

375—380 Caturaśra and Tryaśra forms of Tāla are prescribed separately or jointly in these limbs. This is all about the Tāla of songs of the seven types prescribed by me. Dhruvās are to be known as Caturaśra and Tryaśra. The rules of their Tālas relate briefly to six kinds. Of these the Aḍḍitā and Utthitā are Caturaśra in form consisting of four Sannipātas in the Cañcatpuṭa. At the end of the Supratiṣṭhā there should be Sannipāta. Apakṛṣṭa should be in Tryaśra Tāla depending on Cāpapuṭa. It is combined with four Sannipātas at the end of the Pāda. The Ākāśagraha of all these will be Cañcatpuṭa. Vilambita Dhruvā will be Tryaśra and it will be followed by these two and it is to be joined with the Cañcatpuṭa beginning Niṣkrāma.

381—385 The two Pādas known as the pair, at the end of Pādas in the Sannipāta are to be regularly connected with the

Cañcatpuṭa of two Kalās. Śīrṣakas one to be applied with the Pañcapāṇi i.e. Caturaśra Tāla in two different manners. Along with four Sannipātas quite at the end of the Pāda one should apply two final Mātrās of the Tāla. These two Mātrās in their time are to be made equal to Jhaṁkāras. If there is a Kalā in the Dhruvā, without any excess, an expert in dramatic production should make it of equal Matrās by reduction or prolongation. Alongwith the increase of Varṇas there should be an increase of the form of Tālas. A new Kalā in the syllables of the Niryukta songs will be Jhaṁkāra. This is called Śuṣkakuṭṭana because there is connection with Kalā and Tāla.

386—389 A proper Kalā and Tāla are to be observed in all the Dhruvas. The principal Tāla should be regularly observed in the case of Natkuṭas. In its Kalāpāta it will be in the Cañcatpuṭa Tāla. This Tāla will be Tryaśra in the Khañjaka Dhruvā. The limb will be Ākrīḍita. The limbs which are applied in the Dhruvās are to be made up of eight or six Kalās. This is all about the Tāla prescribed by me.

390—395 *Catuṣpadā.* I shall now speak of rules its at the end of a discussion on the Catuṣpadā. The Tāla of the dance which begins with delicate movements and relates to the erotic (Śṛṇgāra) sentiment and which has been created by the goddess Pārvatī will now be discussed after due description. The song known as Catuṣpadā should be performed by women and it is of two kinds Tryaśra and Caturaśra. The Catuṣpadā will be of three kinds according as it relates to the speech of one, two or many. It abounds in the Śṛṅgāra sentiment. It will again be of three kinds viz. Sthitā, Pravṛttā and Sthitapravṛttā. Its Tāla shall be Niṣkrāma Śamyā, Tāla, Śamyā preceded by Niṣkrāma and followed by Sannipāta. There are twenty eight varieties of Catuṣpadā.

396—402 I shall speak of these varieties in due order, The Catuṣpadā of the Sthitā class will have a quick tempo and that of the Pravṛtta class a slow tempo and the Catuṣpadā or the Sthita Pravṛtta class will have a medium tempo and the Tāla there will be the Cañcatpuṭa as well as the Cāpapuṭa. Their Pātas will be in double Kalās. The varieties of Catuṣpadā are—Bahvakṣarā, Vipulā, Māgadhī, Ardha-Māgadhī,

Samākṣara Padā, Viṣamākṣarā, Ādyantyā Paharaṇā, Anīkinī, Avasānāpaharaṇā, Antāpaharaṇa, Abhyantarāpaharaṇā, Ardhanatkuṭa, Ardhakhañjā, Miśrā, Śīrṣaka, Ekāvasānā Niyatākṣarā and Ardha Pravṛttā. Now listen to their characteristics.

403—410 That song which has its words fully expressed consisting mostly of short syllables is uttered quickly and is sung in quick tempo. It is called Bahvakṣarā. The song which mostly consists of long and prolated syllables and includes short sentences and words and observes successively three different tempos is called Vipulā. It is connected with the practice of delicate dance. The song which observes three tempos and three Yatis and includes three kinds of syllables in equal measure a requires a Talā of thirty one Talā is called Māgadhī. The song which consists of long and short syllables above and observes quick and medium tempos and has half the number of Kalās required for the Māgadhī is called the Ardhamāgadhī. The song that has a regular number of short and long Mātrās in its padas, and its padas, Varṇas tempo and Tāla are regular is called Samākṣarapadā. The song which has an irregular number of syllables and Mātrās and has the feet irregular in number and which observes no regular tempo and Tāla is called Viṣamākṣarapadā. That song which requires the final Sannipāta and the final Anusvāra is called Ādyantāpaharaṇā made of Anusvāra. The song which has in its middle, beginning and end, syllables with Anusvāra and the remaining Pādas are without any such restriction is called Anīkinī. The song with no fixed number of syllables in its Pādas is always called Avasānāpaharaṇā.

411—418 A song that has an Anusvāra and is quick in tempo is called Antāpaharaṇa. The song which has its second Kalā in Sannipāta and has syllables in its middle is called Abhyantarāpaharaṇa with Anusvāras. The song which is divided into halves is called Ardhanatkuṭa. When followed by Tryaśra Tāla it is called Ardhakhañja. When in a song the Khañja and the Natkuṭa have been mixed up and it is sung in the Tryaśra or the Caturaśra Tāla it is called Miśra. The song of which the half is suddenly commenced and finished and is adorned with Śirṣa is called the Śīrṣaka. The Catuṣpadā song, of which one Pāda ends with help of the Varṇas is called

Ekāvasāna. It should have only long short syllables in the previous Pāda. The Eka Pādāvasāna song which is furnished with a Śīrṣaka in each of its Pāda is called the Niyatākṣara. The song in which the Sthitā or Pravṛttā is half applied is called Ardhapravṛttā and it is created by both of these two. The Grāhana Tāla in the Catuṣpadā Niṣkrāma, Śamyā, Tāla, Śamyā, Āvâpa and Sannipāta.

419—422 There are three kinds of Upohana in the delicate kinds of dance. Its Pratyupohana consists of two Kalās in the minimum and three Kalās in the maximum. Its final Kalā named a double one (Dvikala) will end in Sannipāta. This song will have Sannipātāpaharaṇa in its middle and end and it may be completed in two or in many sentences. It may consist of one, two, three or four Pādas but not more.

423—426 Making it full of numerous Pādas is not conducive to beauty. Further it removes the nature of the Varṇas and obstructs the expression of limbs. Hence the Sthita is always to contain two Pādas and it should be also performed in one Pāda and the Pravṛttā is to consist of four Pādas. The Pādapātas there will have one form and will consist of one Pāda and its Kalās will be twenty two to the maximum. It shall contain a Sannipāta in its Pāda. In its medium size it is known as having three Pādas. On account of the Sannipāta it should be sung in a medium tempo.

427—435 *The Lāsyas.* I shall now describe for you in due order the characteristics and application of the lāsya of which I spoke to you before. It is said that the Lāsya is so called because of its shining (Lāsana). It relates to mutual attraction of men and women. Like the Bhāṇa, it is to be performed by one person. Its subject matter also should be suitable. That its theme may have one or many topics has been mentioned in connection with its different Aṅgas. It has ten such types. I shall define them. The types of Lāsya are Geyapada, Sthitapāṭhya, Āsīnapāṭhya, Puṣpagaṇḍikā, Pracchedaka, Trimūḍhaka, Saindhavaka, Dvimūḍhaka, Uttamottamaka, Vicitrapada, Uktapratyukta and Bhāvita. The Āsīnapāṭhya should be performed carefully by a woman while she is seated. The Sthita Pāṭhya should include the earthly Cārīs (Bhaumīcārī) at the time of dance and of playing of instruments and at the beginning and closing of songs. The rules which hold good at the time of ordinary dance and of the playing of instruments should generally be followed in the Lāsya. Types of the Lāsya are briefly ten in number. I shall now speak of their application and characteristics.

436–440 *Geyapada.* After the musical instruments, have been placed in the proper order and the screen has been drawn away and the flour offerings have been made to the seat of Brahmā, and the drums have been tuned and the Trisāman Mantra has been chanted the wise should perform the Śuṣka Āsārita to the accompaniment of three flutes. Then the Āsārita should be performed in the Tāla prescribed for the Mārgā Sārita. Upohana follows it in the Tryaśra Tāla of two Kalās and afterwards the three Parivṛttis. This should be the conclusion of the preliminaries. The experts should then observe the conclusion with Parivṛttis. During the Parivṛtti male voice (sentence) should be uttered at the outset. An aggregate of three sentences is male whereas that of four sentences is female. This should be done for attaining the Nirvahaṇa at the conclusion.

441—446 This is what is known as the first type of Lāsya called the Geyapada · *Stihtapāṭhya.* I shall now speak of the Sthita Pāṭhya. One or two Vṛttas (Parivartas) should be sung in the Pañcapāni Tāla, and the two Khañjakas are to be sung in the Cañcatpuṭa Tāla of two Kalās. This Tāla shall be of the Yathākṣara class and should include eight Sannipātas. It should end in the Cañcatpuṭa of two Kalās in a quick tempo. *Āsīnapāṭhya*—After adopting the Tryaśra Tāla the Āsīnapāṭhya should properly be performed with a song composed in metres of long feet expressing wholly manly feelings. Thus the Āsīnapāṭhya should be performed in the four feet of its song expressing the meaning sung in the Pañcapāṇi Tāla.

447—451 In the Āsīnapāṭhya one should employ a Śīrṣaka consisting of eight Sannipātas and of Tālas etc. This should be in the Yathā-Kṛarapañcapāṇi Tāla. In its second Parivarta when the eighth Sannipāta is over one should then sing a Śloka in the Caturaśra Tāla. The playing of drums performed in the Āsīnapāṭhya should agree with the movement of limbs made in it. One should then sing eighteen or twelve Padas and the

Nirvahaṇa should afterwards be performed in the Uttara Tāla. This is the rule regarding the Āsīnapāṭhya.

452—456 *Puṣpagaṇḍikā.* Now listen about the type of Lāsya called the *Puṣpagaṇḍikā* which is adorned with various kinds of metres, and in which singing and playing of instruments are done alternately and during the singing of every foot of songs these should be appropriate Aṅga Hāras and the playing of instruments. One should sing there a song in a male metre of the Samavṛtta class. At the time of singing each foot there should be a suitable dance and the playing of instruments in the Cañcatpuṭa Tāla with four Sannipātas. Then the two songs of metres of the Khañjanatkuṭa class should be sung and at the end of their Nirvahaṇa there should be a Śirṣaka in the Pañcapāni Tāla and the dance in it should be performed in the Āviddha Cārī and with expressive Aṅga Hāras.

457—463 *The Pracchedaka.* An expert in the performance of Lāsyas should know that the Pracchedaka consist of three relates to the joy of a heroine on seeing the face of the lover in moonlight in a temple or in a mirror the expert should know that it is the Pracchedaka in which, dance predominates and which is rich in games and is besides adorned with different expressions of passion (Helā). Its games should be performed in the Cañcatpuṭa Tāla and with a song of regular feet in the Mātrā Vṛtta and with eight Sannipātas or it should include a song in the Toṭka metre of many syllables and meanings, and should be performed in the Pañcapāṇi Tāla of two Kalās or of one Kalā or both of them mixed with each other. Its Śīrṣaka should be made up mostly of heavy (Guru) syllables and it should be performed in the Tryaśra Tāla of the Yathākṣara kind including eight Sannipātas. The Lāsyāṅga called the Pracchedaka should include games and be performed with songs combined with Vivadha and Ekaka and these should relate to the Kaiśikī Jāti.

464—471 *The Trimūrdhaka.* The Trimūrdhaka consisting of soft words devoid of harshness, sung in the Gāndhārī Jāti should be performed in the proper Mārga and with proper number of Kalās with Tāla and with much Vidārīs and Vivadha it should have in it sixtyfour Sannipātas. But there should not be in it Aṅga Hāra and Viṣkambha. The recitation here connected with the play should be delivered in the attitude of a male person and the Natkuṭa and the Khañjakas are to be performed in this way. Thus has been described the Trimūḍhaka which has in it many sentiments.

Saindhavaka. This should be known as a performance without very clearAṅga Hāras and without many Recakas and it should be in the dialect of Sindhu. Accompanied by instrumental music it should be in an energetic metre. The recitation in at should not be short and the instrumental music in it should be rich in Vitasta and Ālapti and it should mostly include Guru syllables and be followed by many mild Aṅgahāras. The Saindhavaka should be performed in the Caturaśra Tāla with Ākrīḍita Bhāgas. *Dvimūḍhaka* should have Mukha and Pratimukha in the Cāpaputa Tāla which should contain twenty Sannipātas.

472–479 It should have a theme with more than one set of events and with many meanings and it should relate to manly feelings and should consist of one limb or Śīrṣaka as limb. *The Uttamotta.* In the Uttamottamaka one should first of all sing the Natkuṭa and then a Śloka with various meanings. Then the theme of the song should be in the Aparāntakhe Śākhā and the Śīrṣaka in it should be in the Yathāksara Pañcapāṇi Tāla and the performance should be adorned with the expression of passion (Helā) *Uktapratyukta.* The Uktapratyukta is alway described as abounding in references to anger and its pacification and its always characterized by beautiful dialogues and censuring actions. Its Tāla should be in the half-measure of the of the Vastu of the Prakarī. Afterwards it should perform the Sīrṣaka in the Pañcapāṇi Tāla. The Vastu and Sampiṣṭaka of these should be in the Tryaśra Tāla. This the Uktapratyukta should end in pacification. This is the Lāsya of ten types which I have finished decribing and these ten types may oceur in the same manner in a Prakaraṇa.

480—487 *Importance of the Tāla.* A break in the Lāsya is known as the Sañcāra because of its inversion. These are the schemes of Tālas of songs in the Lāsyas. In observing these, one ought to make great efforts for a dramatic performance (Nāṭya) is based on the Tāla. The same rule holds good in case of playing all the musical instruments in a dramatic performance for the Tāla relating to the timing always gives it proper measure or a song deficient in a Varṇa or having a superfluous Varṇa is held within measure by the Tāla. Hence this should be carefully studied by the producers of the plays. The seven types of traditional songs such as Ṛk, Gāthā Pāṇikā etc. and the Prakīrṇaka Catuṣpadā and Vardhamāna are all recognized by their Tāla. Hence one should with every effort ascertain their Tālas. One cannot be a singer or player of instruments unless one knows the Tāla. Hence one should observe the rules given above. Yati, Pāṇi and Laya are remembered as the limbs of Tāla. There are three kinds of Laya such as Druta, Madhya and Vilambita. This tempo is made manifast in different Mārgas of songs and playing of instruments. It is the very soul of these two (namely singing and playing on instruments). In these Mārgas three Yatis related to Laya.

488—494 That which is known as completion of metres, syllables and words is called the Laya or Māna depending on the variation of timing in Kalās in its Tāla.

The three Yatis. The Yati which is of three kinds such as Samā (Even), Srotogatā (flowing like current) and Gopucchā (cows-tail is the regulation or the duration of words Varṇas or syllables in relation to songs and to playing of instruments. If the Yati has the same tempo in the beginning, middle and in the end or Varṇas and words it is called Samā. It is used in the Citra Mārga and it predominates generally in the playing of instruments. While traversing the path of musical sounds, if the Yati is sometimes start, and sometimes running it is called Srotogatā. It is used in the Vṛtti Mārga. If the syllables are in this manner cannot be distinguished as long or short it is Gopucchā Yati. It is a prolonged one and is generally used in songs.

The three Pāṇis. The Pāṇis relating to songs and playing of instruments are of three kinds, Samapāṇi, Avapāṇi, and Uparipāṇi. The playing of instruments which is simultaneous with the start of Laya is called Samapāni.

495—502 That which preceds the start of Laya is called the Avapāṇi. The playing of instruments which follows the start of Laya is called the Uparipāṇi. The totality of syllables penultimate to the Yati will indicate the tempo and from the tempo the measure of these will change. A decrease of Kalās should be made in other Pāṇis. In the slow tempo there should be one Sannipāta, in the medium tempo two Sannipātas and in the quick tempo the number of Sannipātas should be four. That which is indicated by this difference is called the quick and the medium tempo and the Avapāṇi is dependent on a medium tempo. When the Tālas of one Kalā be come the Antarakalās played in quick tempo, it is called the Uparyupari Pāṇi. There is no provision for Kalās bigger than thus. Yatis, Pāṇis and Layas should be observed in due manner by experts after considering the application of songs. This is the rule of Tāla for the Dhruvās, when the Tāla is to be observed in their cases. I shall therefore speak about the limbs of the Dhruvās.

Notes

Verse 1. The word Tāla is used in various meanings. It is traced to the root Tal to establish (Dhātupātha 32-58). The word means clapping the hands together musical tune or measure, a dance, a cymbal, a variety of metre etc etc. See Verse 32 also.

Verse 8. The terms Cañcatpuṭa etc appear to be mere in memonics without special significance.

14 - 15 Kallinātha explains Pāta as the audible and Kalā as inaudible ones. The former is Dhruvā etc.and the latter Āvāpa etc.

16 Pāṇikā is a type of very primitive songs.

24 The term Saṁparkeṣṭāka has many variants viz. Saṁpakveṣṭāka, Saṁpatkeṣṭāka, Saṁpadvestāka etc.

31 The two different sets of gestures were probably brought together to facilitate the indication of developed time measures. They helped the musicians to avoid the confusion that is bound to happen if only one is in vogue.

47 The Dhruvā, used in connection with the performance of the Nāṭakas were apparenlty very early types of Indian

songs; for their schemes of time measure consisted of six or eight Kalās only whereas in the later songs the number of Kālās is much greater.

48—50 Why should the fingers be used to indicate the time measure in base of land gestures? It is probably the influence of the practice of the chanters of the Sāmans who indicate different notes by means of fingers alone.

59 Kallinātha specifies the differcnce in meanings of the word Kalā. It is usually used identically with the word Mātrā. Whereas in the case of the words. Ekakala, Dvikala and Catuṣkala Tālas the word Kalā implies a long syllable.

78 Piṇḍī Bandhas are group dances. See ante V/13.

114 The original connection of dance and drama with the worship of Śiva is examplified through these eulogies of Śiva cited as examples for different types of Āsāritas.

139 Kallinātha supplements the explanation here by mentioning that the Upohanas of the four parts of the Vardhamāna consist of five, six, seven and eight Kalās.

147 Tāla of the Saṁgatā īs Niṣkrāma, Śamyā Tāla, Śamyā, Niṣkrāma, Sannipāta. In the case of the Tālɛ of the Sunandā these will be added to the preceding Tāla.

180—190 The original Mss. text has evidents various omissions. Some scholars have suggested some plausible pieces. These are corrupt texts later too.

217 See Kallinātha on Saṅgītaratnākara V-87.

220 Later Indian music does not adopt these seven types of songs.

404 ff Refer chapters 29 and 32.

427 Refer ante chapter 20-132 ff.

32

Dhruvā Songs

1 Understand from me the details of those types of songs called Ḍhruvā by Nārada and other twice-borm ones.

2—6 The Ṛks, Pāṇikas and Gāthās as well as the seven traditional types of songs having seven different measures are called Dhruvās. They shall be discussed in different metres in as much as they attain the status of Dhruvās as they are created from those types. They have the limbs (Aṅgas) viz. Mukha Pratimukha, Vaihāyasaka, Sthita, Pravṛttā, Vajra, Sandhi, Saṁharaṇa, Prastāra, Upavarta, Māṣaghāta, Caturasra, Upapāta Praveṇī, Śīrṣaka, Sampiṣṭaka, Antāharaṇa and Mahā Janika eighteen in number altogether.

7 Dhruvās are songs consisting of one Vastu; Parigītikā of two Vastus; Madraka of three Vastus and Catuṣpadā of four Vastus.

8 Since in the Dhruvā songs, words, Varṇas, Alaṁkāras, tempo, Jāti and Pāṇis are connected with one another regularly the term Dhruvā is justified.

9—16 *The types of Dhruvās and their Aṅgas.* These are five types of Dhruvās based on different conditions. I shall explain their seven limbs (Aṅgas) too. Upaghāta Pravṛtta, Vajra and Śīrṣaka are the Aṅgas of the Prāveśikī Dhruvā. The Aṅgas of the Aḍḍitā Dhruvā are Prastāra, Māṣaghāta, Mahā Janika Praveṇī and Upapāta. The Avakṛsta, Dhruvā has the Aṅgas Mukha and Pratimukha while the Aṅgas Vaihāyasa and Antāharaṇa belong to the Sthitā Dhruvā. The Aṅgas Saṁharaṇa and Caturaśra belong to Khañja-Nātkuṭā Dhruvā. The Antarā Dhruvā has the limbs Prastāra and Sandhi. Appropriate types of metres are employed to represent the Aṅgas and the Kalās included in the songs. It has already been mentioned that the Tāla in a Dhruvā should consist respectively of six or eight Kalās when Tryaśra and Caturaśra. The limbs of all songs mentioned before are Vṛtta, Vivadha and Ekaka.

17—22 Vidārī is that part of the song which completes the Pada and the Varṇa. I shall explain the rules in regard to their application to the different characters in a play. The Vṛtta class of Aṅgas apply to the superior characters, the Vivadha to the middling ones and the Ekaka to the inferior types of characters. The Yoga (application) of the Tāla may be Tryaśra or Caturaśra. One shall therefore perform the Āvasasānikī Dhruvā in its proper measure. This Dhruvā should have the feet of metres resting between Gāyatrī (six syllables and Atiśakkvarī (fifteen syallables). If the Āvasānikī Dhruvā falls between Śakvar (fourteen syllables) and Atikṛti (twenty-five syllables) metres it should consist of a foot and a half of these. The foot of Āvasānikī Dhruvā should be made up of short and long syllables according to the rules of Yati, metre and its measurement in Mātrās.

22—27 The Āvasānikī Dhruvā should necessarily be Caturaśra in regard to the middling and superior characters when it shall be Tryaśra in the case of inferior characters. Vṛtta should be applied in the Dhruvā of it is full of meaning in all its parts. On the strength of Vṛtta the Dhruvā should be Āvasānikī. Dhruvās originating in various metres are of five kinds. According to the Rasas which they contain they can be termed Uttamā Madhyamā and Adhamā Dhruvās are of three classes viz. Kaniṣṭhikāgrahā, Sannipātāgrahā and Apagrahā. The first Dhruvā Prāveśikī (entering), the second one Ākṣepikī (indicating), the third one Prāsādikī (calming), the fourth one Antarā (transitional) and the fifth one is Naiṣkrāmikī (departing). Their metres are being explained.

28—32 The Vastu of the Gandharva mentioned before as consisting of notes Tāla and words is called Pada in as much as it reflects notes and Tālas. Pada consists of everything made up of syllables. If it is regularly composed it is Nibaddha and other wise Anibaddha. It is again of two kinds; if it conforms to a time measure it is called Satāla and if it is other wise it is Atāla. For the purpose of the Dhruvā it must of necessity conform to time measure and is to be Nibaddha. A Pada conforming to no time measure and which Anibaddha, is connected with the Karaṇas and it embellishes the playing of all instruments. A regularly composed Pada is furnished with a fixed number of syllables. It has a metre including caesure (Yati) and has a time measure and tempo for its syllables.

33—36 The irregularly composed Pada has a free metre and caesure. It has no fixed number of syllables. It has no prescribed time measure and tempo. If the syllables are not regularly composed, they will be outside the Jāti songs and one should describe their performance along with the Karaṇas of the musical instruments. irregularly composed Padas with no time measure furnished are connected with the musical instruments which they are meant to embellish. Padas regularly composed in pursuance of the rules of syllables in a metre are called Dhruvās. Their characteristics are being explained.

37—43 The three Tryaśra classes of metre to be applied in the Sthitāpakṛṣṭā Dhruvā are the Atyuktā (2 syllables) Madhyā (3 syllables) Pratiṣṭhā (4 syllables) and Gāyatrī (6 syllables). The Yugma class of metres to be applied in the Prāsādikī Dhruvās are the Uṣṇik (7 syllables), Anuṣṭup (8 syllables), Bṛhatī (9 syllables) and Paṅkti (10 syllables). The classes of metre known to be as use in the Dhruvās of speed are the Anuṣṭup, Udgatā and Dhṛti (18 syllables). Now listen about the class of metres for the Prāveśikī Dhruvās in the case of energetic characters. The class of metres applicable to such characters are Paṅkti, Triṣṭup, Jagati, Atijagati and Śakvari. Three kinds of syllabic metres have been prescribed for all these classes. They may be mostly in Guru or in Laghu syllables or may equally have both. The Apakṛṣṭā Dhruvās should be in metres mostly with Guru syllables and the Drutā Dhruvās should be in metres containing mostly Laghu syllables and the remaining Dhruvās should be in metres having both in almost equai numbers.

44—48 The metres to be applied in the Mukha are those with odd number of syllables. In the Drutā Dhruvās, metres made up of short syllables of even number. In the Drutā Apakṛṣṭā as well as in the Akṣepikī Dhruvās, metres with a small number of syllables and hence know as small metres are to be applied. In the Sthitā Dhruvā one usually applies metres with long syllables while those beginning with Laghu syllables are employed in the Drutā Dhruvā. Ākṣepikī Dhruvā are to be made with metres with odd and even numbers in alternate feet. A metre consisting of short and even number of syllables or of odd and small number of syllables are to be applied in the Ākṣepikī Dhruvās. If the Varṇas are desired to be increased they should include Śamyā in their Tāla. I shall now describe all the classes of metres with exambles of their patterns and according to their names extent and use Listen.

49 *Metres used in the various Dhruvās.* Hrī. The metre with a long syllable in every foot is called Hrī e.g. Yo Gaṅgāśrit. He who has offered succour to Gaṅgā.

50 Atyuktā there are two long syllables in every foot. I adore lord and master Śarva.

51 Taṭī. There are three syllables in every foot and the middle one is Laghu e.g. Śaṅkaraḥ Śūlabhṛt Pātu Mām Lokakṛt May Śaṅkara weilding the Trident and the creator of the words protect me.

52 Dhṛti. There are three syllables in every foot of which the first syllable is Laghu e.g. Umeśaḥ Surendraḥ Tavāyur Dadātu (Let the consort of Uma give you long life. He is the chief of gods).

53 Rajanī—Of the three syllables the first two are short and the last long. The metre is Rajanī. Love burne greetly when in separation).

54 Another name for Rajanī is Madhyā. These Dhruvās are all of the Vṛtta class. Those of Pratiṣṭhā and the Supratiṣṭhā classes shall be described now.

55 Pratiṣihā—four syllables in every foot. If the second is short it is Pratiṣṭhā. If the third and the fourth too are short it is Supratiṣṭhā.

56 The wind dries up the limbs and blows the scent of the flowers.

57—63 The examples are in the Prākṛta Bhramarī—This metre has the first two short and the next two long in every foot of four syllables. (When the sytam region is in bloom the isolated elephant is distressed). Jayā—This metre has in every foot of four syllables two pairs of Laghu and Guru syllables, one followed by the other) (When the forest region is struck with frost this elephant has entered at) Vijayā—If in the above metre the third syllables becomes short it is Vijayā metre. (At the advent of the clouds the peaeocks dance all round).

64—71 Vidyuḍ—Bhrāntī—this metre has five syllables in every foot. All of them are long. These clouds have arrived roaring, pouring water and enveloping the universe). Bhūtala—Tanvī—the second and the third syllables are short (On seeing the sky covered with clouds the wife of the man in exile is drenched in tears) Kamalamukhī—the final syllable in every foot is long (The rain bearing cloud drafted by the wind passes through the sky like a serpent). Guru—in every foot the first the third and the last are long. Another name of the metre is Vāgurā. (Having lost its lustre on being covered by the cloud this moon is always dim).

72—80 Śikhā—in every foot of the Supratiṣṭhā chandas the second the fourth and the last ones long. (The sky is assailed as it were by the roaring clouds all round). Ghana—Paṅkti—In this metre in every foot the first two syllables are short. (The sky appears to shed tears through the torrents of water when covered with clouds and brightened with lightning). The above are the classes of Dhruvā known as Supratiṣṭhā. We shall take up the Gāyatrī types. Tanumadhyā—This metre has six syllables in every foot. It belongs to the Gāyatrī class. The first two and the last two syllables are long. This lord of mountains got its head struck by the thunderbolt when he was down with the heat of fever. He sinks as it were into the earth) Mālinī. If the first, the fourth and the earth) Mālinī. If the first, the fourth and the last syllables are long the metre is Mālinī. (In the east the full moon is seen in conjunction with the moonlight).

81—90 Makaraka Śirṣā—If in every foot the last two syllables are long it is Makaraks Śirṣā. (The wind is blowing in the pleasure garden her in this winter that excites passion). If the fourth and final syllables are long the metre is Vimalā) In to the lotus ponds,the abode of bees the elephant in its rut enters). If the first three syllables and the last one be long the metre is Vīthi. (In the charming rainy season the clouds rumble the peacocks dance and the bees hum). If the first three and the fifth also of the syllables in every foot are short the is Girā. (On hearing the rumbling of the cloud the elephant apprenends that there is a rival elephant in the forest. Hence he trumpets). If in every foot the following syllables viz. the the first two, the fourth and the last one are long the metre, is Jalā. (On seeing this tree struck with frost and having the leaves scathered the females even weeps).

91—100 If the fourth syllables are Guru the metre is Ramyā. (These frightening black clouds that rumble and overspread the world produce alarming agitation). The metre in which the first,fourth,fifth and the sixth syllables are long is called Kāntā. (Why are you O darling, angry ? Adopt excellant behaviour and attitude. You don't see (me) long associated with you and possessed of good intention). The metre in which the following syllables viz. the first three and the last one are long is called Paṅkti. (This bride of sevan though pricked (with thorn etc.) in the forest is eager to contact her lover). The metre in which two Laghus and one Guru are repected twice is Nalinī. (The young trees at the time of the out come of the flowers appear to be smiling). The metre that has the second syllable Laghu and all the others long is called Nīlatoyā. (The bearable wind that scathers the group of clouds appeas to be one that makes the trees dance).

101—109 These metres belong to the Gāyatrī, I shall now describe the metres in the Uṣṇik chandas. The metre that has seven syallables in every foot and has only the last one long is Capalā, It is also called Drutagāti. (This face of yours produces my mad excitement. It has beautful eyes and is embellished with clusters of excellant jewels). The metre in which the third, the fifth and the final syllables are long is called Vimalā. Like a lover this breeze of the spring season blows pleasanlty exciting passion). The metre is which the Laghu alternate with Gurus called Kāminī. Having seen the spring arrived the southern breeze flows,shakes the arrived the southern breeze blows shakes the tree). The metre in which the first two and the last two syllables are Guru is to known as Bhramaramāla. (In this autumnal season the water in the lake charming with the advent of the swans and apearing with the Kāśa flowers, is pleasing).

110–119 The wherein the first fourth and the last are long is called Bhogavatī. (In this pure water the female ruddy goose moves about with the assistance of her lover) The metre where the first two and the final one are long is called Madhukarikā. (The Priyaka creeper embellished with charming ornaments has come into full bloom in the season that inspires excess of passion). The metres with the second, fourth and the penultimate syllables long is called Subhadrā. (The elephant in its rut has come to the forest bereft of its female companion. The frost has struck he forest and the mud water has vanished). If the last two syllables are Guru and the remaining ones Laghu the metre is Kusumavatī. It the root of the mountain where the clouds have collected the elephent moves about in the company of its female companion). If the second, the third and the last two syllables are Guru the metre is called Muditā. A great owning of clouds has been fitted into the firmament when the chain of cranes very terribly.

120—128 The fourth the sixth and the final syllables are long and then the metre is called Prakāśitā (A pleasing wind wafss the odour of the blossoms laden with particles of water as it blows to excite love). If the first and the fifth are short and the rest are long the metre is Dīpitā. In the winter the wind that carries the fragrance of flowers blows creating terror in me but exciting passion too). If the second the fourth and the last two syllables are Guru the metre is Valambitā. (The water-less rivers almost dried up. From them the birds have been scattered and the Cakravāka has departed. They therefore do not shine). If the first the fifth and last syllables are long the metre is Ceñcalagati. (The full moon shines in the court yard of the firmamen, coming out of the dirt of clouds). The above are the metres to be applied in the Prāsādhi Dhruvas. I I shall now explain those in the Anuṣṭubh class.

129—138 Every foot contains eight syllables. If the third and the last ones are long the metre is called Vimalajalā. (A bird is wandering in the vast expanse of clear water white lotuses smile and the bees hum). If the fifth and the last syllables ae long the metre is Lalitagati. (This bride of sevan is wandering in the garden of the pleasure grove perfumed with odour of the blossoms exciting passion). If the sixth and the eighth syllables are long the metre is Mahī. (The female swams accompanied by here mate roam, about in the lotus pond adorned with flowers). If the first six syllables are short and the other long the metre is Madhukara Sadṛśā. (In the autumn the wind blows over many forests; it has the sweet fragrance of the lotuses; it causes the bloom of the lilies as well). The metre in which the fifth and the final syollables are long is called Nalinī. (The female stork that lives in the lotus lake is proceeding to the bode of her dearest one on the beach of the river.

139—147 If the first and the final syllables are long the metre is Nadī. (The female bee is wandering about in the forest abounding in swams and resounded with the noise of the storks. The bees therein are intoxicated). The above ones are the Prāveśikī Dhruvā of the Anuṣṭubh class applicable in the case of ladies of the highest and middle classes. Now understand the Apakṛṣṭā varieties of Dhruvās. In the Bṛhati Chandas of nine syllables, if the first, the fourth and the final two syllables, are long the metre is called Rucirāntā. (On coming to know that the moon in the sky is deprived of its beauty due to the eclipse of Rāhu the stars too wcap, as it were, shedding tears in the shape of thes radiance). In the Paṅkti Chandas of ten syllables used in Avakṛṣṭā Dhruvās. If the third, the fifth and the last three are long the metre is called Pramitā. The moon bereft of lustre thrown in amongst the clouds and abscured in its beauty due to the rays of the morning sun does not shine while it movcs in the vast area of the sky). In the Jagatī Chandas of eleven syllables in every foot if the sixth and the final two syllables are long the metre is called Gataviśokā. (The moon has its body covered with the awning of the clouds. It has been robbed of its beauty by the rays of the sun. It is luster-less due to the advent of the morning. It enters the mountain of setting quickly).

148—158 If the foot has twelve syllables and if the first two the fourth, the eighth and the tenth and the final too are long the metre is called Viślokā Jāti (The moon along with the night has set. It is with in the clouds, it is struck by the rays of the sun, it has been separated from the galaxy of stars, and it is strick by the morning rediance). If the first, fourth, eighth, tenth and the final syllables are long the metre is called Lalitā. This lordly elephant flees into the forest of great beauty. Its head is shaking because it is in rut. He is shaken by the wind that blows over the forest in bloom. His feet are tied with cords and it followed by other elephants. In the Atijagati Chandas of thirteen syllables if the third, the fifth, the ninth, the eleventh and the last are long it is called Vilambitā. The moon rises in the evening amidst the forests blackened by the advent of darkness. Hence it does not shine,well. It appears to have shortened its light by dimming it). These are the classes of metres in the Dhruvās of the Prāveśikī Sthitā class. I shall explain those of the Ākṣepikī Apakṛṣṭa class. Metres of the Supratiṣṭhā class are to be applied in the Apakṛṣṭā Dhruvās. Atyuktā and others are employed in the eulogy of gods. If the Yatis and the Pāṇis are dragged on by the arrangement of syllables it shall be called Apakṛṣṭā. The Apakṛṣṭā should have Sthāyi Varṇas Sthita Layas proper number of syllables in the different Kalās, Samapāṇi Samayati. The Syllables in the Kalās and the Antarakalās of the Apakṛṣṭā Dhruvās should be in accordance with the rules of the Vṛtta metres.

A short Vastu and Pada are indispensible in the Apakṛṣṭā Dhruvā. In the Prāveśikī Dhruvā the Vastu is necessarily shortened since the Karaṇāṅga is taken up. These are to be understood as the metres of the Vṛtta class for the Apakṛṣṭā Dhruvās. I shall hence forth explain the metres of the Drutā Dhruvās. At the outset there shall be the Toṭaka metre. The remaining shall consist of short syllables. The rest may have short syllables in alternate positions. There shall be different types of metres of the Jagati and Atidhṛti Chandas.

163—170 Every foot consists of twelve syllables. In the first nine and the last syllables are long the metre is called Vikrāntā. This cloud **resembling** a smoke column rumbles. Equipped with thunderbolt it pierces the surface of the earth as it were. It is terrible and resembles an elephant pouring water and covering the entire world). In the Atijagati Chandas of thirteen syllables if the first eight and the final syllables are long the metre is called Madanavatī. (It is also known as Vinyunmāla). This cloud resembles forelocks of hair. It rumbles.

It has the lightning on a par with moonlight. It pierces (?) and wonders quickly). In the Chandas of fourteen syllables, if the first five syllables as well as the eighth the ninth and the last long the metre is called Vimalagati. (The lovely crescent moon is free from clouds. It has brightways. With its fascinating body it shines above. It has been thrown up as if were by the carrier of the Gaṅgā sportingly. In the month of Jyeṣṭha under the Mūlā star of rises and dwells in the sky with the large body). The metre in which the ninth, twelfth, the thirteenth and the last are long is called Vibhramā. (O beautiful maiden, the moon, the friend of the full-blown Kumuda flowers, is shining near the silver-mountain It is your heart's delight. It rises in the sky where the dense darkness has vanished and the bright stars have begun to appear.

171—181 In the Atiśakvari Chandas of fifteen syllables if the first, fourth, fifth, sixth, the ninth, the tenth and the last are long the metre is called Bhūtalatanvī. (The strongly flouring wind, striking the lops of the trees with incessant ruslte, moving about at the foot of the mountain and raising up dusts red and brown is running along as though he is very furious). In the Chandas of sixteen syllabled feet if the first, the fourth the seventh the tenth and the last are long it is called Sukumārā. The expanse of the sky shines with an awning spread by the cluster of clouds, with water filling it up and with the middle briliant by means of the rain bow). In the Aṣṭicchandas of sixteen syllables in every foot if the metre has the third, the fourth, the seventh the eighth, the ninth the twelfth, the thirteenth and the last long it is called Skhalitavikramā (This moon is seen rising in the cluster of lilies like the sun in the sky during the day. Its shape is like that of the disc and mirror. When the sky is free of clouds it scatters the autumnal moonlight very much. It is naturally gentle according graceful pleasure. It moves about quickly (as it were). If the metre has seventeen syllables in every foot and the fifth, eighth, the eleventh, the twelfth and the last are long it is called Ruciramukhī. (This mountain appears to be laughing through the music of notes of the cuckoo among the Campaka trees. It is bowers are resorted to by diverse kinds of birds. Its ridges reverberate with the sounds of the streams coming out of its caves. Many of the groves of the groves of the trees therein are sturck by thunder, The clouds on its top appear to be obstructed). In in the foot of a metre there are eighteen syllables and the fifth, the eighth, the thirteenth and the last are long it is called Drutacapalā. (The water in this take in which the lotuses have been turned down by the wind, and to which the petals of those lotuses have given sweet small and in which the moving waves have broken the Kumuda flowers is sending forth a call as it were by the cries of birds which have been agitated).

182—192 In an Atidhṛti Chandas of nine... syllables of the metre has in every foot the thirteenth the fourteenth and the last long it is called Kanakalatā. (O fair-bodied one the beautiful moon of silver splendour surrounded by the bright planets and free from the scattered clouds dispelling darkness by means of its cluster of rays is moving about like a plough bearer in the autumnal sky). The metre that has the fifth, the twelfth and the last syllables long is called Mukhacapalā. (Look at the sky where moves the young heavenly damsel who changes, her face quickly and has made it beautiful by her passion. These eight are the principal classes of metre for Dhruvās. From these have been developed the metres of odd and even number of syllables in the feet and the metre of these two kinds mixed up. These are the classes for Dhruvā, of the Drutā types. They relate to the comparison of divenities and royalties. The metre with seventeen syllables in every foot where in the third the fifth, the eighth, the eleventh and the seventeenth are long is Kṣiptakā. That Dhruvā is called Drutā where the initial syllable may be short or long, where the metre may have even, uneven or mixed Vṛtta types and where it is enshrined. Thus the Tryaśrā Dvipadās are explained. I shall hereafter explain the Caturaśrā Dvipadā. If the metre has sixteen syllables in every foot and all of them are long it is called. Mālā. (The clouds well up in the sky roar loudly, put forth lighting rays and pour water coving the earth.

193—205 The metre in which the fourth and sixth syllables constitute a Jagaṇa (i.e. v—v) and all the other syllables are long is called Prabhāvatī. (The example is corrupt and does not confine to the rule). In the Atidhṛti chandas of nineteen syllables if the first three, the fourth and the sixth are

Laghu and the remaining ones are Guru it is named Citra. Excited on hearing the rumbling of the clouds the elephants in the midst of his female companions rushes through the forest smashing the trees). (Incomplete defintion). If in the Kṛti Chandas of twenty syllables there are three Jagaṇas with a Gaṇa of Laghus in the beginning they call it Mālakitā. (Maddened by the songs of the cuckoos, the forests appear to dance on being agitated by the wind of the pleasing winter), In the Jagati Chandas of twelve syllables if the first, the fourth eighth, tenth and the last are long it is called Surabhimukhī. (This row of intoxicated birds equipped with the fragrance of the lotuses appears like the collection of flames in combination with fragrant winds. These are the Caturaśra classes of metres for the Vilambitā Dhruvās. I shall hence forth explain the classes of metres for the Drutā Dhruvās. If in the Ākṛti Chandas of twenty two syllables there are some Gaṇas of Sagaṇa or Jagaṇa types and there is Guru in the end the metre is called Manojña Gamanā. (In the autumn the female swan is bathing in the water of the sweet smelling lotus pond and sporting with her lover in front). In the Vikṛti Chandas of twenty three syllables in a foot there are five Sagaṇas followed by one Jagaṇa and the last syllable is long and the remaining one short. Then the metre is called Lalitagati. (In view of the contact with the spring the wind is filled with fragrance. It generates exceedingly great elation in the garden).

206—216 If in the Saṁskṛti Chandas of twenty four syllables the sixth the tenth, the thirteenth, the sixteeth and the last are long the metre is called Rati in the Dhruvā song. The example is corrupt. If in the Atikṛti Chandas of twenty five syllables the metre has the sixth seventh tenth, seventeenth and the final one long it should be known as Bhujaga Mukhi. O friend, this fragrant wind that comes along with the clouds and has been made agitated by the god of love generates passion, kills sleep and is hence helpful to women. In the Utkṛti Chandas of twenty six syllables if there is Jagaṇa in the even feet and the last syllable is Guru the metre is called Druta-Padagā is accordance with the meaning of the term. The humming of the bees appears to declare that the lotus pond which has recently blossomed and opened its lotus like face shines on being surrounded by lovers. These are the Caturaśra classes of metres prescribed for Drutā Dhruvas. I shall henceforth explain the metres for Uddhatā Dhruvās. In the Bṛhatī Chandas of nine syllables if the metre has the first two and the last three long it is called Kanaka Latākṣiptā. O friend a terribly big cloud is seen in the sky. It rumbles drenching the earth with fresh showers of water. In the Tpiṣṭup Chandas of eleven syllables if the metre has the first two and the last three long it is called Surucira Citrā. This blue cloud is like a mountain. It is frightening. It fills the earth with it torrential showers. Its sound is rumbling. It moves along the sky filled with water.

217—227 In the Bṛhatī Chandas of nine syllables if the metre has the fifth and the last long it is called Śaśi Rekhā. With the form of an elephant that roams about in the mountain and the rumbling sound of great agitated ocean, the clusters of clouds shaken by the wind moves on. The metre that has the sixth and the final two syllables long is called Śalabhavicalitā. The night shines like a youthful maiden. It has the rays of the moon for the hanging pendant, the stars as the head ornaments and the other planets to increase the beauty. In the Bṛhatī Chandas of nine syllables if the first eight are Laghu the metre is called Maṇigaṇani Karakṛtā. The night with the stellar galaxy for floral embellishment and the planets decorative spots on the face is proceeding to the moon.

In the Bṛhatī Chandas of nine syllables if the first four and the last long it is called Siṁhākrāntā. Shaking the surface of the earth and the vast expanse of the firmament, this cloud equipped with plenty of waters and lighting streaks proceeds ahead. These are the different metres of the Bṛhatī Chandas. I shall now explain those of the Paṅkti group. In the Paṅkti Chandas at the first the fourth and the last are long the metre is called Suradayitā. The young Swan white like the moon and resembling Kunda flower moves about in the pure water among the clusters of lotus, followed by Sārasakas.

228—238 *Cranes.* The metre with ten syllables in every foot which has the first three and the last long is called Kusumasamuditā or Kumudinī. O friend, the joyous evening hour of the spring has come. Enriched by the out come of the flowers at causes the withering up of those people who are separated from their dear ones. The metre that has the first, the fourth, the sixth, the seventh and the last long is called Vṛtta. On hearing the peals of thunder arising in the sky this elephant is burning furiously and moves about restlessly in the forest. The metre used in the musical setting which has the first three the sixth the ninth and the last long is called Kṛtoddhata. Over cast with rain clouds fringes whereof are illuminated by the streaks of lightning the sky maddens the herd of elephants shaken by the gusts of wind and trembling much. If the metre has ten syllables in every foot and has the first the fourth the fifth, the sixth and the last long it is called Puṣa Samṛddhā. On seeing the columns of cloud occasionally illuminated by the streak of lightning and against which the rows of cranes fly, the elephant has become wrathful. It rushes against the birch forest with loud trumpets.

The metre that has the fifth the eighth, the ninth and the last long is called Vipulabhujā. Due to the flow of ichor the elephant has become restless. It is agitated on hearing the volley of thunderous peals. In its anger it rushes to the forest and moves on with violent and proud strides. Briefly these are the metres of the Paṅkti Chandas. I shall now explain those of the Triṣṭubh group.

239—250 In the Triṣṭubh Chandas of eleven syllables in every foot if the metre has the first two and the last long it is called Capalā. These terrible clouds have gathered together in the sky. They are equal to great mountains. Their rumbling sound resembles that of the huge drums. The blue and black birds form a girdle round them. If the metre has the fifth, the sixth and the last long it is called Rucitamukhī or Kamaladalākṣī. The moon rises in the sky while climbing the mountain Vdaya it shakes the cloth of rays. It is the kins man of galaxy of the stars and a companion of the Kumuda flower. The metre that has the fifth the eighth and the last long is called Drutapādagati. After pushing aside the screen of clouds (like a dancer) the moon appears in the sky. It is adorned with myriad rays and is about to traverse the path of the heavens. The metre in which the two middle ones (i.e 5th and 6th) and the last are long is called aticapalā. In the early autumn many flowers do open. The wind is **permued** with their fragrance. It makes the trees dance. It roves about among the lotus flowers of the pleasure park. The metre that has the third the fifth the sixth, the seventh, the seventh and ıe last long is called Vimalā. The lake is full of to **this** and ; strown with flowers. The bees buzz about the flowsrs in the lake. **In the** clear water the birds enjoy themselves and the eleplant in ıts rut is **moving** about. The metre that has the fourth, the penultimate and the last long is called Rucirā. The wind flows on quicly like a wrathful one. It moves the canopy of the clouds. It shakes the cluster of Kumuda flowers and it **scatters** the masses of water.

251—264 The metre has thirteen syllables in every foot and if only the last syllable is long it is called Tvaritagati or Laghugati—Aticapalā. Unparellaled in his brightness the sun is the crown of the Udaya mountain. It is adored by **Brahmins** and the excellent sages. He moves in the sky after shaking off the clouds as though they are black cloths. The metre that has the fifth and the final two long is called Madakalita. Here comes the moon which is similar in form to the silver mountain. It is like the clusters of great crystals. It rises up on the sky wandering **every** where in the fresh advent of the autumn. There are the Triṣṭubh metres. Now listen to those of (Ati) Jagati class. In the Ati Jagati Chandas of thirteen syllables in every foot if the metre has the ninth and the last long it is called Kamalalocana. Its lustre and radiance is adored by the groups of **Brahmins** and the sages. Thousands of rays appear to be closely tying him. Shaking off the cloth of darkness the sum the britliant lamp of the **Universe** rises quickly in the sky. The metre of eleven syllables in every foot which has the seventh, the ninth and the final long is called Aparavaktra. Moving about near the side of the mountain this cloud appears to shake the earth with the rumble of the thunder with cleverly made music it comes down rapidly. These are the metres to be employed in the entering Dhruvās (Prāveṣikīs) of the Drutā variety. I shall explain the Vardhamāna class. Definition of all the metres beginning with Pratiṣṭhā has been given before with an analysis of their feet Pratiṣṭhā—(Example in the **text**) (Tr). On hearing the loud report of the thunder in the early **autumn** the huge elephant **becomes** angry. Supratiṣṭhā—

The star be-reft sky weaps incessantly for it has been beaten by the wind with lightning streaks for its lashes Gāyatrī. In the sky the luminaries have been checked and the sun has been obscured. After being perturbed by peals of thunder it appears weak Uṣṇik. Surrounded by its mates the he sevan roams about in the pleasure park where the trees in full bloom are shaken by the sweet smelling wind.

265—275 These are the Vardhamāna metres of the Tryaśra type. I shall explain those of the Caturaśra type Listen. The gentle moon rises in the sky scattering the cloths of clouds. The kinsman of the stars is embellished with thousands of rays. Anuṣṭubh Bṛhatī—This pair of birds roams about in the forest of Sumeru sung about by the Devas and the Sindhas. It habitually wanders in the highly fragrant forests.

Paṅkṭi. On fair bodied one, perfumed by the chor of elephants the forest wind blows on to shake the tree tops and to make the garden trees dance.

Triṣṭubh—The moon of clear says is rising in the sky. Adorning the Kumuda flowers it throws aside the curtain of the clouds and climbs the eastern mountain.

Jagati—The sun's body is as radiant as the molten gold. It is praised by the Brahmins and the sages. After quickly ascending the dome of the sky it will be roaming there very soon. These are the metres of the Caturaśra Vivardhita class. I shall explain the metres on the basis of the Mātrās. The final foot of the Supratisṣṭha metres consists of two and a half Gaṇas whereas all the four beet together can contain only six Gaṇas. In the same way the Apakṛṣṭā Dhruvās should have the final foot consisting of two and a half Gaṇas and the entire song ten Gaṇas. In the case of the Āḍḍitā the last foot as three and a half Gaṇas even as the entire song consists of fourteen Gaṇas. The Dvipadas of the Tryaśra class should have its final foot consisting of six and a half Gaṇas even as the entire song contains eleven Gaṇas.

276—286 The ultimate foot of the Caturaśra Dvipadas should contain eight and a half Gaṇas even as the entire song contains, fifteen Gaṇas. Each Gaṇa consists of one long and one short syllable. In the feet of the Caturaśras the Gaṇas should not be less than two and more than nine. In the Tryaśra such Gaṇas should never be less than five and more than nine, in the other feet of the Caturaśra the Gaṇas are not less than seven and more than ten.

If the Gaṇas consist of Guru syllables, in Caturaśra they should be not less than five and more than nine of they are all sport. On they may be not less than seven if they are all long and more than thirteen if they are all short. In the case of all the Dhruvās the rule regarding the total number of syllables is the same. Now the different parts of the Dvipada and the number of Gaṇas therein. The first foot in the Tryaśra Dhruvas shall consist of eleven and the last one of twenty one Gaṇas. These Gaṇas are made up of long syllable followed by a short one. The first foot in the Caturaśra Dhruvā will consist of sixteen Gaṇas. The last foot shall have twenty Gaṇas made up as usual. There is no rule regarding the feet in the case of the Śīrṣakas. There shall be two long syllables in the beginning the middle and the end, followed by a short syllable. The Sannipāta in the Tryaśra Dhruvā should be of five Gaṇas while in the Caturaśra Dhruvā it it is of eight Gaṇas. The Dhruvās have two Pādas and Sannipāta. They shall be other than Druta and Śīrṣakas Gaṇas in the Tryaśra are not less than five and more than nine. In the Caturaśra they are not less than eight and more than thirteen.

287—298 If the Gaṇas consist of Guru Syllables, in Caturaśra Dhruvā they should be not less than five and more nine if they are all Laghu. Or hey may consist of not less than eight and more than thirteen. An expert in the Dhruvās should know these Gaṇas. I shall now explain the distribution of Gaṇas and Mātrās in the Drutā Dhruvās. The Sannipāta of the Drutā Dhruvās should consist of six Gaṇas and a half. These are to be made up of twenty two Mātrās in long and short syllables. In the Śīrṣakas these should be rules regarding their Pādas. Of course they are to be made of different metres. Gaṇas beginning with long syllables, or with short syllables or having all short syllables should be employed in them. They will vary from the previous metre. The Śirṣaka will have Pādas consisting of seven and a half Gaṇas and they will include thirty Mātrās in Pādas of even or odd number of syllables. In the Śirṣaka there should be not less than twenty one and more than twenty six syllables in each foot. In the four feet there should be even and odd number of syllables mixed up and according to the rules there should be collection of short syllables in the Śīrṣaka. If there are three short Gaṇas in the beginning, three such in the end, and two long Gaṇas in the middle then the Śīrṣaka is called Capala. In the first half these should always be four short and four mixed Gaṇas and the rest will be a collection of short syllables. Virāmas (cessations) of the Dhruvās to be made by the Prāsādikī, Antara and Ākṣepikī Dhruvās should have the duration of one, two, three, four, six or eight Kalā. The Pause (Virāma) in the Tryaśra Dhruvā will be of three Kalās and in the Caturaśra at will be of four Kalās. This is the rule in the Prāveśikī as well as the Naiṣkrāmikī Dhruvās.

299—309 The pause in the Antarā Dhruvā is of two Kalās duration and the pause in the Antarā is at the end of a Pāda. In the Sthitā and the Prāsādikī Dhruvās the Virāma will be at the end of half of the Pāda and the Kalās will be as described above increased by half a Kalā and they will consist of short and long syllables. The Sthitā Dhruvā should have mostly long syllables and the Drutā Dhruvā mostly short syllables and the Drutā Dhruvā mostly short syllables and the Prāsā Dikī and the Antarā Dhruvās an admixture of short and long syllables (in equal measure). Thus should be made metres of the Dhruvās originating in the Vṛtta class. I shall next describe the definition of the various Śīrṣakas. In the Pravrti Chandas of twenty one syllables, of the metre has the first the third, the fifth, the seventh the eighth and the last long it is called Śyenī. O fair bodied lady, moving swiftly like a chariot this pleasani wind shakes the sea, strikes the mountains creates unprecedented terror amongst the trees and raises dust to soften the sharp rays of the sun. It proceeds ahead exciting passion in the common folk. The metre in which there are twenty two syllables in every foot and the following syllables are Guru viz. the first five, the eighth, the ninth and the last, is called Krauñcā. It is recited by groups of Brahmins and sages. O fair bodied one, this moon has the body without impurities, it is the enlightener and the delight of the world; it is followed by the groups of stars and planets it appears to cover the mansions with great white sheets of cloths. It gladdens the worlds after tossing about the dense darkness as though it is a big curtain black in colour. It thus move about ine sky. The metre that has twenty three syllables of which the first six the ninth the tenth and the final are long is called Puṣpasamṛddhā. It is recited by groups of **Brahmins** and sages. O fair bodied lady, the forest wind moves on violently with great noise in the midst of the trees at the foot of the mountain. It drives away the clouds raising an awning of clouds that scatters petals of lotus. It gives rise to a rustling sound in the waters of the lakes.

310—320 The metre that has twenty four syllables in the Samskṛti Chandas and has the fifth, the sixth, the seventh the tenth and the last long is called Saṁbhrāntā. In the early autumn there rises in the sky the moon lhe lover of Rohiṇī.

It is the *kinsman* of the groups of planets. It brightens the world. It is white like the big mass of the Kumuda flowers. Its white lustre resembles that of the crystal gems stars and other lumaniries follow it. It scatters myriads of rays in order to awaken the Kumuda flowers whom it be friends. The metre that has twenty three syllables or which the first eight and the last are long is called Mattākrīdā as well as Vidyunmālā. O beautiful one of excellar-creeper like body, this cloud is as huge as a mountain. Its rumbling sound resembles the sound of the thunderbolt and the drums Muraja Paṭaha. It is brightened up by many hightning streaks. It is followed by dense clouds. It is of diverse colours. It pours down waters and moves about. Beautiful flowers are kept at the head. Like the clusters of moving mountains it moves about covering the world. In the Saṁskṛti Chandas of twenty four syllables if the metre has the first, the fourth, the seventh the tenth, the eleventh and the last long the Śīrṣaka is named Skhalita. The ripples and the waves have been raised by the wind. The water is beautiful resembling the cluster of crystal gems waves after waves have produced a terrific noise. The violent gust of wind has made the flight of birds agitated. The frightening billows have been agitated by the brood of fishes. The sound of the sea resembles the rumbling of thick dense sets of clouds. Thus the ocean appears to be angry restraining the pride of even lofty mountains. In the Prakṛti Chandas of twentyfive syllables if the metre has the fifth the eighth, the eleventh the twelfth and the last long it is Capalā. O fair lady; with its body as bright as the molten gold the sun removes the dark screen of the heavens. It rises to awaken the masses of lotus flowers in to full bloom. With its thousands of rays it gives joy unto the world. The Yatis and sages sing songs of praise. The augment its rays through offerings. In the Utkṛti Chandas of twenty six syllables, if the metre has the fifth, the twelfth the thirteenth and the last long it called Vegavatī. The moon, the lamp of the Universe comes up with its rays as white as masses Kumuda flowers. If ascends the dome of the sky with all the stars and the planets following close behind. Its body can be likened to the silver mountain. It spreads a counterpane of its rays all over the world. Appearing as white as the face of Balarāma it causes intoxication of everyone. It is a friendly ally of young maidens.

321—330 These are the eight metres of the Śīrsakas. Understand those of the Natkuṭas. The basic metres here too are eight. Their definitions and examples are given now. They are Rathoddhata, Budbudaka, Udgatā, Vaṁsa Patraka Pramitākṣarā, Ketumatī, Haṁsāsyā and Toṭaka. In the Triṣṭubh Chandas of eleven syllables if the metre has the first the third, the seventh, the ninth and the last long it is called Rathodhata. The female bee has her abode in the lotus. Her fee are beautifully coloured with pollen dust she then flies over the lake with an affectionate hum in quest of her mate. In the Atijagatī Chandas of thirteen syllables of the metre has the third the tenth the eleventh and the last long it is called Budbuda. The example in the Mss is very corrupt. In the Aṣṭi Chandas of sixteen syllables of the third the third the fifth, the ninth, the twelth, the fourteenth and the last long, it is called Udgatā. At the advent of the antumn this lake where the lotuses in full bloom abound along with cackling geese appears like the sea made turbid by herds of big elephants. It is now softly giving rise to constant sounds in harmony with the humming of bees that fly over its flowers.

331—346 In the metre of seventeen syllables in every foot, if the first, the fourth, the sixth the tenth and the last are long it is called Vaṁśapatrapatita. The cuckoo has the voice sweet to the ears always. In the vernal forest abounding in Cūta, Ticaka, Kuruvaka and Aśoka trees in full bloom it roams about. The flowers attract the humming bees and create intoxecation in the young maidens. In the Jagati Chandas of twelve syllables if the metre has the third the fifth the ninth and the last long it is called Pramitākṣarā. The young swan wandering for a long time with its young mate and imbiding Āsava form her mouth is swimming now in the lotus pond which is fragrant due the flower, in bloom or. O fair lady, after wandering for a long time in the lotus pond the bee is flying through the odorous Cūta forest adorned by the spring. It is desirous of tasting the Āsava from the very mouth of its female companion. If the metre has fourteen Mātrās in the first foot and sixteen Mātrās in the remaining feet it is called Ketumatī, After smashing the lover the young elephant went to the lake where the lotuses are in full blooms. The young bee with its female companions left the lotuses, to roam elsewhere. The metre in its first three feet often syllables, the fifth and the last long and in the last foot of ten syllables, the fourth and the sixth syllables long, it is called Dhvajinī. The female bee is tempted by the flowers. It then sports among the lotuses and after surfthy drinking honey she is becoming rest less for joy. In the Jagati Chandas of twelve syllables if the second, the fourth the sixth the tenth and the last syllables are long it is called Haṁsāsya. The fragrant wind blowing over the charming lake with its waves and lotuses in full bloom is tempting the bees as well as birds.

Another type of Haṁsāsya. If the metre in its feet of twelve syllables the third, the fourth the sixth, the seventh, the tenth and the last long at is called Haṁsāsya. It belongs to to the Natkuṭa class of Dhruvās. A swarm of bees after constant flying in quest of honey of flowers over the lotus pond where swans and other birds have come is now moving among the lotus leaves. If the metre has in its feet of twelve syllables, the third, the sixth, the ninth and the last long it is cālled Toṭaka. At the close of night the terrible owl which had a fearful booting has behind it a group of chasing crows and it is now hastly searching after its own hollow of the tree.

347—359 These in brief are the metres for the Natkuṭa Dhruvās. I shall now speak of the metres for the Khañjaka Dhruvās. They are the three metres viz Pramoda, Khañjaka and Matta Ceṣṭita for the Khañjaka Dhruvā. In the Ākṛti Chandas of twenty two syllables, the first, the fourth, the sixth, the tenth, the twelfth the seventeenth and the last long it is called Pramoda. This cuckoo is oscillating here and there in the garden full of flowers in full bloom in the months of spring. There are many birds in full inebriety. There are mango blossoms and so there are swarms of bees which they follow. The metre that has nine syllables in every fcot a l the first, the third, the fifth and the seventh and the last are long it is called Bhāvinī. Coming out from the flowers the bee is inebriated due to the drinking of the honey from the Jāti flowers.

The metre that has eight syllables, the first, the third, the fifth and the seventh are long, than that metre called Maṭṭa Caṣṭita. The nightangle is going towards forest when other birds are also assembled. The trees are full of flowers and Natkuṭa forms these metres. Others that have even or odd numbers of syllables, or unequal numbers of syllables comes out from these Dhruvās have sixty four primary classes. Some of them are made of equal numbers of syllables. Dhruvās are of three types —even or odd number of Mixed feets or odd feet are made of even numbers and odd number syllables or half odd and half even numbers. Dhruvās having even numbers of syllables in the meterial feet are one hundred eighty five in numbers and those of partially even numbers are one hundred ten and similar is the number of uneven number of syllables. Dhruvās of unequal length feet or words of unequal number of feet are also generally made and the names of these Meters may be given according to one's will.

360 363 *Five Aspects of Dhruvās.* The above are the classes of Dhruvās arising out of various metres. I shall henceforth explain the different as pects due to five causes—Jāti (class), Sthāna (location), Prakāra (Variety), Pramāṇa (Measure) and Nāma (name). The Number of syllables in the metre of a Dhruvā constitutes its Jāti. The fact that these

numbers may be even or odd gives rise to its Prakāra (Variety). The Tāla constitutes their Pramāṇa. It may be of six or eight Kalās as observed in the Dhruvās. Men are given names in accordance with their Gotra, Kula or Ācāra (traditional convention). Similarly names are applied to Dhruvās according to their dependance on the Sthānas (Occasions).

364—375 *Five Sthānas of Dhruvās.* The Sthānas in connection with the Dhrvuās are five viz—Praveśa (Entry), Ākṣepa (diversion), Niṣkrāma (Exit), Prasādana (Calming) and Antara Transition). Themes of various Rasas sung at the time when persons enter the stage are called Prāveśikī Dhruvās. In the course of a dramatic performance, when songs are sung at the end of Acts while the characters stage their exit they are called Naiṣkrā Mikī Dhruvās. Sometimes experts disregard to rules governing the Laya. They may have a Dhruvā of medium or of slow tempo (Laya) sung in a quick tempo. It is called Antarā Dhruvā. After a sudden distraction, the audience in the auditorium enjoying a different Rasa has to be calmed down in regard to their feelings. This calming or Prasadanas through the Prāsādikī Dhruvā. The Antarā Dhruvās are the songs sung during these occasions—the principal characters are gloomy absent-minded, angry, asleep, inebriated, enjoying the association of others, groaning under heavy weight, loss of consciousness, swooning as a result of being poisoned, having committed blunders, adjusting or fixing garments and ornaments, covering up their slips in acting etc. I shall now explain the Sthānas (occasions) along with the Rasas and Bhāvas where all the Dhruvās are to be sung carefully. The Sthānas are of two types, that which relates to one's own self and that which relates to others. Listen and understand from me the Sthāna connected with Ākṣepa. The Apakṛṣṭa Dhruvā in the Kruṇa Rasa should be sung at the time when are (i.e. the Principal Character) is captured, restrained fallen over whelmed with ailments, dead or in the state of Swoom. Dhruvā in a slow tempo should be sung when one is impatiantly eager, tendancy to dissimulate, anxios, lamentation, fatigue, depression and despair. Further, in these Bhāvas and in pathetic reports the Dhruvā is sung in a Druta Laya (quick tempo)furnished with a rapid movement.

376—386 The Dhruvās should be in a Vilambita Laya when depicting the direct witnessing of the slaughter or wounding of any one along with the sorrow resulting therefrom. The Rasa shall be Karuṇa. The Dhruvas should be sing Dṛuta Laya in case of the witnessing of a calamity, intolerance, supernatural being utter desperateness, carelessness, anger, tempestuousness as well as direct report of Vīra, Bībhatsa and Bhayānaka and similar Rasas. Prāsādikī type of Dhruvā should be employed in the Madhyalaya in the following cases. Propitations, requesting some one, recollecting near and dear ones, in exaggerated aration, meeting of the lovers on the first occasion, joyous moments, begging, supplicating, seeing something peculiar in regard to love making etc. The Antarā Dhruvā is employed incessantly in depicting physical distress, anger, aiming a missile against some one etc. No Dhruvā is to be employed to weeping or singing persons are on the point of entry, in hurried arrivals, in the announcement of something, on the occurrance of calamity or excessive surprise. The rules regarding themes, places, times and seasons involved should be taken into consideration before appling the Druvās. The characters in the play and the indication of the Bhāvas are also to be considered. There are six types of (other) Dhruvās viz. Śīrṣaka, Uddhatā Anubandha, Vilambitā, Aḍḍitā and Apakṛṣṭā. That which is at the head of things (events) is called Śīrṣaka. If a Dhruvā is sing in an elevated (Uddhata) manner it is termed Uddhatā. If the Dhruvā is employed in a sportful manner with all the attendant features of Nāṭya and adopts the requisite tempo it is called Anubandha.

387—396 The Vilambitā Dhruvā is that which does not move very quickly in accordance with the dramatic convention. A Dhruvā becomes very pleasing when it is employed in the Śṛṅgāra Rasa with some intrinsic extraordinary quality. It is called Aḍḍitā. A Dhruvā is called Apakṛṣṭā it for reasons other than that with which it is begun it is continued to be sung in other Bhāvas. The excited Prāveśikī Dhruvā should be employed only in the case of men characters if the movement is restrained or delayed. The Prāsādikī Dhruvā in the case of women should be of the Aḍḍitā type, provider it is in a slow tempo and it will be Apakṛṣṭā. That which is not Drutā will be Vilambitā. The following are called the Prakāras (aspects) f entry in as much as Laya, Vādya, Yati (pause) Pada (words), Varṇas (letters) and Akṣaras (syllables) accompany a song. Kings and gods have to be provided with Śīrṣaka and Aḍḍitā types of Dhruvā and Aḍḍitā is employed in the case of women divinity, royalty and courtezans. At the entry of Madhyama (middling) characters the Dhruvā should be of the Drutavilambitā type and in the case of inferior characters it should be of the Natkuṭa and Khañjaka types. These two latter will be for bringing joy to the occasion. Why should it be so? Since these two belong to comic and Śṛṅgāra Sentiments (Rasas). In the case of the base and mean characters as well as of those dead there should be Anubandha with the relevant Laya. In the case of women of the Kṣatriya and Vaiśya castes there should be Apakṛṣṭā Dhruva in proper Laya (tempo).

397—406 The Tāla with four Sannipātas is employed in the Prāveśikī Dhruvā. The remaining ones are to have two Sannipātas and the Śīrṣakas are to have six Padas. In the case of inferior characters no sensible person sings Aḍḍitā with a Vilambita Laya. One should sing Natkuṭa Dhruvāa in their (i.e. inferior ones) movements relating to all the Bhāvas. The inferior characters can have only the three Bhāvas dependent on Hāsya (laughter), Śoka (grief) and Bhaya (fear). The Dhruvā shall be in view of this fact alone. The sensible ones always take into consideration the Vastu (theme), the Prayoga (performance) the Prakṛti (characters) in a play, the Rasas, the Bhāvas, the Ṛtus (seasons), the age the locality, time and mental condition. Thereafter the relevant Dhruvā is employed. The Vastu arises from the Deśa (locality) in relation to a city or a forest region. The Prayoga (performance) may relate to mortal beings or gods. The Prakṛti dramatics personal) in a play are of three kinds the superior, the middling and the inferior Rasas and Bhāva's have already been explained. The change of time causes the seasons (Ṛtus). The Vayas (Age) consists of infancy, youth and senility. Deśa (locality) is of diverse kinds based on zonal and other divisions. Day and night cause the change of time. So also the fortnights cause the change of time. So also the fortnights and the months. The mental Avasthā (condition) depends upon joy and sorrow. These are the salient features of the Sthānas (situations). They are to be employed by the sensible ones after the due consideration of Rasas and Bhāvas. Things and events impossible or forbidden to be expressed in words and ordinary speech should be presented through songs since Rasa Pāka (the ripeness of Rasa) is enjoyed as meanings of word become powerful.

407—416 *Contents of the Dhruvās.* Dhruvās should relate to objects comparable to superior, middling or inferior men and women characters in regard to quality. In case of the gods and kings such comparable objects are the moon, the fire, the sun and the wind; in the case of Daityas and Pākṣasas they are clouds, mountains and seas. In case of Siddhas, Gandharvas and Yakṣas the comparable objects are the planets stars and bulls and for all these persons engaged in the performance of austerities the comparable objects are the sun, the fire and the wind. In the case of the Brahmins and others engaged in austerities the comparable object is fire. For their womenfolk the same can be the comparable objects, comparable to the heavenly beings are the lightning, meteor and solar rays. Objects befitting gods apply to the case of kings too. Elephants, lions and bulls are not objects befitting heavenly beings. But elephants, serpents and lions are used in the case of kings. Mischievious beings such as Yakṣas, Rākṣasas and Bhūtas are comparable to the buffalo, Ruru, deer, lions and other beasts of prey with regard to the portrayal of different Rasas superior characters are compared to an elephant in rut and swans. Objects with quality entitling them to a comparison with middling characters are Sārasas (cranes) peacocks, Krauñca (heroine) ruddy geese (Cakravāka) and lakes with Kumuda flowers. The Cuckoo bee, crow, osprey, owl, crane, pigeon and Kadamba are comparable to inferior characters.

417—421 Now listen and understand from me the objects comparable to the womenfolk of superior, inferior and middling characters. The night, the earth, moonlight lotus pond female elephants and the rivers have qualities entitling them to be compared with women of royalty. A lakye, ospre, creeper, female crane, pea, hen and female deer are always to be compared with women of middling characters as well as with courtesans. A hen, bee, crow, cuckoo, and our of the female species are to be mentioned in the Dhruvās connected with the womenfolk of inferior characters comparison about going and other movements should be indicated by means of the Prāveśikī and Naiskrāmikī Dhruvā.

422—426 *Dhruvās to suit time and occasion.* Events happening in the forenoon are to be indicated through Prāveśikī Dhruvā songs. The Naiṣkrāmikī Dhruvās may serve in general for occurrences throughout the day or night. Saumyā Dhruvās (gentle ones) are to be sung in regard to the forenoon and Dīptā (excited) Dhruvās are to be sung in regard to the moon while Karuṇa Dhruvās are to be sung in case of afternoon and evening Prāveśikī Dhruvās are employed to express any report about going where as Ākṣepikī Dhruvās are employed with regard to the stationary ones. The Ākṣepikī Dhruvās are all to be sung in a Druta as well as Vilambita Laya. The same in the case of Dhruvās when they arise in connection with anger and intolerance and the following Rasas are portrayed viz. Karuṇa, Adbhuta and Bhayānaka. All objects of the terrestrial globe connected with a corpse, god etc. are to be mentioned in the Dhruvā song with suitable comparison.

427—431 *Dhruvās indicative of moments.* Comparable objects in regard to stationary things should themselves be stationary. If they move they should be compared with only moving objects. Bhāvas in regard to joy and sorrow should be related to qualities in their objects of comparison. In the case of chariots, arrows, horses, elephants, heavanly cars, deer, birds, palankeens and aerial Cars the experts should make Dhruvās with a view to their movement and progress. The experts should compose the Dhruvā with words and syllables capable of being expressed quickly in the case of chariots, horses, arrows, elephants, heavenly cars, swings and birds used as vehicles. In the case of bills, elephants, lions and bears, the Dhruvā should be made up of Guru syllables that are to be uttered with force. The Dhruvās should be made of Laghu syllables with swift movement and Guru syllables with slowness of movement in the case of crows, monkeys, swans and peacocks. This being the case one should apply Dhruvās after knowing the relevant Bhāvas.

432—439 *Metres for Dhruvās.* Words of a song cannot be without a metre. After considering the contents of the Dhruvā songs one should couch it in a suitable metre. Hence a Dhruvā to express the movement of a vehicle should be made up of suitable syllables so that the different limbs of the song may agree with the Vādya concerned. The metre prescribed for the foot of a Dhruvā in connection with the movement of a vehicle should also be available in the musical instrument and in should also agree with the movement of all the Aṅgas of a song. The song is to be taken up first than the instrumental music and thereafter the dance movements. A combination of songs and instrumental music (with dance, of course) is called a Prayoga (performance). The Bhāva within the heart should be depicted by means of histrionic representation in all its Aṅgas and the Sūcās of the Nivṛtyaṅkura class. The Prāsādikī Dhruvā arising from the quality of giving pleasure should be employed when there is an eartny person and where there is an aerial speech. The Dhruvā in this case connected with speaking should perfectly suit the meaning of its name when the Dhruvā connected with pleasing or jealousy and anger attains the Śṛṅgāra Rasa it should fit in with the meaning thereof. When there are occasions of pleasing, Dhruvās connected with the different Rasas should be made Prāsādikī to fit in with the meaning of their names.

440—443 *The Language of the Dhruvas.* The language in the application of the Dhruvās should be Śūrasent. Sometimes it can be Māgadhī when the Dhruvās of the Natkuṭa class are to be made. Saṁskṛta songs have been prescribed by the authorities in the case of heavenly beings; and in case of human beings half-Saṁskṛtaı song should be used. Listen about their treatment if the gods who have been made objects of comparison make entrance in a play in course of its action. That which is their Sāttvika Bhāva and constitutes a narration of their deeds should be expressed through a song according to the authoritative rules.

444—457 *Metres of Dhruvās.* In the case of heavenly beings, songs are desired to be in metres of suitable measure. This should relate to their praise or a narration of their exploits. In the feet of Dhruvās one should describe that which relates to the qualities of comparison. In this connection it is suggested that the metres like Mālā, Vaktra, Puṭavṛtta, Viśloka, Cūlikā, Udgatā and Aparavaktra should be used by the producers of the play. I have described the rules of the play. I have described the rules of metres before (Verses 49 ff.). In case of gods these Dhruvās should include words expressing victory or blessing and for them Ṛc, Gāthā and Pāṇikā will be understood as their measure. As these are pleasing to hear they should be applied in the songs. The Jātis including Gāndāra Ṣaḍja, Madhyama, Pañcama and Dhaivata should be reckoned as the suitable form of these songs (Ch. 28—103 ff). Their form befitting the four occasions should be such as Prāsādikī, Sthitā, Naiṣkrāmikī and Prāveśikī. In the various acts of the gods when there is no obstacle Saṁskritshould often be used in the Anuṣṭhup metre. The metres like Mālā Vaktra and Apara Vaktra are suited to Prāveśikī Dhruvā and Puṭa and Cūlikā are meant for Naiṣkrā Mikī Dhruvās. Udgātā metre is applicable in the Prāsādikī Dhruvā and the Anuṣṭup in the Vilambitā Dhruvā. These occasions are to be expressed by one who is an expert in measures. The song which is in the Anuṣṭup metre and is in a slow tempo and relates to a fall due to course, suffering from anxiety and abounds in Guru syllables, notes of pathetic expression and long drawn out Varṇas should have the Sthita Sthāna. For the excitement of human beings and for their roaming over different places, heavenly beings are to resort to songs in the Anuṣtubh metre. In relating the memory of those of heavenly beings who are born among mortals one should resort to suitable songs expressing heavenly Bhāvas. suitable songs relating to the sorrow of these very beings when these are meant to destroy sorrow and anxiety are to deal with a change due to afflicted conditions.

458—470 *Dhruvās suit occasions.* Listen now what are usually done for the rule of Dhruvās occurring to their division of occasion. When the muscial instruments have been placed in order and three Sāmans have been uttered one should apply the Āśrāvaṇa (see V-18) included in the Bahirgīta (see V-30-31).

After the performance of Bahirgīta one should perform the Pūrvaraṅga (see V-726) and Raṅga-Dvāra (V-26-27, 116-119) thereafter. In connection with the entry of characters one should sing the Dhruvā indicating movement and also the Parivarta. (V-65 ff) By taking steps upon the stage while singing or due to some other need one should make six Parivartas. The Dhruvā in this case should be made as in the case of gods and the Pātas there should be twenty one in number. The Dhruvā in its application in drama should be of the Tryaśra or of the Caturaśra type. In case of Tryaśra the Pāda Pāta will consist of three Kalās while in the Caturaśra it will consist of four Kalā. In the case of superior characters the Dhruvā will be Caturaśra and in case of the middling characters Tryaśra type, and in case of the inferior characters it will be of the Khañja and the Natkuta class. This will be the rules about tunes in connection with the movement of feet. In case of hurry, calamity and anger it will consist of one Kalā or half of a Kalā. The movement of feet will consist of one, two, three or four Kalās. At that time there should be a harmony of dance with the instrumental music and not with song. There should be no pause in Dhruvā of one or two Kalās in dance. There should be harmony with the instrument and not with the song. One should know the setting of feet in case of the Bhāva mentioned before depending on the slow or the quick tempo (Laya) and should made harmony with the instrumental music. On account of excessive joy, sorrow or anger the character makes a precipitate entry with a tossing of the curtain. This should be made along with the stipulated durations.

471—480 *Rule of Graha* There are the rules about Parivarta (Ch. 33—180 ff) in a play shall now describe the Grahas in connection with the musical instruments. The song starts without any music of the instrument the Parivarta and in the fourth Parivarta there thould be the Graha of the instrument. Sometimes there should be Sannipāta Graha. Sometimes Tarjanīgraha and sometimes Ākāśa Graha in the Dhruvā songs. As the Graha in the Dhruvā is regulated by Kalā Tāla and Laya it should be observed in the movements, and walks by means of instruments. In the Śīrṣaka of the Uddhata class of Dhruvās the Graha should be by the Pradeśinī and in the

Vilambitā Additā Dhruvā it should be by the Sannipāta and the third finger. In the Natkuṭa, Aḍḍitā and Prāsādakī Dhruvās the Graha will be in Sannipāta and in the Druta Dhruvās the Graha will be from above and in the Naiṣkrāmikī and Anubandha Dhruvās the Graha will be with instruments. For songs there should not be made any repetition by the experts. Natkuṭa Dhruvās should have four Grahas such as Sannipāta, Śamyā, Tāla and Ākāśa. In the entrance of any character with hurry, excitement and joy there should by the Graha with the song and such a Graha is called Udghātya. In case of falling of ornaments, clothes, or of any disorder any loss of memory, fatique and in the general covering of faults there should be the Udghātya Graha of the Antarā Dhruvā.

481—490 *Application of song.* Producers should in this manner apply in their proper places, the Dhruvās required for dance and drama. Just as a well bulb dwelling house does not become beautiful without and colour, so also without any song the drama does not attain the capacity of giving joy. The rule regarding songs have been mentioned in connection with the formalities of the Pūrvaraṅga(Preliminaries) and the worship of gods has also been mentioned there. Hence notes in the two Grāmas and that with Sādhāraṇa (overlaping note) should be applied to plays (poetical composition) which express the diverse Bhāvās. In the opening of the drama there should be the songs of the Madhyama Grāma those of Ṣaḍjagrāma during the progression, in the Garbha (development) the Sādhārita (of overlapping), in the Vimarśa (Pause) the Pañcama and the Kaiśika in the conclusion (Nirvahaṇa). These songs depending on the Sandhi (junctures) and Vṛtta (metres) should be of suitable Rasas and Bhāvas, Dhruvās depending on the Prakaraṇa (contexts) and made to express Rasa suited to the occasion embellish the drama just as the stars brighten the firmament. The Māgadhī is the first Gīti, then Ardha Māgadhi, the Sambhāvītā is the third and the Pṛthulā is the fourth one. Māgadhī is known by the repetition of its Pādas in different tempo and it is in the Citra Vṛtti (ch. 19-77 ff). Similar is the Citra Vṛtti (ch 19—77 ff). Similar is the Ardha Māgadhī which has recourse to repetition turce. Sambhāvitā generally depends on Guru syllables. It is applied in the Vārtika Vṛtti and Pṛthulā consisting of eight syllables in the instrumental music is to be applied in thė Dakṣiṇa Vṛtti.

491—498 These four Gitis are to be applied everywhere in songs by singers. These consisting of appropriate syllables applied in Dhruvās as well. That which includes full notes, is embellished by instruments, relates to the three voice registers, has three Yatis and three Mātrās, gives joy, is harmonious and delicate, contains Alaṁkāras, is performed with ease and has sweetness is called a song par excellance. One should first of all bestow care on songs. For songs have been called the bed (resting place) of the dramatic performance. The song and the playing of musical instruments being well executed the performance of the drama does not encounter any risk.

494—498 *Qualities of singers and players of instruments.* I have described a dequately the salient features of Dhruvā. I shall now explain the essential qualities of singers and players of musical instruments Knowledge is produced by qualities and mind becomes repulsed on account of fauls and defects. Hence one should carefully understand good qualities and defects. The singer should be in the prime of his youth with a loving nature and a throat capable of sweet voice. He must be thoroughly acquainted with Laya, Tāla division of Kalās their measure and application. [Saṅgīta Ratnākara III-13—22]. The Śyāmā woman (one who has not yet borne children) can be the beat female singer she should have good physique, brilliance, courage, sweetness, soft, sweet, resonantly charming harmonious and auspicious voice. She must be able to observe pause (Yati). She must never be nervous she must be an adapt with good knowledge of songs together with Tāla, Laya and Karaṇas which she can regulate in accordance with the musical instruments).

499—500 *Characteristics of the Vīṇā player.* Usually there are two Vīṇā players. They must be perfectly conversant with the use of Pāṇi (ch. 31—494/495) tempo, Yati (pause) allotted to different parts of a song. They should have nimble hands in producing charming sound. All the good qualities of the singers are expected in them. Attentive in mind they must be able to sing well in accompaniment of other instruments too.

They must be able to produce the Karaṇas clearly. They should be industrious and should have pleasing voice and adequate experience. In Vṛttis like **Citra** etc. they must have adequate practice.

501—502 *Characteristics of the flutist.* The flute player is expected to be strong and careful knowing songs and Layas properly. He must be able to sing well in accompaniment of other instruments. He must be capable of producing sweet pleasing and voluminous notes. His breath power must be superb, flute music must be steadily maintained. It should be continuous and expressive of Varṇas and Alaṁkāras. He must be able to cover immediately in case any fault happens in the course of the performance.

503—511 *Difference between male and female musical performance.* Women are naturally capable of singing sweetly while men have recitative ability. The voice of women is naturally sweet and that of men strong. If a woman has has recitative capability and a man sweetness in voice, this should be considered accidental and casual embellishing them without being their intrinsic ability. Should men lead in songs possessing good characteristics except sweetness it does not add to the Śobhā of the song (beauty in the performance). So women's songs and men's recitatives are successful when these are hot indiscriminately attempted there shall never be strained. Dānavas, Asuras, Rākṣasas, Yakṣas and Vāgas as males and females do indulge in many actions and speeches Woman shall therefore play man's parts carefully one graceful movements are their natural features. Men acquire Sauṣṭhava (ch. 11—91) by regular practice and repetition. The movement of the limbs by women are naturally pleasing. With all these things in view man are to instruct the women in songs and musical instruments and recitatives. (Paṭhyas) in regard to different characters in the play. A loss of note in the women's songs and playing of instruments can be condoned. But thus will not be sweet to the ear in cass of men.

512—574 *Qualities of the Ācharya, Śiṣya and the Kaṇṭha* (Voice) A teacher should have the following six qualities—memory, medhā (intelligence). Mati (discriminating judgement) UHa (reasoning positive), Apoha (negative reasoning) and

Śiṣya Niṣpādana (Ability to impart to the disciple). A disciple should have intelligence memory, Ślāghā (Willing ness to serve and gain praise) devotion to work spirit of emulation and enthusiasm. The six qualities of the Kaṇṭha are loudness, compactness, smoothness, sweetness, carefulness and harmony with the three Sthānas.

575—578 Landness is termed Śrāvaka. The voice can be heard from a distance. Compactness is Ghanatva. This occurs when the voice is sweet without being diffused. Snigdhatva (Smoothness) occurs when the voice is loud but not harsh. Madhurya (sweetness) occurs when there is no discordance even at the higest Sthāna. Avadhānavatva (carefulness when voice does not lapse into excess or deficiency. Tristhāna Śobhā occurs when the voice becomes sweet with reference to head, throat and chest which it strikes.

519—524 *Faults of the Singer*. The five faults (a) Kapila (b) Anavasthita (c) Sandaṣṭa (d) Kākī and (e) Tumbakī. In the Kapila the voice is unnatural with a gurgling sound due to being afficted by phlegmatic excess. The voice is anavasthita (unsteady) when there is an irregular excess or want of volume in it or when it is lean. Sandaṣṭa (Bitten). If the musician appears to bite the words as it were it is called Sandaṣṭa. A harsh voice in its enunciation may not properly touch the relevant Sthāna (voice register). It is called Kākī (crow like). Tumbakī is a nasal sound. These are the salient features about the good qualities and defects of voice. They have been adequately explained by me. I shall now describe the Ananaddha (covered) instrument.

525 I have thus described Gāndharva science originally propounded by the grandfather (i.e. Brahmā the crestor). A man who will cause thus to be performed will win the highest credit in this world.

Notes

Verse 1. Nārada is supposed to be one of the original propounders of the science of music as learnt from Brahmā himself.

31 *Karaṇa*. This evidently refers to musical instruments and notes produced therein.

56 Examples given in the text are not repeeted by us. Only translation is given.

87—88 Bhaṭṭıkāvya II-9 gives a similar instance.

161 Toṭaka is the name of a well known metre.

241—242 Ruciramukhi metioned in 178 consists of seventeen syllables in a foot. Here the number of syllables is eleven.

259 *Vardhamāna.* The word indicates the increase in the number of syllables by one two and three in the 2nd, 3rd and 4th feet unlike the regular metre of the same name.

408 Comparable objects given in the examples quoted above in various verses should be noted

504 Good singing appears to be the prerogative of women since very early times in the history of the development of dramas. Maitreya in the drama Mṛcchakaṭika (Act-III) comments adversely on Cārudatta's encomvism given to Revila a male singer. Indirectly Cārvdatta concades the point that women are better singers by saying that if he had been behind the screen Revila could have passed for lady.

33

Avanaddhatodya Vidhanam

Explanation of Avanaddha Instruments (Covered Ones)

1—2 I have already explained thus the Tāla Instruments (strainged ones). I shall now extoll the class of Avanaddha instruments with their salient features, functions etc. in regard to the drums of the types Mṛdaṅga, Paṇava and Dardura.

3 Svāti and Nārada have spoken about the Gāndharva art and the play on musical instruments along with their extended amplitude and similar features and functions.

4—8 *Origin of Avanaddhas.* In emulation Svāti I shall succinctly explain the origin and evolution of the Pauṣkara instruments (Drums etc.). On a holiday in the rainy season when the sky was overcast with dark clouds Svāti went to a great pond for fetching water. Even as he was seated near the lake the chestiser of Pāka (i.e./Vdra) endeavoured to convert the whole universe into a vast expanse of water by means of torrential downpenrs. Thanks to the velocity of the gust of wind, clear sounds were made over the leaves of the lotus clusters by the falling columns of water. On hearing the sound arising from the water colmns falling down considered it a mysterious occurrence and hence observed it carefully.

9—13 He returned to the hermitage with the full knowledge of the high, medium and low sounds made on the lotus leaves as majestically deep, sweet and delightful. After returning to the hermitage he sought the help of Viśvakarman to devise the Mṛdaṅgas, Puṣkaras, Paṇavas and Darduras. The observation of the Dundubhi of the Devas enabled him to make the Muraja, Āliṅgya, Urdhvaka and Āṅkika. Adept that he was in reasoning out with pros and cons he covered these Avanaddhas, the Mṛdaṅgas and Darduras with hide and the Paṇava with strings. He made other drums too such as Jhallarī, Paṭaha etc. end covered them with hide.

14—17 Listen now to such of those musical instruments as should be included as Aṅgas and Pratyaṅgas (main and subsidiary parts) in the performance of the collection of Ātodyas. The Vipañcī and the Citrā are termed Aṅgas among the wooden stringed instruments and Kacchapī, Ghoṣaka etc. are Pratyaṅgas. Among the drums Mṛdaṅga and Dardura among Paṇavas are termed Aṅga and Jhallarī Paṭaha etc. are Pratyaṅgas. Among the Suṣira instruments the Vaṁśa (flute) has the salient features of the Aṅga and the Śaṅkha (Counch shell) and Dakkinī are enumerated as Pratyaṅgas.

18—22 *Use of Drums.* In the ten kinds of Rūpakas no Ātodya is considered as unfit in the performance. Of course consideration of the Rasa and Bhāva is necessary for their inclusion in accordance with the rules. All the Ātodyas are played in the performance of plays depicting festivities, regal procession and comaigns, joyous and auspicious, marriage celebrations, nativity of princes and in the was tumultuous with the participation of many soldiers etc. Limited number of instruments are played during the commonplace domestic occurrences but all the Ātodyas during expeditions, Compaigns and compositions of plays etc. The Bhāṇḍavādya is to be employed for the sake of the harmonious blending of the different Aṅgas, for the covering up of gaps and minor defects, for providing leisure of intervals and for general grandeur.

23—28 *General description of Avanaddhas.* I shall now explain the Avanaddhas giving rise to regular notes equipped with many Karaṇas and Jātis. O excellent Brahmins, Ātodyas of every sort with hide coverings such as Tripuṣkara etc. are remembered as Avanaddhas. Hundreds of varieties do exist among the Avanaddhas but I shall mention the characteristics of Tripuṣkara There is no multiplicity of functions as in others. No production of distinct notes and no regulated strokes. No distinct syllables are available and Mārjanā is not required. Depth of is desired by the playing of Bherī, Paṭaha and Jhañjha as well as Dundubhi and Ḍiṇḍimas due to their slackness and extended surface. These are to be played generally with due consideration of time and occasion. But listen now to the rules regarding the Tripuśkara.

29—35 Sound is airy [i.e. depending on air] and it is considered to be of two kinds one equipped wih Svaras (notes) and the other with Abhidhāna (name-words with meaning). That which is called Abhidhānavān (having words with meaning) depend upon different languages and those called Svaravān depend on diverse kinds of instruments. Seven Svaras (notes) have been proclaimed in the Vīṇā as well as human vocal cords. The same are being produced in the Ātodyas as well. Notes coming out of the human body are transmitted to the wooden Vīṇā, then to the Puṣkara and ultimately to the Ghana (solid instruments i.e. Kāmsya Tāla etc.). Prahāras (strokes) on them by various movements are to be known as based on words. There are in application to the play on Vīṇā in the course of battles etc. There is Vāskaraṇa (mnemonic patterns) as, for example Jhaṇṭu, Sagati Kāt etc. alongwith many Karaṇas. The notes which the singer produces should be by means of musical instruments and these necessarily contain Laghu and Guru syllables showing relevent Yati and Pāṇi.

36—41 *Salient features of Puṣkara instruments.* I shall now explain the rules regarding Puṣkaras as based on Mṛdaṅga Paṇava and Dardura. The following are the features (a) sixteen Akṣaras (syllabic sounds) (b) the four Mārgas (c) Vilepana (d) the six Karaṇas (e) three Yatis (f) three Layas (g) three Gatis h) three Pracāras i) three Yogas j) three Pāṇis k) the five Pāṇiprahatas l) three Prahāras m) three Mārjanās n) eighteen Jātis and o) twenty Alaṅkāra Prakāras. The music of the Puṣkaras should have all these features.

Prose pieces

What has been mentioned as sixteen Akṣaras we shall explain. The sixteen Akṣaras are Ka Kha, Ga, Gha, Ṭa, Ṭha, Ḍa, Ḍha, Ta, Tha, Da, Dha, Ma, Ra, La and Ha. They are to be invariably applied in the Vāṣkaraṇa. The four Mārgas are Ālipta, Aḍḍita, Gomukha and Vitasta *Vilerana* (Application of flour paste) and Vāmaka and Urdhvaka. The six Karaṇas are (1) Rūpa, (2) Kṛtapratikṛta, (3) Pratibheda, (4) Rūpaśeṣa, (5) Ogha and (6) Pratiśuṣka. The three Yatis are Samā, Srotogatā and Gopucchā. The three Layas are Druta, Madhya and Vilambita The three Gatis are Tattva , Anugata and Ogha. The three Pracāras Sama, Viṣama and Samaviṣama. The three Yogas (Saṁyogas) are Guru, Laghu and Gurulaghu. The three Pāṇis are Samapāṇi, Avarapāṇi and Uparipāṇi. The five Pāṇiprahatas are Samapāṇi Prahata, Ardhapāṇiprahata Ardhārdhapāṇiprahata, Pārśva Pāṇiprahata and Pradeśinīprahata. The three Prahāras ore Nigṛhīta (controlled) Ardhanigṛhīta (Semicontrolled) and Mukta (Uncontrolled). The three Mārjanās. are Māyūrī, Ardhamāyūrī and Karmārvī. The eighteen Jātis are Śuddhā Ekarūpā, Deśānurūpā, Deśādapetarūpā, Paryāya, Viṣkambha, Pārṣṇi Samastā, Duṣkarakaraṇā, Urdhva Goṣṭhikā, Uccitikā, Evamvādyā, Mṛdaṅgapaṇavā, Avakīrṇā, Ardhāvakīrṇā, Samplavā and Vidhūta. The twenty Alaṁkāra Prakāras are Citra, Sama, Vibhakta, Chinna, Chinnaviddha, Viddha, Anuviddha, Svarūpānugata, Anusṛta, Vicyuta, Durga, Avakīrṇa, Ardhāvakiṛna, Ekarūpa, Parikṣipta, Sācīkṛta (Sattvīkṛta) Samalekha, Citralekha, Sarvasamavāya and Dṛḍha. The sixteen Akṣaras that have been mentioned before are applicable to Puṣkaras such as Paṇava, Dardura and Mṛdaṅga as well.

Prose pieces

42—43 *The mode of producing Vowels and Consonants in the Avanaddiha* (drums) instruments. The following consonants are to be produced on the right face—Ka, Ṭa, Ra, Ta, Ṭha, Da and Dha. The following on the left face Ga, Ha and Tha. Tha on the Urdhvaka and Ka, Raṇa, Dha, Va and La on the Āliṅgya face. I shall explain the combination of vowels with the consonants The vowels are A, Ā, I, Ī, U, U, E, Ai, O, Au, Am and Aḥ with Ka the vowels A, I, U, E, O and Am can be added thereby getting Ka, Ki, Kukeko and Kam. With Kha the vowels I, U and O can be added thereby getting Khi, Khu and Kho. With Ga the vowels A, E and O can be added thereby getting Gu, Ge and Go. To Gha the vowels A, E and O can be added thereby getting Gha, Ghe and Gho. With Ṭa the vowels A, I, O and Am can be added they getting Ṭa, Ṭi, Ṭo and Ṭam. With Ṭha the vowels A, I, O and Am can be added thereby getting Ṭha, Ṭhi, Tho and Ṭham. With Ḍa the vowels A and O can be added thereby getting Ḍa and Ḍo. With Ṇa the vowels A, I and E can be added thereby getting Ṇa, Ṇi and Ṇe. With Ta and Tha the Vowels A, Ā, I and E can be added thereby getting Ta, Tā, Ti, Te, Tha, Thā, Thi and The. With the consonant Da the vowels A, U, E and O can be added thereby getting Da, Du, De and Do. With Dha the vowels A, I, O and Am can be added to produce Dha, Dhi, Dho and Dham. With Ra the vowels A, Ā, I, and E can be added to produce Ra, Rā, Ri and Re. With La the vowels A, Ā, I and E can be added to produce La, Lā, Li and Le. The consonants H and M are produced without the combination of any vowel. Among these Ka, Gha, Ta, Tha and Dha has Ra as the Anubandha (appendage) to produce Ghrum, Dhra, Kram, Tre, Tram, Thram and Dhram. With Ka, La also acts as Anubandha (Kiam Kle).

Sounds produceable by two hands are made by combining all these Dham is produced in Āṅkika, Mṛdaṅga and two Puṣkaras by the simultaneous strokes of two hands.

Ku is produced by running the finger and Dha by controlling it. When it is half controlled there is Tha. When the back of the hand strokes it there is Kla; from curving the fingers comes Kṣa (Kha) By the simultaneous striking of Urdhuaka and Vāmaka by the two hands there occurs Ham and by striking the forefinger Kle is heard. Some of the sounds are produced from one face of the drum and some from both. Some from three faces of two drums e.g. from all faces Da, Dha from Ālingya and Vāmaka, Ma from Āliṅgya and Dakṣiṇa, Ga from Vāma and Urdhvaka. Dha is sometimes made from Ālinṅgya for the sake of facilities. There should be no prohibition thereof. So much for these combinations.

Pañca Pāṇiprahata. There are Samapāṇi (level handed), Ardhapāṇi (half-handed), Ardhārdhapāṇi (Quarter handed), Pārśvapāṇi (side handed) and Pradeśinī (The index finger). There Pāṇiprahatas (hand strokes) are to be produced with controlled, semicontrolled applications or free of either. Of these Ma is a Prahata of Samapāṇi and Nigṛhīta (controlled) Ga, Da and Dha are Ardhapāṇi and Ardha Nigṛhīta strokes Ka, Kha, Ṭa and Ḍa are with Pārśvapāṇi and controlled Ta, Tha and Ha are Ardhapāṇis and Ardha Nīgṛhītas. Ma, Tha,

Ra, La and Ha, Ṇa are Dvihasta Prahatas and Muktas (free) Klam is a stroke of Ardhapāṇi and Mukta. Drām, Dhram and Klem are two handed Pārśvapāṇi and Mukta. Thus the strokes are made in accordance with the requirements. Only sixteen are the sounds issuing from Avanaddha instruments from which Vāṣkaraṇas are to be produced by sensible people with suitable combinations.

44-45 Prose *Four Mārgas.* The four Mārgas in Avanaddha instruments in regard to the ślokas are Aḍḍita, Ālipta, Vitasta and Gomukha. Aḍḍita Mārga pertains to a combination of Āliṅgya and Mṛdaṅga strikes. Ālipta Mārga pertains to a combination of the Vāmaka and Urdhvaka strokes. The Vitasta Mārga pertains to a combination of Urdhvaka and the right face of Āṅkika strokes. The Gopuccha Marga pertains to the strokes of all Puṣkaras mixed up mostly with those of Aliṅgya Aḍḍita Prahāras (strokes) areas follow—Ghaṭṭam Katthita Ghattam Ghetāmghaṭṭa Gatthimam Gatthi Gatthitthe.

The Ālipta Mārga—Dadhro, Mamadro, Māmmudu Dhem Gudara Nuṇtum Ghumghem Ghendram Ghendrā Maṅ.

The Vitasta Mārra Takitān Takitān Sentām Kintām Ghisam Ketām· Idu Hutaketām. The Gomukha Mārga-Guddham Kladdham Mathikaṭā Ghamghena Chidukhu Khuṇogaga Datthi Maṭam. Ha is produced by pressing the fingers and it is a Mukta stroke and the fingers will have to be crossed and Ardhanigṛhīta on the Urdhvaka and Āṅkika. That is because the level hand (Samapāṇi) is seen to be used on both. Since Ha is produced as mentioned before the following strokes are also to be made viz. Dhittha, Tittha Kitākhaden Khaden Gughum Duleṇṭa Satti Titthan Ghitān Huvaghe. The Vitasta Mārga stokes are devoid of those for La, Ma and Ra. In the Urdhva Marga Speciality is arranged through Gomukhī. The strokes there are Khaṭa Matthi Maṭṭaghaṇṭā Ghurakheṭṭam Khata Mām Vuduṇa Kitti Kitti Kiṭi Mām Khu Khuṇu Ddhe Dhedho Dho. Now the Gomukhavādya Tha Ḍa Ṇa Gheṇṭa Khan. Dulaṅg Hukheṅ Ghaṭa Maṭta Ṭāmṇu Dha Khu Khu Ṇām Tthi Ghaṭam Ghiṭi Mām Kakkuṭāmṇugheṅ Kiṭi Māṅ Ghegbe Ko Ko Ma Strokes produced in the Ālipta Marga can used in all the other Māgas too Groups of Akṣara, Constitute Graha of Mṛdaṅgas.

46—54 I shall give examples thereof in the four Mārgas in due order (a) Ghrṅ Ghṛṅ Ghaṭa Gheṅ Matthi Matthi Maṭā Madāttha Ṭhiṅ Mana Gheṅ Kraṅ Kathi Katāṅ—these in Aḍḍita. (b) Ghā Gha Gendrā Taki Tā Ghṛ Ghṛṅ Dhokaṭi Gheṇṭāṅ Gā N Ghi Kiṭi Ketthā Tha Kutā Kitā Kiri Dām—these in the Vitasta (c) Domāṅ Gudur Gheṅ Ghe Ghaṇṭām Ghe Gha Ṭa Du Mā—these in the Ālipta. They are to be combined thus by those conversant with the same (d) Ghe Ghe Ṭātthi Kaṭām Guṭṭā Ghuṅ Gheṭā Ghaṇṭāṇ Dhima Dhitthi Yamkesaṭe Ghega Gheṇo Ṇam—these in Gomukha. Three are the Pracāras of the Puṣkaras there viz. Sama Viṣama and Sama-Viṣama. In the Vāmaka and Urdhvāka the Pracāra should be Sama as well as of Vāmaka and Savyaka in the Aḍḍita Mārga as well a Āliṗta Mārga. The left hand should be used while striking the Vāmaka Urdhvaka and Madhyaka. The right hand should be used in the Viṣamapracāra in striking the Savya and Urdhvaka. In the Vitasta Mārga, the two hands are to be similarly used in cross wise stroke and the same is produced in the Visama Pracāra. The Pracāra of the hands in the rest of the Mārgas can be in accordance with one's own free will. The Pracāra of the hands should be Sama-Viṣama in the combina- of the Aḍḍita and Gomukha Mārgas. The Vādyas should be played in the Aḍḍita Mārga when Śṛṅgāra and Hāsya Rasas are depicted. When Vīra, Ravdra and Adbhuta are depicted they should be played in the Vitasta Mārga. The Pathetic (Karuṇa) sentiment is depicted with the playing of the instruments in the Ālipta Mārga and the Bībhatsa and Bhayānaka Rasas are depicted by playing them in the Gomukha Mārga. Instruments should be played after careful observation of the dance be fitting the Rasas, Bhāvas, the Sattva of the charactors their gestures, mode of walking and the location of the scene.

55—64 *Playing of Dardura and Paṇava.* The wise and the senseble ones should observe the rule of strokes in accordance with the traditional way. I shall now explain the playing of Dardura and Paṇava. There are three types of playing these drums viz (a) Ativādita (b) Anuvādya and (c) Samavādita. Of these the Ativādita is the playing of drum keeping the Puṣkara in front. When one Mṛdaṅga is played after another at is Anuvādya and when the Mṛdaṅgas are played simultaneously it is Samavādita. The syllabic sounds Ka, Kha, Pa Ṇa,

Pra, Ha, Ṇād, Bra, Hu, Lām, Ghrā Hu, Lām are to be used in playing Paṇava. So also in the playing of Paṇava the sounds Kiri, Ghinṭām, Tho, Tho, Ṇo, Dho, Tra, Avlām, Kiri, Ghinṭām, Ṇo, Ṇo, Ṇa, Ṇṭam, Co, Kiri, Kaṇṭam, Maṭa, Maṭa, Tthi. Te, Ṭe, Ṭe Biduṇṇām are used. The different Karaṇas should be produced by experts by striking the Paṇavas lossely with the tips of the little and the ring fingers. The syllabic funds for colouring Karaṇas are to be produced by the little and the ring fingers. In producing the remaining sounds there be strokes by other fingers. The playing with the Koṇa and the ring finger should be a Śuddha stroke. The playing in irregular Karaṇa comes Taikulaham which is the beginning of the irregular playing. It Continues as Ribhita Karaṇa and Anubandha and to it is added a double Tra. In anubandha of the mixed Karaṇa Dre is produced by striking with the raised hand. This to be specially done by the best player of drums.

Notes which are charming due to their being in the various Karanas are to be produced by the extremity of the small finger. The strokes A Ṇiṇi Ba are also produced by that same finger.

65—71 *Playing of Paṇava.* This should be done by means of the tip of the little finger in a loosely trim drum. The sound Dhattvo Dhvāṇa should be produced by tightly trimmed Paṇavas. In the tightly and loosely trimmed Paṇavas strokes Ka, Ṭha, Ṇa, Ta Ṇa in the tightly trimmed Paṇava. In the loosely trimmed one there should always be strokes, Ta T then Tata. In the trimmed Paṇava Ka Kha and Ta strokes should be produced. They are to be combined with irregular Karaṇas. It is possible to create a resonance of Ṭa in a tightly trimmed Panava. In the same way Hṇa including Ṇa is also possible. This stroke is to be made on the face of the drum held obliquely. The stroke will sound as Kahulām Krak Hulām Krak Hulām. This in brief is the regular playing of Paṇava described by me.

72—77 *Playing of Dardura.* The syllabic stroke, of Dardura are being explained Rakti (Reklii), Tri, Kala Klecadro, Goño Hathiṇṇa—these strokes are included in the free strikes Dardura. So also Tha Na and Ṇṇa. One should make there the stroke, to produce E Ṇaṇakṣāra Gradha by one's right hand and to produce Go Matthā by touching Dardura by the tip of the left hand. Strokes giving Muktollā should be produced by two controlled hands and the sounds being pressed after seizing the drum by freely holding it. Thitten Tra should be produced by pressing the hand ar usual. Special sounds are are produced freely and half free and half-checked ones are produced by arresting the strok. If the sounds are too surftly done or in quick succession they are bound to be wrongly produced. These are the pure strokes not mixed up with strokes of drums of other types. Now for the combined playing of Dardura, Paṇava and Mṛdaṅga.

78—86 *The three Puṣkaras inunism.* When the instruments are played unison some Karaṇas are expressed distinctly whereas some Karaṇas are simultaneously produced and some serially. In such mixed playing the strokes like Ṇa, Ga and Ra and Dheṅ Kākattham Caikho Kahulam Takita are made in the Mrdaṅgas. In the case of Darpura Daṅ Syeṅ Dreṅ Kahulām and Maṭam white in the case of Paṇava Yam Maṭatthi Dām Kahulām Maṭatthi Deṅva. Karaṇas other than these are to be always mixed in production; further, those mentioned previously are also be mixed up in accordance with necessity. Simultaneous production of these Karaṇas in the Paṇava is follows:—Kahulām Ṇna Ṇnām, Kha, Khu, Ṇne, Khe, Dromo, Droṇam, The, Tho, Thim, Dvam. The excellent player gradually produces these Karaṇas—Ṭa, Ṭa, Ṭe, Ghoṇa, Ṇa, Ṇa, Kirini Kiṇi, Kiṇṇā. In the Aṅubandha of Paṇava the Karaṇas should be Ṇṇu Khu, Khu, Ṇa and Kṛtapratikṛta is played in the experts in Mṛdanga and Darpura. Those Karaṇas expected to be produced in Muraja at the time of walking and other movement of the different characters in a play should also be followed in all its syllables in the playing of Paṇava. At the time of walking and similar movements no playing of drums in the Citra Mārga is indulged in by experts. When the setting of feet is not to be seen by the audience the playing of the drum should by Sama-Viṣama.

87—91 The Uparipāṇi should be freely employed while playing Paṇava and Mṛdaṅga. The same should be made by similar strokes. Generally Paṇava should be taken up for playing before all other instruments. Now I shall explain the Prahāras of the Dardura viz. Dasṛk Sentatitā, Tetitsa, Deve, Ramita, Nṛtthā, Matthi. After making these two free and then stopping strokes such as Ṇa, Ṇṇā, Re should be made. strokes like Bhre Dhro Kithi by the right hand and Gudat Him Klam by the left hand. The tips of the hand then make Tatvavṛṣṭi and the two hands should be checked after striking Tam. Further, the stroke Takam should indicate the rest of the Karaṇānubandha.

92—93 *Prose.* The six Karaṇas are Rūpa, Kṛtapratikṛta, Pratibheda, Rūpaśeṣa OGha and the sixth one Pratiśuṣka (a) *Rūpa*—When the Karaṇas reproduced by both the hands. e.g. Gham Khu Khu Ṇa Khu Gham Kramam Tthimam Tyettaram Ghaṭam Ghatthi Methi Gheṇṭā Kaṭa Guddha Raṇa Kiṭi Gham Ghe Kaghaṭam Ghe Ka Kham (b) *Kṛtapratikṛta* When the Tripuṣkara cause of the Udbhāvanā (display) of a Karaṇa it is called Kṛtapratikṛta e.g. Tham Ghu Ṇa Khatham Kramatthi Vaggeṁ Raghaṭām Ghaṭatthi Gham Tsām Idughe Kuhu-lāṇṇam Dodhoṇa (c) *Pratibheda.* When after the two Karaṇas of Mṛdaṅgas have been produced simultaneously the playing takes to Uparikaraṇa (e g.) Dho Dho Ṇā Kho Lā La Ṇā Ṇā Tthi Ṭabhi Ghaṇḍām (d) *Rūpaśeṣa.* When there is absence of the distinction of Karaṇas (e.g. Khu Khu Ṇo Ṇṇā Maṭa Dheṁ Ghentā Maṭa Ghoṭā Mathi Ātlyām Ghom (e) *Ogha.* When the playtng of all the instruments called Caturka (four some) is in tempo and sonant syllables are produced it is Ogha (e.g) Thaṅkiṭi Manthi Hi Kiṭi Dheṅ Ghaṇṭāṇam Gheṇḍā Ghoṇa-ghaṭugoeṅ Gham Ghe Viriṇi Ṇageham Thaithotho Tathai Ghe and (b) *Pratiśuṣka.* When there is Anusvara (Harmonious note) among the players of the Mṛdaṅga, Paṇava and Dardura (e.g.) Ghaṭamatatthi Duṇa Therjakiṭi Kegheṅ Ghoṅ Ghoṇḍā Ghoṇa Kh Kho Kha Kuṭakiṭa Vakatthi Ṇanatthi. Thus the six types of the combination of the Karaṇas have been explained. The Vāṣkara Ṇa should be employed by the sensible in this manner.

Prose and 94—101 *Three Yatis.* The three Yatis are Samā Srotogatā and Gopuccha.. Yati connotes the three ways of combining tempo and Pāṇi. It is of three types i.e. Rāddaa, Viddha and Śayyāgata. The three Layas (tempo) are Druta (quick), Madhya (meduim) and Vilambita (slow). The three

Pāṇis are Samapaṇi Ardhapāṇi and Uparipāṇi Thus the three ways of combining the Karaṇas. The Raddha play occusr when in the performance the Yati happens to be Sama, the Laya Druta and there is Upṇi as well. Smilarly when the musical instruments are given importance with Uparipāṇi Sama Yati but Madhya Laya it is also called Pāddha Vādya. When the Yati is Srotogatā the Laya is Madhya and also Samapāṇi the playing is called Viddha. The Vādya is called Viddha when in the case of characters of superior or middling type its procedure is Vārtika of Dakṣiṇa. When there is Ardhapāṇi stroke, Vilambita Laya and Gopvccha Yati, the playing is called Śayāgata When the singing is given importance and the procedure is Dakṣiṇa the playing of Atyukta instruments is also called Śayyāgata. Their standard arises from the Sthita Laya etc. In other Pāṇis, Kalās are reduced. The Yati, Pāni and the Laya in connection with the playing of instruments should be observed according to one's liking after considering the special performance of plays.

102—107 *Three Mārjantās.* The three Mārjantās are Māyūrī, Ardhamāyūrī and Karmā Ravi. They are known to relate to notes of Puṣkaras notes in the Māyūrī Mārjanā are Gāndhāra in the Vāmaka; Ṣaḍja in the Dakṣiṇā Puṣkara and Madhyama in the Urdhvaka. Notes in the Ardha-Mayūrī are Ṣaḍja in the Vāmaka Puṣkara; Ṛṣabha in the Dakṣiṇa and Dhaivata in the Urdhvaka. The notes in the Karmāravī are Ṛṣabha in the Vāmakapuṣkara; Ṣaḍja in the Dakṣiṇa Puṣkara and Pañcama in the Urdhvaka. On having Mārjanā in Āliṅgya, there should be provision for Niṣāda which is assonant to the notes above-mentioned and which is a note of Jātis. The Ardha Māyūrī Mārjanā is in the Ṣaḍjagrāma the Māyūrī in the Madhyama Grāma and the Karmāravī in the Gāndhāra Grāma. Of course overlapping notes too are included.

108—110 Notes including regular Srotis are fixed and relate to the Marjanās and the remaining are considered Sañcārī (transitory), Accessory notes, should be produced through the Vāmaka and the Urdhvaka by their plastering which will give then slackness or tenseness. Similar treatment should be given to the Āliṅgya and the Āṅkika Players of drums should through their slackness and tenseness as well as of piercing of hides produce these notes.

111—118 *Use of Mṛt (clay) for Mārjanā of Vāmaika and Ūrdhvaka.* This Mārjanā of the Vāmaka and the Urdhvaka should be done through the use of clay. Listen to salient features of the clay used for this purpose. The clay shall shall contain no gravel, sand, grass or husk of grains. It should not stick. It shall not be while, alkaline, pungent yellow, black, sour or letter, This clay is to be used for plastering for the plastering for the purpose of plastering. The blackish clay from a river bank, renders fine and drained of water should be used for Mārjanh. One should use wheat flour or barley flour or a mixture of both, if the clay available spreads very much; it is heavy or unstable, white or black and full of husks or if it does not produce desirable notes. One defect of the mixture of the two flours is that it creates a monotonous around.

Thus it is blackish clay applied for the Mārjanā that will produce proper notes. *There Saṁyogas.* I shall now explain the three Saṁyogas. They are a Gutusaācaya, (b) Laghusañcaya and (c) Guru-Laghu-Sañcaya. *Gurusañcaya.* It has Guru syllables, vilambita Laya and Ogha Pravṛtti e.g. Gheto Ketām Candrām Khetam Dvam Dvam Khetāddham Dvam Dvam Drāghetām Kattām Khetām. *Laghusañcaya.* Only short syllables are used in Drutaloya e.g. Ghaṭa Maṭa Ghata Matthi-Ghaṭu Ghaṭu. *The Guru Laghu Sañcaya.* Laghu Syllables mixed with Guru ones in Druta Laya e.g. Ghaṭa Vimatthi the Mathitham Kimtā Gham Gham. *The three Gatas.* The three Gatas are, Tattva, Anugata and Ogha. In the Tattva playing of drums there should be strokes similar to recoginzed syllables distinctly expressing words and syllables distinctly expressing worns and syllables comforming to the metre of songs and well divided in Karaṇas.

119—20 The Anugata playing of drums should begin with the Sama Pāṇi or the Avara Pāṇi and it should have Karaṇas produced by distinct strokes and it should follow the song. The Anugata playing of drums should begin with Upari Pāṇi and it should not rest on one Karaṇa only it should be quick tempo its Karaṇas should be Āviddha and it should be used extensively **Eight *Sāmyas* (conformities).**

121—129 All playing of drums should have eight Sāmyas (conformities) viz. Ṣarasama (conforming in syllables) (2) Aṅgasama (—in limbs) (3) Tāla Sam (—in Tāla) (4) Layasama (— in Laya) (5) Yatisama (—in Yati) (6) Grahasama (—in Graha) (7) Nyāsopanyāsa (Sama—) and (8) Pāṇi Sama (conforming in Pāṇi). The playing which follows the song in the metre consisting of short and long syllables shows conformity in syllables. The playing which follows the song equally in the three limbs in its beginning (Graha), end (Mokṣa) and in the Kalās and Antara Kalās shows the Sāmya in limbs. The playing which by its measures of Kalās and time, equals the body of the song, shows the conformity in Tāla. The playing of drum which follows the song equally in its performance in slow, medium and quick Layas shows conformity therein. If the playing of the drum follows the Samā, Srotogatā and Gopucchā Yatis of the songs it an example of comformity in Yati. If in the Tata, Avaṇaddha and Vaṁśa Vādyas there is the Graha of similar Śrutis along with the songs it is called the Sāmya in Graha. The playing of Veṇu and Vīṇā in such a way that the notes in their Nyāsa and Apanyāsa may agree to that of the song is an example of the Samya in Nyāsa and Apanyāsa when the Samapāṇi, Avapāṇi and Uparipāṇi playing of instruments follow the song it is an example of conformity in Pāṇi.

Prose+130—141 *The Eighteen Jātis.* What has been mentioned as Eighteen Jātis we shall explain now. They (1) Śuddhā (2) Ekarūpā (3) Deśānurūpā (4) Deśādapetarūpā (5) Paryāyā (6) Viṣkambhā (7) Paryastā (8) Saṁrambhā (9) Pārṣṇi Samastā (10) Duṣkara Karaṇā (11) Urdhva Goṣṭhikā (12) Uccitikā (13) Evamvādyā (14) Mṛdaṅga-Paṇavā (15) Avakīrṇā (16) Ardhāvakīrṇā, (17) Samplavā and (18) Vidhūtā I shall elaborate the features and examples thereof. If the playing of the drums includes Karaṇas of one or two syllables and if it is worthy of being used in all movements it is called Śuddhā. It consists of Kho Kho Kham Kham Khām. It should be known as Śuddhā, the Jāti for the action of the middling and superior women characters when one plays separately Gomukha in the Aḍḍita Ālipta or Vitasta Mārga it is called Ekarūpā as for example Droṅ Ghoṅ Doṅghoṅ Ghegheṅ in the Aḍḍitan Mārga. This Ekarūpā Jāti should be employed in the case of songs of male singers. This Jāti should be used in case of all characters while the Dhruvā is sung in a slow or quick tempo and it may also be used after one has judged adequately the place time and condition of characters in the case of Dhruvas sung in a medium tempo. When all other musical instruments follow one Karaṇa in pursuance of the playing of Mṛdaṅga it is also called Ekarūpā. The Deśānurūpā Jāti played in Aḍḍita Mārga is used in the Śṛṅgāra Rasa of enjoyment of pleasures. Vilambita Laya is to be followed. Mī Matthi Tthamabhū Tthikimā are the syllables in Deśānu Rūpā Jāti. It has to be used in the most excellent Śṛṅgāra of women. Deśād Apetorūpā Jāti [is played in Vāmaka and Urdhvaka in a Druta Laya in Avakṛṣṭa Dhruvās. It is to be employed when Karuṇa Rasa has to be delimated. Ghedrāṅ Ghedrāṅ Gheghem—these are the syllables in the Deśād Apetarūpā Jāti while playing drums. When the same set of Karaṇas as played previously are followed in all three tempos it is Paryāyā Jāti e.g. Ghedāṅ Gheḍeṅ Gudughoṅ played in the Vāmaka and Urdhvaka by the left hand should be employed in the Vīra, Adbhuta and Raudra Rasas.

142—149 Two Gurus two Laghus, one Laghu syllable, three Guru syllables and a laghu syllable such as Siṅ Māṅ Ghaṭa Chendra Gvdu Gheṅ Gheṅ Ghama Tthi Mettham constitute the Viṣkambhā Jāti. It is to be employed in the case of superior women while portraying Śṛṅgāra Rasa. Playing of the drums in all Mārgas with Karaṇas of one syllable and with the Samapracāra of the hands is called Paryastā Jāti. It is to be employed in the case of a quick movement of the chariots, Vimānas Vimānas Vidyā-Dharas, serpents etc. in the sky or in heavy downpour of water, Paryastā Jāti should be used in the slow tempo in the Śṛṅgāra Rasa of superior characters; it is also used in the case of inferior characters Gheṅtāṅ Gheṅ Ṇām these constitute the Samrambhā Jāti, to be applied in case of inferior women. The Jāti which has Karaṇas of Ardhapāṇi and the medium tempo in the beginning and quick tempo in the end is called Samrambhā e.g. Maga Ṭham Kuyuthakim. Pārṣṇi Samastā Jāti should be played on the face of Urdhvāṅkika and Dakṣiṇa by quick strokes in the Vitasta Mārga and it is to be applied in movements of Śṛṅgāra and Hāsyarasas Parṣṇi Samasta Jāti should be played with Karaṇas Tatthim Karam Mamcchi and Dhaun Drāṅ Gudheṅ Gūdhi Tāṅ with the pressure of the Pārṣṇi. This is to be applied to the movement of superior male characters of calm type and of the Dānavas.

150—160 By striking of all the Mṛdaṅgas with the movement of Svastika hands one should play the Duṣkara Karaṇā in all their tempos Duṣkara Karaṇā Jāti should include syllables like Duṇu Duṇu Duṇā Kiṁka Dheṅ Ghoteṅ Madatthi Dughakḥi Dheṅ. Duṣkara Karaṇā Jāti should be applied in case of movements of Daitya kings, chiefs, Bhujagas, Rākṣasas, Piśācas, Gandharvas, Guhyakas etc. Light strokes on the face of Urdhvaka, Āṅkika and Dakṣiṇa in the Vitasta Mārga or striking of Dakṣiṇaka and Vāmaka after beginning with Aṅkika and Urdhvaka (will constitute Urdhavagoṣīhikā) Playing almost violently Adhi Dhṛṅ Dhṛṅ in the Vitasta Mārga will constitute Urdhva Gossṭhikā Jāti. It is meant for the movement of bearenly characters. The playing which includes all the Mārgas connected in an imperceptible chain is called Uccitikā Jāti. This Jāti includes syllables like Kentām Kenām Gaditām and is to be applied in the natural movements of kings. Evamvādyā Jāti should be played with syllables of the Gomukhī and it should have all the strokes of Mṛdanga; and it should be applied in the pantomima of jugglery by persons with or without disguise and it should include the syllables like—Gheṇiā Ṭādau Tāthita Dheṅ Dheṅmaṭa Tthi Ghaṭa Iṅghe. This should be applied in the case of the movement of dwarfs, persons in confusion, lame men and those who suffer from bodily pain or wounds in the feet. The playing of drums in which there is striking of the earth in different sections (Parvans) of Karaṇas is the Jāti which suits all Mañcas (stages).

161—169 Syllables like Dhrom Dhrom Ṭem Tem are included in this Jāti. It is to be applied to women's movements. Avakīrṇā Jāti is the playing of Mṛdaṅga with three fold Karaṇas, when the same is added to the playing of Dardura and Paṇava it is called Ardhāvakīrṇā Jāti. This Ardhāvakīrṇā Jati consists of Kentām Kentāmke Ntām played in the Gomukha Mārga Dardura Paṇava and Mṛdaṅga. should be played by halves in the manner of the Ardihva Kirṇā Jāti and with light syllables included in the suitable Mārga and it should consist of syllables like Thaṅ Gadagheṇḍām. This is called the Samplavā Jāti. The samplavā Jāti produced by using all the fingers and by all the strokes of Mṛdaṅga is to be applied to movement of terrified persons and to any movement of theirs in the sky. The Vidhūtā Jati, produced with various Divya (fascinating) Karaṇas and strokes of Mṛdaṅgas is to be applied in the case of the natural movement of superior persons. It should consist of syllables like Darige Gudu Gheṅ Titthiklāma Ṭatthi Kaṇam Kukrāma. These are the Jātis to be known by the sensible ones for application in the walk and other movements. Those that have not been mentioned here should be understood from the persons concerned with a view to their meaning.

170—174 *Playing of the drums in three Gatas.* Sensible men should play the drums according to the rules specially in walks and other movements of characters in the ten kinds of Rūpakas. (Dramas). In the songs of the seven types and the Āsārita metre it is desired to employ Tattva, Anugata and Ogha playing of drums. If one desires the unison of the two, one should play drums with Guru but small number of syllables at the time of songs indicating walks and other movements. Tattva and sometime Ogha too should be applied in the case of kings because these are natural to their charming conditions. Tattva should be applied to the first song, Anugata to the second and Ogha should be the playing of drum at the time of walking and other movements.

175--180 *Playing of drums in Dhruvās.* In the case of the remaining Dhruvas one should have various manners of playing drums in accordance with one's inclination. In the case of the Sthitāvakṛṣṭā Dhruvā the playing should be of the Anugata. type. In the case of the Prāvesikī Dhruvā (the playing should be Anugata. In the Naiṣkrāmikī and the Antarā Dhruvā the playing should employ all the three Layas. The Prāsādikī Dhruvā should have Druta Laya and Dhruvās in general will be of five types. This will be the playing of drums in the Prakaraṇas. Experts should observe through playing of drums the Mātrās and divisions in the Pāda of Dhruvās at the time of walking and other movements. The producers should thus apply the playing of the drums at the time of walking and other movements. *How to begin the playing of drums.* 'I shall now speak of the manner of beginning the play of drums. According to some this should begin with Śamyā and Tāla and according to others with the middle finger, some say that it should begin with the Ākāśa (empty space) and others with the forefinger.

181—186 In the Niṣkrama (exit) the Graha may also be from Ākāśa. The Āsārita songs will always have the Śamyā Graha and the two Tālas growing from the limbs of Dhruvās. There is no Laya as well as Gīta Graha. But, where the Graha should begin with the index finger, the Śīrṣaka as well as the Graha of Uddhatā Dhruvās should be produced with the index finger. The Graha of the Natkuṭa and Aḍḍitā as well as of Prāsādikī will be Sannipāta and it will consists of divisions one Kalā. The Ākāśa Graha consists of four divisions of two Kalās. Its songs will be composed of limbs suiting it in due order. These are the Grahas relating to the Vādyas to be known by the wise. I shall next speak of the playing of these in dances of energetic (Tāṇḍava) and of delicate (Lāsya) types.

187—197 [Sukumāra] One Parivarta (performance) of the song should be with no accompaniment of instruments. At the end of this the Graha should be the Sannipāta in playing instrument. Or for the embellishment of the dances there should be change of limbs of the performance, together with the change of the Laya of the song. When the limb of the performance requires the employment of gestures there should be no playing of music (in the drum). But when there is the dance consisting of Aṅgahāras there should be music accompanying it when due to the manner of its performance a limb is replated frequently first it should be accompanied by gestures and finally it should be connected with dance. The playing of drums (Vādyas) should be similar in metre to that of the songs. The movements of limbs should be made in conformity to the measures of the songs and those of the instruments. The playing of drums in the Mukha and Upohana should consist of Guru syllables along with the Laghus and this should be Prakṛṣṭa in the production of such Varṇas (letters). The playing of drums along with songs in a Vilambita Laya with the strokes sufficient to produce the syllables and in all these the Uparipāṇi should be observed. In the Tāṇḍava (graceful) dance the playing of the drums by those who are well-conversant with the same and Laya should be harmonious (Sama), pleasing (Rakta), divided into Kalā, distinct (Sphuṭa) produced by simple pure strokes and accompanying the various limbs of the performance. In the performances including dance the Tattva followed by Anugata should be played in drums while in performances with any dance, the Tattva should be followed by Ogha. The drum should be played on these occasions in Vilambita, Madhya or Druta Laya as in the case of a song and the same should be the method of playing drums in the performance of Padas and dance with Aṅgahāras. Rules regarding the Padas as well as Varṇas which apply in the case of songs and playing of instruments, should be observed in dance with Aṅga Hāras in connection with the dramatic performances.

198—204 *Twenty Prakāras and their application.* Thus I have explained the eighteen Jātis in regard to the playing of drums. I shall now explain the Prakāras connected therewith. They are (1) Citra (2) Sama (3) Vibhakta (4) Chinna (5) Chinnaviddha (6) Viddha (7) Anuviddha (8) Svarūpānugata (9) Anusṛta (10) Anusṛtavicyuta (11) Durga (12) Avakīrṇa (13) Ardhāvakīrṇa (14) Ekarūpa, (15) Parikṣipta (16) Sācīkṛta (17) Samalekha (18) Citralekha (19) Sarvasamavāya (20) Dṛḍha. The playing which is performed with the various Karaṇas such as Nirvartita etc. by many kinds of hands and which has the three Layas and the three Pāṇis is called Citra Dardara, Paṇava and Mṛdanga are played with various Karaṇas and this playing combined with Tāla, limbs and flutes is called Sama. When the playing is not very broad in position and it observes equally, syllables, Pāṇi and Laya in its divided Karaṇas, it is Vibhakta. The playing of drums in a quick tempo suddenly stopping when all other instruments are separately played is called Chinna. The playing in which the Mṛdangas are taken up with Avapāṇi and the Paṇava with Upari Pāṇi is called Chinna Viddha. When Paṇavas are played with the Karaṇas used for Mṛdaṅgas and such Karaṇas are the various Sūcivedhas, the playing is called Viddha.

205—213 The playing which is intermixed with Viddha and is seen in connection with all the instruments, is called Anuviddha because of the mutual Anuvedha. When the playing has a simple nature and is done by Samapāṇi and follows its own fixed pattern it is called Svarūpa. When the Paṇava follows the Muraja and Dardara follows the Paṇava the playing is termed Svarūpānugata when, after following these instruments they attain the same Laya and are head simultaneously with these, it is called Anusṛta. When the playing of a drum following another instrument in its own Jāti, passes into another Jāti it is called Anusṛtavicyuta. The playing which being irregular in its movement develops all the Mārgas and is done with undivided syllables, is called Durga. When Mṛdaṅgas are played together with Paṇavas in many and various Karaṇās the playing is called Avakīrṇa. When a Paṇava or Dardara is played in Drutalaya along with Avapāṇi the playing is called Ardhāvakīrṇa when the playing of all the instruments follow one Karaṇa it is called Ekarūpa.

214—221 When the playing in a low round of Mṛdaṅga with undivided syllables is coverged with that of Paṇava it is called Parikṣipta. When various Karaṇas are played in one instrument to follow a dance with Aṅgahāras it is called Sācīkṛta. When a Paṇava and a Muraja, after being played first, take up the Murajas the playing is called Samullekha. When a Paṅava etc. are played together in various ways it is called Citralekha. The playing which follows all the Mārgas adopts all the Pāṇis and Layas is various and is well divided in their syllables is called Sarvasamavāya. The playing which is in a medium tempo, harmonious and has clearly produced syllables and is fit to accompany movements, is called Dṛḍha. These different Prakāras of the playing of drums should be taken up to follow movements and songs after considering the sentiments and Bhāvas involved Prakāras and Jātis apply to all Mārgas. But in movements they are to be in their pure forms

Seating of the Musicians.

226 *Prose passages.* I shall explain the application thereof the members of the orchestra [Kutapas] should be seated on the stage facing the east. Their seats shall be between the two doors of the green room referred to before. The Muraja

player should face the stage the Paṇava player occupies the seat to his right and the Dardara player he seat on his left. Thus is the seating of Avanaddhakutapa. The Gāyana (male singer) faces the north the Vīṇā player sits to his left and the two Vaṁśa players sit to his right. A female singer faces the male singer. This explains the Kutapa Vinyāsa. *Trisaman.* Now the players of Mṛdaṅga, Paṇava and Dardara are porperly seated in the company of male and female singers and also the flute and Vīṇā players. The strings of the Ātodyas are tightened, controlled and sounded duly with relation to proper Grāma, Rāga and Mūrcchanā. The Mṛdaṅgas are struck in quick succession by Nipīḍita (Pressed), Nigṛhīta (arrested) Ardha-Nigṛhīta (Semi-arrested) and Mukta (free) strokes. Thereafter the players place their hands on the best Dardaras and observe at the outset the caremony of Trisāman for the reception of the Devas, their invocation and the ceremonial send off. By means of the first Sāman arising from the mouth of Brahmā the creator, the sustainer and the destroyer of all the living beings mobile and immoble, the singer pleases the moon on the left the serpents on the right and the aquatic creatures in between. By means of the second (Sāman be delights the sages and by the third Bṛhat Sāman the divine beings in general. The Trisāmatva is thus to be known by the sensible ones because, one pleases and delights duly the Daivatas there by. This has been glorified by sages as Trisāma because thereby Brahmā, Keśava and Śiva are resorted to. The Mantra Om is uttered at the outset when the four Vedas are recited. So also the Trisāma is sung in the beginning of all the songs. Three Prakāras are to be observed in this Trisāman. So also the three Layas, the Aḍḍitā Mārga and a division of three or six Kalās to the accompaniment of the drums. Its Ākṣaras should be of three kinds including the Guru and Laghu ones. The latters Au and Ma are to be uttered thrice after trebling than (Prose Passage). The sponsor should make arragements to perform the Bahirgītas at the end of the Trisāman after duly concluding the procedure of the preliminary rites. There shall be three Layas with the drumming which will follow the song in its metre and syllables. At the application of the Āsārita song, one should perform the drumming of the Tattva and Anugata Prakṛti. After the Trisāman when Pratyāhāra etc. reach their end it is the time to begin the drumming. At the outset all the drums are to be played in the following order:—The Vāmaka and Urdhvaka are struck first, then the Āliṅgyaka with the Gopucchā Yati and playing of the Vipañcī should be performed afterwards. If it were to be asked why so?" The answer as drums played at outset are sure to bring about success. Performance of the Dhruvā is first indicated by drums. Then, in the auditorium filled with laymen and women that type of music which is capable of creating their interest should be performed.

(227+prose passages) *Different Tastes of those also listen.* Masters of the art of music are interested in the perfect harmonious unison of all units; the learned Paṇḍitas admire the distinct enunciation of the Padas that constitute the songs, the women love the sweetness of the voice of the singers and the remaining members of the audience are satisfied with Vikruṣṭa (crying loud in the form of full throated singing).

Variety of drumming befitted the occasion. When the playing of drums is concluded the experts in the Mṛdaṅga should produce in their Vādyas perferebly by the touch of their fingers, a music consisting of a collection of light Varṇas and aad relating to the Tāṇḍava at the time of the appearance of the danseuse. The song relevant to the appearance of the danseuse being concluded the orchestra take up the Sannipātas. In the connection thereof a music related to the Karaṇas conforming to the Aṅgahāras of the Lāsya dance should be combined with the Karaṇa Dhātu. Hence is the utterence Samam (Harmonious) Raktam (pleasing). 33—194 Next at the start of the performance music should be played in relation to the Karaṇa of the Ālipta Mārga. It should be ferformed by the striking of the Vāmaka and the Urdhvaka. It shall be as follows—Dheṅ Mati Dhaṅ Mathā Dheṅ Dhiti Ṭit Samkram Kram Kho Kaṇe Devyām Kentām Kiṭ Dheṅ. The change after these two sorts of playing will be to that of pure Jāti in the four Mārеas consisting of Kho Kho Ṇām Kho Kho Ṇām Kho Kho Kho Nā. After their stoppage there should be Kho Kho Kho Do Kho Ka Khe Ṇām Gha Gha Tāgham in the setting of the nenter foot, just as there should bẹ playing of Kondukhon at the time of the entering of the Caturthavāra. This should be played mostly by running the fingers on the drums. In the Utthāpana of the Vastu and in the Apakṛṣṭa Cārī teere, the playing should begin with Ghe Ghentām Gheṅ Ṅo Ghakkhaṇā Doṇām Gho Gea Ghe Gha Ghe. In the Śuṣkāpakṛṣṭā Dhruvā of the Nāndī the playing should be in the Pratiśuṣka Karaṇa and should have Tho Thotho Khekhadho Gheṅ Nādamyaṅ Khoddho Kuṭām Kha Khe Khe Ṇaka Ṇaka Suguka Gheā No Khi Kheṅ Tāṅ Kheṅ Ṇam Kiṭī Kiṭi Gha Gheṅ Ghekaṭu Ka Ghu Dukam Lava Lā Kho Kho Kho Vāghru Teṭām Māliṁ Ṇammām Kiṭi Vatthi. One should take to Sannipāta of the Aḍḍitā Mārga when the Cārī accompanying the Jarjara Śloka is performed during the ceremonies of the Raṅgadvāra! In the Mahācārī connected with this there should be playing of drums in the Vitasta Mārga and the Graha therein shouid be by the fore finger. Similarly during the prelminaries an extra ordinary playing of **drums** suited to Tāṇḍava dance has been recommended and it should have Sannipāta Graha and should be played by the left hand with the following Akṣaras Kho Kho Nām Do Do Dokaḥ Mokaḥ Daheṇaṇā Tho Tho No Gho Gha Ṭama Ṭatḥigham Gho Gho Kaṭha Kaṭha Jham Kho Kho Khitakaṭakaṭām Ghaṭaka Matthi Gho Gho Mitthi Nām Kiṭi Kinām Khakavalam. Next an example of playing of the Ālipta Mārga should be **offered** The Graha of the **Vitasta** Mārga played **shall** be with the fore finger. It is as follows—Nāṇa Kho Kaṇa No Madhuṇam Kho Kho Mathi Takitām Tavitām Kintikitkm Kiṭi Kito Kho Kho Matitā Matihitra Mati Kinnām Kentām Mudrām Garem Garem Klem Ghram Ghram Dā Grām Gḥadre Dram Ghendrām Ghaṅe Kleṅ. From the time of the tossing of the screen there should be the playing of drums during the Catnrasra Pūrva Raṅga Vidhāna to ensure the success of the performance. In the Tryaśra Pūrvaraṅga Vidhāna there should be the same playing without interval time now the directions about the playing of drums shall be given later. They will be those suitable at the time of walking and other movements of the four heroes viz. Dhīrodātta, Dhīroddhata, Dhīra Lalita and Dhīraprasānta in the plays Nāṭaka etc. During the movement of gods ths playing should include Bram, Dhram Dhram Dhrā Dram. During the movement of kings it should have Ghem Tām and in the case of middling men the playing should include Dhram Klam Dhaṭu Gheṅ Geṭ Titthi Duna Kiṭi Drām

Nām Nām Dhra Drām. Now I shall speak about the playing of drums in the Sthitā Dhruvā.

Prose passages

228—232 At that time, the dance steps should be in conformity to the rhythm consisting of three Kalās two Kalās or of one Kalā. And the song should conform to drums. Now I shall speak of the playing of drums in different conditions of characters in a play. In the course of their quick walking the playing should include Vam Vam Gheghe Ṭām and it should be performed by the unequal strokes by fingers. They have been written properly while discussing the movement of fingers. Again I shall describe the rules regarding the playing of drums. In walking and other movements the experts shall provide for playing of the drums with Tālas of three or four Kalās after considering the tempo and manner of walking of the characters concerned. In the playing of the drums there should be no pause of one Kalā or of two Kalās between the Dhruvās. Hence the movements hould be in unison with the playing of drums and not with the songs. In quick walk, walking the Pāta of Tāla should be as described in the case of the walking and other movement. Strokes like Dhraṅ Dhraṅ Gheṅ Gheṅ should be mostly made in this playing. In the case of the movement of boats, chariots and aerial cars, birds moving heavenly bodies the playing of the drums should be by running the fingers on the face of drums or by striking in the Catuṣka by the two hands alternatively. In the case of sorrow, suffering illness, curse, death of dear ones loss of wealth, killing imprisonment, vow austerity and fasting etc. the playing of drums in Utthāpana should be according to the Ālipta Mārga mentioned before. In the case of the walking of Daityas, Dānavas, Yakṣas Rākṣasas and Grahas the playing of drums should include Karaṇas such as Dṛṅ Dhṛṅ Khada together with with Ghaṭu Tutanta Tetondrām. In the walking of the lame, handicapped dwarf, hump backed etc the playing consists of Ghetām Kaṭakām. In the case of the buffoon, Nirmuṇḍakas, Upasthāyakas (servant, Buddhistic disciple) Varṣavaras (enuchs) the Vādya consists of Ghegheṅ Stānoṇṇo Doṇna Nām. Further in the walking of old Śrotriyas, Kañcukins corpulent persons etc. the playing should include Dhrām Dhrom Dhrām

Droṅ Dhiṅ Droṇām Kho Khoṇā. In the case of the movements of elephants horses, asces, camels, chariots and aerial cars the playing should include Vamkiṭi. In all cases of superior, middling and the inferior men the playing of drums should be performed after a consideration of Rasas and Bhāvas in the world. So much about the playing drums in the cases of men. I shall now describe the same in the case of women. In the case of the superior females viz goddesses, the playing will include mostly Vam Gati Kipi Ghameṭa Prathi Ghe. In the case of queens it should include mostly Kathi Kathi Mathi Do Do Khu Khu. In the case of the brahmin ladies it should include Cam Kitti Kitthi Ghaṭa Maṭa Thi Ghe. In the case of middling women who are courtezans female artisants anP actresses the playing should include Gha Khu Khu Ghikiṭa Matthi Kina Toṇām Gho. For inferior women the playing should include Marathi Kule Keḍu Khu Khi Khi mostly. Thus much succinctly in regard to the playing in the case of females. In their special conditions playing in conditions similar to those of males should be performed. It is from these that the general Vibhāvas like fear, suffering sorrow anger etc, srise. Here also there should be playing of drums in proper Mārgas which relate to Rasas and Bhāvas.

Prose

233—239 Moreover he is the best player who observes proper Jāti Mārga and Prakāra in suitable Karaṇas and syllables and then plays drums. The intervening playings are Anuviddha, Viparahārika, Siddhigrahaṇa and Paricchinna. *Anuviddha* e.g. the playing is Khokhoṇeṇegne. *Viprahārika* at the conclusion of the Vādya is Dhram Drām Kho Kho. *Śiddhigrahaṇa* should be played at the attainment of wealth, oblivion, exhaustion and when the clothes are tightened or ornaments are adjusted. This Siddhi should take to proper Mārgas and include Citrakaraṇas. It may consist of five or six Kalās. It should be played also at the stoppage of recitations, at the pause when someone begins to do any thing at the fall of garments, ornaments etc. and when adjusts the head gear or crown. The playing after the beginning of Dhruvā should be clear and should relate to all the drums and should include Ghumghumlka. In the case superior ladies there should be a playing in the Āḍḍitā Mārga which is to include Ṇaṇām Kho Kho Ṅaṇṇām. In the case of the inferior female characters there should be playing suited to Khañja Natkuṭa Dhruvā and should include Saṁ Saṁketa Kiṭi Kiṇṇām. In other conditions they should be reduced by a half. Now about the playing of drums in the Prāsādikī and Prāveśikī, Ākṣepikī and Avakṛṣṭā Dhruvās. The playing in the Prāsādikī (Druvā) should be with Samapāṇi and is to be divided into Karaṇas while this is in quick tempo the plaing should be with the Uparipāṇi in the Citra Karaṇa. In the Sthitā (slow) tempo. In the Avakṛṣṭā Dhruvā in tne Āḍḍitā Mārga there should be Ardhasannipāta. In this manner there should be playing of drums in walking and other movements at the of Prāsādakī and Antarā Dhruvas. As a change, one song without any playing of drums should be sung and at the end of the Sannipāta the drums should be taken up for playing. In the quick and slow tempos there should be strokes Cetelaṣoṣa. In the Āḍḍitā Druvā, Ṇā De De De De Kho Kho Kha. In the Khañja and Natkuṭa Dhruvās Na Nṇā Vuvuṇā Nā Kho Nā Nṇā De De De De Kho Kho Kho Kha. Hereafter the Udghā Tya playing is being explained. It is the playing which is performed at the time of excess of hurry or joy or surprise, excitement or sorrow, or at the time of receiving some gift. Now I shall explain the Mokṣa (Releasing) of playing. It is of two kinds Samihanana and Samasaraṇa. Mokṣa at the Uddhata and the quick Anubandha should include Ghettāmkikiṭi Datta Kettikim Go Gha Ghe Degha Ṭe Gho Ghe Yado. Now the Mokṣa of Khañja and Natkuṭa. It should include Dham Drām Dham Drām Takitām Takitām Gu Du Ghe. The Mokṣa of the same in the Sthita Laya (slow tempo) should include Dhe Dham Dheṭ Maṭa Dhe Dhe Chimaṭam Kaṅta Chi. The Mokṣa of the Āḍḍitā Dhruvā is Kinta Kintām. Mokṣa of the same in the slow tempo should include Ghaṭṭatām. In the Avakṛṣṭā it should be Vavoṭa. These are the beginning and the conclusion of Dhruvā of Niṣkrāma (exit), Praveśa (entrance) Ākṣepikī and Antarā classes. The player of drums should strive in this way with a knowledge of the Tāla, time and the notes on this there are the following complets.

240—250 *Defects of the drummar.* The wise say that the player of drums who does not know about the Tāla, the requisite occasion and the theoretical text there of is merely a Carma-Ghātaka (Hide-injurer) and no drummer. The producer should apply the playing of drums according to these rules. Hence, I shall speak about the salient features of drums. *Salient features of drums.* These are the shapes of Mṛdaṅgas. In shape they are like myrobalan, barley and Cow's tail. The Aṅkī or Āṅkika is like a myrobalan and the Uṛdhvaka is like a barlay. The Āliṅgya resembles a cow's tail. The Mṛdaṅga and the Aṅkika should be three and a half Tālas long and their face eight fingers in diameter. The Paṇava should be made sixteen fingers long and its middle should be thin and the faces should be eight and five fingers in diameter. Its rums should be made half of a finger in thickness. The middle should be hollow and four fingers in diameter. The Dardara should be like a bell sixteen fingers in diameter. Its face should resemble the mouth of a Ghaṭa and should be twelve fingers in diameter. There is a flat lip (rim) on all sides.

250—254 *Characteristic features of the excellent hides.* Hence forth I shall explain the best characteristic features of the hides. These should not be old, torn, crow-pecked, covered with fat or soiled by smoke or fire. Cow's hide free from these six blemishes and the face thereof is like blossoms in colour or is white like snow or Kunda flowers and glossy and free from flesh and is fresh, is good. After procuring such hides with hairs on them, an intelligent person should soak them in water for a night and then take them out.

255—259 *On the making of drums.* One should bind and fix the round Candraka cuttings to the drums after duly rubling them with well cleaned Gomaya (dried cowdung). In these Candrakas one must make Puṣpāvarta of three layers and a Parikara named Kakṣā; So also a Svastika in its Grīvā (neck). One must be able to make three hundred Akṣaras by means of the drums.

Applying Rohaṇa. One should apply to Mṛdaṅgas of fresh manufacture a Rohaṇa consisting of Gingerlly paste mixed with Cow's ghee and oil.

260—271 *Ceremony of installing drums.* After binding the Āṅkika, the Āliṅgya and Uadhvaka with strings in this manner there should be placed on the ground after worshipping the gods. Under the constallation of Citrā or Hastā during an auspicious day of the bright half of the **Lunar mouth** a perfect master of dramatic arts born of a noble family, who is free from passions, who is an adept in the playing of solid instruments, who knows the theory of singing art, who has a sweet temper, with control over the sense organs, has fasted and cut his hairs short and has worn white clothes and has taken strong vow should make three Maṇḍalas (Circular places) with cow-dung free from foul **odor** and assign these three to Brahmā, Śaṅkara and Viṣṇu. At the outset the Āliṅgya is to be placed in the Maṇḍala of Brahmā and the Urdhvaka should be placed in the second Maṇḍala named after Rudra. The Āṅkikā (Utsaṅgikā) should be put **across** Viṣṇu's Maṇḍala. To the Āliṅgya he should make an offering consisting of honey with a mixture of milk pudding along with various kinds of flowers. To the Āṅkika one should give the offering of Apūpa and Locika. **Afterwards** all the offerings should be made to the Urdhvaka in a Svastika to gether with Locikā Apūpa Piṇḍa and Keṇḍarika. This offering is to be embellished with Dhustūra, Karavīra and similar flowers. The oblation is to be scrupulously prepared with blood and pink cloths. To the Āṅkika stationed on the Maṇḍala of Viṣṇu, on circled by Bīja Mantras one should place the offering along with garlands, clothes and unguents of yellow hire. Pāyasa wiih carus of diverse kinds are also offered. The Brahmins are then requested to chant the **Svastimantras** and the monetary gift is offered to them. Gandharvas are then adored before the playing of drums. The Paṇava is then bound on all sides with well prepared strings. The Puṣkarikās are then covered with the hide. In this manner the sponsors should get the Mṛdaṅgas, Paṇivas and the Darduras Made.

272—279 Let me now explain the presiding gods and deities of these Vādyas. The Muraja drums are presided by the deities Vajrekṣaṇa, Śaṅkukarṇa and Mahā Grāmaṇī. The name Mṛdaṅga, is applied because the instrument is made of Mṛt (Clay). The name Bhāṇḍa is derived from the verb Bhrāmayati (moving). Because they are set up right (Urdhvakaraṇa) they are called Murajas. Since they are related to To Dana (striking) they are named Ātodya. We have set down the rules of Bhāṇḍas. Hence forth the rules of Paṇava are being set down Dāru is so called because it Dārayati (Splits it up). The word Dardara owes its origin to the same. After getting the Mṛdaṅga ,Paṇavas and Dardaras made the great sage Svāti brought about a similarity of their notes with those of clouds. The high sounding cloud damed Vidyujjihva gave the note of Vāmaka, the rain cloud named Taḍit to the name of Āliṅgya; the Puṣkara cloud to the name Dakṣiṇa and the cloud Kokka to the name Vāmaka and the Nandi cloud to the drum named Āliṅgya and the cloud named Siddhi to Aṅkika and Piṅgala to the Āliṅgya.

280—284 Those who eagerly wish for success in these performances should offer to these clouds the requisite **oblation** dear to the Bhūtas. After worshiping the deities one should produce the Prekṣā (dramatic performance) on the stage. The Mṛdaṅga should be placed on a heap of dried cowdung. The regular Śānti rites are then performed with the Ātodyas and and Paṇavas that the dancer brought out. In the performance of the Daśa Rūpakas, four Paṇanvas should be used and the same number of Ātodyas are also to be played in the different situations in those Rūpakas. The Mṛdaṅga, Paṇava and Dardara are to be played in the Nāṭaka, Prakaraṇa, Vīthi, Bhāṇa and Ḍima. Thus the wise should understand the characteristic features of the Mṛdaṅgas.

285—292 *The Characteristics of Upahastas.* Hence forth I shall expatiate the characteristic features of Upahastas. They are five viz. Kartari, Samahasta, Hastapāni, Vartanā and Daṇḍa Hasta. The movement of the forefinger and the thumb of both the hands by letting them fall one after the other is called Kartarī. The serial falling in the same Tāla of the two halves of the two palms on the face of the drum is called **Samahasta** The clear falling of the back of the palm and the fingers of the left hand and the falling once of the right palm is called Pāṇi Traya. The four strokes when the right hand falls first and the left thereafter are called Varitnā because they occurly turns. When one takes with strikes by the right hand after beginning the stroke with the left hand, the serial strokes are called Daṇḍahasta. The four qualities of all these hands are eleqance, swiftness, variety and firmness. These are what I had to say about the characteristics of hands.

Prose

293—296 *Characteristics of Good drummers.* I shall explain the characteristics of a good **clapper** of drums. An adept in songs, playing of instruments, Kalā, tempo and one conversant with how to begin a song, to bring it to a finish and has a nimble hand in playing and knows about the various **Panis** |**and** general rules of the success and is an expert in singing **Dhruvās** and who practises Kalās and has a pleasing hand in playing instruments, power of concentration and who can produce pleasing Mārjana and is strong in body and reguler in his physical and intellectual habits and is an accomplished artist is called the best player of drums *Qualities of a good player of the Mṛdanga.* One who know how to give proper plastering to drums, and has underone laborious training in the four Mārgas has earned successes of all kinds, has no defect of limbs, has practised all the Karaṇas well and knows songs, **who** gentle (Saumya), who knows many kinds of Grahas and knows how to perform good music is called a good player of the Mṛdanga because of the above mentioned various good qualities.

297—201 *Qualities of a good player of the Paṇava.* He who does not commit blunders,one an adept in the use of hands and in the observance of time, in covering defects in performance one who is well practised in playing Karaṇas is an expert player or Paṇava due to the above qualites. The player of the Dardara who is firm, clever in his art **swift** nimble knowing all **the** rules of playing and knows to play other instruments as well is praised by everyone.

General rules of drumming

After observing the performance of all kinds of plays the playing of drums has been described after considering the taste of all men. That which has not been specificable mentioned should be devised by good producers after the consideration of the Mārga and the Jāti of the songs.

Qualities of Mṛdanga

The playing of Mṛdangas in which strokes are very clear, well divided, loud but controlled adhering to the palm and including the three Mārjanās and is full of conbination of of pleasing notes is mentioned for it quality.

Indispensability of Drum.

One should first of all be very careful in the play of the drums. This playing has been called the basic bed of the dramatic performance. This playing and the songs being well performed the production of plays does not run any risk.

Notes

Verses

1—2 Mṛdaṅgas are popular all over India. Many South Indian Mṛdaṅga players have become world famous for their scientific precision. Paṇavas are regional instruments made of word. Dardaras appear like large gongs made of bell metro. Some consider these as types of flute.

Verses

5—8 The episode about the origin of drums is fanciful but has some substance.

10 Puṣkaras may be the general term for all types of drums.

15 Kacchapa means tortoise. Evidently tortoise shell is used in making this instrument which has only one string. Ghoṣaka profably is a kind of Tānpūrā.

24 Saṅgīta Ratnākara includes Maroala and Muraja in the term Puṣkara.

34 Vāṣkaraṇa is possibly deribed from "Vācaskaraṇa"

40 Śārṅgadeva uses many of these terms while enumerating Hastapātas.

42 Vāmakas and Dakṣiṇās are termed Bāyān and Dāhinā in modern Hindustani music.

103 Māyūrī Madayati Mārjannī Manāṁsi in Mālavikā Gnimitra (1-24) by Kālidāsa.

34

On Prakṛtis (Type of Characters)

1—5 I shall explain the characteristics of the Various Prakṛtis and the four types of Heroes (Nāyakas). *The three main types*—In a play there are male and female characters. They come under three types (1) the superior or Uttama (2) the middling or Madhyama and (3) the inferior or Adhama. The superior Male character is a man with full control over the sense organs. He is wise and skilled in various arts and crafts. He never utters lie. He is prove to enjoy pleasures. He is willing to help and console the poor people. He is conversant with all Śāstras, grave, biberal, patient and munificent. Such are the salient features of the Uttama. The Madhyava is an expert in understanding the manners of people proficient in arts and also in the Śastras to make a living thereby. He possesses wisdom and sweetness of **manna**.

6—12 *The inferior Male character* uses harsh words. They are ill mannered and base in their mental spirit. They do not hesitate to commit crimes. They are irascible and violent. They engage themselves in useless activities too. Haughty in manner they are even ungrateful. They do not hesitate to dishonour venerable person. They are covelous of women fond of querrel, treacherous and eager to commit sinful deeds. They will steal others Aossess wins. ***Superior female charactor*** is a woman of tender nature. She is never bickle. She speaks similing. She pays head to superior persons' advices. She is never cruel. Bashful by nature and good in her manners she possesss natural beauty nobility and similar qualities. In thing grave she is patient and for bearing.

13—16 *The middling female* character does not have these fine qualities to a greet extent. Further there are defects and faults no plenty. *The inferior* female character is more or less like the inferior male character *Saṁkirrṇa Prakṛtr Mixed character* Maid servants etc. come under this category. The eunuch is also such a one but still inferior. In Drames the Śakāra Vita are also characters of mixed nature.

17—21 *Four types of Nāyakas* only the superior and the Middling ones come under this category (1) *Dhīroddhata* The vehement one with self control (2) *Dhīrodātta.* The frivolous or light hearted possessing self control (3) *Dhīrodātta.* The exalted and esteemed one with self-control and (4) *Dhīra-prasānta.* The quiescent one with self control. The gods are Dhīroddhata. The royal dignitanes are Dhīra Lalita. The minister and the commenders inchief are Dhīrodātta. The Brahmins and **merchants** should be known as Dhīra Prasānta.

22—28 Vidūṣaka or ester of four types. They are the jesters in order of the gods, kings, Ministers and Brahmins viz. the Sannyāsin, the Brahmins, other Dvijas and disciples. They are the confidents of the respective heroes during their Separation from their beloved ones and exibit mastery of good dia· logue *Nāyaka.* If there are many male characters in a play and one of them undergoes greet difficulties and nisenes but, by dint of energetic enterprise ultimatelv attains an exalted position that character is called the **Nāyaka** Sometimes there may be two or more characters answering such description the person who is the better one of the two is the real Nāyaka. *Four types of Heroines.* These are the goddesses, Queen a woman of exalted family and the fourth one the courtezan. As in the case of the heroes these are Dīrās, Lalitās, Udāttās and Nibhṛtā (Quite, modest) The women of noble families are Udāttā and Nibhṛtā. The **courtezan** and the crafts woman may be Lalitā and Udāttā.

29—34 *Two Classes of Prakṛti.* In regard to function the Characters in a play have two types of employment at the Bāhya (External) and the Ābhyantara. The character that has the Upacāra (Service) and dealings with the king is the **Ābhyantara and those dealings with outsiders are called Bāhyas**

Inamtes of the Harem. I shall explain the service of the female characters of the Ābhyantara nature. They are the Mahādevī (Empress), other queens, noble born (Svāminī) the Sthāyinī (permanent wife), Bhoginī (Mistress), Śilpakāriṇī (Crafts woman), Nātakīyā (Actress), Nartaki (danseuse), Anucārikā (Attendant woman), Paricārikā (Chaperon), Sañcārikā (Maid that moves about), Preṣaṇacārikā (Maid for running errands), Mahattarā (Mationly attendant), Pratīhārī (Portress), Kumārī (Virgin), Sthavirā (Old dance) and Āyuktikā (female supervisers).

35—39 *Mahādevī.* She is the female equipped with the following qualities—She has been coronated along with the Emperor. She belongs to an exalted family and possesses good character. Her accomplishments are remarkable. She is a bit elderly. Neutral in respect to kings exacpades. Anger and malice do not find a place in her. She understands sympathetically the workings of the king's mind and shares his ioys an sorrows. Religious rites are constantly performed by her for the good of the husband and the royal household. Calm, affectionate and patient she is kind and considerate to the members of the harem. *Other queens.* They may have most of these qualities. They do not enjoy coronation. They are proud of their royal parentage. They are fastitions in dressing and embellishing themselves. Jealousy of their rivals is prominent in them. They may be elated due to their youth.

40—45 *Svāminī.* The daughters of the ministers other officers and the commander in chief are sometimes the recipients of special attention of the kings. They are honoured and taken into the harem as the favourites by the kings due to their physical charm and merits *Sthāyini.* This is the ordinary wife of the king. She is in the prime of her youth. Violent in sexual intimacy and full of amorous dalliance and gestures, she is an expert in the enjoyment of pleasures. She is jealous of the their rivals. Always alert and unerring, free from lethargy and ruthlessness. She can discriminate between those who should need not be venerated. *Bhoginī.* Although she is only the mistress she is clever and honest in her dealings. Always exalted and brilliant she makes use of unquents, garlands and scents. She scrupulously follows the inclinations of the king and is never envious. She does not expect special distinction. She is gentle and well behaved. Sober humble and forbearing she is never vain.

46—51 *Śilpakāriṇī*. Fully conversant with all arts and crafts she has mastered the art of manufacturing sweet scents, the art of painting in different ways arrangements of making the beds comfortable and easy, preparation of the seats, vehicles and other royal paraphernalia. She is sweet clever and dexterous. Amiable when behaviour she keeps straight forward dealings with everyone. She is humble and gentle too *Nāṭakīyās*. Women with sinnous and seductive charms and selected as Abhinetrīs (Actress). They possess good qualities of head and heart, patience and nice behaviour, Soft sweet and melodious voice and can make voices in the throat. They can portray Helā Bhāva and Sattva. With sweet manners and skill in instrumental music, Tāla, Yati and Laya they are associated with the Ācāryas of dramatic art. They are able to argue and reason in the Uha and Apoha. Youthful in age.

52—60 *Nartakī* (Danseuse). She is a woman of beautiful limbs. She is conversant with the sixty four fine arts and crafts; Constantly gentle in behaviour she is bereft of the ailments common to women. She is bold and is never indolent. Hard work she never shirks. She is skilled in rendering musical compositions. She surpasses all other women in beauty and youthfulness brilliance and can did charm. *Anucārikā* (Attendent woman). She never leaves the king under any condition. Her Upacāra (service) is constant. Paricārikā (Chaperon). The maid of special personal work of the king She looks after the royal umbrella, bed, seat etc. She fans him and massage his body applies sweet scents and unguents. She helps him to put on the garments and ornaments. *Sañcārikās* (Maids for running errands). They roam about in the nooks and corners of the palace, gardens, shrines, pleasure Maṇḍapas, grottos etc. The Yāmas are indicated by them by striking the bells and gongs. They are not depicted as enjoying sexual pleasures. *Preṣaṇa Cārikās*. These are the women whom the king employs in secret missions that have a bearing on the amorous affairs of the royal patron.

61—66 *Mahattarī*. She is the mationly elderly woman for the upkeep of the harem, the kings prosperity, auspicious rites etc. She takes special care and interest in singing hymns to the deities • *Pratīhārī*. She is the female portress of the king who looks after the royal affairs of Sandhi (heavy), Vigraha (war) and the similar ones also. *Kumārikās* (Virgins) They have never tested love's pleasures. They are quiescent and are never rash and impestuous. Modest and bashful they never exhibit excitement. *Vṛddhās* (Sthavirās, old dames). These are the women who are thoroughly conversant with the manners of dead and departed kings duly honoured by them in their days. They should know the characters of all the inmates of the harem • *Āyuktikās* (Female Supervisors). They are entrusted with the affairs connected with the Royal stores, weaponry fruits, roots, grains, testing of cooked food, Scents, ornaments and clothes of the king. They look into all the connected affairs as well as Thus I have explained the different classes of women workers in the harem.

67—78 The characteristics of other inmates with special assignments. They aye never rash, restive, greedy, ruthless and angry. They are quiet, satisfied an forgiving by nature. Self control and absence of passion are their salient features. No ailment affects them. They are devoted to the king. They belong to the various regions of the realm. Womanly infatuations are absent in them. The eunuchs, earlier mentioned as the third Prakṛti should be employed in the harem. Then the following are employed viz. Snātakas, Kañcukīya, Varṣadhara, Aupasthāyika, Nirmuṇḍa etc. in the different parts of the harem. In a Nāṭaka in variable the eunuch or one who is castrated is employed in the harem. *Snātaka*. He is a man with polished manners. He is the Warden of the gate Dvāstha, not of the menial type but of an officer's status. Old Brahmins with skill in various affairs and free from sexual passion should be employed by the king to attend of the needs of the queen *Kañcukīya*. They are learned, truthful, and free from Sexual inclinations. Wise and conversent with various affairs they are to be employed in business connected with polity. *Varṣadharas*. These are also called Varṣavaras and are employed in errands relating to love affairs. The *Aupasthāyika* Nirmuṇḍas are those employed for escorting the royal ladies and quarding maidens and girls. The Anucārikās are employed for receiving women of honour and prestige.

79—83 Women who attend to all the affairs of the king should be proficient in performing all types of dance in the theatre under the authority and jurisdiction of the harem. Varṣanaras are persons of feeble nature with poor vitality. They have feminine qualities but are not defective since naturly. They are eunuchs. The Nirmuṇḍas are also eunuchs bereft of feminine qualities. They have no personal knowledge of Sexual contact. Thus I have explained the eighteen kinds of harem attendants. *Bāhya Male Characters*. These are the kings, chiefs of the Army, priest, Ministers, Secretaries, judges, tutors and wardens of the princes, and members of the Assembly. I shall explain their characteristics.

84—88 *Rājā* (King). The king should be intelligent with perfect control over the sense organs. He must be truthful, clever and powerful with good memory, purity and high mindedness he must be of good character. Energetic in his activities he must be farsighted and grateful. Eloquence and ability to speak sweetly should be remarkable. He must be began to protect his subjects with ability in the different modes of administration. Alerthess without the slightest carelessness must be his sterling quality. He should frequently associate with old and experienced people. He must be a master of Arthaśāstra and the Science of polity. He must be aware of his forbles too and equanimity is to be maintained both in prosperity and decline. He must be aware of the weak points of his enemies and the principles of Dharma. No evil habits should mar him.

89—95 *Commander in Chief*. He should possess a good character, truthfulness and thorough knowledge of Arthaśāstra. He should be active and sweet tongued. He must note the weakned of the enemy and the opportune time to march against him. He should be devoted to the king and honoured by every one. These qualities will end him to be the real leader of the army. *Purohita and Mantrī*. They are high-born intelligent and masters of the Vedic lore and polity too. They must be the inhabitants of the realm of the king. They should be loyal pure and righteous. They should not fall into the temptation of the offer of bribery by the enemies and their agents. They must be disciplined and trust-worthy. *Saciva* (Amātya). He should be intelligent and equipped with mastery of polity. He should be sweet in words and powerful in carrying out the requisite activities. He must have studied the Arthaśāstra. He should be righteous and devout. He must love the people of the realm and their welfare. *Prāḍvivākas* (Judicial officers). They must know the details of the work of litigation. Monetary transactions should be gone deep into by them. Intelligent and well versed in many disciplines and lores they must be pious and impartial. Ability to discriminate between the good and the bad deeds and forbearing control of the sense organs and absence of wrathful venegenceshould be their main qualities They should not be haughty. They must have similar respect for every one.

96—99 *Kumārādhikṛtas* (The tutors and Wardens of the Princes) must be alert and watchful. They should not be indolent or partial. Well versed in polity and the different Śāstras they should not be negatively influenced by passion. They should be aware of reasoning properly. They should be hereditary officials of the royal family. *Sabhāsadas*. Members of the court should be persons of efficiency and practical experience. They are also called Sabhāstāras and their appointment, as enjoined by Bṛhaspati should be carefully done by the king after observing as testing their qualities. Hence forth I shall explain the characteristics of the Bhūmikās (various roles) in different plays.

Notes

3 *Bhogadakṣas*. It need not necessarily be that a Prakṛti should be a recluse when control over the sense organs is enjoined. Desire to enjoy the good things of life legitimately is not prohibited.

5 The similarity in the accomplishments of the superior and the Middling characters is not identity completely. The superior character has the various skills as an accomplishment while the middling character makes professional use of his

mastery of the Science. Unless the middling character is so disposed his sustenance may be jeopardised. (Vide Mṛcchakaṭika Act II)

14–16 Saṁkīrṇa Prakṛti is further explained which 35—Verses 76—78.

31—34 The detailed enumeration of the female inmates and officials of the harem gives us a good idea of the system in Royal house holds in those early days. That the kings took many wives with of course the proviso that their claim on them is limited and different in the different individuals is evident from these Verses.

39 Pratipakṣā Bhyasuyikās (Unable to brook rivals). This rule has not been followed by some playwrights.

49—50 Personal security of the king is the sins qua non of prohibiting male characters as Danseuses.

59 *Bhogavāritas.* They have been precluded from enjoyment of sexual pleasures to prevent their personal involvement in the royal escapades.

73–74 Snātakas are not introduced in later dramas. The *Dvāstha* is not the menial porter but a responsible officer incharge of the ingress and egress of visitors etc.

91 The Mantrī and the Purohita may be the same person or different persons.

95 *Prāḍvivākā.* The root meaning of this word is that he is one who elicits the requisites information knowledge by means of pointed questions asked repeatedly and put in diverse forms.

35

Bhumika Vikalpa
(The different roles)

1—4 I shall now explain how the roles should be assigned carried out by the different male and female characters. *General principles*. The expert sponsor of the play must assign different roles to the different people after carefully observing their mode of walking speaking and moving also be taken into consideration. It necessitates a careful enquiry into the anticedents and accomplishments of the would be actors, lest the sponsor of the play, the director in charge, should come to grief later on. The Acārya therefore ascertains the natural aptitudes of the actors before distributing the roles.

5—14 *Role of Gods*. The person selected should not be wanting in any limb. He should be well informed and be nature. He should not be too stone or too lean. Nor too tall or slow in movement. He must have Vivacity, pleasing voice and appearance. Such a character should be assiged the role of gods. *Role of Rākṣasas*. Bulky ones with large bodies and gruff voice resembling the rumbling of the cloud, furious eyes with knit eyebows should be assigned the role of demons Dānava, and Daityas. Performance of male actors must be inconformity with their limbs and movements. *Role of kings*. Beautiful eye, eyebows, forehead, nose, lips, cheeks, face, neck, and all other limbs too are essential in the character intended to be assigned the role of kings. They must be tall with pleasing steps, good behaviour wisdom and steadness of nature. They should neither be fat nor very lean. The same holds good in the assignment of the role of Princes. *Role of the Army and the Sacivas*. The limbs of these should be perfectly shaped. They, should have distinct speech. They should not be too tall or fat. They must be heroic, eloquent and brave

positively and negatively reasoning a'ɩlity and pre
should be their salient features. *Kāñcukīyas*
are persons with long nose and brown eyes.
short or tall.

15—24 *Role of minor characters.* Role can be assigned at the discretion of the director after considering the age and physical condition of the actor considering the age and physical condition of the actor concerned. Persons who are devarfish, hunch-backed, uncouth and oddfaced can be engaged in the role of slaves. They should be rather fat with expressionless eyes small chin and low nose. Evil nature, deformed body and ugly raiments are also marked characteristics of a slave. *Role af tired persons.* The person should be naturally thin. He can represent a person in utter exhaustion and fatigue. *Healthy ones* can be represented by fat person. *Special cases for the assignment.* If requisite types of persons were to be unavailable the director should exercise his power of discrimination. The Bhāvas and Ceṣṭās (gestures) should be taken into account before the assignment of the role. The natural movements of the people may be good, bad or middling. They can be regulated by the director incharge and the candidate can later properly represent the Bhāvas properly. In other cases also the convention has been laid down. Roles should be assigned after the due consideration of their native places, costumes etc. *Characters with superflous limbs.* Many armed or many-headed characters, persons with uncouth faces, or animal faced ones including beasts of prey, asses, camels etc. the director can cause the masks etc. made with clay, wood, lac or leather. *The entry of a character.* No character shall enter the stage in his natural form or shape. The body should be covered with paints decorations and embellishments.

25—32 In the production of a drama even persons in their natural forms can be employed provided the age, costume etc. do fit in. Just as a creature gives up its nature and body and assumes another body and another nature after entering the body concerned so also the sensible actor should think within himself. "I am that character" and thereby try to represent the Bhāvas of and the person by speech, made of walking gesture etc. *Prakṛti of three types*. Human characters in as much as they are represented on the stage can be classified into three Anurūpā befitting, natural), Virūpā (Not fitting, unnatural) and Rūpānusāriṇī (Close by emulative). Women actresses in the role of female characters and man actors in the of male characters with age etc. befitting the respective roles can be called Anurūpā If a boy plays the part of an old man or *vice versa* it is an example of Virūpā Prakṛti. A man may assume the role of a woman and be successful in imitating the character. This is called Rūpānusāriṇī. In the same manner a woman may assume the role of a man. But an old man or a boy should not emulate each other. *Special suitability of men and women.* Bold men with strength and heroism may be employed in the role of reciters and women in the role of singers. Women naturally befit the songs and men recitatives. Women's voice is naturally sweet and that of men forceful.

35—42 Men may know the theoretical rules and technique of singing in accordance with the tradition thereof yet their songs are bereft of sweetness. They are not charming. Sometimes accidentally there may be merit in the recitation of women and sweetness of voice in men also. This is something contrary to the nature but that can be embellishment. *Women in Men's roles.* In temples, palaces and the abodes of the captains of the army or other prominent persons a dramatic performance is usually held by women in the roles of men. *Women's special merit.* A frail and delicate person's role is always to be taken up by women. Hence in the cases of women as well as gods and men of delicate nature women can assume the roles. Exactly on account of this, Rambhā and Urvasī and other celestral damsels established in the heaven dramas; and imitating then such plays were eracted in the kings' harems on earth *Training of womens* should be carried out by the directors in accordance with the Śāstras but they themselves should not be the actual instructors. Masculine roles should be carefully directed we observe in women natural aniorousness and their naturally graceful limbs are easily graceful limbs are easily accessible to Sauṣṭhava. Sportful nature will be their additional embellishment when they assume a masculine role.

43—46 *Benefit of proper assignment.* When there are similar conditions and behaviour in the characters and the actors representing them through natural limbs and organs thay shall surely embellish a dramatic performance women get musical practice and mastery without difficulty. Dramatic performance attains sweetness and mastery by repeated practice. Woman who are experts in the practice of love and portrayal of love affairs appear like creepers full of charms due to blossoms if the acting on the stage is graceful. So the sponsor of the dramatic performance must bertow undivided attention to befitting women's exercise in dance and music. Without the befitting ones,Bhāvas and Rasas can not be depicted perfectly.

47—56 *Types of dramatic production.* The production of a drama with the depictions of Bhāvas and Rasas is of two types—Sukumāra (graceful) and Āviddha (Energetic). The *production graceful.* Nāṭaka, Prakarṇa, Bhāṇa, Vīthi and Aṅka are the graceful ones and they depend on human beings for the purpose of theme. This graceful type of dramatic production please the kings most. Hence plays of this type with Śṛṅgāra as the Rasa should be produced by women. Women should not be asked to play the dramas in which violent fighting, speedy movement and much excitement occur. They are to be played by men alone. If a play includes no exalted incidents, no hurried or violent movement of limbs with the necessity of proper tempo, Tāla Kalā and regulated utterance of syllables and clearly divided words as well as desired Rasas it should be produced by woman. *The Energetic production.* In these productions the play must consist of Āviddha type of Aṅgahāras to represent cutting, piercing and fighting. They include the use of magic and miraculous acts as well as artificial objects and costumes. The dramates personal include may males and a small number of females. Whose nature is very quiescent. The style may be Sāttvatī or Ārabhaṭī. Saṃvakāra., Ḍima, Vyāyoga and Īhāmṛga come under the category of Āviddha type of dramatic production conducted through Devas, Dānavas and Rākṣasas The assignment of roles has been explained thus. I shall now explain how a play becomes excellent thanks to costumes and make up.

57—65 *Potrayal of the role of a king.* People may wonder how an actor with limited wearing appearely could represent the qualities of the king. In this respect it has already been explained that I have made plays furnished with dramatic conventions when they came into vogue. The actors are covered with paints and embellished with ornaments. So they reveal the significant parts of the king by assuming a grave and dignified attitude. They become then the refuge of the Seven-great divisions of the world (Saptadvīpas). The individual actor maks the movement of the limbs after he has been painted over. Trimmed by the director in accordance with his discretion the actor becomes like a king thanks to the Sauṣṭhava (Perfection) of his limbs. In this manner the king also may be like an actor. Just as an actor is so is the king and just as the king is so is the actor. (It means the king is only an ordinary human acting gravely and in grandaur. Hence he is called the king. In fact he is a supreme actor). Bhāva is given expression to by both of them by means of departments and and Sauṣṭhava of limbs. If he properly carries out the directions of the star manager the actor brightens the stage. So also the king becomes brilliant through his innate qualities. The retinue of the king is similar to that of the divine personage. It is to be introduced with proper costume, language and age. The sponsor of the play must allow the actor to portray naturally his role by means of suitable costume etc. and through the association of the proper make-up and befitting age. It is in this manner that the selection of persons for the portrayal of of the king. I shall now explain the Salient features of the Sūtradhāra.

Prose passage

66—71 *Characteristics the Stage Manager.* At the outset he is expected to possess knowledge of every salient feature of the theatre, desirable exquisiteness of speech, rules of Tāla and the technique of musical instruments and notes in general. One who is an expert in playing the four types of Vādyas, has adequate practical experience, one who is reasonally fully aware of the rites of various heratic religious cults, one who is conversant with polity and Arthaśāstra, the manners and costums of courtezans, the science of erotics, conventional movements and modes of walkings one who thoroughly understands all the Rasas and Bhāvas, one who is efficient in the production of plays, one who is acquainted with all arts and crafts, with the rules of metres and prosody, one who has mastered all the Darśanas, science of the luminaries and planets, the functions of the different parts of the body within and without, one who knows the extent of the earth the continants therein, mountains and seas, the people inhabiting them their manners and customs, the lineage of royal dignatries, one who can understand Śāstra discourses, give practical demonstration of the various rites should be made the Ācārya as well as Sūtradhāra.

72—77 *Natural qualities of the Sūtradhāra* are good memory, intelligence, patiance, liberal mindedness, fixity of purpose, appreciation of poems, absence of ailments, sweet manners, self control, absence of warth, impartiality, truthfulness absence of craving for cheep praise. *The Assistant Director or Pāripārśvik* is of the middling type and somewhat deficient in some of the qualities of his master. *The Naṭa* (Actor) should lively. He has good physique. He is adequetely acquainted with the theatrical accessories and the utility thereof. Possession of intelligence is essential. He should be an expert in his duties with the full knowledge of the rules. *The Viṭa* (Lecher, Parasitic hangeron) is an expert in dealing with courtezans. He must possess all the qualities of the Sūtradhāra in respect to the theatrical production. Impartial poetic and proficient in the Śāstras, he should be capable of seeing the positive and the negative side of arrangements. He must be eloquant and clever.

78—83 The Śakāra is usually the Rājasyāla (the brother of the chief mistress of the king) dressed in gaudy clothes and ornaments. He becomes angry at the slightest provocation and is also pacified easily. An inferior character he speaks the Māgadhi dialect of Prākṛta. His aberrations are too many. The Vidūṣaka (Jester) should be somewhat short in stature, dwarfish with big teeth, hunch back and bald pate. He is tawny eyed and double-longued.

Ceṭa (the Servant, Valet) is found of quarrel. He is uncouth is physical appearance and garrulous. He may be a bounded slave. He is expected to discriminate between persons worthy of being venerated or not. *Courtezan* is the woman constantly attending the Ādārya in the artistic production and the application of the various crafts for that purpose. Amorous movements, Hāva and Bhāva, sweetness of manners, personal discipline etc. etc. are remarkable in her. Conversant with all the sixty four Kalās she is of good temperament and is an expert in dealing with the king. She has no ailments common to women. She is clear in her speech clever and undaunted by fatique.

84—90. *Nāyikā* (Heroine) is a lady endowed with the following attributes. A good physical form, good qualities of the head and heart, character, youthful in age, brilliant with garlands, necklaces etc. sweetness and affection, ability to speak sweetty & mastery of Laya, Tāla, Rasa and Bhāva. *Prakṛti unfit to take up any role* if the women smile out of context, rough in appearance, mode of walking is unnatural and unever, is angry persistantly, is miserable in her look and exhibits haughtiness and fickleness. *The ideal theatrical troupe.* Consists of the following—Bharata (Main Actor), the Vidūṣaka, Tauripa (Songs), the Naṭa Sūtradhāra, Nāṭyakāra, Mukuṭaraka (Maker of crowns), Ābharoṇakṛt (goldsmith, maker of ornaments), Mālākāra (gardener) the Rajaka (washerman, dyer), Citrakāra (Painter), Kāru (craftsman), Śilpī (expert in fine arts), Kuśīlavas (Musicians) and others as well,

91—97 *Bharata.* He is the leader of the troupe and acts in many roles. He can play on many instruments. It is he who provides the others with the necessories. He is therefore called Bharata. *Vidūṣaka.* He is eager to amuse and humour people. He can minicry people and imitate others easily. He mixes freely with women. He is an expert in repartee pleasantry and concealed humour. He can rebuke through his sarcastic words but not wound unbecomingly. *Tauripa* (or Taurika, Instrumentalist). He is an expert in the playing of all types of Ātodyas. He is the lord of Tūra (musical accessories) and is always mindful of the triple symphony. *Naṭa.* The root Naṭ means to act. Since this member acts again and again the stories of people with Rasa, Bhāva and Sattva he is called by the name Naṭa. *Nāndī* is the benedictory Verses. It is through this that the advance is pleased. Hence the name Nāndī. It May have Saṁskrita and Prākrit recitatives.

98—102 *Sūtradhāra* is one who knows the Sūtras (principles) thanks to the instruction from Śaṣtras. He knows the principles of songs, Vādyas, Pāṭhyas (Recitatives) in their union. Hence Sūtradhāra. *Nāṭyakāra* (Playwright) is so called because he puts is different Rasas, Bhāvas, Sattvas as enjoined in the Śāstra in the different characters of the play. *Naṭa* (Actor) is the person who produces the play in accordance with the injunction of the Śāstra as well as his own reasoning faculty. He can introduce all the four kinds of Ātodya. *Nāṭakīyā* (Actress) is the woman conversant with Laya and Tāla. She is fully aware of the technique of drum play. She is very lovely in her limbs and has mastered the portrayal of Rasa. *Mukuṭakāra* (Crown manufacturer and mender). He makes the diverse kinds of marks, head wear and garments of various kinds as suitable to the different occasions.

103—109 *Āmbharaṇakṛt* (Ornament maker) should produce ornaments as enjoined in the Śāstra. The names of the various officials involved in this should specify the article dealt with by them *Mālakāra* (garland maker & gardenar) makes the five different kinds of Mālās (As explained in XIII—10). The *Veṣakāra* is the person in change of make up and dressing Citrakāra etc. (Painter and others). He who paints is the Citrakāra. The dyer of clothes is Rajaka because he does the work of dyeing. One who makes articles out of the substances of lac, stone, metal and wood is called a Kāru.*Kuśīlava* is the expert in playing musical instruments. He employs the principles of instrumental music suitable. Since he is Kuśala (Clever) Avadāta (Cultured and refined) and Avyatuita (bereft) of fatique) he is called Kuśīlava.*Other members.* The persons who are employed in the various other activities of art and craft and production and experts in the respective fields are called the suitable names. That is the description of the hereditary members of the troupe in accordance with the rules of Nāṭyavidhi engaged in the production of the play. I have thus concluded the description of assignment of roles according to the injunctions of Dramatic art. O Sages what else shall I explain ?

Notes

22—24 The rules, and further details regarding Ahārya Abhinaya are explained in the 23nd Adhyāya. How to tackle the characters of ugly end distorted faces or plurality of faces can be understood therefrom.

26—27 Saubhar and other Yogins are reputed to be capable of taking up many bodies simultaneously in order to wipe off Prārabdha Karmans. Śaṅkarācārya could not defeat an objector because he had no personal knowledge of love in physical exercise. In order to master that piece of knowledge the sage entered the body of a dead king and remained in his harem for sometime.

33—34 See XXXII 504—508.

48 The various types of dramatic compositions are defined explained in XX-10 to 115.

78 The Rājaśyāla was in the habit of boasting about his connection with the king but the people dared not laugh at him openly. They did laugh derively behind his back.

81—83 Courtezans of those days enjoyed analevated status in the society due to their accomplishments. They were not roadside prostitutes.

92—93 How Viduṣaka is to breated etc. are explained in XXII.

102—104 Rules about Mukuṭas, Mālyas costumes etc. are explained in XXIII-ff.

106 Kuśa and Lava song Rāmāyaṇa in sweet voice. Hence, later the word Kuśīlaya must have come to mean "clever in singing".

107 The theatrical troupes must have had various kinds of Artisans with them for ready mending of damaged accessories etc.

36

Nāṭyāvatāra (Incarnation of the Science of dramatic performance)

1—6 The sages assembled were the following viz. Ātreya, Vasiṣṭha, Pulastya, Pulaha, Kratu, Aṅgiras, Gautama, Agastya, Manu, Ātmavān (self-possessed, Prudent), Viśvā-Mitra, Sthūlaśiras, Samvarta, Pratimardana, Uśanas, Bṛhaspati, Vatsa, Cyavana Kāśyapa, Dhruva, Durvāsas, Jamadagni, Mārkaṇḍeya, Gālava, Bharadvāja, Raibhya, Vālmīki Bhagavān (Venerable one), Sthūlākṣa, Śaṅ Kulākṣa, Kaṇva, Medhātithi, Kuśa (or Kṛśa), Nārada, Parvata, Suśarman, Ekadhanvin, Niṣṭhyūti, Bhavana, Dhaumya, Śatānanda, Kṛtavraṇa, Rāma the son of Jamadgni, Jamadagni and Vāmpna. These delighted sages said these words to Bharata who knew everything, with eagerness.

7—15 You have explained in detail the science of dramatic performance and we have fully comprehended them with concentration of the minds. But, O Venerable Sir, we have certain doubts which you will kindly clarify. Indeed no one else knows the Nāṭya Veda decisively. It is for further enlightenment that we enquire now, but not for any distrust, rivalry or intention to dispute. This question has not put earlier lest there should be interruption in your narration. Now do expatiates exhaustively the mystery of drama. Explorts of men, you have mentioned earlier make by the dramatic performances. Hence what is not fully revealed to the laymen may kindly be explained. O excellant, Twice born mention the characteristics of the deity appearing in the Pūrvaraṅga. Why Ghoṣa '(sound of musical instrument) supposed to be relevant? What is the purpose served on being put into use? Which god is delighted thereby? What does he do on being delighted? The Sūtra Dhāra is performing cleaning rites again why? O Sir, how did Naṭya descend to the earth from the heaven (How your race become established in the name of Naṭa? O great sage mention everything factually, On hearing these words of these sages, the sainlty Bharata spoke again to them for the purpose of clarifying the confidential matter Bharata said.

16—29 I shall explain, O Brahmins, of excellent vows, what you have you have enquired regarding the Pūrvaraṅga, Listen and understand.Earlier I had mentioned it as the thing that causes the destruction of Obstacles In continuation thereof the Pūrvaraṅga had been described. The body is covered with the coat of mail for avoiding the attack of missiles. So also Homa is performed to Subdue the sin present in all. By worshipping gods with Japa, Homa adoration of the deities utterance of words of blessings and enlogy I warded off the sins and destroyed obstacles songs about their benign activities were sung. The instuments were played. The gods were delighted and they said, Your performance has pleased me. Since it pleases the people after propitiating the deities and the Asuras this performance shall hence forth be known as Nāndī (Verse of benediction). If the Kākusvana (Emphetic mutter) in initation and succession of vocal and instrumental music is auspiciously made it shall quell sins and be conducive to auspiciousness in the whole region neither the Rākṣasan nor Vighnavināyakas (Malevolant) will ever stay in the region covered by the sound of the instruments. On the utterance of Nāndī people hear it in the course of Āvāha (marriage ceremony at the groom's place) and Vivāha (The same at the bride's place) & Yajña performed for bringing in the prosperity of the being all types of violance are always destroyed. The Pāṭhya (the passages recited),Nāṭya, Geya (song) and Vāditra (Instrumental music) will be on a par with the exposition of the meanings of Vedic Mantras. It has been heard factually from Śaṅkara the lord of the Devas that the sacred song and instrumental music more conducive to the welfare than thousand of holy ablutions and Japas. No inauspicious thing will ever occure in that place here,there are dramatic performances and the auspicious Sound of the instruments and vocal songs. It is for thus that I devised Pūrvaraṅga ceremony consisting of the eulogy of the deities and Verses and Mantras.

30–35 *Sutradhāra's ablution on the stages.* The head gets tired by frequent bowing on the stage. Hence the rule permitting (or rather enjoining) the Sūtradhāra to bathe at with water. Subsequent to the ablution the Sūtradhāra is to worship the Jarjara with Mantras. Hence Ablution is glorified. I shall now explain how dramatic performance happened to descend to the earth from the heaven I have to mention everything without with-holding anything. Bharata's sons offended the sages. All these sons of mine became naughty due to their mastery of the Nāṭyaveda. They wantonly began to practise in course of time an art that vexed all the people by means of Prahasanas intended to provoke laughter In an assembly of spectators they performed a play cancaturing the sages. It was not approved because it was unacceptable and replete with incked acts encouraging obscene and rustic activities The poem was a ruthlessly inauspicious ones.

36–42 *The sages curse the sons of Bharata.* On hearing thus the sages became excassively furious and agitated. They spote to the Bhāratas as though they were fires burning all of them—"O Brahmins enough of these pranks. It is not proper that we should be caricatured in this manner. What is this insult for? Why is this act disapproved by us? You have become maddened due to your (professed) knowledge. you have become rude and impolite. Hence this biased knowledge will get destroyed. You will become persons with activities similer to those of Śūdras after having left off all Brahamical rites in the group and assembly of sages and Brahmins you are sure to become mere Sūdras taking up their activities. Those successors in your line will also become impure. The posterity of the all will turn out to be dancers worshipping other deities along with their womenfold and sons". On coming to know of the occurrance of this course on my sons, the gods became worried They rushed to the sages.

43–54 *Gods plead on behalf of the sons of Bharata.* The Devas with Indra as their head averred—"A great calamity has happened now. This Science of dramatic performance is doomed. The songs said—"This will not perish, but everything also will transpire in the manner uttered by us". *Bharata's sons approach the father.* On hearing the words of the sages of fiery brilliance my sons became beurldered and wished to kill themselves. They came to me and said. "We have been utterly destroyed by you. As a result of the deficiency of drama we have been converted into persons with Sūdra behavious and activity." *Bharata consoles them.* By way of assuaging their grief, said—O sinless ones, do not be grief stucken. This arrangement has been caused by Kṛṣṇnta (fate) in regard to us. The words of those sages will never go in vain or be untrue. Thus consoled by me avert your minds from the thought of self- immoltion You know fully well that the Nṛtya science has been initially propounded and set in motion by Brahmā himself. By demonstrating the same, give instruction therein to the disciples and others. Dramatic art has been evolved and set in practice with greet difficulty. Let it not be ruined. Actually it has a greet basis. It is highly meritorious. It has originated from the Vedas, their ancillaries Aṅgas and their further subdivisions. Impart unto the celestial damsels this Nāṭya, explained by me on the basis of what has been heard by me and thereafter perform atonement rites."

52—63 *Nahuṣa invites divine Artistes to the earth.* As time elapsed an earthly king named Nahuṣa obtained the lordship of the divine kingdom thanks to his political acumen, intelligence and exploit. After attaining divine prosperity he administered the same duly. He witnessed the dramatic performance and the musical programme of the Gandharvas and so ponderes thus—"How can the performance of drama demonstrated this by the Devas be held in my houses? With palms joined in reverence the king said to the 'Devas for the sake of performance thereof—? Let this drama of the Apsaṛas be performed in our abode too? *Gods reject.* He was duly given a reply by the Devas with Bṛhaspati as their leader." There cannot be an association of the divine damsels with human beings here. Since your highness is the lord of the heaven what is beneficial and befitting must be mentioned by us. May the Ācāryas go there. After going there let them carry outwhat is beneficial to you. *Nahusa pleads to Bharata.* The king pleaded to him with palms joined in reverence—"O Vanerable Sir, I wish that this dramatic art should be established on the earth. Earlier it has been assured to me that your service as instructor is possible. O excellent Brahmin, now it has been manifestly obtained from your presence. *Urvasī and the dramatic performance.* In the mansion of my grandfather (Purūravas) the performance of a drama based on the composition of my grandfather had been demonstrated by Urvaśī before the inmates of the harem. When she vanished, the king (my grandfather) died of sheer madness and the inmates harem too died. So this art got lost. We wish that this esteemed art should be manifested on the earth again. It shall be conducive to auspiciousness at the rites of the Yajñas performed on different lunar days plays comprising of many characters shall be produced in my abode with the graceful movements of women. They will add to your renown".

64—74 *Bharata Concedes.* I said to king Nahuṣa "Let it be so". My sons were called together along with the Devas. They were consolingly told thus by me. This king Nahuṣa requests me with palms joined in reverence that you all should go to the Earth in a body in order to perform the dramatic Compositions. Once the drama is performed there I shall see that the course upon you too is ended. You will no longer be despicable unto the kings and the brahmins. Go therefore to the Earth and perform the art duly on the Earth. I can not say may to the importunity of the king. The self form lord Brahmā has already said that we and the noble king Nahuṣa will achieve fulfilment through authoritative instructions. What remains further to be related will be narrated by Kohala in the Uttaratantra (the supplementary treatise) including the demonstration, memonic verses and proper derivations of terms used. As an instrument of pastime this treatise has been established by me in the heaven through the collaboration of the celestral damsels and the sages Svāti and Nārada. *Demonstration of the drametic art on the Earth.* Then O twice form ones, they descended to the Earth. In the abode of Nahuṣa they fixed programmes of the woman in due order. My sons procreated through human bodies many sons and fixed many other programmes with diverse themes. After begetting sons and arranging dramatic performances duly my sons returned to the heaven with the permission of Brahmā. Thus, evidently due to a curse the dramatic art was brought into vogue on the Earth and the future race of Bharatas was set in motion.

75—83 By Kohala and others along with Vātsya, Śūṇḍilya and Dhūrtila this Śāstra was adopted and furthered. As man they stayed there for some time and promoted the Śāstra that increased the intellect of human beings. This Śāstra dealing with the activities of all the three worlds can be considered a model for all other Śāstras. *The greatness of the Nāṭya Śāstra.* This Śāstra with its practical application has been uttered by the Self born lord Brahmā. It is conducive to auspiciousness. It is gracefully regulated. It is meritorious, sacred and destructive of sins. He who listens to this, he who performs this and witnesses it with attention shall attain that goal which is reputed to be the goal of the Vedic scholars, that goals of those who perform Yajñas and the goal of those who make gifts oemingly. Of all charitable and pions rites this has been mentioned as the producer of great benefits. Indeed the gift of a visual art is praised more than all other gifts. When worshipped with scents, unguents and garlands gods do not get as much pleasure as with the performance of dramas. The man who perfectly looks after the arts of music and dance attains the meritorious goal along with Brahmanical sages. In connection with the dramatic performance we have described many other Śāstraic rites. If any thing is left unsaid it should be understood by people conversant with practices imitating the usage in the world. Let the earth be full of greenary. Let it be free from ailments. Let there be peace of cows and **Brahmnis** Let the king rule the entire earth, Nāṭyaśastra concluded.

Notes

1—6 The long list of the sages is in accordance with the Dīrghapāṭha. 1-2 there is the mention of a few beginning with Ātreya.

12—14 In V-50-53 fuller details of Pūrva Raṅga are available.

17 Vighna Vāraṇa (Warding off obstacles) through divine grace is mentioned in V-70 ff.

31 Obeisance to the Jarjara is mentioned fully in V-118-119.

41 Laws of the land are comprehensive and those governing "Defamation, libel etc." can bring about the prosecution of the dramatist and the players.

50 Regarding the Vedic origin of the Nāṭya Śāstra there are divergent opinions. Further elucidation can be seen in the introduction.

68—69 There is Uttara Stnāna in medical treatises as in the Suśṛuta Samhita. Kohau treatise has not been published, it seems.

80 Financing the schemes for the furtherance of the theatrical art, dramalurgy etc. has come an essential feature of our budgets both at the centre and the States.

83 The author does not want a cent percent adherence to the rules laid down by him. Playwrights and sponsors of plays can use their discretion based on the extra scientific knowledge and later inventions etc.

Index